Product Innovation through Knowledge Management and Social Media Strategies

Alok Kumar Goel
CSIR Human Resource Development Centre, India

Puja Singhal
Amity University, India

A volume in the Advances in Marketing, Customer Relationship Management, and E-Services (AMCRMES) Book Series

Published in the United States of America by
Business Science Reference (an imprint of IGI Global)
701 E. Chocolate Avenue
Hershey PA, USA 17033
Tel: 717-533-8845
Fax: 717-533-8661
E-mail: cust@igi-global.com
Web site: http://www.igi-global.com

Copyright © 2016 by IGI Global. All rights reserved. No part of this publication may be reproduced, stored or distributed in any form or by any means, electronic or mechanical, including photocopying, without written permission from the publisher. Product or company names used in this set are for identification purposes only. Inclusion of the names of the products or companies does not indicate a claim of ownership by IGI Global of the trademark or registered trademark.

Library of Congress Cataloging-in-Publication Data

Names: Goel, Alok Kumar, 1971- editor. | Singhal, Puja, 1978- editor.
Title: Product innovation through knowledge management and social media
  strategies / Alok Kumar Goel and Puja Singhal, editors.
Description: Hershey : Business Science Reference, 2016. | Includes
  bibliographical references and index.
Identifiers: LCCN 2015037481| ISBN 9781466696075 (hardcover) | ISBN
  9781466696082 (ebook)
Subjects: LCSH: Knowledge management. | Social media. | Technology transfer.
  | New products--Management.
Classification: LCC HD30.2 .P756156 2016 | DDC 658.4/038--dc23 LC record available at http://lccn.loc.gov/2015037481

This book is published in the IGI Global book series Advances in Marketing, Customer Relationship Management, and E-Services (AMCRMES) (ISSN: 2327-5502; eISSN: 2327-5529)

British Cataloguing in Publication Data
A Cataloguing in Publication record for this book is available from the British Library.

All work contributed to this book is new, previously-unpublished material. The views expressed in this book are those of the authors, but not necessarily of the publisher.

For electronic access to this publication, please contact: eresources@igi-global.com.

Advances in Marketing, Customer Relationship Management, and E-Services (AMCRMES) Book Series

Eldon Y. Li
*National Chengchi University, Taiwan &
California Polytechnic State University, USA*

ISSN: 2327-5502
EISSN: 2327-5529

Mission

Business processes, services, and communications are important factors in the management of good customer relationship, which is the foundation of any well organized business. Technology continues to play a vital role in the organization and automation of business processes for marketing, sales, and customer service. These features aid in the attraction of new clients and maintaining existing relationships.

The Advances in Marketing, Customer Relationship Management, and E-Services (AMCRMES) Book Series addresses success factors for customer relationship management, marketing, and electronic services and its performance outcomes. This collection of reference source covers aspects of consumer behavior and marketing business strategies aiming towards researchers, scholars, and practitioners in the fields of marketing management.

Coverage

- Online Community Management and Behavior
- CRM strategies
- Electronic Services
- B2B marketing
- Social Networking and Marketing
- Legal Considerations in E-Marketing
- Cases on CRM Implementation
- Cases on Electronic Services
- Mobile services
- Web Mining and Marketing

IGI Global is currently accepting manuscripts for publication within this series. To submit a proposal for a volume in this series, please contact our Acquisition Editors at Acquisitions@igi-global.com or visit: http://www.igi-global.com/publish/.

The Advances in Marketing, Customer Relationship Management, and E-Services (AMCRMES) Book Series (ISSN 2327-5502) is published by IGI Global, 701 E. Chocolate Avenue, Hershey, PA 17033-1240, USA, www.igi-global.com. This series is composed of titles available for purchase individually; each title is edited to be contextually exclusive from any other title within the series. For pricing and ordering information please visit http://www.igi-global.com/book-series/advances-marketing-customer-relationship-management/37150. Postmaster: Send all address changes to above address. Copyright © 2016 IGI Global. All rights, including translation in other languages reserved by the publisher. No part of this series may be reproduced or used in any form or by any means – graphics, electronic, or mechanical, including photocopying, recording, taping, or information and retrieval systems – without written permission from the publisher, except for non commercial, educational use, including classroom teaching purposes. The views expressed in this series are those of the authors, but not necessarily of IGI Global.

Titles in this Series

For a list of additional titles in this series, please visit: www.igi-global.com

Trends and Innovations in Marketing Information Systems
Theodosios Tsiakis (Alexander Technological Educational Institute of Thessaloniki, Greece)
Business Science Reference • copyright 2015 • 455pp • H/C (ISBN: 9781466684591) • US $225.00 (our price)

Capturing, Analyzing, and Managing Word-of-Mouth in the Digital Marketplace
Sumangla Rathore (Sir Padampat Singhania University, India) and Avinash Panwar (Sir Padampat Singhania University, India)
Business Science Reference • copyright 2016 • 309pp • H/C (ISBN: 9781466694491) • US $200.00 (our price)

Strategic Customer Relationship Management in the Age of Social Media
Amir Khanlari (University of Tehran, Iran)
Business Science Reference • copyright 2015 • 333pp • H/C (ISBN: 9781466685864) • US $200.00 (our price)

Maximizing Commerce and Marketing Strategies through Micro-Blogging
Janée N. Burkhalter (Saint Joseph's University, USA) and Natalie T. Wood (Saint Joseph's University, USA & Edith Cowan University, Australia)
Business Science Reference • copyright 2015 • 354pp • H/C (ISBN: 9781466684089) • US $225.00 (our price)

Analyzing the Cultural Diversity of Consumers in the Global Marketplace
Juan Miguel Alcántara-Pilar (University of Granada, Spain) Salvador del Barrio-García (University of Granada, Spain) Esmeralda Crespo-Almendros (University of Granada, Spain) and Lucia Porcu (University of Granada, Spain)
Business Science Reference • copyright 2015 • 404pp • H/C (ISBN: 9781466682627) • US $200.00 (our price)

Engaging Consumers through Branded Entertainment and Convergent Media
Jose Marti Parreno (Universidad Europea de Valencia, Spain) Carla Ruiz Mafe (Universidad de Valencia, Spain) and Lisa Scribner (University of North Carolina Wilmington, USA)
Business Science Reference • copyright 2015 • 354pp • H/C (ISBN: 9781466683426) • US $205.00 (our price)

Handbook of Research on Integrating Social Media into Strategic Marketing
Nick Hajli (Newcastle University Business School, UK)
Business Science Reference • copyright 2015 • 440pp • H/C (ISBN: 9781466683532) • US $310.00 (our price)

Customer Relationship Management Strategies in the Digital Era
Süphan Nasır (Istanbul University, Turkey)
Business Science Reference • copyright 2015 • 322pp • H/C (ISBN: 9781466682313) • US $200.00 (our price)

www.igi-global.com

701 E. Chocolate Ave., Hershey, PA 17033
Order online at www.igi-global.com or call 717-533-8845 x100
To place a standing order for titles released in this series, contact: cust@igi-global.com
Mon-Fri 8:00 am - 5:00 pm (est) or fax 24 hours a day 717-533-8661

Testimonial

This book will act as a practical guide to the companies and academics involved in the area of innovation, knowledge management, social media and new product development. It intends to present different types of innovations, situations in which they may be useful, the role of KM and different social media tools and technologies to support it. The book is meant to serve business practitioners, academicians and management students.

Dr. Daisy Selematsela
National Research Foundation of South Africa, South Africa

The topics presented in this collection address important issues in organizational learning, innovation, and knowledge management—particularly regarding the interactions among factors including social networks, social media, work environments, organizational processes, and innovation.

Mark C. Harris, Ph.D.
U.S. Air Force (AFOTEC), USA

Editorial Advisory Board

Mark Harris, *U.S. Air Force (AFOTEC), USA*
G. S. Krishnan, *Government of India, India*
Neetu Jain, *Indian Institute of Public Administration*
Atul Rai, *IBM, Singapore*
Mahesh Singh Rana, *National Institute of Technology Patna*
Santosh Rangnekar, *IIT Roorkee, India*
Renu Rastogi, *IIT Roorkee, India*
Eric Tsuai, *The Hong Kong Polytechnic University, Hong Kong*

List of Reviewers

Amitabh Anand, NEOMA Business School, *France*
Luisa Dall'acqua, *Scientific Lyceum (ITA-EU), Germany*
Gunjan Gupta, *CCS University, India & New Age International Publishers, India*
José G. Hernández, *Universidad Metropolitana, Venezuela*
Annika Lorenz, *Hasselt University, Belgium*
Judith Mavodza, *Zayed University, UAE*
Flor Morton, *Tecnológico de Monterrey, Mexico*
Joana Coutinho Sousa, *Brainiac, Portugal*
Bandi Srinivas, *CSIR Human Resource Development Centre, India*
Teresa Treviño, *Tecnológico de Monterrey, Mexico*
Laura Zapata-Cantú, *Tecnológico de Monterrey, Mexico*

Table of Contents

Foreword xvii

Preface xix

Acknowledgment xxvii

Testimonial v

Section 1
Social Media Strategies and Knowledge Management

Chapter 1
Best Practices in Social Media for Knowledge Management: With Special Reference to
Communities 1
M. K. Prasanna Iyer, PromptKPO, India

Chapter 2
Cultural Barriers to Organizational Social Media Adoption 31
Amir Manzoor, Bahria University, Pakistan

Chapter 3
Social Media as Elements of Shared Workspaces: The Multifactory Case Study 46
Giulio Focardi, Osun Solutions, Italy
Lorenza Victoria Salati, Bigmagma, Italy

Chapter 4
Social Aspects of Reverse Logistics and Knowledge Management 65
José G. Hernández, Universidad Metropolitana, Venezuela
María J. García, Minimax Consultores, Venezuela
Gilberto J. Hernández, Minimax Consultores, Venezuela

Chapter 5
Graph Mining and Its Applications in Studying Community-Based Graph under the Preview of
Social Network 94
Bapuji Rao, VITAM, India
Anirban Mitra, VITAM, India

Section 2
Knowledge Management Approaches and Innovation Process

Chapter 6
Implementing KM Lessons from the Frontline 148
    Rusnita Saleh, University of Indonesia, Indonesia
    Niall Sinclair, Independent Researcher, Thailand

Chapter 7
How to Improve Knowledge Exchange by Using Internet Technologies: An Empirical Study in
Small and Medium-Sized Enterprises 176
    Simona Popa, University of Murcia, Spain
    Pedro Soto-Acosta, University of Murcia, Spain

Chapter 8
Mapping the Enterprise Social Network (ESN) Spectrum in Knowledge Management and Product
Innovations 193
    Aparna Venugopal, Indian Institute of Management Kozhikode, India
    T. N. Krishnan, Indian Institute of Management Kozhikode, India

Chapter 9
Digital Technologies as Media to Transfer Knowledge in IT Firms 204
    Laura Zapata-Cantú, Tecnológico de Monterrey, Mexico
    Teresa Treviño, Tecnológico de Monterrey, Mexico
    Flor Morton, Tecnológico de Monterrey, Mexico
    Ernesto López Monterrubio, Vector Casa de Bolsa, Mexico

Chapter 10
Orientism Management (OM): A New Framework to Manage Decisions and Hyper Dynamic
Knowledge Process in a Multi-User Network 218
    Luisa dall'Acqua, Scientific Lyceum TCO, Italy & PHSG, Germany

Chapter 11
Relationship between Knowledge Management and Academic Integrity in a Middle Eastern
University 241
    Judith Mavodza, Zayed University, UAE

Section 3
New Product Development and Managing Innovation

Chapter 12
Managing Innovation within Organizations 266
    Achilleas Boukis, Sussex University, UK

Chapter 13
Start-Up: A New Conceptual Approach of Innovation Process 291
    Joana Coutinho Sousa, Unlimited-Hashtag, Portugal
    Jorge Gaspar, Unlimited-Hashtag, Portugal

Chapter 14
Learning, Using, and Retaining Deep Domain Expertise: Working in Smart R&D
Organizations 317
    Anders Hemre, interKnowledge Technologies, Sweden

Chapter 15
Creating Product Innovation Strategies through Knowledge Management in Global
Business 330
    Kijpokin Kasemsap, Suan Sunandha Rajabhat University, Thailand

Chapter 16
Innovation Landscape Idea to Product Development 358
    Alok Kumar Goel, CSIR Human Resource Development Centre, India
    Puja Singhal, Amity University, India

Compilation of References 370

About the Contributors 411

Index 418

Detailed Table of Contents

Foreword xvii

Preface xix

Acknowledgment xxvii

Testimonial v

Section 1
Social Media Strategies and Knowledge Management

Chapter 1
Best Practices in Social Media for Knowledge Management: With Special Reference to
Communities 1
    M. K. Prasanna Iyer, PromptKPO, India

The spirit of Social Media is in community building, and they have enriched the practice of Knowledge Management in very exciting ways. CoPs and Forums are ideal platforms to share experiences and lessons learnt. Communities are extremely valuable because of their informal, just-in-time, increasingly real-time advantage and cannot be replaced by structured KM platforms. It is this aspect of communities, that new Social Media enhances, in spirit as well as in tools support. Social Media provides multiple user-friendly tools to make it easy to share experiences and Lessons Learnt as they happen, as well as in a curated form. Best practices developed by this author and other practitioners are presented, so that other communities can benefit from them. Cases and anecdotes from organizations across industry sectors enliven the discussions. Emerging trends and innovative use of Social Media, are introduced as benchmarks.

Chapter 2
Cultural Barriers to Organizational Social Media Adoption 31
    Amir Manzoor, Bahria University, Pakistan

Before they became a part of our social lives, most communication technologies were introduced with a business function in mind. Private individuals quickly adopted social media technology as an extension of their personal life. Due to this reason, many organizations are struggling to understand how this technology can benefit their mission, while many more worry that it will devastate productivity and security. Individuals who wield the power of expansive social media networks can significantly alter an organization's credibility and fiscal health. Organizations who harness the massive data warehouses behind these social media networks have the ability to significantly alter individual lives and society at large; for better or worse. However, barriers to organizational social media adoption are more cultural than technical. This chapter analyzes what cultural barriers are being raised against social media adoption and how can management re-align their understanding of social media to better utilize resources and take advantage of the opportunities this technology presents.

Chapter 3
Social Media as Elements of Shared Workspaces: The Multifactory Case Study 46
Giulio Focardi, Osun Solutions, Italy
Lorenza Victoria Salati, Bigmagma, Italy

Shared workplaces are becoming very common within Europe. Multifactories are shared working environment that combine traits of a Coworking Space, a Fab Lab and a Makerspace. One of the traits that characterize a Multifactory is how knowledge exchange brings to innovation. This chapter has its focus on a case study that shows how a traditional SME and a multifactory can work together in order to develop an innovative idea and how Social Media can be parts of an overall strategy set to product innovation.

Chapter 4
Social Aspects of Reverse Logistics and Knowledge Management 65
José G. Hernández, Universidad Metropolitana, Venezuela
María J. García, Minimax Consultores, Venezuela
Gilberto J. Hernández, Minimax Consultores, Venezuela

The main contribution of this chapter is the study of the generation and management knowledge, emphasizing the social aspects, from an area of the Logistic Model Based on Positions (LoMoBaP). The area to use is the Inverse logistics, which is integrated for the Reverse logistics manager, the Compilation and Reception manager and the Classification and use manager. The analysis will be done via dynamic knowledge, studying the upward spiral of knowledge creation, tacit to explicit to tacit. To do this will be constructed tables where the functions of these three positions will be identified and will be discussed, as these functions are involved in the process of management and generation of knowledge, following the processes of Socialization, Externalization, Combination and Internalization, simultaneously that are located in the Ba and knowledge assets are analyzed: Experimental, Conceptual Systemic and Routine Knowledge.

Chapter 5
Graph Mining and Its Applications in Studying Community-Based Graph under the Preview of
Social Network 94
Bapuji Rao, VITAM, India
Anirban Mitra, VITAM, India

One of the fundamental tasks in structured data mining is discovering of frequent sub-structures. These discovered patterns can be used for characterizing structure datasets, classifying and clustering complex structures, building graph indices & performing similarity search in large graph databases. In this chapter, the authors have discussed on use of graph techniques to identify communities and sub-communities and to derive a community structure for social network analysis, information extraction and knowledge management. This chapter contributes towards the graph mining, its application in social network using community based graph. Initial section is related literature and definition of community graph and its usage in social contexts. Detecting common community sub-graph between two community graphs comes under information extraction using graph mining technique. Examples from movie database to village administration were considered here. C++ programming is used and outputs have been included to enhance the reader's interest.

Section 2
Knowledge Management Approaches and Innovation Process

Chapter 6
Implementing KM Lessons from the Frontline 148
    Rusnita Saleh, University of Indonesia, Indonesia
    Niall Sinclair, Independent Researcher, Thailand

While the KM initiative highlighted in the case study in the previous section is still in its formative stages, it would be safe to say that the majority of KM implementation projects are likely to take anywhere between one to three years to even begin to have any significant impact on the organizations involved. In other words, KM is something that takes time to embed itself into the working fabric of the organization, and so anyone who thinks that KM implementation is going to be a short-term affair is fooling themselves; as well as setting a dangerous and unattainable level of expectation in any potential stakeholders. Overall, there are many barriers that stand in the way of successfully implementing KM, whether it is a lack of access to current information, a lack of clear communications, difficulty in transferring knowledge and information, difficulty in maintaining the relevance and currency of knowledge and information, lack of support from senior managers, or limited resources – both in time and personnel.

Chapter 7
How to Improve Knowledge Exchange by Using Internet Technologies: An Empirical Study in
Small and Medium-Sized Enterprises 176
    Simona Popa, University of Murcia, Spain
    Pedro Soto-Acosta, University of Murcia, Spain

This paper seeks to extend previous studies on the use of Internet technologies and knowledge management by analyzing factors affecting Web knowledge exchange in small and medium-sized enterprises (SMEs). More specifically, by drawing on the technology-organization-environment framework, a model to examine how distinct contextual factors influence Web knowledge exchange in SMEs is developed. The hypotheses are tested by using structural equation modelling on a large sample of Spanish SMEs from different industries. Results suggest that IT expertise and commitment-based human resource practices positively affect Web knowledge exchange, with the latter being the strongest factor in our proposed model. In contrast, a negative relationship is found between competition and Web knowledge exchange.

Chapter 8
Mapping the Enterprise Social Network (ESN) Spectrum in Knowledge Management and Product Innovations... 193

Aparna Venugopal, Indian Institute of Management Kozhikode, India
T. N. Krishnan, Indian Institute of Management Kozhikode, India

This book chapter unravels the difference brought into traditional knowledge management due to the use of enterprise social networks (ESNs). The advantages and barriers to the use of ESNs in organizations are also explained. The ESN spectrum and the corresponding knowledge management practices and innovation types are clearly delineated in this chapter. There are myriads of human as well as social factors affecting the usage and implementation of ESNs in organizations. This book chapter explores these factors too. Organizations may require special mechanisms to utilize the knowledge shared via ESNs and transform them into innovations. The book chapter suggests a few of these mechanisms. In this book chapter we use the theory of technology acceptance and works testing the theory of media richness to understand the varied uses of ESNs in knowledge management and innovation in organizations.

Chapter 9
Digital Technologies as Media to Transfer Knowledge in IT Firms.. 204

Laura Zapata-Cantú, Tecnológico de Monterrey, Mexico
Teresa Treviño, Tecnológico de Monterrey, Mexico
Flor Morton, Tecnológico de Monterrey, Mexico
Ernesto López Monterrubio, Vector Casa de Bolsa, Mexico

During the last decade, improvements in information and communication technologies have made possible the transformation of knowledge transfer processes from purely informal to increasingly formal and more diverse communication mechanisms that enrich intra-organizational communication channels. In this chapter, the authors followed a case study approach to analyze three Mexican companies with the objective of understanding how companies in the IT sector are implementing digital technologies to achieve knowledge transfer in their organizations. The findings suggest that workers seek and choose tools that can be personalized and customized to adapt to their own needs. New digital technologies are proving to be a new and relevant channel of communication among people: therefore, these should be considered to be one possible way to motivate knowledge transfer at work.

Chapter 10
Orientism Management (OM): A New Framework to Manage Decisions and Hyper Dynamic Knowledge Process in a Multi-User Network... 218

Luisa dall'Acqua, Scientific Lyceum TCO, Italy & PHSG, Germany

The model of learning/training in the 21st century requires the evaluation of new and better ways to measure what matters, diagnosing strengths and weaknesses, to improve people performance, and to involve multiple stakeholders in the process of designing, conducting and use of knowledge. The thesis is that the orientation, today, is no longer limited only to outline the direction of a professional career, but it concerns "Life designing" over which "Work designing". This chapter intends to describe a new interpretative paradigm, Orientism, to understand and manage fluid nature of knowledge, but at the same time to seize and manage the unpredictability and risks of the dynamics of knowledge management in relationships complex environment, in a society. Element of news are 5 key factors and criteria to direct and motivate people in choosing process, and following 10 different and key relationships between them. They define areas of management to improve own personal leadership and success. The concept becomes the conceptual base of an Instructional Design Model (PENTHA 2.0).

Chapter 11
Relationship between Knowledge Management and Academic Integrity in a Middle Eastern University 241
Judith Mavodza, Zayed University, UAE

The difference between knowledge sharing as enabled in a knowledge management (KM) environment, and academic honesty continuously needs clarification and reinforcement in academic institutions. Teaching includes getting students to realize that knowledge is an asset that can be ethically used for creativity and innovation, resulting in the enhancement of the corporate image and effectiveness of a university. Studies have confirmed that academic dishonesty is an ethical challenge facing many academic institutions of higher learning. In the Middle East, the use of English as a second language is often cited as a contributing factor to students' plagiarizing, but the problem extends to the use of Arabic language sources too. Conflicts in approach may arise because KM works well in an environment of sharing, and yet acknowledging academic productivity of others may not always happen spontaneously. This is a challenge faced in MOOCs and by institutions of higher learning the world over.

Section 3
New Product Development and Managing Innovation

Chapter 12
Managing Innovation within Organizations 266
Achilleas Boukis, Sussex University, UK

The management of innovation projects within organisations forms the focal point of this chapter. First, the role of various intra-organizational contingencies that affect innovation performance is addressed. Second, several appropriate management practices are identified which play an important role for innovation success. Third, various ways that customer knowledge can successfully be integrated in innovation efforts are discussed. Fourth, top management's role in innovation projects is analysed. Fifth, the importance of interfirm collaborative partnerships for innovation success is described. Finally, various innovation benefits are identified so that organizations are able to prioritize between different innovation outcomes.

Chapter 13
Start-Up: A New Conceptual Approach of Innovation Process 291
Joana Coutinho Sousa, Unlimited-Hashtag, Portugal
Jorge Gaspar, Unlimited-Hashtag, Portugal

Nowadays, we are witnessing an increase of innovation both on start-up and SME. The implementation of innovation has a strong impact in the knowledge of economy. The ability of human being in creating it can be defined as a basic skill in a global economy, involving learning as an essential dynamism of the competition. Furthermore, the research and development activities are very important not only for universities and companies but also for the global economy. This paper presents a new conceptual approach for innovation process in start-ups and a new methodology to know how long the innovation process must take. The conceptual approach proposed is divided into seven interactive steps: 1) Have an idea (product, service, process, business/marketing; 2) Analyze the state-of-the-art and the market; 3) R&D activities and Intellectual Property; 4) Listen the market; 5) Define a flexible business plan; 6) Find a business partner; and 7) Go-to-market. Regarding the time of innovation, the presented methodology is based on five Porter's Forces.

Chapter 14
Learning, Using, and Retaining Deep Domain Expertise: Working in Smart R&D Organizations 317
Anders Hemre, interKnowledge Technologies, Sweden

New product development is a knowledge intensive undertaking. It involves creative exploration, skilled task execution and complex problem solving. For such activities to be effective, relevant domain expertise is required. Knowledge and expertise are not the same. Expertise is not the expert's knowledge, but the superior ability to put acquired knowledge and experience to work in a professional domain. Knowledge can be transferred, but expertise has to be learned. Organizations need to be aware of the difference when making deliberate efforts to maximize the operational value of their knowledge and expertise. This chapter explains the nature of domain expertise, how it is acquired and its crucial role in new product development.

Chapter 15
Creating Product Innovation Strategies through Knowledge Management in Global Business 330
Kijpokin Kasemsap, Suan Sunandha Rajabhat University, Thailand

This chapter aims to create product innovation strategies through knowledge management (KM) in global business, thus explaining the theoretical and practical concepts of product innovation strategy and KM; the significance of product innovation strategies and KM in global business; and the creation of product innovation strategies through KM in global business. The capability of product innovation strategies and KM is significant for modern organizations that seek to serve suppliers and customers, increase business performance, strengthen competitiveness, and attain regular success in global business. Modern organizations should establish a strategic plan to create product innovation strategies through KM. The chapter argues that creating product innovation strategies through KM has the potential to improve organizational performance and achieve strategic goals in global business.

Chapter 16
Innovation Landscape Idea to Product Development 358
Alok Kumar Goel, CSIR Human Resource Development Centre, India
Puja Singhal, Amity University, India

This study seeks to address various phases, challenges and the principles influencing transforming an idea into a product innovation. This study is particularly relevant in light of the driving role given to small scale enterprises by the supporting policies and practices in the process of transforming India into an innovation-oriented nation and leading 'Make in India' program. Based on a multi-disciplinary the framework discussed in this study highlights a number of internal processes and external network attributes, their interactions and moderating relationships as related to their impact on Indian small scale enterprises' product innovation capabilities. This study offers an overview of the factors that affect product innovation capabilities, with particular reference to entrepreneurial orientation of Indian Small and Medium Enterprises (SMEs). This study showcase provocative views that considers the concept of innovation ecosystem and new product development central to its philosophy and objectives.

Compilation of References 370

About the Contributors 411

Index 418

Foreword

Knowledge Management (KM) encompasses a range of practices used by organizations to identify, create, preserve, represent and share knowledge for reuse, business intelligence, awareness and continuous learning to ensure process continuity among other KM possibilities. Trends in social media are changing the face of personal interactions and the manner in which business operations are conducted. The perceived interlinking relationship between innovation as part of generation of new knowledge, knowledge management and social media is seen as an approach that may influence knowledge management to collect new ideas and measure their acceptanceas part of the contribution to the knowledge economy and societal impact. This however, depends on the ability of individuals and groups to progressively develop and radically innovate functional processes, products and services. Social media tools are intuitive to use and allow people to share information, collaborate, discuss common interests and build relationships. The digital element of social media is used more increasingly both internally and externally to the enterprise in the context of its business and customers, which facilitates the generation of volumes of structured, semi-structured and unstructured content and data including metadata. With this trend well underway, business and in particular small medium enterprises (SME's) or "starter companies"are beginning to explore how social media can help them enter new markets, grow and improve profits, attract and gain new clients and not just with common practices such as outbound marketing, but to enhance business interactions also as part of the innovation and product development process. Taken together, this building block of a digital enterprise generates a lot of information, which enhances innovation capabilities and fostering collaboration and partnerships across different stakeholders. This enables the formation of distributed Communities of Practices (CoPs) and special interest groups with the added advantage of bringing new insights and enabling sophisticated analysis on top of the generated information by the peers.

Innovation in this book implies new products, processes and services undertaken by organizations, which may be attained through interacting knowledge processes. These processes comprise the engagement of prevailing knowledge from the external environment, the generation of new knowledge through innovative thinking and interchange of ideas, the rapid dissemination of ideas and visions through knowledge networking. The aim of this book is to explore the possible use of knowledge management and social media within organizations as a catalyst for enhancing product innovation, competitive intelligence and for remaining relevant in the 21st century.

There is a perceived need for the development of a strategic *'Knowledge Innovation'* framework that will assist in gathering and sourcing stimulating ideas inside an organisation (participative innovation) and outside (open innovation) and between organizations (global innovation). This book intends to fulfil this missing approach. The proposed framework aims to address approaches to handling the innovation ecosystem, including the measurement of outputs on a regular basis, the capacity to innovate and the resulting benefits. That is why this book is contemporary and timely. Furthermore, the book aims to share a different perspective on innovation practices, KM processes in relation to social media applications and tools that are perceived to set the groundwork for an innovative and successful product development.

Social media enables new modes of communication between an organization's employees and facilitates knowledge-sharing. It's goal is to improve communication, organizational efficiency, and individual effectiveness. In discussing social media as a vehicle of transformational leadership this book will reveal untapped benefits of social media in knowledge sharing and innovation context and examine where and how it could be adopted. Organizational leaders are now seeking ways to share knowledge with both internal and external stakeholders driven by concerns such as innovating new products, the impending retirement of baby boomers, the embracing of the technocrats "Y-generation" and a host of other organizational challenges. Social media is perceived to address these challenges as it provides flexible, agile, and intuitive solutions for connecting people, facilitating coordination, communication, and collaboration. This book will also elicit perspectives from the current KM and social media technologies which consider the concepts of knowledge sharing, innovation ecosystem and product development central to its philosophy and objectives. It aims to shed light on how the next wave of social media can be harnessed to further innovation.

This book illustrates in depth the theories and techniques of social media and KM in its possible applications to organizations to enhance innovation efforts and productivity. The book is intended to highlight emerging research and practice at the dynamic intersection of these fields, where individuals, organizations, industries and nations are harnessing innovation to achieve and sustain growth in contribution to knowledge generation and contribution to the knowledge economy. The methodologies and tools explained in the book are applicable to academics, managers, ICT, information and business students, Technology Transfer Offices (TTO) and consultants to examine specific aspects of knowledge management and knowledge creation in the organization and in future studies of innovation.

Daisy Selematsela
National Research Foundation of South Africa, South Africa

Daisy Selematsela *is Executive Director of the Knowledge Management Corporate, National Research Foundation of South Africa.*

Preface

In 21st century global environment, knowledge is considered to be the most important strategic resource in organizations (Uziene, 2010) and the management of this knowledge is considered critical for innovation and to attain competitive advantage (Drucker, 2001). To remain innovative managing knowledge successfully has become one of the greatest organizational challenges today. Organizations operate in all the areas through people and it is their skill and knowledge which need to be cultivated and then leveraged to create new innovative product. Knowledge exists and is shared at different levels in organizations. Knowledge acquires greater value when it forms part of knowledge creation or transfer process. The success or failure of an organization is directly related to the way in which knowledge is managed (Rana and Goel, 2015). If organizations have to capitalize on the knowledge they possess, they have to understand how knowledge is created, shared, and used within the organization. Knowledge specific to organizations, such as what employees know about organizational processes, products, customers and their competitive environment is called organizational knowledge. Organizations generally do not manage knowledge well and they behave "much like individuals because they too know more than they put to use" (Wellman, 2009). Any organization's success will finally depend on the speed at which it can generate, capture and disseminate new knowledge and then use this knowledge to develop capabilities that cannot easily be copied by competitors.

In organizations, there are two types of knowledge, namely explicit (tangible) and tacit knowledge (intangible). Nonaka (1990) described four knowledge conversion processes viz. socialization, externalization, combination, and internalization, in the form of SECI model. Each process involves converting one form of knowledge (tacit or explicit) into other (tacit or explicit). Knowledge Management (KM) is a systematic and integrative process of coordinating organization-wide activities of acquiring, creating, storing, sharing, diffusing, developing, and deploying knowledge by individuals and groups in pursuit of major organizational goals (Rastogi, 2000). Every organization has its own way of dealing with data, information and knowledge and it creates its own structures, jobs and systems for that purpose (Nonaka et al., 2000). Therefore, there are no standard methods for leveraging knowledge; the best way is to start with the existing structures and methods and then apply them effectively to create new products and services to achieve the organization's business objectives' (Goel et.al., 2010a).

Knowledge management involves all aspects of an organization - social, technological and human. To develop new product in organizations, managers must continue to develop new knowledge, skills, and experience within their workforce. Infact, we can say that knowledge management is an important factor for the product innovation in any organization in present era of knowledge economy. Knowledge management is being defined into three dimensions viz. KM processes, KM effectiveness and socio-technical support (Lin, 2007). KM processes are further categorised into four factors namely knowledge acquisition (driven by strategy in which an organization determines what knowledge is needed, what it has and then fills in the gap by developing new knowledge or acquiring it); knowledge conversion (involves organizing, structuring, storing, combining, and linking digital storage such as documents and images with knowledge units); knowledge application (process of making knowledge active and relevant for the firm in creating value) and knowledge protection (ability to protect organizational knowledge from illegal or inappropriate use or theft).

Effective management of the knowledge is considered essential to success in contemporary organizations (Chen and Chen, 2005). Knowledge management effectiveness is categorized into two factors viz. individual-level effectiveness (measures whether employees receive and understand the knowledge required to perform their tasks) and organization-level effectiveness (improving organizational innovativeness and performance). KM effectiveness is measured in terms of realizing successful outcomes of KM processes, including generating, sharing and applying knowledge, increasing knowledge satisfaction and enhancing organizational performance (Gupta and Govindarajan, 2000; Chou et. al, 2005). The present book discusses as to how successful social media resource strategies pave way for knowledge management and promote creativity and innovation within and among employees in the organization.

Knowledge is first acquired in the human brain and then transmitted within the organization. According to Nonaka (1994) knowledge creation is a spiral process of interactions between explicit and tacit knowledge. These two forms of knowledge are complementary to each other and both are crucial to knowledge creation. The interactions between them lead to creation of new knowledge. The combination of the two categories makes it possible to conceptualize four conversion patterns. The four modes of knowledge conversion interact in the spiral of knowledge creation. The spiral becomes larger in scale as it moves up through organizational levels and can trigger new spirals of knowledge creation. Nonaka (1990) described four knowledge conversion processes in the form of SECI model that is socialization, externalization, combination and internalization. Each process involves converting one form of knowledge (tacit or explicit) into other (tacit or explicit). Knowledge conversion is a social interaction among individuals and is not confined within an individual. The ability to create new knowledge enables organizations to respond quickly and effectively to a changing environment.

Socialization involves capturing knowledge through physical proximity. Knowledge is acquired from outside the organization through direct interactions with suppliers and customers. Capturing tacit knowledge embedded within the organization by walking around inside the organization is another process of acquiring knowledge. In this way, organizations achieve success if they create new knowledge spread across the organization and incorporate it into new technologies and products (Nonaka and Takeuchi, 1995). In his study Rai (2011) developed a theoretical integrative framework for organizational knowledge management. He presented a new framework by modifying the 'competing value framework' and added a new dimension which represents ethical and trusting culture and then integrates it with the SECI model of knowledge creation and conversion. He identified the conceptual parallels between the two frameworks and analyzed the interaction effects between the dimensions. The two modes of knowledge creation which employ explicit knowledge as an input represent 'exploitation' processes. The other two modes which use tacit knowledge as an input represent 'exploration' processes.

In the present book authors have addressed the theme based on the premise that in the present knowledge economy, knowledge is converted through social media also i.e. Facebook, Twitter, YouTube, wiki, communities, blogs, and LinkedIn, etc., and social media strategies play a vital role in new knowledge creation and establishing the knowledge networks which is an important stage for product innovation. Social media has transformed and revolutionized the whole scenario of knowledge creation, transfer,

Preface

sharing, protection and dissemination. It has integrated all the stakeholders of innovation eco-system at one platform.

In the present juncture creation of new knowledge has undergone sea change vis-a-vis the concepts propounded by Nonaka (1990) and Rai (2011). In our opinion during all phases of knowledge creation and conversion either in 'SECI' processes as explained by Nonaka (1990) or in 'exploitation and exploration' processes as inunciated by Rai (2011), social media has started playing pivotal role as far as connecting innovator to manufacturer to supplier to seller to consumer to innovator is concerned as shown in conceptual framework of social media enabled SECI process given below. The whole book is based on this proposition.

Socio-technical support is further defined in the form of organizational support and IT-diffusion. Social media enables new modes of communication between an organization's employees and facilitates knowledge-sharing. Its goal is to improve communication, organizational efficiency, and individual effectiveness. In discussing social media as a vehicle of transformational leadership this book reveals untapped benefits of social media in knowledge sharing and innovation context and examine where and how it could be adopted. Organizational leaders are now seeking ways to share knowledge with both internal and external stakeholders driven by concerns such as innovating new products, the impending retirement of baby boomers and a host of other organizational challenges (Rana and Goel, 2014). Social media addresses this problem head-on and provides flexible, agile, and intuitive solutions for connecting people with people and facilitating coordination, communication, and collaboration. Knowledge management and the role of social media strategies in product innovation are still in their infancy.

Goel and Rastogi (2011) examined the role of social media as to how it helps in sharing knowledge among knowledge workers particularly within the Indian knowledge intensive organizations and whether creating an environment that encourages and supports knowledge sharing among employees provides an organization with competitive advantage. They also investigated the reasons and circumstances that result in impediments for employees seeking to share their working knowledge. The study offered very useful insights as to how social media provides a user friendly interface helping individuals and project groups to share and enhance knowledge. Some of the salient features of using ICT in knowledge management in Indian knowledge intensive industries were: Wiki; Content Repository; Communities; Search; Forums; Ask an Expert; Blogs; Videoconferencing etc. (Goel et al., 2009). To explore the power of collaborative documentation Wikis are created and maintained to share knowledge. The details available in Wikis are very user friendly and all the needed data/details are listed in Wiki. Information and communication technologies are used to provide a search engine on KM portal which can find the match to key words from all sites or even from specific locations like communities, blogs etc. within the organization (Goel et.al, 2010b; Tiwana, 2003).

The emerging global economy has increasingly put a premium on the ability of firms to quickly and accurately evaluate new market opportunities, new products and other strategic business decisions. Social media sharing plays a key role for such coordination in knowledge sharing. Knowledge management research is still relatively new and knowledge management literature focused primarily on the relevance of knowledge, the contribution of knowledge workers and the advancement of knowledge-based organizations. There is not enough literature which refers to all the dimensions of knowledge management and social media strategies and their inter-relationship with the dimensions of product innovation. A research gap has been observed to explore knowledge management and social media strategies along with their variables. This book will fulfil this gap and showcase pertinent views that derive from the current knowledge management and social media technologies which consider the concepts of knowledge shar-

Figure 1. Conceptual framework of social media enabled SECI process
(Source: Editors, Alok Goel and Puja Singhal, 2015)

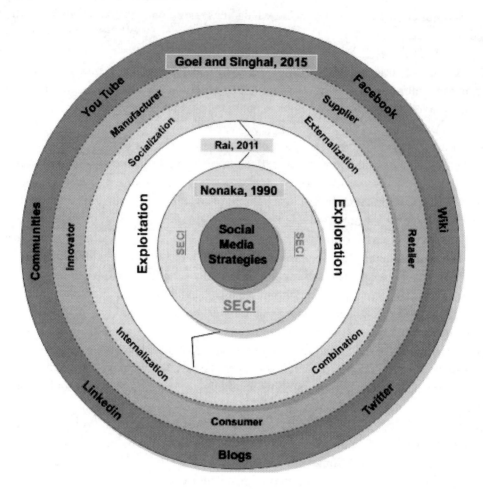

ing, innovation ecosystem and product development central to its philosophy and objectives. It focuses on how the next wave of social media can be harnessed to further innovation.

ORGANIZATION OF THE BOOK

The book is organized into sixteen chapters. A brief description of each of the chapters follows:

Chapter 1

This chapter emphasizes the spirit of Social Media in community building. Communities are extremely valuable because of their informal, just-in-time, increasingly real-time advantage and cannot be replaced by structured KM platforms. It is this aspect of communities, that new Social Media enhances, in spirit as well as in tools support. Best practices developed by this author and other practitioners are presented in this chapter so that other communities can benefit from them. Cases and anecdotes from organizations

Preface

across industry sectors enliven the discussions. Emerging trends and innovative use of Social Media, are introduced as benchmarks.

Chapter 2

This chapter analyzes what cultural barriers are being raised against social media adoption and how can management re-align their understanding of social media to better utilize resources and take advantage of the opportunities this technology presents.

Chapter 3

This chapter establishes the need of Shared workplaces which are becoming very common within Europe. Multifactories are shared working environment that combine traits of a Coworking Space, a Fab Lab and a Makerspace. One of the traits that characterize a Multifactory is how knowledge exchange brings to innovation. This chapter has its focus on a case study that shows how a traditional SME and a multifactory can work together in order to develop an innovative idea and how Social Media can be parts of an overall strategy set to product innovation.

Chapter 4

The main contribution of this chapter is the study of the generation and management knowledge, emphasizing the social aspects, from an area of the Logistic Model Based on Positions (LoMoBaP). The area to use is the Inverse logistics, which is integrated for the Reverse logistics manager, the Compilation and Reception manager and the Classification and use manager. The analysis has been done via dynamic knowledge, studying the upward spiral of knowledge creation, tacit to explicit to tacit.

Chapter 5

In this chapter, the authors have addresses the issues related to the use of graph techniques to identify communities and sub-communities and to derive a community structure for social network analysis, information extraction and knowledge management. This chapter contributes towards the graph mining, its application in social network using community based graph.

Chapter 6

In this chapter authors discusses about many barriers that stand in the way of successfully implementing KM, whether it is a lack of access to current information, a lack of clear communications, difficulty in transferring knowledge and information, difficulty in maintaining the relevance and currency of knowledge and information, lack of support from senior managers, or limited resources - both in time and personnel.

Chapter 7

This chapter seeks to extend previous studies on the use of Internet technologies and knowledge management by analyzing factors affecting Web knowledge exchange in small and medium-sized enterprises

(SMEs). More specifically, by drawing on the technology-organization-environment framework, a model to examine how distinct contextual factors influence Web knowledge exchange in SMEs is developed.

Chapter 8

This book chapter unravels the difference brought into traditional knowledge management due to the use of Enterprise Social Networks (ESNs). The advantages and barriers to the use of ESNs in organizations are also explained. The ESN spectrum and the corresponding knowledge management practices and innovation types are clearly delineated in this chapter. In this book chapter authors have used the theory of technology acceptance and works testing the theory of media richness to understand the varied uses of ESNs in knowledge management and innovation in organizations.

Chapter 9

In this chapter, the authors followed a case study approach to analyze three Mexican companies with the objective of understanding how companies in the IT sector are implementing digital technologies to achieve knowledge transfer in their organizations.

Chapter 10

This chapter intends to describe a new interpretative paradigm, Orientism, to understand and manage fluid nature of knowledge, but at the same time to seize and manage the unpredictability and risks of the dynamics of knowledge management in relationships complex environment, in a society. Author also explains an Instructional Design Model (PENTHA 2.0).

Chapter 11

This chapter uses a KM approach in discussing the academic integrity topic. The view is that good academic conduct or academic integrity helps students learn, and the academe guides them in order to attain high quality qualifications. Thus, the better the quality of perceived products of a university, the more likely employers are encouraged to provide internship opportunities, hire the graduating students, and the more the reputation of the university is perceived to be superior.

Chapter 12

The management of innovation projects within organisations forms the focal point of this chapter. Like the role of various intra-organizational contingencies, effect of several appropriate management practices, various ways that customer knowledge can successfully be integrated in innovation efforts are discussed.

Chapter 13

This paper presents a new conceptual approach for innovation process in start-ups and a new methodology to know how long the innovation process must take. The conceptual approach proposed is divided into seven interactive steps: 1) Have an idea (product, service, process, business/marketing; 2) Analyze

Preface

the state-of-the-art and the market; 3) R&D activities and Intellectual Property; 4) Listen the market; 5) Define a flexible business plan; 6) Find a business partner; and 7) Go-to-market.

Chapter 14

This chapter discusses the nature of domain expertise, how it is acquired and its crucial role in new product development. According to the author Organizations need to be aware of the difference when making deliberate efforts to maximize the operational value of their knowledge and expertise.

Chapter 15

This chapter aims to create product innovation strategies through knowledge management (KM) in global business, thus explaining the theoretical and practical concepts of product innovation strategy and KM; the significance of product innovation strategies and KM in global business; and the creation of product innovation strategies through KM in global business. The chapter also argues that creating product innovation strategies through KM has the potential to improve organizational performance and achieve strategic goals in global business.

Chapter 16

This study offers an overview of the factors that affect product innovation capabilities, with particular reference to entrepreneurial orientation of Indian Small and Medium Enterprises (SMEs). This practitioner oriented paper is build upon a case study, which explores the product innovation process at an Indian SME and integrates the findings with contemporary knowledge on knowledge creation and innovation. This study showcase provocative views that considers the concept of innovation ecosystem and new product development central to its philosophy and objectives.

Alok Kumar Goel
CSIR Human Resource Development Centre, India

Puja Singhal
Amity University, India

REFERENCES

Chen, M., & Chen, A. (2005). Integrating option model and knowledge management performance measures: An empirical study. *Journal of Information Science, 31*(5), 381–393. doi:10.1177/0165551505055402

Chou, T. C., Chang, P. L., Tsai, C. T., & Cheng, Y. P. (2005). Internal learning climate, knowledge management process and perceived knowledge management satisfaction. *Journal of Information Science, 31*(4), 283–296. doi:10.1177/0165551505054171

Drucker, P. F. (2001). The next society - A survey of the near future. *The Economist, 361*(8246), 1-5.

Goel, A., Gupta, N., & Rastogi, R. (2010b). Role of virtual organization in knowledge management. In *Management: Concepts, cases & models*. Excel Publishers.

Goel, A., Rana, G., & Rastogi, R. (2009). Knowledge management implementation in Indian public sector. In *Enhancing organizational performance through strategic initiatives*. Macmillan Publishers India Ltd.

Goel, A., & Rastogi, R. (2011). Knowledge sharing and competitiveness: a study from Indian IT industry. In *Positive initiatives for organizational change and transformation*. Macmillan Publishers India Ltd.

Goel, A. K., Sharma, G. R., & Rastogi, R. (2010a). Knowledge management implementation in NTPC: An Indian PSU. *Emerald International Journal of Management Decision*, *48*(3), 383–395. doi:10.1108/00251741011037756

Gupta, A. K., & Govindarajan, V. (2000). Knowledge flows within multinational corporations. *Strategic Management Journal*, *21*(4), 473–479. doi:10.1002/(SICI)1097-0266(200004)21:4<473::AID-SMJ84>3.0.CO;2-I

Lin, H. F. (2007a). A stage model of knowledge management: An empirical investigation of process and effectiveness. *Journal of Information Science*, *33*(6); 643–659. doi:10.1177/0165551506076395

Nonaka, I. (1990). *A theory of organizational knowledge creation*. Nihon Keizai Shimbun-sha.

Nonaka, I. (1994). A dynamic theory of organizational knowledge creation. *Organization Science*, *5*(1), 14–37. doi:10.1287/orsc.5.1.14

Nonaka, I., & Takeuchi, H. (1995). *The knowledge-creating company: How Japanese companies create the dynamics of innovation*. Oxford University Press.

Nonaka, I., Toyama, R., & Konno, N. (2000). SECI, Ba and leadership: A unified model of dynamic knowledge creation. *Long Range Planning*, *33*(1), 5–34. doi:10.1016/S0024-6301(99)00115-6

Rai, R. K. (2011). Knowledge management and organizational culture: A theoretical integrative framework. *Journal of Knowledge Management*, *15*(5), 779–801. doi:10.1108/13673271111174320

Rana, G., & Goel, A. (2014). Ethan learns to be a learning organization. *Human Resource Management International Digest*, *22*(6), 12–14. doi:10.1108/HRMID-08-2014-0114

Rana, G., & Goel, A. (2015). Stars of the future give Bhushan Power and Steel the edge. *Human Resource Management International Digest*, *23*(1), 15–17. doi:10.1108/HRMID-12-2014-0158

Rastogi, P. N. (2000). Knowledge management and intellectual capital - The new virtuous reality of competitiveness. *Human Systems Management*, *19*(1), 39–48.

Tiwana, A. (2003). *The knowledge management toolkit: Orchestrating IT, strategy and knowledge platforms*. Prentice-Hall.

Uziene, L. (2010). Model of organizational intellectual capital measurement. *The Engineering Economist*, *21*(2), 151–159.

Acknowledgment

We would like to acknowledge the help of all the people involved in this project and more specifically, the authors and reviewers who took part in the review process. Without their support, this book would not have become a reality.

First, we would like to thank each one of the authors for their contributions. Our sincere gratitude goes to the chapter's authors who contributed their time and expertise to this book. It gives us immense pleasure to express our deepest sense of gratitude and heartiest thanks to Prof. Renu Rastogi and Prof. Santosh Rangnekar, Faculties, Department of Management Studies, IIT, Roorkee, India and Prof. Wim Vanhaverbeke, Prof. Nadine Roijakkers, Faculties, Hasselt University, Belgium for their invaluable guidance, constant encouragement and moral support in bringing out this book.

We as editors wish to acknowledge the valuable contributions of all the reviewers and Dr. Mark Harris, Divisional Manager, Knowledge Management Applications Development, Technology Centre, USA and Dr Daisy Selematsela, Executive Director, Knowledge Management Corporate, National Research Foundation of South Africa regarding the improvement of quality, coherence, and content presentation of chapters. Most of the authors also served as referees; we highly appreciate their double task.

We wish to acknowledge the very valuable help we received from our Seniors, Colleagues and friends who came forward to extend their support. We wish to place on record our deep appreciation and thanks to Mr. Keith Greenberg, Managing Editor and Ms. Caitlyn Martin and Ms. Eleana Wehr, Book Development Editors, IGI Global for their support, cooperation and attention to details to bring out the publication of this book in time.

Lastly, we wish to thank our families for their understanding and support in providing us all the necessary facilities and affectionate environment to enable us to complete our work and above all we are immensely thankful to the Almighty.

Alok Kumar Goel
CSIR Human Resource Development Centre, India

Puja Singhal
Amity University, India

Section 1
Social Media Strategies and Knowledge Management

Chapter 1
Best Practices in Social Media for Knowledge Management:
With Special Reference to Communities

M. K. Prasanna Iyer
PromptKPO, India

ABSTRACT

The spirit of Social Media is in community building, and they have enriched the practice of Knowledge Management in very exciting ways. CoPs and Forums are ideal platforms to share experiences and lessons learnt. Communities are extremely valuable because of their informal, just-in-time, increasingly real-time advantage and cannot be replaced by structured KM platforms. It is this aspect of communities, that new Social Media enhances, in spirit as well as in tools support. Social Media provides multiple user-friendly tools to make it easy to share experiences and Lessons Learnt as they happen, as well as in a curated form. Best practices developed by this author and other practitioners are presented, so that other communities can benefit from them. Cases and anecdotes from organizations across industry sectors enliven the discussions. Emerging trends and innovative use of Social Media, are introduced as benchmarks.

INTRODUCTION

The practice of Knowledge Management is enriched by Best Practices developed within the context of each organization and its strategic priorities. The spirit of Social Media is in community building; and they have enriched the practice of Knowledge Management in very exciting ways. Communities of Practice (CoPs) and Forums have been potent tools to organically foster sharing of expertise and experience, actionable learning, innovation, process improvement and engagement. The wide ranges of social media available today, are enablers in this endeavour. Best practices developed by this author and other practitioners are presented so that other communities can benefit from them. Beginning with a real-life scenario to introduce the nitty-grittys of community building, several learnings, and Best Practices and theoretical underpinnings are explained.

DOI: 10.4018/978-1-4666-9607-5.ch001

Imagine this scenario: Saritha is an engineer working on two projects within a business unit. These are prestigious and demanding projects and she wants to give her best to each project. She has two project managers, whom she respects immensely; and teammates, who have not worked on a similar project before. Some of her teammates are located in the US, others are constantly implementing on client sites in Ontario and Tel Aviv. The team also has to consult some subject matter experts on the go.

The primary project manager is convinced that social tools can help improve the project timelines in requirements gathering, planning, documentation, communication with all stakeholders.

There are several challenges and Saritha feels she needs the help of trusted, though not authorized partners. When Saritha faces a problem that stretches her knowledge, she turns to people like Partha, Chiranjeev, Thulasi and ex- manager Arup. Even though they work on their own projects in other business units, they are her real colleagues. They all go back many years. Saritha believes Arup has been there, done it all.

Arup had a successful experience with project wiki. His team member has offered to set up the wiki for the current project. The team had earlier used Google Drive to collaboratively document the project. For informal sketches, they used OneNote. With a wiki, they could save 50% of documentation and communication time. On hind-sight, it can be said that the wiki helped the team the most in requirements gathering. There was greater clarity and commitment for the project team and the client team. And, it helped when requirements changed all the time, which is how all projects are!!In addition, they could track changes made by any team member; there was the advantage of an early start and greater clarity for everybody concerned.

The primary project manager also works well with Arup. At first he needed some convincing that it would help the project if they learned from the experiences of Arup's team, instead of re-inventing the wheel.

It can be safely concluded, that this collaboration helped Saritha and the entire team in their learning on a new domain. Teammates also learnt a lot on practices and processes. Arup's team members were happy with their mentoring opportunity. Saritha also felt comfortable to bring valuable innovations that she had been thinking about for a long time.

In fact, Saritha had earlier in her student days moderated a community of Solid Works designers for the automobile industry. The current project was for the aerospace industry; and there were many similarities. Saritha used best practices from TWIN- a community of technical writers in India.

Now, going back to Aerospace Design Community, Saritha built a forum where all of these members were included. As she was learning about aerospace domain, she prepared PowerPoint presentations, which she hoped she could use for training new project joiners. She also found a number of YouTube, Vimeo, Webinars and Slideshares and shared the links with new forum members. As these new members also began sharing industry news, standards, diagrams, tips and tricks, small tools that they could use, the forum was fast becoming a learning community.

As Saritha reported- most members understand her style of approaching the project, how she learnt, issues she may face and were ready to *explore new ideas* with her. Arup, as her first PM actually taught her how to understand a new project, and even Razi, who now works for one of the sister concerns, is only a phone call away. These are the people with whom Sarithacan discuss domain knowledge, ask very basic questions in the domain; the latest developments in the field and discuss pros and cons of each other's most difficult design challenges. Through the Aerospace Design Community, Saritha felt comfortable just sounding off an idea; or validating an improvement or innovation. She understood that most of her *introvert team members* felt the same way. They felt a sense of belonging and so opened up more easily. This was an unexpected benefit. One daresay, this COP was a better teambuilding exercise than many others that one has undergone.

BACKGROUND

The community or Forum such as the above-mentioned Aerospace Design Community is technically called, a CoP or Community of Practice in its evolved state. Etienne Wegner, who is the seminal authority on CoPs, defines it as:

Communities of Practice as groups of people who share a concern(such as Quality or Safety), a set of problems (such as Cost-reduction), or a passion about a topic (such as Knowledge Management) and who deepen their knowledge and expertise in this area by interacting; and learning from each others' experience on an ongoing basis. In a CoP, members are "drawn by common interests to engage in sense-making activities though sharing, learning and solving problems (Lave and Wenger, 1991; Brown andDuguid, 1991).Members of communities share their experiences and knowledge in free-flowing and creative ways that foster new approaches to problems. They may be charged with a structured goal- say, to shorten business process cycle or introduce Agile software development or introduce a new line of business. The emphasis is on setting up these processes, piloting them, documenting and making them available to the organization in user-friendly formats (visual, checklists, training, and so on) and promoting their adoption. This is also a very potent tool to incentivize and promote innovations and their adoption.

A CoP may be any Tech Club or Study Group or Learning Network, Networks of Excellence (they are generally not called CoP), where members brainstorm and seek ideas, request for information/ experience, "can you help me tweak this proposal to suit XYZ client", discuss new trends, developments, tools, collaborate, fill in gaps in documenting or reporting, and so on.

One categorization of Forums and communities is:

1. **Blogs:** generally, one-to-many communication, sharing tips, experiences, progress, announcements.
2. **Forums:** generally many-to-many discussing problems and solutions; asking and replying to questions.
3. **Wikis:** Many–to-public or specific audience; for indepth collaboration, documentation and publication.
4. **Communities:** Many-to-many expert or knowledgeable professionals or practitioners communicating and sharing experiences and practices.
5. **Networks of Excellence:** Apart from knowledge sharing, they may promote Quality, Safety, Balanced Scorecard and other interests of organizational development.
6. **Professional Networks:** Many-to-many or public networks with strong core group and other passive members. They may be professionals from several companies or organizations. There may be multiple networks within the parent network.
7. **Network of Practitioners:** Many-to-many or public networks, generally using virtual tools.

Key Application: Lessons Learnt Sharing

There are several applications of CoPs and Forums. This author has chosen to highlight how CoPs can embed Lessons Learnt by a team or Project or a business unit or even an organization into the Business.

Needless to emphasize (as the literature does) CoP is the best way to communicate Lessons Learnt from diverse disciplines. Members profiles of KM LinkedIn Groups (KM Practitioners Group) are a case in point. Those in the field of Software Development can learn from the experiences of Education or Mathematics. Social Media is also a potent tool for KM because not all lessons learnt can be documented using formal text. They can be better captured as audio or video podcasts, File Notings, Lab Notes, Mind Maps, Sticky Notes, and so on. Effective knowledge management aided by social media also adds to the social capital of the organization, which is defined by the 'strength of weak ties' ie. Less-known and unknown participants of a social network (Seebach, 2012) by providing novel and non-redundant knowledge especially recommendations and opinions, as well as factual knowledge. All this adds to the richness of answers to specific problems; as well as new perspectives approach a project.

Lessons Learnt is not just a log item. *When communicated while the project is on, the community mentioned in the scenario, implemented the lessons while on the current project itself.* Also, with multiple inputs received within the community, Lessons Learnt was an enriched experience. One caveat though- *sometimes extremely valuable feedback have been received as anonymous lessons learnt inputs.* Such a facility should be provided in the community, not as a norm, but as an exception.

Lessons learnt documented and disseminated within the organization, improves the organization's capability. They also provide inputs to organizational process assets, at other times the context in which the process was developed. As KM professionals, we know that, to be harvested by others, providing the project, problem, community and organizational *context is of paramount importance.*

Lessons Learnt through failures should invariably, (in fact, even at the cost of success stories) be documented and discussed in communities. This is to be viewed within the big picture of KM as a problem-solving and project management tool.

Many knowledge management researchers have presented CoPs as a compelling form of informal organizational structure which produced remarkable outcomes:

Cases:

1. A successful case study by Wenger and Snyder, shows how Hewlett-Packard (HP) succeeded in standardizing sales processes and established a Model pricing scheme using a Community of Practice which shared knowledge and ideas through monthly teleconferences. This community of isolated product delivery consultants was formed by the KM team for such a purpose. In Wenger's reference to the legendary Goose that Lays Golden Eggs- the team gave lasting value to the success of HP- the goose that lays them.
2. Glennie and Hickok give another example of the CoP at the US Navy and the Defense Acquisition University. It has grown to 3,200 members and attracted around 9,000 online contributions (Glennie and Hickok, 2003).
3. American Management Systems, a consultancy found that CoPs have helped the company win the war (or at least some of the battles) for talent. A valuable consultant, *who was planning to leave the company, decided to stay after peers at a community forum found project opportunities for her that were tailor-made to her interests and expertise.* Six other valuable consultants would have followed suit, had they not been invited to join a prestigious CoP that would enable them to develop skills and find new clients.

Best Practices in Social Media for Knowledge Management

4. Another case study, which proves that CoPs should make an effort *to focus on specific strategic or tactical outcome* is given below. Before creating an online COP Michael Behounek, KM director at Halliburton, a $1.25 billion oil and gas company identified the worst points of pain facing the business units. He says, "I go to the business VP of a unit and I say, 'Give me your top five issues.' Then I make a determination: If people communicated better on this issue, would it have a big impact?" If so, Halliburton attacks the problem in a relevant COP. As he remarks about CoP members - "They must get a good answer for little effort."

The details follow:
Behenouk illustrates a successful CoP at Halliburton with electronic technicians representing more than 80 countries. It was created for electronic technicians who needed to be connected to experts and to each other so that the experience of the entire group could be used to troubleshoot and solve problems. This is a better idea than relying on the limited knowledge of one individual who is isolated at a customer's oil or gas well site. The group developed a collaborative, problem-solving community to provide 24/7 peer-to-peer training, troubleshooting and support.

In his words:

The team defined the community and processes required for the technicians to discuss issues and share good practices. The group developed an easy-to-use portal interface, which was designed around a collaboration tool, which allows the community to share its knowledge and get answers to questions. The interface also provides access to vital documents and contact information for leading experts on various pieces of hardware to ensure immediate answers to urgent technical questions. The community was launched in December 2001 and today is a thriving knowledge-sharing network of more than 200 users in numerous locations around the world. Interestingly, the number of users is greater than the actual number of electronic technicians within the community.

Through collaboration and problem solving between employees in Halliburton outposts around the world, faster response time and increased service quality have produced an estimated $20m of benefits per year. In 2003, individual instances of knowledge sharing generated, in one way or another, over $1.4m for Halliburton. In addition, electronic technicians report time-savings of approximately 20 per cent due to the community. This has allowed the company to meet the demands of business growth without employing additional technicians. The technicians it currently has are also better trained and more effective than ever. They have reduced the number of repeat repairs, measured through SAP work orders, from 30 per cent to virtually zero.

Additional business gains that could be directly attributed to knowledge management, including:

- *Reduced 'request for service' tickets per month. On account of the community answers to Supply Chain questions and experiences, the experts in the help centre say they are saving at least ten hours a month, worth $1,000;*
- *The community has acted as a source of training and has also provided mentoring, which has led to reduction in the cost of unreconciled inventory in Saudi Arabia from $700k to $250k;*
- *A single instance of collaborative working saved over $10,000 in one shipping event in the Middle East.*

Overview of Benefits

In the long term, a mature Community of Practice organically provides personal and professional development and professional identity to its members. It also improves professional marketability for its members. For the organization, it provides strategic capabilities. It helps the organization keep abreast with new innovations. Talent retention is also another benefit which has been reported.

To sum up the benefits of communities see Table 1:

The short term value of communities for the members are- it helps with challenges of access to experts. An expert would trust and become accessible to his community members rather than to an occasional email writer seeking advice. In the long-term, members can exploit their expertise for meaningful work within the organization. It brings about best results and problem-solving culture, because problem-solving contexts excite experts. Where such a culture exists, it is possible to reuse valuable talent and business resources for competitive advantage. A knowledge sharing plan is a less desirable but useful way to force a larger number of members to agree to share their experiences within business units.

Tools

During the project in the current scenario, described in the earliest section, something interesting happened. A newcomer came to me after a Kickoff meeting and said- "If only you had more time for these kinds of interactions... If I were you, I would create a forum for all of these people" A forum for interaction among some old trusted friends; some newcomers; some geographically distributed team members; mentors. "I would also use Twitter, GDrive, and so on". For learning from this team, this author would use Cisco WebEx, GoToMeeting, etc. There are a plethora of communication tools (Free, such as FB Groups, Google+ hangouts and Enterprise Tools within SharePoint, Confluence). We were, in fact using enterprise tools. It does feel very satisfying, when your own ideas come back to you from a GenY team-member. That is the spirit of KM.

All these set of configurations are being done by *GenYers in the Scenario CoP, because they are more than happy to contribute while senior experts prefer to focus on domain and experience sharing.* This arrangement helps harness member strengths and mutual mentoring opportunities create such a

Table 1. Benefits of community

	Short Term Value	**Long Term Value**
Members	Help with challenges Access to expertise Validation of innovations Confidence Social capital Work becomes more meaningful	Personal Development Reputation Professional identity Network creation Visibility/ Marketibility
Organization	Problem solving becomes easier Time saving Knowledge sharing Synergies across business units Reuse of business resources	Strategic capabilities Keeping abreast Innovation Retention of Talent New strategies are organically developed

bond among new joinees and other team members that all these efforts have paid off better than any team-building exercise.

Most discussions begin with what tools are appropriate. Depending on objectives, potential CoP size, geographical distribution, security concerns, budget availability and existing systems and tools, each CoP has a wide choice of tools; In fact, this is the most exciting time for exploring the variety of community tools being introduced each day.

Tools are potent enablers, but much less important than the spirit and dynamics that should be developed first. The cultural aspect of the community beats all other aspects, every time. The key lies in "igniting the fire", according to Johannes Müller of Siemens'. "The best theoretical concept cannot replace excitement. Seimen's Com ShareNet and Reference+ are pioneering icons in the history of enterprise KM and Enterprise CoP.

The ideal tools would be:

- Trustworthy
- Always available
- Support Conversation As it happens - so it is a perpetual conversation
- Serves as Corporate memory
- It reuses earlier template or framework and maintains continuity
- It helps organically find like-minded people serendipitously

Best Practices

Several Best Practices in KM using Social Media and CoPs, have been shared in previous sections. In the following sections, are shared, several learnings and Best Practices from other KM practitioners and those learnt over several months the Company in the scenario has been using communities and forums in a big way. These Best Practices are categorized as follows:

- Best Practices related to People
- Best Practices related to Process
- Best Practices related to Governance

Best Practices Related to People

Learning Community

It is appropriate to highlight that there has to be, among the participants, an attitude of learning, re-learning, problem solving and sharing. As Alvin Toffler has famously said- "The illiterates of the Twenty First Century will not be those who cannot read, but those who cannot learn, unlearn and relearn."

The best neurosurgeons don't rely simply on their own brilliance; they read peer-reviewed journals, attend conferences in which their colleagues discuss new research, and travel great distances to work alongside surgeons who are developing innovative techniques. According to a KM expert in Healthcare, KM "is more than a database, it is a new spirit,"

Some companies have found that communities of practice are particularly effective arenas for fostering professional development. At IBM, communities of practice hold their own conferences, both in person and on-line. Presentations, hallway conversations, dinners, and chat rooms are opportunities for members to exchange ideas, build skills, and develop networks.

In fact, it is a good idea to build the KM strategy using a CoP of KM champions.

Face-To-Face Meetings

While the importance of face-to-face interactions in the lifecycle of the CoP cannot be overemphasized, that is the most difficult to organize. From my experience, organizing a kickoff event, a larger KM event for all CoPs and other KM events are ideal. Not only does it provide the required momentum for the CoPs, it provides a *branding and marketing opportunity for all stakeholders.*

Many researchers have rated media from highest to lowest in terms of richness, most rate face-to-face, as the richest and email and memos at the low end. In describing what makes face-to-face a rich medium, Olson and Olson explain, "It provides more clues in terms of tone of voice, facial expression, body language, etc. all of which assist the person speaking to make quick adjustments in their message in order to head off misunderstandings and disagreements. It also provides those listening greater ability to immediately clarify or add perspective before the topic moves on." Olsen and Olsen's research has shown that tightly coupled work is difficult to do remotely because of the absence of those characteristics that are found in face-to-face interaction.

Focused meetings often do not happen for want of quorum, as was the failure experience shared by Alton Chua about Holden College CoPs. The CoP of Instructional Designers had some opportunities to meet face to face, but found it difficult to organise meetings partly because - people other than core members did not identify with the specific topics of discussion instantly (without marketing); and so did not prioritize it. Therefore the discussions fell back on electronic communication. In subsequent meetings, critical mass was far greater for CoPs that interacted online on a regular basis, and the fate of the Holden College CoP changed. This is possibly the trend, we will see in future. Possibly, generic discussions are not appreciated, when work pressure is high.

What worked best for this author has been a bi-yearly KM Fair, Once people know each other as fellow practitioners or experts or meet in an informal setting and develop trust, knowledge sharing begins to happen. *Thereafter, face-to-face meetings take place at calenderized intervals and at well-publicized events.*

Induction is good time to network KM enthusiasts and new joinees- new professionals as well as veterans who are enthusiastic about mentoring them.

Put People at the Centre

The idea is to put PEOPLE at the centre of KM. Another best practice has been to *enlist early adopters or enthusiasts in the beginning. This gives the community the Can-Do culture. It serves like a good internal PR and to neutralize the nay-sayers.*

A successful implementer of communities is Booz Allen Hamilton, the award winning consulting firm. Steven Walling reports that they used evangelists:

"When many people think of an evangelist, they think of an individual or two that take up the mantle of enterprise 2.0 on an ad-hoc basis. But Booz Allen went about it in a much more directed way by bringing together a cross-functional team" to develop and deploy the Community tool called hello.bah .com. In this context, there is a choice to be made- whether to have multiple tools to run the Enterprise 2.0 or a one-stop-shop. What really worked for Booz Allen was to create a true one-stop shop for information that included individual profiles, communities, forums, blogs, wikis, and social bookmarking.

Another best practice is a Profile Page for each employee (most organizations used profiles of experts or senior leadership only). On the Profile page, an employee list professional projects and work interests (e.g., biodata or resume, documents that he owns, and major clients) as well as personal hobbies, interests (e.g., personal tags), and associations. The following Availability Display is embedded thus creating a data-rich context for colleagues to think about not only availability, but also fit.

Booz Allen's Availability Display (an improvement on Outlook):

Recognition vs. Rewards

A pertinent question which is frequently asked is: What is in it for me? Therefore, a community can determine and spell out the intangible, tangible, monetary benefits of joining in the welcome document itself. Some remarkable reward statements are given in Table 2:

At ConocoPhillips, Archimedes Awards are a great source of KM success stories.

Give, Grab, Gather and Guts Awards are given to the business units or regions which has successfully created a collaborative community through applying, and sharing knowledge. Individuals, teams or Networks of Excellence are eligible to win Success Story of the Year or Networks of the Year.

Purpose

It must be emphasized that communities need to *focus on organizational pain points- ideally focused on the challenges that can provide the greatest opportunity for growth.* Unstructured ideas and suggestions do not have a "home" in communities and create noise. On the other hand, well-articulated questions, structured as innovation challenges are best seeds for communities. This will motivate employees, especially experts and loyal employees; as well as benefit the organization.

Another perspective of Social Media as Knowledge Management resources is:

Figure 1. Booz Allen's availability display

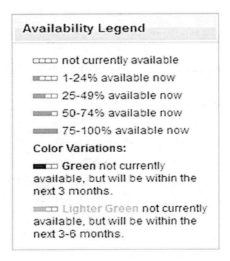

Table 2. KM participation as reward/ recognition

Reward	Remarks
Formalising in performance appraisal (most powerful)	Encouraging people to be a Knowledge Champion. Recognition not reward - when recognized as one. Knowledge Champion must be able to put his/her achievements in his performance appraisal. "The minute a measure becomes a target, it ceases to be a measure" (Goodhart's Law). Formal inclusion of KM work into performance appraisal and bonus schemes has often led to knowledge scoring or even knowledge theft - claiming credit for the work of less politically aware contributors.
Sponsored attendance at an external training or conference of their choice	Ideal KM rewards as they respond like for like, but they need to be dispensed by managers as privilege, rather than entitlement.
Giving them access to a mentor / coach normally only available to senior executives	Helps them develop into valuable experts to align with organizational requirements and improves their career path.
Organization's "Drona" award; Coach Title; 'Turtle' award for people who stick their neck out for the good of the organisation	
Funding (partially / fully) a project that is important to this person where the project is not necessarily work-related -- it could be a cause he supports etc -- so he/she gets the opportunity to extend the reward forward to something important to him/her. The funding need not be monetary either but also in time.	
Profile on intranet	In the long run it may become a standard expectation of being a Knowledge Champion, In the long run it acts as an incentive for others to get more active (which is good but not 'rewarding' the Champion)
"Photo-ops" with senior managers	Not just a photo, but being seen as being truly appreciated by high-level managers as part of those managers' efforts to walk the talk and remain actively involved in the KM effort

Just in time and Just in Case: When there is a question or problem or crisis, there are two alternatives- you ask people or you search a database. The social inclinations of most professionals are to ask trusted individuals or groups (earlier called your invisible college; now referred to as your network). The advantage of People for answers is that it is often quicker, has a ripple effect within the group. It in fact, energizes the group; leading to referrals and redirects. Some people help rephrase and reframe the question, leading to multiple and richer conversations. Plenty of peripheral issues get raised and lead to innovations, even disruptive innovation. Some cases follow:

1. At Buckman Labs, members of communities of practice from around the world routinely respond to practice-specific queries within 24 hours. In one case, an employee trying to help a pulp mill customer in the Pacific Northwest solve a dye-retention problem, received many ideas within hours of posting it from expert and peers in Europe, South Africa, and Canada—and one response provided the exact solution to match the customer's need.
2. Siemens' ShareNet has become a case study at Harvard Business School. On ShareNet, on average, about 80% of the 'Urgent Request' receives at least one answer, most of them within 24 hours. Any 'Urgent Request' is a pressing demand for information and is clearly marked as urgent for 14 days. In additionally, the latest 'Urgent Requests' are shown on Com ShareNet's Home Page.
3. In China, domestic vendors such as Huawei or ZTE heavily attack foreign vendors. The competition situation was serious and Siemens stood at a very disadvantageous position. Some questions

Best Practices in Social Media for Knowledge Management

      where posted in Seimens' ShareNet regarding integrated microwave solution using Siemens outdoor BTS BS41. The Italian colleagues answered exactly the key blocking point for the project and the customer could be convinced for the Siemens solution. The contract value was about US$ 4 million.
4. In a famous case study at Caterpillar, (Manufacturer of Heavy Engg machinery): Stuedemann (erstwhile KM Chief), says the impact of an ineffective mechanic calling on a customer will provide a much greater impact on the bottom line and the customer. He was referring to the impact of Communities of Practice at Caterpillar.
5. Tech clubs at DaimlerChrysler meet regularly to discuss questions in 11 areas of product development, including body design, electronics, and vehicle development. They analyze variations in practice and set standards. Engineers who participate in the clubs are responsible for developing and maintaining an Engineering Book of Knowledge, a database that captures information on compliance standards, supplier specifications, and best practices.
6. Seth Kahan's Business Performance Community is not far from realization. Kahan is the author of Building Beehives: A Handbook for Creating Communities that Generate Returns (Performance Development Group, 2004).

Best Practices in CoP Process

Innovation or success in KM also stems in deliberately designed processes. It must be highlighted at the outset that CoP processes are not tightly built. There are trial and error and iterations after iterations. The processes involved in identifying the goals, identifying success and failure factors, designing the community experience- all of these are processes that can make or break the whole framework The Silicon Valley phenomena is not only about individuals with brilliant products; it is in fact a story of start-ups learning from the success and failure of its predecessors. There is an invisible, even visible community phenomenon that this geographical cluster has benefitted from. On similar lines, are built Innovation Hubs at MIT, IITs and IIMs, ISB. Similarly, Entrepreneurial Ventures within companies like Google, HP, Infosys, and Wipro.

In fact, all Social Media aim at cultivating communities, be it Facebook or LinkedIn, Twitter, or Scoop.it or Wikipedia. Some of the benefits and motivators for individual community members are:

- Giving knowledge in turn for reusing others' knowledge,
- being a part of a community,
- pride of excellence,
- demonstrating expert status – around the world,
- cooperation within a team by the help of ShareNet (e.g. team-internal use),
- reducing the time known experts spend answering standard questions, and
- the Quality Assurance and Reward System.

For the organization, the benefits listed are:

- reduces costs and improves quality by making all relevant knowledge available,
- helps to avoid "re-inventing the wheel",
- saves time by providing reusable modules, presentations, key selling arguments, etc.,

- increases skills by providing a wide range of proven selling methodologies, best practices, competencies, tips and tricks,

For all this to happen, communities have to be designed. Wegner's definition itself contains many of these design elements. Communities of Practice as groups of people who share a concern(such as Quality), a set of problems (such as cost-reduction), or a passion about a topic (such as Knowledge Management) and who deepen their knowledge and expertise in this area by interacting; and learning from each others' experience on an ongoing basis.

The definition signifies a life-cycle too. A forum or CoP can be temporary, such as, during a CMMi certification process or setting up a KM initiative. Many CoPs and Forums lose their steam after the sense of urgency has gone; which is part of its life-cycle. Communities have a lifecycle not dissimilar to the lifecycle of a plant- begins with sowing the seed; germination; nurturing the sapling, cultivating the crop; harvesting it; and perhaps renewal or exit. It is remarkable that he calls it "sowing the seed", "nurturing" and "cultivating" in the book "Cultivating Communities".

Life Cycle Approach to CoP

A life-cycle approach is best suited for KM initiatives in general, and CoPs in particular. It is not easy to build and sustain communities of practice or to integrate them with the rest of an organization. The organic, spontaneous, and informal nature of communities of practice do not allow for manager supervision and interference. It was found that managers cannot mandate communities of practice. Instead, successful managers bring the right people together, provide an infrastructure in which communities can thrive, and measure the communities' value in nontraditional ways. These tasks of cultivation are not easy, but the harvest they yield makes them well worth the effort.

Another quote about the value of people and networks and communities is worth noting: "Assets make things possible. People make things happen." Any number of assets in an organization would not bring alive a vision or a goal. It is when people use these assets to fulfill a process or workflow and then deliver the output in a usable form that a goal is achieved. It is when such goals are married with quality and excellence that a higher goal or vision is fulfilled. In this context, "nurturing" and "cultivating" are appropriate.

It is also necessary to differentiate between a Team and a Community. The following table is self explanatory:

Table 3. Community vs team

	Team	Community of Practice
Purpose	Tasks Processes Outcomes	Learning/ sharing Ad-hoc Emergent
Members	Defined roles	Informal/ self-selected roles
Manage	Manager Manages	Facilitator facilitates
Participation	Required participation High interdependency	Encourages participation Trust
Tools	Tools define or control teamwork	Community defines how tools are to be used

Forum and Community Design

As Nancy White shares her experiences: *Short-term communities have a discernable beginning, middle and end around a specific purpose, outcome or activity. For example, when there is a major event or initiative and a community is set up around that event. There is a very clear target audience and a defined set of activities. These time-delimited communities can be very successful because people are more easily willing to commit for set action items within defined time ranges. They have a sense of their ability to say yes. These can also be seeds for longer-term communities if there is sufficient attention to relationship and evolving with and to member needs over time, or they may simply be ended and archived. Both are realistic strategies.*

According to Vestal (2003), for a successful community one of chief traits is a "clear business value proposition for all stakeholders". At some point in the life of the forum or community, it is critical to define and measure the outcomes expected; or the business drivers for its activities. In corporate contexts, gaining buy-in from decision –makers and stakeholders is a prime requirement. Contextual factors- organizational culture, leadership dynamics, relationships and interactions among members and other such issues affect best-laid plans.

Most CoPs, esp. primarily electronic and content communities start open-ended, with a broad topic and a wide invitation to participants. This strategy often builds on the aggregation of content that might be useful in this topic area and people come, browse content and some interact. Or members can begin to interact more actively with others interested in the topic.

But once the community is established, there is a critical strategic choice to be made- continue as a content hub (as a service) or begin to cultivate and weave relationships to move people from content browsing to some other kinds of interactions. This might be identification of sub-communities of interest, attracting experts who might be willing to share their knowledge, etc. The key thing about this approach is within about a year, there needs to be an assessment and decision about the next phase or you end up simply providing content.

There is another best practice from the general KM strategy. This useful but less common way forward is piloting a community with one of the active and strategic subset of the network. This strategy is good for complex or emerging situations where KM team can sense an opportunity for engaging people and solving significant business problems. The team facilitates people designing and doing small community experiments with each other – generally time- delimited with a clear beginning, middle and end. As in any KM initiative, a useful practice is to do a mid-point review and support changes and iterations. At the end of the experiment, KM team and other stakeholders evaluate what works and stop what isn't working. This is a useful form for places of both uncertainty and where you want to foster both innovation and member ownership. Sponsor goals are looser and more flexible.

Wenger had proposed that there are seven design principles. E.g. a budding community should not be forced to adopt a fixed structure but be allowed to evolve organically as it grows. Also, different levels of participation in the community should be invited so that all members have a role to play based on their varied degree of commitment and interests. Winkelen and Ramsell (2003) also contend that the key to a successful community of practice is to align the values among members' motivation to participate and the organisation's need to support the community.

Participation

Community discussions are often very informal. As Wegner et al (Cultivating Communities of Practice) shares his experiences at Shell, the Oil & Gas major:

Typically, a member poses a question or problem he or she is having and the group makes observations and suggestions. A coordinator, who helps people explicate the logic or assumptions behind their observations, lightly facilitates the discussions. When a speaker seems to be defensive and closed to the ideas of others, the coordinator reminds him that the purpose of the meeting is to surface many different ideas. When the group seems to be "grilling" a speaker, asking him many detailed questions without offering any alternate ideas, he reminds them that they owe the speaker some ideas of their own. He then suggests they shift focus and discuss other ways the speaker could approach the problem. These community discussions seem very spontaneous, but this spontaneity is more deliberately planned than it appears. Between meetings the coordinator "walks the halls." He drops in on community members, follows up on meeting items, asks people about hot issues to discuss at the next meeting, and informally lets others know about upcoming meeting topics he would particularly like them to participate in.

Nancy White suggests that we use an Activity Orientation tool to review the community:

Figure 2. Community Orientation

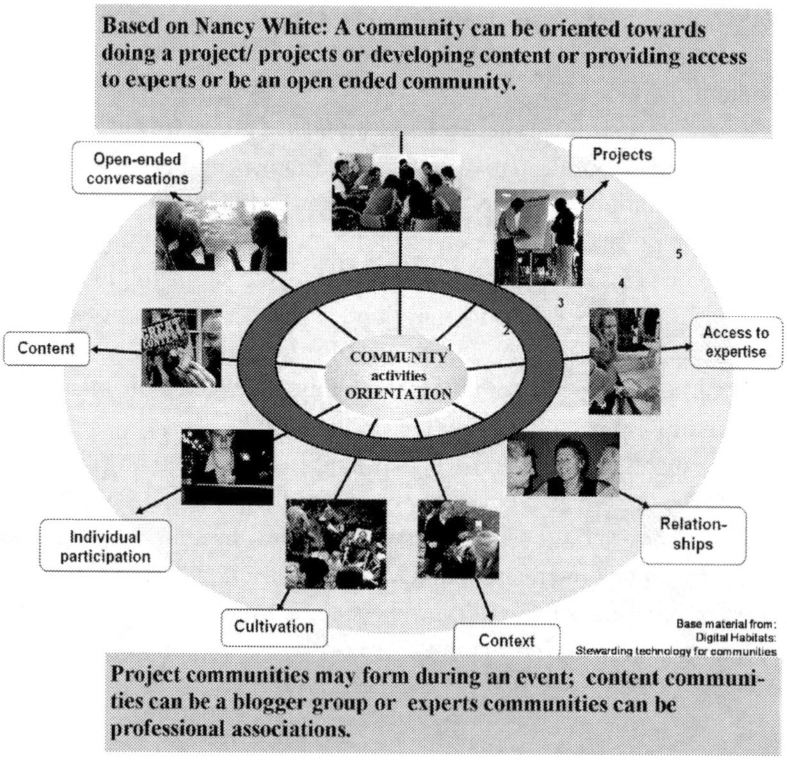

Best Practices in Social Media for Knowledge Management

As opposed to "I think therefore I am", CoP moves the professional to "I participate therefore I am". So it is experiential learning; it is invested learning. What things do members do offline already that they might do online? What do they want/need?

("Start where people are now.")

1. Ask & answer questions
2. Share resources
3. Share case stories
4. Do "peer assists"
5. Create things together
6. Practice new skills together
7. Learn about each other
8. What is the "rhythm" of these activities?
9. What size of group is involved?
10. How are the activities supported or facilitated?

She uses the following diagram to identify the particular orientation of the communities she facilitates. This helps her understand the strengths and weaknesses or characteristics of the community.

Figure 3. Community Orientation Template

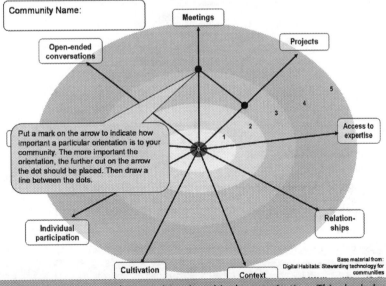

It is important to remember that the frequency of activity is not the success criteria. The "Pareto" principle states that 10% of a community represents 90% of the community activity. Actually, in very large, open communities, that may be as much as 99% !

White cautions against interference; and suggests exploration and subtle catalysis or Adaptive Action, as she calls it (stimulation to explore additional activities and possibly switch to them):

- *Observe. Don't waste a good surprise. Pause and wonder when something unexpected arises. It may be the weak signal foreshadowing something important to come.*
- *Connect. Nothing co-evolves in isolation. The key is connecting in inquiry with the environment, with current and historical patterns, and with other thoughtful people.*
- *Question. Our assumptions blind us to the world around and lock us into our long-held problems and their failed solutions. A good question can break through the expected to discover the possible.*

Try it out. Of course, expectations based on past experience will make us question anything we haven't experienced. To see something new, we really have to see it. Try a new idea out, see what happens, adjust and try again. We call this adaptive action. Reward thoughtful risk taking.

Best Practices in CoP Governance

It is ideal to strategize about all aspects of CoP governance, including how it will be introduced within the organization, strategy to be followed, how it is going to be structured, lead, facilitated, monitored and reported to all stakeholders. *A Stakeholder's communication plan is a Best Practice, which helps get sustained support.*

Strategy

Early on in the community, a Core Group emerges or can be facilitated. In the beginning, leadership needs to focus on the outcomes or the Big Picture rather than details. *It is a good idea to present a vision, if not specific outcomes. Goal setting is also a good community exercise early on.*

Leadership

It is appropriate to plan a governance structure for KM itself, as well as each program, even community governance. An integrated structure for all KM activities is recommended. The greater the role clarity, the lesser conflict there will be; as well as realizing the full potential of each member. One benchmark in KM governance has been that of Seimens. The leadership structure is described thus by Muller:

Seimens' ingredients for success in the roll-out have been based around people:

1. Executive support by 'The King' – At least one top manager needs to give their support for the roll-out across a division.
2. Platform support by 'The Guide' – Johannes Müller from the Building Technologies Division is the owner and very active community administrator for the platform and he constantly supported the Smart Grid Division throughout the whole process.

3. Project led by 'The Roll-outer' – Through the support of top management, JarenKrchnavi was given the time it takes to communicate the platform internally through face-to-face meetings, webinars, creating widgets on the intranet, news releases, and, by starting a contest to gain more members and project contributions.
    - *Listen to the needs of 'The Workers' – The platform was slightly modified to take into consideration the needs of the employees in the Smart Grid Division.*
    - *Search for 'The Supporters' – Motivate and empower those who support the platform to help it succeed.*
    - *Convince 'The Naysayers' – There will always be people within an*
    - *Organisation who do not like change so it is important to be prepared to actively defend KM ideas and projects.*

From Shell's experience, it can be learnt:

It is axiomatic that people issues are the thorniest aspect of any technology initiative. KM is no exception. And don't expect getting individuals involved to come cheap. Shell's van Unnik estimates the annual cost of the KM system at about $5 million, with the majority of that sum going toward engaging community members. "The cost is man power," he says, including two to three full-time employees per major online COP (of which Shell has 12). But with an estimated annual return of more than $200 million, the investment is more than sound.

That kind of investment needs committed business acumen and leadership qualities to pursue every stakeholder.

FACILITATING

A CoP leader is a subject matter expert, but a facilitator need not be a subject matter specialist or expert. Facilitation skills are important. Knowledge Management professionals, trainers, librarians have always been Facilitator. Now they can easily transfer their facilitation skills to this community and online community spaces. The idea is to create a comfortable and inviting online space, where professionals feel comfortable discussing their experiences with voluntarily-assembled like-minded professionals. Of course, now there is a choice of technology enablers to make these spaces user-friendly.

If we want like-minded professionals to find each other and collaborate we must create conditions for them to organically find each other; the ambiance must build trust and openness; and conversations lead to understanding mutual interests and productive output.

Nancy Dixon developed a Best Practice: Before the meeting the facilitator and session leader come together to *prepare a list of questions they want answered in the session and to figure out and gather the information that will be needed to answer those questions* at the meeting. *Another one:* "Some people talk about what can be done, but not what should be done. People don't have to speak and there are always some who speak less or almost nothing. All these tendencies have to be overcome.

The following slide from Hatch Associates brings out the dynamics of creating a vibrant community. An example of a conversation follows:

Figure 4. I create online spaces, not CoPs

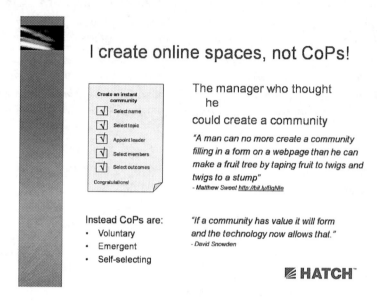

Figure 5. Global Village – a conversation
Straits Knowledge (www.straitsknowledge.com) and **ACTKM** (www.actkm.org) have aptly portrayed the KM facilitator's attributes as follows:

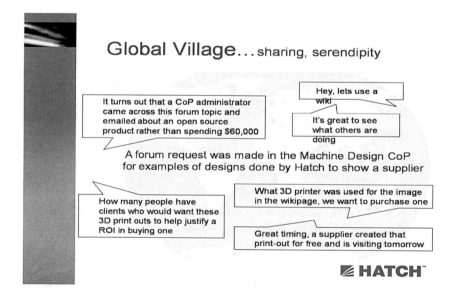

First Steps

Pilot: It is a good practice to check if there are some known/ unknown communities in the organization. If so, they can be used as pilots or prototypes. They can be used to demonstrate what the CoP will look like. It is advisable to study how they function, in fact, what makes them tick? How do they currently share, communicate, and coordinate? Do they use email? Meetings? Lunch time chats? Other tools?

Figure 6. KM facilitator's attributes

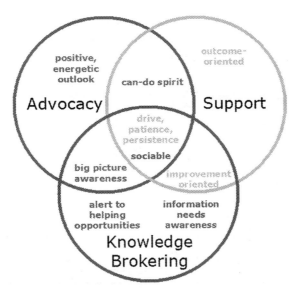

Check out whether there are other people who may want to form similar Communities. or if the current Community members want to form a sub Community.

If senior management wants to form communities, the facilitator, can conduct a work-shop along With a subject matter expert or a senior technical manager. It is better to have conversations with interested participants about a meaty enough topic to cover in initial sessions. Well begun is half done, as the saying goes? It may be a good idea to have an informal forum instead of a full-blown community. Events are Great Energizers. Some initial activities could be a Coffee Corner; Theme for the Month; Personal Stories; Blog Carnivals, Polls, etc.

Following are a few lessons (some in their own words, which are more powerful than reports) which have been successful in KM friendly companies:

DOs

(Adapted from Melinda Bickerstaff, vice president of knowledge management for Bristol-Myers Squibb -BMS, a drug manufacturing MNC):

2. **Tell Stories:** KM practitioners know that tacit knowledge (which is 85% of human understanding in people's heads not in documents or databases) is complex. Bickerstaff encourages storytelling about professionals' experiences (such as winning Federal Drug Administration approval for Sustiva, an anti-HIV medicine) as a way to exchange lessons learned. Multiple stories like this reveal the complexity of these experiences, more than any report can. Nor will professionals enjoy writing such reports, as compared to recording a story in comfortable surroundings or even writing it on a blog. Every time a story is retold, there is richness added.
3. **Context-Building:** At the same company, in-house writers/ PR professionals took detailed notes and then wrote up a report or articles, not a PPT. How the precedents or context is built is important too. As Bickerstaff says, "There are 16 dimensions to a story and only one or two to a PowerPoint,"

Writing an article weaves together several themes into a complex whole that more fully reflects the tacit knowledge of the people who worked on the problem. This is how context is rebuilt. That is an important component of experience-sharing and Lessons Learnt.

4. **Focus on Lesson, Not Name:** The facilitators of Lessons Learnt sessions at BMS begin by ensuring that participants reach a trust and comfort level by saying that the notes from the meeting will never be seen by any outside person.

"The facilitators steer the conversation away from "XYZ screwed up," says Alyson Krumwiede, of BMS, who has participated in three lessons-learned sessions. "With this, you're not looking for names. You're looking for what you learned from this experience that you can apply next time." The approach appears to be paying off. This year, BMS has received FDA approval on two new drugs with a third pending, which is an amazing coup in an industry where one approval per year is considered good.

5. **Recognize Contributions Immediately:** "The most powerful incentive for sharing is peer recognition," according to Peter Engstrom, Vice President for Corporate Knowledge Creation at Science Applications International Corp. (SAIC), a research and engineering company that helps organizations adopt KM. Shell and Giant Eagle give informal recognition by mentioning knowledge sharing and innovation related accomplishments in an immediate e-mail or newsletter or meeting. Halliburton has a sports metaphor of "most valuable player" and acknowledges the person with the best idea every month. Many of these companies also factor in knowledge sharing into employees' formal job reviews. KM practitioners emphasize that it important to make a clear statement that the enterprise appreciates knowledge-sharers.

6. **Create In-Person Knowledge Forums:** BMS had atleast five different knowledge-sharing forums and plans new ones regularly. A winning idea, borrowed from the NASA Jet Propulsion Lab, is called My BMS Experience. The origin was a company veteran's talk looking back on his 34 yr career. "It's like going back to the campfire, letting people tell their story, creating opportunities for people to share what they know. That's a huge side of managing knowledge." She expected about 100 to give up their lunchtime leisure to hear the talk, but around 250 employees showed up. Thereafter, My BMS Experience became a regular event.

7. **Create a Model:** US Federal Government encourages projects, which can be used as Models or benchmarks. It encourages expertise and mastery. That approach is true for Communities too. At SAIC, a group, which had experience with creating a system for granting credentials to physicians in the state of Florida became the Model or de facto team on all state government projects. After a project is complete, team members meet to analyze what worked and what did not. At the end of each workday, project teams meet to examine the gap between their to-do lists and what actually got done. This helps in benchmarking and standardization.

8. **Build Trust:** Although time consuming and expensive, an organization cannot take a short-cut to getting people become comfortable sharing knowledge. It is like a new habit, which takes say, 21 days to become part of their culture. Says SAIC's Engstrom, *"You have to systematically embed knowledge sharing into the culture as opposed to overlaying it on top. You cannot bolt it on and force people to use it. The atmosphere of trust has to be there first."*

Nick Milton quotes the thought-provoking "Don'ts Best Practices" listed by Asif Devji of the Com-Prac community. It is his list of the top ten worst practices, or "what not to do to have a successful CoP".

DON'Ts:

1. Expect a CoP to change your organizational culture
2. Incorporate a CoP into an unstable organizational environment
3. Use a CoP to filter down organizational talking points
4. Be exclusivist in your selection of CoP members
5. Fail to recognize employee participation in your CoP
6. Control the discourse in your CoP
7. Leave your CoP to its own devices
8. Use a CoP to colonize knowledge (ie lurk in there, and steal ideas).
9. Commodify a CoP for profit
10. Expect a quick quantifiable ROI from your CoP

Day-to Day tasks are important too:

Hatch has also charted tasks and activities during the different stages of CoP development as follows:

Sometimes COPs form and then break apart once the immediate issue is resolved. This is a natural cycle. CoPs can also evolve into other forms; or to solve other issues or goals.

Behounek of Halliburton once created a community to devise performance enhancements for a particular 2,000-horsepower pump used in the company's oil refineries. While it was an urgent matter at the time, the community's activity rapidly decreased because the essential business problem had been solved. "There was nothing more to be gained from it, so we saw the usage numbers fall off," says Behounek. His group relaunched the COP to cover all equipment in that business unit. With the broader focus, usage picked up again.

Monitoring and Measurement

An important aspect of CoP leadership is to track the time, investment and effort spent on KM and Social Media. According to this author the Balanced Score Card (BSC) is ideally suited to set KM goals and measure them. However, there is a huge change and investment involved. For current purposes, Patrick Lambe's KM Measures have been found accessible and easy to implement.

Patrick Lambe's KM measurement based on KPIs (Key Performance Indicators for a role or department or a business unit) is highly valuable in this context. There are several approaches available, but the following approach is planned for implementation by this author. One limitation that should be

Table 4. Visible and invisible tasks

Visible Tasks	Invisible Tasks
Publishing, Blogging, Curating what transpires in the CoP	Back channel to encourage participation/ discuss preferences
Whitepapers, podcasts	
Guest speakers	Build relationships with Key Members and stakeholders
Managing Events	Planning campaign calendars
Policy formation, tools	Advocacy for value of the community
Branding efforts	Measuring and monitoring usage, contributions, value and ROI

Figure 7. Living and Breathing – stages of CoP development

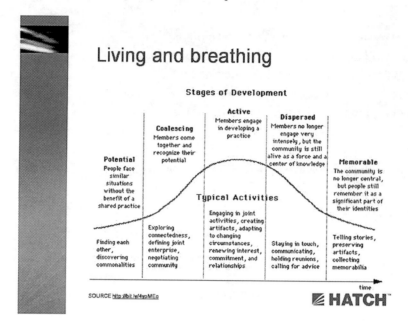

explained upfront – the following model focuses on documented sharing of knowledge and experience. There will be a large number of incidences of informal sharing which are equally valuable. However, the KM team plans to capture this informal sharing in the next phase of monitoring of CoP engagements. The plan is to use this approach to:

- *Communicate* with stakeholders and retain their support and involvement- metrics related to number of stakeholders with buy-in; quality and impact of strategy documents; quality and impact of promotional material (posters, video, events, presentation in organizational or business unit events)
- *Monitor* implementations for progress of CoPs and Forums, compared to plans; number of contributions and contributors; member time spent on them.
- *Gather* number and evidence of beneficial impact of communities
- *Control* the focus of KM efforts for new phases and KM tools
- *Learn* from past activity to feed into new plans- we plan a PDCA cycle (Plan, Do, Check, Act cycle)

Finally, in Andrew Carnegie's wise words:
"The only irreplaceable capital an organization possesses is the knowledge and ability of its people. The productivity of that capital depends on how effectively people share their competence with those who can use it." This can be discerned, not necessarily measured. It is KM leadership function to help management discern the increased effectiveness and competence.

Table 5. Activity and investment related metrics:

Operational KPIs	Comments
Number of contributions and member and stakeholder contributors % of members and non-members accessing the forums per month Awareness and membership metrics	Activity – CoP meetings do not need to be frequent but they do need to establish a regular and consistent pattern of meetings. Activity - A membership drive and its results are important.
No. of stakeholders Quality of Strategy documents % of members contributing to the forums	Activity logs – participation rates
Number of events and coverage Member time spent on forums and communities	Investment – through survey
Number of new topics/threads per month	Activity – currency and freshness of discussions
Number of posts per month	Activity – enables tracking of cycles of activity
Average number of posts per topic	Activity – extent of discussion
Average number of replies per posting	Activity – depth of discussion
No. of Templates, Job Aids, other process assets shared	Activity – depth of discussion
No. of improvement suggestions	Activity – depth of engagement
% of lurkers per forum	Activity – lurkers are people who are viewing but not actively contributing – they are very likely picking up valuable knowledge; however too few active contributors, and the community will decline
Ratio of experts to practitioners to novices per forum	Too few experts and they will find little incentive to participate; too few practitioners, and experts will be annoyed by naïve questions from novices
Number of divisions represented among the contributors	Activity – cross boundary sharing
Number of new members/ subscriptions per month	Activity – enables tracking relevance of forums
Number of cancelled subscriptions per month	Activity – enables tracking relevance of forums
Number of links to knowledge assets published in forums	Activity – guiding member to relevant knowledge assets

Emerging Trends in Communities

Emerging trends and innovative use of Social Media are introduced as benchmarks. *Some areas which impact global, national, organizational, sector productivity and innovation are mentioned below.*

Standards Development

An industry-wide or pioneering company community can set standards for their discipline. Pioneering Telecom companies, like Motorola; and Healthcare organizations, like Mayo Clinic, Sloan Kettering, and CDC are cases in point. Veteran professionals can use their influence and bring about consensus through their personal relationships. In the early stages of community development, these relationships are based on validating each other's ideas and practices. In a mature community, they are based on mutual sense of responsibility for stewarding a practice. This typically involves creating standards, influencing industry trends and practices, and educating new community members. Capturing gems from these knowledge exchanges is complex and difficult. Either the community coordinator needs to follow up or the people involved need to document their gems for the community as a whole. Excellent Curation skills are called for.

Table 6. Impact KPIs

KPI	Comment
Number of Knowledge assets created	Output
Frequency of use of knowledge assets created	Indicates reuse value
Average age of knowledge assets created	Indicates currency and updating
Number of expertise-related questions answered via forums Number of requests to the knowledge base Number of Reusable applications or R&D components	Indicates knowledge transfer and continuity
Increase in orders Reduction in labour costs Reduction in production costs Lower training expenses Reduced IT investments	Indicates ROI- KM may be one of the factors
Members' assessment of forums value for work effectiveness and/or knowledge development	Via survey
Relevance of discussion topics for the business generally	Via survey
Relevance of discussion topics for critical knowledge areas	Via survey
Degree to which forums are felt to promote cross divisional knowledge sharing	Via survey
Examples of impact of forums on work effectiveness and/or knowledge development of member	Collected via "Most Significant Change" or "anecdote circles"

Mentoring

At Shell, the Petrophysicist CoP/ community pioneered a mentor program for this niche area of practice. While the organization already had a formal mentoring program, most of the mentoring burden fell to a few senior petrophysicists. When the community took on mentorship, they were able to distribute the work of mentoring more evenly among the members. This shows how a well-planned mentoring program within a CoP helps in mentoring, recruitment from a small pool of talent, nurturing rather than poaching talent- and thus is beneficial to the organization, as well as the industry. Mentoring also helps attract new talent and branding of the profession or practice. APQC, SPIN, HYSEA and NASSCOM, software industry communities in India, are excellent examples of such initiatives. Silicon Valley Angel investors are well-known to mentor and fund promising technology startups. Similarly, several companies develop women leaders through mentoring communities. Ashoka Fellowship program is a community of leaders in Social Enterpreneurship.

Customer Focused Innovation

CoP nirvana is Marketing or Field Sales inputs becoming part of product planning in say, the Pharma industry. There are many success stories of Customer Service Organizations learning from CSAs or customer facing retail employees. Many software service companies have benefitted too. Similarly, Aerospace or even automotive engineering teams can have learning communities with the Supply Chain or outsourcing partners. Product companies in many industries can learn from communities. In fact, DFSS activists like Subir Chowdhury advocate that product development teams should begin with Customer Focus Groups (Voice of Customer). These are opportunities to build perpetual Customer–Product Communities.

At the very least, companies can continuously improve their product or service; employee engagement and entrepreneurial and consulting abilities of its experts. Lord Browne, Chief Executive Officer of BP once said, "Most activities or tasks are not onetime events. Whether it is drilling a well or conducting a transaction at a service centre, we do the same things repeatedly. Our philosophy is fairly simple: Every time we do something again, we should do it better than the last time". There is no better source of customer feedback and innovation inputs than one's own customers.

Collective Sense-Making: KM Impact within Social Networks

The knowledge impact or value creation of the social network of the community is a relatively new perspective in KM. It is well-recognized that in these complex times of fast changes, no one individual is smart enough to address the challenges organizations face. It is the time for drawing on the collective intelligence of the network to generate both strategy and action. This is called *Collective Sense-making*.

It is time to start leveraging the collective knowledge of the community to create new knowledge or innovation. *The process consists of Listening, Organizing and then Presenting.* Listening provides us new ideas but as long as those ideas are just swimming around in our heads, they are neither fully formed nor implementable. It is only when a knowledge worker puts an idea together in a way that allows him or her to explain the idea to others, that the idea takes shape for the knowledge worker, as well as for the person the knowledge worker is talking with.

Researchers at the University of Minnesota, have shown that we organize information in a different way when we are preparing to explain our thinking to others. The information not only becomes more logically organized, but new connections are made, often in the act of speaking. It is fair to say, "We don't learn when we listen, we learn when we speak," or write, or even create a visual representation of our understanding. Giving professionals in the community, the time needed to put their thinking into words, and then presenting this predigested and reflected knowledge creates new knowledge.

Open Innovation, Crowd Sourcing and Other Community Excitement

Even the most discreet professions are finding value in openness, community involvement, and learning across disciplines. Since 9/11, US Military has been working with other govt. agencies, corporates etc. using wikis, cloud applications such as Google Docs, and collaboration software such as Adobe Connect, Cisco Systems' WebEx, and Citrix Online's GoToMeeting. In addition to using collaboration IT services, the Army has adopted the concept CoPs, in which professionals with roles and interests in security, intelligence, cultural studies and so on, to share information. These COPs are called Army Professional Forums, and consist of more than 200,000 members. The well-sustained DISA Defense Connect Online (DCO), a 380,000-user network lets service personnel exchange unclassified and secret information with authorized mission partners. DCO uses Adobe Connect Pro for Web conferencing and Cisco Systems' Jabber chat technology. There is the example of explosives experts who may have met earlier in their careers and maintained a professional association- they came together to help with 9/11 investigations. Ramon Barquin who provided IT strategy for this community says:

"These communities were formed because, for instance, somebody who is now with the New York Police Department used to be with the FBI and went to the same classes with others in this area, so they have already established a community of trust," Barquin said. "Now 10 years into their careers, they are still a part of communities of practices or interests."

Policing and Intelligence work are characterized by knowledge that involves discretion, sensitivity and tacit understanding, on-the-job and case-based cooperation are critical. *"They in turn mentor new kids on the block,"* Barquin said, *"and they become a part of these communities of interest."*

As Communities and Collaborative come of age, in this golden age of Social Media, the following path-breakers are worth noting:

P & G Connect and Develop: Partnering with innovators(for Crest Spinbrush), suppliers (penta-peptide, a compound added to develop winning product Olay Regenerist), university-based ventures, partnering with competitors and other organizations(Febreze, a billion-dollar new brand; Swiss Precision Diagnostics, a joint venture), helped P&G grow into unexpected (50% of its products) businesses. Many other companies are inspired by P&G experiences.

Innocentive and Other Grand Challenges: are crowd-sourced innovation platforms for global innovators, who compete to provide ideas and solutions to important real-world business, social, policy, scientific, and technical challenges. Innocentive reports that Exxon Valdez spill in 1989 was solved in November 2007 by an oil industry outsider, John Davis, who used his expertise in the concrete industry to come up with the $20,000 award for his creative solution.

Leading organizations like, Astra Zeneca, Booz Allen Hamilton, Cleveland Clinic, Eli Lilly & Company, NASA, Nature Publishing Group, Procter & Gamble, *Scientific American*, Syngenta, *The Economist*, Thomson Reuters, The Department of Defense, and several government agencies in the U.S. and Europe have used these platforms to develop cost-effective and time-saving solutions.

Co-Creation Communities: Other open source innovation communities aim at co-creation. Collectively they produce a new product or products. Some excellent examples are:

Linux: Open Source Software

- Wikipedia: peer produced encyclopedia
- NineSigma: technology problem solving community
- Innovation-community.de: Community of innovators, creators, designers & thinkers (made by Hyve)
- OpenIDEO: collaborative design platform
- Challenge.gov: crowd-sourcing community for government problems
- Lumenogic: collective intelligence markets
- Ushahidi: crowdsourcing crisis information
- Quirky + GE: co-creating platform by Quirky & General Electric
- InnovationJam*: IBM's idea generation project
- Dell IdeaStorm: external idea sourcing
- Betavine: Vodafone's mobile app community

These are the Best Practices to be learnt from successful innovation communities. A couple of such communities are introduced in the following section. Board of Innovation has benchmarked several Innovation Communities such as the following:

harKopen brings together electronics professionals to create projects, services, webtools and so on fort the world to interconnect digitally. They are very active in building the 'Internet of Things'. Local "Hackerspaces" provide face-to-face opportunities for these professionals.

Best Practices in Social Media for Knowledge Management

Figure 8. harKopen platform

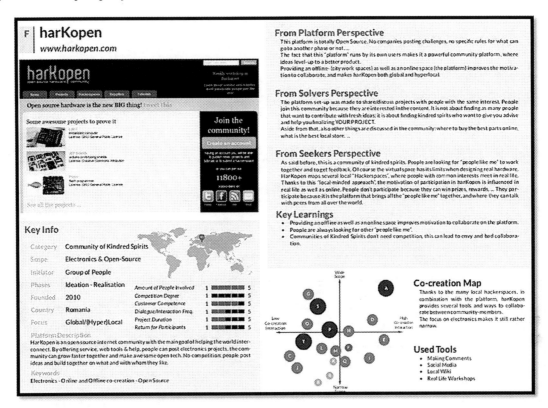

OScar is an online community of people who co-create an innovative car- collectively plans and develops a new car. The idea is about the goal to develop a simple and innovative car, as also an innovative way this goal is achieved. They would like to convey the idea of Open Source to "hardware" The project insists on high competence in the selected contributors.

Bottom-Up Design using Conversations, FaceBook, Hangouts, Blogs,

With a majority of GenY employees, organizations are leveraging social media conversations in a seamless manner. For example, FaceBook for Enterprises, with rich media tools, is considered a benchmark in bottom-up design for communities. It is a reflection of New Age organizations like Google, FaceBook, Teach For America and so on. A designed community experience described by Nancy Dixon is described below: ProQuest's has consistent and seamless conversations going on throughout the year: *At ProQuest, face-to-face meetings are called "Summits." In between Summits, team members are in constant communication with each other using various forms of social media. They Scrum several times a week over Google Hangout or Skype, hold Hangout meetings between individual members or small groups to address problems, and use Flowdock as their group chat room.*

They brainstorm to ask- What do we want to discuss? What are the larger things that will come up in the next four months? What is not yet actionable? … find a date and location …ask the team what

Figure 9. OScar Platform

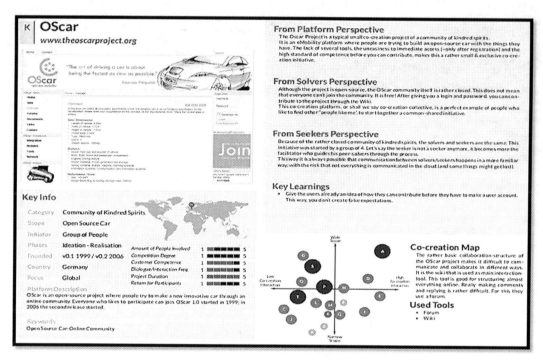

do you want to talk about? What sessions we should have? What needs to be whiteboarded? A team member might respond with a topic like, "We should talk about becoming more international so we can sell in China".

When people actually see that what they suggested is on the agenda, then they know their response and ideas will impact the agenda. This is powerful. Dixon quotes Mark Baloga, principal researcher at Steelcase, who thinks that creating physical and virtual spaces where shared visual images, audio, text and data can be explored together is often the key to producing breakthrough thinking. "It gives each member the power of reviewing thoughts at a glance. It is an instant reminder of what the team is doing and what it has accomplished. It is the group's thinking on display."

Coming back to the ProQuest example, (in the light of "Collective Sense-Making", discussed about 5 sections earlier).

The ProQuest team appears to have developed this capability, employing face-to-face for the design meetings, using Google Hangout and Skype for problem solving, and Flowdock for the transmission of errors and customer comments. The researchers also note that part of that capability is team members delaying raising difficult issues until the next scheduled face to face meeting, understanding that the nature of the issue requires a richer medium. Taco Ekkel, the Team Lead of the Summit studied by Dixon explains, *"We often (and largely unconsciously, I think) delay discussions around features of a certain magnitude until the next Summit, knowing we'd never really effectively get them conceptualized without the richness of face-to-face contact coupled with sketching."* Matching the conversation or task to the suitable social media is faciliated regularly through calenderized schedules. This is a Best Practice as opposed to having as-needed collective sense-making meetings, because this practice makes sure that there is consistency and team members know there will be an opportunity to address the more difficult issues.

As suggested by Chatti et al. (2007), *"social media supports a bottom-up building of communities and networks"*. By using appropriate social media technologies, it can enhance the social motivation of the users in pursuing knowledge management.

Blogs are commonly used by most progressive organizations, but researchers (and very likely users) have found Facebook more conducive for community building. Chan of Hong Kong University explains:

Facebook users are more likely to express social support on the platform. The results clearly indicated that Facebook is a more effective social media in building a culture of support, thereby facilitating the social-collaborative process of knowledge management. As a social networking platform, Facebook comprise more interactive and collaborative features (e.g. group notification, private messaging), and provides more channels to demonstrate social support (e.g. giving "Like"), not necessarily having to substantiate or defend why they "Like".

Facebook lets users within a community form tighter social bonds through "where they come from" i.e. their hobbies, interests, local associations, offline loyalties and such multidimensional view, which is a real-life reflection of themselves. Thus it "cultivates", within the network, a favorable culture for online and offline knowledge management by increasing motivation to participate in knowledge-sharing within and without using the tool. In general observation, this author found that Facebook users showed a high degree of safe, non-judgemental engagement in reflecting on knowledge, capturing daily/professional experiences and providing feedbacks that support knowledge transfer. Community development comprises not only the tools and conversations; but also social support

CONCLUSION

The Best Pactices recommended are as follows:

- An integrated KM strategy for all KM programs is recommended. Organizational pain-points are the best seeds for developing communities and other KM initiatives. Focus on specific strategic or tactical outcomes helps achieve visible, measurable outcomes, which should be communicated in a consistent manner.
- Enlisting early adopters and getting early successes- through piloting gives momentum. A lifecycle approach to community building is useful.
- Make it personal. Regular recognition for engaging experts or knowledge sharers rather than rewards for contributions are recommended.
- CoPs and Forums are ideal platforms to share experiences and lessons learnt. Communities are extremely valuable because of their informal, just-in-time, increasingly real-time advantage and cannot be replaced by structured KM platforms.
- Social Media provides multiple user-friendly tools to make it easy to seamlessly converse, share experiences and Lessons Learnt as they happen; as well as in a curated form. Regular Face-to-face meetings are crucial.
- Sharing of lessons learnt and innovation (process innovation, customer and partner driven innovation and breakthrough innovation) are best benefitted from collaboration and co-creation in Communities.
- Lessons Learnt through failures should invariably, (in fact, even at the cost of success stories) be documented and discussed in communities.

- Community leadership (SME), role-clarity and community facilitation reflecting trust, the spirit of learning and problem solving are ideal to engage Experts and novices.
- Monitoring and Measuring the activities, business benefits and impact of communities and forums helps sustain them.
- Collective sense-making and curation help the organization in harvesting and branding, resulting in lasting competitive advantage.
- Challenges (competitive and non-competitive) are great energizers for breakthrough innovations. Co-creation is community nirvana.

REFERENCES

Board of Innovations. (2011). *Open Innovation and Crowd-sourcing Examples*. Retrieved 12 November 2014 from, http://www.boardofinnovation.com/list-open-innovation-crowdsourcing-examples/

Chan, R. C. H., Chu, S. K. W., Lee, C. W. Y., Chan, B. K. T., & Leung, C. K. (2013). Knowledge management using social media: A comparative study between blogs and Facebook. *Proceedings of the American Society for Information Science and Technology, 50*(1), 1–9.

Chatti, A., Klamma, R., Jarke, M., & Naeve, A. (2007). *The Web 2.0 driven SECI model based learning process*. Paper presented at the International Conference of Advanced Learning Technologies (ICALT-2007), Japan. doi:10.1109/ICALT.2007.256

Chua, A. Y. K. (2006). Starting a Community-of-practice at Holden College: A Reflection of the Experience. *OR Insight, 19*, 3–8.

Milton, N. (2012). *Quantified KM success story number 30: Halliburton Electronic Technicians Community*. Retrieved on November 12, 2014, from http://www.nickmilton.com/2012/05/quanitified-km-success-story-number-30.htmlnumberixzz3HcelCSrV

ProQuest Case Study. (2014). *Using the Oscillation Principle for Software Development Conversations Matter Blog*. Retrieved on 21 November 2014 from http://www.nancydixonblog.com/

Vestal, W. (2003). Ten traits for a successful Community of Practice. *KM Review, 5*(6), 6.

Walling, S. (2009). *Becoming an open enterprise: five lessons from Booz Allen Hamilton*. Retrieved November 13, 2014, from http://Readwrite.com/2009/06/26/Becoming-An-Open-Enterprise-Five-Lessons-From-Booz

Wenger, E., McDermott, R., & Synder, W. (2002). Cultivating Communities of Practice: A guide of Managing Knowledge. Boston: Harvard Business School Press.

Wenger, E. C., & Snyder, W. M. (2000). Communities of Practice: The Organizational Frontier. *Harvard Business Review, 78*(1), 139–146. PMID:11184968

Wilken, C. V., & Ramsell, P. (2004). Building Effective Communities. In E. Truch (Ed.), *Leveraging Corporate Knowledge* (pp. 55–60). Burlington, VT: Gower Publishing.

Chapter 2
Cultural Barriers to Organizational Social Media Adoption

Amir Manzoor
Bahria University, Pakistan

ABSTRACT

Before they became a part of our social lives, most communication technologies were introduced with a business function in mind. Private individuals quickly adopted social media technology as an extension of their personal life. Due to this reason, many organizations are struggling to understand how this technology can benefit their mission, while many more worry that it will devastate productivity and security. Individuals who wield the power of expansive social media networks can significantly alter an organization's credibility and fiscal health. Organizations who harness the massive data warehouses behind these social media networks have the ability to significantly alter individual lives and society at large; for better or worse. However, barriers to organizational social media adoption are more cultural than technical. This chapter analyzes what cultural barriers are being raised against social media adoption and how can management re-align their understanding of social media to better utilize resources and take advantage of the opportunities this technology presents.

1. INTRODUCTION

The biggest hurdle to social media adoption by businesses is culture. In a 2011 global study by IBM, four barriers were identified that prevented companies from social media adoption: Security, Adoption, Compliance, and Culture. According to Information Week, "Command-and-control culture" was the number one obstacle among the Top 10 Enterprise Social Networking Obstacles. In his 12 social business predictions for 2012, Dion Hinchcliffe from the Dachis Group predicted that social intranets will continue to struggle not from a technology perspective but from lack of collaboration between internal teams like IT, Human Resources, Marketing, etc. This is a culture challenge (Perficient.com, 2011).

DOI: 10.4018/978-1-4666-9607-5.ch002

Paul Otlet an entrepreneur, visionary envisioned a mechanized system of shared knowledge based on a system of hyperlinks, which not only bound information together but also expanded on the understanding of the information by providing context (Rayward, 1975). The birth of World Wide Web in 1993 brought a milestone of the system envisioned by Paul Otlet. The final component was to add context to the hyperlinks so that the information could be turned into social knowledge.

The dawn of social media started the realization of context through a combination of metadata and machine awareness. Social media sites use metadata and network awareness to provide suggestions to users for new friends with whom they might want to connect. Search engines like Google are combining traditional indexing structures with social media networking data transfers to add further context to searches. This understanding of context also improving the learning of network of machines that makes up our inter-connected world. However, a world of freely shared, contextual information is still a dream that faces significant cultural than technological challenges to come true.

According to a study by the PulsePoint Group (PulsePoint, 2012), the average return on social engagement was calculated to be between 3-5 percent. The most engaged businesses are reporting a calculated 7.7 percent business impact specifically from social engagement, which is four times the performance of the lowest performers who only achieved a 1.9 percent estimated return.

The growing popularity of social media is making its mark on companies as well as individuals. Facebook enjoys more than 500 million members. This number alone is enough for organizations to realize that social media is the next place where they would find their customers, future employees and other stakeholders. Social media can provide multiple benefits to the organizations such as customer contact, facilitation in knowledge work, fast and easy information exchange, and increased departmental collaboration (Fuchs-Kittowski et al. 2009). Despite the possibilities, many companies still haven't leveraged social media due to various challenges and problems associated with its adoption and use (Bughin et al. 2008). These challenges may arise due to the fact that social media, being a web 2.0 tool, is a paradigm shift in how users connect and communicate with each other. Social media can enable collaboration and break down information silos to help aggregate and publish information (Mande and Wigand, 2010). Social media provides a platform for content production where consumers and other external stakeholders become active content producers and consumers at the same time. Some companies are becoming open organizations and using social media to relinquish some of the historical control they have had on the content they produced. Such organizational shift marks a big change in the organizational culture.

The barriers to enterprise social media adoption are far more cultural than technical. The objective of this chapter is to discuss the cultural barriers to social media adoption in the organizations. Within most organizations, there lies a wealth of information locked away due to both technological and cultural constraints. For the purpose of this chapter, cultural constraints are those organizational habits, leadership and management styles, policies and procedures that significantly hinder adoption of social media usage.

2. FACTORS UNDERLYING THE CULTURAL BARRIERS

According to (Miller, 2010; Michael Silverman, 2013; Beth Kanter, 2009; Jones, 2010; Coye Cheshire, 2011; Michael Brito, 2012; Hunt, 2013) the following cultural barriers hinder organization's adoption of social media.

- **Fear**: Fear refers to the apprehension caused by uncertainty. It could include fear of failure, fear of change, fear of employee abuse, fear of reputational damage, fear of security violations, fear of accountability of one's actions, fear of productivity reduction due to social media usage, fear of maintaining one's relevancy with the new technology, fear of security in sharing information through social media, fear of legal reporting requirements, and fear of changing organizational structure. Concerns about employees compromising the environment have gated adoption of social technologies in numerous ways. Organizations may be slow to adopt based on these concerns. They may adopt in pockets but be hesitant to deploy to the broad enterprise. They may deploy broadly but curtail the scope of the effort to exclude communication in areas where there is potential risk.
- **Business Case:** It refers to absence of a well-grounded business case or rationale for implementing social technologies and difficulty in measuring return on investment.
- **Uncertainty**: It could include loss of control over subordinates or project scope, and loss of competitive advantage.
- **Knowledge and Understanding:** A lack of knowledge and understanding about the wider use of social media and what can be done in practical terms to facilitate implementation.
- **Leadership:** Senior management lacking skills and awareness about social media that stifles their views of tangible organizational benefits, prevents leaders from driving change and make them dismissive and distrusting.

The various barriers mentioned above do not work in isolation and they may overlap and interconnected. For example, lack of knowledge and understanding may be an antecedent of fear. Similarly, lack of knowledge and understanding by leaders can result in overestimation of risks by thee leaders. Organizations should review these barriers and their relationships with regard to their specific purpose and organizational context.

There can be several factors underlying these cultural barriers. Such factors may include loss of employment, family and even financial security due to over exposure through social media. Transparency issues, requirements for greater transparency as well as those for greater privacy have resulted in private and public institutions being forced to respond to expensive and embarrassing cases of exposure. To maintain trust should organizations hide from social media? Should organizations cut their employees off from these interactions before these problems arise? Social media networks do make it easier than ever for inappropriate connections to be made. Facebook boasts 400 million active users (Facebook 2010). The ability for so many people to connect to an individual's online content and repost that content creates a multiplication factor of previously unheard of proportions. This exponential reach is what presents us with both risk and opportunity and management needs to look for the opportunities to be found in this level of individual outreach. Those opportunities are often positive ways to mitigate the risks. The organizations that ignore social media are often the ones finding themselves blindsided. In all cases, we see that these cultural barriers are an attempt at risk management. But we need to see whether the risk actually exist or its just perceived risk. However, to suggest that this is merely an issue where removing the technology is the solution would be severely underestimating what is happening within our culture. Social media has become integral to many people's daily lives and removal of it would be tantamount to removal of phone access.

During the short lifespan of social media, we already have several examples of people losing employment, family and even their financial security due to over exposure through social media. Transparency issues, loss of reputation, requirements for greater transparency as well as those for greater privacy have resulted in private and public institutions being forced to respond to expensive and embarrassing cases of exposure. Let's take an example. In Spanierman v. Hughes, 2008 U.S. Dist. LEXIS 69569 (D. Conn. Sept. 16, 2008), Jeffrey Spanierman, a teacher at Emmett O'Brien High School in Ansonia, Connecticut, created a page on MySpace (a popular social media network), ostensibly "to communicate with students about homework, to learn more about the students so he could relate to them better, and to conduct casual, non-school related discussions." (Jeffrey D. Neuburger, 2008). The page contained, among other things, pictures of naked men with "inappropriate comments" underneath them. Spanierman used this page to have personal conversations with the students. This case highlights several risks that organizations and individuals face due to the highly transparent nature of social media use. One of Spanierman's school colleagues became concerned about the page and she convinced Spanierman to remove the page. Spanierman subsequently created a new MySpace page, however, that included similar content and similar personal communications with students. When the colleague learned of the new page, she reported it to the school administration, which placed Spanierman on administrative leave and ultimately declined to renew his teaching contract for the following year. Mr. Spanierman claims that he had a right to use his MySpace profile both for his own personal pursuits as well as for communicating with students. The courts ultimately did not agree with him and his dismissal was upheld. This case highlights several risks that organizations and individuals face due to the highly transparent nature of social media use.

A resolution of this issue required involvement of many individuals and the facts surrounding the case were damaging for both the school and career of Mr. Spanierman. Many parents raised questions about the health and safety of their children. Though school took action to resolve the situation but this action was reactive and not preemptive. As a result, school lost trust of parents. This case raised some serious questions for organizations. In order maintain customer trust should organizations not maintain their social media presence? Or should organizations pro-actively monitor their employees interactions on social media before any problem arises? (Miller, A. 2010).

Back in April 2013, the Guardian Newspaper reported that a Freedom of Information request revealed that the Metropolitan Police investigated 75 officers for potentially misusing Facebook and other social networks in the past five years. Three community support officers and four police officers were dismissed following disciplinary investigations since 2009. A further six community support officers and 2 staff resigned or retired after facing complaints about their misuse of social media. Of the 75 officers investigated, 38 had complaints proven against them and 25 were cleared. A further six were investigated further. Of those 38 officers, three were sacked, 18 were given written warning, six received some form of management action, six retired or resigned and further five received "management advice". Out of 12 police civilian staff investigated, four were sacked, two resigned, four received written warnings and two were formally reprimanded over their use of social media (Elspeth Buck, 2013).

In 2009, Domino's employees posted a disgusting video of what they did to pizzas before delivery. The video soon went viral. The company's initial response was limited with a small social presence – a release on the website, a video from the CEO and a makeshift twitter feed to respond in real time. But more importantly, the company took this experience to heart and developed ways to improve their customer relationship. Domino's spent months getting feedback from surveys and focus groups, and decided they needed an entire product overhaul. They created "The Pizza Turnaround" campaign to market their new pizza. Not only did they push this campaign on social sites, but searched for creative ways to truly engage. Domino's showed social media feedback on a billboard in Times Square, asked people to snap pictures of their pizza, and even created an innovation hub. In 2006, Dell was just starting in social media when one of their computers spontaneously caught on fire, and the accompanying video went viral. The chairman of Dell at the time released a very transparent blog post telling their customers they did not yet know what the cause was. Customer reaction to this post was overwhelmingly grateful for the honesty. After this experience, Dell created a strategic, transparent infrastructure to develop better relationships in the future. They reached out to bloggers like Jeff Jarvis who had previous bad experiences with Dell, and asked for ways to improve. In 2011, they even launched a social media command center powered by Radian 6. With a tactical focus on listening, they invested greatly in empowering their employees to engage with customers on the social web. Today, 1/3 of all Dell employees are trained on social media literacy, over 4,000 are certified to engage with customers (Research Team, 2012).

An incident at O'Hare International Airport provided United Airlines an opportunity to experience the online exponential reach of individuals and its potential impact on company's image and reputation. Sons of Maxell, a little-known Canadian country and western music duo, claimed that their Taylor acoustic guitar had been damaged by United Airlines baggage handlers at Chicago's O'Hare airport. The band was involved in a vain year-long attempt to win compensation from United. After several months of requesting a settlement from United Airlines, the company chose to deny the claims based on technicalities. The Sons of Maxell then developed and released a song named *United Breaks Guitars* to describe their situation. This song became a YouTube sensation and provided the band with the biggest hit of their career. The song had almost 4 million hits on YouTube. Once the video appeared and became a YouTube hit, United sat up and took notice. It offered to pay the cost of repairing the guitar and flight vouchers worth $1,200 (£700) but the band refused the offer. Other airlines offered the band free trips to experience their customer service. United, which has seen its share price tumble, could have spared itself this public relations humiliation if it had followed its own policy on customer service (Tran, 2009; Carroll, 2009).

While United lost their image despite having a large public relations department, southwest airlines shined by expanding their customer service to the online world. The agents of southwest airlines continuously observed social media for any conversations about southwest and offered assistance where possible and gratitude when positive comments were made. All of this was made possible by simply empowering the workforce to do the right thing. Southwest achieved consistently higher levels of customer satisfaction with very low rates of customer complaints (US Department of Travel, 2009).

The extension of the Southwest customer service to include social media was a move that was closely monitored by its competitors and many companies followed suit. The key point of this customer service model is that it provided help to the customers when they wanted it and in the environment they preferred. Social media provided an opportunity to the companies discover people in need based on their content and then reach out to them directly to solve their problem. This very much informal process didn't require traditional helpdesk or PR staff but required a broader base to cover this type of extensive, proactive outreach effort.

The current social media users have a great deal of comfort with these pseudo-informal processes that companies like South west Airlines employed to maintain their organizations reputation. This is because they used these same sorts of strategies for maintaining their own reputations online. According to Palfrey and Gasser (2008) these users grew up with no direct experience to the pre-internet enabled digital world. This always-connected always-sharing environment makes these users comfortable with freely shared intellectual property, mass collaboration, decentralized leadership, and broad transparency. This culture lends itself to creative problem solving and greater innovation – in all aspects of life.

Social media innovators are taking advantage of these online cultural traits and using them to create products and solutions not because they are charged with some sort of traditional position of power to make these things happen; they are instead doing it based on a burning desire to see it happen and the free or cheap resources to do it. Historically 3M has been a leader in supporting experimentation by its research employees, giving them time to work on projects they find personally interesting. A culture of innovation has been built at 3M. To foster creativity, 3M encourages technical staff members to spend up to 15 percent of their time on projects of their own choosing. Also known as the "bootlegging" policy, the 15 percent rule has been the catalyst for some of 3M's most famous products, such as *Scotch Tape* and *Post-it* Notes (3MCulture, 2009). When those projects look like they might have a marketable application 3M gives more time and resources; the company understands that innovation can come from unexpected places if you just let it. This is exactly how the ubiquitous *Post-It* Note came to be. This shows the value of exploration and experimentation in product design even in highly vertical organizational structures. In traditional organizations, staff members strictly work according to assigned job roles and develop a myopic vision about innovation duet to the lack of opportunity for experimentation and innovation. The middle management of many organizations follow similar culture. The online social media is much more about communication, collaboration and innovation. One great example is Twitter that provides a convenient way for internal employees to communicate. A realignment of workers and workgroups, based on a loose definition of their job roles, can actually provide them with sense of empowerment and opportunity to follow personal desire and curiosity. This, in turn, can bring significant increase in worker productivity.

Social media tools provide higher efficiency and broad collaboration even in traditional management structures. These tools provide ease of communication and can help develop searchable and linkable digital knowledgebase. A study estimated that ineffective collaboration and knowledge transfer could result in a potential net loss of $485 million and a use of better social media collaboration tools and implementing a culture of collaboration could turn this loss around (Microsoft, 2009). However, management and shareholders also see a major downside to productivity and efficiency gains achieved by using social media, namely loss of direct control over intellectual property. The management and shareholders share the perception of (Kelly, 2008) that Internet is a media that provides uncontrollable and indiscriminate sharing of anything made available online.

The culture of free sharing of intellectual property over the social media (whether legal or illegal) has provided a mass of cheap products. This culture of sharing deeply engrained in social media is posing serious threats to the viability of historical culture of patents, trademarks and copyrights. There is predominant thinking that anything digital will eventually become free. The philosophy behind this thinking is that abundance of computing power and availability of many individuals willing to do knowledge work for free should provide digital content which is free. This system of "freeconomy" however is a transactional ecosystem than a traditional one-way market where sellers bring something to sell to the buyers (Anderson, 2009). This free sharing culture provided by social media provides retention of the value of intellectual property but provides different ways to realize this value. According to Lessig (2004), historically the intellectual property has been made free when the greater good provided by it increased. With digital technologies bringing this shift across many industries, this issue of free sharing has become more controversial. Google is the company most criticized in this debate of free sharing due to Google's mission of organizing the world's information and make it universally accessible and useful (Google, 2009). Google doesn't charge individuals for the services it provides. Google earns through advertising and selling services to corporate customers. One controversial services of Google is the one that publishes online orphan works of media. Google Books stored 10 million book in digital format and made them freely available. This free access was considered by many as a theft of intellectual property and Google faced many law suits (Google, 2010). Following the similar line of arguments, new services argue that Google's attempt to aggregate their content by search engine is not only a theft of intellectual property but also damaging to their revenue from web advertisements. Technology behind targeted advertising is another controversy that companies using this technology face (such as Google). In order this technology works most efficiently require a massive database of users' online activities (such as use of social media and online searches). How companies (such as Google) collects this information and whether such information collection violates any privacy laws is another controversy. This discussion leads us to a very important question as to how organizations can establish a big-brother relationship with the society in which and possibly contribute to a society citizens rapidly lose all privacy. The answer to this question has serious implications for citizens, clients and competitive advantage of the organizations. It is still unknown whether the rapid adoption of social media by general public will bring a culture of transparency in private organizations where most have still not adopted social media networks. It is interesting to see whether private organizations will be able to establish the big-brother relationship with the society or consumers will force a culture of transparency in such organizations (Miller, 2010).

3. CONVERTING BARRIERS TO SOCIAL MEDIA OPPORTUNITIES

The removal of barriers can result in various opportunities/advantages for organizations. These opportunities can be viewed from three perspectives namely employees, customer engagement, and external partners.

Benefits to employees include speedier access to organizational knowledge, speedier access to internal expertise, greater collaboration opportunities, reduced internal communication costs, improved training processes, and improved recruitment of new employees. Benefits in terms of customer engagement include ability to mine and analyze customer data more effectively, ability to personalize marketing activities based on customer interests, and better product development. Benefits to external partners (including suppliers and other business partners include, speedier access to external knowledge and improved information sharing, reduced external communication costs, and improved collaboration and innovation opportunities.

The themes below are suggested as the most relevant when an organization is considering deploying social media and want to address the barriers to adoption (Coye Cheshire, 2011).

3.1. Find a Champion

A champion is a super user or a powers user who uses a new technology for the sake of trying out something new (Moore, 1991). This person is a regular user of social media tool and can drive the adoption of social media. Since they understand the importance of social media they are strong candidates to sell social media within organization. This is because these users have the additional power of influence and can convince others of the utility of the social media. They see social media as a source of competitive advantage and desire to be the harbinger of change. These champions should be the people well-known in the organization with established significant internal networks that they can use leverage these fairly easily. A champion should preferably have knowledge of both the technology and business. A thought leader is the one who is recognized from outside world for its deep understanding of business, the needs of customers, and the broader marketplace in which the organization operates. Several large corporations have thought leadership initiatives. These initiatives/programs can be a starting point to look for these champions. For smaller companies, this may be a slightly more difficult task.

3.2. Define a Use Case

To ensure success of social media adoption within organization, organizations should first identify specific and measurable goals of social media adoption. Organizations should not first implement social media and then wait for users to find a use of it. The majority of users need to be convinced about the genuine reason because of which they must use social media (Moore, 1991). To establish social media as an organizational asset a clear and well-defined use case is required and non-technical people of organization play a very important role in this regard. These people need to define how social media can be used in the organization.

3.3. Understand Your Target Audience

A deep understanding of organizational users of social media is important to determine the possible attributes that can be used to analyze the population of users who may be using social media. Following are some examples of some of these attributes. There may be other attributes that may exist when looking at additional firms.

3.3.1. Age

Age has a clear influence on the propensity to use social media (Brzozowski, Sandholm, & Hogg, 2009). Reverse mentoring (an initiative in which older executives are paired with and mentored by younger employees on topics such as technology) can be used to overcome the age barrier. However, there exist risk that older populations of users will never see the value in social media.

3.3.2. Departmental Affiliation

Departmental affiliation often create different needs for users because this affiliation sets the context in which populations of users exist. These different needs can impact users' choice of social media. Users are generally interested to use that tools of social media that are more relevant and helpful in doing their day-to-day job.

3.3.3. Culture

The internal culture of an organization can largely impact how social media is adopted. The clients of organizations often have very different cultures and priorities. Organizations need to understand these priorities in order develop use cases aligned with these cultures and meaningful and attractive to the workforce. Incentives and reward structures are a good example of a culture component. Organizations should implement social media with a targeted initiative to collectively reward participation and knowledge sharing.

3.3.4. Geography

Organizations have different geographical distributions, and this plays into their specific needs for social media. To understand needs of their target audience, organizations need to understand their pain points. Once those pain points are identified, use cases of social media could then be created or modified directly address those problems. If social media use cases do not directly address a pain point in a measurable way the attention of the workforce cannot be obtained. For example, if sales managers of an organization are struggling to get timely updates on what's happening in the field, an appropriate use case would provide a suitable social media tool to address this need. With understanding of their target audience, the organizations can determine key problems that keep target audience from accomplishing their work and find measurable ways to address those problems with social media.

3.4. Right Mix of Bottom-Up and Top-Down Influence

Social software is bottom-up by design and this design enable the architecture of participation. Executive support is needed for the social media implementation to succeed. Rather than mandating and governing usage of social media, organizations should let their employees to discover the right ways to use the social media themselves. If the key decision makers are not sold on to the idea early on, it will slow down, or even result in unsuccessful adoption. Executive support can be more important when the company successfully implements the first use case and tries to push for cross-unit collaboration.

3.5. Approach Adoption as a Lifecycle

Technology adoption life cycle (Bohlen & Beal, 1957) is a model that describes the adoption of any new product and every step of the adoption process brings on users that have key defining characteristics. Every step brings forth a new kind of user and different sets of users have different needs. User groups can be divided into innovators, early adopters, early majority, late majority, and laggards. Rogers (1962) identified some key reasons that influence the end-user's decision to adopt or reject a process. To apply this concept on social media adoption we need to answer few question such as relative advantage (i.e. how is use of social media better than the previous way of doing this), compatibility (i.e. how compatible is the social media with present way of doing business, complexity (i.e. how easy is it to use social media in the intended way), trialability (i.e. the ability to experiment with social media easily, without committing to it early on), and observability (i.e. who are the existing users of this technology and what are their perceptions about this technology). The strategies for pushing adoption differ from stage to stage. Towards the end of a stage technology usage tends to plateau indicating that a new strategy is needed to push technology adoption further.

3.6. Harvesting Social Knowledge

Harvesting can also be used to provide social content. Social media collaboration tools can provide high level of transparency by recording every move a user makes on his/her system. In an organization where such transparency is maintained workers are well-placed to the positions they deserve while the ones not working transparently can be exposed and repositioned. This transparency provides organizations an opportunity to re-align their workforce according to current requirements and gain increase in worker productivity and innovation. However, organizations should use this transparency cautiously and find a balanced approach in which transparency is encouraged as a means to achieve positive change for both organization and employees. Sunshine laws in United States provided US citizens with a level of government transparency. Through sunshine laws, administrative agencies are required to do their work in public, and as a result, the process is sometimes called "government in the sunshine." While similar laws are implemented in other countries as well, most private organizations worldwide face few requirements to implement transparency in their conduct of business. The culture of transparency in the organization can be directly affected by transparency laws and the individuals administering those laws. One example can be taken from the government of former US president of United States, George W. Bush. The Bush administration blocked many attempts by watchdog groups to invoke transparency laws (Miller, 2010).

3.7. Crowdsourcing

Crowdsourcing is the process of soliciting contributions from a large group of people (especially experts belonging to an online community) in solving a problem and creating something new. Social media has provided a platform for individuals to experience the power of crowdsourcing where they can exploit very basic social knowledge at home and in their communities. The significant driver behind participation in crowdsourcing is the personal passion. One drawback of crowdsourcing is the loss of direct control over a project. However, crowdsourcing is a very efficient way to empower participants and provide learning and collaboration in the organizations that could ultimately result in increased organizational efficiency and innovation.

3.8. Organization-Wide Collaboration

Use of social media for collaboration provide reduced hierarchal levels in organizations and change command and control structures of projects. Any individual can scrutinize this collaboration that can provide an added competitive advantage by gaining opportunities to make significant changes in company's products and services. Wider collaborations can result in development of superior goods and services. One good example is Wikipedia. Wikipedia is very flexible and doesn't sacrifice the accuracy of the content to provide this flexibility (Giles, 2005). A business needs to foresee such products and services that can be developed and marketed as a result of collaboration. In future, secrecy of product will become less important in gaining competitive advantage than the quality of organization-wide collaboration.

4. ORGANIZATIONAL USE OF SOCIAL MEDIA: IMPLICATIONS/RECOMMENDATIONS

Use of social media by organizations to grow, capture and reuse the social knowledge can make these organizations more efficient, innovative and successful. Social media use by individuals appears to be penetrating organizations enough. The cultural issues are as important to reference and detail as the technology surrounding them. The various cultural barriers in the way of wide-spread social media adoption by organizations vary but are similar to the ones faced by organizations while adopting any technological advancement. For successful implementation and sustainable use of social media, organizations need to take up first various cultural barriers that may hinder the organizational social media adoption. Organizations must realize that social media is a tool and just as the case of any other tool users need certain time to become comfortable at using it. A solid cultural foundation among social media users is necessary and organizations must take this responsibility on priority basis. Some defining characteristics of this cultural foundation should include openness to sharing, a clear understanding of transparency, individuals with collaborative approach, and a clear understanding of the new working of social media. Failing to provide such cultural foundation, organizations may run into deep-rooted issues while implementing social media use. Many a times organizations may not recover from the pitfalls and end-up failing to achieve the desired results of social media adoption.

The current ongoing economic downturn is forcing organizations to use knowledge workers as a source of competitive advantage. Social media has provided organization a platform to support distributed work environments. The existing tools, such as email, are so overburdened that they are losing their effectiveness even for the purposes they were invented for. To better utilize knowledge workers and communities in core business processes, existing applications are integrating social media capabilities in their core feature set.

The first step of building the required cultural foundation for organizational social media adoption is to provide internal work groups and staff opportunity to engage in understanding the utilization of social media. This is because there could be some people already familiar with social media tools and how they could be efficiently utilized within organizations. Organizations can also strengthen this cultural foundation by arranging participant led cross-functional meetings. These meeting can provide an avenue to discover the experts of social media within the organization. By utilizing face-to-face interaction techniques that remove hierarchy the true wisdom of the organization can be found. Social knowledge harvesting is ultimately the focus of these meetings, which can then provide content for the social media tools being used. Knowledge capture through social media not only provides a source of quick reference but also strengthen the internal network of organization. This is because organizational use of social media helps achieve strong buy-ins from all organizational stakeholders because now everyone is socially connected. While such organization-wide social media adoption provides many advantages there also exist disadvantages. There is a need to bring individuals, government and private organizations on to same page with respect to developing guiding principles over transparency in social media use.

This chapter contributes to better understanding the nature of enterprise social media adoption as not only a technological deployment, but as an enabler of a much larger change in how we think about and do business and work. For businesses and managers, this chapter represent an illustration of what kinds of issues should be considered before adopting social media and what are the possible ways to overcome these issues for transformation to become a truly social business.

5. FUTURE RESEARCH DIRECTION

One area that needs further research is the risks to organizational adoption and use of social networking and social media technologies. Future research is needed to ascertain whether such risks are theoretical or not. With respect to these risks, further research is needed to ascertain whether there are certain types of industry or organization that are especially prone to risk in terms of the adoption and use of these technologies. Future research is also needed to analyze which of the risks associated with social networking and social media platforms could be addressed through organizational or governmental policies.

This chapter did not attempt to address the question of whether or not social media was truly effective within the workplace. This is another relevant area of research that deserves future work.

6. CONCLUSION

Implementing social media is not a 'plug-and-play' solution. Barriers to adoption exist but the relevance of any given barrier is unique within each organization, use case, or user population. It is imperative that stakeholders identify those barriers that matter the most in the given scenario. A "one-size-fits-all approach" is ineffective. The overarching message is that any competitive benefits that social media offers cannot simply be purchased. Social media only enable those benefits. Organizations must be willing to do the work to identify their key barriers to adoption and to implement strategies that address those barriers. The discussion of barriers, provided in this chapter, provides a starting point for organizations who are interested in capitalizing on social media. It is possible that other barriers to adoption (outside of those mentioned in this chapter) exist.

The key to successful implementation and sustainability of social media in any organization is to realize that the cultural changes must be considered up front. Social media is merely a tool. Like any new tool, there is a necessary adjustment period where the user has to grow into a comfort level with it.

While there are many pitfalls to avoid along the way to embracing social media the reward of navigating this cultural and technological shift appears to be well worth the risk.

REFERENCES

3MCulture. (2009). *3M – A Culture of Innovation*. Retrieved from http://www.3m.com/us/office/ postit/pastpresent/history_cu.html Anderson, C. (2009). *Free: the future of a radical price*. New York: Hyperion.

Aral, S., Dellarocas, C., & Godes, D. (2013). Introduction to the Special Issue—Social Media and Business Transformation: A Framework for Research. *Information Systems Research, 24*(1), 3–13. doi:10.1287/isre.1120.0470

Bower, B. (2010). *Wired Science Online: No Lie! Your Facebook Profile Is the Real You*. Retrieved from http://www.wired.com/wired- science/2010/02/no-lie-your-facebook-profile- is-the-real-you/

Bridges, K. (2013). Use of Social Media by Catholic Organizations. *New Theology Review, 26*(1), 1–10.

Brito. (2012, January 4). *Lessons from IBM: 4 Barriers To Social Business Adoption*. Retrieved from http://www.socialbusinessnews.com/lessons-from-ibm-4-barriers-to-social-business-adoption/

Buck, E. (2013, July 30). *Can I dismiss for an employee for making comments on a social media?* Retrieved from http://fpmblog.co.uk/2013/07/30/can-i-dismiss-for-an-employee-for-making-inappropriate-comments-on-a-social-media-site/

Carr. (2011). 10 Enterprise Social Networking Obstacles. *InformationWeek*. Retrieved from http://www.informationweek.com/social-business/social_networking_private_platforms/10-enterprise-social-networking-obstacle/232301139

Carroll, D. (2009). *United Breaks Guitars*. Retrieved from http://www.davecarrollmusic.com/story/united-breaks-guitars/

Coye Cheshire. (2011). *Enterprise Social Software: Addressing Barriers to Adoption*. Retrieved on October 29, 2014, from http://www.ischool.berkeley.edu/programs/mims/projects/2011/enterprise

Curtis, L., Edwards, C., Fraser, K. L., Gudelsky, S., Holmquist, J., Thornton, K., & Sweetser, K. D. (2010). Adoption of social media for public relations by nonprofit organizations. *Public Relations Review*, *36*(1), 90–92. doi:10.1016/j.pubrev.2009.10.003

Dilenschneider, C. (n.d.). *Inspiring Institutions to Embrace Social Strategies: A Formula for Change*. Retrieved July 28, 2014, from http://colleendilen.com/2011/06/13/inspiring-institutions-to-embrace-social-strategies-a-formula-for-change/

Dispatch, C. (2010). *One of the Best Values Around– Only in the Dispatch*. Retrieved from http://www.dispatch.com/live/content/faq/exclusive.html

Electronic Frontier Foundation. (2010). *Panopti- click*. Retrieved from https://panopticlick.eff.org/

Facebook. (2010). *Facebook Statistics*. Retrieved from http://www.facebook.com/press/info.php?statistics

Forcier, E., Rathi, D., & Given, L. (2014). Tools of Engagement for Knowledge Management: Using Social Media to Capture Non-Profit Organizations' Stories. *Proceedings of the Annual Conference of the Canadian Association for Information Science*. Retrieved from http://www.cais-acsi.ca/ojs/index.php/cais/article/view/823

Gantz, J. F., Chute, C., Manfrediz, A., Minton, S., Reinsel, D., Schlichting, W., & Toncheva, A. (2008). *The diverse and exploding digital Universe*. An IDC White paper. Framingham, MA: IDC

Giles, J. (2005). *Nature International Weekly Journal of Science – Special Report: Internet encyclopedias go head to head*. Retrieved from http://www.nature.com/nature/journal/v438/n7070/full/438900a.html

Google. (2009). *Corporate Information – Com- pany Overview*. Retrieved from http://www.google.com/corporate/index.html

Google. (2010). *Google Books Settlement Agreement*. Retrieved from http://books.google.com/googlebooks/agreement/faq.html

Holtzblatt, L. (2013). Evaluating the Uses and Benefits of an Enterprise Social Media Platform. *Journal of Social Media for Organizations*, *1*(1).

Huang, J., Baptista, J., & Galliers, R. D. (2013). Reconceptualizing rhetorical practices in organizations: The impact of social media on internal communications. *Information & Management*, *50*(2–3), 112–124. doi:10.1016/j.im.2012.11.003

Hunt, C. (2013). *4 Big Barriers to Social Media Adoption: Key Research Findings.* Retrieved July 28, 2014, from http://www.recruitingblogs.com/profiles/blogs/4-big-barriers-to-social-media-adoption-key-research-findings

Jones, C. (2010, January). *Organization Culture: Barriers to 2.0 Adoption.* Retrieved from http://source-pov.com/2010/01/11/culture/

Kanter, B. (2009, April). *What lies beneath social media stress, fear, and barriers to adoption in nonprofits? - Beth's Blog: Nonprofits and Social Media.* Retrieved October 29, 2014, from http://beth.typepad.com/beths_blog/2009/04/what-lies-beneath-social-media-stress-fear-and-barriers-to-adoption-in-nonprofits.html

Kelly, K. (2008). *Better Than Free* [e-Book]. Retrieved from http://changethis.com/search?action=search&query=better+than+free

Leonardi, P. M., Huysman, M., & Steinfield, C. (2013, October). History, and Prospects for the Study of Social Technologies in Organizations. *Journal of Computer-Mediated Communication, 19*(1), 1–19. doi:10.1111/jcc4.12029

Lessig, L. (2004). *Free Culture: How Big Media Uses Technology and the Law to Lock Down Culture and Control Creativity.* New York: The Penguin Press.

Maes, P., & Mistry, P. (2009). *Retrieved from TED talks – Pattie Maes and Pranav Mistry demo SixthSense.* Retrieved from http://www.ted.com/talks/pat-tie_maes_demos_the_sixth_sense.html

Marlow, D. C. (2009). *Primates on Facebook.* Retrieved from http://www.economist.com/sciencetechnology/displayStory.cfm?story_id=13176775

Microsoft. (2009). Oil and Gas Pros View Social Media as Important for Productivity, Collaboration; Yet Few Firms Have Tools in Place. *New Survey Reports.* Retrieved from http://www.microsoft.com/presspass/press/2009/feb09/02-18OGSocialMediaPR.mspx

Miller, A. (2011). Cultural Barriers to Organizational Social Media Adoption. *Social Knowledge: Using Social Media to Know What You Know,* 96-114.

Moloney. (2011). *12 Social Business Predictions for 2012.* Retrieved from https://blogs.perficient.com/portals/2011/12/21/12-social-business-predictions-for-2012/

Neuburger. (2008, October 15). *Teacher Fired for Inappropriate Behavior on MySpace Page | Mediashift | PBS.* Retrieved from http://www.pbs.org/mediashift/2008/10/teacher-fired-for-inappropriate-behavior-on-myspace-page289/

Palfrey, J., & Gasser, U. (2008). *Born Digital: Understanding the First Generation of Digital Natives.* Cambridge, MA: Basic Books.

PulsePoint. (2012). *The Economics of A Fully Engaged Enterprise.* Retrieved July 28, 2014, from http://www.pulsepointgroup.com/services/social-media-accelerator

Rapp, A., Beitelspacher, L. S., Grewal, D., & Hughes, D. E. (2013). Understanding social media effects across seller, retailer, and consumer interactions. *Journal of the Academy of Marketing Science, 41*(5), 547–566. doi:10.1007/s11747-013-0326-9

Rathi, D., Given, L., Forcier, E., & Vela, S. (2014). Every Task its Tool, Every Tool its Task: Social Media Use in Canadian Non-Profit Organizations. *Proceedings of the Annual Conference of the Canadian Association for Information Science*. Retrieved from http://www.cais-acsi.ca/ojs/index.php/cais/article/view/905

Rayward, W. B. (1975). *The Universe of Information: The Work of Paul Otlet for documentation and International Organisation*. Chicago, IL: University of Chicago.

Research Team. (2012, May 14). *How Domino's and Dell Rebuilt Trust After a Social PR Crisis*. Retrieved from http://pivotcon.com/how-dominos-and-dell-rebuilt-trust-after-a-social-pr-crisis/

Sharif, M., Davidson, R., & Troshani, I. (2013). Exploring Social Media Adoption in Australian Local Government Organizations. *CONF-IRM 2013 Proceedings*. Retrieved from http://aisel.aisnet.org/confirm2013/29

Silverman. (2013, September 10). *4 Big Barriers to Social Media Adoption: Key Research Findings*. Retrieved from http://denovati.com/2013/09/barriers-to-social-media-adoption

Treem, J. W., & Leonardi, P. M. (2012). *Social Media Use in Organizations: Exploring the Affordances of Visibility, Editability, Persistence, and Association* (SSRN Scholarly Paper No. ID 2129853). Rochester, NY: Social Science Research Network. Retrieved from http://papers.ssrn.com/abstract=2129853

Chapter 3
Social Media as Elements of Shared Workspaces:
The Multifactory Case Study

Giulio Focardi
Osun Solutions, Italy

Lorenza Victoria Salati
Bigmagma, Italy

ABSTRACT

Shared workplaces are becoming very common within Europe. Multifactories are shared working environment that combine traits of a Coworking Space, a Fab Lab and a Makerspace. One of the traits that characterize a Multifactory is how knowledge exchange brings to innovation. This chapter has its focus on a case study that shows how a traditional SME and a multifactory can work together in order to develop an innovative idea and how Social Media can be parts of an overall strategy set to product innovation.

INTRODUCTION

Many people say do it yourself, we say do it together, make things together and share knowledge. Parade, M. (2013, July 15). Personal interview.

The shrinkage of product life cycles is a very well known issue and is a problem that companies have to face since a long time. Traditionally, companies used to change or renew products quite often and to have in their R&D departments several new products at different development stages. Product innovation is also traditionally linked to the idea that when someone in a company has a good idea, this has to be protected, kept as secret as possible, internally developed within the company or with a help from very reliable partners and brought to the market only when transformed into an exclusive product/service, ready to face the market. Nowadays, the life cycle of ideas, products, and services is so fast that it's less important to protect them. It's much more important to develop them as fast as possible, in a very reliable, cheap, and flexible way, to release the product on the market as soon as possible.

DOI: 10.4018/978-1-4666-9607-5.ch003

Social Media as Elements of Shared Workspaces

This chapter focuses on Multifactories, which are shared workspaces dedicated both to the development of services and to the production of material goods.

Multifactories are a type of collaborative environment where innovation comes from free access to common resources, contamination, mutual support and free exchange of knowledge.

Multifactories are multi-competency environments, where the concepts at the base of Sharing Economy apply to physical places and allow for a creative reuse of competencies that leads to product innovation.

A Multifactory is a system that generates more value than the sum of its node's individual values, also due to the social use of Social Media as constitutive elements of an overall strategy.

But a Multifactory is also an economic agent that interacts with other agents, like traditional companies are. When this happens, from the interaction and contamination of these different agents can come out a completely new way to product innovation, where Social Media take an important part.

THE RESEARCH PROJECT

Bigmagma, the multifactory that worked with Nuova Ferrari & Zagni in order to develop Grinding Project, is the result of the experimental stage of a research project carried out by Focardi and Salati from 2012 to 2015. The research started with the aim to visit and study workplaces with three characteristics: to have a great heterogeneity within people working in them, to include a part of production of goods, and to have a bottom-up governance system, at least partially. The research was as an on-field research that took place in five European Countries (Italy, Spain, Portugal, United Kingdom, and Germany), making use of a visual anthropology method and assuming an ethnographic point of view.

The first step of the research took place in North Italy and was to analyze the Made in MAGE of Sesto San Giovanni (Milan). Made in MAGE is a project hosted in a former steel factory, born in 2011 as a temporary reuse project and evolved as a community project. The Made in MAGE experience is interesting for what concerns the interaction of the project with the territorial stakeholders and how companies manage their relationship.

The second step of the research took place in South Italy and was to analyze the Progetto Microfiliera in the Pollino Natural Park. The Progetto Microfiliera is a project promoted by the regional agency for the agricultural development, born in 2011 to help local farmers to create a network and to establish a long term relationship with EVRA, a local factory that produces vegetable extracts. The Progetto Microfiliera experience is interesting for what concerns how a value chain management can result in a cross-skills exchange.

Table 1. Crowdworkers' voice on EXPECTATIONS

"In a way, MOB is a channel for me to get closer to people related to innovation and open collaborative systems, and that's why it makes sense for me being into MOB. I didn't have any expectations, at the beginning. I was working at home, but I realized it was too hard to spend so much time at home, alone, I was completely isolated and I was completely out of the world. I was spending 14 hours a day in my living room. It was unhealthy. At first, I started looking for an office, then I found MOB, and I felt it was different. My expectations were like a coworking space, with many people going around, but then, I think, MOB has exceeded my expectations in many ways. Especially for the workshops, and then I started getting familiar with these Makers, a movement I was completely ignorant about. Like in a way you're working, but while working you keep yourself updated and connected to the world, so that's the part that's exceeding my expectations." Rius, C. (2013, September 10). Personal interview.

The third step of the research took place in United Kingdom and was to analyze Building Bloqs, a "Coworking space for those in practical professions" as its coordinator defined it. Building Bloqs takes form as a Public Interest Company and was born in 2012 in Tottenham (London). Building Bloqs experience is interesting for what concerns the construction of a governance system.

The fourth step of the research took place in Lisboa, Portugal, and was to analyze Balneário and Oficina Colectiva. Balneário and Oficina Colectiva are the smallest shared working environments visited during the research and were founded by two groups of architects. Balneário is interesting for what concerns what happens when the coordinator of the space is also one of the workers of the space. Oficina Colectiva is interesting for what concerns the exchange with the neighborhood.

The fifth step of the research took place in Germany and was to analyze Agora, in Berlin. Agora is a Coworking facility for artists, but opens to other categories of workers. Agora experience is interesting for what concerns the study of interactions and exchanges between workers hosted by the project and the collective that runs it.

The sixth step of the research took place in Germany, in Potsdam, and was to analyze FreiLand, a huge project supported by the local municipality. FreiLand experience is interesting for what concerns the interactions between the project and the local government.

The seventh step of the research took place in United Kingdom and was to analyze again Building Bloqs, after six months, as the first visit to Building Bloqs took place when it was at a very early development stage.

The eighth step of the research took place in Spain, in Potsdam, and was to analyze MOB, Makers of Barcelona. MOB is a project run by a private company, and is interesting because of the mix between a coworking facility and a community working on Digital Fabrication.

The main characteristics of the places:

- **Made in MAGE:** Multifactory of 15 companies near Milan, in Sesto San Giovanni (IT), in a 2,000 square meters space previously part of the Falk steel factory. It can accommodate up to 50 people. Most of Litefactories are artisans, companies and freelancers.
- **Pollino:** Multifactory system located in Basilicata (IT) and geographically spread over a dozen municipalities, consisting of about 20 production facilities involving about 100 people. It's an example of Multifactory mainly made of companies in the agricultural market.
- **Building Bloqs:** Multifactory located in London (UK), in a 1,000 square meters space. It can accommodate up to 100 people, most of them are artisans or artists.
- **Balneário:** Multifactory located in Lisbon (PT), in a 300 square meters space, which is part of LX Factory, a former industrial complex. It can accommodate up to 20 people (artisans, artists and freelancers).
- **Oficina Colectiva:** Multifactory located in Lisbon (PT), in a 200 square meters space (a former industrial bakery) in the city center with windows on the street. Oficina Colectiva includes 8 different LiteFactories (artisans, companies and freelancers) and accommodates 16 people.
- **FreiLand:** Multifactory located in Potsdam (DE), situated in a 15,000 square meters area formerly owned by the local gas and water company. Freiland includes companies, artisans, artists, makers, associations, a FabLab, a café, a club for concerts and events, a guest house, an area for conferences and workshops. Freiland includes 40 different LiteFactories and it can accommodate up to 120 people.

- **MOB (Makers of Barcelona):** Multifactory located in Barcelona (ES), in an 800 square meters space (a former warehouse). MOB includes a café, a FabLab and accommodates up to 120 people. MOB is highly focused on Makers, digital fabrication and smart manufacturing.
- **Agora:** Multifactory located in Berlin (DE), in an 800 square meters space, includes a café and an event space. In Agora most of Litefactories are freelancers and artists, but there is also a workshop for manual works. Agora can accommodate up to 80 people on four floors.

As stated by Focardi & Salati (2015), the places visited during the research project "were not built on an existing model, following given guidelines. They are totally self-made, mainly on a trial and error basis, and developed by people who never met and who didn't know anything about each other. So, it was somehow surprising to discover that the Multifactories faced the same problems and they presented many similarities in structure, organization and governance. Moreover, also the self-perception of people involved in different Multifactories is very similar, as is the overall ethical point of view.

None of the Multifactories included in the research wrote anything about their experience, and they never theorized anything on their intervention scheme. Sometimes they have some theoretical reference models coming from the US, but these models were completely changed as the socio-economical environment is radically different. As a matter of fact, all of the analyzed Multifactories are managing their growth by themselves, as if they have no idea that there are other similar places to compare with.

On one hand, this has been a great advantage for the research development, as Multifactories always were very welcoming, and it was possible to make shootings and interviews without restraints. It was possible to freely move inside the Multifactories and to see the everyday life for several days, and this allowed for a deep understanding of their characteristics. Moreover, as each Multifactory didn't know anything about others, the answers from interviewed people are expressions of truly personal points of view.

On the other hand, it was also clear that the lack of reference models leads the Multifactories to carry forward their own projects on a trial and error basis, so a systemization of these experiences and the development of a coherent model should have been very helpful to support the establishment of new ones, especially because places similar to the eight included in the research are in project or under construction, or open to the public every month, and a unifying intellectual framework could help their development."

With the trip to Barcelona the on field phase of the research project ended. The on field phase aimed to understand how these places work and their characteristics. After the on field phase, the development of the Multifactory Model took place. To develop the Multifactory Model started systemizing the collected data, and understanding, underlining, and categorizing the main common characteristics of the visited places. The Multifactory Model describes the key elements that constitute a Multifactory, their roles and the dynamics that take place in it. From the Multifactory Model was developed The Multifactory Intervention Model, that describes the steps to establish a Multifactory.

Table 2. Crowdworkers'voice on MODELS

"We arrived through a process of many months of brain cuddling and mind maps and discussions." Parra-Mussel, A. (2013 February 26). Personal interview.
"My dream is that we create something here which proves to be so useful, so beneficial, so interesting, and innovative that is only a question of time before we ourselves or somebody else builds the next BB so we can spread the benefit of what we are achieving here as fine as well as possible we will not necessarily be employing people directly as an organization but what we are doing is job creation and this is so necessary here right across the UK, but also right across Europe now." Nichols, A. (2013, February 27). Personal interview.

BIGMAGMA

As the final phase of the research, all the ideas and suggestions included in the intervention model were tested in an experimental environment. Focardi and Salati also point out (2015) that "researchers have an enormous responsibility, as in case their assumptions are wrong, or they are not able to properly manage unexpected dynamics, their intellectual failure means also an economical and personal defeat for many people, who not necessarily have all the instruments to correctly evaluate in advance the risk of joining an experimental project based on an innovative, not fully tested intervention model.

Under this point of view, the necessity to make predictions as accurate as possible is a moral need, and thought that all the socio-economic environments are complex systems, characterized by emerging behaviors that are impossible to forecast with intuition, the use of Simulation Environments to support the development and management of these social experiments seemed to be an innovative and effective way to reduce the risk of failure and to fully accomplish the social role that Researchers have to play.

But this was not enough. Each new idea, each new model related to Social Innovation needs to be tested. This lead to set up an experimental environment, based upon the Multifactory Intervention Model, where several people decided to work and somehow to risk on their own, and to establish their own activities.

This environment is called Bigmagma and is a self-financed, self-regulated Multifactory based in Milan and built following the Multifactory Model, as it was defined by this research.

Bigmagma was an experiment to check if it would have been possible to build a Multifactory from scratch, and if that environment should effectively support the growth of the Litefactories which compose it. People who joined Bigmagma are small entrepreneurs, designers, craftsmen, musicians, a drawer, an oenologist and an artist. Researchers who developed the Multifactory Model are part of it, and contribute to the community of workers exactly as every other member.

After one year, Bigmagma is a fully functional Multifactory, which has grown from four to ten Litefactories and is still growing. All the Litefactories which are part of Bigmagma are going quite well on the market and self sufficient. All the activities are self organized and regulated by few democratic concepts, which were formalized in a collective Manifesto. Bigmagma is also part of a free exchange program within Multifactories, aimed to support the exchange of experiences and knowledge, which allows people from Multifactories to spend working periods in other ones for free."

Multifactories, Innovative Working Environments

A Multifactory is a shared working environment made by several different economic agents aimed at the production of goods and the supply of services. A Multifactory is a System made by many different economic subjects which are heterogeneous, and interact in several different ways. They are heterogeneous in terms of dimensions, experience on the market, industry. They can product or distribute of physical goods, or they can operate in services, so they can be free lancers, small or very small enterprises, craftsmen, or creative companies. They all have separate properties and are fully autonomous under an operational, fiscal, commercial, and strategic point of view. According to Focardi & Salati (2015), "they are open to new opportunities and able to make changes very fast, according to the situational needs. They are flexible, innovative, sustainable, and "thin" under dimensional, strategic, operative, and structural points of view. Their competitiveness is mainly based on their immaterial assets and on a mix of quality, innovation, customer care, and the construction of a network of partner companies. They are companies that by structure, style and perspective are in a grey zone between the word of craftsmanship, the free lances, and the SMEs. They are a new class of economical subjects that refer to past productive categories, but at the same time express specific characters. To identify these companies in one word, the choice was to introduce the term "Litefactory." It effectively expresses the "lightness" and flexibility of these economic agents, joint in their propensity to act in the production field.

In a Multifactory the presence of some artistic or creative Litefactories is very common, but a Multifactory is not an ensemble of creative companies; it's a system of companies that act in a creative way."

People who run the Litefactories own a wide range of skills, which are part of the immaterial assets of their companies, but lack many others. Old craftsmen often have experience and technical skills, but don't know anything about marketing or Social Networks, while young entrepreneurs or free lancers are comfortable with digital age technologies, but lack most of the practical skills. The knowledge exchange that these subjects can establish is very wide and goes from Digital Fabrication skills, like 3D modeling and printing, laser cutting, fast prototyping in general to traditional manufacturing techniques like soldering, woodworking, sewing, and so on, to immaterial skills like copywriting, project writing, proofreading, to other technical skills like video-making, music composing, event organization, web design, SEO.

The continuous exchange of knowledge and professional suggestions coming from people with different experiences helps Litefactories to find creative solutions to everyday problems, but is also a way to establish professional relationships, reinforced day by day. When this happens, after a while companies involved in this process become able to cooperate and share resources in such an integrated way that they can operate as if they were divisions of a single huge company, an "Invisible Factory," made by independent companies that can, when needed, operate as a single entity.

Main Constitutive Parts of Multifactories: the Litefactories

Focardi & Salati (2015) underline that "the average dimension of the companies included in a Multifactory ranges from micro to small, as they are often start-ups.

One day you make a thing, another day you do something else, but I can use the same stuff I learnt at the University to have a different perspective on what I'm doing. - Oliveira, F. (2013, May, 3). Personal interview.

People who establish and animate the Litefactories have a high level of personal commitment, show a medium-high to very high education level, and they usually come from very diversified previous work experiences. They face challenges as opportunities for growth and believe it is important to have satisfaction in what they do, regardless of the economic return, which is generally relegated to second place with respect to the return in terms of quality of life.

Table 3. Crowdworkers' voice on DIVERSITY

"I think I'm really lucky that I can work in a space were everyone is different and has got his own specialty and I can learn from them." Lapo. (2013, May 3). Personal interview.
"There are people doing different things here at Oficina Colectiva, and we're very different. They have stuff we don't have, 'cause they're more rational, more organized than we're here upstairs. Downstairs they're more logical, and they think much better than us. And this infects us in a good way. I think we both inspire each other in some way. It's really good to see the reactions: if we start putting post-it on the walls, they first react a little bit strangely to that, and after a month you see they're doing the same thing. If they start doing a commercial work, we think "damn, we should do a commercial work also" and we start following them and they start following us. It's a kind of a really healthy competition when they do something we have to positively react and do something good, and it's the same for them. It's a kind of creating that feeling like "let's move, let's move let's move, let's do stuff, let's do things!!" This is the kind of feeling I feel here." Quinta, R. (2013, May 5). Personal interview.

Table 4. Crowdworkers' voice on MULTIFACTORY'S ADVANTAGES

> "Money in its basic form is about exchange: a token for some work and some work for a token and in this form it's a great thing. But it has been taken a funny road. BB is a great opportunity for people to exchange skills, rather than money." Nichols, A. (2013, February 27). Personal interview.
>
> "People like to share their knowledge, so we do a lot of workshops where members present themselves, and maybe someone says "oh, you're an expert in social media, could you help me with this project?" and they start to collaborate.
> There are situations where someone from the outside says: "I have a product, I just came up with this new wine, but I need a team, can you put a team together? So we say, yes, what do you need? I need a photographer, a graphic designer, a marketing person, and we have all of that here, in MOB. So we build a team and sell it as a package." Then there's a third kind of collaboration when someone has just a really brilliant idea and just writes it on a board asking who is interested in it. It's very organic, we don't really have rules and instructions, people just grow as they like, and this was pretty effective until now." Tham, C. (2013, September 18). Personal interview.
>
> "…Then other collaborations, trivially common interests in trade fairs, sharing costs and making a joint logistics. Then there are thousands of examples in everyday life, trivialities perhaps, as exchange information on the suppliers, or on the development of a small solution that is implemented thanks to the intuition of a neighbour and maybe it's something that for you alone it would have required days of study. Or a mutual exchange of instruments and equipment. These are aspects that you don't even notice, because they are part of the daily." Colombo, S. (2012, October 13). Personal interview.

In general, the entrepreneurial spirit is very strong, as is the idea to achieve something concrete, So is the awareness to be social actors, both as promoters of culture rather than as individuals able to give employment and generate well-being.

In most cases, they are not entrepreneurs or artisans by vocation or family tradition, but in response to the crisis in the labor market. Some of them are reluctant to accept a subordinate position as an employee, but many were expelled from the labor market, or never had the opportunity to enter it. In general, they are people who, after evaluating several other options, chose to try to make their passion a profession.

Some of them have solid theoretical and practical skills, others only partial specific ones, supported by good will, commitment and a strong personal network.

All, however, are reluctant to be framed in precise patterns. Formally are entrepreneurs, artisans, professionals, but when they work together they continuously mix roles, areas of expertise, and methods.

So, we decided to refer to these people as "Crowdworkers", as they usually share and mix skills and resources between Litefactories, and their products and services come from a continuous confrontation with others".

Table 5. Crowdworkers' voice on LEARNING

> "I don't think I have to go to workshops or courses of illustration to improve my job but I think I have to do a lot to make experiments, it's like a trial, I say "Ok it works, or it doesn't work", I find that producing and drawing every day and trying different things I can learn more than if I would go to any courses." Lapo. (2013, May 3). Personal interview.
>
> "I watch tutorials. I see how people do things, and then I try to do the same, and I try, I try until it works." Oliveira, F. (2013, May, 3). Personal interview.
>
> "This is an open space and open space means also open knowledge. People should try to transfer their knowledge to other people. It's not so important to have very expensive tools, as you can't use these tools if you don't understand how to operate them. This is for us very important: we try to make a new way to find new technologies and open these technologies to other people, and we're not alone in doing this". Parade, M. (2013, July 15). Personal interview.
>
> We like to promote peer-to-peer learning, we work with university abroad and they send us their students, they come to study inside our facility instead of going to university, they actually look for a non academic environment and instead of teachers we pair them up with members. It's not exactly coworking, it's not exactly a school; it's a kind of a new environment for learning. Tham, C. (2013, September 18). Personal interview.

Knowledge Sharing in a Multifactory

As stated by Focardi & Salati (2015), "a crucial issue in a system where free exchange of knowledge is an important aspect of how relationships are regulated between nodes is that whoever spreads competencies, or suggestions, should have some form of non-monetary return.

In most cases, the "knowledge exchange" also requires some labor, sometimes the use of their equipment and machines, and at least the use of an (many times small) amount of time.

Many people, in their private lives, share knowledge for philanthropic reasons, or because it's something that belongs to their values, or beliefs, or just use it as a way to spend some spare time. In this sense, the return of sharing could also be just the proud of being part of a movement, or the consciousness of being useful for someone else. This obviously should not apply to entrepreneurs, professionals, or artisans; at least not as a strategy of growth.

At first sight, the return should be intended as a mere exchange of professional services, a way to offer and get services without money, or a kind of barter: "I have a need, I looked for a skill, I found it, I offer something in change."

This is something that happens, but there is something hidden much more interesting, that's the capability of the system to increase through knowledge sharing the opportunities of growth of the Companies that are part of the system.

What happens is that availability of competencies enables and leads people to think in a different way. They know that when they face some problems, or professional challenges, they can count on a wide range of capabilities and skills that are available and reliable, and this constant, continuous availability of resources enables entrepreneurs to think in a wider way.

It's a buffet of skills. Entrepreneurs know which resources are available and how to get them. Maybe they don't need them for a long time, but they are aware of the availability and this leads them to take on big projects because they know that they will have access to all what they will need.

So, when they put knowledge into the system, what they're doing is raising the global potential of the system by itself, and if everyone in the system offers something different, the result is that every node in the system can grow faster and steadier.

It's a way to build a system where all the players give their contribution to increase the capabilities of every single node of the system itself.

Table 6. Crowdworkers' voice on SHARING

Often I go to other people here and I ask for help, or for ideas, I'm not alone. Ribbe, S. (2013, July 14) Personal interview.
It's not about me, us, we live in a network society, we're all networked, but we don't have a place to meet. This is a perfect place to establish discussions about any topic and we do that a lot, it's a different way to educate yourself. Tizzi, C. (2013, July 12). Personal interview.
"We've access to internet and to every single tutorial you can imagine, we've access to very cheap technology, we've access to knowledge, and if you combine them, every individual has the power to manufacture things that are mind blowing. I googled "nuclear reactor" and there are the instructions to build your own, in your kitchen. This would be impossible 50 years ago, you wouldn't be able to do this. This is the direction we're moving towards and this is the way to get out of our crisis, nowadays, with 55% of youths in Barcelona and in Spain who are unemployed. I think, instead of giving them a job, we teach them the tools, we give them the knowledge, we give them the resources that they need to invent their own jobs, I think this is the only way. Tham, C. (2013, September 18). Personal interview.

This is an emerging property of the system, which comes from the interaction between elements of the system, and that increases the possibilities of each node of the system to afford new and bigger projects, which means an increased possibility for success on the market".

An Interaction between a Multi-Factory and a Traditional Company: The Grinding Project

In places like Multifactories innovation comes from contamination and there is a direct linkage between social innovation, process innovation and product innovation. This happens while Litefactories work together, and is possible because they know each other very well and have everyday interactions. But, as obvious, Multifactories are part of a larger economic system. So, an interesting question is how that approach to innovation can coexist and integrate with more traditional companies.

An interesting case to answer this question is Grinding Project. Grinding Project is as a side activity of the an Italian family company, Nuova Ferrari & Zagni of Fiorano Modenese, a small city near Modena and very close to Maranello. Nuova Ferrari & Zagni is a grinding facility, and their main business is to restore engines changing the internal parts. This brings them to have many used parts that are usually thrown away as special wastes. These parts are mainly valves, made of steel, pistons, made of aluminum, and metallic bushing, but there are also other less common parts like turbines and rods.

Nuova Ferrari & Zagni was in search for innovative ideas to boost the business and in 2012 Alessandra Zagni, one of the actual owners of the company, went to "Fà la cosa giusta", an Italian fair on sustainable lifestyles, where she came in touch with the Multifactory Bigmagma. This is a first interesting point: the first contact took place in a very conventional way: a fair. Alessandra Zagni in 2011 had an idea for an upcycling project, then abandoned. The main guideline from Nuova Ferrari & Zagni was to develop this upcycling project with a direct linkage to the main business. The first step was to define a series of prototypes, in order to verify the technical feasibility of the idea. At this stage, there was no clear idea of what kind of products Grinding Project could build, also if the indications coming from the designers involved in this phase suggested that they could have been jewels and objects for the home or office. Bigmagma proposed to Nuova Ferrari & Zagni to develop the idea starting a low budget project, using suggestions, instruments and methods referring to Sharing Economy and Network Economy.

Nuova Ferrari & Zagni accepted and this is the idea that Bigmagma was asked to develop: "In addition to the concept of reuse, I would like to emerge the concept of changing perspective. The perception of objects, that in our case were made for a specific function, but which are now "altered" to "do" something else. This is a metaphor of how to reinvent ourselves to survive in the world of work, to face the changes of the labor market in recent years." *Zagni, A. (2014, March 5). Personal communication.*

The name of the project was chosen in order to resemble this concept:

"When I started to color the pistons, to make my small and insignificant experiments on my own, I called this "thing" Grinding Project, which recalls a term well known to us, indicating a change in a metamorphosis of the surface, a correction ...." *Zagni, A. (2014, March 5). Personal communication.*

Then a logo was created and a Facebook page was opened, to set up the base for the communication actions that had to follow. It was March 2014 and Grinding Project was starting. It was not by chance that the first communication channel was Facebook, and that at first a website didn't exist. The project started with the idea to be a community project, and social media were chosen to be not only a place for exploitation if the project, but to build it from the scratch in a participative way. The first action was to organize an open event, a 24 hours marathon aimed to collect ideas for new products. The event took place in Sesto San Giovanni (Milan) in the Bigmagma headquarter and had the technical sponsorship by Vectorealism.com, a laser cut service well known in North Italy. The formula of the marathon was very simple, this is the text of the call:

"Creativity Marathon, to give a new life to old rods, pistons, turbines, bearings and bushings.

A white night dedicated to students, designers, architects, designers, Nerd, Makers.

Subscriptions is free:

http://www.eventbrite.com/e/registrazione-designers-vs-mad-scientists-in-cosa-trasformerai-un-vecchio-motore-11200714639

Purpose: To design various objects to be produced in small series, starting from parts coming from rectified engines.

Output: Projects selected will be funded through a crowdfunding campaign and if there will be an enthusiastic response from the audience, they will be put into production in small series.

Of course, intellectual property of the authors will be protected with regular contracts.

Constraints:

1. Objects must be possibly made with the fewest number of modifications of the raw material (to be better reproducible)
2. Objects must be able to be manufactured in series even if raw material is of variable size time to time (pistons, connecting rods and all the rest can be different from time to time)

Available Ingredients: Some boxes will be prepared in advance. Each box will contain more or less the same pieces (same number of pistons, rods, valves, ...), with some surprise. The content of boxes will be visible in advance. On may 16 each team will have a box, assigned among those present.

How to Participate: The pre-registration is required. You can subscribe by yourself or in a group. Those registering alone will be merged into an existing group, or you will create a group of singles.

Categories: You can enroll in two categories: DESIGNERS or MAD SCIENTISTS.

Subscribe as a designer, if you want to have in your fellow group people who prefer the form to function.

Sign up as a mad scientist, if you want to have in your fellow group people who prefer function with form.

Theme: There will be a "guiding theme", very generic, that will be unveiled only May 16, at the time of distribution of boxes.

Timing: From the time of delivery of boxes, the prototypes will be ready in 24 hours.

Permitted Modifications: Materials in the boxes can be modified in any way, by hand or machine, adding other pieces, special materials. Vectorealism will provide its laser cut to create special parts, if you feel you need.

(retrieved from: https://www.facebook.com/events/543935185719336/)

The Creativity Marathon was promoted on Facebook and by a participation of Bigmagma at "Fà la cosa giusta 2014", where 2500 flyers were distributed in three days.

On May 2014 the first "Creativity Marathon" took place, the marathon started on May 16, 2014 at 7:00pm and ended one day after. The event was covered on Facebook and some parts were covered with a streaming. Two of the products developed by participants were later put into production.

The production is made following a scheme that resembles much more a network, rather than a chain. All products are made in Italy by artisans and SMEs, which are autonomous and independent production nodes. Nuova Ferrari & Zagni ships the used motor parts cleaned, sanded and free of oils and carbon residues, to the production nodes, which then produce the finished products. Even logistics is based on a widespread system of small and decentralized logistic centers. The aim is to make production flexible, economical and at the same time minimize the environmental impact resulting from the storage and handling of goods. Quality control is structured on the basis of an Integrated Quality System, in which quality is seen as a product of the system and all the actors have an overall responsibility on final quality.

This production system is completely different from the traditional production chain used by the company, and was set up following the same logical scheme of a social network.

Immediately after the marathon, Bigmagma contacted the headquarter of L'Ecolaio, an Italian franchising network of shops selling products related to sustainability and ethical lifestyles, who accepted to distribute products by Grinding Project. They were convinced by the overall design of the project, rather by the inner quality of the products, and in particular by "the social innovation and the attention to social and environmental sustainability".

To sustain the launch of the products, it was chosen also to start a crowdfunding campaign on indiegogo.com, that started on December 2014 and ended on January 2015.

The campaign didn't have the main goal to raise funds, but to explore the potentialities of crowdfunding platforms as a social way to intend a press office. The idea at the base was that the fact to have an active crowdfunding could help to contact newspapers, blogs and magazines, as there was a "news" with a precise content to share, that means something much more interesting than the simple fact that a new product was on the market. This worked and the overall response was interesting, but most of all the fact to have an active crowdfunding was the occasion to contact other partners of Nuova Ferrari & Zagni, and this sparked interest in the eV-Now Foundation which had a stand at the Motorshow of Bologna and offered to host Grinding Project. The participation of Grinding Project to the Motor Show had then a full coverage on Facebook. So, the crowdfunding campaign was used not as a way to collect money, but as a tool used in conjunction with other social networks like Facebook to spread in a social way the fact that the project was active and the products were on sale in the shops. At the same time, Grinding Project was recognized as an innovative experience by the Club for the Corporate Social Responsibility of Modena and Nuova Ferrari & Zagni was accepted as a member, together with companies which are two orders of magnitude larger.

Table 7. Crowdworkers' voice on WORKING TOGETHER

"Oficina Colectiva is not a Company, it's a place. But when we work together on the same projects, we don't even have to separate the teams, as we're from the same space, the same environment. We don't have to say: "these are the guys from Toyno; these are the guys from Nambana". Quinta, R. (2013, May 5). Personal interview.
"We collaborate with other people here, we use our experience to help them, and they do the same.
We had a side project when we first came here, we were redesigning the brand for a restaurant and we needed someone who designed the interiors of the restaurant, so we cooperated, they designed the restaurant interior and in exchange we're redesigning their brand for the notebook." Quinta, R. (2013, May 5). Personal interview.
"MOB is a strange beast, in a sense that from the very beginning we wanted to apply this mentality of the Makers, as a mentality, not simply as the act of making, so as we know makers are people making manual things, actually using their hands, physically building something, which is great, but want a kind to define it on a different level, meaning that we want to change into an attitude. While changing people attitude, you can change movements, and society." Tham, C. (2013, September 18). Personal interview.

CONCLUSION

Product Innovation is a crucial point in order to increase competitiveness of a Company, but also to keep it on the market. To be a player on a market that evolves in such a fast and unpredictable way requires the capability to develop new products, and sometimes to change industrial sector, or at least to explore diversification strategies. At the same time, the uncertainty of the markets, the shortening of product life circle and the reduction of margins and profitability raise the risk related to the development of a new product. While this risk can be somehow managed by large companies and corporations, it can be fatal for small business. This leads SME's to innovate less than they used to be, also because their overall resources are more limited than once, but if they don't innovate they lose competitiveness, and this can trigger a downward spiral from which is almost impossible to exit. So, it's very important for them to find different ways to make innovation, which can help companies to innovate in a faster and more effective way. Methods and ideas that come from Sharing Economy can help them to innovate, but they also require a change of perspective and a change of attitude.

Sharing Economy is based on dynamics that take place in a social environment, but this can happen only if all the nodes of the system act in a social way, and companies that want to innovate their products using the opportunities offered by Sharing Economy need to rethink themselves as social agents. This is very hard to do for companies that are structured and used to act in a traditional way. Multifactories are shared working environments that are based on concepts that are deeply linked with principles from Sharing Economy. This helps, and somehow forces, people who work in a Multifactory, like artisans, entrepreneurs, or free lancers, to act in a social way. This brings them to cooperate, to share, to cross-contaminate and the result is innovation, both in terms of products and methods. So, product innovation comes from a social behavior and this also involves social media, which are part of the system. When a Multifactory gets in contact with a traditional company, this innovative way to interact between Litefactories somehow can infect also the traditional company. This doesn't mean that the traditional company has to change its overall structure, but at the same time it means that the traditional company has to accept to establish the R&D project of that specific product in a different way. When this happens, also traditional companies can develop innovative products in a social way. So, in a way Multifactories can be seen as rams' heads of Sharing Economy and can convey traditional Companies on that field. Product innovation through participative methods can be faster and cheaper, but when a company, regardless of whether it is traditional or not, starts to develop a new product in a social way it has to be credible. This means that every aspect of the development of a new product has to be rethought in order to be social and participative. Social Media are a key point of this operation. Traditional Companies often tend to think to Social Media as if they were a modern interpretation of traditional media, like television or newspapers. Most of the companies are on Social Media, but they are not able to interact with the rest of the social system and simply communicate on Social Media in a top-down manner. To innovate in a social way, companies have to understand that Social Media are not only the way to communicate, but a constitutive part of the development environment, and they have to build a system in which all the nodes are aware of what is happening and can take crucial decisions. While managing a research project that involves Social Media, it's very important to use them in a real social way and to set multiple goals for every action that takes place on them. When a company is able to build a system like that, Social Media can really make the difference, as they can leverage the initial inputs. On the other hand, to get this result is not easy, and traditional companies don't have the skills and habits to use Social Media in such a way. This gap can be filled establishing an interaction between traditional companies and innovative working environments based upon participative principles, like Multifactories are.

Future Research Directions

Multifactories are a particular kind of working environments, and proved to be capable to incorporate new ideas, and to experiment new ways to develop and produce goods and services. Multifactories can also help traditional companies to innovate the way they innovate, defining new paths to imagine and develop innovative products together.

Multifactories are working places based on a participative governance system, and could give strong suggestions to traditional companies, usually base on a top-down scheme. A further step is to study if and how a Multifactory can be a model to innovate the structural asset of a traditional company and, If this would be possible, how this new structural asset could affect product innovation.

Background

Obviously, there isn't any specific reference on Multifactories, as it is a completely new concept. The general framework assumed as background refers to Sustainable Development, with particular regard to:

- Creative Industries
- Workplace Innovation
- Sharing Economy

The basic assumption of the work presented in this chapter is the need for a change from a Taylorist work organization; characterized by task specialization, a pyramidal hierarchical structure, and a centralization of responsibilities; to a holistic organization, featuring flat hierarchical structures, job rotation, flexi-time, self-responsible multi-skilled teams, worker empowerment, and the change from vertical to horizontal organization models.

The labor market changes reflect not only an economic crisis but also a social one, and the international *World of Work Report (2013)* gives a wide view about the social impact of the rise of long-term joblessness and problems related to job quality in Europe. It also composes the general framework to be considered, which include the official European Commission legislation and reports as *A European strategy for smart, sustainable and inclusive growth (2010)*, the *Agenda for new skills and job (2010)*, and *Social innovation as part of the Europe 2020 strategy (2010)* as well as the International Institute for Labor Studies Working towards sustainable development: *Opportunities for decent work and social inclusion in a green economy (2012)*.

Creative Industries

According to John Howkins, The Creative Economy is a comprehensive kind of new economy, based on creative people, creative industries, and creative cities. That means revitalizing manufacturing, services, retailing, and entertainment industries, leading to a change of where people want to live, work and learn, where they think, invent and produce. Howkins (2005) recognizes all kinds of creativity, not only the arts, as major cultural and economic processes. *"Success in the creative economy will come to the organizations that recognize and reconcile the personal, the spiritual, and the economic."*

Living out the debate on which activities have to be included in the concept of "creative industries," there are interesting concrete platforms to apply this concept in concrete projects such as URBACT, an European exchange and learning program promoting sustainable urban development.

The URBACT Creative Clusters Project analyzes the crossroad between the creative economy and the economy of culture. Multifactories are an example of successful creative-based strategies on local public policies and how those strategies, trying to promote a local creative ecosystem, rapidly take the shape of a social innovation strategy. *"Creative industries is not limited to arts and culture, it extends to fields where creative individual, managers and technologists meet together. Moreover, the creative entrepreneur comprises much more than people working in cultural and creative industries."* (Rivas, 2011, p. 92)

Referring to Nordström and Ridderstrale (2007), the Multifactory model is an example of a creative-based business model and proposes new ways of organizing work in general, rather than focusing on how creative class is exploring new ways of working. Most of the interviewed people can be considered part of the creative class, but not because they do creative jobs, as this is not the most relevant characteristic: the focus is not to be creative or not, but to be productive in a creative way, as a Multifactory is aimed to economic development, rather than to cultural development.

Workplace Innovation

A lot of literature is focusing on workplace innovation as directly linked to the technological changes. More in general, one can say that there is a strong correlation between the introduction of new technologies and work reorganization. The development of information technology has induced managers to rethink the way work has traditionally been organized (Beblavy, Maselli, & Martellucci, 2012) and this is an important framework that has to be kept in consideration.

To the extent of the Multifactory Model, Workplace Innovation is intended in the way Pot (2011) suggests, *"the idea behind is to combine economic and social goals."* As Cressey and Kellher (2003, p. 93-107) pointed out, innovative work practices represent a radical change in the production process. This implies the shift from a static type of organization, where tasks and processes are continually replicated, to a transformative learning organization, where relationships and connections matter, and the action is the core of the processes. *"Transformative action requires a focus on human beings and the organization must be viewed not as a machine but as 'living' entities."*

Sharing Economy

The sharing economy business models are an answer to a rising need to make businesses cooperate and share. The most common examples of sharing economy are the Crowdfounding platforms (such as Kickstarter and Indiegogo), which are instruments often used by Litefactories, or the Multifactory by themselves, but sharing economy is a concept that can refer to a much wider range of experiences, as can be a Multifactory, that is a small community, like a village, and a natural place for sharing resources, competences, and experiences within all the involved agents.

There are recent interesting studies about the collaborative economy, commissioned by the newest giants of P2P marketplaces and synergic platforms on the web (as Airbnb), as well as studies in general about social media (Maineri, 2013).

Talking about sharing experiences related to work, there are many different models and answers, from the territorial networks to the shared working places. The first ones have existed a long time and take form as associations of enterprises, industrial districts, and corporations. Shared working places can take many forms, as Coworking places, Maker Spaces, Creative Hubs, Fab Labs, or Startups Farms, and are new answers to the disintegration of the labor market. They are experiencing dramatic growth and increasing structuring, assuming well-defined specificities that are very clear to those who are part of these cultural movements, but often escape the understanding of those who are not directly involved and engender errors and misunderstandings.

Usually, shared environments for workers are a solution for work-at-home professionals, independent contractors, or people who travel frequently who end up working in relative isolation. Unlike a typical office environment, those places are not employed by the same organization. They are also the social gathering of a group of people who are still working independently, but who share values and who are interested in the synergy that can happen from working with like-minded talented people in the same space. The most studied is the coworking movement that has roughly doubled in size each year since 2006. The latest *Global Coworking Survey* (2012) carried out by Deskmag shows there are now more than 1100 spaces worldwide.

As said before, at first sight the MF could seem similar to a coworking space, but every time the Multifactory Model was presented to people involved in the coworking movement they refused every similarity.

During the National Day of Social Security 2013, a public debate was organized at the Milan Stock Exchange between the developers of the Multifactory Model and the founders of the three main coworking spaces in Milan and they affirmed they could not link the Multifactories to their experience or, at least, they associated more to a new kind of working space for the new craftsmen (GNP, 2013) which is in line with the theoretical frame well underlined by Stefano Micelli (2011).

Another confirmation came from the interview to the founder of *deskmag.com*, the most relevant European on-line magazine about coworking that is based in Betahaus, the most famous coworking space in Berlin, as the Multifactory Model wasn't absolutely comprehensible from his point of view, *"It is not possible for me, that I have to write at the computer all day long, to share the space with a carpenter who produces dust." Deskmag founder, (2013, July 13). Personal Interview, Betahaus.*

REFERENCES

Cressey, P., & Kelleher, M. (2003). The Conundrum of the Learning Organisation - Instrumental and Emancipatory Theories of Learning. In B. Nyhan, P. Cressey, M. Kelleher & R. Poell (Eds.), Learning Organisations: European perspectives, theories and practices. Luxembourg: CEDEFOP.

Deskmag, C. E. (2012). *The 2nd Global Coworking Survey*. Retrieved from http://www.deskmag.com/en/first-results-of-global-coworking-survey-171

Focardi, G., & Salati, L. (2015). A New Approach to Knowledge Sharing, the Multifactory Model. In O. Teràn & J. Aguilar (Eds.), *Social Benefits of Freely Accessible Technologies and Knowledge Resources*. IGI Global. doi:10.4018/978-1-4666-8336-5.ch009

GNP. (2013). *Tem(p)i e luoghi del lavoro flessibile*. Retrieved from http://www.giornatanazionaledellaprevidenza.it/terza-giornata-gnp2013

Howkins, J. (2005). Enhancing creativity. In Creative Industries. A symposium on culture based development strategies. New Delhi: Malvika Singh Editor.

Maineri, M. (2013). *Collaboriamo! come i social media ci aiutano a lavorare e a vivere bene in tempo di crisi*. Milano: Hoepli.

Micelli, S. (2011). *Futuro artigiano*. Venezia: Marsilio Editore.

Nordström, K. A., & Ridderstrale, J. (2007). *Funky Business Forever: How to enjoy capitalism*. Pearson Education.

Pot, F. (2011). *Social innovation of work and employment, Challenge Social Innovation*. Paper presented at the meeting workshop: Social innovation at work, Wien, Austraia.

Rivas, M. (2011). *From creative industries to the creative place. refreshing the local development agenda in small and medium size towns*. URBACT creative clusters project final report.

ADDITIONAL READING

Aigrain, P. (2014). *Sharing: Culture and the Economy in the Internet Age*. Amsterdam, The Netherlands: Amsterdam university press.

Amidon, D. M., Formica, P., & Mercier-Laurent, E. (2005). *Readings on Knowledge Economics: Emerging Principles, Practices and Policies*. Estonia: Tartu University Press.

Anderson, C. (2010). How web video powers global innovation. *TEDGlobal*. Retrieved June, 12, 2013 from http://www.ted.com/talks/chris_anderson_how_web_video_powers_global_innovation.html

Anderson, R. (1999). *Mid-course correction: toward a sustainable enterprise*. Chelsea, MA: Green publishing Company.

Anderson, R. (2009). The business logic of sustainability. *TEDX*. Retrieved July, 2013, from http://www.ted.com/talks/ray_anderson_on_the_business_logic_of_sustainability.html

Antagata, W., (2007). *Libro Bianco sulla creatività*. Roma: Commissione sulla Creatività e Produzione di Cultura in Italia/Ministero per i Beni e le Attività Culturali.

Ariely, D. (2012). What make us feel good about our work. *TED talk. Rio de la Plata*. Retrieved July, 2013, 23, from http://www.ted.com/talks/dan_ariely_what_makes_us_feel_good_about_our_work.html

Bettoni, M. C. (2003). *The Essence of Knowledge Management: A Constructivist Approach* (pp. 1–6). Basel, Switzerland: Institute for Methods and Structures.

Bollier, D. (2008). *Viral spiral. How the Commoners Built a Digital republic of their Own*. New York, NY: The new Press. Published under creative commons licence and available at http://www.viralspiral.cc/sites/default/files/ViralSpiral.pdf

Broderick, D. (2001). *The spike: How Our Lives Are Being Transformed by rapidly Advancing Technologies*. New York, NY: Tom Doherty Associated.

Caves, R. E. (2000). *Creative Industries, Contracts between Art and Commerce*. Cambridge, MA: Harvard University Press.

Chapain, C., Comunian, R., & Clifton, R. (2011). Location, location, location: exploring the complex relationship between creative industries and place. *Creative Industries Journal*, 1(3), 5-10. Retrived from http://www.ingentaconnect.com/content/intellect/cij/2010/00000003/00000001/art00002

Christopher A., & Dominique C. (2007). The strength of weak cooperation: an attempt to understand the meaning of web 2.0. *International journal of digital economics*, 65, 51-65.

Communication from the Commission to the European Parliament. the Council, the European economic and social Committee and the Committee of the regions. (2011). *A renewed EU strategy 2011-14 for Corporate Social Responsibility*. {COM(2011) 681 final}, Brussels: EU. Retrieved from http://eur-lex.europa.eu/LexUriServ/LexUriServ.do?uri=COM:2011:0681:FIN:EN:PDF

Communication from the Commission to the European Parliament. the Council, the European economic and social Committee and the Committee of the regions. Social Business Initiative. (2011). *Creating a favourable climate for social enterprises, key stakeholders in the social economy and innovation*. {SEC(2011) 1278 final}, Brussels: EU. Retrieved from http://eur-lex.europa.eu/LexUriServ/LexUriServ.do?uri=COM:2011:0682:FIN:EN:PDF

Communication from the Commission to the European Parliament. the Council, the European economic and social Committee and the Committee of the regions. (2011). *An Agenda for new skills and jobs: A European contribution towards full employment*. {26.11.2010 COM(2010) 682 final/2} Strasbourg, EU. Retrieved from http://eur-lex.europa.eu/LexUriServ/LexUriServ.do?uri=COM:2010:0682:REV1:EN:PDF

Coy, P. (2010), The creative economy. Which companies will thrive in the coming years? Those that value ideas above all else. *Business Week magazine*.

CREATIVE METROPOLES. Situation Analysis of 11 Cities: Final Report. (2010). Retrieved from Creative Metropoles Interreg IVC Programme web site www.creativemetropoles.eu

Drew, J., Sundsted, T., & Bacigalupo, T. (2009). *I'm Outta Here: How Coworking is Making the Office Obsolete*. Austin, TX: NotanMBA Press.

Drucker, P. (1993). *Post-Capitalist Society*. Oxford, UK: Butterworth Heinemann.

Eck, J. (2005). Struggling with the creative class. *International Journal of Urban and Regional Research*, 29(4), 740–770. doi:10.1111/j.1468-2427.2005.00620.x

European Commission. (2010). Green Paper. Unlocking the potential of cultural and creative industries. Brussels, EU: COM (2010).

European Commission. (2010). Europe 2020. A European strategy for smart, sustainable and inclusive growth. Brussels, EU: COM (2010).

Gansky, L. (2012). *The Mesh: Why the Future of Business Is Sharing*. New York, US: Portfolio Trade, Penguin Group.

Genevieve, V. DeGuzman & Andrew, I., (2011). Working in the UnOffice: A Guide to Coworking for Indie Workers, Small Businesses, and Nonprofits. San Francisco, CA: Night Owls press.

Gordon, R., & Brynjolfsson, E. (2013). The future of work and innovation debate. *Ted2013*, Retrieved July, 15, from http://blog.ted.com/2013/04/23/the-future-of-work-and-innovation-robert-gordon-and-erik-brynjolfsson-debate-at-ted2013/

Howkins, J. (2001). *The Creative Economy: How People Make Money From Ideas*. New York, US: Penguin Group.

Jackson, T. (2005). *Motivating Sustainable Consumption: A Review of Evidence on Consumer Behavior and Behavioral Change, Paper published by the Centre for Environmentl Strategy,* University of Surrey www.epa.gov/sustainability/workshop0505/5d_Jackson_Tim.pdf

Jacobs, J. (1961). *The death and life of great American Cities*. New York, US: The Random House.

Kurki, L., & Manoliu, M. (2011). Opinion of the European Economic and Social Committee on Innovative workplaces as a source of productivity and quality jobs (own-initiative opinion) *Official Journal of the European Union* (2011/C 132/05) Retrieved from http://eur-lex.europa.eu/LexUriServ/LexUriServ.do?uri=OJ:C:2011:132:0022:0025:EN:PDF

Miroslav, B., Maselli, I., & Martellucci, E. (2012). *Workplace Innovation and Technological Change*, Brussels, BG: Centre for European Policy Studies Special Reports. Forthcoming. Retrieved July 15, 2013, Available at SSRN: http://ssrn.com/abstract=2147619

Morace, F. (2011). I paradigmi del futuro. Lo scenario dei trends. Busto Arsizio, IT: Nomos Edizioni.

Rombie, D. (2010). *The Entrepreneurial Dimension of the Cultural and Creative Industries. A report commissioned by the European Commission*. Utrecht School of the Arts.

Rushkoff, D. (2011). *Life Inc: How Corporatism Conquered the World, and How We Can Take It Back*. New York, US: Penguin Random House Trade Paperbacks.

Shirky, C. (2008). *Here Comes Everybody: The Power of Organizing Without Organizations*. New York, US: Penguin Group.

Tapscott, D., & Williams, A. D. (2007). *Wikinomics: How Mass Collaboration Changes Everything*. New York, US: Portfolio Penguin Group.

Towse, R. (2002). Book Review of Creative Industries. *Journal of Political Economy, 110*(1), 234–237. doi:10.1086/324388

Van Heur, B. (2010). *Creative Networks and the City: towards a Cultural Political Economy of Aesthetic Production*. Bielefeld: Transcript. doi:10.14361/transcript.9783839413746

Verwijnen, J. (1999). The Creative City's New Field Condition. Can Urban Innovation and Creativity Overcome Bureaucracy and Technocracy? In J. Verwijnen & P. Lehtovuori (Eds.), *Creative Cities. Cultural Industries e Urban Development and the Information Society*. Helsinki, FI: UIAH Publications.

KEY TERMS AND DEFINITIONS

Crowdworker: People who run the Litefactories and who usually put their skills together to run joined projects.

Litefactory: Every Company, Craftman, Freelance, Artist, Association which is constitutive part of a Multifactory.

Multifactory: Self regulated shared working environment for both those into intellectual jobs and practical professions.

Sharing Economy: An economical paradigm based upon the opportunity and potentialities of sharing knowledge, ideas, equipments and resources.

Social Business: A business whose aim is to address wealth for investors and shareholders, and to gain social improvements for Society and stakeholders.

Sustainability: While running a Company, a condition that is reached when the economical situation of the company is good, the company has good development opportunities, people who work in and for the company are safe, personally satisfied and paid according to their needs, the company respects the environment, doesn't create pollution and doesn't waste non-renewable resources, customers are given high value for money products and services.

Work Life Balance: The balance between the aspects related to work and to private life. Crowdworkers usually agree to shift the balance towards private life aspects.

Chapter 4
Social Aspects of Reverse Logistics and Knowledge Management

José G. Hernández
Universidad Metropolitana, Venezuela

María J. García
Minimax Consultores, Venezuela

Gilberto J. Hernández
Minimax Consultores, Venezuela

ABSTRACT

The main contribution of this chapter is the study of the generation and management knowledge, emphasizing the social aspects, from an area of the Logistic Model Based on Positions (LoMoBaP). The area to use is the Inverse logistics, which is integrated for the Reverse logistics manager, the Compilation and Reception manager and the Classification and use manager. The analysis will be done via dynamic knowledge, studying the upward spiral of knowledge creation, tacit to explicit to tacit. To do this will be constructed tables where the functions of these three positions will be identified and will be discussed, as these functions are involved in the process of management and generation of knowledge, following the processes of Socialization, Externalization, Combination and Internalization, simultaneously that are located in the Ba and knowledge assets are analyzed: Experimental, Conceptual Systemic and Routine Knowledge.

INTRODUCTION

The enterprise logistics is related to practically all the areas of an organization. This is an advantage and a disadvantage. Is an advantage, because, since the same it can study the organization as a whole. But at the same time, it is a disadvantage, because the enterprise logistics study is complex.

DOI: 10.4018/978-1-4666-9607-5.ch004

These two topics, the relationship of the enterprise logistics with the entire organization and the complex that it is to study the enterprise logistics, it can see through some aspects of great social impact, as:

The Quality. Since the late twentieth century Anderson, Jerman & Crum (1998), present the impact of quality in logistics. They reflect the social impact, linking the impact of logistics in customer service.

Later indicate Van der Vorst, Tromp & Van der Zee (2009), the relationship of the quality and logistics through the quality in the food industry. And to relate its social impact not only through the quality required to food, but in the sustainability and especially the environmental impact of the supply chain in the food industry.

The maintenance. Some authors (García, Escobet & Quevedo, 2010; Luna, 2009) manage a concept that relates the logistics and maintenance and the social impact, of the Prognostics and Health Management (PHM). Although obviously in this case Health, does not refer to the health of the staff, if not to the equipment and parts.

The relationship with the social is given because equipments which makes it a suitable maintenance, generates fewer problems for the employees in its environment, while generally more environmentally benign.

The industrial design. In different sections of their book Järvinen & Koskinen et al. (2001), draw attention to the sociological aspects of industrial design, which should be focused on the man. Among other aspects it must consider the logistics, either in the use of the designed, as in the logistics for its creation. In this way it can see the close relationship between logistics, industrial design and the social aspects.

Although they focus more on the market that the logistics, Van Gent et al. (2011), to present the technical Experiential Design Landscapes (EDL), show how the design is a social problem. And again it is clear that the design and logistics could ensure greater social comfort. They understand that the current design must do trying to minimize consumption of energy and minimizing the environmental impact.

The Human resources. A term that immediately relates logistics, human resources and the social is Humanitarian logistics, which clarify Tomasini & Van Wassenhove (2009), it is directed to vulnerable people. While this concept is intended to alleviate the deficiencies of people affected by a disaster, it covering aspects such as: transportation, planning, procurement and warehousing, which are specific terms of business logistics.

In some cases, the private organizations take part in works of Humanitarian logistics, not only for social commitment, but to learn managerial aspects of these experiences (McLachlin & Larson, 2011; Tomasini & Van Wassenhove, 2009). These last authors clarify, that between the differences between the business logistics and the Humanitarian logistics is emphasizes in collaboration.

Through business logistics directly, or through the Humanitarian logistics, it can see the close relationship between logistics, human resources and social aspects. In any case, the companies will take all this relationship through the human resource management.

It could show more examples for each of them. But with these four aspects there has been only a brief overview about how logistics is related with the whole organization, at the same time as influences in their social impact.

By all this complexity and multiple interactions, to facilitate the understanding of the business logistics have been created in the academy four models qualitative-quantitative, which study it from different approaches.

Under this scenario of logistics, in this chapter will cover three main aspects: Analyze business logistics through a qualitative-quantitative model, studying the same focus on the roles who have positions associated with it; select an area of this model and see through this area can generate and manage knowledge and third, show how through this dynamic knowledge generated, enterprises can increase their social impact.

It will use the area Inverse logistics of the Logistic Model Based on Positions (LoMoBaP [MoLoBaC]), which is composed of three managers: the Reverse logistics manager and his two subordinates the Collection and reception manager and the Classification and use manager. Through the functions of these three positions, it will analyze the generation and management of dynamic knowledge, using the spiral model proposed by Nonaka, Toyama & Konno (2000).

But in any case, taking advantage of reverse logistics has great environmental and social impact, the analysis of the generation and management of knowledge will be made by measuring especially its social impact.

From the above, the general objective of the chapter will: Show, as it can generate and manage knowledge in a dynamic organization, based on the functions of managers of the area of Inverse logistics of the MoLoBaC, while this knowledge is expressed by emphasizing its social components.

This general objective generates three specific objectives:

Present the MoLoBaC and with it one of its areas, Inverse logistics and its three positions, the Reverse logistics manager, the Collection and reception manager and the Classification and use manager; Define the main functions of these three positions of LoMoBaP and finally to show since thorough these functions generates a base of dynamic knowledge, allowing the organization to a efficient knowledge management and with a great social impact.

To achieve these objectives will follow the Integrated-Adaptable Methodology for the development of Decision Support System (IAMDSS, in Spanish, Metodología Integradora-Adaptable para desarrollar Sistemas de Apoyo a las Decisiones [MIASAD]) (García, Hernández & Hernández, 2014a; Guerrero et al., 2014).

Although IAMDSS arises for the developed of Decision Support Systems (DSS), as shown in García, Hernández & Hernández, (2014a), by its flexibility can be adapted to different types of investigation, where it can select from its twenty basic steps, only those who are deemed indispensable at the time of its application.

In a manner similar to what has been done in other research (García, Hernández & Hernández, 2014b; Guerrero et al., 2014) for this work, the following steps shall be:

1. To define the problem, that, as is indicated in the objectives is show, as it can generate and manage knowledge in a dynamic organization, based on the functions of managers of the area of Inverse logistics of the LoMoBaP, while this knowledge is expressed by emphasizing its social components,
2. To prepare a first prototype, where is identify the users of the final product. Being a scientific paper, end users will be the main readers of the same. These readers are all studious of business logistics, essentially those interested in social approach and in the global vision of it. Especially those interested in learn of the reverse logistics and its different perspectives. In addition those interested in understanding the relations of the logistics with the entire organization and they are willing to use new models qualitative-quantitative. But on all those who seek to have new tools for the generation and management of knowledge.

Also, with the first prototype, it sets out the structure of the article, which in addition to this introduction and the background, where will present the antecedents of the logistic models to use; it will consist of three sub-chapters central.

In the first of these sub-chapters will be presented the importance of the generation and management of dynamic knowledge, in the second Inverse logistics area of the MoLoBaC will be presented, doing insistence mainly in the functions of the positions associated with it and in the last and principal sub-chapters, it will illustrate how it can build and manage the dynamic knowledge of an organization, through the functions of the positions assigned to the area of Inverse logistics of the MoLoBaC;

3. Obtain data, on all available sources, especially journals and books. In this case on generation and management of the dynamic knowledge, logistics models, reverse logistics and functions of the managers associated with inverse logistics;
4. Establish alternatives, that would be the ways that could generate and manage dynamic knowledge, a society oriented approach, from managers associated with reverse logistics area and that in a certain way will be given by the functions that should play these managers;
5. Evaluate alternatives, in the sense to see the feasibility of the proposed alternatives to achieve the desired objectives. Taking as element for evaluation the possibilities and facilities to generate and manage dynamic knowledge with social content, that have each of the functions, of the managers associated with the inverse logistics;
6. Select the alternative, according to the previous evaluation and considering the secondary objectives, whether they are tacit or explicit. The alternative selected can be a group of functions;
7. Implement the best alternative, to establish all the mechanisms that allow that the select alternative could take to the practice, illustrate with a hypothetical vision and with a few functions of managers of the Inverse logistics, as it can create and manage dynamic knowledge with a social focus and
8. Establishing controls, which would be mechanisms to recognize if the solution or solutions achieved remain relevant over time.

It should be emphasized that in this work, a chosen alternative, does not have to be a function, but in general, is going to try a set of functions.

It is also important to emphasize, with regard to limitations and scopes, there will be no field work, but that will be the illustration of the generation and management of dynamic knowledge with social content, following a hypothetical view, to thereby provide a more general approach.

BACKGROUND

This chapter will cover three main aspects: Analyze enterprise logistics business through a qualitative-quantitative model, studying the same focus on the functions who have positions associated with it; select an area which make this model and see how through this area it can construct and manage the knowledge and third, to make clear like through this dynamic generated knowledge, companies can increase their social impact.

It is important before entering these details the origins of the present model to use.

It was commented that the high relationship of logistics to the different areas of business activity, constitutes an advantage and a disadvantage, the latter is determined by how hard it is to teach logistics. To minimize the difficulty of teaching logistics, in academia have been created, four qualitative-quantitative models (García, Hernández & Hernández, 2014b; Hernández, García & Hernández, 2012a), which were created to cover most of the areas and aspects that are related to business logistics, while trying to facilitate the teaching of the same.

As shown in Hernández, García & Hernández (2012a), these four models have been based, mainly, in the most relevant aspects of logistic:

Supplying, (Öberg, Huge-Brodin & Björklund, 2012; Xavier & Martins, 2011);

Production and productive process (Anttonen, 2010; Gold & Seuring, 2011; Sloan, 2011); Distribution, including transportation (Cholette & Venkat, 2009; Iannone & Thore, 2010; Le-Anh, Koster & Yu, 2010; Roth & Kaberger, 2002) and

Inverse logistics (Gnoni & Rollo, 2010; Ilgin & Gupta, 2010; Jack, Powers & Skinner, 2010; Pokharel & Mutha, 2009; Srivastava, 2007; Xanthopoulos & Iakovou, 2009).

These models are:

- The model Supply, Production, Distribution and Inverse Logistic (LSPDI, in Spanish el modelo Logístico, Abastecimiento, Producción, Distribución e Inversa [LAPDI]) model, centered in the logistics flows (García, Hernández & Hernández, 2013; Hernández, García & Hernández, 2012b);
- The Logistic Model Based on Positions (LoMoBaP, in Spanish Modelo Logístico Basado en Cargos [MoLoBaC]), studies logistics through the functions performed by the managers in logistic positions in an organization (Hernández, García & Hernández, 2012a; 2013);
- The Logistic Model Based on Indicators for Positions (LoMoBaIPo, in Spanish Modelo Logístico Basado en Indicadores de Cargos [MoLoBaICa]), which have a strong relationship with MoLoBaC and measures enterprise logistics through indicators (Guerrero et al., 2014; Hernández, García & Hernández, 2013) and
- The Logistic, Strategic, Tactical, Operational with Inverse Logistics Model (STOILMo, in Spanish Modelo Logístico, Estratégico, Táctico, Operativo con logística Inversa [MoLETOI]), which analyzes logistics through normal stages of administrative analysis: Strategic, Tacit and Operative (García, Hernández & Hernández, 2013).

It is necessary to clarify that in the quotations relating to these four logistic models, as well as in the MIASAD, has sought only to present the latest works that relate to the topic and they are preferably written in English. Therefore it is recommended, who wants more details on these topics, reviewing the citations of these works and in turn the citations of these and so on to find the original sources of the same, according to their respective interests.

The second of these four models, MoLoBaC, consists of forty-four positions, which are grouped into twelve areas and these together into six stages. One of these areas, Inverse logistics will be the focus of this work.

Through the positions of MoLoBaC has studied the generation and management of knowledge (García, Hernández & Hernández, 2014b; Hernández, García & Hernández, 2012a), some of these works only available in Spanish (Barreto, 2012; Jeney, 2014).

In the work of Hernández, García & Hernández, (2012a) it was the analysis of knowledge management illustrating it with the functions of the Customer service manager and was left open a line of research.

In this chapter will continue this line of research, but did not make use of a position but an area MoLoBaC, in addition to highlighting the social content of the generation and management of dynamic knowledge.

Another important aspect of this work is knowledge management. To continuation make a few brief comments on the dynamic knowledge.

BRIEF COMMENTS ABOUT THE GENERATION AND MANAGEMENT OF THE DYNAMIC KNOWLEDGE

Knowledge is present in the development of any field of human endeavor. And in the business world it can be noted that it is critical to the performance of organizations and that can acquire and accumulate knowledge from many sources: Customers, the related, of the proper processes and innovations and above all of human resources, thus forming a large intellectual capital, which will be useful in the critical decisions (Shang, Lin & Wu, 2009).

To leverage the knowledge in decision-making, adequate knowledge management needs.

It is important to emphasize, that a vital element in the management of knowledge is the knowledge sharing, which also approximates the generation and knowledge management to a social approach (Ibragimova, et al., 2012).

There are basic aspects, as is the need to share knowledge, particularly among members of the same organization (Teh & Yong, 2011), that contrast with the need for organizations to protect their knowledge, especially in organizations where a high competition occurs (Steinicke, Wallenburg & Schmoltzi, 2012).

It is important to note, as stated Grundstein (2008), in the knowledge society, when speaking of generation and knowledge management, there is little that has focused on man. It was possible to say that the society of the knowledge, takes little in account to the principal element of the society, the man.

Although it has been said that it can accumulate knowledge, really the most important thing is to harness the flow of knowledge, which is profit that knowledge generally, is often dynamic.

Many authors coincide, as pointed for Maracine & Scarlat (2009), that the essence of dynamic knowledge it is in turning tacit knowledge in explicit and this convert in tacit.

For those interested in the main topic of this chapter, the generation and knowledge management are encouraged to review Hernández, García & Hernández, (2012a), thence through a set of authors, among which are Nonaka & von Krogh, (2009) and Wan et al. (2010) is revised the exchange and creation of knowledge to passing of tacit knowledge to explicit and again to tacit and thus increasingly.

In particular for this chapter will focus on the work of Nonaka, Toyama & Konno (2000), those who focus the process of creation and knowledge management, in a dynamic spiral, that covers three main dimensions: SECI, Ba and Knowledge assets. Although the basic principles of the spiral dynamic of knowledge, had already been exposed a few years before by Nonaka, Reinmoller & Senoo (1998).

Figure 1. shows a conceptualization of this model.

The Socialization, Externalization, Combination and Internalization processes are recommended to check at the original source Nonaka, Toyama & Konno, (2000), or according to the approach followed in this chapter in Hernández, García & Hernández (2012a).

The Ba it may be, perhaps, a more difficult concept to transmit and it is related to the context necessary to create the knowledge, which must be specific, in the sense of those who are involved and as participating in the creation of knowledge. From there a first approximation to the Ba it is equated with place, understood as a shared place in which knowledge is created, shared and used (Nonaka, Toyama & Konno, 2000), what leads to the Ba is not necessarily only analyzed as physical space, but that is a close relationship space-time.

In this condition the Ba unifies the physical space, the virtual and the shared space, as it could be this latter, the ideas shared by an organization, from there that the key to understanding the Ba be interaction and its condition of being open and changing.

Social Aspects of Reverse Logistics and Knowledge Management

Figure 1. Conceptualization of the model of Nonaka, Toyama & Konno.
Source: Barreto (2012), based on Nonaka, Toyama & Konno (2000), following the interpretation of Hernández, García & Hernández (2012a).

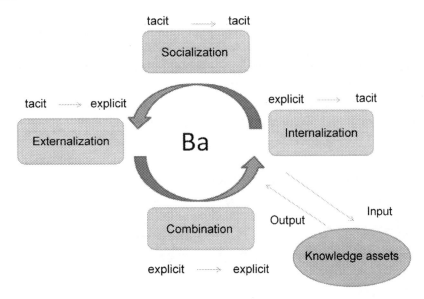

Finally when referring to the Knowledge assets, Nonaka, Toyama & Konno (2000), the categorized into four types: Experimental, Conceptual Systemic and Routine Knowledge assets, which can also be reviewed in Hernández, García & Hernández (2012a) or directly in Nonaka, Toyama & Konno (2000).

In this chapter, to perform a good management of knowledge and to understand the dynamic knowledge, should follow the spiral of these authors (Nonaka, Toyama & Konno, 2000), based on SECI, Ba and Knowledge assets.

Before closing this section, presents a definition of dynamic knowledge: It is an intangible resource, that works as the center of gravity of the creation and is itself the process of creation, diffusion, transference, internalization and absorption of the knowledge, departing from the transformation and conversion of the tacit knowledge in explicit knowledge and continuously through a spiral, that makes this last explicit knowledge generated, in tacit knowledge, restarting the cycle. For all this, the dynamic knowledge is expansive and complex and is one of the most important sources of competitive advantage of organizations (Hernández, García & Hernández, 2012a). For this chapter business logistics will be used, particularly reverse logistics for the management and acquisition of dynamic knowledge with social content, therefore, reference will be made to reverse logistics from the standpoint of the MoLoBaC.

Inverse Logistics and the Logistic Model Based in Positions

It will depart from the concept of enterprise logistics. Of the many and very good existing definitions, it will use the submitted by Hernández, García & Hernández (2013), since it is better suited to the objective in this chapter.

There to be told that the enterprise logistics is centered in searching and achieving a greater satisfaction, present and future of the final costumer, and includes socio-environmental and ethical-legal aspects, organization planning, execution and control of all related activities related to the attainment, flow, gathering and maintenance of materials, products and services, since the raw material source, including there the costumers through inverse logistics, to the sale point of the finished product local or international, massive or enterprise, in a more effective and efficient, maximizing performance and the expected quality, minimizing waste, times and costs and using modern information technologies.

The different areas of knowledge identified in the concept of business logistics, have been forced to create different approaches to study. One of these approaches is the four models mentioned above. Of these models for this chapter will be used MoLoBaC, which in its current version is consists of forty four positions, as can be seen in figure 2, that is the presented in Hernández, García & Hernández (2012a), with a slight modification in the position identified with the number 18, now corresponds to Systems of information and networks manager (Jeney, 2014). As can be seen in this figure, each of the positions is identified by a number.

These positions of the MoLoBaC, as explained in Hernández, García & Hernández (2012a; 2013), are grouped into twelve areas that meet in six stages:

1. Supplying, with an area, Procure, which is pure, while being conformed by positions that belongs to a single stage;
2. Production, conformed by two pure areas, Maintenance and Inventories;

Figure 2. Logistic Model Based on Positions (LoMoBaP [MoLoBaC])

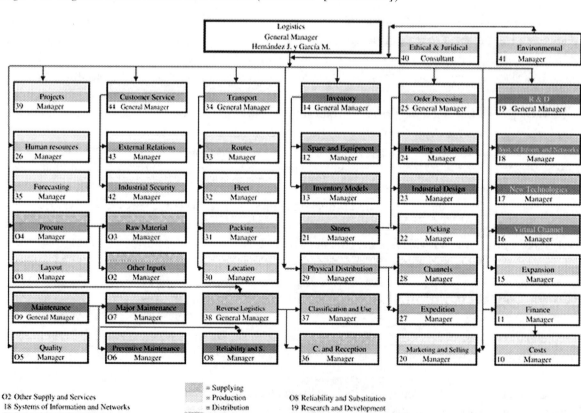

3. Distribution, with four areas, Order processing, is considered a mixed area, since integrates positions of different stages, Physical distribution, a pure area, Transportation, which it is a mixed area and the area that is the reason of being of the MoLoBaC, Costumer service, which is pure;
4. Inverse, formed by a unique pure area, Inverse logistics and that is the area in which this work is focused;
5. General to the company, with three areas, all pure, Intrinsic to logistics, Supported by logistics and Supporting logistics and
6. Information (General to information), formed by a mixed area, Information.

The area Inverse logistics is itself conformed for three positions: the 36, Collection and reception manager, 37, Classification and use manager, too designed how Utilization manager (Hernández, García & Hernández, 2012b) and 38, Reverse logistics general manager. As this area of Inverse logistic and its positions, is the focus of this work, then make some comments on the same.

Inverse Logistics Area in MoLoBaC

Taking the concept of business logistics as a starting point and integrating aspects of Díaz, Álvarez & González (2004) and Leite (2003), it is possible to construct a definition of inverse logistics, noting that involves three main protagonists: consumers or market, the economic future of the organization and perhaps the most important, the environment.

Therefore the reverse logistics seeks to recover value for the company, while it is a way to improve the present and future customer satisfaction, from there that needs to be carried out in the most effective and efficient manner, minimizing costs and waste and making use of modern information technologies, also covers the socio-environmental, ethical-legal aspects, the planning, organization, execution and control of all activities related to obtaining, flow, storage, maintenance and better exploitation of materials, products or parts of them, that have reached the end consumer and that by various causes or reasons must be returned to the supply chain of the organization that produced, either after being partially or totally consumed the main product or with no or few modifications on the part of customers.

On having read this concept, there is no doubt in affirming that the managers of the area Inverse logistics, these are responsible for ensuring that all materials, products or parts of them, that returning to the organization, having been in the hands of customers, are utilized in the best possible way.

This implies handle so they represent an added value for the organization and that can be exploited to the maximum, both from a financial point of view, such as environmental and market. To perform this operation, it must ensure the greatest satisfaction, present and future of consumers, costs should be minimized and should use the most appropriate technologies. The meet these conditions, it will define the functions that each of these managers must perform.

Before starting mentioning the functions of the managers associated with the area Inverse logistics, it is important to clarify than in inverse logistics, although frequently spoke of materials, to refer to the components of the products, the concept of product is a broadened concept (Brito, Flapper & Dekker, 2002), which may cover the products themselves and their components, that is to say, from a small piece, part of a product or a minor equipment, up to a big machine or part of a plant or an industrial complex. For this reason, when it speaking of product, in inverse logistics, will be referring to this expanded concept.

On the functions of the positions of the area Inverse logistics, is clear that among the three positions must meet a number of functions very linked together. This close relationship may suggest that many of these functions are common. This chapter will attempt to distinguish, if possible, the functions of each of the positions.

In the Tables 1, 2 and 3 it is separately presented some of the functions performed by each of the three managers of the area Inverse logistics. And those functions that might seem to be repeated in another position, have tried to avoid, minimizing the number of total functions. Anyway it will try to highlight those functions which may represent a social component.

Before continuing it is important to briefly comment on Social logistics. Following the statement by Twaróg, Szoltysek & Otreba (2012), it can say that social logistics is understood external to the company

Table 1. Some functions of the Collection and reception manager of the MoLoBaC

	Intrinsic to the Position
01	Establish policies and norms relating to the C&R of the organization.
02	Ensure compliance with the rules and regulations, to help the environmental protection.
03	Analyze for each PRL, its real possibilities of collection.
04	Generate the mechanisms that facilitate the customers to collaborate with the collection.
05	Apply an approach following the techniques of environmental economics to define the C&R.
06	Keeping up with new technologies to facilitate the collection.
07	To define clearly the zones of collection, when this field activity is realized directly by the organization.
08	Provide guidance to consumers on the separation of the PRL, when necessary.
09	Ensure that consumers will have the tools and instruments needed for separations which go beyond the normal conditions.
10	Conduct studies to ensure that they can receive each PRL, interest.
11	To condition inside the organization, the areas for the reception.
12	Track the PRL collected and received.
13	Inform to the organization of any change in the C&R.
14	To prepare the organization for the C&R of the PRL that needs special conditions.
15	To create or to take part in the creation of the best conditions for the reception.
16	Classify the PRL, according to their potential to pollute the environment.
17	Create incentives for the collection, which motivate staff and consumers, and go beyond the legal requirements.
18	To determine for which PRL, it is necessary to establish special campaigns for his collection.
19	Do consumers understand that the collection can be a first step to recycling?
20	Getting external, financial and promotional incentives for the activities of C&R.
21	Disseminate, inside and outside the organization, the benefits of a well-conducted collection.
22	Improve the reputation of the organization through good performance in collection.
23	Be alert to changes in the approaches of consumers that may affect the C&R.
	Related to other Positions of MoLoBaC
24	Ask the advice to the Quality manager to include aspects of quality in the C&R.
25	Working with the Layout manager to define appropriate spaces for reception.

continued on following page

Table 1. Continued

26	Maintain a permanent exchange of information with the Procurement manager and his subordinates for them take into account the PRL that are received.
27	Ensure, through the general manager of maintenance and their subordinates, the equipment for the C&R receive the necessary maintenance.
28	Coordinate with the manager of cost, to perform the C&R at a minimum cost.
29	Participate, together with the Cost manager, in the minimization of costs of the organization.
30	Receive the collaboration of the R&D manager and their subordinates, in order to maximize the contribution that the new technologies of the information they can provide to the C&R.
31	Ensure that the C&R should be considered in all the expansion plans of the organization.
32	Work with Inventories and Warehouse managers, to the best location of the PRL.
33	Coordinate with the MHM, the movement of products received through the C&R.
34	Assist the Industrial design manager to design products that are easy to separate.
35	Contribute to the IDM to generate products whose parts are easily collected.
36	Use with the help of the M&SM, C&R, as a tool to promote the organization and its products.
37	Ensure, by the RHM, the C&R staff has the necessary training.
38	Leverage, in collaboration with the RHM, the C&R, to encourage staff.
39	To prepare, together with the managers of HR and IS&IR, to the whole personnel of C&R, to confront the industrial accidents and catastrophes of natural origin.
40	Provide, together to the IS&IR Mgr., the staff of C&R of the protection and the necessary equipment and instruments for the achievement of their work.
41	Generate with the Project manager, in projects on C&R that benefit the whole organization.
42	Working in close collaboration to the Environmental manager, to establish policies that support the environment through the C&R.
43	Check, together to the E&JC the legal framework on C&R to comply with it fully.
44	Collaborate with the CSM to convert the C&R, in a best service.
Related to MoLoBaICa, LAPDI, MoLETOI and the Enterprise Logistics in General	
45	Ensure that the staff of C&R promotes the vision, mission and rectors principles.
46	Help generate management indicators that measure the performance of C&R.
47	Studying the flow of all the products managed in the C&R.
48	Ensure that the C&R staffs participate in the strategic and tactical aspects, in addition to the operational.
49	Integrate to the C&R, with the other logistical aspects of the organization beyond the IL.
Related to SCM and the Enterprise and its Environment as a Whole	
50	Integrate to the distribution channels in the process of collection and even the reception.
51	Establish partnerships with the other members of the SCM, to facilitate the collection process.
52	Take advantage of any variation or change in the environment that will enhance the C&R.
53	Maintain a permanent contact with consumers to improve the C&R.
54	Ensure that the staff of C&R has a positive impact on society as a whole.
55	Help build campaigns that encourage recycling and with this will help the collection.
56	Promote the reduction of energy consumption in the work of C&R.
57	Establish partnerships with institutes of education, to promote the C&R through them.
58	Create campaigns that will allow them to integrate to the staff of C&R with neighboring communities.

Table 2. Some functions of the Classification and use manager of the MoLoBaC

	Intrinsic to the Position
01	Establish policies for classification and subsequent use of all the PRL.
02	Ensure that all the PRL, will be given the best utilization.
03	Maximize the value added in all the PRL.
04	To watch that in the C&U there are fulfilled norms and regulations, which help to the environmental protection.
05	To promote, inside and out of the organization, the benefits of the C&U.
06	To acquire new technologies that facilitates the classification and better later use.
07	To take part in the creation of better conditions for the classification and later use.
08	To do pursuit of the products already classified to guarantee his best use.
09	Create mechanisms that would improve the performance in C&U.
10	Generate mechanisms within the organization for the management of products that require special conditions, for their classification or later use.
11	Manage external incentives, financial or promotional, associated with the C&U.
12	Gain a reputation for the organization through the C&U.
13	Be open to new ideas of the staff relating to C&U, in particular to the use.
14	Define the conditions for a PRL can be considered Resalable.
15	Establish the circumstances under which a PRL should be Reconditioned.
16	Deciding when a PRL should be Repairable.
17	Analyze that PRL can be converted into Renovated.
18	Create, if needed, the spaces of manufacturing, in order to be able to carry a PRL to conditions of Resalable, Reconditioned, Repairable or Renovated.
19	Ensure that any intervention on a PRL, generate a value-added.
20	Set up situations in which an LRP is carried to Reprocessed.
21	Apply the models and techniques necessary to know whether a PRL is Reusable.
22	To define in what point of the chain of production there joins a PRL that is Recyclable.
23	To create the mechanisms that allows that a PRL, which cannot offer another possibility of use, should be turned into Redirected.
24	Minimize, without altering the quality of the production, the PRL that end as Waste.
25	To guarantee that the Wastes are eliminated in a most suitable way.
	Related to other Positions of MoLoBaC
26	Condition, together with the managers of Layout and of C&R, the areas inside the organization, to take the process of classification.
27	Establish, along with the managers of Layout, of Stores and Materials handling, the routes of circulation and storage of the PRL.
28	Facilitate, with the collaboration of the managers of Layout, of Stores and the Procure manager and his subordinate, the discharge of the PRL and the later classification of the same.
29	Receive the support of the Quality manager, especially to classify the PRL, considering, between other aspects, his quality of origin.
30	Keep informed the Procure manager and his subordinates, about the volumes and the direction that the PRL will take.
31	Work together with the Cost manager to minimize costs in the whole C&U.
32	Generate a constant flow of information, with the Maintenance manager and their subordinates, in order to maintain operational all machinery and equipment needed to perform the classification and later a better use of all the PRL.
33	Define with the Inventory manager and subordinates, the spaces to store the PRL.

continued on following page

Table 2. Continued

34	Inform the Spare and Equipment manager, of all those PRL that will be converted Reusable, Recyclable, Redirected and that could serve as spares and parts.
35	Achieve, together the Expansion manager and other managers involved, the C&U, is a vital part in all the expansion plans of the organization.
36	Track, together the M&SM, changes in consumer behavior that may affect the C&U.
37	Set together the M&SM, markets into which flow the PRL.
38	Provide information to the IDM, obtained when disassembling PRL.
39	Set with the Packing manager, needs and management of packaging and packaging for all PRL.
40	To keep informed the Packing manager, of any material that could be used as packing or wrapping, from the PRL.
41	To guarantee, together the HRM, the good training of the personnel of C&U.
42	Check with the managers of Forecasting and of Projects and with the support of the HRM, the projects of progress that involve the PRL.
43	Guarantee, along with the IS&IR Mgr., that the handling of the PRL realizes with the most advanced norms of safety.
44	Train to the personnel of C&U, with the help of the IS&IR Mgr. and of the HRM, to confront any industrial accident or catastrophe of natural origin.
45	Working jointly with the Environmental manager, to minimize any environmental impact, especially caused by waste.
46	Check permanently, together the E&JC the legal framework which would affect the C&U.
47	Ensure, together CSM and their subordinates, the PRL, will be located, organized and managed, in the form of ensuring the best service to the end customer.
Related to MoLoBalCa, LAPDI, MoLETOI and the Enterprise Logistics in General	
48	Create indicators to see the evolution of each of the groups in which the PRL are classified.
49	To monitor and correct, if necessary, flow of PRL.
50	Convert the C&U a strategic element for the organization.
51	Set all tactical aspects of C&U.
52	Integrate C&U, with the other logistical aspects of the organization, beyond IL.
Related to SCM and the Enterprise and its Environment as a Whole	
53	Making the best use of PRL, minimizing energy consumption.
54	Establish partnerships with other members of the SCM, to make better use of C&U.
55	Exploit any variation or change in the environment that will improve the C&U.
56	Maintain regular contact with customers to improve C&U.
57	Getting that the C&R staff have a positive impact in society.
58	Create campaigns that integrate the staff of C&R with neighboring communities.

and is the effective management of flows of materials and information, associated with a social value, with the sense of creating a major well-being to the society as whole. And just as with Humanitarian logistics, Social logistics, often serve as a means of training to improve their logistics. It is important to note here that when talking about Humanitarian and Social logistics, it is usually referred to the relationship between reverse logistics and risk management.

However in this chapter, mainly for reasons of space, this aspect can be presented from many different points of view, intentionally this topic, risk management, will not be covered in spite of all the interest that can wake up.

Table 3. Some functions of the Inverse logistics manager of the MoLoBaC

	Intrinsic to the Position
01	Establish all the political and norms relative to the IL of the organization.
02	Promote environmental protection through the IL.
03	Apply to each of the products, the model of the 11Rs, or any similar, to decide its IL.
04	Establish parameters that define if a PRL belongs to the AIL or BIL.
05	Make effort to ensure that the maximum of the PRL to the BIL.
06	Minimize the number of PRL to be the AIL.
07	Maintain a clear classification of PRL, as coming from Post-sale or Post-consumer.
08	Establish mechanisms for maximum recovery of the products coming from Post-consumer.
09	Perform permanently proposals that encourage and enhance IL.
10	Set the sphere of influence of the organization as regards IL.
11	Involving consumers as much as possible in all aspects of IL.
12	Conduct studies to improve all stages of reverse logistics.
13	Caring that IL, respond beyond the expectations that consumers have.
14	Measure the resources invested in IL, are rewarded with benefits.
15	Ensure that IL meets finance, market and legal-environmental aspects.
16	Keep constant track of all PRL.
17	Using IL as a source to determine substitutes and complementary products.
18	Analyze potential markets for PRL: Resalable, Reconditioned, Repairable, Renovated, Reprocessed and Reusable.
19	Consider getting the most out of the PRL: Recyclable and Redirected.
20	Devise strategies to achieve rid of the waste with the least environmental and economic impacts possible.
21	Create or participate in creating the best possible conditions for the IL.
22	Submit PRL, constant revision from the point of view of the environment.
23	Create incentives for IL, beyond the legal, environmental or economic.
24	Do consumers understand the importance of IL has for them.
25	Spread within and outside the organization, the benefits of IL.
26	Enhance organization reputation by performing in IL.
27	Pay attention to changes in consumer habits that may affect IL.
	Related to other Positions of MoLoBaC
28	Collaborate to achieve those products, by-products and its parts, from the inverse logistics they are a part of the regular sources of supplying of the organization.
29	Provide information to the Procure manager and their subordinates, in order to reduce their purchases of those products that are received by IL.
30	Offer, together the General maintenance manager and their subordinates, the maintenance that may require some PRL, prior to joining his definitive use.
31	Coordinate with the Cost manager, to perform all the processes of IL at a minimum cost.
32	Achieve, together the Costs manager, that IL be a source of savings for the organization.
33	Create by Inventory models manager, the models that best suit IL.
34	Exchange information with the managers of Spare and equipment and of Inventories, to incorporate into the inventories the obtained products of the IL.
35	Taking care the Spare and equipment manager, can ensure the equipment and parts needed to perform the activities of IL.

continued on following page

Table 3. Continued

36	Working with Inventory and Stores managers for the best location of the PRL.
37	Reach agreement with IDM to design products that are easy to handle from the point of view of the IL.
38	Set together with the Expansion manager possibilities offered management policies of PRL in future expansions of the organization.
39	Establish agreements with marketing channels, with the support of Channel manager for the best management of Post-sales products.
40	Participate in establishing strategies that enable production and distribution processes, minimize the AIL.
41	Work together with the Packing manager, to take advantage of the IL in this area.
42	Ensure that the Location manager, consider the IL by studying a new location.
43	Generate and participate with the project manager, in projects on IL that benefit the whole organization.
44	Working in close collaboration to the Environmental manager, to establish policies of IL, in favor of the environment.
45	Ensure, together the E&JC, that the legal framework on IL is fully meets.
46	Provide, together the IS&IR Mgr., the staff of IL of the protection and the necessary equipment and instruments for the achievement of their work.
47	Regulate, with the help of the CSM, which PRL of Post-sale can be received and what is not, still maintaining, high levels of customer service.
48	Become, with the help of the CSM, IL, in a best service.
49	With the help of HRM ensure that all personnel from area IL are ready to face any natural disaster or industrial accident that may occur.
Related to MoLoBaICa, LAPDI, MoLETOI and the Enterprise Logistics in General	
50	Generate or help generate management indicators that measure the performance of the IL.
51	Keep up to date and in constant review these indicators.
52	Set all the flows relating to the IL.
53	Prepare the organization to manage the IL of the PLR which require special conditions.
54	Establish the strategic, tactical and operational aspects of the IL.
55	Integrate the entire organization in managing IL.
Related to SCM and the Enterprise and its Environment as a Whole	
56	Integrating distribution channels in IL.
57	Conduct, where possible, activities of IL in conjunction with other members of the SCM.
58	Promote changes in the environment that facilitate and enhance IL.
59	Exploiting variations or changes that occur in the environment to enhance IL.
60	Seek the cooperation of consumers to enhance IL.
61	Working for all staff IL, has a positive impact on the social environment.
62	Create campaigns that encourage BIL, while minimizing the AIL.
63	Improve, where possible, energy consumption in the process of IL.
64	Make some studies to convert waste into energy.
65	Manage campaigns to integrate IL staff with neighboring communities.

However, for each of the studied charges are included functions related to risk management. In particular risk management for disaster or industrial accidents.

In the Table 1 there will be included the functions related to the Collection and reception manager, that particularly, from the point of view of the MoLoBaC, it is responsible for establishing policies relating to that product and under what conditions is going to receive from the hands of consumers and how to do is to take the process of collecting the same.

Further on, before submitting Table 3, there will be some comments of the model 11R's (Hernández et al., 2011), however, for a better understanding of Table 1, is necessary to take this model a couple of definitions Collection and Reception.

Understanding the Collection as: the initial process of the inverse logistics, that is define the policies of the organization to remove from hands of the client materials and products that will be the reverse flows of the organization. And about the Reception it will be said that it is the second process of the inverse logistics, which begins just on having finished the collection and is to establish policies to receive goods that arrive by reverse flows, those who must subsequently be classified according to the greater utility that can provide (Hernández et al., 2011).

For the three table, the functions presented there, although not expressed textually are inspired or have been extracted principally of Baker, 2004; Díaz, Álvarez & González, 2004; Leite, 2003; Peterson, 2005; Pishvaee, Farahani & Dullaert, 2010; Ravi, Shankar & Tiwari, 2005 or Shevtshenko et al., 2012. Additionally some functions were inspired in concepts that took of Hernández et al. (2011).

In these tables will make use of some abbreviations like C&R, by collection and reception; C&RM, by C&R manager; C&U, by classification and use; C&UM, by Classification and use (Utilization) manager; CSM, by Customer service manager; E&JC, by Ethical & Juridical consultant; HR, by human resources; HRM, by Human Resources manager; IDM, by Industrial design manager; IL, by Inverse logistics; IS&IR, by Industrial Safety and Internal Relations; Mgr., by Manager; MHM, by Material Handling manager; M&SM, by Marketing and Sales manager; PRL, by product of reverse logistics; R&D, by Research and Development and SCM, by Supply Chain Management. Some of these abbreviations will still be used in the remaining work.

In the three tables, but in particular in Table 1, it is understood that when speaking of receipt and collection, reference is made to the products that returning through the reverse logistics and that is making use of the broad concept of inverse product, as noted earlier.

To facilitate the understanding of the Tables 1, 2 and 3, but especially the first two, there are some general comments made below.

When speaks about intrinsic functions of the position, as its name indicates, it refers to functions that are proper of the position and that in certain way identify it. Of there that in these functions emphasize all those regulative aspects that the respective manager must handle. In particular in the Table 3 will be mentioned functions that are general to the planning of the reverse logistics as a whole.

While in the Table 1 will be placed on functions that are specific to the collection and receipt of the goods that arrive through the reverse logistics. In Table 2, it will be more emphasis on functions that are related to the end use will give these products from reverse logistics.

By the above, it is also common to find in Table 3, functions that have more to do with the fields of application of reverse logistics, with their ability to generate added value and in particular adverse reverse logistics and benign reverse logistics, which will be discussed later, just before submitting Table 3. Equally, in the Table 3, for being proper of the Inverse logistics manager there will be functions that relate it to two general types of inverse logistics that they usually present, the logistic inverse post-selling and the logistic inverse post-consume, on which also they will comment before presenting this table.

The functions grouped down related to other positions of the MoLoBaC, meanwhile let see how the respective managers are interrelated.

Thus in Table 1, looks like there are many functions of the Collection and reception manager that have direct effects on the remaining positions, either because they influence the performance of the remaining positions or because they can influence and collaborate on them. Likewise in Table 2, these relations are seen with the remaining positions of the MoLoBaC, but this time through the use that you can give to the products that arrive by means of reverse logistics.

In Table 2, are some of the functions of the Utilization manager, in particular, are responsible for classifying and search for the best utilization of all the materials that returns to the organization through the reverse logistics.

It should be noted, that in addition to the sources mentioned above, for this post is mainly used to Hernández et al. (2011) and Hernández, García & Hernández (2012b) and the works, on the subject, quoted by them. In particular of 11R's model (Hernández et al., 2011) it took the terms: Collection (Recolección in Spanish), Reception, Resalable, Reconditioned, Repairable, Renovated, Reprocessed, Reusable, Recyclable, Redirected and Waste (Residuos in Spanish), which will be briefly discussed at the end of the Table 2.

Before presenting the functions of the Inverse logistics manager, there will be a few brief comments of the 11-Rs presented by Hernández et al. (2011).

But it must have been previously clarify that these authors make use of the concepts of Adverse Inverse Logistics (AIL) and Benign Inverse Logistics (BIL), to differentiate that reverse logistics that generates direct costs, that which creates valued added.

On many occasions, that a PRL is finally classified as BIL or AIL, often depends on whether it is a product of post-sale or post-consumer.

Leite (2003) indicates that the inverse channel of Post-consumption is that constituted by the flows reverses of a set of PRL, that return to the productive cycle after having finished, in hands of the final client, its original utility; meanwhile the channel reverse of Post-selling it is constituted by the different forms and possibilities of return of a set of PRL, that with little or no use they flow, from the consumer towards the manufacturer.

It is noteworthy, that in general the Post-consumer logistics is often associated with the BIL, while the reverse logistics Post-sales is more related to the AIL.

Following the 11-Rs, the first two, Collection and Reception, already they were submitted, before the Table 1, therefore only comment Rs nine, remaining.

It should be noted that 11-Rs corresponds to the initials of each of them in Spanish, what does not indicate that English these terms also begin with R, so that at the side of each definition, has placed the term in Spanish.

- **Resalable (Revendible):** Most of these products should be of Post-sale, although it is not discarded that any products of Post-consumption are included. These are products that will return to the original market, and very few times to one less, they do not need that on them any modification is realized, at most a process of general cleanliness and in few cases pack them again.
- **Reconditioned (Reacondicionable or Reacondicionado):** Just like the previous case in general, they are products of Post-sale, although it could have some Post-consumer. These products typically need a thorough cleaning, without major changes, with the exception of the wrapping, the packaging or both that can be replaced. Also tend to go back to its original market and with exceptions to a market less.

- **Repairable (Reparable or Reparado):** It will also seek mostly products of Post-sale, with a lower percentage of products Post-consumer. The repair implies that these products require the replacement of smaller parts, a cleaning process and probably a re-packaging. Generally they are aimed at a lower market and rarely return to their original market.
- **Renovated (Renovable or Renovado):** Like the above three types of products, are located in a large majority among the products of Post-sale, with minor participation of products of Post-consumer. Just like the Repairable are products that require replacement parts, although higher than them, In other words can be understood as products that require a major repair, Involving a greater cleaning and probably a major change in the packaging. Often return to a market less than its original market.
- **Reprocessed (Reprocesable or Reprocesado):** They are still products of Post-sale, although there may be in similar amounts of post-consumer products. Here it is not a replacement of minor parts, but additionally these products often require major parts are replaced, thus involving an increase in the cost and time. In general they return only to markets lower than its market of origin.
- **Reusable (Reutilizables):** Mostly they come from the markets of Post-consumer. To just as the products to re-condition usually need cleanliness and some minor repair, only that now usually is not the original product, but a part of it or its packaging, wrapping or pack. The process of reuse involves integrating them into the productive chain, within a new product of the same species of the initial product that took it to the reverse logistics process. In general it could return to their original market.
- **Recyclable (Reciclable):** As Reusable mostly comes from Post-consumer market. Usually complete or nearly complete products, that suffer a process of disassembly or cannibalization, as mentioned Díaz, Álvarez & González (2004), to retrieve the parts that are still useful, which in general are converted to product to reuse and rarely go to other industrial markets, to give a similar use to that played before returning by the reverse logistics process. Similar to reusable, they can also return to their original market.
- **Redirected (Re-dirigible or that can Redirigir):** They can be products of Post-sale or Post-consumer, in integral form or only some of its parts. These products are already not useful to keep on redeeming his initial function, nevertheless, as everything or some of his parts, they still have practical utility in other means, they are transformed to be integrated to the new functions that they must redeem. In general they go to markets of minor value, which can be very different from his markets of origin.
- **Waste or in occasions Residues (Residuos):** They can have its origin in Post-sale, but mainly they are of Post-consumption, probably already have gone through any of the eight previous Rs and they no longer have any value, practical or aesthetic. Mostly must be incinerated or fit in some landfill and only tend to be a cost to the organization, which should be responsible for them to fulfill their social responsibility, whether voluntary or imposed by any environmental law.

In the Table 3, introducing the functions of the Inverse logistics manager, will notice that many of them are related to the post-sale and post-consumer, as well as AIL and the BIL.

Although there are other functions, for each of the three positions of Inverse logistic area, these will be sufficient for an analysis of how IL can generate and manage knowledge, encompassing social aspects.

GENERATION AND MANAGEMENT KNOWLEDGE AND REVERSE LOGISTICS

The analysis that will do next will be based, principally, on the functions of the three previous tables. To avoid creating long explanatory, avoid confusion and for reasons of space, the table number be used before any function. If it presents the function 119, it will be making reference to the function 19 in Table 1.

Not only is it wants to study the generation and management of knowledge, but wishes to emphasize its social content. To emphasize this social content will emphasize those functions that facilitate its handling.

On the other hand it is necessary to remember that the knowledge to generate, to identify or to acquire is a dynamic knowledge and to illustrate this process will be used to model submitted by Nonaka, Toyama & Konno, (2000) and will be made via the three essential elements of the model: SECI, Ba and Knowledge assets. As it wish to emphasize the social components, is not surprising that the process of socialization, the model is the one with the greatest impact.

Similar to the approach followed by García, Hernández & Hernández (2014b), which also follow the model Nonaka, Toyama & Konno, (2000), relationships are presented witch.

In the Tables 4 to 12 a summary of all the functions that are most relevant to each of the aspects of the model will be presented. In particular in the Tables 4, 5, 6 and 7 will do the relation with the processes: Socialization, Externalization, Combination and Internalization, respectively.

In the Table 8 will be collected the functions related to the Ba and in the Tables 9, 10, 11 and 12 will be introduced to the functions that in some way reflects the Knowledge assets: Experimental, Conceptual Systemic and Routine, respectively.

Inverse Logistic and Social Aspects

In the Tables 4 to 12, shown as the area Inverse logistics of the MoLoBaC, allows generation and knowledge management. However, for reasons of space and to meet the objectives, below will only are a brief discussion of those topics, in the generation and knowledge management, which are more closely related to social aspects.

Already in the Tables 4 to 12 has endeavored to select only those functions, which in one way or another had a high social content. In the analysis below this area of interest will be further reduced.

Table 4. Management of the Socialization through managers of inverse logistics area

SECI (Socialization)	
Aspects	Functions that do
Share experiences:	
With his subordinates.	113; 117; 121; 207; 213; 220 to 223; 208; 321.
With other positions of MoLoBaC.	113; 124 to 144; 226 to 247; 328 to 349.
With external entities.	104; 107; 108; 109; 116; 117; 119; 120; 121; 122; 123; 150; 151; 152; 153; 154; 155; 157; 158; 204; 205; 211; 212; 214 to 217; 224; 225; 237; 254 to 258; 302; 303; 310; 311; 313; 318; 320; 322; 324 to 327; 339; 344; 348; 356 to 360.
Exchange of information.	102; 110; 112; 114; 115; 156; 208; 210; 218; 230; 232; 234; 238; 240; 249; 209; 329; 334; 352; 353.
Frequent meetings.	Are routinely made and therefore not explicitly contemplated.

Table 5. Management of the Externalization through managers of inverse logistics area

SECI (Externalization)	
Aspects	Functions that do
Crystallizes the knowledge.	102; 104; 116; 118; 123; 201; 206; 302; 307; 317 to 322; 325; 342 to 344; 356 to 364.
Transformed into explicit the tacit knowledge.	106; 117; 119; 125; 202; 214 to 225; 227; 324; 350 to 355.
Articulated work.	102; 108; 112; 113; 114; 115; 124 to 144; 150 to 158; 204; 226 to 247; 253 to 258; 309; 328 to 349; 356 to 364.
Forms the basis of new knowledge.	103; 107; 110; 146 to 149; 207 to 210; 213; 248 to 252; 303; 304; 312.

Table 6. Management of the Combination through managers of inverse logistics area

SECI (Combination)	
Aspects	Functions that do
Systematized knowledge.	102; 109; 112; 115; 118; 123; 201; 209; 219 to 223; 253 to 258; 302; 303; 308; 314; 321; 324 to 327.
Convert explicit knowledge into more explicit knowledge.	110; 114; 119; 146 to 149; 202; 206; 208; 214 to 218; 224; 225; 248 to 252; 304; 309; 312; 317 to 320; 350 to 363.
Help to process, combine, edit and convert knowledge into new knowledge.	104; 108; 113; 116; 121; 124 to 144; 150 to 154; 204; 207; 210; 213; 226 to 247; 311; 316; 322; 328 to 349.

Table 7. Management of the Internalization through managers of inverse logistics area

SECI (Internalization)	
Aspects	Functions that do
Integrates knowledge.	103; 110; 114; 123; 147; 149 to 153; 207; 213; 249 to 258; 302 to 307; 311; 327; 355 to 364.
Converts explicit knowledge into tacit knowledge.	107; 112; 116; 119; 146; 156; 210; 214 to 223; 248; 309; 312; 350 to 354.
Spread the new knowledge.	104; 108; 113; 115; 120; 121; 124 to 144; 155; 157 to 158; 205; 225 to 247; 317 to 321; 324; 325; 328 to 349.

Table 8. Management of the Ba through managers of inverse logistics area

Ba	
Aspects	Functions that do
Offer: Space. Time. Conditions. Space-time.	The managers of the area of inverse logistics, do not generate explicitly the Ba, nevertheless, in the following functions it is possible to see its presence: 101; 107; 110; 111; 114; 115; 117; 124 to 144; 153; 201; 207; 210; 214 to 223; 225 to 247; 255; 301; 302; 307; 310; 318; 319; 321; 327 to 349; 353; 358, 359.

Table 9. Knowledge assets Experimental through managers of inverse logistics area

Knowledge assets (Experimental)	
Aspects	Functions that do
Emotional and affective.	All the functions. Here participate all the positions of the MoLoBaC, highlighting the relationships with subordinates.
Tacit knowledge shared and re-built.	Participate, practically all the functions, but it is still proper to each organization.

Table 10. Knowledge assets Conceptual through managers of inverse logistics area

Knowledge assets (Conceptual)	
Aspects	Functions that do
Images and symbols.	Practically all the functions, it stand out those who use the model 11Rs.
Explicit knowledge.	101; 104; 107 to 109; 114 to 116; 119; 121; 146 to 149; 154; 156; 201; 204; 209; 210; 214 to 218; 220 to 225; 248 to 253; 301; 302; 304 to 306; 308; 310; 317 to 319; 322; 324; 325; 350 to 364.
Shared knowledge.	124 to 144; 226 to 247; 311; 328 to 349.

Table 11. Knowledge assets Systemic through managers of inverse logistics area

Knowledge assets- (Systemic)	
Aspects	Functions that do
Explicit knowledge organized, systematized and legalized.	More visible of the Knowledge assets. Practically all the functions, especially the related to the E&JC: 143; 246; 345.
Easy to understand and to transmit.	All the functions of three positions.

Table 12. Knowledge assets Routine through managers of inverse logistics area

Knowledge assets (Routine)	
Aspects	Functions that do
Organizational culture.	It is essentially practical. Participants all functions of all three positions. It is also proper to each organization.
Tacit knowledge is implanted and embedded in the daily work of the organization.	

Therefore, the analysis is primarily focused in Table 4, although, of course, also are incorporated functions appearing in other tables.

These functions of social content can be divided into three groups, not necessarily disjoint: those relating to the organization, related to the society as a whole and those who seek to benefit the environment.

As interest is focused on the social impact of the organization to the outside world, there will not be made major comments of the internal functions to the organization. In these functions internal to the organization include all those relating to other positions of MoLoBaC, there are the functions: 124 to 144, 226 to 247 and 328 to 349.

Again for reasons of space and to facilitate the reading, the other two areas are presented through Table 13.

Of the Tables 4 to 13, but especially the Table 13, it can see how the area of reverse logistics can be an excellent starting point to generate knowledge, which goes beyond the organization. Without making more analysis, for reasons of space, it can be seen that the reverse logistics, not only has an environmental impact, but incorporating the rest of society in the productive process to achieve goals of high social content.

What is important, for organizations, is to determine and analyze those functions that facilitate this exchange with the society, to empower them. The great advantage is that it does not require a greater effort, since they are functions that normally must be made in the organization, to achieve a better performance.

FUTURE RESEARCH DIRECTIONS

This chapter has focused on the functions of managers of the area of reverse logistics of the MoLoBaC. There has been only a collection of some of them and have been classified, according to the social impact that can offer, to generate knowledge. For this generation and management of dynamic knowledge, it has been used an adaptation of the model Nonaka, Toyama & Konno (2000). This has made it possible to highlight that functions more influence in the SECI, the Ba and the Knowledge assets, by separating the first and last in each of its components, according to the mentioned authors.

For reasons of space and escape from the objectives of this work has not been performed, any kind of quantitative measurement of the impact of these functions, both in the generation of knowledge, as in society. However, following the approach of the work of Hernández, García & Hernández (2012a), it could apply some multicriteria model, in particular the Matrixes Of Weighing (MOW), to have a measure of this impact. This is a line of research that is recommended to follow.

Another line of research, in this case it is recommended to continue, is continue to analyze the management and generation of knowledge, from the point of view of the positions and areas of MoLoBaC.

Hand in hand with this line of research as a continuation of this work, recommended, as to what was done here, not only measure the potential of generating and managing knowledge, but to measure what impact has this knowledge in society.

Additionally, the knowledge provided in this work, about the relationship of logistics to practically all areas of a company, it is recommended to apply the positions of the MoLoBaC, to study other aspects, such as they could be enterprise diagnoses. And not only the application of the MoLoBaC is recommended, but also other models here mentioned: LAPDI, to measure flows, MoLoBaICa to measure performances and MoLETOI to have a study of the strategic, tactical and operative aspects.

Table 13. Impact on society of the functions of the area Inverse logistics of the MoLoBaC

Social Impact of the Inverse Logistics Area	
Impact on	Functions that do
Society as a whole.	103; 104; 107 to 110; 117; 121; 123; 126; 134; 135; 139; 144; 152 to 158; 202; 205; 237; 238; 244; 247; 253; 255 to 257; 303; 308; 310; 311; 313; 323 to 325; 327 to 329; 341; 353; 358 to 365.
Specifically the environment.	102; 116; 119; 142; 143; 204; 214 to 218; 220 to 225; 234; 245; 246; 302; 315; 318 to 320; 322; 337; 344; 345.

Obviously another line of research would be to continue to exploit is the model of dynamic knowledge management here used, which is a permanent source of research in what generation and utilization of the dynamic knowledge refers.

In this chapter only discusses the relationship between the reverse logistics and risk management. It is recommended to deepen in this aspect, which offers different viewpoints to be treated.

Finally it is advisable to open lines of investigation that integrate the material presented in this chapter, with the aspects studied in other chapters of the book and thus to make use of these synergies.

CONCLUSION

Through a hypothetical display, to ensure greater generality, this chapter showed, that the generation and management of knowledge through the area Inverse logistics of the MoLoBaC, can reveal the social components of this process.

To get the revelation of these social components in the generation and knowledge management, previously it was necessary to present the MoLoBaC. In particular the three positions of Inverse logistics area are discussed. These positions of the MoLoBaC were presented, principally through its functions.

In addition, it presented a model for the generation and management of knowledge, to facilitate the construction of dynamic knowledge. This model among their main components presents: the Socialization, Externalization, Combination and Internalization, in addition to the space-time, where this generation of knowledge is carried and which is recognized as the Ba. And in addition to this generation and knowledge management are reflected their knowledge assets summarized in: Experimental, Conceptual, Systemic and Routine Knowledge assets.

All these parameters were used to detect the social components of interest.

Finally through tables were presented the functions that were most important in the knowledge management and that in turn offered greater social component. This was completed to meet the objectives.

REFERENCES

Anderson, R. D., Jerman, R. E., & Crum, M. R. (1998). Quality Management influences on logistics performance. *Transportation Research Part E, Logistics and Transportation Review*, *34*(2), 137–148. doi:10.1016/S1366-5545(98)00008-8

Anttonen, M. (2010). Greening from the Front to the Back Door? A Typology of Chemical and Resource Management Services. *Business Strategy and the Environment*, *19*, 199–215.

Baker, P. (2004). Aligning Distribution Centre Operations to Supply Chain Strategy. *International Journal of Logistics Management*, *15*(1), 111–123. doi:10.1108/09574090410700266

Barreto, O. E. A. (2012). *Gestión del conocimiento a través del Gerente de Proyectos de un modelo logístico*. (Magister dissertation). Universidad Metropolitana, Caracas, Venezuela.

Cholette, S., & Venkat, K. (2009). The energy and carbon intensity of wine distribution: A study of logistical options for delivering wine to consumers. *Journal of Cleaner Production*, 1–13.

de Brito, M. P., Flapper, S. D. P., & Dekker, R. (2002). *Reverse logistic: a review of case studies.* SMG Working paper EI 2002-21, Econometric Institute Report, Erasmus University.

Díaz, A., Álvarez, M., & González, P. (2004). *Logística inversa y medio ambiente.* Madrid: McGraw Hill.

García, C. M., Escobet, T., & Quevedo, J. (2010). PHM Techniques for Condition-Based Maintenance based on Hybrid System Model Representation. *Annual Conference of the Prognostics and Health Management Society.*

García, G. M. J., Hernández, G. G. J., & Hernández, R. J. G. (2014a). A Methodology of The Decision Support Systems applied to other projects of Investigation. In *Encyclopedia of Information Science and Technology* (3rd ed.). Hershey, PA: IGI Global.

García, G. M. J., Hernández, G. G. J., & Hernández, R. J. G. (2014b). Knowledge management through the Material Handling Manager. In G. Dukic (Ed.), *Proceedings ICIL'2014.* University of Zagreb.

García, M. J., Hernández, G. J., & Hernández, J. G. (2013). Enterprise diagnosis and the STOILMo. In Delener et al. (Eds.), Fifteenth annual International Conference Global Business And Technology Association. GBATA.

Gnoni, M. G., & Rollo, A. (2010). A scenario analysis for evaluating RFID investments in pallet management. *International Journal of RF Technologies, 2,* 1–21.

Gold, S., & Seuring, S. (2011). Supply chain and logistics issues of bio-energy production. *Journal of Cleaner Production, 19*(1), 32–42. doi:10.1016/j.jclepro.2010.08.009

Grundstein, M. (2008). Assessing Enterprise's Knowledge Management Maturity Level. *International Journal of Knowledge and Learning, 4*(5), 415–426. doi:10.1504/IJKL.2008.022060

Guerrero, M. L. E., Hernández, G. G. J., García, G. M. J., & Hernández, R. J. G. (2014). Indicators and the Picking manager of the Logistic Model Based on positions. In *Proceedings ICIL'2014.* University of Zagreb.

Hernández, J. G., García, M. J., Hernández, G. J., & De Burgos, J. (2011). Once Erres (11-Rs) en la Logística Inversa. In Actas CAIP'2011. Universitat de Girona.

Hernández, J. G., García, M. J., & Hernández, J. G. (2012a). Dynamic knowledge: Diagnosis and Customer Service. In N. Delener (Ed.), *Service Science Research, Strategy, and Innovation: Dynamic Knowledge Management Methods* (pp. 558–584). Hershey, PA: IGI Global; doi:10.4018/978-1-4666-0077-5.ch030

Hernández, R. J., García, G. M., & Hernández, G. G. (2013). Enterprise logistics, indicators and Physical distribution manager. *Research in Logistics & Production, 3*(1), 5–20.

Hernández, R. J. G., García, G. M. J., & Hernández, G. G. J. (2012b). The Utilization manager and logistic flow. In *Proceedings ICIL'2012.* University of Zagreb.

Iannone, F., & Thore, S. (2010). An economic logistics model for the multimodal inland distribution of maritime containers. *International Journal of Transport Economics, 37*(3), 281–326.

Ibragimova, B., Ryan, S. D., Windsor, J. C., & Prybutok, J. C. (2012). Understanding the Antecedents of Knowledge Sharing: An Organizational Justice Perspective. Informing Science: the International Journal of an Emerging Transdiscipline, 15, 183–205.

Ilgin, M. A., & Gupta, S. M. (2010). Environmentally conscious manufacturing and product recovery (ECMPRO): A review of the state of the art. [PubMed]. *Journal of Environmental Management, 91*(3), 563–591. doi:10.1016/j.jenvman.2009.09.037

Jack, E. P., Powers, T. L., & Skinner, L. (2010). Reverse logistics capabilities: Antecedents and cost savings. *International Journal of Physical Distribution & Logistics Management, 40*(3), 228–246. doi:10.1108/09600031011035100

Järvinen, J., & Koskinen, L. (2001). *Industrial Design as a Culturally Reflexive Activity in Manufacturing*. Saarijärvi, Finland: Gummerus Printing.

Jeney, A. (2014). Impacto del Gerente de Sistemas de Información y Redes del Modelo *Logístico Basado en Cargos en la gestión del conocimiento de una organización, medido a través de una Matriz De Ponderación*. (Magister dissertation). Universidad Metropolitana, Caracas, Venezuela.

Le-Anh, T., Koster, R. B. M., & Yu, Y. (2010). Performance evaluation of dynamic scheduling approaches in vehicle-based internal transport systems. *International Journal of Production Research, 48*(24), 7219–7242. doi:10.1080/00207540903443279

Leite, P. R. (2003). *Logística reversa. Meio ambiente e competitividade*. Prentice Hall.

Luna, J. J. (2009). Metrics, Models, and Scenarios for Evaluating PHM Effects on Logistics Support. *Proceedings of Annual Conference of the Prognostics and Health Management Society*.

Maracine, V., & Scarlat, E. (2009). Dynamic Knowledge and Healthcare Knowledge Ecosystems. *Electronic Journal of Knowledge Management, 7*(1), 99–110.

McLachlin, R., & Larson, P. D. (2011). Building humanitarian supply chain relationships: Lessons from leading practitioners. *Journal of Humanitarian Logistics and Supply Chain Management, 1*(1), 32–49. doi:10.1108/20426741111122402

Nonaka, I., Reinmoller, P., & Senoo, D. (1998). The 'ART' of Knowledge: Systems to Capitalize on Market Knowledge. *European Management Journal, 16*(6), 673–684. doi:10.1016/S0263-2373(98)00044-9

Nonaka, I., Toyama, R., & Konno, N. (2000). SECI, Ba and leadership: A unified model of dynamic knowledge creation. *Long Range Planning, 33*(1), 5–34. doi:10.1016/S0024-6301(99)00115-6

Nonaka, I., & Von Krogh, G. (2009). Tacit knowledge and knowledge conversion: Controversy and advancement in organizational knowledge creation theory. *Organization Science, 20*(3), 635–652. doi:10.1287/orsc.1080.0412

Öberg, Ch., Huge-Brodin, M., & Björklund, M. (2012). Applying a network level in environmental impact assessments. *Journal of Business Research, 65*(2), 247–255. doi:10.1016/j.jbusres.2011.05.026

Peterson, A. J. (2005). *An examination of reverse logistics factor impacting the 463-L pallet program*. (Master dissertation). Air University, Dayton, OH.

Pishvaee, M. S., Farahani, R. Z., & Dullaert, W. (2010). A memetic algorithm for bi-objective integrated forward/reverse logistics network design. *Computers & Operations Research, 37*(6), 1100–1112. doi:10.1016/j.cor.2009.09.018

Pokharel, S., & Mutha, A. (2009). Perspectives in reverse logistics: A review. *Resources, Conservation and Recycling, 53*(4), 175–182. doi:10.1016/j.resconrec.2008.11.006

Ravi, V., Shankar, R., & Tiwari, M. K. (2005). Analyzing alternatives in reverse logistics for end-of-life computers: ANP and balanced scorecard approach. *Computers & Industrial Engineering, 48*(2), 327–356. doi:10.1016/j.cie.2005.01.017

Roth, A., & Kaberger, T. (2002). Making transport systems sustainable. *Journal of Cleaner Production, 10*(4), 361–371. doi:10.1016/S0959-6526(01)00052-X

Shang, S. S. C., Lin, S., & Wu, Y. (2009). Service innovation through dynamic knowledge management. *Industrial Management & Data Systems, 109*(3), 322–337. doi:10.1108/02635570910939362

Shevtshenko, E., Bashkite, V., Maleki, M., & Wang, Y. (2012). Sustainable design of material handling equipment: A win-win approach for manufacturers and customers. *Mechanika, 18*(5), 561–568. doi:10.5755/j01.mech.18.5.2703

Sloan, T. W. (2011). Green renewal: Incorporating environmental factors in equipment replacement decisions under technological change. *Journal of Cleaner Production, 19*(2-3), 173–186. doi:10.1016/j.jclepro.2010.08.017

Srivastava, S. K. (2007). Green supply-chain management: A state-of-the- art literature review. *International Journal of Management Reviews, 9*(1), 53–80. doi:10.1111/j.1468-2370.2007.00202.x

Steinicke, S., Wallenburg, C. M., & Schmoltzi, Ch. (2012). Governing for innovation in horizontal service cooperations. *Journal of Service Management, 23*(2), 279–302. doi:10.1108/09564231211226141

Teh, P., & Yong, Ch. (2011). Knowledge sharing in IS personnel: Organizational Behavior's Perspective. *Journal of Computer Information Systems, 51*(4), 11–21.

Tomasini, R. M., & Van Wassenhove, L. N. (2009). From preparedness to partnerships: Case study research on humanitarian logistics. *International Transactions in Operational Research, 16*(5), 549–559. doi:10.1111/j.1475-3995.2009.00697.x

Twaróg, S., Szoltyseck, J., & Otreba, R. (2012). Shaping alumni's sensitivity to issues of social logistics. In *Proceedings of the Management, Knowledge and Learning International Conference 2012.*

Van der Vorst, J. G. A. J., Tromp, S., & Van der Zee, D. (2009). Simulation modelling for food supply chain redesign; Integrated decision making on product quality, sustainability and logistics. *International Journal of Production Research, 47*(23), 6611–6631. doi:10.1080/00207540802356747

Van Gent, S. H., Megens, C. J. P. G., Peeters, M. M. R., Hummels, C. C. M., Lu, Y., & Brombacher, A. C. (2011). *Experiential Design Landscapes as a Design Tool for Market Research of Disruptive Intelligent Systems. 1st Cambridge Academic Design Management Conference.*

Wan, J., Zhang, H., Wan, D., & Huang, D. (2010). Research on knowledge creation in software requirement development. *Journal of Software Engineering & Applications*, *3*(05), 487–494. doi:10.4236/jsea.2010.35055

Xanthopoulos, A., & Iakovou, E. (2009). On the optimal design of the disassembly and recovery processes. [PubMed]. *Waste Management (New York, N.Y.)*, *29*(5), 1702–1711. doi:10.1016/j.wasman.2008.11.009

Xavier, W. S., & Martins, R. S. (2011). Logistic strategy and organizational structure in Brazilian Small and Medium-sized Enterprises (SMEs). *Organizations and Markets in Emerging Economies*, *2*(4), 91–116.

ADDITIONAL READING

Anand, G., Ward, P. T., & Tatikonda, M. V. (2010). Role of explicit and tacit knowledge in Six Sigma projects: An empirical examination of differential projects success. *Journal of Operations Management*, *28*(4), 303–315. doi:10.1016/j.jom.2009.10.003

Do Nascimento, S. P. C. (2010). *The knowing work practice as situational creation of meaning*. Doctoral dissertation, University of Tampere, Tampere, Finland.

García, M. J., Hernández, G. J., & Hernández, J. G. (2014). Logistics flows through the functions of the Cost Manager. In Delener et al. (Eds.), Sixteenth annual International Conference Global Business And Technology Association, Reading Book: USA, GBATA, 185-192.

Giunipero, L. C., Hooker, R. E., Matthews, S., Yoon, T. E., & Brudvig, S. (2008). A decade of SCM literature: Past, present and future implications. *Journal of Supply Chain Management*, *44*(4), 66–86. doi:10.1111/j.1745-493X.2008.00073.x

Gu, H., & Rong, G. (2010). A two-stage discriminating framework for making supply chain operation decision under uncertainties. *Chemical & Biochemical Engineering Quarterly*, *24*(1), 51–66.

Hernández, R. J. G., García, G. M. J., & Hernández, G. G. J. (2014). Shelter Selection with AHP Making Use of the Ideal Alternative. In Mehdi K. (Ed.), Encyclopedia of Information Science and Technology, Third Edition: Hershey, PA: IGI Global, V3, 2003-2015.

Leistner, F. (2010). *Mastering organizational knowledge flow: How to make knowledge sharing work*. USA: John Wiley and Sons.

Mills, P. K., & Snyder, K. M. (2010). *Knowledge services management. Organizing around internal markets*. New York, NY: Springer.

Miralbell, O. (2014). Knowledge exchange in social networking sites. Perspectives on Social Media: A Yearbook, 11.

Retzer, S. (2010). Inter-organisational knowledge transfer among research and development organizations: Implications for information and communication technology support. Doctoral dissertation. Victoria University of Wellington, Wellington, New Zealand.

Shi, Y., Cai, S., & Song, Y. (2010). Study on non-redundant storage technology of dynamic knowledge in real-time diagnosis. *Computer Engineering and Applications, 46*(9), 246–248.

van Helden, G. J., Aardema, H., ter Bogt, H. J., & Groot, T. L. C. M.Helden van. (2010). Knowledge creation for practice in public sector management accounting by consultants and academics: Preliminary findings and directions for future research. *Management Accounting Research, 21*(2), 83–94. doi:10.1016/j.mar.2010.02.008

Wang, M., & Sun, Z. (Eds.). (2010). *Handbook of research on complex dynamic process management: Techniques for adaptability in turbulent environments*. Hershey, PA: IGI Global; doi:10.4018/978-1-60566-669-3

KEY TERMS AND DEFINITIONS

Enterprise Logistics: Is focused in searching and achieving a greater satisfaction, present and future of the final costumer, and includes socio-environmental and ethical-legal aspects, organization planning, execution and control of all related activities related to the attainment, flow, gathering and maintenance of materials, products and services, since the raw material source, including there the costumers through inverse logistics, to the sale point of the finished product local or international, massive or enterprise, in a more effective and efficient, maximizing performance and the expected quality, minimizing waste, times and costs and using modern information technologies.

Inverse Logistics: It should be noted that involves three main protagonists: consumers or market, the economic future of the organization and perhaps the most important, the environment. Therefore the reverse logistics seeks to recover value for the company, while it is a way to improve the present and future customer satisfaction, from there that needs to be carried out in the most effective and efficient manner, minimizing costs and waste and making use of modern information technologies, also covers the socio-environmental, ethical-legal aspects, the planning, organization, execution and control of all activities related to obtaining, flow, storage, maintenance and better exploitation of materials, products or parts of them, that have reached the end consumer and that by various causes or reasons must be returned to the supply chain of the organization that produced, either after being partially or totally consumed the main product or with no or few modifications on the part of customers.

Knowledge Dynamic: It is an intangible resource, that works as the center of gravity of the creation and is itself the process of creation, diffusion, transference, internalization and absorption of the knowledge, departing from the transformation and conversion of the tacit knowledge in explicit knowledge and continuously through a spiral, that makes this last explicit knowledge generated, In tacit knowledge, restarting the cycle. For all this, the dynamic knowledge is expansive and complex and is one of the most important sources of competitive advantage of organizations.

Knowledge Management: It is a key feature for organizations that raise their level of competitiveness and is to create, transform, preserve, protect and make useful knowledge that they possess, including it being responsible for creating the environment spatiotemporal and coordinate the process of amplifying and make available the knowledge created by individuals and the organization as a whole, and crystallize it and connect it to the system of organizational knowledge in all fields.

Logistics Model Based on Positions (MoLoBaC): Studies enterprise logistic through the functions relative to the positions. MoLoBaC is composed of forty-four positions, which are grouped into twelve areas and these together into six stages.

Logistics Model: Will all those created, explicitly or accidental, to justify and understand the business logistics. In particular for this chapter are of interest four models qualitative-quantitative created to explain the logistics: Logistics of Supply, Production, Distribution and Inverse (LSPDI); Logistics Model Based on Positions (LoMoBaP); Logistics, Strategic, Tactical, Operational with Inverse Logistics Model (STOILMo) & Logistics Model Based on Indicators for Positions (LoMoBaIPo).

Social Logistics: It can say that the social logistics is understood external to the company and is the effective management of flows of materials and information, associated with a social value, with the sense of creating a major well-being to the society as whole.

Chapter 5
Graph Mining and Its Applications in Studying Community-Based Graph under the Preview of Social Network

Bapuji Rao
VITAM, India

Anirban Mitra
VITAM, India

ABSTRACT

One of the fundamental tasks in structured data mining is discovering of frequent sub-structures. These discovered patterns can be used for characterizing structure datasets, classifying and clustering complex structures, building graph indices & performing similarity search in large graph databases. In this chapter, the authors have discussed on use of graph techniques to identify communities and sub-communities and to derive a community structure for social network analysis, information extraction and knowledge management. This chapter contributes towards the graph mining, its application in social network using community based graph. Initial section is related literature and definition of community graph and its usage in social contexts. Detecting common community sub-graph between two community graphs comes under information extraction using graph mining technique. Examples from movie database to village administration were considered here. C++ programming is used and outputs have been included to enhance the reader's interest.

INTRODUCTION

Social network can be defined as the set of relationships between individuals where each individual is a social entity. It represents both the collection of ties between people as well as the strength of those ties (Mitra, Satpathy, Paul, 2013). In a general way, Social network is used as a measure of social "connectedness", within the social networks for observing and calculating the quality and quantity of informa-

DOI: 10.4018/978-1-4666-9607-5.ch005

tion flow within individuals and also within groups. Hence, from author's point of discussion, a social network can be defined as structure comprises of social actors (consisting of either group of individuals or organization) and the connectivity among them. Further, such structured network can also be called as social structure.

Network comprising of social entities becomes active when the relationships get established in course of regular interaction in the process of daily life and living, cultural activities such as marriage, thread ceremonies, different communities yearly celebrations, engagements, etc. and so on. Among vast examples, regular interaction may be a household requesting another for help, support or advice, creation of new friendship or choice of individuals to spend leisure time together; and many more. Sometimes a relationship can be a *negative*, i.e. hostility or alliance, alienation as against mutuality or integration with even having the security aspect as an important factor (Tripathy & Mitra, 2012).

To extract information or pattern of interaction between two or more social entities or between two or more social group, one needs to look deep into the properties of social network and the interactions. To analyse the above said process, the authors have put the network into mathematical model using the concept and properties of graph theory. About one of the properties on interaction, the Social networks show strong community relationships for interaction of people, such that, these interaction may be limited with in specific group or community or exceed outside the virtual boundary of the community or group. Relationships between communities can be analyzed using the basic algebraic concept of *transitivity*. Considering a simple example of three actors (say A^1, A^2 and A^3), there is a high possibility that if A^1 and A^2 are friends, A^2 and A^3 are friends then most likely A^1 and A^3 are also friends (however, the degree of their friendship may differs and can be easily demonstrate using weighted graph) . Further, the property of transitivity can be used to measure the *Clustering coefficients*.

Due to the property of strong community effect, the actors or the social entities in a network form a group which is closely connected. These groups are termed as modules or clusters or communities or even sub-groups. The authors have observed that individuals interact more frequently within a group. To detect similar groups within a social network, which is also known as similar *community detection* is a major challenge in analyzing the social network. To extract such type of communities helps in solving some more tasks, that are associated with the analysis of social network. Several works in terms of definitions and approaches are available in the area of community detection.

One of the most important processes in structured data mining is to discover frequent sub-structures. Authors have initiated the work with a discussion on various available techniques. Once we find at least one similar vertex between two sub-structures, then it is easy to merge both the sub-structures to form a larger structure. For this purpose the authors follow the simple graph techniques to identify at least one community between two villages community sub-structure and merge both to produce a larger community structure. The authors propose a new algorithm which merges two community sub-graphs in an efficient, easier and faster way. As each community sub-graph is represented as an adjacency matrix form which only contains 0s and 1s. Though, the adjacency matrix of both the community sub-graph contains 0s and 1s, which can be represented as a bit-matrix which substantially occupies less space for a larger community graph. In later section the authors discuss about the algorithm, memory management, and some examples related to the proposed algorithm which shows merging of two community sub-graph and produces one community graph having with at least one common community between those community sub-graphs.

With available set of graphs, discovering frequent sub-structures can be considered as graph patterns. Such patterns in the graph plays important role in various applications like characterizing graph sets, analyzing the difference among various groups of graphs, classifying and clustering graphs and building graph indices. Two of the fundamental steps that are followed for discovering of frequent sub-structures are firstly to generate frequent sub-structure candidates where and secondly to check the frequency of each candidate. The recent work by other researchers focuses on discovering various methods for frequent sub-structures. This step is further followed by the process of graph isomorphism, a NP-complete problem.

AGM is considered as initial frequent sub-structure mining algorithm, was proposed by Inokuchi et al. (Inokuchi, Washio, and Motoda, 2000), which has similar characteristics with the Apriori-based item set mining (Agrawal and Srikant, 1994). The other algorithms are FSG (Maniam, 2004) and the path-join algorithm (Vanetik, Gudes, and Shimony, 2002). These algorithms follow a join operation to merge two (or more) frequent sub-structures into one larger sub-structure. They distinguish themselves either by using vertices, edges, and edge-disjoint paths. In frequent sub-structure mining, Apriori-based algorithms have two sets of overheads: (i) joining two size–k frequent graphs (Vanetik, Gudes, and Shimony, 2002) to generate size –$(k + 1)$ graph candidates, and (ii) checking the frequency of these candidates separately. These overheads are the drawbacks of Apriori-based algorithms.

The Apriori-based approach follows breadth-first search (BFS) strategy because of its level-wise candidate generation. To determine whether a size –$(k + 1)$ graph is frequent; then it has to check all of its corresponding size –k sub-graphs to obtain its frequency. Before mining any size –$(k + 1)$ sub-graph, the Apriori-based approach starts mining of size –k sub-graphs. Therefore, BFS strategy is essential in the Apriori-like approach. In search method the pattern growth approach is more flexible. In graph search, both breadth-first search (BFS) and depth-first search (DFS) are used.

The present world can be called as a digital world with information highways and speed connectivity. In this digitization world, new methods are exploded for creation and storing of amount of structured and unstructured data (Infosys, 2013). The size of datasets of big data is beyond the ability for database software tools to capture, store, manage and analyse. The information which cannot be processed or analyzed using traditional processes or tools, there big data applies for extraction of information. There is no specific definition of big data. So we can define big data as "data is too big, moves too fast, or does not fit the structures of existing database architectures" (Infosys, 2013).

The organization of this chapter is as follows. The authors have initiated the chapter with a general overview followed by mentioning related definitions and notations on graph theory and big data with few of its characteristic. The next section discussed on Aspects of Graph Mining and authors have explained using examples of Movie Database and representation of World Wide Web followed by analyzing the proposed approach. Graph Representation Techniques is one of the important steps in the process of knowledge extraction from graphs. Various graph representation techniques like sequential representation and linked list representation are discussed. Sub-structure and graph matching for various kinds of graphs have been mentioned in due course of literature. The next section focuses on Apiori and Non-Priori based techniques and Pattern Growth Approach followed by implementation of those techniques using algorithms. Other than graph representation techniques as a step in extraction of knowledge, graph grouping and Community or Group Detection has also its own importance. Various community detection technique, its implementation and analysis have been discussed in the followed section. The last section gives an overview on application of graph theoretic concepts in big data analysis followed by the conclusion.

DEFINITIONS AND NOTATIONS ON GRAPH THEORY

Social network, its actors and the relationship between them can be represented using vertices and edges (Cook and Holder, 2007). The most important parameter of a network (i.e., a digraph) is the number of vertices and arcs. Here the authors have denoted n for number of vertices and m for number of arcs. When an arc is created by using two vertices u and v, which is denoted by uv. Then the *initial vertex* is u and the *terminal vertex* is v in the arc uv.

- *Digraph:* A digraph $G = (V, A)$ with $V = \{V_1, V_2, \ldots, V_n\}$ can be represented by its adjacency matrix A. This is the $n \times n$ square matrix $((a_{ij}))$ where a_{ij} is 1 or 0 depending on $v_i v_j$ is an arc or not. Note that $a_{ii} = 0$ for all i.
- *Sub-Digraph:* A sub-digraph of G to be (V_1, A_1) where $V_1 \cup V$, $A_1 \cup A$ and if uv is an element of A_1 then u and v belong to V_1.
- *Converse of Digraph:* The converse of a digraph $G = (V, A)$ is the digraph H with the same vertex set V, uv being an arc in H if and only if vu is an arc of G. Note that the adjacency matrix of the converse of G is the transpose A^T of the adjacency matrix A of G.
- *Null Graph and Complete Digraph:* A digraph G is said to be **null** if no two vertices of G are adjacent. G is said to be **complete** if, for any two distinct vertices u and v, at least one of uv and vu is an arc. Clearly a null graph on n vertices has no arcs and any complete digraph on n vertices has at least $(n|2) = (n(n-1)/)2$ arcs.
- *Symmetry in a Digraph:* A digraph G is said to be symmetric if vu is an arc whenever uv is an arc. G is symmetric if and only if its adjacency matrix is a symmetric matrix. G is said to be asymmetric (or anti-symmetric) if vu is not an arc whenever uv is an arc.
- *Out-Degrees and In-Degrees:* The arcs in a digraph G may not be evenly distributed at the different vertices. So one considers the out-degree $d^+_g(u)$ of a vertex u in G, defined as the number of vertices v such that uv is an arc. It is the number of vertices u is joined to. In a social network, $d^+_g(u)$ usually indicates the *expensiveness* of u. So the out-degree sequence of a digraph with vertex set $V = \{v_1, v_2, \ldots, v_n\}$ is $\{d_1, d_2, \ldots, d_n\}$ where $d_i = d^+(v_i)$ for all i. The in-degree $d^-_g(u)$ of a vertex u in G, defined as the number of vertices w such that wu is an arc. In a social network, $d^-_g(u)$ usually indicates the *popularity or power* of u. So the in-degree sequence of a digraph with vertex set $V = \{v_1, v_2, \ldots, v_n\}$ is $\{e_1, e_2, \ldots, e_n\}$ where $e_i = d^-(v_i)$ for all i.
- *Graph-Based Data Mining:* Mining graph data is also known as *graph based data mining* which can be explained as the process for extracting meaningful and useful knowledge from a set of data which is represented as a graph (Cook and Holder, 2007). In this technique the knowledge is extracted from a graph generates a graph. Therefore, this *knowledge* is sometimes referred as *patterns (or sequence)*, which is extracted from the graph data and are also called as sub-graphs or graphs.

ON BIG DATA

- **Definition:** According to Dumbill (Dumbill, 2012), the big data is that amount of data that any conventional database systems fails to process due to limitation in capacity or size of handling the data. Hence, author can conclude that the data is too big having the characteristic of fast transaction and movement and does not fit into the standard structures of existing database architectures.

Moreover, IEEE has further explained (ieee, 2014) on big data that it is a collection of large and complex data sets so such that processing it using conventional database management tools or traditional data processing applications is of great challenge (ieee, 2014).

According to Manyika (Manyika, 2014), when the data cannot be process by a typical database software tools for capturing, storing, managing and analyzing the data due to its size, is known as big data (Manyika, 2014).

- **Characteristics of Big Data:** The characteristic of big data is explained in four simple points using 4V, i.e. Volume, Velocity, Variety, and Veracity (ieee, 2014).

In "Big Data", the meaning of "big" means *Volume*. So volume is a relative or fuzzy word. For smaller-sized organisations, data in size of gigabytes or terabytes may be called voluminous where as for bigger organization; data size may vary from petabytes to exabytes. For many organisations, the size of datasets are limited to terabytes range but is expected to reach in terms of petabytes or exabytes in the future.

The *velocity* of data is in terms of generation of frequency of data and its delivery. The term, Velocity under the domain of big data is about fastness of the data arrival, storing it efficiently and retrieving it again with in response time. Velocity of data can also be expressed as the speed of flow of the data inside the domain. The advancement in information processing, streaming and the increase in sensors through network have allow the data to flow at a constant or specific pace.

Data can arrive from a *variety* of sources (which includes internal source as well as external source) and in different types and structures. Due to advancement in techniques and with proper hardware supports, the arrived data can easily be segregate and retrieve in form of structured traditional relational data as well as *semi-structured* and *unstructured* data.

- **Structured Data:** The structured data are those Data that can be grouped into a schema (consists of finite rows and columns in database) or simply relational scheme.
- **Semi Structured Data:** It is a kind of structured data that is not limited to an explicit and fixed schema or scheme. The data is inherently self-describing and contains tags or other markers to enforce hierarchies of records and fields within the data. Examples include weblogs and social media feeds.
- **Unstructured Data:** Data consists of formats which cannot easily be indexed into relational tables for analysis or querying. Examples include images, audio and video files.
- **Veracity:** The data mainly biases, noise and abnormality. Veracity in data analysis is the biggest challenge when compares to volume and velocity of data. The quality of the data being captured can vary rapidly. So the accuracy of analysis completely depends on the veracity of the source data.

Above two figures, Figure 1 and Figure 2 gives an overview and relation of the big data and its logical components (Rao, Mitra, ichpca, 2014), (Batagelj and Pajek, 2003).

Figure 1. 3V's in Big data

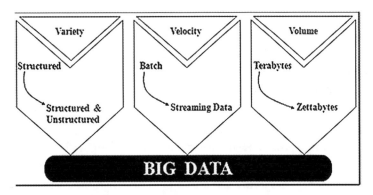

Figure 2. Types of Input data for 3V's

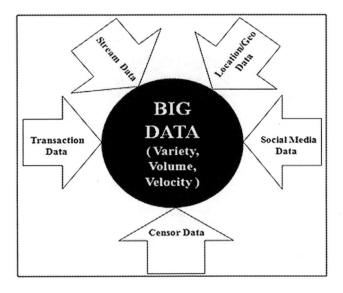

ASPECTS OF GRAPH MINING

Graph representation is a collection of nodes and links between nodes and supports all aspects of the relational data mining process. The graph easily represents entities, their attributes, and their relationships to other entities. As, one entity can be arbitrarily related to other entities in a relational databases. Graph representations typically store each entity's relations with the entity. Finally, relational database and logic representations do not support direct visualization of data and knowledge. So, that relational information stored in this way can be easily converted to a graph form for visualization. Using a graph for representing the data and the mined knowledge supports direct visualization and increases comprehensibility of the knowledge. So, we can say that mining graph data is one of the most promising approaches to extracting knowledge from relational database.

Representation of Movie Database

Three domains of mining graph data are the Internet Movie Database, the Mutagenesis dataset, and the World Wide Web. Several graph representations for the data in these domains were proposed. These databases serve as a benchmark set of problems for comparing and contrasting different graph-based data mining methods (Corneil and Gotlieb, 1970).

To represent movie information as a graph, relationships among movies, peoples, and attributes can be captured and included in the analysis. The cited figure here (Figure 3) shows one possible representation of information related to a single movie. Here each movie as a vertex, with links to attributes describing the movie. Similar graphs could be constructed for each person as well. With this representation, one can perform the following query: What are the commonalities that one can find among movies in the database? The answer to this query gives us the required knowledge.

In the above movie graph, we can report large fraction of sub-graphs. These sub-graphs may discover such as movies receiving awards often come from the same small set of studios which is shown in the figure 4 or certain director/composer pairs work together frequently as shown in the following figure 5.

By connecting people, movies, and other nodes that have relationships, a connected graph can be constructed. The cited in the figure 6 shows how different movies may have actors, directors, and can be produced by a common studio. Similarly, different actors may act in the same movie, forming a relationship between these actors. By analysing this connected graph one may answer questions such as:

Figure 3. Graph representation of single movie

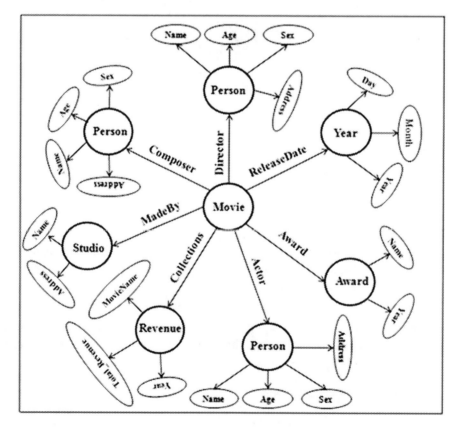

Figure 4. One possible frequent sub-graph related to awards

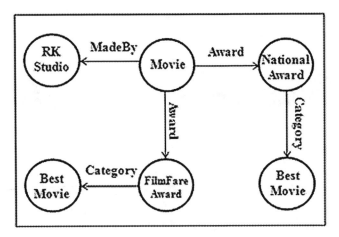

Figure 5. Another possible frequent sub-graph related to background artists

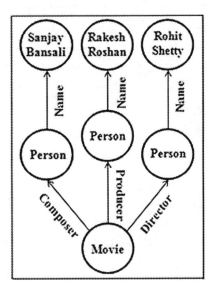

The authors can easily analyse about the common relationships between objects in the movie database. For the above movie graph, a discovery algorithm may find a pattern that movies made by the same studio frequently also have the same producer. Jensen and Neville (Jensen and Neville, 2002) mention another type of discovery from a connected movie graph. In this case, a successful film star may be characterized in the graph by a sequence of successful movies in which he or she stars as well as by winning one or more awards.

Ravasz and Barabasi (Ravasz and Barabasi, 2003) analyzed a movie graph constructed by linking actors appearing in the same movie and has found graph of hierarchical topology. Movie graphs can also be used for classifications. The patterns can be mined from structural information that is explicitly provided. However, missing structure can also be inferred from this data. Mining algorithms can be used to infer missing links in the movie graph. For example, to know number of actors who starred together in

Figure 6. Movie Graph with data points used as labelled edges

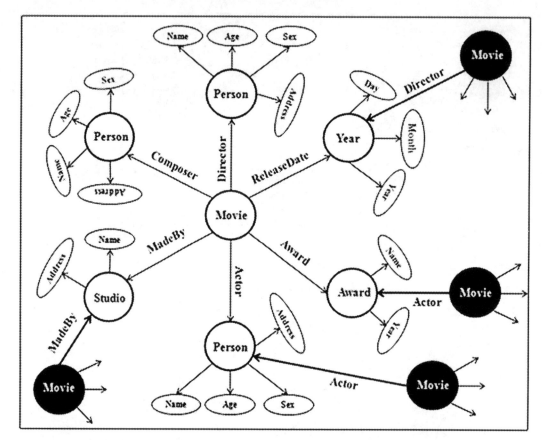

a movie, link completion (Goldenberg and Moore, 2004), (Kubica, Goldenberg, Komarek, and Moore, 2003) can be used to determine who the remaining actors are starred in the same movie. The same link completion algorithms can also be used to determine whether one movie is a remake of another (Jensen and Neville, 2002).

Representation of World Wide Web

World Wide Web is a valuable information resource that is complex, dynamic contents, and rich in structure. Mining the Web is a research area that is almost as old as the Web itself. According to Etzioni, *Web mining* (Etzioni, 1996) is referred to extracting information from Web based documents and web based services. The types of information that can be extracted are of variable in nature. So it has been refined to three classes of mining tasks, i.e. Web content mining, Web structure mining and Web usage mining (Kolari and Joshi, 2004).

Web content mining algorithms is attempting to mining types of patterns from the content of Web pages. The most common approach is to perform mining of the content that is found within each page on the Web. This content generally consists of text occasionally supplemented with HTML tags (Velez and Sheldon, 1996), (Chakrabarti, 2000). Using text mining techniques, the discovered patterns forms

Graph Mining and Its Applications

a classification of Web pages and Web querying (Mendelzon, Michaila Milo, 1996), (Zaiane and Han, 1995), (Berners-Lee, Hendler and Lassila, 2001).

When structure is added to Web data in the form of hyperlinks, analysts can then perform Web structure mining. In a Web graph, vertices represent Web pages and edges represent links between the Web pages. The vertices can be labelled by the domain name (Cook and Holder, 2007) and edges are unlabeled or labelled with a uniform tag. Additional vertices can be attached to the Web page nodes that are labelled with keywords or other textual information found in the Web page content. The figure 7(Figure 7. Graph representation of web text and structure data) shows a graph representation for a collection of three Web pages. With the inclusion of this hypertext information, Web page classification can be performed based on structure alone (Cook and Holder, 2007) or together with Web content information algorithms (Gonzalez, Holder and Cook, 2002) that analyze Web pages based on more than textual content can also potentially learn more complex patterns.

Other researchers focus on the structural information alone. Chakrabarti and Faloutsos (Cook and Holder, 2007) and others (Broder, Kumar, Maghoul, Raghavan, Rajagopalan, Stat, and Tomkins, 2000), (Kleinberg and Lawrence, 2001) have studied the unique attributes of graphs created from Web hyperlink information. Such hyperlink graphs can also be used to answer the question for finding the patterns in the Web structure. Again, the answer will be an extraction of knowledge.

The authors have observed about frequent discovering of sub-graphs in the above topology graph (Cook and Holder, 2007). How new or emerging communities of Web pages can be identified from such a graph (Cook and Holder, 2007)? Analysis of this graph leads to identification of topic hubs (overview

Figure 7. Graph representation of web text and structure data

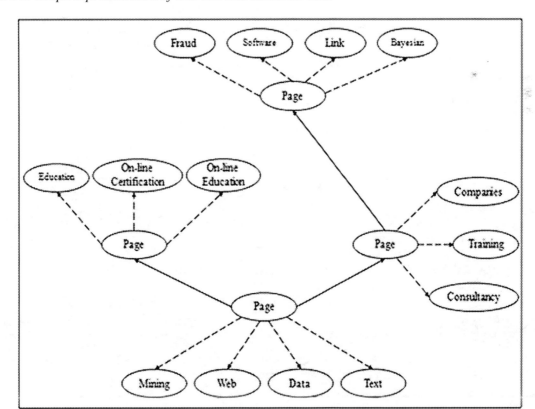

sites with links to strong authority pages) and authorities (highly ranked pages on a given topic) (Kleinberg, 1999). The Page Rank program (Kleinberg, 1999) pre-computes page ranks based on the number of links to the page from other sites together with the probability that a Web surfer will visit the page directly, without going through intermediary sites. Desikan and Srivastava (Desikan and Srivastava, 2004) proposed a method of finding patterns in dynamically evolving graphs, which can provide insights on trends as well as potential intrusions.

Web usage mining is used to find commonalities in web navigation patterns. Mining click stream data on the client side has been investigated (Maniam, 2004), data is easily collected and mined from Web servers (Srivastava, Cooley, Deshpande and Tan, 2000). Didimo and Liotta (Cook and Holder, 2007) provide some graph representations and visualizations of navigation patterns. According to Berendt (Berendt, 2005), a graph representation of navigation allows the construction of individual's website. From the graph one can determine which pages act as starting points for the site, which collection of pages are navigated sequentially, and how easily pages within the site accessed are. Navigation graphs can be used to categorize Web surfers and can assist in organizing websites and ranking Web pages (Berendt, 2005), (McEneaney, 2001), (Zaki, 2002), (Meo, Lanzi, Matera and Esposito, 2004).

Figure 8. Community Graph of village

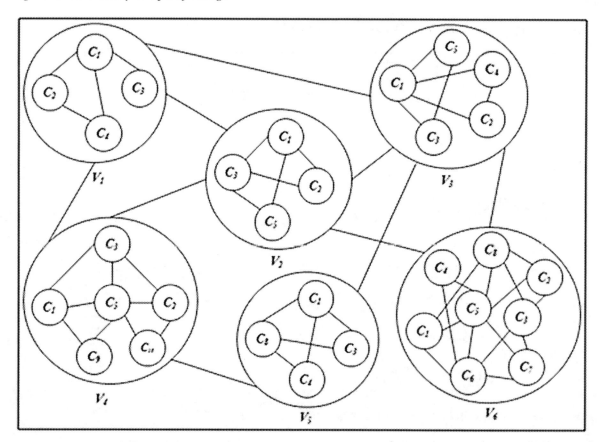

Graph Mining and Its Applications

ANALYSIS ON THE PROPOSED APPROACH

Given the importance of the problem and the increased research activity, the graph mining is needed to extract knowledge from the social community network, which is defined as a complex graph, and each unit is an individual, village, household, country, etc. so the social community graph may be defined as a set of villages $V = \{V_1, V_2, ..., V_n\}$ and between villages there is a set of links or connectivity or edges $E = \{E_1, E_2, ..., E_n\}$. The figure describes the community graph (Figure 8). Each village has a set of communities and connectivity among communities forms a community sub-graph (Rao and Mitra, Oct-2014). From literature survey, analysis and discussion, authors have the solution to the below listed queries. Here the authors have proposed a social community network which is being shown as a Graph, with respect to Movie and World Wide Web Graph.

Applying the *graph data management algorithms* on the above proposed social community network using earlier referred figure (Figure 9), one can mine the following knowledge (Rao and Mitra, Oct-2014):

- On applying *Indexing and Query Processing Technique*, the authors can mine similar communities and isolated communities.
- On applying *Reachability Queries*, the authors can find path between villages by BFS or DFS techniques.
- On applying *Graph Matching*, the authors can detect similarity between sub-graphs.

Figure 9. Connected graph by dotted lines

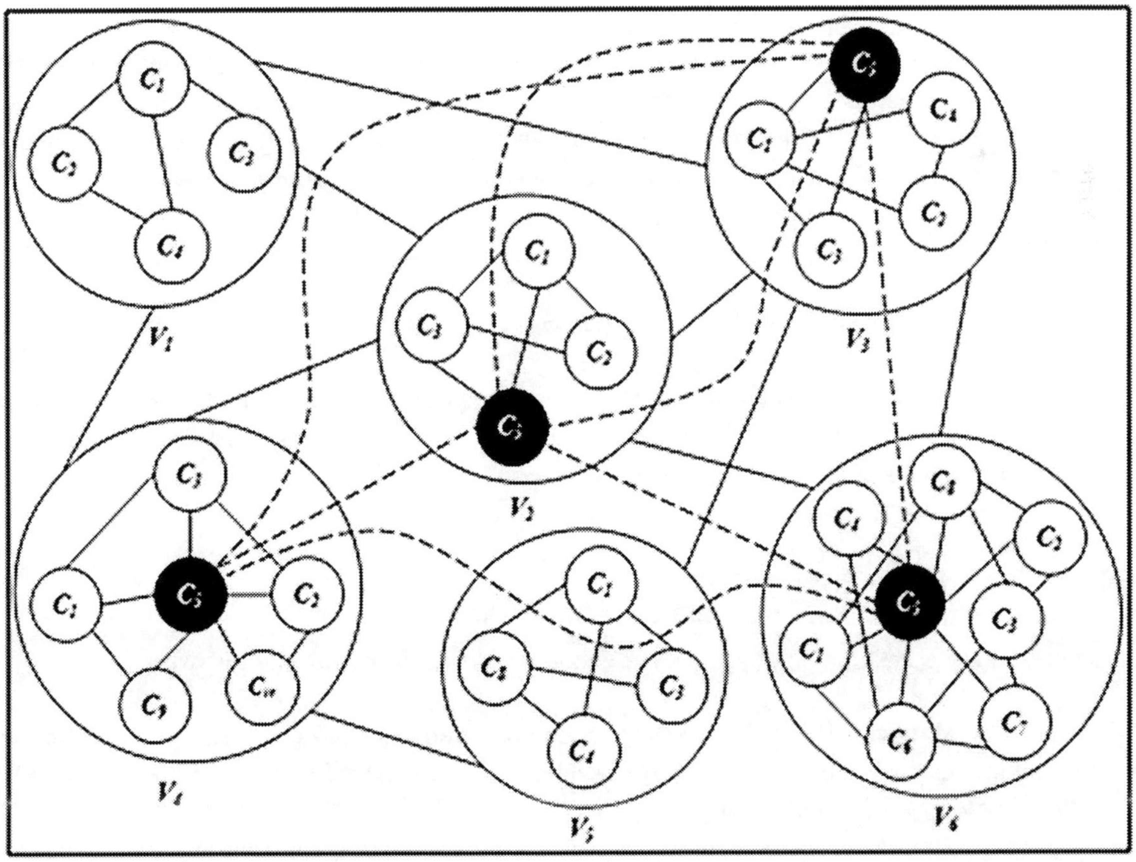

Figure 10. Community detection graph for C5

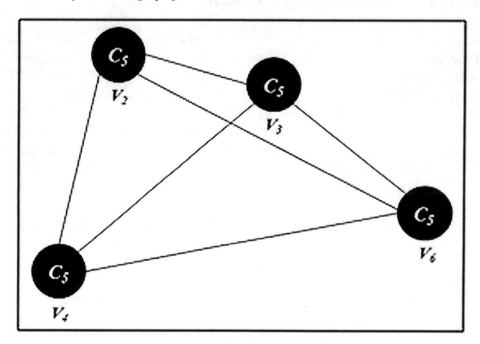

- On applying *Keyword Search*, the authors can find the community name which forms a community detection sub-graph is shown in the earlier figure. In the authors example a community detection sub-graph for C_5 has been shown here in Figure 10.
- On applying *Synopsis Construction of Massive Graphs* (Brandes, Kenis and Wagner, 2003), (Brandes and Erlebach, 2005), (Batagelj and Pajek, 2003), the authors can respond to any query for sufficient information and maintain in a smaller space. It means a graph can be represented as a square matrix having consists of 0s and 1s, which substantially occupies less space.

GRAPH REPRESENTATION TECHNIQUES

A graph can be represented in two different ways (Seymour, 1999), (Mitra, Satpathy and Paul, 2013), (Rao and Mitra, Oct-2014), (Rao and Mitra, ichpca-2014), (Rao and Mitra, iccic-2014). These two representations are explained in details as follows.

SEQUENTIAL REPRESENTATION

The sequential representation of graphs in the memory is further classified into two ways.

- **Adjacency Matrix:** Let G be a graph with n nodes or vertices $V_1, V_2,...,V_n$ having one row and one column for each node or vertex. Then the adjacency matrix $A = [a_{ij}]$ of the graph G is the nXn *square matrix*, which is defined as:

Graph Mining and Its Applications

Figure 11. Graph and adjacency matrix

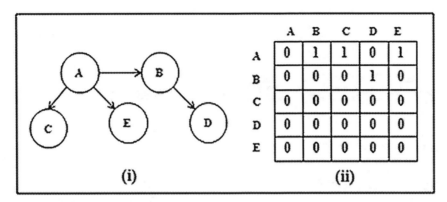

$a_{ij} = 1$ if there is an edge from V_i to V_j

Else

$a_{ij} = 0$ otherwise.

This kind of matrix contains only 0s and 1s is called bit matrix or boolean matrix. In undirected graph, the adjacency matrix will be a symmetric one. For example in the given digraph *G* has vertices *V = {A, B, C, D, E}* in (i) of the figure 11 and the set of edges *E = {(A, B), (A, C), (B, D), (A, E)}*. Then the adjacency matrix of the graph *G* is shown in (ii) of same.

- **Path Matrix:** The path matrix of graph *G* having *n*-vertices is the *nXn square matrix*, which is defined as:

$p_{ij} = 1$ if there is a path from V_i to V_j via V_k

Else

Figure 12. With Path matrix

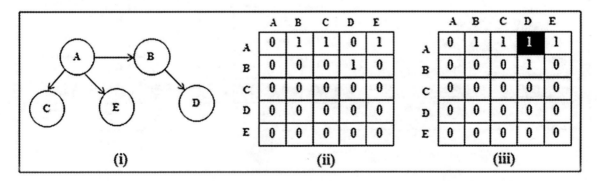

107

$p_{ij} = 0$ otherwise.

The path matrix only shows the presence or absence of a path between a pair of vertices. It only says about the presence or absence of a cycle at any vertex. It cannot count the total number of paths in a graph. Let us consider a graph *G = {A, B, C, D, E}*. Its adjacency matrix and the final path matrix *P* in adjacency matrix is shown here Figure 12. The presence of edge between *A* to *D* in (iii) of the same figure is the indication of presence of path in the graph.

Linked List Representation

It this representation two types of lists is used. They are *node list* and *edge list*. The node of node list is a double linked list kind. The node consists of three parts: *Info, Next,* and *Adj. Info* is the information part of a node or vertex, *Next* is a pointer which holds address of next node of node list, and *Adj* is a pointer which holds address of node of edge list where the actual adjacent is present. The node of edge list is a single linked kind. The node consists of two parts *Node* and *Edge. Node* is a pointer which holds address of node of node list where the adjacent is present and *Edge* is also a pointer which holds address of next node of edge list.

Let us consider a graph *G = {A, B, C, D}*. The adjacency matrix and adjacency list for the graph *G* is shown in Figure 13. By using adjacency list is in (iii) of the same figure, one can draw its equivalent adjacency list with the help of edge list and node list.

Incidence Matrix

There are two types of incidence matrix, (i) Un-oriented incidence matrix and (ii) Oriented incidence matrix. In the next sub section, we have discussed about them.

Unoriented Incidence Matrix

The incidence matrix of undirected graph is called as unoriented incidence matrix. The incidence matrix of an undirected graph *G* is a $v \times e$ matrix *(MAT_{ij})*, where *v* and *e* are number of vertices and edges re-

Figure 13. Diagraph, adjacency matrix and list

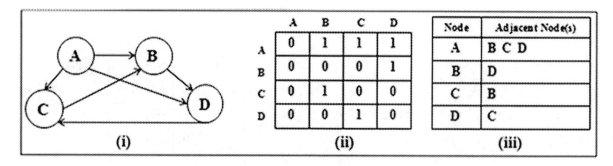

Graph Mining and Its Applications

Figure 14. Unoriented incidence

	e_1	e_2	e_3	e_4
V_1	1	1	1	0
V_2	1	0	0	0
V_3	0	1	0	1
V_4	0	0	1	1

spectively, such that $MAT_{ij} = 1$ if the vertex v_i and edge e_j are incident. $MAT_{ij} = 0$ If there is no incident between v_i and e_j.

Let us consider a *graph* $G = \{V_1, V_2, V_3, V_4\}$ whose unoriented incidence matrix is shown in (i) figure 14. The order of unoriented incidence matrix in (ii) of the same figure is 4 (number of rows) X 4 (number of columns).

Oriented Incidence Matrix

The incidence matrix of directed graph is called as oriented incidence matrix. The incidence matrix of a directed graph G is a $v \times e$ matrix (MAT_{ij}), where v and e are number of vertices and edges respectively, such that $MAT_{ij} = 1$ if the edge e_j away from vertex v_i, that $MAT_{ij} = -1$ if the edge e_j pointing to the vertex v_i, and $MAT_{ij} = 0$ if there is no edge at all.

Let us consider a graph $G = \{V_1, V_2, V_3, V_4\}$ whose oriented incidence matrix is shown in (i) Figure 15. The order of unoriented incidence matrix in (ii) of the same figure is 4 (number of rows) X 4 (number of columns).

Figure 15. Incidence matrix

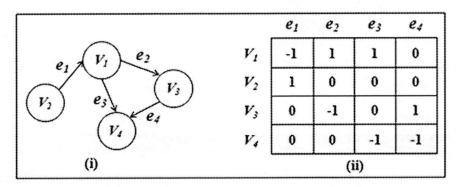

APIORI AND NON-PRIORI BASED ALGORITHMS

Algorithm Frequent Sub-Structure Mining proposed by Inokuchi et al. (Inokuchi, Washio and Motoda, 2000) and algorithm Apriori-Based Frequent Itemset Mining developed by Agrawal and Srikant (Agrawal and Srikant, 1994) have similar characteristics where searching starts from bottom to top and generating candidates with an extra vertex, edge, or path. Different kinds of candidate generation strategies are:

1. AGM (Inokuchi, Washio and Motoda, 2000) is a vertex-based candidate generation method that increases the sub-structure size by one vertex for each iteration. Two *(size–k)* frequent graphs are joined only when the two graphs have the same *size – (k – 1)* sub-graphs. Here *size* is the number of vertices in a graph. The newly formed candidate includes the common *size – (k – 1)* sub-graphs and the additional two vertices from the two *size–k* patterns.
2. An edge-based method adopts by FSG proposed by Kuramochi and Karypis (Kuramochi and Karypis, 2001) increases the sub-structure size by one edge in each call. Two *size–k* patterns are merged together if they share the same sub-graph having $k - 1$ edges. The same sub-graphs are called *core*. Here *size* means the number of edges in the graph. The newly formed candidate includes the core and the additional two edges from the *size–k* patterns.
3. The disjoint-path method based on Apriori-based proposed by Vanetik (Vanetik, Gudes Shimony, 2002) uses a more complicated candidate generation procedures. A sub-structure pattern with $k + 1$ disjoint path is generated by joining sub-structures with k disjoint paths.

The discovery of Non-Apriori based algorithms due to considerable overheads at joining two *size–k* frequent sub-structures to generate *size–(k + 1)* graph candidates. Most of the Non-Apriori based algorithms adopt the pattern growth methodology (Han, Pei and Yin, 2000), which extends patterns from a single pattern directly. Pattern-growth based discovers a frequent sub-structure. It recursively discovers frequent sub-graph and embeds. Finally produces a final sub-graph until it does not find any more frequent sub-graph. It discovers the same graph more than ones. This detection of duplicate graph leads workload to the algorithm. To avoid duplicate graphs for discovery, other algorithms gSpan (Yan, Zhou and Han, 2005), MoFa (Borgelt and Berthold, 2002), FFSM (Huan, Wang and Prins, 2003), SPIN (Prins, Yang, Huan and Wang, 2004) and Gaston (Nijssen and Kok, 2004) are evolved. Among this gSpan algorithm is the efficient one and adopts DFS traversing.

Closed Frequent Sub-Structure

According to the Apriori property, all the sub-graphs of a frequent sub-structure must be frequent. A large graph pattern may generate an exponential number of frequent sub-graphs. A frequent pattern is *closed* if it does not have a super-pattern. A frequent pattern is *maximal* if it does not have a frequent super-pattern.

Approximate Sub-Structure

To reduce the number of patterns, it mines approximate frequent sub-structures that allow minor structural variations. In this technique, one can approximate one sub-structure from several frequent sub-structures having slight differences. For mining approximate frequent sub-structures, Holder et al. (Holder, Cook and Djoko, 1994) proposed a new method which adopts the principle of minimum description length (MDL), called *SUBDUE*.

Contrast Sub-Structure

For a predefined set of two graphs, the contrast patterns are sub-structures that are frequent in one set but infrequent in the other set. It uses two parameters, one from the positive set of a sub-structure which is the minimum, called as *minimum support* and the other one from the negative set of the sub-structure which is the maximum, called as maximum support. This algorithm is called as MoFa algorithm (Borgelt and Berthold, 2002).

Dense Sub-Structure

Relational graph is a special kind of graph structure where each node label is used only once. These structures are widely used in modelling and analyzing massive networks. For this Yan et al. (Yan, Zhou and Han, 2002, 2005) proposed two algorithms, *CloseCut* and *Splat*, to discover exact dense frequent sub-structures in a set of relational graphs.

Graph Matching

Graph matching is one-to-one correspondence amongst the nodes between two graphs. This correspondence is based on one or more of the following characteristics. (i) The labels on the nodes in the two graphs should be same. (ii) The existence of edges between corresponding nodes in two graphs should match each other. (iii) The labels on the edges in two graphs should match each other.

Such problems arise due to different database applications such as schema matching, query matching, and vector space embedding. Its detailed explanation can be seen in (Riesen, Jiang and Bunke, 2010). *Exact graph matching* determines one-to-one correspondence between two graphs with an edge exists between a pair of nodes in one graph, and the same edge must also exist between the corresponding pair in the other graph.

Inexact graph matching detects the natural errors during the matching process. A proper method is required to quantify these errors and the closeness between different graphs. A function called *graph edit distance* is used to quantify these errors. The *graph edit distance* function determines the distance between two graphs by measuring the cost of the edits required to transform from one graph to other. So it may be a node or edge insertions, deletions or substitutions. The cost of the corresponding edits between two graphs judges the quality of the matching. The concept of graph edit distance is to finding a maximum common sub-graph (Bunke, 1997).

Frequent Graph

Given a labelled graph dataset, $D = \{G_1, G_2, ..., G_n\}$, where frequency($g$) is the number sub-graphs in D. A graph is frequent if its support is not less than a minimum support of nodes or vertices.

EXAMPLE:

Let us consider three graphs are shown in Figure 16, which is considered as three datasets $D = \{G_1, G_2, G_3\}$. The authors depict three frequent sub-graphs from the datasets D, which is shown in Figure 17.

Figure 16. Graph dataset G1, G2, G3

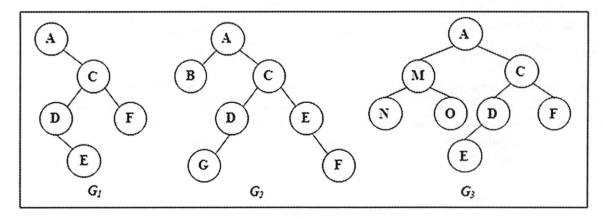

Figure 17. Frequent Graphs

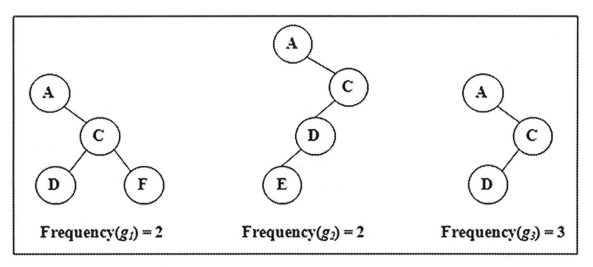

So the three frequent sub-graphs are { g_1, g_2, g_3 } and their frequencies are {2, 2, 3}, which is shown in the same figure.

APRIORI-BASED APPROACH

Apriori-based frequent item set mining algorithms developed by Agrawal and Srikant (Agrawal and Srikant, 1994). Searching of frequent graphs having larger sizes follows bottom-up manner by generating candidates having an extra vertex, edge, or path.

In the algorithm S_k is the frequent sub-structure set of size k. It follows a level-wise mining technique. The size of newly discovered frequent sub-structure is increased by one for each iteration. The new sub-structures are generated by joining two similar but slightly different frequent sub-graphs that are discovered in the previous iteration. So Line 4 of algorithm is the candidate generation logic. Then the frequency of newly formed graphs is checked. The detected frequent sub-graphs are merged together to generate larger candidates in the next round. The algorithm is listed below.

```
Algorithm  Apriori(D, min support, S_k)
Input: A graph dataset D and min support.
Output: A frequent substructure set S_k.
1: S_k+1 ← ∅;
2: for each frequent g_i (is element) in S_K do
3: for each frequent g_j (is element) in S_K do
4: for each size (k + 1) graph g formed by the merge of g_i and g_j do
5: if g is frequent in D and g ∉ S_k+1 then
6: insert g to S_k+1;
7: if S_k+1 ≠ ∅ then
8: call Apriori(D, min support, S_k+1);
9: return;
```

Let us consider two frequent item sets of size 3 each i.e. *(abc)* and *bcds)*. It generates a candidate frequent item set of size 4 i.e. *(abcd)*. Here two item sets are *(abc)* and *(bcd)* are frequent in candidate frequent item set *(abcd)*. Then we check the frequency of *(abcd)*. So, the candidate generation problem in frequent sub-structure mining becomes much harder than frequent item set mining since there are different ways of joining two sub-structures.

Another kind of candidate generation strategies AGM (Inokuchi, Washio and Motoda, 2000) proposed a vertex-based candidate generation method that increases the sub-structure size by one vertex at each iterations. The complete algorithm is listed below. Two size-k frequent graphs are joined only when two graphs have same size−$(k−1)$ sub-graph. Here size means the number of vertices in a graph. The newly formed candidate includes the common size−$(k − 1)$ sub-graph and the additional two vertices from the two size−k patterns. If there is an edge connecting the additional two vertices, then only we can form two candidates. FSG proposed by Kuramochi and Karypis (Kuramochi and Karypis, 2001) adopts an edge-based method that increases the sub-structure size by one edge in each call also follows the listed below algorithm. Two size−k patterns are merged if they share the same sub-graph that has $k−1$ edges, which is called the *core*. Here size means the number of edges in a graph. The newly formed candidate includes the core and the additional two edges from the size−k patterns.

Other Apriori-based methods such as the disjoint-path method proposed by (Vanetik, Gudes and Shimony, 2002) use more complicated candidate generation procedures. A sub-structure pattern with $k + 1$ disjoint path is generated by joining sub-structures with k disjoint paths. Apriori-based algorithms have more overheads while joining two size-k frequent sub-structures to generate size-$(k + 1)$ graph candidates. To avoid such overheads, the authors need to follow non-Apriori-based algorithms.

PATTERN GROWTH APPROACH

A graph can be extended by adding a new edge. The edge may or may not introduce a new vertex to the newly formed graph. The extension of new graph may extend is in a *forward* or *backward* direction. Its algorithm is listed below.

```
Algorithm: PatternGrowth(g, D, min support, S)
Input: A frequent graph g, a graph dataset D, and min support.
Output: A frequent substructure set S.
1: if g_i ∈ S then return;
2: else insert g to S;
3: scan D once, find all the edges e such that g can be extended to g';
4: for each frequent g' do
5: Call PatternGrowth(g', D, min support, S);
6: return;
```

The above algorithm is simple but not efficient. It is inefficiency during extending the graph. It discovers the same graph again and again. This repeated discovery consumes more time and space. It has to be avoided. Let us consider an example that there exist n different $(n-1)$–edge graphs can be extended to the same (n–edge) graph. It ignores the repeated discovery of the same graph. Line 1 of the above algorithm creates duplicate graphs whereas Line 2 discovers that *duplicate graph*. So the generation and detection of duplicate graphs may require additional workloads. To reduce the generation of duplicate graphs, each frequent graph should be preserved. This principle leads to the design of several new algorithms such as gSpan (Batagelj and Pajek, 2003), MoFa (Borgelt and Berthold, 2002), FFSM and SPIN (Prins, Yang, Huan and Wang, 2004), and Gaston (Nijssen and Kok, 2004).

AUTHORS PROPOSED APPROACH

The authors have studied the scenario of a social graph, which consists of various villages in a panchayat (panchayat is an Indian term for administration of villages). In a village different types of communities live together and have connectivity. Taking this scenario into mind, one can compare two community graphs for finding a similar sub-graph from it. For such case the authors have proposed an algorithm for detecting frequent sub-graph between two community graphs. A simple technique using graph theory is employed to detect the frequent sub-community graph between two community graphs in two villages. The proposed algorithm has been given below.

```
Algorithm Frequent_Graph_Inbetween_2_Graphs (V_1, S_1, V_2, S_2)
V_1 [1:S_1, 1:S_1]: Adjacency matrix of Social Graph-1.
V_2 [1:S_2, 1:S_2]: Adjacency matrix of Social Graph-2.
Result[1:Size, 1:Size]: Global 2D-Array for representation of frequent graph's
adjacency matrix.
Size: The unique communities from villages V_1 and V_2.
1. [Assign 0's to Result[][] Adjacency Matrix of Frequent Graph]
   Repeat For i=1, 2,........., Size
     Repeat For j=1, 2, ......., Size
         Set Result[i][j]:= 0.
     End For
   End For
2. Set  i:= 2.
```

```
        Set  j:= 2.
3. Repeat While i<=S₁
    Do
       (a) Repeat While j<=S₂
            Do
               If V₁[i, 1] = V₂[j, 1],
               Then
                     (i) Call Column_Compare(V₁, S₁, i, V₂, S₂, j).
                     (ii) i:=i+1.
                     (iii) j:=j+1.
               Else
                     (iv) j:=j+1.
               End If
            End While
       (b) Set j:= i.
       (c) i:=i+1.
    End While
4. Exit.
```

Procedure Column_Compare (V_1, S_1, r_1, V_2, S_2, r_2)

```
1.  Set c₁:= 2.
    Set c₂:= 2.
2. Repeat While c₁<=S₁
    Do
       (a) Repeat While c₂<=S₂
            Do
               (a.1) If V₁[1, c₁] = V₂[1, c₂],
                     Then
[Edge between same pair of communities in both the graphs]
                        If V₁[r₁, c₁] = V₂[r₂, c₂] = 1,
                        Then
[Finding actual row position of village in Result[][] Matrix]
                           (i) Set row:= 2.
                           (ii) Repeat While TRUE
                                Do
                                   If V₁[r₁, 1]=Result[row, 1],
                                   Then
                                      Break.
                                   Else
                                      Row:= Row+1.
                                   End If
                                End While
[Show edge of same pair of communities in the Result[][] Matrix]
                           (iii) Set p:=1.
                           (iv) Repeat While TRUE
```

```
                    Do
        (iv.a) If V₁[1, c₁]=Result[1, p],
               Then
                  (I) Set Result[row, p]:= 1.
                  (II) Break.
               End If
        (iv.b) p:=p+1.
               End While
             End If
   (a.2) c₁:=c₁+1.
   (a.3) c₂:=c₂+1.
   Else
   (a.4) c₂:=c₂+1.
   End If [close of if(a.1)]
 End While [close of while (a)]
     (b)Set c₂:= c₁.
(c)c₁=c₁+1.
```

Figure 18. Adjacency matrix and village sub graph

C	1	2	3	4	5
1	0	1	1	0	0
2	1	0	0	1	0
3	1	0	0	0	1
4	0	1	0	0	0
5	0	0	1	0	0

(i)

C	1	2	3	5	9	10
1	0	0	1	1	1	0
2	0	0	1	0	0	1
3	1	1	0	1	0	0
5	1	0	1	0	1	1
9	1	0	0	1	0	0
10	0	1	0	1	0	0

(ii)

C	1	2	3	4	5	9	10
1	0	0	0	0	0	0	0
2	0	0	0	0	0	0	0
3	0	0	0	0	0	0	0
4	0	0	0	0	0	0	0
5	0	0	0	0	0	0	0
9	0	0	0	0	0	0	0
10	0	0	0	0	0	0	0

(iii)

$V_3 = \{C_1, C_2, C_3, C_4, C_5\}$, $C_{tot1} = 5$,
$V_5 = \{C_1, C_2, C_3, C_5, C_9, C_{10}\}$, $C_{tot2} = 6$,
Size = $V_3 \cup V_5 = 7$.
So unique communities are
$\{C_1, C_2, C_3, C_4, C_5, C_9, C_{10}\}$

(i) Adjacency matrix of village V3,
(ii) Adjacency matrix of village V5.
(iii) Initial adjacency matrix Result of common community sub-graph between villages V3 and V5

Graph Mining and Its Applications

```
End While [close of while (2)]
3. Exit.
```

Let us consider a community graph for villages V_1, V_2, V_3, V_4, and V_5 which is shown in earlier in figure (Rao and Mitra, ichpca-2014). For village V_1 the communities $VC_1 = \{C_1, C_2, C_3, C_4\}$. Similarly for village V_2 the communities $VC_2 = \{C_1, C_2, C_3, C_5\}$, village V_3 the communities $VC_3 = \{C_1, C_2, C_3, C_4, C_5\}$, village V_4 the communities $VC_4 = \{C_1, C_3, C_4, C_8\}$ and village V_5 the communities $VC_5 = \{C_1, C_2, C_3, C_5, C_9, C_{10}\}$ respectively.

Now the authors have to detect the frequent sub-community graph by considering two community graphs. In this example the authors have considered two villages' V_3 and V_5's community graph which is shown in (i) and (ii) of the figure18.

And its adjacency matrix is shown in (iii) and (iv) of the same figure. The above algorithm has to pass four parameters such as V_3, 5, V_5, and 6. Then the authors have to union both the communities of the villages V_3 and V_5. Now, the authors are able to find the order of resultant adjacency matrix by finding the total number of unique communities. In this example it is 7 and the adjacency matrix must be created which is shown in (iii) of the figure 19. Based on the algorithm, the final resultant matrix is formed and shown in (i) of figure 20. (Figure 20. Common community sub grapg between V3 and V5). By using the resultant matrix, the authors are able to draw the frequent sub-community graph. In this example the sub-community graph is shown in (ii) of the same figure.

Figure 19. Common community sub graph between villages

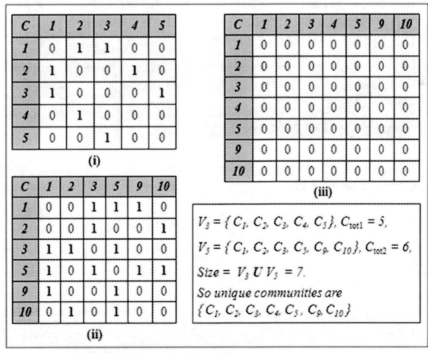

(i) Adjacency matrix of village V3,
(ii) Adjacency matrix of village V5.
(iii) Initial adjacency matrix Result of common community sub-graph between villages V3 and V5

Figure 20. Common community sub grapg between V3 and V5

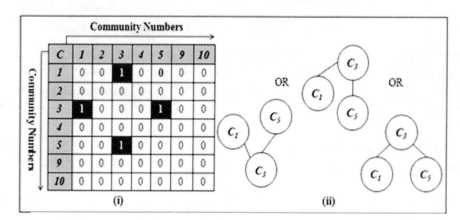

(i) The final adjacency matrix Result of common community sub-graph between villages V3 and V5.
(ii) The drawn common community sub-graph from villages V3 and V5

Figure 21. First Screenshot of program's output

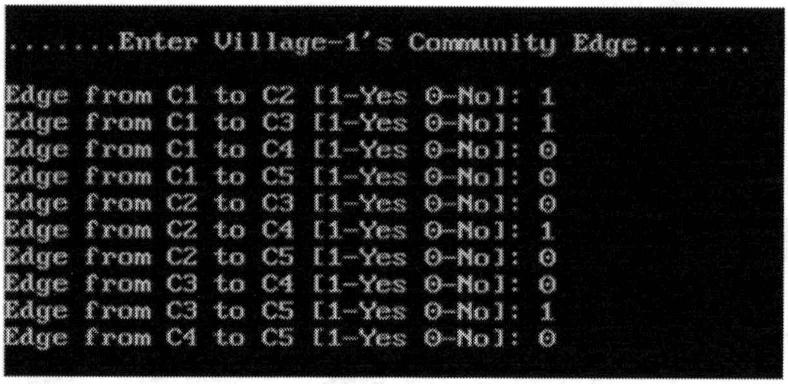

```
.......Enter Village-1's Community Edge.......
Edge from C1 to C2 [1-Yes 0-No]: 1
Edge from C1 to C3 [1-Yes 0-No]: 1
Edge from C1 to C4 [1-Yes 0-No]: 0
Edge from C1 to C5 [1-Yes 0-No]: 0
Edge from C2 to C3 [1-Yes 0-No]: 0
Edge from C2 to C4 [1-Yes 0-No]: 1
Edge from C2 to C5 [1-Yes 0-No]: 0
Edge from C3 to C4 [1-Yes 0-No]: 0
Edge from C3 to C5 [1-Yes 0-No]: 1
Edge from C4 to C5 [1-Yes 0-No]: 0
```

OUTPUT FOR THE EXAMPLE

The screenshots of the output are given in sequence in the following figures 21, 22, 23, 24, and 25.

MERGING OF GRAPHS

Merging of two sub-graphs at a time to form a large graph having at least one common vertex or node between those sub-graphs.

Graph Mining and Its Applications

Figure 22. Second Screenshot of program's output

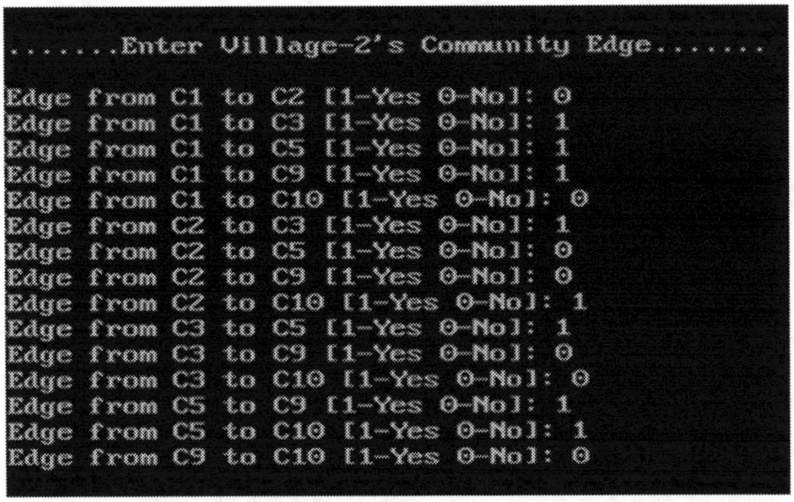

```
........Enter Village-2's Community Edge.......

Edge from C1 to C2 [1-Yes 0-No]: 0
Edge from C1 to C3 [1-Yes 0-No]: 1
Edge from C1 to C5 [1-Yes 0-No]: 1
Edge from C1 to C9 [1-Yes 0-No]: 1
Edge from C1 to C10 [1-Yes 0-No]: 0
Edge from C2 to C3 [1-Yes 0-No]: 1
Edge from C2 to C5 [1-Yes 0-No]: 0
Edge from C2 to C9 [1-Yes 0-No]: 0
Edge from C2 to C10 [1-Yes 0-No]: 1
Edge from C3 to C5 [1-Yes 0-No]: 1
Edge from C3 to C9 [1-Yes 0-No]: 0
Edge from C3 to C10 [1-Yes 0-No]: 0
Edge from C5 to C9 [1-Yes 0-No]: 1
Edge from C5 to C10 [1-Yes 0-No]: 1
Edge from C9 to C10 [1-Yes 0-No]: 0
```

Figure 23. Third Screenshot program's output

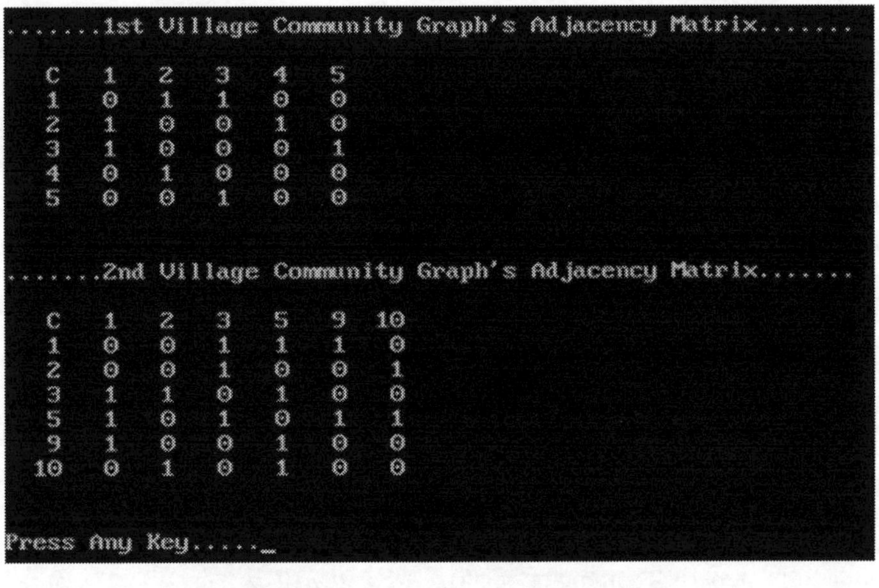

```
........1st Village Community Graph's Adjacency Matrix.......

 C  1  2  3  4  5
 1  0  1  1  0  0
 2  1  0  0  1  0
 3  1  0  0  0  1
 4  0  1  0  0  0
 5  0  0  1  0  0

........2nd Village Community Graph's Adjacency Matrix.......

 C   1  2  3  5  9  10
 1   0  0  1  1  1  0
 2   0  0  1  0  0  1
 3   1  1  0  1  0  0
 5   1  0  1  0  1  1
 9   1  0  0  1  0  0
 10  0  1  0  1  0  0

Press Any Key....._
```

Figure 24. Fourth Screenshot of program's output

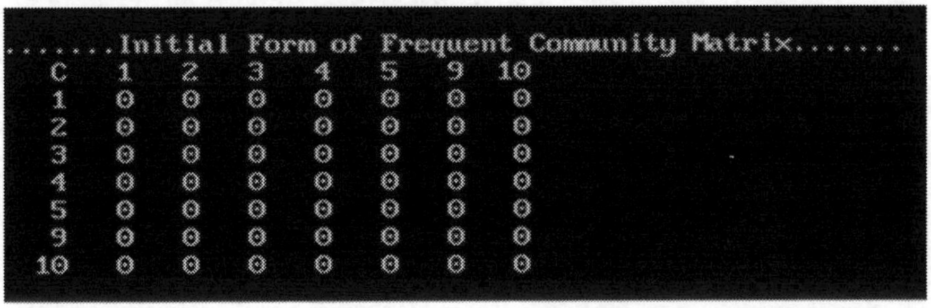

```
........Initial Form of Frequent Community Matrix.......

 C   1  2  3  4  5  9  10
 1   0  0  0  0  0  0  0
 2   0  0  0  0  0  0  0
 3   0  0  0  0  0  0  0
 4   0  0  0  0  0  0  0
 5   0  0  0  0  0  0  0
 9   0  0  0  0  0  0  0
 10  0  0  0  0  0  0  0
```

Figure 25. Fifth Screenshot of program's output

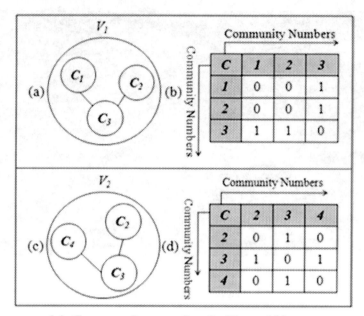

(a) Community graph of village V1
(b) Adjacency matrix of village V1
(c) Community graph of village V2
(d) Adjacency matrix of village V2

AUTHORS PROPOSED APPROACH

The authors propose here for merging of two community graphs into a larger community prior to at least one common community between these community graphs (Rao and Mitra, iccic 2014). The authors have followed graph matching technique by matching one-to-one correspondence communities of the two community graphs which is for merging. Here the authors represent a community graph (an undirected graph) in memory as an adjacency matrix. Finally the authors have proposed three algorithms for merging of two community graphs.

Algorithm-I explains about finding the order of merged communities of two villages. And make available of initial form of merged community matrix. *Algorithm-II* explains about creation of adjacency matrix community graph of village. These adjacency matrices of community graph of villages are used in *Algorithm-III*. *Algorithm-III* explains about creation of merged community adjacency matrix. Finally from this adjacency matrix the authors can construct the merged community graphs of two villages.

```
Proposed Algorithms
(I) Algorithm for finding order of merged communities of two villages.
```
Algorithm $Order\_of\_Merged\_Commuity\_Matrix$ (CV_1, N_1, CV_2, N_2)
CV_1 $[1:N_1]$: Village-1's communities 1, 2, 3, ……., N1.
CV_2 $[1:N_2]$: Village-2's communities 1, 2, 3, ……., N2.
CMV $[1:N_1+N_2]$: Global array to hold the merged community arrays CV_1 and CV_2.

MV [1:size, 1:size]: Global 2D-Array for representation of initial form of merged community matrix.

size: The size of merged array.

1. Merge CV1 and CV2 and store in CMV.
2. Arrange CMV in ascending order.
3. Set size:= N1 + N2.
4. [Remove the repeated community from CMV[ ]]
    Repeat for I = 1, 2, ……., size-1:
    (i) If CMV [I] = CMV [I+1],
        Then
           [Shift one step left all communities]
Repeat for J = I+1, I+2,……., size:
    Set CMV [J-1]:= CMV [J].
 End for
Set size:= size-1.
Set I:= I - 1.
End if
     End for
5. [Initial representation of merged community matrix of order sizeXsize]
    Repeat for I = 1, 2, ……, size:
      Repeat for J = 1, 2, ….., size:
         Set MV [I][J]:= 0.
      End For
    End For
6. Return

(II) Algorithm for Adjacency matrix creation for village's community graph

Algorithm *Adjacency_Village_Community_Matrix* (*CA*, *Size*, *CMatrix*)

CA [1:Size]: Community array of a village of dimension Size.

CMatrix [1:Size+1, 1:Size+1]: Community matrix of village V of order (Size+1) X (Size+1).

1. [Community number assignments at row and column places in community matrix CMatrix[][]]
    Repeat for I = 1, 2, ……, Size:
     a) Set CMatrix [1][I+1]:= CA [I].
     b) Set CMatrix [I+1][1]:= CA [I].
    End For
2. [Adjacency Matrix Creation through community matrix CMatrix[][]]
    Repeat For I = 2, 3, ….., Size+1:
      Repeat For J = 2, 3, ……, Size+1:
        If Edge from CMatrix [I][1] to CMatrix[1][J] = True,
        Then
           Set CMatrix [I][J]:= 1.
        Else
           Set CMatrix [I][J]:= 0.

               End If
          End For
     End For
3. Return

Note-i. To create a community graph $CV_1[1:N_1]$'s adjacency matrix as $V_1[1:N_1+1, 1:N_1+1]$ then follow the given statement:
Call *Adjacency_Village_Community_Matrix* (CV_1, N_1, V_1)

Note-ii. Here CV_1 village-1's community array having $1, 2, 3, \ldots.., N_1$ communities.

V_1: Adjacency matrix of the community graph of village-1 of order (N_1+1) X (N_1+1)]

(III) Algorithm for merging two villages' community adjacency matrices and represent in the
merged community adjacency matrix MV of order sizeXsize.

Note-iii. The initial state of matrix *MV [1:size,1:size]* has been created in Algorithm-1.

Algorithm *Merge_Community_Graphs* (V_1, N_1, V_2, N_2)

V_1 *[1:N_1+1, 1:N_1+1]*: Adjacency community matrix of order (N_1+1) X (N_1+1).
V_2 *[1:N_2+1, 1:N_2+1]*: Adjacency community matrix of order (N_2+1) X (N_2+1).
(Above both matrices formed from Algorithm-II)

MV [1:size, 1:size]: Global 2D-Array (formed from Algorithm-I) for representation of merged community matrices V_1 and V_2, of order sizeXsize.

1. [Adding adjacency matrices V_2[][] with merged community matrix mv[][]]
   Repeat for i = 2, 3, ……,N_1+1:
    Repeat for j = 2, 3, ……., N_2+1:
     Repeat for m = 2, 3, ……..,size:
        Repeat for n = 2, 3, ……,size:
      If MV[m][1]=V1[i][1] And MV[1][n]=V1[1][j],
      Then
          i) Set MV[m][n]:= MV[m][n] OR V_1[i][j].// logical OR
                                           //operation
         ii) Break.
      End If
        End For
     End For
    End For
  End For

2. [Adding adjacency matrices V_2[][] with merged community matrix MV[][]]
    Repeat for i = 2, 3, ……,N_1+1:
      Repeat for j = 2, 3, …….., N_2+1:
        Repeat for m = 2, 3, ……..,size:
          Repeat for n = 2, 3, ……,size:
        If MV[m][1]=V_2[i][1] And MV[1][n]=V_2[1][j],
        Then

```
                i) Set MV[m][n]:= MV[m][n] OR V₂[i][j]. // logical
                                                    //OR operation
            ii) Break.
        End If
            End For
        End For
    End For
    End For
```
3. The matrix MV [][] is the resultant merged community matrix. From it we can draw the merged community graph.
4. Exit.

EXAMPLE AND ANALYSIS FOR AUTHORS PROPOSED APPROACH

Let us consider an example which consists of villages $V = \{ V_1, V_2, V_3, V_4, V_5 \}$. Each village consists of a community network known as sub-community graph. The villages' unique community list is given in seed table of villages in Table 1. The total number of communities in a village is termed as its *seed*.

Table 1. seed table of villages

Village	Seed	Communites
V_1	3	C_1, C_2, C_3
V_2	3	C_2, C_3, C_4
V_3	4	C_4, C_5, C_7, C_8
V_4	4	C_1, C_2, C_4, C_8
V_5	6	$C_2, C_3, C_7, C_8, C_9, C_{10}$

Figure 26. Community graph and adjacency matrix

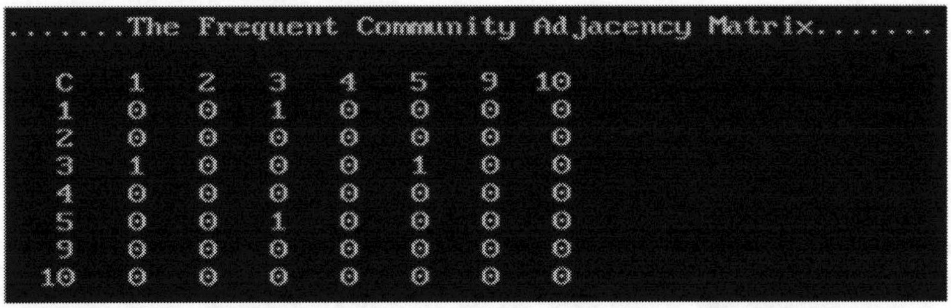

```
.......The Frequent Community Adjacency Matrix.......
    C   1   2   3   4   5   9   10
    1   0   0   1   0   0   0   0
    2   0   0   0   0   0   0   0
    3   1   0   0   0   1   0   0
    4   0   0   0   0   0   0   0
    5   0   0   1   0   0   0   0
    9   0   0   0   0   0   0   0
    10  0   0   0   0   0   0   0
```

When two villages community graph are to be merged for a larger community graph, then there must

Figure 27. Merged graph and respective matrix

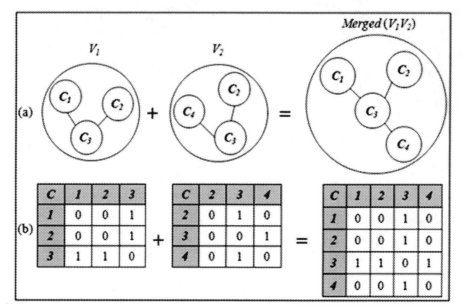

(a) Merged community graph of villages V1 and V2
(b) Merged adjacency matrices of villages V1 and V2

Figure 28. Another example for Community graph and adjacency matrix

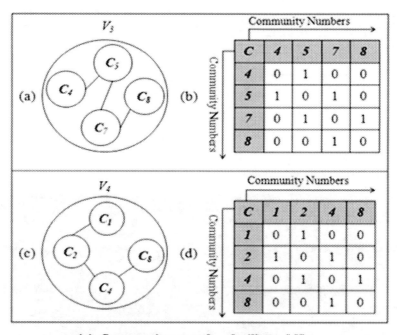

(a) Community graph of village V3
(b) Adjacency matrix of village V3
(c) Community graph of village V4
(d) Adjacency matrix of village V4.

Graph Mining and Its Applications

Figure 29. Another example of Merged graph and respective matrix

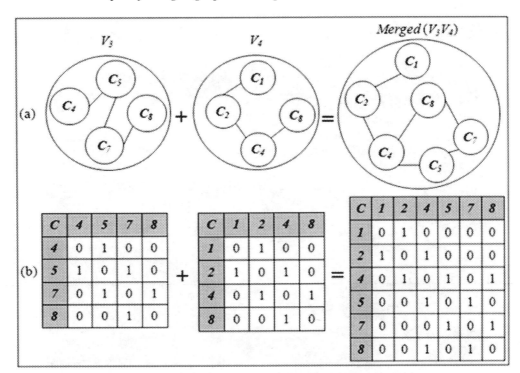

(a) Merged community graph of villages V3 and V4
(b) Merged adjacency matrices of Villages V3

Figure 30. First screenshot for output of program

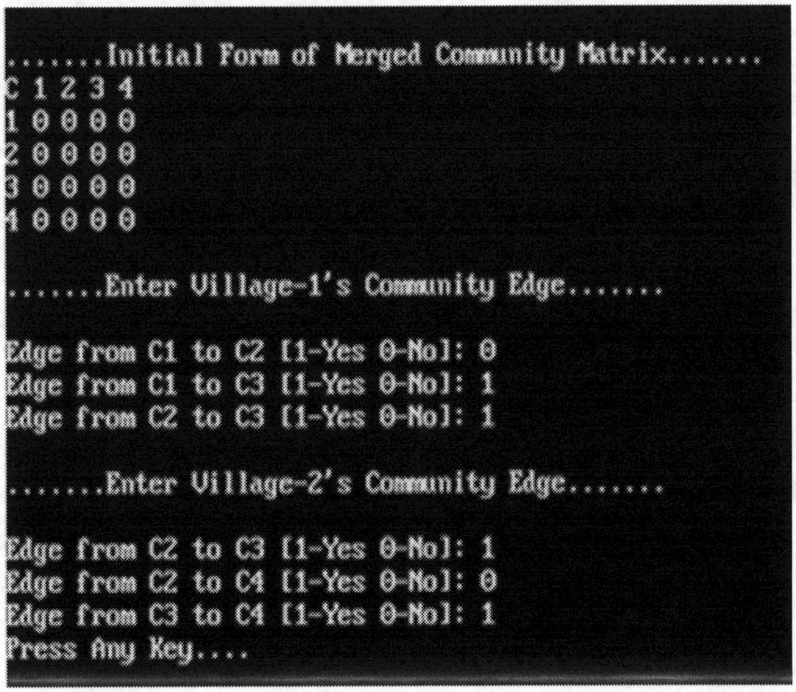

```
......Initial Form of Merged Community Matrix.......
C 1 2 3 4
1 0 0 0 0
2 0 0 0 0
3 0 0 0 0
4 0 0 0 0

......Enter Village-1's Community Edge.......

Edge from C1 to C2 [1-Yes 0-No]: 0
Edge from C1 to C3 [1-Yes 0-No]: 1
Edge from C2 to C3 [1-Yes 0-No]: 1

......Enter Village-2's Community Edge.......

Edge from C2 to C3 [1-Yes 0-No]: 1
Edge from C2 to C4 [1-Yes 0-No]: 0
Edge from C3 to C4 [1-Yes 0-No]: 1
Press Any Key....
```

Figure 31. Second screenshot for output of the program

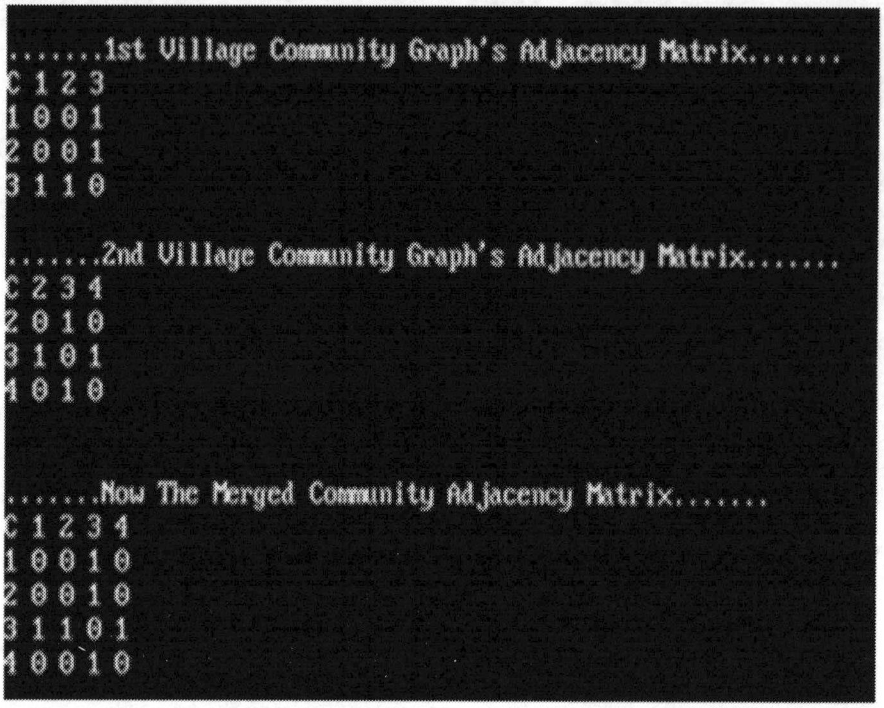

Figure 32. First screenshot for output of program

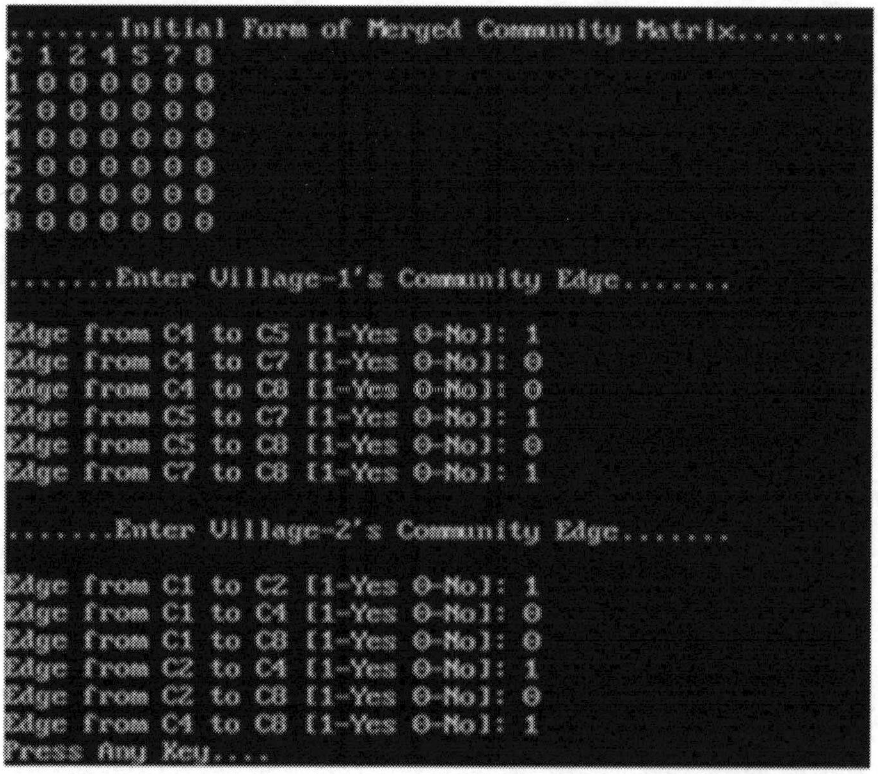

Figure 33. Second screenshot for output of the program

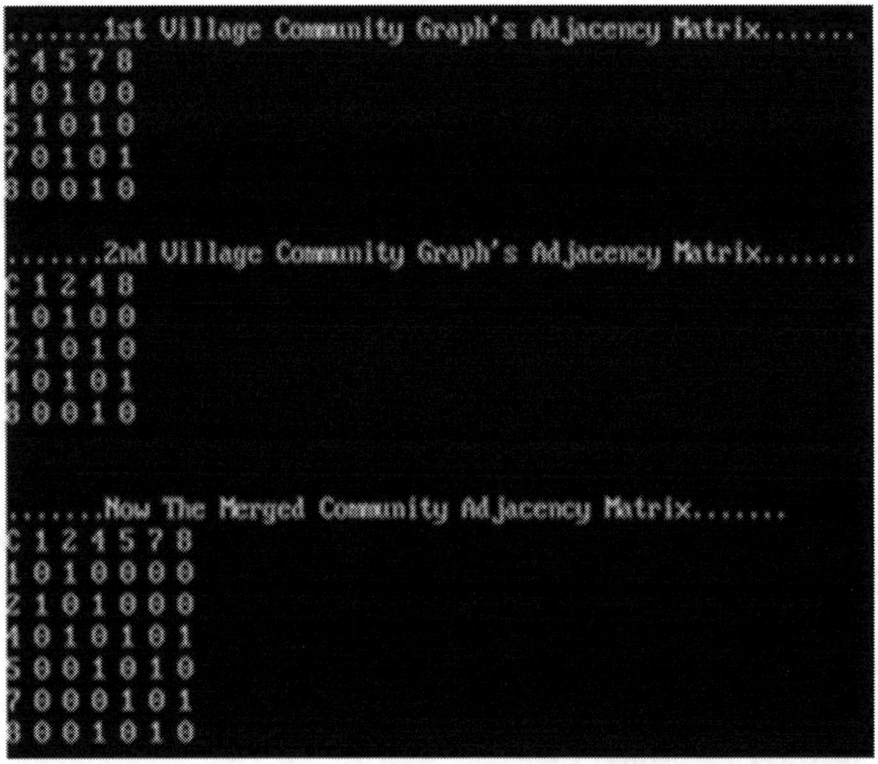

be at least one common community between those community graphs. Taking the help of seed table, the authors can find the common communities between the villages whose community graph are to be merged. *Algorithm-I* (Rao and Mitra, iccic 2014) says about the common communities to be used as the order of merged community adjacency matrix (*MV [ ][ ]* matrix). Finally *Algorithm-I* creates the initial form of the merged community adjacency matrix which initially assigns with 0 (zero) values.

Algorithm-II (Rao and Mitra, iccic 2014) for adjacency matrix creation for village's community graph and *Algorithm-III* (Rao and Mitra, iccic 2014) for merging of two villages' community adjacency matrices. *Example-1* and *Example-2*'s data is being used as sample data in our algorithm to reach to a conclusion that the algorithm is being worked out properly. *Example-1* is shown in figure 26 and 27, whereas *Example-2* is shown in figures 28 and 29. Its' sample output are listed in *Results-1* and *Results-2*. The algorithm is being implemented in C++ programming language.

Results in form of output screen for Example-1is mentioned in Figure 30 and 31.
Results in form of output screen for Example-2 is mentioned in Figure 32 and 33.

CRITERIA FOR GROUPING

The criteria of groups can be classified node-centric category, hierarchy-centric category group-centric category and network-centric category and. Some methods that are available for grouping are listed in the below.

NODES-CENTRIC COMMUNITY DETECTION

To detect a community using node-centric criteria "each node *in* a group requires satisfying certain properties which includes *mutuality, reachability, or degrees*. Some grouping based methods are briefly explained below.

- **Groups Based on Complete Mutuality:** A sub-graph is formed by considering more than two nodes and all are adjacent to each other which are termed as a *clique*. The existence of a complete bipartite in a community graph from a directed graph is given in (Kumar, Raghavan, Rajagopalan and Tomkins, 1999).
- **Groups Based on Reachability:** It says the reachability between two actors or nodes in a community. Two nodes can be considered as part of one community if there is a path between these two nodes. So the connected component is said to be a community (Kumar, Novak and Tomkins, 2006).
- **Groups Based on Nodal Degrees:** It checks actors within a group to be adjacent to a relatively large number of group members or not. Two commonly studied sub-structures are: k-*plex* and k-*core*.
- **Groups Based on Within-Outside Ties:** It only detects and selects node which has more connections to nodes that are within the group rather than outside the group.

GROUP-CENTRIC COMMUNITY DETECTION

It only focuses connection of nodes only inside a particular group. One such example is density-based groups. It has no guarantee whether the reachebility for each node in a group. In (Abello, Resende, and Sudarsky, 2002), maximum γ-dense quasi-cliques are discussed.

NETWORK-CENTRIC COMMUNITY DETECTION

It only detects the complete connection of the whole network. It partitions the actors into a number of small disjoint sets. It never defines independently a group.

HIERARCHY-CENTRIC COMMUNITY DETECTION

Based on the network topology, it builds a hierarchical structure of communities. Basically there are three types of hierarchical clustering: divisive, agglomerative and structure search.

- **Divisive Hierarchical Clustering:** Divisive clustering first partitions the actors into several disjoint sets. Then each set is further divided into smaller ones which contain only a small number of actors. A divisive clustering based on edge betweeness is proposed in (Newman and Girvan, 2004).

Graph Mining and Its Applications

- **Agglomerative Hierarchical Clustering:** The clustering starts with each node as a separate community and merges them successively to form a larger community. The hierarchical clustering is based on modularity which uses criterion (Mewman and Moore, 2004).
- **Structure Search:** It starts from a particular hierarchy and searches for similar hierarchies to generate the network (Vismara, Battista, Garg, Liotta, Tamassia and Vargiu, 2000). A random graph model for hierarchies is defined in (Moore, and Newman, 2008).

GROUP DETECTION

Group detection refers to the discovery of underlying organizational structure from a large structure which consists of selected individuals which related each other.

Best Friends Group Detection Algorithm

It passes user-defined parameters which finally form an initial group. Every group has begin node is said to be a "seed" node. The instructions for running Best Friends Group Detection either interactively or through TMODS batch scripts can be found in (Moy, 2005).

Terrorist Modus Operandi Detection System

It searches for and analyzes instances of particular threatening activity patterns. Its distributed Java software application can be found in (Moy, 2005). Graph matching is sometimes called as sub-graph isomorphism (Paugh and Rivest, 1978), (Diestel, 2000). Graph matching finds subsets of a large input graph and returns a true value if it is found.

TMODS EXTENSIONS TO STANDARD GRAPH MATCHING

It extends to standard sub-graph isomorphism problem to provide additional capabilities and able to detect a sub-graph in a large graph.

- **Inexact Matching:** TMODS able to find and highlight activity that exactly matches that pattern, as well as find the close pattern, but not an exact match by following sub-graph isomorphism.
- **Multiple Choices and Abstractions:** TMODS supports how various patterns can be instantiated. TMODS defines various alternative graphs for each pattern, called choices.
- **Hierarchical Patterns:** TMODS allows defining patterns that are built from other patterns. Rather than describing the entire pattern, TMODS modularizes the patterns.
- **Constraints:** TMODS allows defining constraints between attribute values on nodes and edges. Constraints restrict the relationships between attributes of actors, events, or relationships.

ALGORITHMS

The exhaustive algorithms those that authors have listed in the earlier sections will be able to solve the problem in reasonable time for particularly large graphs (Messmer, 1995), (Corneil and Gotlieb, 1970), (Cordella, Foggia, Sansone and Vento, 2011) practically. Non-exhaustive techniques are used for practical implementations to achieve results faster. TMODS follows two major algorithms, the merging matches' algorithm and the fast genetic search.

- **Merging Matches:** It builds up a list of potential matches. The initial entries of the list match a node from the input pattern to one node in the pattern graph. This way the merging matches take place.
- **Genetic and Distributed Genetic Search:** When the input patterns are large, then the merging matches' algorithm is not feasible for searching task. TMODS adopts a Genetic Search algorithm efficiently solving the above problem. TMODS allows a genetic search over several processes to increase the speed and completeness of the search. Each process is assigned with a limited search domain, which actually runs on different computer systems.

AUTHORS ANALYSIS AND WORK

The authors have studied the scenario of a social graph, which consists of various villages in a panchayat (A panchayat is an Indian term for administration of villages). In a village different types of communities live together and have connectivity. The authors have proposed a community graph given in figure. How a same community shares their social values, feelings, and activities with the same community living in other villages of the same panchayat or different panchayat? Taking this scenario into mind, one can find the community match graph (Rao and Mitra, Dec-2014). For such case the authors have proposed an algorithm to detect the same community and find the graph which is underlying in the original large community graph. It is a simple technique using graph theory to detect a particular community from various villages. The new proposal of algorithms (Rao and Mitra, Dec-2014) for creation and detection as follows:

`Algorithm` Community Incidence Matrix Creation ()
(Algorithm conventions (Seymour, 1997))
`n:` No. of villages.
`vno[1: n]:` Global array which holds 'n' village numbers in ascending order.
`nc [1: n]:` Global array which holds number of communities (i.e. seed number) for 'n' villages, which is arranged with respect to vno[ ].
`cno [1:nc[1], 1:nc[2], ......, 1:nc[n]]:` Global dynamic matrix which holds list of community numbers for 'n' villages against village seed number.
`rcno[1:`$\sum_{i=1}^{n}\left(nc[i]\right)$`]:` Global dynamic array which holds merged community numbers of size, S = [Summation (from i=1 to n)(nc[i]). Assume it is arranged in ascending order and removed the duplicate community numbers.

Graph Mining and Its Applications

CIMatrix [1: n+1, 1: S+1]: Global matrix of order 'n' villages X 'S' unique communities.

1. [Initial form of community incidence matrix]
   Repeat For I = 2, 3, 4,………., n + 1:
      [Village number assignment]
      i) Set CIMatrix [I][1]:= vno [I-1].
   Repeat For J = 2, 3, 4,……..., S + 1:
      [Community number assignment]
      ii) If I=2, Then: Set CIMatrix [1][J-1]:= rcno [J-1]. [Assign 0's to all villages and their respective communities]
      iii) Set CIMatrix [I][J]:= 0.
      End For
   End For
2. [Final form of community incidence matrix]
   Repeat For I = 1, 2, 3, ……..., n:
      Repeat For J = 1, 2, 3,……..., nc [I]:
         Repeat For K = 2, 3, 4,……..., S+1:
            If cno [I][J] = CIMatrix [1][K],
            Then
   a)   Set CIMatrix [I+1][K]:= 1.
   b)   Break.
            End If
         End For
      End For
   End For
3. Exit

Algorithm Community Detection (Cno)

(Algorithm conventions (Seymour, 1997))

Cno: Community Number, vno[1: M]: Global array which holds 'M' village numbers in ascending order.

Cno_Array[1: M]: Global Array for assignment of true(1) value for detected community number Cno; otherwise false (0) value for M villages.

CIMatrix[1: M, 1: N]: Global Matrix which shows the existence of communities for M villages and N number of unique communities.

1.   Repeat For I = 1, 2, 3, ……..., M:
   [Initializes 0 to M villages in Cno_Array.]
   Set Cno_Array[I]:= 0.
   End For
2.   Repeat For I = 1, 2, 3, ……..., N:
   [To find community number Cno in matrix CIMatrix[][]; when found assign 1 to the corresponding village in the array Cno_Array[ ]]
3.   If CIMatrix[1, I] = Cno, Then:
4.   Repeat For J = 1, 2, 3, ……, M:
      If CIMatrix[J, I] = 1, Then: Set Cno_Array[I]:= 1.

Figure 34. Displaying Community Heads

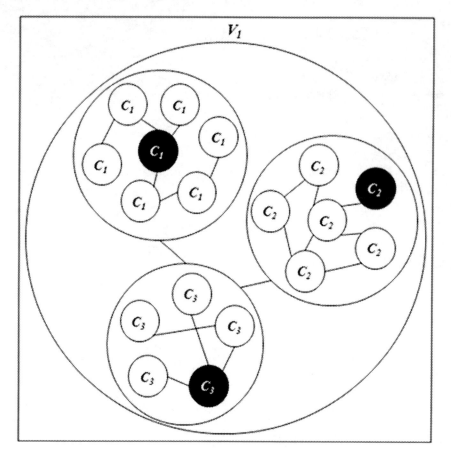

```
      End For
    End If
End For
5.          Repeat For I = 1, 2, 3, …….., M:
    [Output the array vno[] for community matched villages]
       If Cno_Array[I] = 1, Then: Write vno[I].
     End For
6.          Exit.
```

EXAMPLE:

Let us consider a community graph for villages V_1, V_2, V_3, V_4, and V_5 which is shown in figure (Rao and Mitra, ichpca-2014). For village V_1 the communities are C_1, C_2, and C_3. Here C_1 indicates the community head. Village V_1's extracted view is given in figure 34. In this case the black filled circles are the community heads. It is represented as one node or vertex or community in figure, labeled as V_1, V_2, and so on for individual community. So the seed number of village V_1 is **3**. The villages seed number

Graph Mining and Its Applications

Figure 35. Seed table of villages

Village	Seed	Communities
V_1	3	C_1, C_2, C_3
V_2	4	C_4, C_5, C_7, C_8
V_3	3	C_2, C_4, C_6
V_4	4	C_1, C_2, C_4, C_8
V_5	6	$C_2, C_3, C_7, C_8, C_9, C_{10}$

Figure 36. Community incidence matrix

Villages/Nodes/Vertices	C_1	C_2	C_3	C_4	C_5	C_6	C_7	C_8	C_9	C_{10}
V_1	1	1	1	0	0	0	0	0	0	0
V_2	0	0	0	1	1	0	1	1	0	0
V_3	0	1	0	1	0	1	0	0	0	0
V_4	1	1	0	1	0	0	0	1	0	0
V_5	0	1	1	0	0	0	1	1	1	1

Figure 37. Community detected array

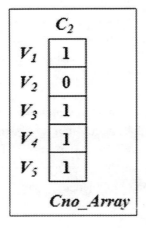

Figure 38. Connected graph of community

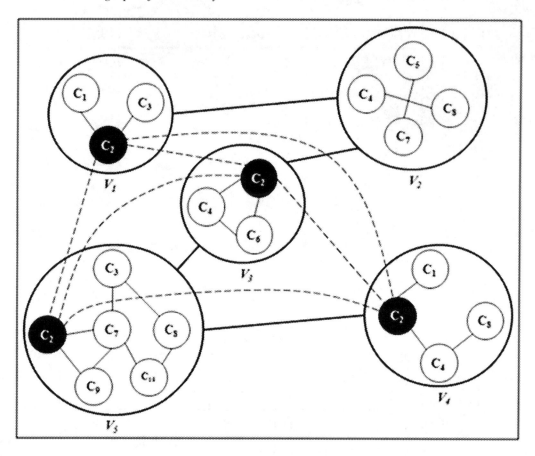

and communities are mentioned (Figure 35). The unique communities from villages V_1 to V_5 are C_1, C_2, ..., C_{10}.

To represent the community graph in figure using incidence matrix, the order would be (*'Number of villages' X 'No. of distinct Communities'*). Thus, the order of the above community graph in figure is **5 X 10**. Its incidence matrix representation is shown in Figure 36. The final incidence matrix only holds boolean values 1 and 0. This matrix is said to be the *community incidence matrix* because it shows the presence (*1*) or absence (*0*) of a community for a particular village.

Now the detection of community number **Cno** is being carried out on Community Incidence Matrix **CIMatrix[ ][ ]**. If **Cno** found, then assign 1 to the corresponding village in community detection array **Cno_Array[ ]**. For the above example the community number is C_2. And the **Cno_Array[ ]** is shown in Figure 37. So the indication of 1 against those villages is the same community detected i.e. C_2 in this example.

Using **Cno_Array[ ]**, the authors can show the community detected graph which is shown in figure 38. The dotted path is the underlying graph for community C_2 which is said to be the community detection graph for the nodes (or villages) V_1, V_3, V_5, and V_4. From the above cited figure, we can draw our community matched graph as a digraph which is shown here in figure 39. Finally, it is possible to detect the isolated communities in the community incidence matrix.

Figure 39. Another example for community detection graph

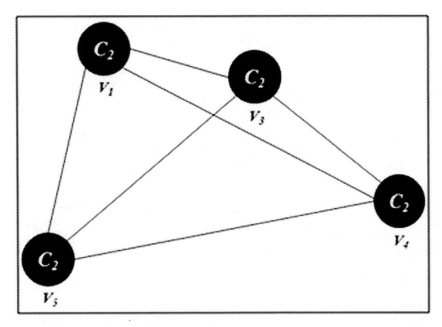

Figure 40. Displaying isolated communities

Communities →

Villages/ Nodes/ Vertices ↑

	C_1	C_2	C_3	C_4	C_5	C_6	C_7	C_8	C_9	C_{10}
V_1	1	1	1	0	0	0	0	0	0	0
V_2	0	0	0	1	1	0	1	1	0	0
V_3	0	1	0	1	0	1	0	0	0	0
V_4	1	1	0	1	0	0	0	1	0	0
V_5	0	1	1	0	0	0	1	1	1	1

Black filled circles indicate isolated communities

In the authors example, the isolated communities are $\boldsymbol{C_5}$ in village $\boldsymbol{V_2}$, $\boldsymbol{C_6}$ in village $\boldsymbol{V_2}$, and $\boldsymbol{C_9}$, $\boldsymbol{C_{10}}$ in village $\boldsymbol{V_5}$. The isolated communities are black filled circles which are shown figure 40.

Authors have presented the results in form of output screen in sequence Figure 41, 42, 43, and 44. The results in form of output screen for *COMMUNITY DETECTION FOR* $\boldsymbol{C_2}$: is mentioned here in order in Figure 45 and the results in form of output screen for *COMMUNITY DETECTION FOR* $\boldsymbol{C_8}$: is mentioned in Figure 46.

Figure 41. First screenshot of output

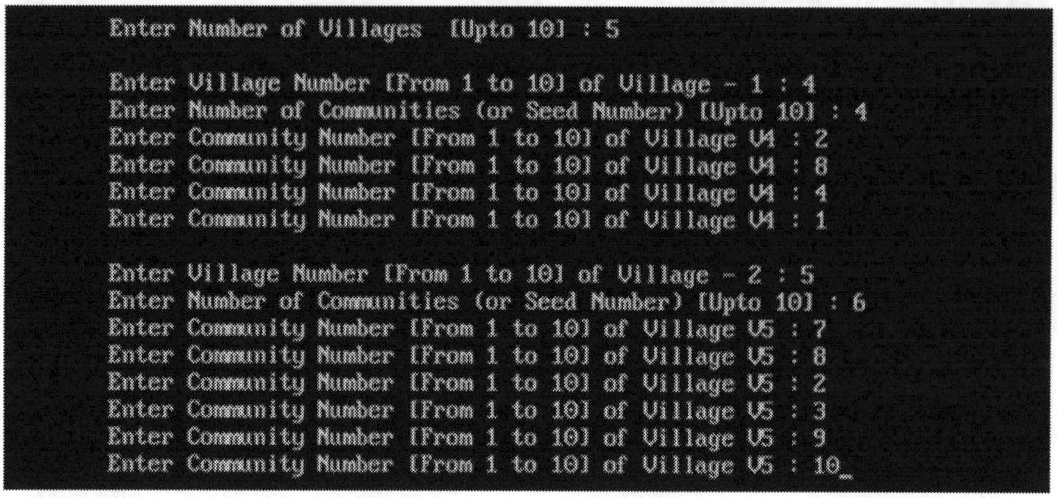

```
        Enter Number of Villages  [Upto 10] : 5

        Enter Village Number [From 1 to 10] of Village - 1 : 4
        Enter Number of Communities (or Seed Number) [Upto 10] : 4
        Enter Community Number [From 1 to 10] of Village V4 : 2
        Enter Community Number [From 1 to 10] of Village V4 : 8
        Enter Community Number [From 1 to 10] of Village V4 : 4
        Enter Community Number [From 1 to 10] of Village V4 : 1

        Enter Village Number [From 1 to 10] of Village - 2 : 5
        Enter Number of Communities (or Seed Number) [Upto 10] : 6
        Enter Community Number [From 1 to 10] of Village V5 : 7
        Enter Community Number [From 1 to 10] of Village V5 : 8
        Enter Community Number [From 1 to 10] of Village V5 : 2
        Enter Community Number [From 1 to 10] of Village V5 : 3
        Enter Community Number [From 1 to 10] of Village V5 : 9
        Enter Community Number [From 1 to 10] of Village V5 : 10_
```

Figure 42. Second screenshot of output

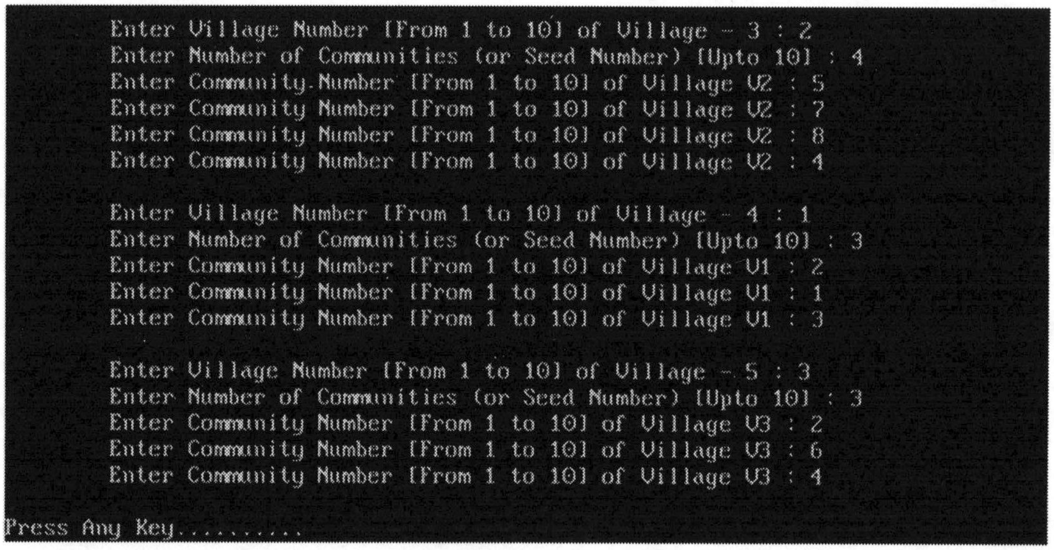

```
        Enter Village Number [From 1 to 10] of Village - 3 : 2
        Enter Number of Communities (or Seed Number) [Upto 10] : 4
        Enter Community Number [From 1 to 10] of Village V2 : 5
        Enter Community Number [From 1 to 10] of Village V2 : 7
        Enter Community Number [From 1 to 10] of Village V2 : 8
        Enter Community Number [From 1 to 10] of Village V2 : 4

        Enter Village Number [From 1 to 10] of Village - 4 : 1
        Enter Number of Communities (or Seed Number) [Upto 10] : 3
        Enter Community Number [From 1 to 10] of Village V1 : 2
        Enter Community Number [From 1 to 10] of Village V1 : 1
        Enter Community Number [From 1 to 10] of Village V1 : 3

        Enter Village Number [From 1 to 10] of Village - 5 : 3
        Enter Number of Communities (or Seed Number) [Upto 10] : 3
        Enter Community Number [From 1 to 10] of Village V3 : 2
        Enter Community Number [From 1 to 10] of Village V3 : 6
        Enter Community Number [From 1 to 10] of Village V3 : 4
Press Any Key.........
```

SOME ISSUES ON GRAPH ANALYTICS

- **Single path analysis:** The goal is to find a path through the graph, starting with a specific node. All the links and the corresponding vertices that can be reached immediately from the starting node are first evaluated. From the identified vertices, one is selected, based on a certain set of criteria and the first hop is made. After that, the process continues. The result will be a path consisting of a number of vertices and edges.
- **Optimal path analysis:** This analysis finds the 'best' path between two vertices. The best path could be the shortest path, the cheapest path or the fastest path, depending on the properties of the vertices and the edges.

Graph Mining and Its Applications

Figure 43. Third screenshot of output

```
Village   Seed   Communities

  V4       4     C2 ,C8 ,C4 ,C1

  V5       6     C7 ,C8 ,C2 ,C3 ,C9 ,C10

  V2       4     C5 ,C7 ,C8 ,C4

  V1       3     C2 ,C1 ,C3

  V3       3     C2 ,C6 ,C4

Before Sort. Press Any Key..........
```

Figure 44. Fourth screenshot of output

```
Village   Seed   Communities

  V1       3     C2 ,C1 ,C3

  V2       4     C5 ,C7 ,C8 ,C4

  V3       3     C2 ,C6 ,C4

  V4       4     C2 ,C8 ,C4 ,C1

  V5       6     C7 ,C8 ,C2 ,C3 ,C9 ,C10

After Sort. Press Any Key..........
      C1 C2 C3 C4 C5 C6 C7 C8 C9 C10
  V1   1  1  1  0  0  0  0  0  0  0
  V2   0  0  0  1  1  0  1  1  0  0
  V3   0  1  0  1  0  1  0  0  0  0
  V4   1  1  0  1  0  0  0  1  0  0
  V5   0  1  1  0  0  0  1  1  1  1
```

Figure 45. First screenshot of output

```
        Enter a Community Number [From 1 to 10] for Detection : 2

        Village Names with Community C2
Village-1
Village-3
Village-4
Village-5
```

Figure 46. Second screenshot of output

```
            Enter a Community Number [From 1 to 10] for Detection : 8

        Village Names with Community C8
Village-2
Village-4
Village-5
```

- **Vertex centrality analysis:** This analysis identifies the centrality of a vertex based on several centrality assessment properties:
- **Degree centrality:** This measure indicates how many edges a vertex has. The more edges there are, the higher the degree centrality.
- **Closeness centrality:** This measure identifies the vertex that has the smallest number of hops to other vertices. The closeness centrality of the node refers to the proximity of the vertex in reference to other vertices. The higher the closeness centrality is the more number of vertices that require short paths to the other vertices.
- **Eigenvector centrality:** This measure indicates the importance of a vertex in a graph. Scores are assigned to vertices, based on the principle that connections to high-scoring vertices contribute more to the score than equal connections to low-scoring vertices.

APPLICATION OF GRAPH ANALYTICS

In the finance sector, graph analytics is useful for understanding the money transfer pathways. A money transfer between bank accounts may require several intermediate bank accounts and graph analytics can be applied to determine the different relationships between different account holders. Running the graph analytics algorithm on the huge financial transaction data sets will help to alert banks to possible cases of fraudulent transactions or money laundering.

The use of graph analytics in the logistics sector is not new. Optimal path analysis is the obvious form of graph analytics that can be used in logistics distribution and shipment environments. There are many examples of using graph analytics in this area and they include "the shortest route to deliver goods to various addresses" and the "most cost effective routes for goods delivery".

One of the most contemporary use cases of graph analytics is in the area of social media. It can be used not just to identify relationships in the social network, but to understand them. One outcome from using graph analytics on social media is to identify the "influential" figures from each social graph. Businesses can then spend more effort in engaging this specific group of people in their marketing campaigns or customer relationship management efforts.

An Example on Use of Graph Analytics

For analytical purposes, a social network is visualized as a *digraph* (in a graph if the relationship has no direction) (Bandyopadhyay, Sinha and Rao, 2006). So in a digraph, one unit may be an individual, a

Figure 47. A digraph

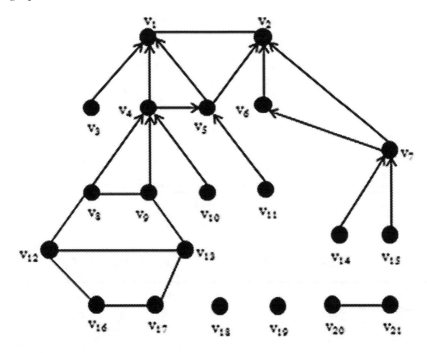

family, a household, a village, an organization in a village is called a *node* or *vertex*. A tie between two nodes indicates the presence of a relationship. No tie between two nodes is the absence of a relationship. A tie with a direction is called an *arc* and tie without direction is called an *edge*. The weight of a tie is the value or volume of flow. If the *arc* or *edge* is labeled with any weight then the graph is termed as *weighted graph*. In social networking we concentrate only the *presence* (1) or *absence* (0) of the relationship. We also assume that ties have directions.

Let us denote G is a digraph. The set of vertices of G can be denoted by $V(G)$ and the set arcs can be denoted by $A(G)$. If uv is an arc, then diagrammatically it can be shown as an arrow from vertex u to vertex v. if both uv and vu are arcs, then we sometimes represent these two together by a line without arrow heads joining vertex u and vertex v.

For the figure 47, we have considered a digraph G. The vertex set is $V = \{v_1, v_2, \ldots \ldots v_{21}\}$. The different arcs are $v_1v_2, v_2v_1, v_3v_1, v_4v_1, v_4v_5$ etc., but v_1v_3 and v_2v_3 are not arcs in the graph G.

Representing Social Network Using Properties of Graph Theory and Matrices

The 1st network illustrates that everybody goes to everybody else. The 2nd network, the ties are reciprocated but the network is highly fragmented. The 3rd network is connected but highly centralized and shows concentration of power lies in only one node or vertex. The 4th network is connected cyclic i.e. everybody can go to everybody else through a large number of intermediaries. The 5th network illustrates a strong hierarchy, things flow only in one direction. The number of vertices and number of arcs constitute the most basic data in a social network.

Let us consider an example for the 4th network in the figure 48, suppose there are six households in a neighborhood connected in a circular way. Here each of household goes to exactly one among the

Figure 48. Five different networks

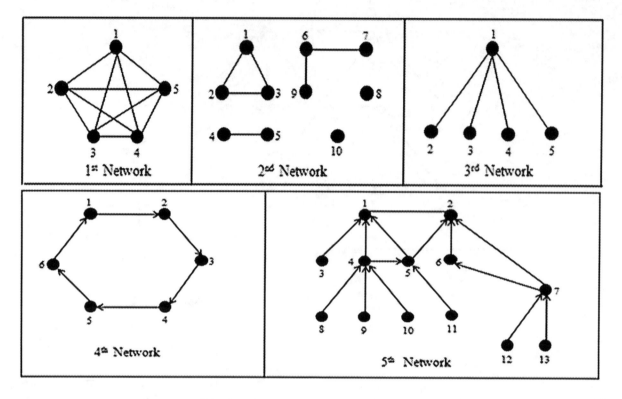

Figure 49. Three different patterns

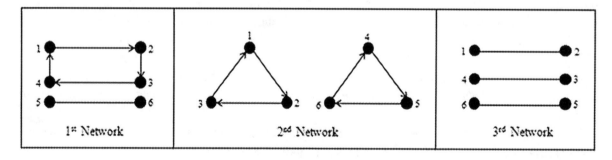

remaining five and only one of the remaining five comes to it. If we impose this condition further, there three other patterns possible besides that the 4th network of the same figure. These patterns are:

From the figure mentioned in Figure 49, we understand that a few parameters cannot determine completely the structure of a social network.

AUTHORS OBSERVATIONS AND PREDICTIONS

Considering a state is one large community graph. The authors combine India's 29 states together to form a very large community graph (Rao and Mitra, Oct-2014, Dec-2014).

From such a large community graph (Rao and Mitra, 2014) - how big data can be mined so that the standard of living of a particular community can be analyzed? For this we can apply distributed mining technique to discover the very big data which is in *4V*. From it the authors try to select the desired itemset so that prediction can be taken place on those big data.

A Brief Case Study on Application of Big Data on Social Media

Social Media usages among its consumers are growing at exponential pace thus resulting in huge amount of data created at every minute. General users are no more restricted in using the Internet, rather usage of Smart phones', location based apps and other Internet of Things, has lead to generation of data in a much faster pace. Looking at the basic statistics on the social data growth, one can easily observe that more than 250 million tweets are generated in a day and it is increasing at a high speed. Further, at an average of 30 billion pieces of content are shared on Facebook per month. It is predicted that data will grow over 800% in the next 5 years and 80% of these data will be unstructured (Infosys, 2013).

While handling such huge volumes of data is big challenge as well as it also provides numerous opportunities and competitive edge for the enterprises to acquire, store and manage the data for information and knowledge extraction. Thus, the need for a robust platform is a necessity, which cans efficient handle hardware challenges that are common in case of Big Data.

A high performance scalable architecture is essential component of the infrastructure for processing big data. Segregating or storing the unstructured data from different sources within minimum response time for query processing with accuracy remains a software challenge for such an environment. Providing security and safety and thus extracting pattern, meaning or sense from the huge stored data is the ultimate challenge for the big data environment.

The analysis of Big Data will help in combining social media data streams with enterprise applications in a powerful way to derive meaningful insights on the social conversations. Progress can be made in analysis the opinion and sentiments employee based on their interaction with social media.

Further, the developed analysis agent can be build so as it can process huge volume of data at a higher speed and can identify sentiment, buzzword, predictive, correlation and influencer data.

The knowledge extracted from analysis of big data of social media has many important advantages. The organization can easily detect and respond to a social outburst before negative sentiments go viral in the social world. Decisions can be easily taken after analysing the customer's sentiments and purchase pattern. Identifying and engaging key influencers who are impacting the increase or decrease of sales is now easy, as the decision is based on the information extracted from the huge data.

CONCLUSION

The initial sections of this chapter give an overview of modeling basic representation of social network using the concepts of graph theory, especially using digraphs. Foundation of graph mining has been discussed thoroughly. Two existing examples from social network background have been considered and proposed social community networks have been represented using the graph theoretic concepts to focus on the discussed concepts. A brief outlining on the process and steps for extracting knowledge by using graph mining techniques has been mentioned.

Community network can be analyzed using the concepts of graph technique, especially incidence matrix of an undirected graph. Further, the chapter gives an overview on various representation techniques for any graphs.

Breadth-first search (or simply BFS) is used in Apriori-based approach for generating level-wise candidate. The authors have studied earlier algorithm and have proposed the present technique, which is also based on Apriori-based approach. The authors have observed that the proposed technique by them is little bit efficient compared to the earlier algorithms. The derived properties with the proposed techniques work perfectly on specific cases. The related sample output and have hence justified. An example of social community graph of undirected kind is considered for better understanding. Further, literature on community detection followed by technique for detection of community with example from social network background has been discussed using the graph theoretic concepts. Thus extraction of knowledge i.e. particular community detection as well as isolated communities by using graph mining techniques is achieved.

Sub-structures are helpful for analysis and extraction of information. The related sections discussed on merging of sub-structures to form a larger structure which can be used for information extraction. Further, authors have proposed three algorithms which merge two community sub-graphs in an efficient and simpler manner. The first algorithm explains about finding the order of merged communities and to make available of initial form of merged community matrix, the second one explains about creation of adjacency matrix community graph and the third one uses the adjacency matrices of community graph and explains about creation of merged community adjacency matrix. Stepwise implementation of proposed algorithms and obtained satisfactory and acceptable results are presented.

Fundamental concepts of big data and its characteristics have been discussed as a case study. This part of the chapter is conclusive in nature and focuses on issues of Graph Analytics and its applications in Big Data

REFERENCES

Abello, J., Resende, M. G. C., & Sudarsky, S. (2002). Massive quasi-clique detection. doi:10.1007/3-540-45995-2_51

Agrawal, R., & Srikant, R. (1994). Fast algorithms for mining association rules. In *Proceedings of 1994 International Conference Very Large Data Bases* (VLDB'94).

Bandyopadhyay, S., Sinha, & Rao. (2006). Social Network Analysis, a handbook. Sage Publications Inc.

Batagelj, V., & Mrvar, A. P. (2003). Analysis and visualization of large networks. In M. Junger & P. Mutzel (Eds.), Graph Drawing Software. Springer Verlag.

Berendt, B. (2005). The semantics of frequent subgraphs: Mining and navigation pattern analysis. In Proceedings of WebKDD. Chicago: Academic Press.

Berners-Lee, T., Hendler, J., & Lassila, O. (2001). The semantic Web. *Scientific American*, *279*(5), 34–43. doi:10.1038/scientificamerican0501-34 PMID:11681174

Borgelt, C., & Berthold, M. R. (2002). Mining molecular fragments:Finding relevant substructures of molecules. In *Proceedings of 2002 International Conference on Data Mining* (ICDM'02). Academic Press.

Brandes, U., & Erlebach, T. (Eds.). (2005). Network Analysis: Methodological Foundations. Lecture Notes in Computer Science, 3418.

Brandes, U., Kenis, P., & Wagner, D. (2003). Communicating centrality in policy network drawings. *IEEE Transactions on Visualization and Computer Graphics, 9*(2), 241–253. doi:10.1109/TVCG.2003.1196010

Brandes, U., & Wagner Visone, D. (2003). Analysis and visualization of social networks. In M. Junger & P. Mutzel (Eds.), *Graph Drawing Software* (pp. 321–340). Berlin: Springer Verlag.

Broder, A., Kumar, R., Maghoul, F., Raghavan, P., Rajagopalan, S., Stat, R., & Tomkins, A. (2000). Graph Structure in the Web: Experiments and models. In *Proceedings of the World Wide Web Conference*. Amsterdam, The Netherlands: Academic Press. doi:10.1016/S1389-1286(00)00083-9

Bunke, H. (1997). On a Relation between Graph Edit Distance and Maximum Common Subgraph. *Pattern Recognition Letters, 18*(8), 689–694. doi:10.1016/S0167-8655(97)00060-3

Chakrabarti, S. (2000). Data mining for hypertext: A tutorial survey. *SIGKDD Explorations, 1*(2), 1–11. doi:10.1145/846183.846187

Clauset, A., Mewman, M., & Moore, C. (2004). *Finding community structure in very large networks*. Arxiv preprint cond-mat/0408187.

Clauset, A., Moore, C., & Newman, M. E. J. (2008). Hierarchical structure and the prediction of missing links in networks. *Nature, 453*(7191), 98–101. doi:10.1038/nature06830 PMID:18451861

Cook & Holder. (2007). Mining Graph Data, Electrical Engineering and Computer Science. John Wiley & Sons, Inc.

Cordella, L. P., Foggia, P., Sansone, C., & Vento, M. (2001). An improved algorithm for matching large graphs. In *Proceedings of the 3rd IAPR-TC-15 International Workshop on Graph-based Representations*.

Corneil, D. G., & Gotlieb, C. C. (1970). An efficient algorithm for graph isomorphism. *Journal of the ACM, 17*(1), 51–64. doi:10.1145/321556.321562

Desikan, P., & Srivastava, J. (2004). Mining Temporally Evolving Graphs. In Proceedings of WebKDD.

Diestel, R. (2000). *Graph Theory*. New York: Springer.

Dumbill, E. (2012). *What is big data?* [Online] Available from: http: //radar. oreilly.com /2012/01/what-is-big-data.html

Etzioni, O. (1996). The World Wide Web: Quagmire or Gold Mine? *Communications of the ACM, 39*(11), 65–68. doi:10.1145/240455.240473

Goldenberg, A., & Moore, A. (2004). Tractable learning of large Bayes net structures from sparse data. In *Proceedings of the 6th International Conference on Machine Learning*. doi:10.1145/1015330.1015406

Han, J., Pei, J., & Yin, Y. (2000). Mining frequent patterns without candidate generation. In *Proceedings of 2000 ACM-SIGMOD International Conference on Management of Data* (SIGMOD'00). Dallas, TX: ACM.

Holder, L. B., Cook, D. J., & Djoko, S. (1994). Substructure discovery in the subdue system. In *Proceedings of AAAI'94 Workshop Knowledge Discovery in Databases* (KDD'94). Seattle, WA: AAAI.

Huan, J., Wang, W., & Prins, J. (2003). Efficient Mining of Frequent Subgraph in the Presence of Isomorphism. In *Proceedings of 2003 International Conference on Data Mining* (ICDM'03). doi:10.1109/ICDM.2003.1250974

IEEE. (2014). ieee.bigdata.tutorial.1.1slides.pdf. IEEE.

Infosys. (2013). *Infosys – Connect Architecture, Big Data Spectrum*. Infosys Ltd.

Inokuchi, A., Washio, T., & Motoda, H. (2000). An apriori-based algorithm for mining frequent substructures from graph data. In *Proceedings of 2000 European Symposium Principle of Data Mining and Knowledge Discovery* (PKDD'00). doi:10.1007/3-540-45372-5_2

Jensen, D., & Neville, J. (2002). *Data Mining in Social Networks*. Paper presented at the Workshop on Dynamic Social Network Modeling and Analysis, Washington, DC.

Kleinberg, J., & Lawrence, S. (2001). The Structure of the Web. *Science*, 294–322. PMID:11729296

Kleinberg, J. M. (1999). Authoritative sources in a hyperlinked environment. *Journal of the ACM*, *46*(5), 604–632. doi:10.1145/324133.324140

Kolari, P., & Joshi, A. (2004). Web mining: Research and Practice. *IEEE Computational Science & Engineering*, *6*(4), 49–53. doi:10.1109/MCSE.2004.23

Kubica, J., Goldenberg, A., Komarek, P., & Moore, A. (2003). A comparison of statistical and machine learning algorithms on the task of link completion. In *Proceedings of the KDD Workshop on Link Analysis for Detecting Complex Behavior*.

Kumar, R., Novak, J., & Tomkins, A. (2006). Structure and evolution of online social networks. In *KDD '06: Proceedings of the 12th ACM SIGKDD international conference on Knowledge discovery and data mining*. New York: ACM. doi:10.1145/1150402.1150476

Kumar, R., Raghavan, P., Rajagopalan, S., & Tomkins, A. (1999). Trawling the web for emerging cyber-communities. *Computer Networks*, *31*(11-16), 1481–1493. doi:10.1016/S1389-1286(99)00040-7

Kuramochi, M., & Karypis, G. (2001). Frequent Subgraph Discovery. In *Proceedings of 2001 International Conference on Data Mining* (ICDM'01). doi:10.1109/ICDM.2001.989534

LaPaugh, A. S., & Rivest, R. R. (1978). *The subgraph homeomorphism problem. Annual ACM Symposium on Theory of Computing, Proceedings of the tenth annual symposium on Theory of Computing*, San Diego, CA.

Lipschutz, S. (1997). Schaum's outline on Data Structures. Tata McGraw-Hill Publishing Company Limited.

Maniam, A. (2004). *Graph-based click-stream mining for categorizing browsing activity in the World Wide Web*. (Master's Thesis). University of Texas at Arlington.

Manyika, J. (2014). *Big data: The next frontier for innovation, competition, and productivity*. Retrieved from http://www.mckinsey.com/insights/mgi/research/technology_and_innovation/big_data_the_next_frontier_for_innovation

McEneaney, J. E. (2001). Graphic and Numerical Methods to assess Navigation in Hypertext. *International Journal of Human-Computer Studies*, 55(5), 761–786. doi:10.1006/ijhc.2001.0505

Mendelzon, A., Michaila, G., & Milo, T. (1996). Querying the WWW. In *Proceedings of the International Conference on Parallel and Distributed Information Systems*, (pp. 80–91). Academic Press.

Meo, R., Lanzi, P. L., Matera, M., & Esposito, R. (2004). Integrating web conceptual modelling and web usage mining. In Proceedings of WebKDD.

Messmer, B. T. (1995). *Efficient Graph Matching Algorithms for Pre-Processed Model Graphs*. (Ph.D. Thesis). Institut fur Informatik und Angewandte Matheatik, Universitat Bern, Switzerland.

Moy, M. (2005). Using TMODS to run the Best Friends Group Detection Algorithm. 21st Century Technologies Internal Publication.

Newman, M., & Girvan, M. (2004). Finding and evaluating community structure in networks. *Physical Review E: Statistical, Nonlinear, and Soft Matter Physics*, 69, 26–113. PMID:14995526

Nijssen, S., & Kok, J. A. (2004). Quickstart in frequent structure mining can make a difference. In *Proceedings of 2004 ACM SIGKDD International Conference on Knowledge Discovery in Databases* (KDD'04). Seattle, WA: ACM.

Prins, J., Yang, J., Huan, J., & Wang, W. (2004). Spin: Mining maximal frequent subgraphs from graph databases. In *Proceedings of 2004 ACM SIGKDD International Conference on Knowledge Discovery in Databases* (KDD'04). Seattle, WA: ACM.

Rao, B., & Mitra, A. (2014b). A new approach for detection of common communities in a social network using graph mining techniques. In *High Performance Computing and Applications (ICHPCA), 2014 International Conference on*. doi: .2014.7045335 doi:10.1109/ICHPCA

Rao, B., & Mitra, A. (2014a). *An approach to study properties and behavior of Social Network using Graph Mining Techniques*. In DIGNATE 2014: ETEECT 2014, India.

Rao, B., & Mitra, A. (2014c). An Approach to Merging of two Community Sub-Graphs to form a Community Graph using Graph Mining Techniques. *2014 IEEE International Conference on Computational Intelligence and Computing Research* (ICCIC-2014). IEEE.

Rao, B., & Mitra, A. (2014d). *An Approach of Mining Big-Data from a very large community graph for analysing of economic standard of communities using Distributed Mining Techniques*. CCSN 2014, Puri, India.

Ravasz, E., & Barabasi, A.-L. (2003). Hierarchical Organization In Complex Networks. *Physical Review*, 67. PMID:12636753

Riesen, K., Jiang, X., & Bunke, H. (2010). Exact and Inexact Graph Matching: Methodology and Applications. In Managing and Mining Graph Data. Academic Press.

Srivastava, J., Cooley, R., Deshpande, M., & Tan, P.-N. (2000). Web usage mining: Discovery and applications of usage patterns from web data. *SIGKDD Explorations*, *1*(2), 1–12. doi:10.1145/846183.846188

Tripathy, B. K., & Mitra, A. (2012). An algorithm to achieve k-anonymity and l-diversity anonymisation in social networks. IEEE – CASoN, Brazil. doi:10.1109/CASoN.2012.6412390

Vanetik, N., Gudes, E., & Shimony, S. E. (2002). Computing Frequent Graph Patterns from Semistructured Data. In *Proceedings of 2002 International Conference on Data Mining* (ICDM'02). doi:10.1109/ICDM.2002.1183988

Vismara, L., Di Battista, G., Garg, A., Liotta, G., Tamassia, R., & Vargiu, F. (2000). Experimental studies on graph drawing algorithms. *Software, Practice & Experience*, *30*(11), 1235–1284. doi:10.1002/1097-024X(200009)30:11<1235::AID-SPE339>3.0.CO;2-B

Weiss, R., Velez, B., & Sheldon, M. (1996). HyPursuit: A hierarchical network search engine that exploits context-link hypertext clustering. In *Proceedings of the Conference on Hypertext and Hypermedia*. doi:10.1145/234828.234846

Yan, X., & Han, J. (2002). gSpan: Graph-based substructure pattern mining. In *Proceedings of 2002 International Conference on Data Mining* (ICDM'02).

Yan, X., Zhou, X. J., & Han, J. (2005). Mining closed relational graphs with connectivity constraints. In *Proceedings of 2005, ACM SIGKDD International Conference on Knowledge Discovery in Databases* (KDD'05). doi:10.1145/1081870.1081908

Zaiane, O. R., & Han, J. (1995). Resource and knowledge discovery in global information systems: A preliminary design and experiment. In *Proceedings of the 2nd International Conference on Knowledge Discovery and Data Mining*.

Zaki, M. J. (2002). Efficiently Mining Frequent Trees in a Forest. In *Proceedings of the 7th International Conference on Knowledge Discovery and Data Mining*. doi:10.1145/775047.775058

Section 2
Knowledge Management Approaches and Innovation Process

Chapter 6
Implementing KM Lessons from the Frontline

Rusnita Saleh
University of Indonesia, Indonesia

Niall Sinclair
Independent Researcher, Thailand

ABSTRACT

While the KM initiative highlighted in the case study in the previous section is still in its formative stages, it would be safe to say that the majority of KM implementation projects are likely to take anywhere between one to three years to even begin to have any significant impact on the organizations involved. In other words, KM is something that takes time to embed itself into the working fabric of the organization, and so anyone who thinks that KM implementation is going to be a short-term affair is fooling themselves; as well as setting a dangerous and unattainable level of expectation in any potential stakeholders. Overall, there are many barriers that stand in the way of successfully implementing KM, whether it is a lack of access to current information, a lack of clear communications, difficulty in transferring knowledge and information, difficulty in maintaining the relevance and currency of knowledge and information, lack of support from senior managers, or limited resources – both in time and personnel.

1. BACKGROUND

Every organization which attempts to implement knowledge management (KM) faces a unique challenge. There are many obstacles, both organizationally as well as individually, facing those who are tasked with embedding KM into the working fabric of any organization. However, after decades of such implementations it is apparent that certain issues remain constant, and certain outcomes appear to happen on a regular basis, if not always exactly duplicating previous outcomes. So, what are the key issues that need to be recognized, planned for, and dealt with when undertaking a KM initiative, and will describing them prove to be of use to those preparing to take on the challenge of implementing KM-based organizational change? The answer of course is yes, but a yes with a caveat: that caveat being that all business-related lessons are context-specific, and maybe more importantly, no context ever

DOI: 10.4018/978-1-4666-9607-5.ch006

exactly duplicates a previous one. Why is this so important? Because, no two environments are ever the same, each organization, and indeed each individual employee within each organization, functions in a different way, with different objectives and different motivations, both personal as well as business, dictating their preferences and actions.

However, whatever the business circumstances of the organization and environment you work in, there are two key pieces of information you simply must know if you want to implement KM successfully. The first is exactly what KM actually means to the organization you are trying to implement it in, and the second is what will succeed for that organization within its own business context and environment. In other words, you need to find out what works!

Therefore, this chapter is mainly focused on helping KM practitioners to find out what usually works in KM implementations and why it works. It contains insights based on 20 years of real-world experience in implementing KM in numerous private and public organizations in a variety of countries and cultures on three different continents (Europe, North America and Asia) around the world.

2. THE REALITY CHECK

The items in this section provide an overview of some crucial organizational issues that need to be recognized and planned for in KM initiatives; and together they should provide a useful checklist of items which KM practitioners need to be aware of if they want to avoid some of the more obvious pitfalls awaiting them during KM implementation projects.

Although no two business environments are ever a complete match, all of the following issues are quite likely to be repeated in any working environment where KM implementation is going on. Why? Because they are all linked by that most over-riding of driving forces behind all organizational decision-making and commitments to change; that is, human nature itself.

So, based on this context, here in no particular order are 8 issues you need to be aware of before you start planning and implementing any KM initiatives.

a. What Is KM Exactly, And Does It Really Matter What It Is?

If someone asked you what KM is, you'd probably be able to reel off an answer pretty quickly. Now repeat that question with every individual and organization you encounter, and soon the number of answers is multiplying fast into the hundreds, thousands and tens of thousands of definitions. In fact if you Google the question 'what is knowledge management?' you'll get something like 15 million responses. So, which is the right definition? The answer is simple, they all are!

In his book 'Stealth KM: Winning Knowledge Management Strategies for the Public Sector', Niall Sinclair (2006) devotes a whole section to describing what he calls the 'definitional warfare' surrounding the term KM. 10 years later and nothing much seems to have changed and you will still find the same kind of warfare going on, and the same types of individuals promoting the same types of views about what KM is, or isn't. In fact, these types of individuals do know what KM is, at least from their own perspective, but then so does anyone else who has an interest in the topic and sees it through an entirely different lens. So, the first lesson any smart KM practitioner should learn is that KM is way too broad and way too deep to ever be constricted by a singular view of what it is, and how it should function.

Probably the worst mistake any practitioner charged with implementing KM can make is to assume that they know the answer to the question 'What is KM?', particularly as it relates to the organization they are trying to implement it in. And yet you'd be amazed at just how may do exactly that before even finding out how the organization works and what is actually important to it! So, if you're ever asked the question, especially in front of a group of senior managers, then the best response is to say that it doesn't matter what you think it is, it's what the organization thinks it should be that's important. However, you can say that the objective of KM work is to help facilitate the creation, collection, sharing and re-use of useful organizational knowledge. That is a basic overview which can be used as a baseline position for strategy and planning purposes, yet leaves plenty of room for organizations to create and refine actual KM processes and procedures in a way which suits them best. In other words, flexibility is a key attribute of successful KM initiatives.

Based on this context, the starting point of any KM initiative should really be a period of evaluation where what KM actually means to the organization is being assessed; and this needs to happen long before any actual KM-related work activity is even contemplated. It's amazing just how profound a step this is, and how often KM practitioners fail to grasp its significance. What comes out of this exercise is not just a better understanding of how people and teams view what knowledge is actually important to them, but also the background information necessary to address strategy, planning and communication issues surrounding the best use of KM in support of the organization's business goals and objectives.

However, there is a difference between understanding all of the various organizational views and definitions of KM and actually trying to address them all in an implementation plan. The reality is that if you try and accommodate everything you'll likely spread your efforts way too thin, and probably end up not changing much of anything. Therefore, the real point of the assessment exercise is to help inform the priorities and choices of those attempting to implement KM, so that they are able to recognize key organizational targets which KM can align with and provide support to. Without this alignment KM will struggle to establish any organizational traction, and more importantly, any sense of relevance to the workforce.

Key Take-Away Item

Don't get sucked into the KM definitional wars. Get to understand what KM means to the organization and why and where they see it as being important, and strategize, plan and implement KM activities in that context.

b. Three Times the Fun

Because of the ever-changing nature of the KM landscape, many organizations are becoming confused as to what exactly KM is anymore, and where exactly they should focus their efforts if they want to implement KM successfully.

It's obvious that over the last few years a new paradigm for KM has emerged, one with a focus on the individual rather than on the organization. New technologies have caught up with the real requirements of knowledge workers and personal computing is now the norm, not the exception. As well, there have been enormous changes in the working demographic as new generations (Y's and Millennials) of workers have entered the workforce, and brought with them an entirely new understanding of how technology should work (i.e. for them) and new attitudes about how and why the work environment should allow them to use technology in the same way that they use it in their social environment.

Because of this evolution, the reality of today's working environment means that there is no longer just one version of KM which needs to be considered and planned for. In fact, KM has evolved into three distinct business varieties, each with its own individual operational characteristics. These three types of KM are:

1. Personally-based KM; or PKM (Personal KM) as it is known.
2. Community-based KM.
3. Organizationally-based KM; or Corporate KM as it is known.

All of which means there may well have to be some re-assessment by many organizations as to what type of KM they have actually invested in, or want to invest in, and how they can maximize that investment. So, to help KM practitioners to understand and plan for this environment, here's a quick overview of these three types of KM, and some of the issues and opportunities associated with them.

1. Personal KM

The advent of more personalized technology offerings such as Twitter, and the uses that many of today's workforce have for such technology, has supported an increase in the growth of a more personalized version of KM. The search for, and use of, knowledge through social media tools has become a reality for the modern knowledge worker.

The main challenge that PKM presents to an organization is in how to manage to support the individual employee's knowledge needs whilst still ensuring that they are being a team-player and remaining compliant to corporate guidance and requirements for knowledge-based activities. *The bottom line here is that organizations will always prioritize security over individuality, so PKM will likely be viewed with suspicion from a corporate standpoint.*

2. Community KM

Communities (of Practice, Interest etc.) were the beneficiaries of the initial wave of KM technologies, with group-ware, inter-active online management tools, threaded discussion tools, and many others, providing a sound platform for the propagation and management of expert groups and communities. This is where the roots of KM have taken hold, and is where the discipline of KM is best represented in most organizations.

Indeed, knowledgeable individuals have always formed specialist areas of organizational expertise, and have been the guardians of corporate wisdom and corporate continuity long before the advent of KM and the label of communities of practice became popular. It is no wonder then that this layer of community and social networks is a fertile ground for KM activity, and will remain the bed-rock of many organizational KM efforts.

The main challenge of Community KM for organizations is how best to create, coordinate and promote knowledge not only for the benefit of the community itself, but to the benefit of the organization as a whole.

The bottom line here is that many managers overlook and underestimate the power of communities when initiating KM projects. In fact communities are the real custodians of important corporate knowledge and with a little help they can play a key role in creating, sustaining and sharing important knowledge throughout the organization.

3. Corporate KM

Most of the larger KM efforts are still focused at this corporate level, with many senior managers (especially in the public sector) seeing KM as just another program-sized endeavour, to be planned for and managed at that scale. However, the larger the scale of work, the greater the likelihood of over-commitment, and the more fraught with dangers the work becomes as it progresses. Based on this reality, many organizations have begun to step back from this all-or-nothing mentality, yet still tend to see KM as solely an enterprise-level activity, and consequently struggle to implement it and make it relevant to their workforce. The problem for many organizations is that with all the added KM complexity now in play, they are unsure if they have invested wisely to date, and whether they can still benefit from what they have already done or will now need to start all over again. Despite these concerns, there has of course already been significant investment in corporate KM activity, and there is still an expectation that KM can play a valuable role in helping individuals and organizations to better achieve their business goals and objectives.

Of course there is no reason why Corporate KM initiatives can't succeed, especially where there is a strong leader involved, and/or an easily defined and measurable pay-back (as in some private sector organizations with clear goals and an unrestricted pathway to changing working models and attitudes quickly).

The real challenge of corporate-level KM for organizations is how to keep it relevant at both a corporate and individual level, and how to manage and maintain it in a way that allows for the inevitable fluctuations in business focus and commitment to it, both from individual employees as well as senior managers.

Each of the three KM domains has a unique dynamic that drives it, and a unique set of needs associated with the work it does. Once this is understood, it is possible to plan for and maintain a more robust KM environment, one with a working balance in place between the various interests and objectives involved.

The bottom line here is that most organizations still have a top-down mindset, whereas a bottom-up operational model suits KM better.

Key Take-Away Item

KM begins at the individual level, flourishes at the grass-roots or community level, and struggles to remain relevant at the enterprise level; and as Community KM is the glue that holds everything together organizationally, it's there that you need to provide the maximum encouragement and support.

c. Are Lessons Learned and Best Practices a Waste of Time?

It has become something of a received truth that knowing about the lessons learned and best practices of other organizations should be an important component of any KM initiative. The case for extraneous lessons and practices being of such importance is often voiced by those who have never actually had

Implementing KM Lessons from the Frontline

to implement KM in an organization themselves, academics or executives newly tasked with delivery of KM change for example. However, the reality is that while some external lessons and practices may indeed have value, the vast majority of them are of little, if any, real value to those looking at them from a later viewpoint. Why is this, and perhaps more importantly, what are the lessons and practices that are really worth learning from?

Firstly, it all depends what kind of an operational model you are dealing with as an organization. If you are looking at external lessons and practices from a tactical standpoint, for example in trying to improve a repetitive and stable process such as product delivery or dealing with customer queries in call centres, then finding out how others have dealt with similar issues and responded to them successfully may well prove valuable to you for planning and training purposes. However, if you are looking at external lessons and practices from a purely strategic standpoint, trying to find out how an organization planned for and implemented KM for example, then the likelihood is that you will find a lot less of value. Why should this be? Well, primarily because lessons and practices are context specific and that means that the chances of being able to repeat that exact same context are low at best. Every organization operates differently, with a different culture and operational model which influences and directs its actions. More importantly, every organization is comprised of individuals who have differing methods of working and differing rationales for their interests and likes. As a result, trying to apply the results of lessons and practices from one organization into another organization may well prove to be difficult at best, and may be a completely unnecessary drain on resources and time at worst.

All of which doesn't mean you can't find value in others' lessons and practices, but keep an open mind about just how effectively you can emulate them. In fact, the reality of others' lessons and practices is that you may have to really dig out the pieces that may be relevant to you, rather than being able to assimilate everything in one piece. The real value in examining external lessons and practices may prove to be that they can help you to find some proven approaches and guiding principles which you can then apply to your own KM planning and implementation decisions. At the same time, don't forget that knowing what others didn't do, or even how they have failed, can be useful to you as well. In fact, knowing what you definitely don't want to do may eventually prove to be a more useful tool to you than knowing what you might want to do is!

The bottom line here is that external lessons and practices should be treated with caution, unless there is an obvious and seamless fit into the operational requirements of the organization.

Key Take-Away Item

Don't spend a lot of time trying to learn from external lessons and practices, rather focus on capturing important internal lessons and practices which are specific to your own organization and ensure that they get captured, shared, and most importantly, updated, in order to keep them relevant and useful.

d. Think Small

Whoever it was that first coined the phrase 'small is beautiful' must have had KM in mind. If any of you has had the experience of trying to implement KM in a large organization, say of 30,000 people, then you will no doubt wholeheartedly echo my sentiments and hopefully feel my pain!

Not that there's anything wrong in thinking big, in fact most KM initiatives have probably sprung from someone's ability to see the big picture. However, there is a world of difference between being able to see the big picture and being able to fit KM neatly into that big picture.

Most executives and managers feel comfortable in running large enterprise-scale programs, which are often quite well aligned with KM, such as IT projects or information management for example. So, it is quite natural that senior managers expect that once they have initiated KM it should perform and be managed in the same way as every other program that they are in charge of. The reality of course is that KM just doesn't conform to such narrow definitional parameters and tends to work in reverse to what managers are used to, that is, it begins at the individual level, flourishes at a community level and may need little actual management control over it in order to gain organizational traction.

All of which presents a challenge; how are you going to get management support for something which itself appears to be a challenge to their very sense of how a program should work? Well, here are some ideas to get you started:

1. Never pitch KM as being a new way of doing business, or as a solution to the operational problems the organization faces. Rather pitch KM as being something which the organization has always done, but now needs a more structured approach (i.e. the discipline of KM) to in order to be better managed. Usually, a good example of this can be shown in how the knowledge created by expert groups and communities/teams has always played a key role in business operations, but has previously not been connected and leveraged for the advantage of the organization as a whole.

2. Never ever pitch KM as being a primary business function, such as IT, but rather always pitch it as being a primary support function, without which the key business functions of the organization won't operate as well as they should. In this way you can easily align KM to whatever key business functions the senior managers care about (almost certainly not KM!) and are responsible for. This was exactly the organizational situation which leads to 'Stealth KM' being written. After having tried to manage KM as a full-blown program for a while it became apparent that there was just no real organizational traction being achieved. The answer was to re-focus KM as a support function at a business unit (rather than enterprise) level, finding out what was important to line managers and providing support to their individual teams and objectives. In this way organizational momentum was gathered through localized partnerships. All of which remained mostly invisible to the senior managers, hence the birth of the Stealth KM descriptor.

The main challenge with the Stealth approach is that it can be fairly labour intensive, at least to begin with, as you have to focus on individual problems rather than the big picture one. However, a train the trainer approach where individuals in each business unit being dealt with are identified and given KM coordination and liaison responsibilities, will help ease the demands once the initial work has been completed. The long-term goal of this approach being to create a whole group of self-managed KM-focused units within the organization. This is the essence of the small is beautiful view of KM implementation.

3. Manage the small KM-related projects/partnerships and don't worry too much about the big picture. As long as you can highlight the high-level goals and objectives of the KM initiative, greater sharing and usage of knowledge for example, for senior managers, they shouldn't worry too much about the details of what you're doing. They'll be more interested in results, and for that you can use the line managers you are working with to showcase the benefits of KM to the rest of the organization.

The bottom line here is that keeping the objectives and scope of any KM initiative as small as is realistically possible will give it the best chance of being successful.

Key Take-Away Item

It's far better to under-promise and over-deliver than the other way round, so make sure you pitch KM at the appropriate level and above all ensure that senior manager's expectation levels are managed and kept realistic.

e. Build It and They Probably Won't Come

The early KM implementations often came with a heavy technology wrapper attached to them, usually a new IT infrastructure of some sort such as an organizational knowledge repository or similar type of database. In the beginning it all seemed so simple. Build a KM system and people will see the benefits of using it. In other words, build it and they will come. Unfortunately, this scenario tells you more about the dominance of IT thinking within organizations over the last forty years, than it does about their ability to understand that a fundamental change has occurred in the working environment during that time. That change being that it is abundantly clear that the best and most viable and sustainable KM systems are those built from the ground up and not those imposed from the top down any more.

One large multi-national consulting agency in Canada in the early 2000's spent over a million dollars building a huge repository of organizational knowledge only to find that few, if any, employees actually used it after it went online. The post mortem revealed that while the project was fueled by good intentions it was also fueled by an IT mindset which believed that building something so all-encompassing would guarantee its usefulness to the workforce. It also became apparent that building something which people hadn't asked for, and which they had no influence over by way of identifying what their real needs were, was a recipe for disaster; a very costly disaster in this instance.

The lesson was/is obvious; it's not so much the scale and type of technology that's used that's the problem, it's the assumption that if you build something that will be of benefit to people then they will use it. This lesson is as relevant today as it ever was, people will only use a new KM-related technology if (a) they were involved in identifying the need for it in the first place, and (b) were involved in all the phases of its scoping and developing; and even then there may only be a very small number of committed users of what has been developed! So, if you are thinking of building and deploying a new KM technology tool, think about the pros and cons of doing so very hard before you get in too deep.

Whether you are planning a new technology roll-out or not, it is a fact that most people like to communicate with each other, and to share their knowledge with others. But it is also a fact that most people don't generally want to manage that knowledge in an overly formal or structured way. So, go into any technology evaluation and rollout plan with that thought foremost in your mind. The new wave of IT tools will allow for more knowledge to be created and shared, but will likely lead to less time or willingness by users to follow structured rules for managing content. People just don't keep everything, so it is imperative that if organizations deploy new KM technology, they accompany that deployment with some sort of guidance as to what is important, and what should/must be kept. That implies that we can finally dispense with the notion that we should keep what we have in order to understand what we know. The 'let's put everything into a repository for future reference' mindset has led to an overload of corporate information, most of which will never be accessed or used. From a corporate perspective, it is really all about devoting the necessary time and resources to understanding what is important knowledge, and more importantly, what isn't, and in finding out what really needs to be retained and disseminated. Accordingly, organizations need to decide just how much of their knowledge needs to be 'managed' (i.e.

maintained centrally) and how much just 'is' and will remain that way. Above all, organizations need to be flexible in their approach to community based tools, such as intranets and wikis. Trying to impose strict IT-centred rule-based approaches to managing these types of platforms is likely to result in low take-up and lack of community ownership. However, allowing a more de-centralized and community-based approach to managing and maintaining the platform will likely lead to a higher take-up rate and a more dedicated user base.

The bottom line here is that you need to exercise caution before committing to any organization-wide KM-related technology rollout. If there is an overwhelming business imperative for it, or its been mandated by the senior manager(s) then you should already have the traction needed, but if not, then you need to work out exactly what the user community's needs really are, and exactly how much of a commitment they have to what you are proposing. Otherwise you may be in for a tough time trying to get any meaningful take-up for the proposed new technology.

Key Take-Away Item

Exercise caution before implementing new KM-related technology; and if a decision has already been taken to implement it, then strongly advocate a limited trial deployment, often called a pilot project, in order to assess the real state of community commitment and take-up. Above all, use the pilot phase as a way to gather user feedback on their likes and dislikes of the technology, and then ensure that such feedback gets acted on before any further deployment is contemplated. This assessment period can also be used as a means to shut down the rollout (this option is often referred to as the 'off-ramp') if it becomes necessary due to negative community reaction.

f. The Most Important Question in the KM Universe

If someone asked you, 'what is the most important question you need to be able to answer if you want to implement KM successfully', what would your answer be? I imagine that everyone who was asked this question would probably have a different answer. However, every one of those answering would also have filtered that question through their own personal perspectives before answering. It is human nature to look at the world this way, and therein lays the clue to what is the most important question you will need to be able to answer if you want to be successful at implementing KM.

In the end, the success of any KM initiative is dependent on just one overriding factor, and that is the willingness of those individuals impacted by the initiative to make a commitment to the methods and objectives of the project.

Without this human connection and commitment all the stated goals and hoped-for benefits of the initiative are not going to be achieved. This holds true for any business project of course, but is of particular significance to knowledge management projects, as they are usually attempting to bring a new dimension of business discipline (KM) into an organization. And this is where the biggest challenge to a successful KM implementation lies; how can you expect individuals to agree to something which seems to imply significant change, a new set of responsibilities, and a possible additional workload is coming their way?

In fact, if you want to succeed with any KM implementation plan then you need to be ready and able to answers three fundamental questions, and these are:

1. What are You Planning to Do?

This question may come in many guises: maybe in a direct question from a senior management team or perhaps in a casual remark from someone over a coffee. Either way, you had better be prepared to provide a reply that captures the heart of what you are trying to do, the goals and objectives, as well as how you are planning to do it, the outputs and outcomes you are expecting to achieve. And all of this in a format which is both short and to the point, and above all, is easy to understand. One way to gauge if you have got such an overview ready is whether you can give it to a complete stranger, and preferably someone who has no previous knowledge of KM, and they are fully able to understand it. If however you don't feel you are able to provide such an easily understood overview, then quite frankly you're not ready to start your project!

2. What Do You Want/Expect Me To Do?

The second fundamental question deals with your preparedness to provide a more detailed assessment of what you are planning to do, and is directly fuelled by that most human of reactions, fear! Why fear? Because, everyone whom your project is likely to impact on will have exactly the same initial mental reaction, "I hope this doesn't mean more work for me!" This is basic human nature, and even if you don't hear it expressed openly you can be assured that it is there beneath the surface.

So, the answer to this question needs to be carefully thought through, as it is both an opportunity as well as a potential hazard. If you itemize a long list of expected outcomes then that will automatically equate to a long list of new work in most people's mind, and you will already have created a negative impression on the very people you will need to be relying on for your success. On the other hand, if you don't have a clear idea of what's going to be expected of employees then your project will be seen as lightweight and unimportant.

The best approach is to promote any targeted KM activity as being an extension of work already being undertaken by employees, rather than it being an additional work overhead. For example, the day-to-day activities of most employees will already include the creating, capturing, sharing and usage of knowledge. Thus, KM can be promoted as being a way to help put more support behind these activities, and in doing so KM can then help both individuals and organizations to leverage their knowledge resources in order to become better and more effective at what they do. Thus, by highlighting KM as a key support activity to the organization's already established work processes you can position it in a positive light. Additionally, you should always try to reassure your potential KM workforce that nothing is going to be imposed on them that they don't understand and agree to. To do this, you will need to make time to talk with business units and find out what's important to them and how KM can best support them in achieving their business objectives. Establishing these types of business partnership, where the organization's KM function supports the organization's business unit functions, will be essential if you want to gain acceptance and traction for your KM implementation project.

However, it never ceases to amaze me the number of KM implementations I've seen where no-one has even talked to the workforce before deciding what they will implement and how they will do it. This is back-to-front thinking and a sure recipe for alienating employees, the very people you will need to rely on for your success. It is far better to have had some sort of consultations, maybe a stakeholders' workshop, where you can discuss things before nailing down the final details of your implementation plan.

And finally, here's the most important question in the KM universe:

3. What's in It For Me?

The single strongest motivational factor behind any successful organizational change, and also the one element that all KM implementations have in common, is that of human nature. And human nature dictates that the vast majority of people are going to be primarily interested in one thing above everything else, themselves! Of course, the question 'What's in it for me?' may come in many different guises, but however it comes you need to be able to answer it, and at the very least have a high-level understanding of what exactly is in it for those who are asking.

Therefore, if you want to get any buy-in for your KM initiative you had better have something to offer your potential KM community before you start trying to implement anything. By something, I mean something tangible, not just airy promises and platitudes. And in order to be able to do that you will need to have a good grasp on what is important to the employees in the organization, and why, before you start planning any implementation activity. This is not as difficult as it may sound, and doesn't imply that you will need to talk to everyone in the organization and get to know what they do, and what they need in order to do it, before you can get started. In fact, you can get a fairly good overarching sense of the business objectives which will be important within the organization by examining the various strategic components which underpin its existence and future viability. For example: the mission statement and strategic vision will tell you what they are trying to achieve as an organization; the business plan will tell you what they are trying to accomplish from a business perspective; and the organization chart will tell you how they are organized to achieve all of this and who is responsible for doing the types of work that are necessary to support the overall business goals. From all of this you can gather a reasonable high-level overview of what specific types of information and knowledge are required to keep the organization viable. Once you have an idea of what the key organizational roles and responsibilities are, then you can begin to map out where and how KM activity can play a role in supporting the organization's strategies and business objectives. This knowledge will help you form the foundation for your KM planning, and will enable you to talk to employees about what should be in it for them.

The bottom line here is that the level of employee buy-in will likely dictate whether your KM initiative succeeds or fails, so make sure you have done your homework well before you start talking to the workforce.

Key Take-Away Item

There are going to be many items that you will need to have a good knowledge of if you want to succeed at implementing KM, but ensuring that you properly understand the business needs of the organization should be a priority item for you. Once you fully understand the business needs then you can position KM activity as a key enabling/support activity for the organization, and properly align it with both grass roots level needs as well as senior management level needs.

g. Strong Leaders; Who Needs Them?

It seems like it has become something of an accepted truth that you will need a strong leader, usually a senior manager, involved if you want to be successful at implementing KM. Well, the reality is that it all depends, and sometimes you don't need a single senior strong leader at all.

Strong leaders come in many shapes and forms, and from a KM perspective they are few and far between. This is because KM is usually a low priority item for a senior leader in any organization and accordingly if you do find a strong senior leader they are likely to be one of two sorts: firstly, a founder/owner/CEO who sees KM as important, and who will mandate their organization to adopt KM practice; and secondly, someone who has been persuaded about the virtues of 'doing' KM and who wants to lend their support to the KM cause. Both of these types of leader are a welcome addition to any KM implementation, but come with a strong cautionary note attached to them. Why? Well, because in the case of the first type, the whole adoption and buy-in for KM has come from a top-down mandate by one individual and if that individual is removed from the picture, or decides to re-focus their (and their organization's) attention elsewhere, then the momentum for KM may well slacken, or even stop entirely. In the case of the second type of senior leader, they can also have a short shelf-life, particularly if they are in the public sector, and may be removed from the picture before you've even had a decent chance to utilize their leverage within the organization. A good example of this being the case of the Public Works and Government Services department in Canada (35,000 employees). All were enthusiastic about supporting KM, and all were replaced within a matter of weeks, leaving the KM initiative back at square one without a senior strong leader to back it! All of which taught a lesson worth learning, treat senior manager support with caution, and utilize it immediately if you're lucky enough to find it in the first place.

So, given this context, are strong KM leaders still worth having? Most definitely yes is the answer, but you will probably need to look beyond the senior management strata if you want to find something reasonably practical and long-lasting. So, where will you find these strong leaders? The answer is simple, they are all around the organization and it is just a question of targeting the right sort of individuals and groups in order to find them.

You can start by identifying teams, groups and committees who have expertise and responsibilities which align with key KM practices, such as the creating and sharing of knowledge. Subject experts, communities of interest and practice, and committees tasked with information management activity, fit this profile really well. However, there is no restriction to where and how you might find a good KM leader, but one thing is sure you will have to engage the workforce in dialogue if you want to find them. By building business partnerships with the aforementioned individuals and groups you should find that some individuals are enthusiastic about the virtues of KM, and are willing to lend their support to it. Now, this support may be at a low-level or it may be of a more robust kind, but either way what you are doing by engaging these individuals is building a KM support network within the organization, one which will include strong leaders.

By using this approach of engaging individuals and groups, you can build momentum for your KM initiative, although it may be one piece at a time and localized rather than total and organizational-wide, at least to begin with. However, this is a safer long-term bet than putting all your money on a single strong leader. The localized approach is a sound one because the community-focused structure of KM reflects the way that people actually work best. These communities are in reality their own little enterprises. It is here that real knowledge exchange takes place, and where access to knowledge and the need to disseminate and share knowledge is assessed. Communities know where knowledge resides corporately and are able to maintain, support and grow those knowledge sources.

Therefore an emphasis on community-based leadership of KM activity encourages a healthy focus on addressing individual pieces of the organizational KM challenge, rather than on trying to fix the whole problem all at once i.e. an incremental approach to change. This appeals to both individuals and teams, as it means they can focus on the tactical (real-world daily problems) rather than on the strategic vision of the organization (large-scale structure and stricture, i.e. most enterprise-style KM programs) for KM activity. It also appeals to line-managers who want to see something practical and visible by way of KM activities and deliverables.

The bottom line here is that nurturing KM support at the grass-roots level is likely to prove to be a better investment of time and energy than targeting the support of a single senior leader or leaders.

Key Take-Away Item

If you want to build a solid foundation of support for KM within an organization, then focus on building that support at a community, rather than at an individual, level. There is nothing wrong in looking to engage a single strong leader in the organization, but be realistic as to how practical and long-term that strategy will prove. In the long run, it is better to have many grass-roots KM supporters (hopefully with some leaders among them) than one single strong senior leader.

h. Nothing Can Beat Experience

The Roman's had an expression, *Caveat Emptor*, which meant 'buyer beware'. If you are looking for external help in implementing KM then you need to beware, or at least be aware. There is a huge pool of vendors and consultants out there just waiting for you to give them the nod so they can provide assistance to you in successfully delivering your KM initiative. However, the following experience, gained from some previous implementations, might prove to be useful to you before making any decisions regarding external help.

a. *One size doesn't fit all* – KM Systems (KMS) still hold an allure for many planners and managers. Often the thinking is that if everyone in the organization has access to a KMS then they will use it to help achieve organizational KM objectives. And this may well prove to be the case depending on the needs of the organization and/or workforce; for example, if everyone is reliant on one knowledge source to become more effective at delivering a service or a product. However, in the majority of cases there won't be a single focus for the organization, and the fragmented nature of its processes and business lines will make it difficult to maximize the use of any one system.

So, exercise caution before committing to any new technology solution unless there is a very compelling business reason to use it. Most enterprise level solutions will likely need to be customized in order to fit the organization's existing working model, or alternatively may require changes to be made to how the organization operates before they can be properly utilized.

Remember that supporting communities and groups is going to be the most effective strategy for embedding KM practice into an organization, and the likelihood is that there are going to be several different technologies employed by these different communities. And while integrating all these technologies may be a desired end state for the organization's IT folks, if that integration means communities actually end up not using the integrated technology solution anyway, then you have actually taken an organizational step backwards, not forwards.

b. *Power to the people* – the need to leverage external expertise may be a necessary step for your KM initiative, but any such arrangement comes with an additional unseen challenge; how to ensure that the knowledge that is bought into the organization by outside experts remains there. If there is no knowledge transfer accomplished during the consultancy then the organization has missed a significant opportunity to improve its own KM capability. Therefore, try and ensure that there is plenty of liaison and opportunity to affect knowledge transfer between external experts and the internal workforce. This growth of organizational KM capacity is essential if you want to provide a solid support infrastructure for future KM growth. That doesn't mean that every employee needs to become a KM expert, but the more people who understand what the discipline is all about and are comfortable with providing support to its objectives, the better shape KM will be in from an organizational perspective.

c. *Yes, but are you experienced?* – as with the technology solution providers, there are plenty of KM consultants who can help you implement your KM plan. However, there is a world of difference between a consultant who has KM expertise and a consultant who has both KM expertise and real KM experience. There is no hard and fast rule that you can apply here, but I would suggest that unless the consultant has at least half a dozen implementation projects behind them then they do not really offer a broad range of experience to you. Every KM implementation project has unique aspects to it, and every implementing organization has its own unique business context and unique set of challenges to overcome. What being involved in many different implementation scenarios gives a consultant is not only real and useful experience, but also the ability to recognize what works, and more importantly what isn't likely to work, in similar situations. This experience through actual hands-on work is invaluable to an organization and can not only save them time and resources, but also give them the best possible chance of success for their implementation project. Don't get fooled by those who may well be able to talk authoritively on the subject of KM, such as academics, but who have never had to actually run a business or implement a major project themselves. What you need is someone who has been-there, done-that, in the real world of business, not just once but several times.

The bottom line here is that external expertise may be exactly what you will need if you want your KM initiative to be successful. However, some initial short-term caution before engaging any external expertise may save you some longer-term problems.

Key Take-Away Item

Don't get taken in by sales pitches from those who are probably going to cause you more problems than they solve. If you do decide to invest in either a KM technology or external KM expertise then make sure that any prospective provider can show you clear evidence of their experience with multiple implementations of a similar nature to yours. And, always ask for details of previous clients and then check with those clients to see whether what you have been told by the provider matches with what actually happened from the client's perspective.

3. THE CASE FOR KNOWLEDGE SHARING

The three basic activities which underpin any knowledge management initiative are the creating, collecting and sharing of knowledge. But while the creating and collecting of knowledge are undoubtedly important, it is the third activity of sharing which is the key to achieving anything substantive from a KM perspective, and is the real organizational pay-off for doing the first two.

So, Why is Knowledge Sharing so Important?

Knowledge management is an important part of any organization's program management operation, as it leverages know-how across the organization to help improve decision making, innovation, partnership, and overall organizational results. Fundamentally, KM is all about making the right knowledge, or the right knowledge sources (including people), available to the right people at the right time; and knowledge sharing is one of the most important aspects of this objective, since the vast majority of business processes depend upon it to be effective. It is the enabler for the transfer and creation of knowledge, and its crucial importance to an organization's well-being has been addressed directly by many researchers and authors over the years.

However, the bottom line is that in order to make knowledge management initiatives work in practice the employees within an organization must first be willing to share their knowledge with others. At the same time, the leaders of the organization will need to fully understand the prevailing working culture, both at an organizational as well as community level. And while culture often exists on an organizational level, each individual community within the organization will also have its own norms, perspectives, and collective understandings. The community's willingness to share and to seek knowledge will be influenced by these collective views. Therefore, an organizational culture that encourages sharing and transferring of ideas, opinions and experiences among the staff is a key factor for knowledge management success.

One major influence on a culture's knowledge sharing willingness is the issue of reciprocity. This refers to the individual's need to perceive a current or future return on the knowledge they choose to share. This could be in the form of direct compensation of some kind, or it could be in the form of something more intangible like the enhancing of the individual's reputation; but it can also be the knowledge that the favour will be returned the next time that the individual requires assistance.

One thing is certain though, and that is that an organizational culture of knowledge sharing doesn't happen overnight. It takes time for new ideas and new commitments to become embedded in any organization's work practices, and particularly so in the case of knowledge sharing which involves a practice which may seem counter-intuitive to some — that sharing your knowledge with others is a way to increase your own store of knowledge. Above all, a knowledge sharing culture cannot just be imposed on an organization, it has to grow organically and be driven by employee or client needs rather than by management design. The key to success is in creating a viable organizational support infrastructure that facilitates knowledge sharing and provides the mechanisms and incentives which will encourage and support employees in collaboration and sharing activities, both internally as well as externally. At the same time getting senior managers interested and involved is a key to helping align knowledge sharing activity with the organization's vision, mission and business objectives.

Knowledge sharing in the organization is not only the internal sharing of individual and team experiences on project work, good practices and lessons learned, but also the external sharing of work outcomes with partners, peers and miscellaneous stakeholders and communities. This external sharing is a two-way process as it is also an opportunity to have a dialogue with subject experts and practitioners from around the world to learn from their expertise, experience and recommendations.

Overall, it is essential to any organization's well-being and ability to perform efficiently that individuals and teams are prepared to share knowledge of what they have done, what they have learned, and how they will use what they have learned to manage their work more effectively in the future.

The bottom line here is that if you want to be effective at 'doing' KM then you need to ensure that knowledge sharing activity is supported and prioritized within your organization. However, sometimes this is easier said than done. And while it is human nature to want to share what we know with others, either to impress them or just to let them know how knowledgeable we are, there are often hidden barriers, such as culture and trust, in the way of a more effective organizational knowledge sharing model.

Key Take-Away Item

The key challenge for KM implementers is going to be in finding ways to promote knowledge sharing activity so that it is seen as being as beneficial to the individual who shares as it is to those who receive. So, focus on facilitating trust-building meetings between individuals and teams and provide them plenty of opportunities for the exchange of knowledge, either in-person or remotely.

4. FINDING THE BEST WAY TO ENHANCE COLLABORATION THROUGH KNOWLEDGE SHARING: AN INDONESIAN GOVERNMENT AGENCY CASE STUDY

Context for KM in Indonesia

Knowledge Management in Indonesia really only got started in the 2000s and was pioneered mostly by private and state-owned companies who were recognized for their progressive works in helping performance improvement in their employees. These companies included PT Indosat, Unilever, and Astra, and were then followed by Bank of Indonesia, The Army School, Police Academy and others. The involvement of universities in supporting the KM movement had a significant impact on its progress. For example, in 2004, the University of Indonesia established a special KM study under the Psychology Department which recognized KM as a behaviour change enforcer, while the Institute of Technology Bandung was focusing more on KM as an IT based infrastructure.

However, from the 1990s Indonesia was already on the way towards developing into a knowledge society and in attempting to create such a knowledge society Indonesia developed a number of national strategies and goals, such as; the "Terwujudnya Masyarakat Telematika Nusantara Berbasis Pengetahuan di tahun 2020" (Creating a Knowledge Based Telematic Society in 2020) which is the vision statement of the KTIN (Kerangka Teknologi Informasi Nasional), the National Framework for Information Technology. The document is broad-based, extending from support for e-business to good governance and e-democracy. This vision and the appended action plan is, however, directed at information technology (IT) and not at knowledge per se, on which information technology has to be based. Some academics, mostly with IT and library science backgrounds, have helped to support the momentum for the implementation of KM though the emphasizing of knowledge works, mostly focused around IT-based solutions, rather than seeing KM as a comprehensive strategy. Thus, people in Indonesia tend to associate KM as being part of IT instead of as a leaning tool. Despite this narrow focus, the overlapping of the information society with the knowledge society is happening all the time.

Since 2005, the practice of including a KM strategy in development work has been supported by many INGOs, including the World Bank, the UNDP, and others, where KM has been seen as a tool for sharing and capturing knowledge for better decision making, including through the sharing of best practices and lesson learned. In 2014, Bappenas (National Development Planning Agency Republic of *Indonesia*) promoted organizational learning and knowledge sharing works among its stakeholders, and gave examples of the importance of knowledge sharing for development work.

Background to This Case Study

In 2012 a newly formed department of the Indonesian government decided to implement a knowledge management strategy and action plan for the organization. Although the organization was a new one, and had a possibly limited life-span, the decision was taken that investing time and resources in improving the management of its knowledge assets would be both prudent as well as empowering for the organization. Accordingly a senior KM advisor and KM leader to staff a KM Office were hired and a KM strategy and action plan created.

However, starting from scratch with a new discipline in a new organization is doubly challenging and presents those trying to implement KM with some unique challenges. So, what sort of challenges did the new organization's KM Office have to face?

Initial Challenges

Some of the key challenges faced were — *culture, awareness, capability, infrastructure, operational model*, and *governance*.

So, let's examine these 6 challenges in more detail.

1. **Culture:** The issues relating to culture have an impact on KM implementation at various levels. The first and most obvious issue relates to organizational culture and how it effects peoples' ability to take decisions and implement them; personal empowerment in other words. To a great extent, effective KM practice depends on how effective individuals and teams can be in collaborating and sharing what they know with each other. And in order for them to fully embrace this activity they need to feel that they are empowered to freely share (within known security and business constraints of course) without worrying about having to seek approvals and directions from those above them in the organization's hierarchy. If the organization doesn't have this kind of culture of empowerment then gaining traction for KM is made much harder.

    The second issue relates to how culture permeates a society and helps to shape the way its people interact with each other. Asian cultures in particular are based around respect for others, especially those in positions of authority, and the avoidance of open and direct criticism of individuals. At the same time, KM is to some extent reliant on the ability of employees to embrace feedback from others as a mechanism for work dialogue aimed at improvement, both personally as well as organizationally. Unfortunately, from a cultural standpoint feedback can sometimes be seen as being a negative force, and disrespectful of others. Accordingly, a major cultural challenge can lie in finding a way for people to share openly without disrespecting the prevalent culture.

2. **Awareness:** The issues relating to awareness are directly linked to the ability of a KM project to gain organizational traction. In the case of KM, it is important to create an awareness of what KM is, and what it does, at every level of the organization. At a senior level it is important to estab-

lish a good high-level understanding of what kinds of activities are involved in KM practice, and where KM can support the organization's business strategy and objectives. At a management and employee level it is important to create an awareness of the specific ways that KM can be aligned with current work activity and how it can play a significant support role in achieving business line goals.

3. **Capability:** The issues relating to capability will have a direct impact on the scope and speed of any KM implementation. Very often, as was the case in this study, employees will be able to grasp the fundamentals of 'doing' KM, but will not yet understand the ways and means they can utilize in order to meet KM objectives. So capability needed to be raised in two key areas: firstly, personal competence in the creating, sharing and re-using of knowledge; and, secondly, personal competence in the using of available, and new, technology to achieve KM objectives.

4. **Infrastructure:** The issues relating to infrastructure have a direct impact on how well KM can be supported and sustained in an organization. In reality there are two dimensions involved in creating an effective KM support infrastructure; the first deals with the technology necessary to provide a technological platform from which to support organizational KM activity, and the second deals with the organizational processes (policies, guidelines, governance etc.) necessary to provide some structure to the management of organizational KM activity. The challenge for the new KM Office was in finding out what was already in place, what was still needed to be put in place, and what would be the best way to embed new technologies and processes into the organization without causing a significant disruption to what was already in place.

5. **Operational Model:** The issues relating to operational models have a significant impact on KM implementation, as how the organization works, and its established business practices, are what new KM practices will need to align themselves with. In this case the reality was that the operational model was one of highly stove-piped operational groups, all more or less operating independently of each other and with dislocated staff often working outside of the operational HQ area.

6. **Governance:** The issues relating to governance have an impact on KM implementation in a number of ways. A proper governance structure can help provide checks and balances within the organization for planned KM activity, and also provide needed guidance for employees and teams looking to improve their KM competence and build internal KM capability for future implementations. In this case the challenge for the KM Office was to find what governance already existed within the organization, and then to find ways of merging needed KM governance within already existing operational practices.

Phase 1 (Months 1 to 3) - Initial Responses from the KM Office to These Challenges

1. **Culture:** To start with it was important for the KM Office to get a sense of how well employees would adapt to a new discipline which requires a degree of independent thinking, and which encourages an open and non-hierarchical system of feedback and honest evaluation.

To achieve this it was necessary to talk to most of the managers (senior and line) and business units, as well as those who held responsibility for key organizational functions, such as IT, to evaluate how open they would be to growing their opportunities to meet with others across the organization.

Once this was accomplished it became apparent that while there was a certain reluctance to accommodate anything requiring additional workload, there was an obvious willingness to try new broad-based approaches to information exchange which could help make individuals and teams more effective at what they did. However, an obvious impediment to this was the lack of opportunity employees had for meeting with others outside of their immediate working environment.

2. **Awareness:** Starting from scratch with an organization that had no previous history with KM activity meant that in this case there would be the need to proceed with a thorough awareness program, while at the same time recognizing that time was of the essence, and that KM would likely not figure highly on anyone's business agenda.
3. **Capability:** Given that capability needed to be raised in two key areas, personal competence in KM activity and personal competence in the use of technology to achieve KM objectives, it was decided that the initial KM Office focus should be on raising personal competence in KM while at the same time evaluating the technology environment to assess the potential for the use of current solutions and for the possibility of the use of new technologies in the future.
4. **Infrastructure:** In order to make an assessment of what was already in place and what approaches different teams took in their business processes, it was decided that a series of meetings with each business unit would be undertaken. There would be a formal meeting with the head of each unit, to allow them to describe what their team did and what their vision for achieving their business goals was, and a less formal meeting with members of each team to get them to describe how they worked, and what sort of challenges they faced in meeting their business objectives.
5. **Operational Model:** The meetings described in the previous section were also used as a means to gaining an understanding of how each functional arm of the organization operated, and of whether there were any inter-dependencies and over-laps between the work of the various units in the organization.
6. **Governance:** Governance, in the form of oversight, approvals and guidance, is an often neglected area of KM implementation, but is something which needs to be addressed if you want to succeed at KM. In this case it became apparent that there was no organizational governance in place which could be used in support of KM, so the KM Office would need to think about how to build something appropriate itself.

So, based on the KM Office's initial evaluations, as well as feedback from employees as Phase 1 progressed, a long-term KM Strategy was created for the organization. This strategy focused on three key business activities: a) improving information management b) improving knowledge management, and c) leveraging information technology to maximize the return on the first two elements. Accompanying the KM Strategy was a KM Action Plan which contained specific activities which would/could be implemented over a 1 to 3 year period. However, the main initial objective of the KM Action Plan was to build enough organizational momentum in the first year to ensure that KM would have a chance of being successful in the long-term.

Phase 2 (Months 3 to 12): Implementation of the Initial KM Action Plan Items

Based on the known challenges, here are some of the activities which the KM Office focused on during the first year of the implementation project:

1. **Culture:** It was decided that the promoting and endorsing of knowledge sharing would be the most effective means of building a knowledge-focused organization, and that by facilitating a culture change through the embedding of KM work practices into business processes would help produce a slow change of emphasis in the workplace from a 'Me' mindset to a 'We' mindset.

Accordingly, the KM Office started building organizational knowledge-sharing capacity by facilitating and encouraging individual, team and group conversations, both internally and externally, through the sharing of business objectives, best practices, lessons learned and other relevant knowledge products from all the organization's business units.

2. **Awareness**: As the organization had no previous exposure to KM, and because of its relatively small size, it was decided that the KM Office would make sure that every employee received at least a basic level of KM training. This would take the shape of briefings and presentations to individuals and teams which would explain the basic objectives of KM, what sort of practices it involved, and what the KM Office was working on towards achieving an effective KM implementation.

At the same time, a short KM/IM orientation training package was prepared for future new employees.

3. **Capability**: Individual and organizational KM capability would determine whether or not the KM implementation would be a success or not. Therefore, this was the most crucial area that the KM Office would need to focus on, and the one which would require the most commitment in terms of time and resources.

Therefore, the main focus for the KM Office's activity was on encouraging and supporting enabling business practices that would grow individual competence and skills, and allow the business to operate more effectively. In particular, the key business activities that would be focused on were: 1-Collaborating, 2-Sharing, 3-Learning.

Specific KM-related activities in the first year included the following:

- A weekly knowledge sharing session hosted by the KM Office. This was promoted as being a personal-enrichment and people awareness program on subjects or programs related to the organization's business activities. Individuals and teams were asked to talk about their work and share what they had learned and what had worked best for them. As the popularity of these sessions grew the list of presenters was expanded to include external practitioners working in related fields.
- The KM Office started to circulate knowledge-related updates to the organization, including: reviews of items of interest, notifications of items of interest; the facilitating of inter-change opportunities between employees; and, the highlighting of group-wide events and opportunities to learn and share from others. The objective of this service was to provide informal sharing opportunities for people, with the driving force being that sharing can be an unplanned-for trigger for all sorts of ideas in support of a knowledge sharing culture within the organization.
- The building of an 'Information Services' function within the KM Office was prioritized. These Services included the following: the creation of virtual and hard-copy library facilities, with accompanying guidelines and protocols for the depositing, withdrawing and returning of library items; the acquiring, classifying and cataloging of information collections (e.g. publications, pre-

sentations, white papers, project documentation etc.); the development of procedures to facilitate information exchange among employees, e.g. the dissemination of inventories and the notification of the availability of products, and for the requesting of specific items of interest.
- The creating of collaboration tools and collaboration opportunities, including: making reporting tools available to business units to help them capture and share high-level details about their projects; the development of an infographic tool used to capture details of each of the organization's programs, such as what each program does and what its purpose and goals are, and make that information available to everyone.

Additionally, there were two key activities which the KM Office focused on that would not only give the organization some initial KM traction, but would lay the foundations for the future viability of the KM initiative, and these were:

a. The Creation of an Initial KM Stakeholder Community to Ensure Buy-in and Gather Momentum for the Initiative.

To do this the KM Office talked with each business manager and asked them to nominate at least one person from their unit to represent their team at a weekly meeting of a KM/IM/IT Working Group that would help to provide input and oversight to the KM Office's activities dealing with KM, IM and IT issues in support of the KM Action Plan. In this way, the business units could feel that they were directly helping to shape and influence the KM rollout, and the KM Office could know that they weren't working in isolation and that a common understanding of their work, and the requirements of the KM implementation, was being achieved.

The participation of working group members was constantly encouraged, and their work was promoted by the KM Office as the most effective way for the organization to socialize recommendation for efficient business process procedures and as a way to evaluate current practices and suggest better ones where possible.

b. The creation of a technology platform to facilitate organization-wide collaboration and sharing.

As no collaboration platforms existed, it was decided by the KM Office that a sharing and collaborating technology in the form of an intranet would be an essential component if a culture shift to becoming a knowledge managing organization were to be achieved. The proposed intranet was promoted by the KM Office as being a key potential knowledge enabler for the organization, i.e. a community meeting place that would allow for a more participatory approach by employees and which would contain information and knowledge resources, collaboration tools and knowledge sharing media available to all employees. Accordingly, funding was sought and granted in order to create the intranet, and an overall design, functional look and feel, and content, was created and approved with the help of the KM/IM/IT Working Group. The KM Office took on the task of core administrator for the new intranet, and the various business units, as represented by the KM/IM/IT Working Group, agreed to feed content to it. Additionally, an Intranet Task Force, comprised of business unit representatives, was created to assist the KM Office in intranet design, content, navigation and on-going maintenance and management issues.

4. **Infrastructure:** The KM Office focused on two technology elements to help provide traction for KM: firstly, providing the organization with a technology platform for collaboration and sharing purposes; and secondly, providing a technical mechanism for integrating key business functions such as e-mail, and organizational and intranet applications.

Based on evaluation and feasibility studies by the IT team and the KM Office, it was decided to invest in two new technologies; Sharepoint (for intranet development, information management development, and community support), and Office 365 for daily business process integration purposes.

Intranet: Awareness and training were the two elements targeted by the KM Office. Awareness was addressed through the constant promotion of the availability, functions and content of the planned-for intranet. At the same time the KM Office prepared a core administrator to actually provide for the management of the intranet, and began a program to provide for employee training on the intranet's applications and tools. Additionally, training for localized (business line) administrators was provided; in essence, a train the trainers model. The objective of this training was to arm these local administrators with the knowledge needed in order to be able to program the application, and to perform simple troubleshooting to assist the wider user community.

Office365 (An Integration System for Email, Organizational and Intranet Apps)

Key activities the KM Office focused on were:

- Socialization of Office 365 through regular training and information mail-outs.
- Assisting users (in collaboration with the IT team and the Intranet Task Force) in preparing for migration into the new system, including installing Microsoft Outlook apps and socialization of the new integrated intranet and communication system environment.
- Overseeing additional vendor activities, including: knowledge transfer of technical operation; providing trouble shooter documentation; and, training for administrators on using the system.
    5. **Operational Model:** While it would be impossible to change the operational model to any significant extent, the KM Office decided that promoting and facilitating opportunities to exchange information and knowledge would be the most effective means of helping to break down, or at least lessen, the existing stove-piped nature of the organization's operations.
    6. **Governance:** As there was no formal KM governance in place at the start of the KM project, and no natural home for overall KM governance under the existing organizational structure, the KM Office focused on two key elements to help provide a governance foundation for KM implementation. The first of these was the creation of an oversight checks and balances implementation mechanism, in the shape of the KM/IM/IT Working Group, and the second was the creation of a number of guidance tools, in the shape of various KM-focused guidelines, procedures and policies.

The KM/IM/IT Working Group - was formed in order to provide input and oversight to corporate KM/IM efforts, and to provide a de-centralized implementation mechanism for KM/IM outputs from the KM Office. The creation of the KM/IM/IT Working Group helped to provide a mechanism for community engagement and support, as well as a means of ensuring deployment and take-up of KM/IM tools and procedures.

Corporate Guidance – a number of high-level guidance tools were created to help employees understand and manage their responsibilities to manage information and knowledge more effectively, including the following: procedures and templates for capturing Best Practices, Lessons Learned and managing After Action Reviews; guidelines for Managing Knowledge and Information; Operating Principles for Knowledge Management and Information Management; and, a draft corporate KM/IM Policy for future consideration and possible deployment.

Additionally, a corporate Taxonomy Guide was developed. This was intended to be an aid for implementing meta tag and taxonomy rules on information-related activities within the organization.

Phase 1 Short-Term Deliverables

Overall, there were a number of key KM-related items delivered to the organization during the first 12 months of the KM implementation project, including:

- A corporate intranet.
- A reference Library (virtual and hard-copy).
- An information brokerage service.
- A number of corporate KM/IM guidance tools (procedures, guidelines, templates etc.).
- A regularly scheduled organization-wide knowledge sharing session.
- A new KM-focused technology platform and associated tools (Sharepoint and Office 365).
- A governance structure to provide oversight to corporate KM activities.
- Information management support tools, such as the corporate taxonomy and meta tags.
- A formalized KM stakeholder community body (the KM/IM/IT Working Group).

Progress Report and Some of the Lessons Learned from the Phase 1 Implementation

While there were several advances in terms of overall corporate KM/IM capability and competence during the first year of the project, the results and feedback from the Phase 1 implementation were mixed, as would be expected in any new KM initiative. In particular, here are some of the issues and reactions which were noted as being significant and seen as both future challenges and items which could/should be addressed in Phase 3 planning and activity.

Information Management and Brokerage Services: Lessons Learned and Up-Coming Challenges

- Setting up some corporate guidance (procedures, guidelines, templates etc.) for managing information has been beneficial to the organization's need to manage its information resources more effectively.
- Information management support tools, such as a corporate taxonomy and meta tags, are now being used in all the publications produced by the organization. The subject headings and keywords are being used in the corporate knowledge repository catalogues, both in the intranet and the library itself.

- Procedures and guidelines for publishing, reporting, and capturing lessons learned were produced by the central KM Office. These have been adopted and customized (based on specific team functions) by individual teams as necessary.
- The information brokerage service (the producing and disseminating of information products and resources) has grown steadily and has been recognized as a useful support tool by the organization's various business units. Additionally, the central KM Office has produced a number of statistics, based on take-up, performance and outputs, showing the beneficial impact of this service for use in organizational reports.

Library and Information Sharing: Lessons Learned and Up-Coming Challenges

- Getting users to share and up-load their assets for access by others is a challenge. Regular training and intensive promoting are likely key factors in being able to recruit more contributors.
- The use of online collections is growing, with most of the materials needed by researchers available for free; though paying for specialist materials is also an available option. Having a wide network, both nationally and internationally, assists the library in getting access to free resources.

Knowledge Sharing Sessions: Lessons Learned and Up-Coming Challenges

- The building of informal conversations, the growing of segmented audiences, the selecting of trending subjects (and contributors), and the providing of promising networks and collaborations have been key factors in ensuring the success of organizational knowledge sharing activity.
- The creation of a formalized knowledge sharing session was a great success within the organization. It was initially scheduled for once every two weeks, which quickly became once a week, and sometimes even more.
- It soon became apparent that this session would provide the organization with a new set of business attributes by providing a platform where: individuals and teams could get instant feedback on team-work in progress; conference speakers could 'test-drive' their proposed presentations, get feedback from peers, and help to strengthen their points of view; and, proposed publications could be show-cased and strengthened through participant input and feedback.
- As with many new success stories, initial interest in the knowledge sharing sessions waned somewhat after the first 6 months and eventually settled into a regular monthly schedule which is probably more in line with the organization's needs. However, the biggest plus side is that now there is a forum where such meetings can be held, and if the need for an unscheduled important or ad-hoc session arises, there is an appropriate setting to hold it in.
- The implementation of a new system (Office365) is a key opportunity to gain more participants both in knowledge transfer and in building bridging networks between parties.

Intranet: Lessons Learned and Up-Coming Challenges

- The intranet has proved popular at both an individual and team level. Individually, employees are using it as the go-to place for their administrative tasks; for example booking rooms and accessing

HR forms dealing with items such as insurance, taxes, permission slips etc. From a team perspective, the intranet is being used as a collection site for team documents and reports, as well as a collaboration site where teams can exchange knowledge with other teams.
- The intranet is also now the primary portal to access all presentations, books and publications produced by the organization and other related stakeholders.
- As the use of the intranet grows, so do the requests and issues around its features. However, it is proving a stretch due to the limited resources being available to perform maintenance tasks.
- Requests to modify and meet specific team's needs are currently being postponed as there are no resources available to maintain the system regularly. Currently, the KM Office has to depend on the Intranet Task Force teams, who only have a limited knowledge of the system, to troubleshoot problems.

Technology (Office 365/SharePoint) Rollouts: Lessons Learned and Up-Coming Challenges

- Using technology (SharePoint and Office 365) as KM tools is one thing but finding the resources to manage and maintain them is another thing entirely and needs to be planned for and managed on a timely basis.
- The absence of funding for a developer and technical support is a big issue as user's requests and expectations cannot be properly met, while at the same time they are beginning to find out that the technology can become the answer to some of their current daily work management problems.
- While SharePoint has been mainly used as a collaboration tool and Office 365 as a communication tool, the lack of funding for development and maintenance personnel has meant that the full functionality of both SharePoint and Office 365 has not been fully utilized. Currently, the new technology is mainly being used for daily email, Microsoft office works, chatting/conference calls, booking rooms, booking drivers, downloading forms and recent regulations, etc

Managing Knowledge Products (Documenting-Publishing-Disseminating etc.): Lessons Learned and Up-Coming Challenges

- The KM Office's focus on formally publishing products, either as hard-copy or online items, has resulted in a decrease in the amount of informal open dialogue sharing across the organization.
- Though the organization contains many researchers and policy designers, capturing their knowledge and producing publication materials has proved to be a difficult task. The lack of a systemic mechanism for producing publications, and the absence of any proper rewards and recognition in this area, appeared to create some hesitancy in the workforce to get fully engaged with publication activity.
- Additionally, the overall quality of the writing showed that capability building among prospective writers needs to be addressed, and that dedicated resources (such as writers, editors) are needed to help with capturing, editing, and proofreading activities as an urgent requirement.

As well as the aforementioned items, there were a number of over-arching observations from the Phase 2 implementation which are worth mentioning, including:

Implementing KM Lessons from the Frontline

1. Social collaborations tools are popular due to the fact that they facilitate collaboration and knowledge transfer.
2. Communities will come together in order to ask questions, share information and analyze project outcomes, but they need to be given support, guidance and the tools necessary to facilitate these types of interaction.
3. By analyzing the amount of data that is produced as a consequence of community interaction and the use of social interaction tools, it is possible to spot common problems in various projects, ranging from management issues to specific technical scenarios. Additionally, in some cases, it is possible to spot some repetitive problems that project teams might be facing.
4. Facilitating knowledge transfer is just as important as analyzing data in order to continuously improve the work environment
5. KM can capitalize on social data – feedback streams, forums, micro-blogging etc. Often this data can be distilled and combined with other information, such as business insight, lessons learned analysis etc., in order to provide a more powerful and insightful understanding of the situation at hand.
6. A formalized KM stakeholder community body (in this case a KM/IM/IT Working Group) will flourish if given the right environment and support. Additionally, such a community provides an ideal environment for establishing internal inter-divisional connections and the growing of individual and team knowledge networks.

Longer-Term (Phase 3 Onwards) KM Activities for Further Consideration

The next phase (months 12 to 24) of the KM implementation project will look to build on the momentum already established through the first two phases, and to consolidate the depth and scope of KM activity, and competence, throughout the organization.

One key issue which will determine the viability of the work done during Phase 2, and the longer-term prospects for maintaining of KM progress and traction, will be the effective use of the information gathered from the stakeholder community during the first 12 months of work. This is an important issue for any KM initiative and those in charge of a KM project will do well to ensure that they have effective feedback mechanisms, and almost more importantly corrective action mechanisms, in place if they want to be successful.

In the case of Asian organizations this can present a harder challenge than in their European or North American equivalents, as direct and open feedback is often hard to extract due to cultural sensitivities surrounding giving the impression of being critical of superiors and work colleagues. However, in the Asian context, if the subject is approached sensitively, and questions are couched in organizational terms rather than in personal terms, it is possible to deduce useful information concerning what works well and what needs to be changed, or at least amended appropriately.

Given this context, Phase 3 work will focus on some key activities aimed at providing support and tools to the growing KM stakeholder community. These activities will include the following:

- The improvement of individual and organizational competence in knowledge management and information management practice.
- The on-going support of individual and organizational knowledge needs.

- The evolution and support of knowledge communities e.g. online communities (via the intranet), and work-based communities (of interest or practice).
- The creation of, and accessibility to, corporate information/knowledge resources, such as lessons learned/best practices repositories etc.
- Providing increased information brokerage services to individuals and teams based on identified information needs and profiles.
- The growth of organizational knowledge networks through partnering e.g. by finding individuals and organizations to participate in internal and external information-sharing activity.

5. CONCLUSION

While the KM initiative highlighted in the case study in the previous section is still in its formative stages, it would be safe to say that the majority of KM implementation projects are likely to take anywhere between one to three years to even begin to have any significant impact on the organizations involved. In other words, KM is something that takes time to embed itself into the working fabric of the organization, and so anyone who thinks that KM implementation is going to be a short-term affair is fooling themselves; as well as setting a dangerous and unattainable level of expectation in any potential stakeholders.

Overall, there are many barriers that stand in the way of successfully implementing KM, whether it is a lack of access to current information, a lack of clear communications, difficulty in transferring knowledge and information, difficulty in maintaining the relevance and currency of knowledge and information, lack of support from senior managers, or limited resources – both in time and personnel. However, there is no reason why KM implementation cannot be a success, given the right approach and the creation of a sustainable KM support infrastructure. And while there are no guaranteed solutions to the types of organizational problems highlighted above, there are approaches which have been proven to be successful over time in many organizations, including the following:

- Focusing on supporting individual and community (including teams and work groups) efforts to create, share and maintain knowledge will always pay organizational dividends. For example, the creating of knowledge sharing networks is key to enriching organizational conversations and in connecting various stakeholders—employees, managers, practitioners, partners etc.—and in providing opportunities for them to interact and engage with each other. These types of knowledge networks will play an especially important role where seekers and providers of working solutions come together with specific business issues to resolve.
- Self-empowerment within teams and projects will always help to promote learning and knowledge sharing, which in turn assists individuals and teams to perform more flexibly and effectively.
- Knowledge sharing events and communities of practice (or interest) are the most effective ways to share the knowledge within an organization and also to engage the largest number of people at the same time. Additionally, supporting knowledge sharing around specific solutions, rather than simply providing technical assistance, will enable comprehensive partnerships to grow among different knowledge providers and stakeholders.
- It is important to acknowledge and leverage the use of social media tools in the workplace, as these are what most young workers use in a 'peer to peer' fashion in order to share knowledge and to learn from others.

- Creating an organizational knowledge sharing platform, such as an intranet, is a key enabler for organizational knowledge sharing and collaboration. However, it needs to be designed and maintained by the stakeholder community if it is to gain real traction within the organization.
- Finding the right balance concerning senior management involvement in KM implementations is extremely important. Management support and incentives will help bottom-up knowledge generation as they have a significant impact on the way that knowledge workers are perceived by organizations. In particular, management needs to assure workers that they value their knowledge contributions and are committed to allowing workers to spend time on their knowledge sharing activities.

Finally, there is no such thing as a one-size-fits-all approach to KM. Each organization has its own lens through which it sees and approaches KM activity. The smart KM practitioner will understand this and make the adjustments necessary to keep KM both flexible and relevant in the eyes of the organization. The bottom line is that it is more important to recognize and understand what works regarding KM as far as the organization is concerned, than it is to believe that you already know how it should work from your own previous understanding of KM.

REFERENCES

Sinclair, N. (2006). *Stealth KM: Winning knowledge management strategies for the public sector.* Db Butterworth Heinemann.

Chapter 7
How to Improve Knowledge Exchange by Using Internet Technologies:
An Empirical Study in Small and Medium-Sized Enterprises

Simona Popa
University of Murcia, Spain

Pedro Soto-Acosta
University of Murcia, Spain

ABSTRACT

This paper seeks to extend previous studies on the use of Internet technologies and knowledge management by analyzing factors affecting Web knowledge exchange in small and medium-sized enterprises (SMEs). More specifically, by drawing on the technology-organization-environment framework, a model to examine how distinct contextual factors influence Web knowledge exchange in SMEs is developed. The hypotheses are tested by using structural equation modelling on a large sample of Spanish SMEs from different industries. Results suggest that IT expertise and commitment-based human resource practices positively affect Web knowledge exchange, with the latter being the strongest factor in our proposed model. In contrast, a negative relationship is found between competition and Web knowledge exchange.

1. INTRODUCTION

With the advent of the Internet and open standards technologies and the associated reduction of communication costs, firms are migrating toward the Internet platform (Zhu et al. 2006) and cloud computing environments (Hsu et al., 2014). As a consequence, effective adoption and use of Internet technologies have become management concerns (Soto-Acosta and Meroño-Cerdan, 2008; Meroño-Cerdan et al., 2008b).

DOI: 10.4018/978-1-4666-9607-5.ch007

How to Improve Knowledge Exchange by Using Internet Technologies

The characteristics of rapid search, access, retrieval and exchange of information make Internet technology suitable for collaboration and knowledge exchange between organizational members (Lucio-Nieto, et al., 2012). One of the main characteristics of the Internet-based digital platform is that it is founded on the democratization of knowledge, so it facilitates the appearance of natural flows of collaboration and knowledge which, in turn, may favour creativity and innovation (Lucio-Nieto, et al., 2012; Pérez-López and Alegre, 2012). Thus, it is important to understand the key factors that facilitate and motivate the use of Internet technologies for knowledge exchange within firms. Competitive pressure has been defined in various studies as a key determinant of firm's readiness to accept new technology (Bayo-Moriones and Lera-Lopez, 2007; Sila, 2013; Teo et al., 2006). At the same time, the literature considers that technological factors are important drivers for the adoption and implementation of IT innovations (Aboelmaged, 2014; Ramdani et al., 2013). However, beyond technological and the environmental factors, research has recognized the importance of organizational factors in influencing Internet technologies adoption and use (Aboelmaged, 2014; Gu et al. 2012; Lian et al., 2014; Sila, 2013). Organizational factors may restrict or facilitate the implementation and usage of Internet technologies. In this sense, the literature suggests that organizational human resource (HR) practices that create a commitment-based environment influence the interactions, behaviours and motivation of employees (Collis and Smith, 2006). HR practices may therefore affect the organizational social climate that motivates employees to work together and exchange knowledge by being organizational enablers of technology use.

Furthermore, small and medium-sized enterprises (SMEs) are of great importance for economic growth, employment and wealth creation. For example, in Europe, SMEs represent around 99% of the total number of firms (Lopez-Nicolas and Soto-Acosta, 2010). However, studies in the literature tend to examine Internet technology adoption and use in large businesses, with very few recent studies analyzing Internet technologies adoption and use in SMEs (e.g. Aboelmaged, 2014; Chang et al. 2012; Chong et al. 2009; Lopez-Nicolas and Soto-Acosta, 2010; Huy et al. 2012; Ramdani et al., 2013). Findings from studies examining large companies are unlikely to be generalizable to SMEs because of various differences between these types of firms (Bhagwat & Sharma, 2007; Lopez-Nicolas and Soto-Acosta, 2010). Moreover, although businesses have extensively adopted Internet technologies, actual use is an important link to business value and such a link has been found to be especially lacking in SMEs (Devaraj and Kohli, 2003).

To respond to the above-mentioned gaps in the literature, this paper develops a conceptual model, grounded on the technology-organization-environment (TOE) framework, to analyze the key factors that facilitate Web knowledge exchange and it uses a large sample of SMEs from different industries for hypothesis testing. The paper consists of six sections and is structured as follows: The next section presents the literature review and hypotheses. Following that, the methodology used for sample selection and data collection is discussed. Then, data analysis and results are examined. Finally, the paper ends with a discussion of research findings, limitations and concluding remarks.

2. THEORETICAL BACKGROUND AND HYPOTHESES

The technology-organization-environment (TOE) theory (Tornatzky and Fleischer, 1990) has emerged as the main theoretical framework to analyze factors which affect the adoption and use of different ITs including: cloud computing (e.g. Hsu et al., 2014; Lian et al. 2014), electronic business (e.g. Bordonaba-Juste et al., 2012, Sila, 2014; Soto-Acosta and Meroño-Cerdan, 2008, Xu et al., 2004), electronic collaboration (e.g. Chan et al., 2012), mobile commerce (e.g. San Martín et al., 2012), enterprise resource planning (e.g. Bradford et al., 2014; Zhu et al., 2010) and information and open systems (e.g. Chau and Tam, 1997; Thong, 1999). The TOE framework conceptualizes the context of adoption and implementation of technological innovations as consisting of three aspects: technological context, organizational context and environmental context. Technological context refers to the characteristics of the technological innovation; organizational context describes characteristics of the organizations; and environmental context involves characteristics of the environment in which the adopting organizations operate (Tornatzky and Fleischer, 1990; Thong, 1999). According to Thong (1999), competition is the business environment in which the business operates. Porter's (1985) five forces refer to horizontal competition (the threat of substitute products, the threat of existing rivals, and the threat of new entrants), and vertical competition (the bargaining power of suppliers and the bargaining power of customers).

The TOE framework has also been extensively used to analyze the factors which affect the adoption and use of Internet technologies. Recent studies have employed this theoretical framework to analyze factors affecting Internet technologies adoption and use (e.g. Bordonaba-Juste et al., 2012; Chan et al., 2012; Gu et al., 2012; San Martín et al., 2012). Thus, drawing upon literature analyzing Internet technology adoption and use, this paper proposes a comprehensive research model based on the TOE framework to study factors that influence Web knowledge exchange in SMEs. The next subsections discuss the hypotheses of the model.

2.1. Technological Context

The extent of Internet technologies use for knowledge exchange would depend on firms' technology competence, since IT plays a pivotal role in supporting organizational knowledge exchange processes. Technology competence refers not only to tangible assets, but also to intangibles resources, which are more likely to create competitive advantages (Aboelmaged, 2014; Bharadwaj 2000; O'Sullivan and Dooley, 2010; Soto-Acosta and Meroño-Cerdan, 2008). With regard to tangible IT assets, technology integration is a factor, within the TOE framework, that has been found to be significant in studies focusing on Internet technologies adoption and use (e.g. Zhu et al. 2006, Zhu and Kraemer, 2005). Technology integration is the degree of connectivity of front-end and back-end IT systems and databases. Front-end integration refers to the degree of integration of the Web site functionalities with databases inside the firm, while back-end integration represents the degree of integration of the legacy systems so as to provide data integration among internal databases (Zhu et al. 2004). Front-end and Back-end integration are built on common Internet technologies in use (intranet, website and extranet...) and are important antecedents of Web knowledge exchange since they enable communications and collaboration. Regarding IT intangibles resources, IT expertise has been identified as one of the main factors that influence the level of e-business use (Bordonaba-Juste et al. 2012). Firms that have IT specialists are more likely to adopt IT innovations because they can develop their IT applications or better adapt them to their organizations (Lin and Lee, 2005). IT expertise provides the technical skills to develop Internet-based applications. Therefore, IT integration and IT expertise may influence the extent to which firms are ready to use Internet technologies for knowledge exchange. This discussion leads to the following hypotheses:

Hypothesis 1: IT integration is positively related to the extent of Internet technologies use for knowledge exchange.

Hypothesis 2: IT expertise is positively related to the extent of Internet technologies use for knowledge exchange.

2.2. Organizational Context

Technology enablers are a necessary but not sufficient condition for employees to collaborate and exchange knowledge through Internet technologies. Knowledge exchange happens when units and members interact, promoting new understanding (Alavi and Leidner, 2001). It is therefore essential for the firm to develop interaction networks. However, besides technology applications, employees need to be willing to collaborate and exchange knowledge. Thus, building a positive social climate may be crucial to motivate employees to work together and exchange knowledge. This is even more crucial when exchanging tacit knowledge, which requires more interaction (Fox, 2000).

Nahapiet and Ghoshal (1998) suggest that cooperation between employees is a key aspect for creating a social climate that drives knowledge exchange within firms. A strong climate for cooperation between knowledge workers positively affects the exchange of valuable and unique knowledge among them (Collis and Smith, 2006). The literature distinguishes between transaction-based HR practices, which focus on individual short-term exchange relationships, and commitment-based HR practices, which emphasize mutual long-term exchange relationships (Tsui et al., 1995). Collins and Smith (2006) found that commitment-based HR practices are significantly related to knowledge exchange among workers. Thus, the following hypothesis incorporates our expectations:

Hypothesis 3: Commitment-based HR practices are positively related to the extent of Internet technologies use for knowledge exchange.

2.3. Competition Context

Early studies on technology diffusion found that competition increases firms' incentives to adopt new technologies so as to remain competitive (Thong, 1999). Competition intensity has been found to be an important driver of Internet technologies adoption (Chong et al., 2009; Sila, 2013; Wang et al. 2010; Zhu et al. 2003; Zhu et al. 2006). Studies have also found that external pressure from customers and suppliers affect e-business adoption (Del Aguila and Padilla, 2008; Wang and Ahmed, 2009). Therefore, competition intensity is expected to drive organizations to adopt Internet technologies for knowledge exchange. However, research (e.g. Chan et al. 2012; Zhu et al. 2006) has also shown that competition may deter firms from using Internet technologies, challenging the traditional wisdom about competition and innovation diffusion. Zhu et al. (2006) found a positive relationship between competition and e-business adoption, but a negative relationship between competition and the extent of e-business use. Similarly, Chang et al. (2012) found that competition intensity is negatively related to the extent of e-collaboration use in SMEs. Thus, Internet technology use is less tied to competition intensity than initially believed in both large and small businesses. Too much competitive pressure leads firms to change rapidly from one technology to another without sufficient time to infuse the technology into the company (Zhu et al., 2006). Porter's (1985) five forces refer to horizontal competition (the threat of substitute products, the threat of existing rivals, and the threat of new entrants), and vertical competition (the bargaining power of suppliers and the bargaining power of customers). Thus, although competition encourages technology adoption, it is not necessarily good for technology use. This discussion leads to the following hypotheses regarding vertical competition and Web knowledge exchange:

Hypothesis 4: Vertical competition from customers is negatively related to the extent of Internet technologies use for knowledge exchange.

Hypothesis 5: Vertical competition from suppliers is negatively related to the extent of Internet technologies use for knowledge exchange.

The set of relationships is illustrated in table 1.

3. RESEARCH METHODOLOGY

3.1. Data Collection and Sample

The organisations selected for this study are SMEs from Spain. Currently, SMEs represent around 99% of the total number of firms in Spain. Nonetheless, to ensure a minimum firm complexity in which ITs may be relevant, only firms with at least 15 employees were used. Data collection was conducted in two stages: a pilot study and a questionnaire were conducted. Five SMEs were randomly selected from a database to pretest the questionnaires. Based on these responses and subsequent interviews with participants in the pilot study, minor modifications were made to the questionnaire for the next phase of data collection. Responses from these five pilot-study firms were not included in the final sample.

The population considered in this study was the set of all Spanish enterprises, with at least 15 employees, located in the southeast of the country whose primary business activity is in one of the following business activities: manufacturing, commercial, services and construction. A total of 2246 were identified and contacted for participation. The survey was administered to the CEO of the companies via personal interview and the unit of analysis for this study was the company. In total, 535 valid questionnaires were obtained, yielding a response rate of 23.8 percent. The dataset was examined for potential bias in terms of non-response by comparing the characteristics of early and late participants in the sample. These comparisons did not reveal significant differences in terms of general characteristic and model variables, suggesting that non-response did not cause any survey bias.

Table 1. Hypotheses

IV -> DV	Path
Technology integration → Web knowledge exchange	H1
IT personnel → Web knowledge exchange	H2
Commitment-based HR practices → Web knowledge exchange	H3
Customer Power → Web knowledge exchange	H4
Supplier Power → Web knowledge exchange	H5

3.2. Common Method Variance

Most researchers agree that common method variance is a potentially serious bias threat in behavioral research, especially with single informant surveys. Two procedures were used to empirically determine whether or not common method bias threatened the interpretation of our results: a) the Harman one-factor test; and b) a confirmatory factor-analytic approach to Harman one-factor test.

The rationale for the first test is that, if common method bias poses a serious threat to the analysis and interpretation of the data, a single latent factor would account for all manifest variables or one general factor would account for the majority of the covariance among the measures. In our case, the one-factor model obtained using principal components analysis revealed several factors in the unrotated factor solution. However, this test is weak, as suggested by Podsakoff et al. (2003). More recently, some researchers using this technique have used confirmatory factor analysis (CFA) as a more sophisticated test. A worse fit for the one-factor model would suggest that common method variance does not pose a serious threat. The one-factor model yielded a $\chi 2 = 222.007$ with 35 degrees of freedom (compared with the $\chi 2 = 30.209$ with 29 degrees of freedom for the measurement model). The fit is considerably worse for the one-dimensional model than for the measurement model, suggesting that common method bias is not a serious threat in our study.

3.3. Measures

Measurement items were introduced on the basis of a careful literature review. Exploratory and Confirmatory factor analysis (CFA) were used to test the constructs. Constructs and associated indicators in the measurement model are listed in the Appendix and discussed below. To facilitate cumulative research, operationalizations tested by previous studies were used. Scales were measured on a 5-point Likert scale with anchors from strongly disagree (1) to strongly agree (5).

Several constructs were operationalized as multi-item constructs. First, Technology Integration was measured by the extent to which the website is connected with back-end information systems and databases, and the extent to which company databases are linked to business partners' systems and databases (Zhu et al. 2006). Second, *Commitment-based HR practices* were operationalized from previous research (Collins and Smith, 2006; Delery and Doty, 1996; Youndt et al. 1996) work. Overall, 5 items were adapted to measure Commitment-based HR practices. *Knowledge exchange through Internet technologies* represents the extent of use of common Internet technologies (Intranet, website, extranet/Internet...) to exchange knowledge with different stakeholders: employees, customers, suppliers, competitors... (Meroño-Cerdan et al. 2008a; 2008b; Soto-Acosta & Meroño-Cerdan, 2006).

There are circumstances when single-item indicators are or must be used for diverse reasons, such as when the construct is simple and single-faceted, making it difficult to create many different items that measure the same construct (Petrescu, 2013; Poon et al, 2002). Bergkvist and Rossiter (2007) showed that single-item measures are equally as valid as multiple-item measures and theoretical tests and empirical findings would be the same if single-item measures are used instead of multiple-item measures. As noted by Baumgartner and Homburg (1996), around 20% of the studies applying SEM in social sciences, use single indicators for examining the relationships among variables. Thus, other variables are directly operationalized by observed variables. First, *IT expertise* was measured by the number of IT professionals (Bordonaba-Juste et al., 2012; Zhu et al. 2006; Zhu et al., 2004). Second, *Customer and Supplier*

Power was measured following two of Porter's (1985) concepts of five competitive forces. This type of operationalization has been used in the IT literature (Thong, 1999; Zhu et al., 2004). The survey items assessed the degree of pressure clients and suppliers exert on business regarding purchasing conditions.

3.4. Instrument Validation

The covariance-based structural equation modelling (SEM) approach, like many other multivariate statistical analyses, requires multivariate normality. The data were examined for kurtosis and skewness to obtain insights about the distributional characteristics. Both Kurtosis and Skewness fell within the acceptable range of -1 to 1 and their absolute values were less than three times their standard error (Hair et al., 2011). The data were therefore close to a normal distribution. Tests for linearity and homoscedasticy were also conducted. To test for linearity, the deviation from linearity test available in the ANOVA test in SPSS was used. Statistical differences (P > 0.05) were not found, which suggests that linearity problems did not exist. To test for homoscedasticity, scatter plots with the variables and the variables' residuals were conducted. No inconsistent patterns were observed, which suggests that data were homoscedastic. Thus, through these analyses normality, linearity and homoscedasticity of data were confirmed.

The unidimensionality and reliability of the dataset was assessed by different procedures. First of all, an initial exploration of unidimensionality was made using principal component factor analyses. In each analysis, the eigenvalues were greater than 1, lending preliminary support to a claim of unidimensionality in the constructs. Following that, CFA was performed to assess the unidimensionality of each construct. In this sense, construct reliability, convergent and discriminant validity were assessed. The measurement model presented a good fit to the data ($\chi^2(29)= 30.209$; CFI = 0.99; IFI = 0.99; GFI = 0.97; RMSEA = 0.04). All traditionally reported fit indexes were within the acceptable range.

Construct reliability assess the degree to which items are free from random error and, therefore, yield consistent results. This study calculated reliability of measures using Bagozzi and Yi's (1998) composite reliability index and Fornell and Larcker's (1981) average variance extracted index. For all the measures both indices were higher than the evaluation criteria, namely 0.6 for composite reliability and 0.5 for the average variance extracted. Convergent validity assesses the consistency across multiple constructs. As shown in table 2, all estimated standard loadings are significant ($p<0.01$) and of acceptable magnitude, suggesting good convergent validity (Sethi and King, 1994).

To assess the discriminant validity – the extent to which different constructs diverge from one another – Forell and Larcker's (1981) criterion that the square root of average variance extracted for each construct (diagonal elements of the correlation matrix in Table 3) should be greater than the absolute value of interconstruct correlations (off-diagonal elements) was used. All constructs met this criterion, suggesting that the items share more variance with their respective constructs than with other constructs.

This study measures commitment-based HR practices as a single construct made up of two dimensions: Training support and employees' interest and career plans and evaluation reporting. A second-order factor analysis demonstrated that the two dimensions reflect a higher-order construct (see Table 4).

4. RESULTS

This paper performs SEM to test the hypotheses, using maximum likelihood estimation techniques to test the model. The fit of the model is satisfactory ($\chi^2(51)= 54.085$; RMSEA=0.040; CFI=0.99 IFI=0.99

Table 2. Measurement model: confirmatory analysis and scale reliability

Construct	Indicators	S. Loadings	t-value	Reliability
Technology integration	TI1	0.651	--	CR = 0.71
	TI2	0.82	4.18	AVE = 0.55
IT professionals	ITP	na	na	na
Training support and employees' interest	HR1	0.749	--	CR = 0.75
	HR2	0.806	6.56	AVE = 0.61
Carreer plans and evaluation reporting	HR3	0.542	--	CR = 0.81
	HR4	0.806	6.58	AVE = 0.60
	HR5	0.926	6.44	
Customer power	CP	na	na	na
Supplier power	SP	na	na	na
Knowledge Exchange through Web technologies	WKE1	0.835	--	CR = 0.76
	WKE2	0.746	4.23	AVE = 0.58
	WKE3	0.697	4.24	

Fit statistics for measurement model: $\chi2(29) = 30.209$; CFI = 0.99; IFI = 0.99; GFI = 0.97; RMSEA = 0.048.
(--): Fixed items; CR: Composite reliability; AVE: Average variance extracted;
na. Loadings, CR and AVE are not applicable to single-item constructs.

Table 3. Descriptive statistics and discriminant validity

Constructs	Mean	Standard deviation	Correlation matrix						
			(1)	(2)	(3)	(4)	(5)	(6)	(7)
1. Technology integration	2.67	1.22	**0.74**						
2. IT expertise	0.73	2.79	0.11**	na					
3. Training support and employees' interest	3.88	0.90	0.09**	0.02	**0.77**				
4. Career plans and evaluation reporting	3.18	0.91	0.33***	0.04	0.33***	**0.78**			
5. Customer power	3.61	1.09	-0.06***	-0.04	0.04	-0.01	na		
6. Supplier power	3.03	1.08	0.08	-0.01	-0.02	0.06	0.22**	na	
7. Knowledge Exchange through Web technologies	3.52	0.79	0.05	0.12***	0.17***	0.21***	-0.09	00.06	**00.76**

Significance levels: $p<0.05**$; $p<0.01***$; na. Variance extracted is not applicable to the single-item constructs.
Diagonal values in bold represent the square root of the AVE

GFI=0.96), suggesting that the nomological network of relationships fits the data and the validity of the measurement scales (Churchill, 1979). The model explained substantial variance of Web knowledge exchange.

Table 5 shows the standardized path coefficients with their respective significant levels. Hypothesis 1 did not find support, indicating that technology integration is not related to Web knowledge exchange in SMEs. Hypothesis 2 was supported (0.13, p<0.05), a result that shows that hiring specialized IT person-

Table 4. Second-order confirmatory factor analysis of HR commitment practices

First-order construct	First-order			Second-order	
	Indicator	Loading	t-value	Loading	t-value
Training support and employees' interest	HR1	0.674	--	0.910	9.626
	HR2	0.858	7.23		
Carreer plans and evaluation reporting	HR3	0.456	--	0.466	6.546
	HR4	0.784	9.80		
	HR5	0.875	9.50		
Fit statistics: $\chi 2(3)= 6.701$; CFI = 0.99; IFI = 0.99; GFI = 0.99; RMSEA = 0.04; (--): Fixed items					

Table 5. Results of the Path Modelling

IV -> DV	Path Coefficient
Technology integration → Web knowledge exchange	n.s.
IT personnel → Web knowledge exchange	(0.13, p<0.05)
Commitment-based HR practices → Web knowledge exchange	(0.55, p<0.01)
Customer Power → Web knowledge exchange	(-0.23, p<0.01)
Supplier Power → Web knowledge exchange	n.s.

Note: n.s. = not significant

nel in the firm is an important factor for knowledge exchange through Internet technologies. Hypothesis 3 was confirmed (0.55, p<0.01), with commitment-based HR practices being the strongest factor in the proposed model. This indicates that the presence of commitment-based HR practices is a critical factor driving Web knowledge exchange. Hypothesis 4 was supported (-0.23, p<0.01), while hypothesis 5 did not find support, indicating a negative relationship between customer power and Web knowledge exchange and a non-significant relationship between supplier power and Web knowledge exchange through Internet technologies. The implications of these results are discussed in the next section.

5. DISCUSSION

The effects of five TOE factors on Web knowledge exchange are analyzed using a data set of SMEs. The empirical results reveal that factors have differential effects. Regarding the technological context, not only tangible but also intangible resources have been incorporated in our model: technology integration and IT expertise. The results suggest that though IT expertise is positively associated with Web knowledge exchange, a non-significant relationship was found for the relationship between technology integration and Web knowledge exchange. The first finding confirms recent research (Aboelmaged, 2014; Bordonaba-Juste et al. 2012), which found that IT expertise is one of the main factors that affect the extent of e-business use. However, the second finding counters existing research (e.g. Zhu et al., 2006, Zhu and Kraemer, 2005), which found that technology integration is positively related to the extent of e-business use (Zhu et al, 2006) and positively associated to e-business value (Zhu and Kraemer,

2005). A possible explanation may be that previous studies have focused on aggregate measures of the organizational adoption and use of Internet technologies and, within that context, technology integration may be more crucial. In contrast, within the specific context of SMEs and knowledge exchange, intangible IT resources (Bharadwaj 2000; O'Sullivan and Dooley, 2010) such as hiring specialized IT personnel seem to be the major technological drivers of knowledge exchange through Internet technologies. These results support the idea that IT per se do not create value, because every firm can purchase IT in the marketplace. Rather, IT value creation depends more on intangible IT assets (Soto-Acosta and Meroño-Cerdan, 2008).

Regarding the organizational context, the effect of commitment-based HR practices on Web knowledge exchange is analyzed. Results show a positive relationship between these two constructs, with commitment-based HR practices being the strongest factor in our model. This finding supports previous studies (Collins and Smith, 2006) which, though not focusing on Internet technologies, found that commitment-based HR practices were significantly related to knowledge exchange among workers. Thus, SMEs should focus on commitment-based HR practices, rather than on transaction-based HR practices, in order to create a social climate which promotes Web knowledge exchange. With regard to the environmental context, results suggest a negative relationship between customer power and Web knowledge exchange and a non-significant relationship between supplier power and Web knowledge exchange. These findings partially support recent research (Chan et al. 2012; Zhu et al. 2006), which found that competition may deter firms from using Internet technologies. Thus, although external pressure from customers and suppliers affects e-business adoption (Del Aguila and Padilla, 2008; Wang and Ahmed, 2009), competition is not necessarily good for technology use. Too much competitive pressure leads firms to change rapidly form one technology to another without sufficient time to use the technology (Zhu et al., 2004; Zhu et al., 2006). Our findings also confirm previous research using SMEs. In this sense, Chang et al. (2012) find that competition intensity is negatively related to the extent of e-collaboration use in SMEs. Thus, this finding demonstrates that Internet technology use for knowledge exchange does not emerge from external pressure.

6. CONCLUSION, LIMITATIONS AND FUTURE RESEARCH

Organizations' survival and success depend on the effort and interactions of employees since they carry the skills and generate knowledge to transform new ideas into innovations. Since firms are increasingly adopting Internet technologies for business processes (Soto-Acosta and Meroño-Cerdan, 2008), it is essential to assimilate Internet technologies to support information sharing and knowledge exchange within firms. Hence, it is important to understand which factors influence the use of Internet technologies for knowledge exchange. This study examines the influence of five contextual factors on knowledge exchange through Internet technologies. Empirical results identified significant factors shaping knowledge exchange through Internet technologies and their effects.

This paper makes several contributions to the literature. First, it analyzes significant factor shaping Web knowledge exchange in SMEs. Previous studies in the literature have tended to focus on large businesses, with very few and recent studies analyzing Internet technology adoption and use in SMEs (e.g. Chang et al. 2012; Chong et al. 2009; Dholokia and Kshetri, 2004; Huy et al. 2012). Based on a large sample of SMEs, this paper favors the generalizability of results to SMEs. Second, using the TOE framework the use of Internet technologies for knowledge exchange is conceptualized within SMEs.

Previous studies have shown the usefulness of the TOE framework for understanding the adoption and use of Internet technologies within firms (e.g. Bordonaba-Juste et al., 2012; Chan et al., 2012; Gu et al., 2012; San Martín et al., 2012). However, much of the existing research is focused on a single aggregate view of the organizational adoption and use of Internet technologies (e.g. Bordonaba-Juste et al., 2012; Gibbs and Kraemer, 2004; Hong and Zhu, 2006; Xu et al, 2004; Zhu et al. 2003; Zhu and Kraemer, 2005). In this paper, we extend previous work by analyzing how Internet technologies use affect a specific activity within SMEs: knowledge exchange. Third, we theorized and tested differential effects of the TOE factors on knowledge exchange through Internet technologies in SMEs. Previous research has found that organizational factors are key drivers of Internet adoption and usage. The high positive influence found suggests that commitment-based HR practices affect the organizational social climate that motivates employees to work together and exchange knowledge.

While the contributions of the present study are significant, there are some aspects which can be addressed in future research. First, the sample used was from Spain. It may be possible that the findings could be extrapolated to other countries, since economic and technological development in Spain is similar to other OECD Member countries. However, similar studies in different countries are likely to show different results, especially when considering high IT advanced countries such as the USA, Finland, and Canada. Thus, in future research, a sampling frame that combines firms from different countries could be used in order to provide a more international perspective on the subject. Second, developing solid instruments in the IT literature is still an ongoing procedure of development, testing and refinement (Zhu et al., 2004; Zhu et al., 2006). Although reliability and validity were empirically tested in our data set, further confirmatory studies are necessary to determine the external validity of the results. Particularly, as discussed in the hypotheses section, competition constructs in our study capture vertical competition, which needs to be enriched in further research to include horizontal competition. Future research designs could consider other important organizational context factors such as organizational strategy and culture. Third, this research takes a static, cross-sectional picture of contextual factors affecting Web knowledge exchange, which makes it difficult to address the issue of how contextual factors and their importance may change over years. A longitudinal study could enrich the findings. These suggestions should be taken into account in future studies to increase the validity of our findings.

ACKNOWLEDGMENT

The authors are very grateful for financial support from the Fundación Cajamurcia.

REFERENCES

Aboelmaged, M. G. (2014). Predicting e-readiness at firm-level: An analysis of technological, organizational and environmental (TOE) effects on e-maintenance readiness in manufacturing firms. *International Journal of Information Management, 34*(5), 639–651. doi:10.1016/j.ijinfomgt.2014.05.002

Alavi, M., & Leidner, D. E. (2001). Review: knowledge management and knowledge management systems: conceptual foundations and research issues. *Management Information Systems Quarterly, 25*(1), 107–136. doi:10.2307/3250961

Bagozzi, R. P., & Yi, Y. (1998). On evaluation of structural equations models. *Journal of the Academy of Marketing Science, 16*(1), 74–94. doi:10.1007/BF02723327

Baumgartner, H., & Homburg, C. (1996). Applications of structural equation modelling in marketing and consumer research: A review. *International Journal of Research in Marketing, 13*(1), 139–161. doi:10.1016/0167-8116(95)00038-0

Bayo-Moriones, A., & Lera-Lopez, F. (2007). A firm level analysis of determinants of ICT adoption in Spain. *Technovation, 27*(6/7), 352–366. doi:10.1016/j.technovation.2007.01.003

Bergkvist, L., & Rossiter, J. R. (2007). The predictive validity of multiple-item versus single-item measures of the same constructs. *JMR, Journal of Marketing Research, 44*(2), 175–184. doi:10.1509/jmkr.44.2.175

Bhagwat, R., & Sharma, M. K. (2007). Information system architecture: A framework for a cluster of small- and medium-sized enterprises (SMEs). *Production Planning and Control, 18*(4), 283–296. doi:10.1080/09537280701248578

Bharadwaj, A. S. (2000). A resource-based perspective on information technology capability and firm performance: An empirical investigation. *Management Information Systems Quarterly, 24*(1), 169–196. doi:10.2307/3250983

Bradford, M., Earp, J. B., & Grabski, S. (2014). Centralized end-to-end identity and access management and ERP systems: A multi-case analysis using the technology organization environment framework. *International Journal of Accounting Information Systems, 15*(2), 149–165. doi:10.1016/j.accinf.2014.01.003

Chan, F. T. S., Chong, A. Y.-L., & Zhou, L. (2012). An empirical investigation of factors affecting e-collaboration diffusion in SMEs. *International Journal of Production Economics, 138*(2), 329–344. doi:10.1016/j.ijpe.2012.04.004

Chang, I., Hsin-Ginn, H., Ming-Chien, H., Ming-Hui, L., & David, C. Y. (2007). Factors affecting the adoption of electronic signature: Executives' perspective of hospital information department. *Decision Support Systems, 44*(1), 350–359. doi:10.1016/j.dss.2007.04.006

Chong, A. Y. L., & Chan, F. T. S. (2012). Radio Frequency Identification (RFID) in the healthcare industry: A multi-stage diffusion analysis. *Expert Systems with Applications, 39*(10), 8645–8654. doi:10.1016/j.eswa.2012.01.201

Churchill, G. A. (1979). A paradigm for developing better measures of marketing constructs. *JMR, Journal of Marketing Research, 16*(1), 64–73. doi:10.2307/3150876

Collins, C. J., & Smith, K. G. (2006). Knowledge exchange and combination: The role of human resource practices in the performance of high-technology firms. *Academy of Management Journal, 49*(3), 544–560. doi:10.5465/AMJ.2006.21794671

Colomo-Palacios, R., Fernandes, E., Sabbagh, M., & Amescua-Seco, A. (2012). Human and intellectual capital management in the cloud: Software vendor perspective. *Journal of Universal Computer Science, 18*(11), 1544–1557.

Delery, J. E., & Doty, D. H. (1996). Modes of theorizing in strategic human resource management: Test of universalistic contingency, and configurational performance predictions. *Academy of Management Journal, 39*(4), 802–835. doi:10.2307/256713

Devaraj, S., & Kholi, R. (2003). Performance impacts of information technology: Is actual usage the missing link? *Management Science, 49*(3), 273–289. doi:10.1287/mnsc.49.3.273.12736

Dholokia, R. R., & Kshetri, N. (2004). Factors impacting the adoption of the internet among SMEs. *Small Business Economics, 23*(4), 311–322. doi:10.1023/B:SBEJ.0000032036.90353.1f

Fornell, C., & Larcker, F. D. (1981). Evaluating structural equation models with unobservable variables and measurement error. *JMR, Journal of Marketing Research, 18*(1), 39–50. doi:10.2307/3151312

Fox, S. (2000). Communities of practice, foucault and actor network theory. *Journal of Management Studies, 37*(6), 853–867. doi:10.1111/1467-6486.00207

Gibbs, J. L., & Kraemer, K. L. (2004). A cross-country investigation of the determinants of scope of e-commerce use: An institutional approach. *Electronic Markets, 14*(2), 124–137. doi:10.1080/10196780410001675077

Gu, V. C., Cao, Q., & Duan, W. (2012). Unified modeling language (UML) IT adoption — A holistic model of organizational capabilities perspective. *Decision Support Systems, 54*(1), 257–269. doi:10.1016/j.dss.2012.05.034

Hair, J. F., Celsi, M., Money, A., Samouel, P., & Page, M. (2011). *Essentials of business research methods* (2nd ed.). Armonk, NY: ME Sharpe.

Hong, W., & Zhu, K. (2006). Migrating to internet-based e-commerce: Factors affecting e-commerce adoption and migration at the firm level. *Information & Management, 43*(2), 204–221. doi:10.1016/j.im.2005.06.003

Hsu, P.-F., Ray, S., & Li-Hsieh, Y.-Y. (2014). Examining cloud computing adoption intention, pricing mechanism, and deployment model. *International Journal of Information Management, 34*(4), 474–488. doi:10.1016/j.ijinfomgt.2014.04.006

Huy, L. V., Rowe, F., Truex, D., & Huynh, M. Q. (2012). An empirical study of determinants of e-commerce adoption in smes in vietnam an economy in transition. *Journal of Global Information Management, 20*(3), 23–54. doi:10.4018/jgim.2012070102

Kuan, K. Y., & Chau, Y. K. (2001). A perception model for EDI adoption in small businesses using a technology-organization-environment framework. *Information & Management, 38*(1), 507–521. doi:10.1016/S0378-7206(01)00073-8

Lian, J., Yen, D., & Wang, Y. (2014). An exploratory study to understand the critical factors affecting the decision to adopt cloud computing in Taiwan hospital. *International Journal of Information Management, 34*(1), 28–36. doi:10.1016/j.ijinfomgt.2013.09.004

Lopez-Nicolas, C., & Soto-Acosta, P. (2010). Analyzing ICT adoption and use effects on knowledge creation: An empirical investigation in SMEs. *International Journal of Information Management, 30*(6), 521–528. doi:10.1016/j.ijinfomgt.2010.03.004

Lucio-Nieto, T., Colomo-Palacios, R., Soto-Acosta, P., Popa, S., & Amescua-Seco, A. (2012). Implementing an IT service information management framework: The case of COTEMAR. *International Journal of Information Management, 32*(6), 589–594. doi:10.1016/j.ijinfomgt.2012.08.004

Meroño-Cerdan, A., Soto-Acosta, P., & Lopez-Nicolas, C. (2008). ª). Analyzing collaborative technologies' effect on performance through intranet use orientations. *Journal of Enterprise Information Management, 21*(1), 39–51. doi:10.1108/17410390810842246

Meroño-Cerdan, A., Soto-Acosta, P., & Lopez-Nicolas, C. (2008b). How do collaborative technologies affect innovation in SMEs? *International Journal of e-Collaboration, 4*(4), 33–50. doi:10.4018/jec.2008100103

Nahapiet, J., & Ghoshal, S. (1998). Social capital, intellectual capital, and the organizational advantage. *Academy of Management Review, 23,* 242–266.

O'Sullivan, D., & Dooley, L. (2010). Collaborative innovation for the management of information technology resources. *International Journal of Human Capital and Information Technology Professionals, 1*(1), 16–30. doi:10.4018/jhcitp.2010091102

Pérez-López, S., & Alegre, J. (2012). Information technology competency, knowledge processes and firm performance. *Industrial Management & Data Systems, 112*(4), 644–662. doi:10.1108/02635571211225521

Petrescu, M. (2013). Marketing research using single-item indicators in structural equation model. *Journal of Marketing Analytics, 1*(2), 99–117. doi:10.1057/jma.2013.7

Podsakoff, P. M., Mackenzie, S. B., Lee, J., & Podsakoff, N. P. (2003). Common method biases in behavioral research: A critical review of the literature and recommended remedies. *The Journal of Applied Psychology, 20*(5), 879–903. doi:10.1037/0021-9010.88.5.879 PMID:14516251

Poon, W.-Y., Leung, K., & Lee, S.-Y. (2002). The comparison of single item constructs by relative mean and relative variance. *Organizational Research Methods, 5*(3), 275–298. doi:10.1177/1094428102005003005

Porter, M. E. (1985). *Competitive Advantage*. New York: Free Press.

Ramdani, B., Chevers, D., & Williams, D. (2013). SMEs adoption of enterprise applications: A technology-organisation-environment model. *Journal of Small Business and Enterprise Development, 20*(4), 89–115.

San Martín, S., López-Catalán, B., & Ramón-Jerónimo, M. A. (2012). Factors determining firms' perceived performance of mobile commerce. *Industrial Management & Data Systems, 112*(6), 946–963. doi:10.1108/02635571211238536

Sethi, V., & King, W. (1994). Development of Measures to Assess the Extent to Which an Information Technology Application provides Competitive Advantage. *Management Science, 40*(12), 1601–1627. doi:10.1287/mnsc.40.12.1601

Sila, I. (2013). Factors affecting the adoption of B2B e-commerce technologies. *Electronic Commerce Research, 13*(2), 199–236. doi:10.1007/s10660-013-9110-7

Soto-Acosta, P., Colomo-Palacios, R., & Perez-Gonzalez, D. (2011). Examining whether highly e-innovative firms are more e-effective. *Informatica, 35*(4), 481–488.

Soto-Acosta, P., & Meroño-Cerdan, A. (2006). An analysis and comparison of web development between local governments and SMEs in Spain. *International Journal of Electronic Business*, *4*(2), 191–203. doi:10.1504/IJEB.2006.009790

Soto-Acosta, P., & Meroño-Cerdan, A. (2008). Analyzing e-Business value creation from a resource-based perspective. *International Journal of Information Management*, *28*(1), 49–60. doi:10.1016/j.ijinfomgt.2007.05.001

Straub, D. W. (1989). Validating instruments in MIS research. *Management Information Systems Quarterly*, *13*(2), 147–169. doi:10.2307/248922

Teo, T. S. H., Ranganathan, C., & Dhaliwal, J. (2006). Key dimensions of inhibitors for the deployment of web-based business-to-business electronic commerce. *IEEE Transactions on Engineering Management*, *53*(3), 395–411. doi:10.1109/TEM.2006.878106

Tornatzky, L. G., & Fleischer, M. (1990). *The process of technological innovation*. Lexington, MA: Lexington Books.

Tsui, A. S., Pearce, J. L., Porter, L. W., & Tripoli, A. M. (1997). Alternative approaches to the employee-organization relationship: Does investment in employees pay off? *Academy of Management Journal*, *40*(5), 1089–1121. doi:10.2307/256928

Wang, Y., & Ahmed, P. (2009). The moderating effect of the business strategic orientation on e-commerce adoption: Evidence from UK family run SMEs. *The Journal of Strategic Information Systems*, *18*(1), 16–30. doi:10.1016/j.jsis.2008.11.001

Wang, Y. M., Wang, Y. S., & Yang, Y. F. (2010). Understanding the determinants of RFID adoption in the manufacturing industry. *Technological Forecasting and Social Change*, *77*(5), 803–815. doi:10.1016/j.techfore.2010.03.006

Xu, S., Zhu, K., & Gibbs, J. (2004). Global technology, local adoption: A cross-country investigation of Internet adoption by companies in the United States and China. *Electronic Markets*, *14*(1), 13–24. doi:10.1080/1019678042000175261

Youndt, M. A., Snell, S. A., Dean, J. W. Jr, & Lepak, D. P. (1996). Human resource management, manufacturing strategy and firm performance. *Academy of Management Journal*, *39*(4), 836–866. doi:10.2307/256714

Zhu, K., & Kraemer, K. (2005). Post adoption variations in usage and value of e-business by organizations: Cross-country evidence from the retail industry. *Information Systems Research*, *16*(1), 61–84. doi:10.1287/isre.1050.0045

Zhu, K., Kraemer, K., & Xu, S. (2003). Electronic business adoption by European firms: A cross-country assessment of the facilitators and inhibitors. *European Journal of Information Systems*, *12*(4), 251–268. doi:10.1057/palgrave.ejis.3000475

Zhu, K., Kraemer, K. L., & Xu, S. (2006). The process of innovation assimilation by firms in different countries: A technology diffusion perspective on e-business. *Management Science*, *52*(10), 1557–1576. doi:10.1287/mnsc.1050.0487

Zhu, K., Kraemer, K. L., Xu, S., & Dedrick, J. (2004). Information technology payoff in e-business environments: An international perspective on value creation of e-business in the financial services industry. *Journal of Management Information Systems, 21*(1), 17–54.

Zhu, Y., Li, Y., Wang, W., & Chen, J. (2010). What leads to the post-implementation success of ERP? An empirical study of the chinese retail industry. *International Journal of Information Management, 30*(3), 265–276. doi:10.1016/j.ijinfomgt.2009.09.007

APPENDIX: MEASURES

Technology Integration

- The website is electronically integrated with back-end systems and databases
- Company databases are electronically integrated to that of business partners (clients, suppliers...)

IT Expertise

- Number of IT professionals (#)

Commitment-Based HR Practices

- Employees' interest are taken into account for decision-making
- Our company support employees willing to take further training
- Our company has established career paths
- Performance appraisals are conducted on a regular basis
- Employees are informed about their performance appraisals

Vertical Competition

- Pressure clients exert on purchasing conditions
- Pressure suppliers exert on purchasing conditions

Web Knowledge Exchange

- The Intranet and other Web technologies are used to exchange knowledge between employees
- Website and other Web technologies are used to exchange knowledge or debate with customers
- The Extranet and other Web technologies are used to exchange knowledge or debate with business partners

Chapter 8
Mapping the Enterprise Social Network (ESN) Spectrum in Knowledge Management and Product Innovations

Aparna Venugopal
Indian Institute of Management Kozhikode, India

T. N. Krishnan
Indian Institute of Management Kozhikode, India

ABSTRACT

This book chapter unravels the difference brought into traditional knowledge management due to the use of enterprise social networks (ESNs). The advantages and barriers to the use of ESNs in organizations are also explained. The ESN spectrum and the corresponding knowledge management practices and innovation types are clearly delineated in this chapter. There are myriads of human as well as social factors affecting the usage and implementation of ESNs in organizations. This book chapter explores these factors too. Organizations may require special mechanisms to utilize the knowledge shared via ESNs and transform them into innovations. The book chapter suggests a few of these mechanisms. In this book chapter we use the theory of technology acceptance and works testing the theory of media richness to understand the varied uses of ESNs in knowledge management and innovation in organizations.

INTRODUCTION

Knowledge management primarily requires that tacit and explicit knowledge be identified and acquired from within or outside the firm and be transformed to innovations. Generally in business enterprises, knowledge is acquired from employees within the firm and from customers, partner institutions, partner universities, research centers and suppliers outside the firms. In our book chapter, we explore the new age ways of knowledge sharing in firms, and its linkages with knowledge management and innovation. We will also explore the barriers, advantages and facilitators to these new ways of knowledge management in firms.

DOI: 10.4018/978-1-4666-9607-5.ch008

In the last two decades organizational researchers (Nicolas & Cerdan, 2011; Carneiro, 2000; Darroch & McNaughton, 2002; & Du Plessis, 2007) have successfully and exhaustively established the linkage between knowledge management and firm level innovation. At the same time, Information Systems researchers have been showing a burgeoning interest in the topic of social media. Enterprises have already built bridges across these disparate realms and started using social media for knowledge management and innovation. To mention a few, Macy's uses Tibbr, T mobile uses Jive, Boral uses Yammer, Nokia uses Social cast, Best Buy uses Kaltura, GE uses Chatter, IBM uses Beehive and Atos uses BlueKiwi (Fee, 2013). These social media platforms used to share content within and sometimes across business and commercial enterprises are called Enterprise Social Networks (ESNs). ESNs are defined as

"Web-based platforms that allow workers to (1) communicate messages with specific coworkers or broadcast messages to everyone in the organization; (2) explicitly indicate or implicitly revealparticular coworkers as communication partners; (3) post, edit, and sort text and files linked tothemselves or others; and (4) view the messages, connections, text, and files communicated,posted, edited and sorted by anyone else in the organization at any time of their choosing" (Leonardi et al, 2013; p. 2). Social media platforms in itself are defined as the platforms used to create, modify, share and discuss internet content in the form of content sharing sites, blogs, social networking sites and wikis (Kietzmann et al, 2011).

The social media phenomenon had started around 1994 with the arrival of Geocities: An internet site that allowed individuals to create their own web pages in cyberspace 'cities' named after commonly used names for industries. Following this, multitudes of social media sites mushroomed across the world. Facebook, WhatsApp, Instagram, Pininterst, Youtube, Linkedin, Wikipedia, MySpace and Flickr are just the tip of the iceberg. And today even business enterprises use social media in the form of ESNs to share classified contents with sensitive and proprietary knowledge.

Knowledge sharing is essential to knowledge management and innovation and knowledge management in turn enhances firm financial performance (Goel et al, 2010). In this new era, the ESN platforms to share information are also pivotal to knowledge management and innovation. Ideally, management research should reflect the real life business situations and amalgamate enterprise issues across disciplines. Yet, in spite of the growing importance of Enterprise Social Networks (ESNs) in enterprises, researchers have not pursued the issues in ESN adoption in firms, or the role of ESNs in knowledge management or innovation extensively. In fact, very few researchers as Swan et al (1999), and Karkkainen et al (2010) have focused on the particular issues of knowledge sharing in ESNs and how it impacts firm level innovation. In this book chapter we intend to unravel

- The changes brought in traditional knowledge management with the adoption of ESNs into it
- The barriers to the use of ESNs for knowledge management and innovation in firms
- The advantages in using ESNs for knowledge management and innovation in firms
- The wide spectrum of social media available in the market today and the corresponding varieties of knowledge management practices and innovation they can encourage.
- The human and social factors affecting the quality and ease of use of the various ESNs for sharing knowledge in firms
- The mechanisms used by organizations to ensure that the knowledge shared via the collaborative tools of ESNs end in fruitful innovations for the firm.

In this book chapter we use the theory of technology acceptance model and works disproving media richness theory to explain the varied use of ESNs in knowledge management and innovation practices in organizations.

How Has Traditional Knowledge Management Changed with the Advent of ESNs?

Traditionally, knowledge management can be viewed using five distinct lenses: the technology used for the knowledge management, the patterns detected from knowledge analyses, the processes, work practices and procedures associated with managing knowledge assets, the algorithms to develop new capabilities from existing knowledge and the network collaborations to create new knowledge (Binney, 2001). Figure 1 depicts these traditional lenses of understanding knowledge management in organizations.

The advent of social media opened an array of new possibilities for collaboration within and across firms for developing knowledge and capability. Along with this, social media drastically changed the landscape of processes, procedures and work practices used in conjunction with the knowledge sharing technologies. In Figure 2 we depict the changes in the traditional knowledge management lenses with the advent of ESNs.

Von Grogh (2012) explains in detail how the knowledge management scenario has changed with the use of ESNs. The knowledge management practices and procedures tend to be more cooperative and collaborative. They are also based on open platforms and enabling services. Di Micco et al (2009) suggests that IBM uses Beehive as a collaborative tool to strengthen weak ties in their organization, more than anything else. The proponents of Beehive expect that it promotes employee collaboration even amongst

Figure 1. Traditional lenses of understanding knowledge management

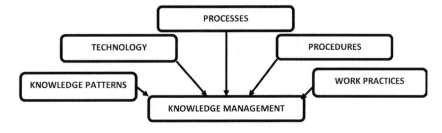

Figure 2. Changes to traditional knowledge management lenses with use of ESNs

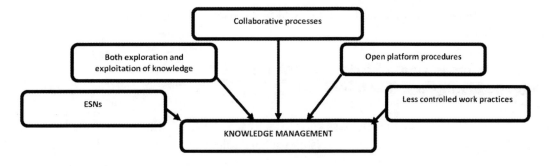

employees who do not know each other, for the success of their projects. An open sharing of knowledge across the organization leads to enhanced exploration of new knowledge across different departments as well as exploitation of existing capabilities.

Barriers to the Use of ESNs for Knowledge Management and Innovation in Firms

The opportunity to share knowledge across these ESN platforms are often riddled with concerns over privacy & security, technically inept employees, unwanted transparency in knowledge sharing, and a negative perception that social network usage is unprofessional. The content beings shared in the ESN is much more sensitive in nature than the content usually shared on the other social media in the web. When a firm starts using ESNs out of the blue, the knowledge sharing efficiency of many of the older employees might actually decrease, due to their technical incompetence. Many firms and managers do not like the added transparency in the knowledge management practices that comes along with the use of ESNs, as they believe it gives away too much information to everyone involved. When everyone in the firm is exposed to the same information, and everyone involved in the issue is aware of it, it can either cause free riding or groupthink. Some firms also believe that the use of social media at work might actually be detrimental to professionalism and might lead employees to while away time. So while implementing ESNs, some of the major barriers faced by organizations, might occur in the form of political and cultural resistances (Cook, 2008).

In his work Cook (2008) suggests that all organizations might not benefit from the use of ESNs. From purely a monetary and technical perspective the ESNs can also be a burden on the allowed bandwidth in the firm. Only organizations willing to cede the control in communications and command lines, and which can agree to the transformation of knowledge management into a facilitating and aggregating role can benefit from the use of ESNs (Balatzis, Ormrod, & Grainger, 2008; Cook, 2008). The use of ESNs might also precipitate other clashes in organizational philosophies. For one, traditional knowledge management did not necessitate the incorporation of diversity into the clusters of knowledge sharing as much as ESNs do (Balatzis, Ormrod, & Grainger, 2008). Hence, an organization which is unwilling to allow diverse opinions to be formulated and floated around in its knowledge management process, might find it difficult to implement and accept ESNs for knowledge management in their organizations. Also, it has been suggested (Brzozowski, 2009) that the targeted use of ESNs might disrupt chances of radical innovation in organizations, as the innovative thought processes of individual employees get more influenced by opinion leaders. Corporate IT might not be in favor of implementing ESNs as they are more prone to cyber attacks and information on the ESNs can be deemed unsecure. The use of ESNs are a heavier burden on the allowed corporate bandwidth too (Balatzis, Ormrod, & Grainger, 2008). Organizations also run the additional risk of unknowingly using content not owned by the firm (Von Krogh, 2012).

The Advantages in Using ESNs in Firms for Knowledge Management and Innovation

Enterprise social networks enable seamless knowledge sharing and coordination in globally distributed, virtual and project based organizations. ESNs play a huge role in sharing content cheap and fast, when organization members are dispersed across the world. Most often we see that project based organizations, developed for one time projects, start WatsApp chats for niche problem solving by bringing in specific experts to the chat group. In spite of increased fragmentation of the work place the ESNs enable enhance collaboration in firms. Even though the employees are extensively detached from the work place and other team members, ESNs provide a platform for collaborative conflict management, comprehensive joint decision making, and information exchange. Organizations use ESNs to enhance, the recreational activities of employees, collaboration among employees, communication channels (Baltatzis, Ormrod & Grainger, 2008). ESNs enable employees to stay in touch, to know what others are working on and most importantly where the niche knowledge sources are. The advantages of ESNs in organizations can be basically drawn from the weak tie theory. The much cited weak tie theory proposed by Granovetter (1983) suggests that the weak ties, that connects an employee with his lesser known group of acquaintances is crucial in drawing information. DiMicco et al (2008) suggested that when using ESNs employees are actually trying to build stronger bonds with their weaker ties, so that they can get to lesser known knowledge sources. Thus the major advantage to the use of ESNs in organizations lies in tapping the otherwise lesser known knowledge sources in the firm. ESNs also give employees an opportunity to manage their identities and impressions about their work in the workplace. This added identity of the self as a part of the organization also motivates employees to contribute more towards the betterment of the firm and collaborate with lesser known employees of the firm (Wang & Kobsa, 2009). On genre analysis Riemer et al (2012) found that Yammer is being used in Deloitte Australia for information sharing, crowd sourcing ideas, finding expertise, solving problems, and building relationships.

The ESN Spectrum and the Corresponding Knowledge Management and Innovation Practices in Firms

In this section we intent to map the links between the various kinds of social media as; content sharing sites, blogs, social networking sites and wikis and the corresponding knowledge management practices and innovations. Each variety of social media might be more suitable for a particular kind of knowledge management practice and innovation. Lopez-Nicolas & Merono-Cerdan (2011) found that personalized modes of knowledge management as in ESNs have higher impact on radical innovations. The traditional modes of knowledge management result in incremental innovation (Swan et al, 1999). With the use of ESNs, knowledge management in organizations can produce both radical and incremental innovations. In a genre analysis of the use of Yammer at Deloitte Australia, Riemer et al (2012) found that it is being used in actively used in all knowledge practices for innovation. Yammer is used by employees to provide inputs, to create new knowledge, to harness existing knowledge and most importantly to build the social fabric a shared cognitive capital to facilitate effective and effortless communication and knowledge sharing (Riemer et al, 2012).

In figure 3, we show the knowledge management practice and the potential type of innovations that can arise from each type of social media in the enterprise. In an analysis of the various ESNs out there, Koplowitz (2010) suggested that organizations looking to reduce administrative overheads should probably adopt IGLOO or blueKiwi, organizations looking for a low cost collaboration and social solution with minimal IT support should probably adopt Jive, Microsoft SharePoint, Newsgator, Novell Pulse or Ramius Sixent and organizations looking for cutting edge innovation should probably adopt IBM Lotus, Mindtouch,Socialtext or Telligent.

While blogs help to evaluate markets and customers quickly, content sharing sites provide useful information about site visitors, social networking sites are good for collaboration, and wikis are benefi-

Figure 3. Enterprise social media, knowledge management practice and potential innovation

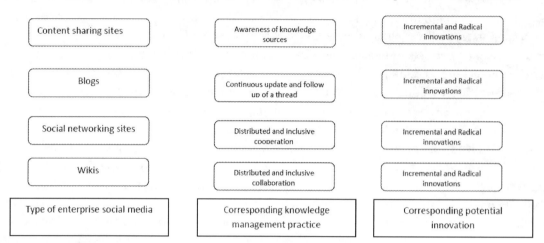

cial for co-development (Safko, 2010). In an attempt to understand why different ESNs should promote different knowledge sharing, innovation, and collaboration patterns, we found literature has often used the media richness theory to explain the varying effects of different media uses. In their seminal paper on media richness theory, Daft & Lengel (1986), suggested that the richness of a media depended upon the personal focus of the medium, ability of medium to transmit multiple cues, language variety, and feedback immediacy (Dennis & Kinney, 1998). According to media richness theory (Daft & Lengel, 1986), team performance improves with use of richer media. Following, this logic, ESNs with richer media should also promote team performances in organization. Yet, like many other researchers (El-Shinnawy & Markus, 1997; Dennis & Kinney, 1998) who contested the validity of the media richness theory, we too suggest that the choice of an ESN and its effectiveness in an organization depends on much more than the richness of media at use. El-Shinnawy & Markus (1997) specifically suggested that the choice of a media in an organization would depend on the communication mode and documentation functionality of the media, more than media richness. Hence, we in this book chapter, we too suggest that organizations should choose ESNs based on their communication modes and required documentation functionalities. Organizations should also consider the broad requirements of the establishment, possible implications of deployment models, and that a single platform might not suffice (Koplowitz, 2010).

Human and Social Factors Affecting the Adoption of ESNs

Davis (1989a; 1993b) in his pioneering work on technology acceptance in organizations suggested that the actual use of any new technology depends on the system characteristics, the subjective norms, the perceived ease of use and perceived usefulness of the technology. In addition to these factors, Legris et al (2003) suggested that the acceptance of any new technology in a firm also depended on many unidentified subjective organizational and social factors. Following the work of Legris et al (2003), we too suggest that the ability of human beings to transcend from the traditional means of communication as emails, instant messaging etc to ESNs plays a key role in the adoption and diffusion of social media in the work place. The social context of the firm i.e the amount of trust, discipline, support and politics in the workplace will also be important in deciding the amount and sensitivity of knowledge being shared across the social media platforms. No firm is going to start sharing knowledge just because ESNs have been provided if distrust crawls deep within the skeletal framework of the firm. When contemplating the question of joining an ESN, employees often fear loss of privacy. These fears are usually triggered by added peer pressure to reveal more about their personal or work related information than they intend to, the efforts required to maintain impression about self and one's work, and unintentional social undermining of one's work (Wang & Kobsa, 2009). Farzan et al (2008) tested the improved participation of employees in IBM's Beehive, by promoting the new bees to busy bees depending on the points they gained for sharing content on the Beehive. Yet, they found that once the employees graduated to senior busy bees they stopped sharing content and some employees refused to join Beehive altogether due to privacy concerns. For example, Burns et al (2011) cite that the social behavior of an organization's employee becomes very important in how comfortable they are in sharing knowledge across social networking sites. Employees need to 'tag' themselves on shreds of information and let the content be 'updated', and then choose to 'follow' the content. Therefore an employee's level of comfort and trust in each other plays a big role in how collective knowledge is built in organizations via social networking sites. On the other hand, authors (Alistoun & Uphold, 2012; Thomas, Kellogg & Erickson, 2001) have already established that the presence of an enterprise social network enhances the level of employee engagement, trust, social capital and cooperation in the organization. Therefore, in this chapter, we understand that enterprise social networks build a better engaged and trusting employee population and this in turn, enhances knowledge sharing via enterprise social networks. The relationship is depicted in Figure 4.

Mechanisms Facilitating Translation of Knowledge Shared via ESNs into Innovations

Firms use adaptive ranking techniques to rank the contents of knowledge available on the ESNs. Using such techniques the knowledge available inside the firm can be prioritized and classified, thereby making it easier to use for innovative purposes. The ESNs also recommend specific individuals to access specific knowledge based on their roles in the firm, or the data they have accessed earlier. Thus the firm is able to identify experts in niche areas using recommender systems. Social media can also help create small communities of likeminded experts with overlapping interests across enterprise boundaries. Such communities help immensely in garnering information from outside the firms (Raghavan, 2002).

Von Grogh(2012) also suggests that organizations should use "knowledge managers" and "knowledge editors" to verify and validate the knowledge available on ESNs. These are some of the mechanisms that can be used by organizations to verify the knowledge available on ESNs and estimate their potential at translating into innovations.

Figure 4. Relationship between ESNs and knowledge sharing among employees

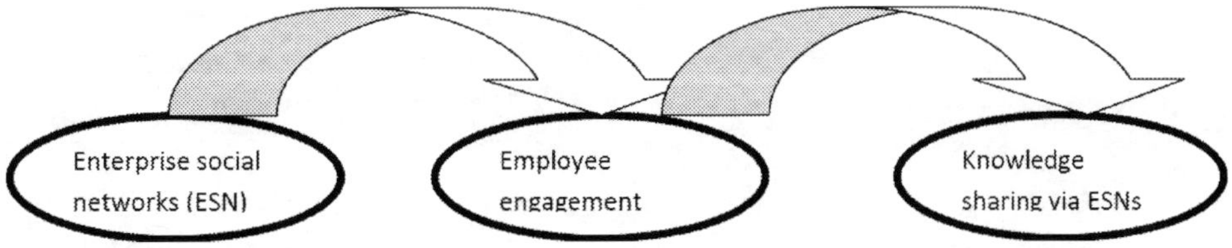

IMPLICATIONS AND FUTURE RESEARCH

The evolutionary journey of ESNs traversed from public sites to private site and now to in-house developed proprietary solutions. ESNs have often been termed as leaky pipes, social lubricants and echo chambers (Leonardi et al, 2013). The communication flowing across ESNs reach unintended receivers and hence the metaphor of a leaky pipe. While this is one of the highly cited negative aspects of ESN usage, ESNs also act as social lubricants bringing varied unknown employees together in an organization and acting as an echo chamber for like-minded people to collaborate with each other by voicing their opinions without conflict.

In this book chapter, we have delineated the exact type of social media and the type of knowledge practice and innovation related to it. Practitioners could develop knowledge management practices according to the social media being used in their organizations. Academicians can explore the possibility of using clusters of knowledge management practices for any one or a mix of social media in an organization.

We have emphasized that the greatest advantage to the use of ESNs in organizations lies in its ability to build strong bonds out of weak ties and then gather knowledge through these weak ties. We have also emphasized that the largest barrier to the implementation of ESNs in organizations lies in the clash of organizational philosophies. In future, researchers could explore the nuances of these barriers on the advantages of using ESNs. In other words, researchers could explore whether the clash in organizational philosophies affect ESN's ability to build strong bonds out of weak ties in organizations. If an organization that has followed a strict control policy in its communication channels till now, suddenly starts using ESN would it able to convert the weak ties of its employees into strong bonds? Thus, through this chapter, we provide clear directions for the future research on the role of ESNs in knowledge management and innovation.

This chapter is of significant importance to today's managers who want to enhance the IT enabled knowledge sharing options in their firms. A vivid description of the specific links between each variety of social media being used in firms and appropriate modes of knowledge management and innovation, will open doors to future researchers who want to explore knowledge management in the new era.

In this chapter we have explained the changes in the traditional knowledge management lenses with the use of ESNs. In future, researchers can attempt to understand knowledge management in terms the new lenses, i.e; collaborative practices, open platform procedure, exploration and exploitation of knowledge, and less controlled work practices. Practitioners could also make use of the changed approaches to knowledge management by trying to implement them in their organizations. In this book chapter we have also emphasized that practitioners using ESNs in the future should also employ knowledge managers and editors. We have suggested implications of the varied use of ESNs in organizations based on the technology acceptance model and the works disproving media richness theory. Future researchers could explore further ways to validate, prioritize and convert knowledge being shared in ESNs into potential innovations.

CONCLUSION

With the advent of ESNs, traditional knowledge management changed drastically. With more collaboration, and cooperation and an ability to leverage the weak ties, ESNs enabled organizations to innovate radically and incrementally. ESNs also enhance the trust and social capital in organizations, which in turn result in enhanced knowledge sharing. In this book chapter we unravel the changes in traditional knowledge management with the advent of ESNs, the advantages and disadvantage in its use and the human and social factors at play. This chapter is of significant importance to practitioners looking at potential ways of enhancing knowledge management with ESNs and enabling innovative firms. This chapter also highlights potential areas of future research in the use of ESNs in organizations.

REFERENCES

Baltatzis, G., Ormrod, D. G., & Grainger, N. (2008). Social networking tools for internal communication in large organizations: Benefits and barriers. *ACIS 2008 Proceedings*, 86.

Binney, D. (2001). The Knowledge Management spectrum–understanding the KM landscape. *Journal of Knowledge Management*, 5(1), 33–42. doi:10.1108/13673270110384383

Brzozowski, M. J. (2009, May). WaterCooler: exploring an organization through enterprise social media. In *Proceedings of the ACM 2009 International Conference on Supporting group work* (pp. 219-228). ACM. doi:10.1145/1531674.1531706

Burns, M. J., Craig, R. B. Jr, Friedman, B. D., Schott, P. D., & Senot, C. (2011). Transforming enterprise communications through the blending of social networking and unified communications. *Bell Labs Technical Journal*, 16(1), 19–34. doi:10.1002/bltj.20483

Carneiro, A. (2000). How does knowledge management influence innovation and competitiveness? *Journal of Knowledge Management*, 4(2), 87–98. doi:10.1108/13673270010372242

Cook, N. (2008). *Enterprise 2.0: How social software will change the future of work*. Gower Publishing, Ltd.

Daft, R. L., & Lengel, R. H. (1986). Organizational information requirements, media richness and structural design. *Management Science*, 32(5), 554–571. doi:10.1287/mnsc.32.5.554

Darroch, J., & McNaughton, R. (2002). Examining the link between knowledge management practices and types of innovation. *Journal of Intellectual Capital*, 3(3), 210–222. doi:10.1108/14691930210435570

Davis, F. D. (1989). Perceived usefulness, perceived ease of use, and user acceptance of information technology. *Management Information Systems Quarterly*, 13(3), 319–340. doi:10.2307/249008

Davis, F. D., Bagozzi, R. P., & Warshaw, P. R. (1989). User acceptance of computer technology: A comparison of two theoretical models. *Management Science*, 35(8), 982–1003. doi:10.1287/mnsc.35.8.982

Dennis, A. R., & Kinney, S. T. (1998). Testing media richness theory in the new media: The effects of cues, feedback, and task equivocality. *Information Systems Research*, 9(3), 256–274. doi:10.1287/isre.9.3.256

DiMicco, J., Millen, D. R., Geyer, W., Dugan, C., Brownholtz, B., & Muller, M. (2008, November). Motivations for social networking at work. In *Proceedings of the 2008 ACM Conference on Computer Supported Cooperative Work* (pp. 711-720). ACM. doi:10.1145/1460563.1460674

DiMicco, J. M., Geyer, W., Millen, D. R., Dugan, C., & Brownholtz, B. (2009, January). People sensemaking and relationship building on an enterprise social network site. In *System Sciences, 2009. HICSS'09. 42nd Hawaii International Conference on* (pp. 1-10). IEEE.

Du Plessis, M. (2007). The role of knowledge management in innovation. *Journal of Knowledge Management*, *11*(4), 20–29. doi:10.1108/13673270710762684

El-Shinnawy, M., & Markus, M. L. (1997). The poverty of media richness theory: Explaining people's choice of electronic mail vs. voice mail. *International Journal of Human-Computer Studies*, *46*(4), 443–467. doi:10.1006/ijhc.1996.0099

Farzan, R., DiMicco, J. M., Millen, D. R., Dugan, C., Geyer, W., & Brownholtz, E. A. (2008, April). Results from deploying a participation incentive mechanism within the enterprise. In *Proceedings of the SIGCHI Conference on Human Factors in Computing Systems* (pp. 563-572). ACM. doi:10.1145/1357054.1357145

Fee. (2013). Retrieved from http://mashable.com/2013/06/14/enterprise-social-networks/

Goel, A. K., Sharma, G. R., & Rastogi, R. (2010). Knowledge management implementation in NTPC: An Indian PSU. *Management Decision*, *48*(3), 383–395. doi:10.1108/00251741011037756

Granovetter, M. (1983). The strength of weak ties: A network theory revisited. *Sociological Theory*, *1*(1), 201–233. doi:10.2307/202051

Kärkkäinen, H., Jussila, J., & Väisänen, J. (2010, October). Social media use and potential in business-to-business companies' innovation. In *Proceedings of the 14th international academic mindtrek conference: Envisioning future media environments* (pp. 228-236). ACM. doi:10.1145/1930488.1930536

Kietzmann, J. H., Hermkens, K., McCarthy, I. P., & Silvestre, B. S. (2011). Social media? Get serious! Understanding the functional building blocks of social media. *Business Horizons*, *54*(3), 241–251. doi:10.1016/j.bushor.2011.01.005

Koplowitz, R. (2010). *Enterprise Social Networking 2010 Market Overview*. Forrester Research.

Legris, P., Ingham, J., & Collerette, P. (2003). Why do people use information technology? A critical review of the technology acceptance model. *Information & Management*, *40*(3), 191–204. doi:10.1016/S0378-7206(01)00143-4

Leonardi, P. M., Huysman, M., & Steinfield, C. (2013). Enterprise social media: Definition, history, and prospects for the study of social technologies in organizations. *Journal of Computer-Mediated Communication*, *19*(1), 1–19. doi:10.1111/jcc4.12029

López-Nicolás, C., & Meroño-Cerdán, Á. L. (2011). Strategic knowledge management, innovation and performance. *International Journal of Information Management*, *31*(6), 502–509. doi:10.1016/j.ijinfomgt.2011.02.003

Raghavan, P. (2002). Social networks: From the web to the enterprise. *IEEE Internet Computing*, *6*(1), 91–94. doi:10.1109/4236.989007

Safko, L. (2010). *The social media bible: tactics, tools, and strategies for business success*. John Wiley & Sons.

Swan, J., Newell, S., Scarbrough, H., & Hislop, D. (1999). Knowledge Management and Innovation: Networks and networking. *Journal of Knowledge Management, 3*(4), 262–275. doi:10.1108/13673279910304014

Thomas, J. C., Kellogg, W. A., & Erickson, T. (2001). The knowledge management puzzle: Human and social factors in knowledge management. *IBM Systems Journal, 40*(4), 863–884. doi:10.1147/sj.404.0863

Von Krogh, G. (2012). How does social software change knowledge management? Toward a strategic research agenda. *The Journal of Strategic Information Systems, 21*(2), 154–164. doi:10.1016/j.jsis.2012.04.003

Chapter 9
Digital Technologies as Media to Transfer Knowledge in IT Firms

Laura Zapata-Cantú
Tecnológico de Monterrey, Mexico

Flor Morton
Tecnológico de Monterrey, Mexico

Teresa Treviño
Tecnológico de Monterrey, Mexico

Ernesto López Monterrubio
Vector Casa de Bolsa, Mexico

ABSTRACT

During the last decade, improvements in information and communication technologies have made possible the transformation of knowledge transfer processes from purely informal to increasingly formal and more diverse communication mechanisms that enrich intra-organizational communication channels. In this chapter, the authors followed a case study approach to analyze three Mexican companies with the objective of understanding how companies in the IT sector are implementing digital technologies to achieve knowledge transfer in their organizations. The findings suggest that workers seek and choose tools that can be personalized and customized to adapt to their own needs. New digital technologies are proving to be a new and relevant channel of communication among people: therefore, these should be considered to be one possible way to motivate knowledge transfer at work.

INTRODUCTION

Organizations have always managed knowledge, although they have not always spoken of it in those terms. Early Knowledge Management (KM) initiatives treated knowledge as an object in an attempt to improve worker's productivity from an organizational perspective. Previous research regarding KM and its contribution to an organization's competitive advantage identify three main aspects. First, at the individual level, the employee is responsible for knowledge generation in the organization (Nonaka & Takeuchi, 1995). Second, at the organizational level, knowledge created in the organization should be transferred across the firm. Third, once all the members in the organization have received the knowledge, it should be integrated into the firm's knowledge base (Zárraga & García-Falcón, 2003:81) and improve or innovate organizational processes, activities, products and services.

DOI: 10.4018/978-1-4666-9607-5.ch009

The basic processes of KM include production, distribution, and use of knowledge and information. These KM processes are interrelated and, in many cases, cannot be separated. However, the present chapter focuses solely on analyzing the process of knowledge transfer, which relies on a greater tacit component. Organizations have been struggling to promote knowledge management initiatives within their members as knowledge is recognized as one of the main resources of a firm. However, technology enables individuals to transfer information in efficient ways; enhancing the communication between one another and facilitating the knowledge transfer process.

The most significant element that enables organizations to move toward an operation that facilitates knowledge transfer is the use of diverse communication mechanisms. Improvements in information and communication technologies have made possible the transformation of the knowledge transfer processes from purely informal to increasingly formal and more diverse communication mechanisms that enrich the intra-organizational communication channels (Zapata, Rialp & Rialp, 2009). Informal mechanisms, such as face-to-face communication, meetings, and communication systems that facilitate interaction among members of the organization, can improve the knowledge transfer process. Practice communities, for example, are a good opportunity to share organizational knowledge among members of the firm (O'Dell & Grayson, 1998). Other tools, such as document management systems, can only be helpful to locate specific information. In this type of tool, there is still missing a space where employees can use this information, share it, and discuss it with others. Cognitive and visualization tools, such as mind mapping software, do not address the social context of knowledge creation but are designed specifically for the solitary worker (Efimova, 2004). In addition to that, telecommuting and virtual offices have separated and reduced opportunities for informal face-to-face knowledge sharing. These facts provide us with a framework to suggest that workers seek and choose to use a tool that can be personalized, customized and adapted for their own needs. This preference for customized communication tools has become a challenge for firms that want to find ways for their employees to share their knowledge. New digital technologies can bring employees together to participate actively in a knowledge transfer process.

During the last decade, technology has facilitated knowledge transfer in organizations (Bennett, Owers, Pitt &Tucker, 2010). Furthermore, technology permits the workplace to be a virtual environment (not necessarily a physical place), where employees can work from different locations. The diversity in backgrounds of each individual in a virtual working environment makes knowledge transfer crucial in this type of environment (Wang & Haggerty, 2009).

New online technologies facilitate the human requirements that are essential during the knowledge transfer process; they provide opportunities for both formal and informal interaction, communication and collaboration with partners and customers/suppliers. This is because it is the employees who control the online content. A relative new concept is that of *ba* proposed by Kitaro Nishida; ba is a space that enables the emergence of relationships and the creation or transfer of individual and/or collective knowledge. This space can be physical, virtual, mental, or a combination. From the different classifications of this term, cyber *ba* is a virtual space of interaction in which explicit knowledge is converted to more complex knowledge; this is done through the acquisition of new explicit knowledge transferred throughout the organization (Nonaka & Konno, 1998).

Recent research has addressed the role of new digital technologies and how they have become essential for the knowledge transfer process in organizations. Furthermore, these have been identified as providing new opportunities that may facilitate the process by which experts share tacit and experiential knowledge (Panahi, Watson, & Partridge, 2013).

Considering this, the objective of this study is to understand how organizations use and implement new digital technologies to facilitate the knowledge transfer process. Using a case study approach, this chapter contributes to the extant literature by determining how companies in the IT sector are implementing the use of digital technologies to achieve knowledge transfer in their organizations.

BACKGROUND

Knowledge in Organizations

In the last decades, knowledge workers have comprised the majority of the workforce. While unskilled labor accounted for approximately 90% of the work force at the beginning of the 20th century, that figure was closer to 20% at the begging of 21st century (Brinkley, Fauth, Mahdon & Theodoropoulou, 2009). Taylor showed that manual work consists only of simple, repetitive activities. Knowledge, that is, the way in which these simple, unskilled motions are put together, organized and executed, can make these activities more productive.

The change from factory to knowledge workers represents a significant challenge to managers who traditionally manage workers in more traditional roles. The basic difference is that a greater stock of knowledge supports a far higher level of productivity (Grant, 2000). Different workers use different types of knowledge. This knowledge takes different lengths of time to acquire, and without knowledge, the employee is completely unproductive. In addition to that, it is difficult to compare the knowledge intensity of different occupations. For survival in competitive environments, all employees have always worked to build the best possible knowledge base within their area of responsibility and to ensure that it can be easily disseminated to all organizational levels (Wiig, 2000:3). For instance, the HRM department must provide a type of storage space to ensure all workers can access most of the firm's knowledge. This storage space may be located within the firm's Intranet or a database containing documents that describe important processes and activities. For employees, the Intranet is a convenient means to establish virtual contact with other members of the organization and to remain current regarding the organization's activities.

Knowledge Transfer Process

According to Gooderham (2007:36), knowledge transfer can be referred to as the accumulation or assimilation of new knowledge in the receiver unit. However, researchers such as Minbaeva, Pedersen, Björkman, Fey and Park (2003:587) argue that pure transmission of knowledge from the source to the recipient has no useful value if the recipient does not see the potential of the new knowledge and hence does not utilize it in his or her own activities. Figure 1 depicts the knowledge transfer process, its actors and its organizational elements.

With respect to the actors involved in the knowledge transfer process (the source of the knowledge and the receiver), the model suggests that the source of a resource that is to be transferred often manifests a certain resistance to sharing his knowledge. This resistance can result from the source's fear of losing ownership or a position of privileged power in the firm or of not being adequately compensated for sharing the fruits of his work and efforts (Szulanski, 1996). In contrast, when the source of the activity is not perceived as being very reliable, the information she or he can supply will likely not be considered

Figure 1.

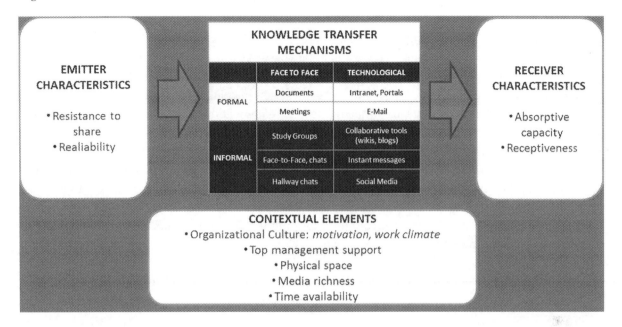

(Minbaeva, 2005). Direct contact is fundamental to developing mutual understanding and to eliminating what is known to be one of the main points of friction that impedes the efficient transfer of knowledge: lack of trust. Trust has been recognized to be a fundamental element for the success of the transfer. In some cases, people do not consider the new knowledge that is obtained to be reliable because they do not trust the person who provided the knowledge (Davenport & Prusak, 2001:115).

Turning to the receiver, Cohen and Levinthal (1990) note that the ability to assimilate knowledge is particularly important when one operates in a dynamic environment. In internal knowledge transfer processes, the receiver often does not have the necessary absorptive capacity to understand and efficiently incorporate a new technology (Zander & Kogut, 1995; Gupta & Govindarajan, 2000; and Tsai, 2001). A further significant barrier to internal knowledge transfer is the lack of openness and receptiveness of the receiver (Ruggles, 1998). The receiver may be unwilling to adopt the new knowledge. This resistance is not only limited to innovations developed by external companies, but may also take the form of a negative attitude of "not invented here", which inhibits the internal transfer of best practices (Szulanski, 1996). It is very common for employees to understand and assimilate new knowledge but continue to refrain from using it for different reasons. The lack of respect for or trust in the source is a key reason. Other reasons are pride, obstinacy, lack of opportunity, and fear of running risks (Davenport & Prusak, 2001:116).

There are also several important contextual dimensions of knowledge transfer. First, firms must seek to operate with an open culture that facilitates knowledge transfer. Other significant contextual elements within the organization include management support and close proximity among employees. As Cummings (2004) comments, great physical distances make communication among members of a group difficult because opportunities for informal contact are reduced. Time is vital for firms that operate in dynamic environments; hence the knowledge to be transferred must be assigned a high priority within the organization. That is, its transfer should be planned similar to all the other important activities of the firm.

Conversely, technology alone is clearly insufficient to induce a person with knowledge to share it with others. Technology can improve access and help bring the right knowledge to the right person at the right time, but this is not sufficient. In addition to technology, an organizational culture is needed that motivates the members of the organization to search for new ways of doing things and where these efforts are facilitated by flexibility and interaction among colleagues. Such a culture should be open to encourage employees to share their knowledge with colleagues even in contexts where time is at a premium.

In addition to informal mechanisms of face-to-face communication such as corridor chats, communication systems that facilitate interaction among colleagues can also improve the knowledge transfer process. For instance, according to O'Dell and Grayson (1998), practice communities provide an opportunity to share organizational knowledge among the members of a group in a bottom-up manner, without any need for intervention by top management. Meetings are another appropriate way to transmit complete messages.

Document management systems are helpful in locating information. Using, sharing, making sense of and discussing information are all done elsewhere. Cognitive tools such as mind mapping software, other visualization tools or personal information management tools are designed for the solitary worker and do not address the social context of knowledge creation (Efimova, 2004). Thus, one tool has become the dominant support for knowledge work: email. Email is successful because it is *personal* and *social* at the same time.

In addition to reaffirming the importance of communication, this suggests that there is another important aspect that influences which tools knowledge workers choose to support their work; they prefer to use *personal* tools, i.e., tools that they can control and customize to their own needs.

Knowledge as part of intellectual capital is the key to competitive advantage in the knowledge economy. Hence, HRM should seek to become an integral part of corporate strategy, enabling knowledge to be managed in the interests of organizational performance (Thite, 2004).

METHODS

The present research used a qualitative approach to understand how knowledge transfer was achieved in organizations. Specifically, a case study approach was followed as a methodological strategy, as proposed by Eisenhardt (1989) and Yin (1989). The data from which we draw our conclusions consisted of the transcripts of four in-depth interviews for each company (12 in total), as well as information found on the company's web page. Particularly, we were interested in understanding how knowledge transfer was achieved by using technological mechanisms. Therefore, we analyzed how companies used several digital tools such as Intranet, e-mail, collaborative tools such as wikis and blogs, MSN Messenger, distribution lists, and social networking sites. The coding and categorization phase was an iterative process because it allowed us to analyze the knowledge transfer process in a deeper form. Later, we crossed the information between companies to find relations among them and conclude with more generalizable findings.

Sample Profile

Three IT companies in Monterrey, Mexico were analyzed to understand how digital technologies and social networking sites facilitate knowledge transfer in organizations. Company A offers IT solutions and services, as well as web solutions and intranets for companies; Company B develops and manages

PC and mobile systems; and finally, Company C, develops software and collaborative portals. The ability to create and replicate knowledge is important for all organizations; for these IT companies, which compete in dynamic environments, it is critical. These companies have relevant technological resources and must demonstrate flexibility and administrative capacity to effectively coordinate their internal competition. For this reason, they need to identify those tools and mechanisms that allow them to generate, accumulate, manage and transfer internal knowledge (See Table 1).

Data Analysis

To analyze the data, the first step was to classify the knowledge transfer tools each company used. For this purpose, we proposed a classification based on the type of interaction, which can be face-to-face or via technological tools, and based on whether they are formal or informal mechanisms (See Table 2).

In this case study, we considered documents and meetings to be face-to-face formal knowledge transfer mechanisms. Any type of file with a specification of the company's process was considered a document. For meetings, we solely considered those formal meetings in the company with the purpose of communicating or transferring knowledge of any area of the company. Furthermore, we classified study groups, face-to-face chats, and hallways chats as informal mechanisms of knowledge transfer. We considered study groups to be informal because, unlike meetings, they derive from an informal chat between more than two employees and the company does not organize these. For the informal mechanisms of face-to-face and hallway chats, we asked for those that had as their purpose explaining or understanding a specific topic regarding the company's processes or functions.

Table 1. Sample profile summary

Company	Creation Year	Initial Employees	Actual Employees	Offered Services
A	2009	5	~17	IT solutions and services, web solutions and Intranets
B	1997	30	~250	Develops and manages PC and mobile systems
C	2004	2	~55	Develops software and collaborative portals

Table 2. Knowledge transfer mechanisms

	Face-to-Face	Technological
Formal	Documents	Intranet, Portals
	Meetings	E-Mail
Informal	Study Groups	Collaborative tools (wikis, blogs)
	Face-to-Face chats	Instant messages
	Hallway chats	Social Media

Cross-Case Analysis KT Mechanisms

We identified the important elements that can influence the usage of each knowledge transfer mechanism. These important elements for knowledge transfer are as follows: (1) top management, where all decisions or processes established by top management for knowledge transfer will have an imperative character; (2) time availability because time plays an important role in knowledge transfer for both the quantity and the quality of knowledge that can be transferred in a company; (3) communication because the more communication channels the company has, the more opportunity for employees to interact and share their acquired expertise on their specific areas of the organization; (4) motivation because employee's attitude on knowledge share and acquisition will determine the degree to which knowledge is transferred in the organization; (5) work climate because the work environment is also an important factor that can determine how knowledge is transferred across the organization, where a poor work climate can undermine motivation and diminish the level and quality of transferred knowledge; and (6) workspace is the physical organization of the company, for instance open workspaces could promote more knowledge transfer than closed workspaces in which every employee is separated from the others.

To compare the data from the three companies and analyze the extent to which knowledge transfer mechanisms are influenced by these elements, a cross-case analysis was conducted based on the information obtained through the interviews.

RESULTS

Company A

Regarding the formal mechanisms used to manage its knowledge transfer, this company recently implemented knowledge transfer meetings by organizing short gatherings between employees, where employees discuss specific topics.

Another formal mechanism to transfer knowledge is the "Induction Program," which is applied to every new member of the organization. This program consists of a course where the new employee is provided with all the basic information and processes of the company. Regarding the informal face-to-face mechanisms, we found that employees indirectly share knowledge at lunchtime. The company supports this practice by offering their employees a subsidy for food and providing them with a specific location and time eat lunch. Another informal mechanism that we found is study groups that derive from hallway chats. By these informal chats, employees identify a specific topic for which they want to obtain more knowledge. Then, the company supports this group of employees by offering the time and place to gather. The main trigger for these study groups has been technological certifications.

Finally, knowledge is transferred by two informal meetings, the annual picnic and the Christmas party. This is described by one of the company's employees:

We are working on this type of thing to develop a favorable work climate in the company. We are working on these type of initiatives, for example, we organize events that enable interaction and networking (between employees), like our annual field trip day or the posada (Christmas party).

Analyzing the technological formal mechanisms to transfer knowledge, we found that all the company's processes are documented on its Intranet, which the company developed internally. This documentation practice assures that all the "know how" is stored and formally documented. Additionally, most of the company's institutional processes are also stored on the Intranet, including training records, evaluations, holidays, payroll information, and sales and billing processes. An important informal tool that is available in this company is a wiki, on which employees express and document what they do. A wiki is considered informal because the company does not require employees to use it; however, there are employees with initiative that use this technology frequently. A common example that is documented in the wiki is when employees find a solution to a problem. They believe that by documenting this information, the next person to encounter the same problem will be able to solve it faster.

In general, we found that the openness and disposition of employees of this company are two factors that allow the successful transfer of knowledge. By having current and well-established processes to transfer knowledge inside the organization, this company has an important level of maturity with respect to knowledge management processes.

Company B

Top management organizes periodic meetings to discuss specific and relevant topics. The organizational climate is very open, and management supports employee interaction and proposal of new ideas; management creates a work atmosphere that facilitates the transfer of knowledge as well.

The physical space in which the employees' work enables many hallways chats. There are also snack and coffee areas, where employees can go at any time to eat or drink at no cost. We found that top management encourages natural and informal interactions by promoting the use of these areas and personally participating in and sharing conversations with other employees.

Regarding the formal technology, this company organizes periodic meetings where all employees gather to discuss a specific topic. Relevant topics in these meetings are how the company is doing, new projects, or new technologies in the market. These meetings are organized with the objective of transferring knowledge through chats, documents, and videos. Interestingly, these meetings are online, through instant messages because the company has operations in both Mexico and USA.

Informally, the employees of this company created a group on a popular instant messaging service. When a new idea, problem, suggestion, or area of opportunity arises, employees share it via an instant message when all online employees. This tool allows people to debate and brainstorm in real time. Additionally, instant messages are also used to inform supervisors that each employee has arrived or left the office, as well as to share documents, experiences, proposals, and notifications.

Another informal tool that employees use is the wiki, in which they store all information regarding customers, internal processes, and other day-to-day issues. All managerial processes such as hiring processes, holidays, expenses reports, planning documents, company rules, and all human resources processes are documented virtually in this tool, as well as past, current and potential projects. The company also has a specialized online tool to manage projects; through this tool, employees can see milestones, task assignments, and other important issues. When someone identifies a process as repetitive, that person creates a document that is stored in the Wiki.

In general, we have identified that this company actively uses technological tools to both generate and transfer knowledge. In general, the most important communication and knowledge transfer tool in this company is an informal technological mechanism: instant messages.

Company C

When a new employee enters the company, there is a formal protocol in which he or she receives all the company's documentation, which includes the basic processes for operation. Another formal mechanism that this company uses is the programmed meetings, in which people can share new knowledge; each week a topic is presented, including technical and nontechnical areas, as well as topics in the forefront that any employee wants to share. When a member of the organization acquires a new certification, he or she develops a course to share this knowledge with other members in these meetings.

Regarding face-to-face mechanisms in the informal category, a new employee visits every area of the company in an informal manner through which other employees share the experiences and processes they follow for each task. This is important for identifying teams, and experts in the different technologies the company uses. Additionally, hallway chats and other informal chats are also present in this company, particularly when a new project is beginning.

Analyzing the technological mechanisms, formal initiatives include the use of SharePoint, in which they try to centralize all processes with their respective documentation. This practice is promoted by the CMMI Level 3 certification that the company has, which establishes that the company must document all of its processes. The firm has as specialized system to manage their projects, which includes customers, deadlines, project deliveries, and bug controls, to complement their knowledge base.

Concerning informal initiatives, employees of this company have developed a blog that can be publicly accessed through its Internet web page. Any other person outside the organization can also consult this blog. As a human resource employee describes,

...Employees write about a specific topic in the blog, about an error for example, and share a solution, step by step. Then anyone can access this blog and see this. This way, people will perceive us as experts in certain areas, and it will also bring us more customers.

Additionally, the company has created an incentive program to motivate employees to increase their own knowledge as well as the company's overall knowledge. Employees can choose how they want to participate: write something on the blog or make a presentation of a topic in the weekly meetings. The organizational culture is very open; this allows employees to learn constantly.

The company also has developed a wiki in which specific topics are documented, including its "Best Practices".

Face-to-Face vs Virtual Technology

The overall results show that both documents and meetings are important to increasing motivation in the company and that hallway chats are significant for both the top management and work climate. This can be identified in the following quote from an employee of Company C:

Every three months, we have a meeting in our office, like a party... after 6:00pm we buy food, drinks, and we invite a musical group or a DJ. In this company we foster this type of interaction because we have a very demanding job; so, we try to relax in some way.

Regarding the technological category, it is clear that the three companies use these tools as a means of communication. This is because these companies mentioned they primarily use these tools to inform, document, and create virtual meetings to transfer both tacit and explicit knowledge.

Knowledge management mechanisms used in the three companies, show that the face-to-face mechanisms are predominant, as employees continue to rely on documents, meetings and face-to-face chats to share important knowledge. Although informal face-to-face mechanisms are important for the integration and networking of employees, the formal mechanisms such as traditional meetings were the most important channels to transfer knowledge inside the organizations. Concerning to technological mechanisms, results suggest that the informal tools such as collaborative wikis or blogs are more important than Intranets and portals (formal mechanisms) to transfer knowledge.

DISCUSSION

Companies' successful transfer of know-how requires communication mechanisms that allow these businesses to quickly and efficiently share their knowledge. The transfer of knowledge in small and medium information technology enterprises is characterized by the use of formal and informal mechanisms of communication, either face-to-face or supported by technology (Zapata, Rialp & Rialp, 2009).

Formal mechanisms are those opportunities to transfer organizational knowledge that is filed in documents or databases; this transfer can be scheduled and approved by the general direction (Hansen, Nohria &Tierney, 1999, and Fiddler, 2000). The present study shows that for face–to=face formal mechanisms, documents and meetings are relevant to the organization as a means to transfer the newly created or acquired knowledge. These are utilized with some frequency, allowing organizations' members to share the progress of ongoing projects and acquire opinions and suggestions from other members of the firm. For O'Dell and Grayson (1998) and Zágarra and García-Falcón (2003), practice communities provide an opportunity to share knowledge among organizational members of a group without the fostering of these communities by top management; instead, their individual members foster these communities. Furthermore, the Fiddler (2000) study notes that the meetings and monitoring are additional appropriate ways to convey entire messages. As the CEO of one of the companies interviewed says,

The advantage of the meetings is that it is the only time that we really are all thinking the same thing and working on the same project.

Documents and meetings are those that have a greater impact on the organization at the time of knowledge transfer; unfortunately, however, there is insufficient time to document relevant issues. Organizations operating in dynamic environments do not have sufficient time to properly transfer their internal competencies (Zapata et al, 2009).

Findings also indicate that the technological mechanisms of companies are primarily based on informal interactions; however, companies also take advantage of several formal mechanisms to complement this knowledge transfer process. For example, one common formal approach is the collaborative work through intranet portals and other Web 2.0 technologies, such as Wikis, that allow employees to have constant interactions between each other. These Web 2.0 tools have the characteristic of having the user as an agent that actively creates content (Matschke, Moskaliuk, & Cress, 2012). For this reason, these tools also serve as a repository for new knowledge that can be accessed by other employees at any time.

Regarding the informal approach, the MSN Messenger and other instant messaging services represented a common form of communication, enabling employees to share new ideas, suggestions or questions in real time. Considering that the studied companies belong to the IT sector, we have identified that they use and take advantage of several digital tools to transfer knowledge inside the organization. Accordingly, we support Panahi, Watson, and Partridge's (2013) propositions. Our findings deliver evidence to suggest that the new digital technologies promote informal communications among employees, provide opportunities for the generation of new ideas, create a visual repository of knowledge, and facilitate the knowledge sharing process.

Digital technologies are proving to be a new channel of communication of increasing use among people; therefore, these should be considered as one possible way to persuade knowledge transfer at work. From a Knowledge Management perspective, we attempt to define these new digital technologies as virtual spaces in the working environment that enable the emergence of relationships, interactions and communication that facilitate the creation and transfer of individual and/or collective knowledge.

CONCLUSION AND FUTURE RESEARCH DIRECTIONS

One of the challenges facing companies operating in dynamic environments is the reproduction of their internal competencies, skills and collective learning that accrue in the company over time. It is important to recognize that although face-to-face mechanisms are the ideal way to share knowledge, this is not always accessible to everyone (Panahi, Watson, & Partridge, 2013). For these reasons, companies understand the importance of utilizing IT mechanisms that will allow them to share and obtain knowledge when needed. For small IT businesses, performing successfully implies that these companies require mechanisms that allow them to quick and efficiently share their knowledge and efficiently disseminate their know-how. These businesses are also aware that technology is not able to enable a person with acquired knowledge to share it with others. Technology can expand access and simplify the problem of delivering the right knowledge to the right person at the right time, but beyond the technology, firms need an organizational culture that encourages members of the organization to seek new ways of doing things, where flexible hours and interaction among members facilitate that search. Additionally, this culture must be open, allowing the CEO to encourage employees to share their knowledge and to facilitate communication between members of the company.

The new information technologies and the role of the employee and carrier initiatives, suggestions, volunteer effort and more commitment, show that organizational structures should be less hierarchical; in addition, a participatory style of management provides the necessary conditions allowing the preservation of the flexibility of individuals.

Thus, important implications arise from these findings. First, with this understanding, managers can support the use of certain social network sites and other digital technologies, promoting these among their employees as new and formal communication channels in their organizations. Second, collaboration, communication and productivity can be improved. If the company promotes SNS as a channel for communication among members of the organization, it will have a higher success rate in the implementation because employees already enjoy using it. Third, employees will be more motivated to ask questions, share useful information, discuss new ideas, reference previously answered questions, discover information and therefore, acquire new knowledge. Finally, issues such as the confidentiality of corporate information should be considered. There is information that should not be shared through other social groups, such as family or friends; therefore, we should find an appropriate SNS that provides security for the organization, yet meets the requirements of employees in a social network site.

Future research can consider the present chapter to be a basis to analyze how the uses of face-to-face vs. technological mechanisms have changed in recent years. As technology has constantly evolved and become more available to companies and people in general, finding significant changes in the use of technological mechanisms for knowledge transfer in organizations is expected.

Overall, this chapter identifies the role of new digital technologies in the knowledge transfer process and provides empirical evidence of how several companies in the IT sector are currently implementing such tools for this purpose as well as the benefits they obtain from their use.

REFERENCES

Bennett, J., Owers, M., Pitt, M., & Tucker, M. (2010). Workplace impact of social networking. *Property Management*, *28*(3), 138–148. doi:10.1108/02637471011051282

Brinkley, I., Fauth, R., Mahdon, M., & Theodoropoulou, S. (2009). *Knowledge workers and knowledge work; A Knowledge Economy Programme Report*. London: The Work Foundation.

Cohen, W. M., & Levinthal, D. (1990). Absorptive capacity: A new perspective on learning and innovation. *Administrative Science Quarterly*, *35*(1), 128–152. doi:10.2307/2393553

Cummings, J. N. (2004). Work groups, structural diversity, and knowledge sharing in a global organization. *Management Science*, *50*(3), 352–264. doi:10.1287/mnsc.1030.0134

Davenport, T. H., & Prusak, L. (2001). *Conocimiento en acción. Cómo las organizaciones manejan lo que saben*. Buenos Aires: Editorial Prentice Hall.

Efimova, L. (2004). *Discovering the iceberg of knowledge work: A weblog case*. Retrieved from https://doc.telin.nl/dsweb/Get/Document-34786/

Eisenhardt, K. M. (1989). Building theories from case study research. *Academy of Management Review*, *14*(4), 532–550.

Fiddler, L. (2000). *Facilitators and Impediments to the Internal Transfer of Team-Embodied Competences in Firms Operating in Dynamic Environments*. (Tesis Doctoral, Boston University). Proquest Dissertation Abstracts.

Gooderham, P. N. (2007). Enhancing knowledge transfer in multinational corporations: A dynamic capabilities driven model. *Knowledge Management Research & Practice*, *5*(1), 34–43. doi:10.1057/palgrave.kmrp.8500119

Grant, R. M. (2000). Shifts in the world economy: the drivers of knowledge management. In C. Despres & D. Chauvel (Eds.), Knowledge Horizonts: the present and the promise of knowledge management (pp. 27-53). Butterworth-Heinemann. doi:10.1016/B978-0-7506-7247-4.50005-7

Gupta, A. K., & Govindarajan, V. (2000). Knowledge flows within multinational corporations. *Strategic Management Journal*, *21*(4), 473–496. doi:10.1002/(SICI)1097-0266(200004)21:4<473::AID-SMJ84>3.0.CO;2-I

Hansen, M. T., Nohria, N., & Tierney, T. (1999). What's your strategy for managing knowledge? *Harvard Business Review*, (March-April), 106–116. PMID:10387767

Matschke, C., Moskaliuk, J., & Cress, U. (2012). Knowledge exchange using Web 2.0 technologies in NGO's. *Journal of Knowledge Management*, *16*(1), 159–176. doi:10.1108/13673271211199007

Minbaeva, D. B. (2005). HRM practices and MNC knowledge transfer. *Personnel Review*, *34*(1), 125–144. doi:10.1108/00483480510571914

Minbaeva, D. B., Pedersen, T., Björkman, I., Fey, C. F., & Park, H. J. (2003). MNC knowledge transfer, subisidiary absorptive capacity, and HRM. *Journal of International Business Studies*, *34*(6), 586–599. doi:10.1057/palgrave.jibs.8400056

Nonaka, I., & Konno, N. (1998). The concept of ba: Building a foundation for knowledge creation. *California Management Review*, *40*(3), 40–54. doi:10.2307/41165942

Nonaka, I., & Takeuchi, N. (1995). *The Knowledge Creating Company*. Oxford, UK: University Press.

O'Dell, C., & Grayson, C. J. (1998). If only we knew what we know: Identification and transfer of internal best practices. *California Management Review*, *40*(3), 154–170. doi:10.2307/41165948

OECD. (2004). *The significance of knowledge management in the business sector*. OECD.

Panahi, S., Watson, J., & Partridge, H. (2013). Towards tacit knowledge sharing over social web tools. *Journal of Knowledge Management*, *17*(3), 379–397. doi:10.1108/JKM-11-2012-0364

Ruggles, R. (1998). The state of the notion: Knowledge management in practice. *California Management Review*, *40*(3), 80–89. doi:10.2307/41165944

Szulanski, G. (1996). Exploring internal stickiness: Impediments to the transfer of best practices within the firm. *Strategic Management Journal*, *17*(S2), 27–43. doi:10.1002/smj.4250171105

Thite, M. (2004). Strategic Positioning of HRM of knowledge-based organizations. *The Learning Organizations: An International Journal*, *11*(1), 28–44. doi:10.1108/09696470410515715

Tsai, W. (2001). Knowledge transfer in intraorganizational networks: Effects of network position and absoptive capacity on business unit innovation and performance. *Academy of Management Journal*, *40*(5), 996–1004. doi:10.2307/3069443

Wang, Y., & Haggerty, N. (2009). Knowledge transfer in virtual settings: The role of individual virtual competency. *Information Systems Journal*, *19*(6), 571–593. doi:10.1111/j.1365-2575.2008.00318.x

Wiig, K. M. (2000). Knowledge Management: an Emerging Discipline Rooted in a Long History. In Knowledge Horizons: the present and the promise of knowledge management (pp. 3-26). Butterworth-Heinemann. doi:10.1016/B978-0-7506-7247-4.50004-5

Yin, R. K. (1989). *Case Study Research: Design And Methods (Applied Social Research Methods)*. Sage Publication.

Zágarra, C., & García-Falcón, J. M. (2003). Factors favoring knowledge management in work teams. *Journal of Knowledge Management, 7*(2), 81–93. doi:10.1108/13673270310477306

Zander, U., & Kogut, B. (1995). Knowledge and the speed of transfer and imitation of organizational capabilities: An empirical test. *Organization Science, 6*(1), 76–92. doi:10.1287/orsc.6.1.76

Zapata, L., Rialp, J., & Rialp, A. (2009). Generation and transfer of knowledge in IT-related SMEs. *Journal of Knowledge Management, 13*, 246–256.

Chapter 10
Orientism Management (OM):
A New Framework to Manage Decisions and Hyper Dynamic Knowledge Process in a Multi-User Network

Luisa dall'Acqua
Scientific Lyceum TCO, Italy & PHSG, Germany

ABSTRACT

The model of learning/training in the 21st century requires the evaluation of new and better ways to measure what matters, diagnosing strengths and weaknesses, to improve people performance, and to involve multiple stakeholders in the process of designing, conducting and use of knowledge. The thesis is that the orientation, today, is no longer limited only to outline the direction of a professional career, but it concerns "Life designing" over which "Work designing". This chapter intends to describe a new interpretative paradigm, Orientism, to understand and manage fluid nature of knowledge, but at the same time to seize and manage the unpredictability and risks of the dynamics of knowledge management in relationships complex environment, in a society. Element of news are 5 key factors and criteria to direct and motivate people in choosing process, and following 10 different and key relationships between them. They define areas of management to improve own personal leadership and success. The concept becomes the conceptual base of an Instructional Design Model (PENTHA 2.0).

INTRODUCTION

The starting point of this research is the statement that, even if the current technological advancement provided or optimized solutions in several sectors of application, it has multiplied the difficulty of understanding the world in which common people, managers, entrepreneurs and researchers operate, making the same 'problems management' more complex, and requiring a mind of decision maker to learn and manage the 'complexity'.

A long tradition of studies analyzed the risk components (i.e. logical-probabilistic, cognitive, regulatory, socio-systemic and socio-cultural), inherent in a decision making process. The multiple variables,

DOI: 10.4018/978-1-4666-9607-5.ch010

able to cause an unstable condition of unpredictability in a decision-making process, found a catalytic function of management in the information factor, or factor 'k', in the regulatory role of external agents (social environment) and the cooperation between action makers.

One change factor is to consider two sequences in the actual knowledge dynamics: on a hand the passage from a received multimediality (such as television and cinema), to an interactive multimediality (such as videogames or virtual reality) to a built multimediality (such as socialnetworking knowledge management tool), to a reflective multimediality (dynamic intelligent and semantic UI). On the other hand, the passage from individual knowledge to global knowledge, multi-user connections, but without losing the subjective component to be managed.

Orientism (see Figure 1) proposes a new scenario of activities, to improve the people's ability of contextual changes in natural-, social-, artificial multi-user environments, with multiple reference points and multi-interpreting paradigms. Furthermore, it proposes a new solution to the demand for "innovative, creative and leadership" education to make choices, to manage own life, relationships and complex environments.

The model is based on intertwined 10 Knowledge Managements typologies, each based on areas of development and improvement of own personal leadership.

In a corporate politics perspective, Orientism Management becomes OMS (Orientism Management Strategy), OMP (Orientism Processes Organization), and OMT (Orientism Management Tools).

Final outcome of this research is the component defining of an e-environment, with new concepts of advanced technological social interactions, enabling an effective capture of the tacit knowledge of employees (e.g., experience, intuition, creativity) that is missed with traditional knowledge management systems,

Figure 1. First typology of change factor in Orientism perspective

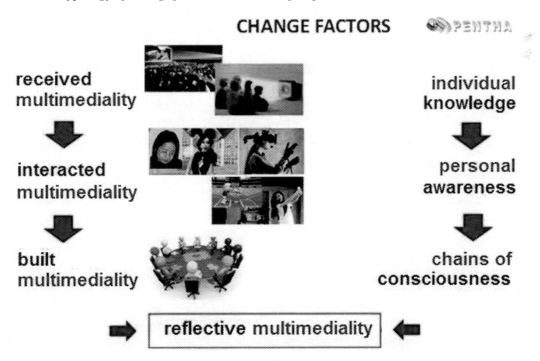

Background

State-of-the-art ICT-enabled, academic knowledge management environments provide an advanced experience where trainee and/or team work are lead figures, and their human and learning behaviours, cognitive preferences and human characteristics are recognised, considered, monitored, recorded, and modelled. This facilitates the capability to personalise, adapt and improve the knowledge management processes in tune with individual preferences, characteristics and preferred learning styles/habits.

Personal Knowledge Management (PKM) is an open question about what are the PKM roles and values in different individual, organisation and social context. The main related literature by different scholars provides insight of the definition and nature of PKM. A valuable synthesis of the more significant designs is the conceptual model of PKM 2.0, developed by Cheong & Tsui (2010). The Authors reviewed the results of a global survey about the roles and values of the main PKM frameworks (Cheong&Tsui, 2010): from mere individual activities to outcome/impact oriented; from information handling skills to personal competencies, sensemaking and self-reflection; from individually focused to a community and social collaborative focused.

This analyzed evolution led the A. towards the design of a comprehensive PKM model that encapsulates the need for personal information management, knowledge internalisation, transferring of knowledge and knowledge creation, and learning, Key identified issue remains an alignment of the appropriate technologies. The outcome was the definition of four core components of PKM: Personal Information Management (PIM), Personal Knowledge Internalisation (PKI), Personal Wisdom Creation (PCW) and Inter-Personal Knowledge Transferring (IKT). The PKM 2.0 framework focuses on the both individual and inter-personal interactions (Cheong&Tsui, 2011)

Methods, strategies and tools to support, enhance, adapt and personalize the training processes to make the action makers aware and having control, step by step, of their own decisional path, is a challenge for designer and trainers.

The Instructional design (ID), the educational methodology of analysis, design, development and evaluation of the training management and effect, acquires a central role: it is the art and science of creating an instructional environment and educational content or experiences, which lead the user from the condition of not being able to accomplish certain objectives to the position of being able to accomplish those objectives.

Historically, ID emerged as a research subject dealing with defining rules and governing choices of appropriate methods of instruction, taking into account the conditions-of-learning (dall'Acqua, 2009, Downes, 2010). A milestone in this respect is Gagné's theory (Gagné, 1985), who introduced the idea of task analysis to instructional design. Through task analysis, an instructional task can be broken down into sequential steps - hierarchical relationship of tasks and subtasks.

Actually, a multitude of models of ID references are in the cultural panorama, where about twenty are considerate internationally relevant:

- Those emphasizing collaborative learning and problem solving approaches – i.e. Constructivist Learning Environments (CLE) of Jonassen (1999), or Collaborative Problem Solving (CPS) of Nelson (1999).
- Those promoting experiential learning/training – i.e. Open Learning Environments (OLE) of Hannafin, Land & Oliver (Hannafin et al., 1999), or Goal Based Scenario (GBS) of Schank, Berman & Macpherson (Schank et al., 1999).

- Those focusing on simple content understanding – i.e. multiple approaches to understanding by Gardner & Hatch (1989) or the Elaboration Theory of Reigeluth (Reigeluth 2004, Reigeluth et al.,2006).
- Those considering and describing the learning environment functionalities, – i.e. Sandberg's Learning Environment Functions (Sandberg, 1994).
- Those proposing a method to manage and introduce new pedagogies – i.e. Activity Theory based expanded learning (Kuuti, 1996).
- Those focusing on an active roles of the agents – e,g. ASSURE, a model designed for trainers when developing their own groups. It incorporates Gagné's (Gagnè, 1985) events of instruction to assure effective use of media in instruction (Marschark et al. 2002) – and in a network of connections – e.g. the PENTHA ID model (acronym of Personalization, Environment, Network, Tutoring/Training, Hypermedia, Activity), which focuses on dynamic relationships and patterns among "complex agents" in the learning process, rather than the static properties of isolated objects (dall'Acqua, 2011).

Quoting Goldsmith: We're trying to manage something-knowledge-that is inherently invisible, incapable of being quantified, and borne in relationships, not statistics […] Our most important work is to pay serious attention to what we always want to ignore: the human dimension (Goldsmith, et al., 2004, 57).

The time to understand knowledge management from a multi-directional perspective has come.

ORIENTISM MANAGEMENT

Orientism Principles

Orientism is an innovative multidimensional knowledge management approach, scientifically based on the following theories.

Design Human Engineering, DHE

It is considered for the definition of criteria to improve the people's ability of contextual changes, to design knowledge/learning strategies to apply.

This theory is the evolution of the well-known NeuroLinguistic Programming (NLP) theory (Bandler et al, 2013):

- While NLP is based on the replication of human behavior (modeling), the DHE is based on the creation of new models.
- While NLP analyzes the sequence of access to certain information, the DHE takes into consideration the simultaneity of how we process information.
- While NLP deals with divide human behavior into smaller and smaller pieces, the DHE is the model by which larger and larger chunks of human experience are put together to achieve success.

Strenght point of the theory is that it not only intends to allow creating of new communication flux, strategies and skills, but also intends to let user create better motivation strategies to accomplish their own tasks.

Nature Knowledge Theory, NKT

It is considered for the definition of Nature and Human Knowledge, to design a semantic interpretation of the knowledge process.

It is a transdisciplinary approach (Md Santo et al., 2014), proposing a holistic vision of the KM process dynamic, and reverses the prospective, proposing a so defined "not management technique": its role is to giving "final touch by blowing spiritual enrichment" to the agents, through contextual interaction of KM components. The organization is interpreted like a living mechanism, having interior own consciousness, wherein each agent works with own specific profile, as well as each tool, works with its specific functions, having to be orchestrated in a "Nature Knowledge continuum", through comprehending the Knowledge Base of a Global Complex System. This approach evolves in Nature Knowledge Theory or NKT.

It is the evolution of the Human System Biology-based Knowledge Management (HSB-KM) model framework. The main goals are: an Establish Taxonomy of Enterprise Process Business (indicating Complexity aspect of Risk Management) based on Process Classification Framework (PCF) method and proceed to strongly recommended Community of Practice (CoP) and Learning Organization (LO), as modern trending issues before developing it to further usual themes of management tools.

Plans of Analysis

The Orientism concept dedicates attention to different "plans" in the decisional process:

- Descriptive plan: how decision makers ("agents") reason
- Prescriptive plan: how they should reason
- Social plan: what type of reasoning motivates the decisional action in terms of efficacy and efficiency
- Communicative plan: what type of reasoning is recognizable
- Management plan: what are the conditions implying a guaranteed "order" in a process, against networking, understanding and learning "chaos"
- Tutoring plan: how the Decision Managers can be supported in their choosing process

Key Points

Key points of Orientism concept are:

- The creation of new models of behavior
- The simultaneity of how we process information
- Larger pieces of human experience are to be put together to achieve success
- The complex interconnection between reference points

Orientism Management (OM)

Orientism view is a new conception of the Knowledge Management: it moves towards a knowledge awareness, extension of own horizon points of perspective and meanings management, in a network of relationships, starting from own strength points and profile, and consciousness transfer in a knowledge interface phenomenon.

New variables, factors and criteria are designed to direct and motivate the mind in the decisional process, in self-reference, to be considered in a lifelong guidance to have success in choices, assumptions of responsibilities and achievement of objectives, over the uncertainty.

The approach is contextualized in the experience of people and their own environment, to enable a person to face the problem positively and to develop strategies to manage situations, to mediate complex relationships through task facing orientation, and it is based on:

- The vision of the decision-making itself like an understanding process, choosing what to learn and the meaning of incoming information, seen through the lens of a shifting reality;
- The management of larger pieces of human experiences to be put together to achieve success;
- The management of a complex network with numerous typologies of nodes/connections, such as information, competences, intelligences, people and interpretations;
- The adaptation of the knowledge management/learning attitude to activate orienting reflex phenomena and to develop a critical mind;
- The definition of the needed supporting learning process; the develop of analytical and aware skills;
- The definition of profile and action modality of supporting human and cognitive tutoring;
- The understanding whether and how an environment, a digital tool, specifically designed, can promote the processes of subjective orientation

Figure 2. Orientism. (Source: dall'Acqua&Md Santo, 2014)

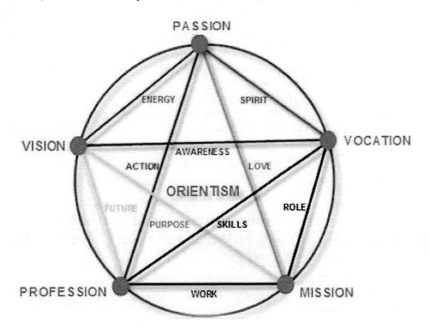

The model is conceptualized in a schema, represented a penthagram within a circle (see Figure 2).

Variables

The Vertices of the penthagram represent the life reference points (variables), to be considered in a lifelong guidance.

The relationships between Vertices represents the added subjective components (factors) to orient, train and activate choice processes. They are 5 (dall'Acqua&Md Santo, 2014):

- **Profession:** Concerning specific knowledge, training and skills towards own employment. It regards the people as Agents.
- **Vision:** Concerning an aware semantic interpretation of reality and/or own will. It leads the thought towards of a meaning schema of actions.
- **Passion:** Concerning powerful emotions of people. It pushes a person towards a target with force and determination.
- **Vocation:** Concerning own talent and strong gifted /professional profile. It is a crucial component in the approach.
- **Mission:** Concerning a statement of intent, considering valuable ideas of useful success, with extended social beneficial outcomes.

The relationship between variables determines a factor of success in the orientism view. They are 10 (see Tables 1 and 2 in the Appendix):

- The relationship between Passion and Vocation variables is the synthesis of own personal investment and powerful being pushed towards a target and own deep feeling and dedication (Spirit factor).
- The relationship between Passion and Vision variables s the synthesis of own personal investment and powerful being pushed towards a target and semantic interpretation of reality (Energy factor).
- The relationship between Passion and Mission variables is the synthesis of own personal investment and powerful being pushed towards a target and own reason to perform (Love factor).
- The relationship between Passion and Profession variables is the synthesis of own personal investment and powerful being pushed towards a target and identity as Agent towards an employment (Action factor).
- The relationship between Vision and Vocation variables is the synthesis of own semantic interpretation of reality and own deep feeling and dedication (Awareness factor).
- The relationship between Vision and Mission variables is the synthesis of own semantic interpretation of reality and reason to perform (Purpose factor).
- The relationship between Profession and Vision variables is the synthesis of own identity as Agent towards an employment and semantic interpretation of reality (Future factor).
- The relationship between Profession and Mission variables is the synthesis of own identity as Agent and own reason to perform (Work factor).
- The relationship between Profession and Vocation variables is the synthesis of own deep feeling and dedication and own identity as Agent towards an employment (Skill factor).

Orientism Management (OM)

- The relationship between Mission and Vocation variables is the synthesis of own deep feeling and dedication and own reason to perform (Role factor)

Orientism and ID

Orientism is adopted as the basic epistemology of the PENTHA Instructional Design Model (vs. 2.0), a theoretical paradigm to interpret the fluid nature of the knowledge, and to analyze the knowledge activities as dynamic, adaptive and self-regulative, based not only on explicit curricular goals, but also on unpredictable interactions and relationships between Agents during the emerging knowledge process, in human and biological, social and cultural environments.

The dimensions are mutual influence between life reference points and factors of Orientism, in a process of building a new knowledge "orienting". They have the purpose to activate dynamic actions toward a goal, to promote awareness with respect to the processes of construction of meanings, and to promote the exploration and mediation of reality. They allow the design of a dynamic cognitive map of activities to lead actions, and a process of self-reference of the individual and group knowledge path.

Following we list the main work/project team's needs, according to the PENTHA 2.0 analysis (dall'Acqua, 2014), to be effective and productive, in addition to activating performance of collaboration and cooperation.

Knowledge Level

This level is focused on

Figure 3. Pentha's Scenario (Source: dall'Acqua, 2010)

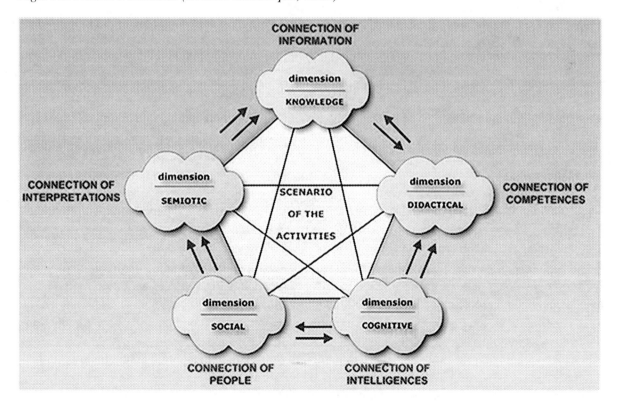

- Generating a significant flux of communications and coordination of actions in order to facilitate the act of processing meaning (by interactions)
- Implementing cooperation through KM strategies, such as: sharing, different level of specialization of the agents, collection or creation of content and sub-division of the work (distributed allocation)
- Managing factual information and access content, as well as procedural knowledge of best practices, working towards a "reduction of complexity"
- Finding related Information and then integrating distributed knowledge
- Realizing and managing re-generation and re-purposing of different knowledge patterns (spirals) emerging in different forms
- Realizing and managing awareness of knowledge and data meaning management in a network of relationships
- Realizing and managing consciousness transfer in an optimised e-learning environment

User(s) Level

This level is focused on:

- Realizing a degree of connectedness, through a high density of connected users, speed and flow of shared information, plasticity and frequency of created connections
- Realizing periodically interaction between all the Agents, to understand problems, mitigate risks and remove the roadblocks
- Managing a complex network with numerous typologies of nodes and connections of knowledge, competences, communication, representations, relationships, technologies and many different paradigms to work

Technology (E-Environment) Level

This level is focused on:

- Facilitating information management by archiving all communications and interactions within an e-environment to access and share for future activities. The environment is a mix of PLE (Personal Learning Environment), PKE (Personal Knowledge Environment), and PWE (Personal Work Environment), able to support social networking activities as well as collaborative learning, supported by an intelligent system
- Enabling an effective capture of the tacit knowledge of Agents (e.g., experience, intuition, creativity) that is missed with traditional knowledge management systems, that focus on document archiving (i.e., explicit knowledge)
- Promoting communication and logistical coordination among (geographically distributed) workforce members through the use of communities of practice (CoPs) and collaboration tools
- Scanning and reporting pathways of individual/social actions
- Facilitating an intelligent and creative learning/business atmosphere that will allow Agents (employees) freedom to capture the knowledge that is up to date and accurate

A Case Study: Knowledge Cafè (K-Cafè) by Comparison

Basically, K-Cafè is "a means of bringing a group of people together to have an open, creative conversation on a topic of mutual interest to surface their collective knowledge, to share ideas and insights and to gain a deeper understanding of the subject and the issues "involved" (source: Regional Gurteen Community Cafes website).

K-Cafè is a useful approach to share tacit knowledge, and it intends to be innovative to connect people to people, people to ideas and ideas to ideas. It challenges people to reflect on their thinking; surfaces new ideas and opens to new connections.

It mainly represents a f2f meeting (Gurteen & Remenyi, 2007), but it was tested in virtual meetings, too (see: The Bamboo project website). It's dedicated to teams and communities of Practice, to facilitate learning from others and gain a deeper collective understanding of a subject through conversation. This approach is suggested to be used for many business ends, such as:

- Turning a traditional "chalk and talk" into an engaging learning event
- Transforming traditional management training courses where younger managers learn from more experienced ones
- As a powerful sales tool, engaging customers in conversation and thus better understand their needs for and them to better understand your product or service
- Surfacing hidden problems and opportunities that exist in the organization or in a department or project - especially ones caused by lack of communication
- Bringing managers and technologists together after a merger to build relationships, surface new opportunities and address cultural issues
- Building and improving relationships, business networking
- Soliciting input and obtain buy-in for a new project or initiative

The model proposes:

- Double flux of information: focus on the topic (from the topic to the roundtables), focus on the groups (from the roundtables to a centric final debate)
- Agents discussions about topics, sharing knowledge, experiences, point of views, interpretations and expertise. The capillary and close sharing allows a better management of the content as well as the communication between agents (same contextualized language, prompt feedback) and group dynamics
- Comparison of own previous knowledge about the topic, updating it through the sharing and acquiring more awareness of it and his/her own capability of management of the content as well as of the relationship in a team work, subject matter dedicated. Each agent become a speaker of own identity as thinker/researcher/worker
- Contribution by speakers from each group, as well as by each agent with a renewed awareness, to the final global debate on the topic. There is not limit of extension

This approach was tested by the Author in a lifelong learning program (Comenius COTTAS 2014), producing the following basic SWOT strategies analysis to improve it (dall'Acqua, 2014).

Strength/Opportunities Analysis

- Leading collaborative dialogue, sharing knowledge and creating possibilities for action in groups
- Leading to action in the form of better decision making and innovation, and thus tangible business outcomes
- Improving open mindset towards renewing thinking and perspective

Weakness/Opportunities Analysis

- Extending the face-to-face meetings using social networking tools
- Extending the environment of application (network of e-environments)

Threats/Strength Analysis

- Making flexible the choices of the group members, monitoring the effective dialogue path

Weakness/Threats Analysis

- Soliciting people to talk openly to one another about theirs specific corporate interests, opportunities and responsibilities

Comparing this approach with PENTHA ID Model in Orientism perspective. This strategy could solve:

- At knowledge level: partially the reinforcement knowledge process and the distributed allocation; potentially the reduction of complexity; re-generation and re-purposing of different knowledge; awareness of knowledge and data meaning management; consciousness transfer
- At User level: degree of connectedness, managing a complex network and potentiality the management of risks and removal of roadblocks
- At technology level: potentially a facilitation of information management via virtual environment; partially an effective capture of the tacit knowledge of Agents; communities of practice and scanning and reporting pathways

Orientism Management Strategy (OMS)

PENTHA 2.0 components are regarded as linked together, through knowledge cicles and energy flows (pathways). The result is an Orientism Management (OM) concept, based on intertwined 10 Knowledge Managements typologies, each based on areas of development and improvement of own personal leadership (see Table 3 in Appendix and Figure 4).

Knowledge Management with Consciousness (Low) (KMC/l)

It focuses on the learning "to know what" that the Agent needs to manage. It is.based on the empower of Energy-, Action-, Future factors (green-yellow-red triangle in the schema), according to Passion, Vision and Profession of the Trainee. To support this knowledge/orientation management PENTHA suggests,

Orientism Management (OM)

Figure 4. Tutoring support (Source: dall'Acqua, 2011)

between others, Fading tutoring/training mode, a method for adjusting and adapting the knowledge/orientation path according to the achievements of the Agent until the proof of his positive capability in full autonomy.

Knowledge Management with Consciousness (Medium) (KMC/m)

It focuses on the learning "to know how" that the Agent needs to manage. It is.based on the empower of Role-, Skills-, Work factors (violet-blue-black triangle in the schema), according to Vocation, Profession and Mission of the Trainee. To support this knowledge/orientation management, PENTHA suggests several tutoring/training modes, such as:

- Scaffolding, a method which favours the adaptation of the knwoledge/orientation path, a reflection on the actions developed by the Agent, stimulated by the Trainer/Tutor
- Modeling, a method according to which the Tutor/Trainer demonstrates how to perform a task
- Performing, a method according to which the Tutor/Trainer motivate the Agent, stimulating his/her own attitude and disposition to the work

Knowledge Management with Consciousness (High) (KMC/h)

It focuses on the learning "to know where" that the Agent needs to manage. It is.based on the empower of Action-, Love-, Work factors (red-orange-violet triangle in the schema), according to Profession, Passion and Mission of the Trainee. To support this knowledge/orientation management, PENTHA suggests, between others, Narrating tutoring/training mode, a method based on a) the basic idea of the tutoring/

training role is to introduce a topic to attract the attention of the Trainees, the appreciation of different learning styles and different forms of intelligence; b) the basic idea of the learning aspect is to encourage the Trainees to verbalize their own experiences, to activate a process of working self-reflection/evaluation.

Knowledge Management with Meaning (KMM)

It focuses on the learning "to know why" that the Agent needs to manage. It is.based on the empower of Purpose-, Future-, Work factors (azure-yellow-violet triangle in the schema), according to Profession, Vision and Mission of the Trainee. To support this knowledge/orientation management, PENTHA suggests several tutoring/training modes, such as:

- Coaching, a method according to which the Tutor/Trainer actively supports the Trainee, primarily motivating and analyzing the Trainees performance, providing feedback, reflecting together on assignments to stimulate discussion about the method adopted
- Norming, a method aimed at high performing guideline, towards effective work and collaborative behavior

Knowledge Management with Feeling (KMF)

It focuses on the learning "to know moving (towards)" that the Agent needs to manage to activate a change of perspective or action. It is.based on the empower of Role-, Love-, Spirit factors (pink, black, orange triangle in the schema), according to Profession, Vision and Mission of the Trainee. To support this knowledge/orientation management, PENTHA suggests, in addition to the above Coaching, Narrating and Fading tutoring/training modes, also to the more specific Reflecting mode, a method based on the pushing the Trainees to compare their own difficulties with an Expert, encouraging them to perform pull actions. Reflection is the vehicle for critical analysis, problem-solving, synthesizing of opposing ideas, evaluation, identifying patterns and creating meanings.

Knowledge Management with Will (KMW)

It focuses on the learning "to know esperiencing", process that the Agent needs to activate and control. It is.based on the empower of Action, Skills-, Spirit factors (red, blue, pink triangle in the schema), according to Profession, Vision and Mission of the Trainee. To support this knowledge/orientation management, PENTHA suggests, the above Fading and Performing.

Knowledge Management with Understanding (KMU)

It focuses on the learning "to know enabling" that the Agent needs to became. It is.based on the empower of Awareness, Skills, Future factors (brown, blue, yellow triangle in the schema), according to Profession, Vision and Mission of the Trainee. To support this knowledge/orientation management, PENTHA suggests, in addition to the above Coaching, Narrating, Scaffolding, Reflective and Fading tutoring/training modes, also to the more specific Exploring mode, which aims to lead the Trainees to solve problems with new or alternative solutions. The construction of knowledge occurs through the observation and the transformation of own or other experiences.

Knowledge Management with Personalization (KMP)

It focuses on the learning "to know changing" for Agent part. It is.based on the empower of Role, Awareness, Purpose factors (brown, black, azure triangle in the schema), according to Vocation, Vision and Mission of the Trainee. To support this knowledge/orientation management, PENTHA suggests, in addition to the above Scaffolding, also to the more specific Storming mode, regards effective communication, and conflict resolution support and training.

Knowledge Management with Availability (KMA)

It focuses on the learning "to know opening" towards people, environment, prospectives and perspectives, interpretations for Agent part. It is.based on the empower of Awareness, Energy and Spirit factors (brown, pink, green triangle in the schema), according to Vocation, Vision and Mission of the Trainee, with high attention to the comparison. To support this knowledge/orientation management, PENTHA suggests the above Scaffolding and Fading tutoring/training modes.

Knowledge Management with Synergy (KMS)

It focuses on the learning "to know devoting" towards work, goals, relationships for Agent part. It is.based on the empower of Purpose, Energy and Love factors (green, orange, azure triangle in the schema), according to Vocation, Vision and Mission of the Trainee, with high attention to the comparison. To support this knowledge/orientation management, PENTHA suggests the above Scaffolding and Fading tutoring/training modes.

Orientism Processes Organization (OMP)

The focus of the Orientism Management is specifically to orient people to manage decisions in unpredictability conditions in multi-user environment context. It intends to propose a new solution to the demand for "innovative and creative leadership" to make choices, to open to the change of perspective, to manage relationships and complex environments, basing on the conception of a new model of behavior and management of the simultaneity of how people process information.

According to HSB-KM model (Md Santo, 2012), the management is comprehensive of three KM dimensions: Technology (KM Tools) analog with human senses, Processes (KM Process Framework) analog with human mind brain and People (KM Standard Culture and Value) analog with human consciousness DNA respectively. The outcome is a living access mechanisms that can be used across any management tool type (such as Total Quality Management / Six Sigma, Learning Organization, HRM, Benchmarking, Process Classification Framework, Business Process Reengineering, Balanced Scorecard, Business Intelligence, Information Management, Library Management, Project Management including Social Media platforms etc.), wherein each with their specific functions to be orchestrated under KM's consciousness.

Figure 5. Comparison between components of KM with KM as Learning Organization

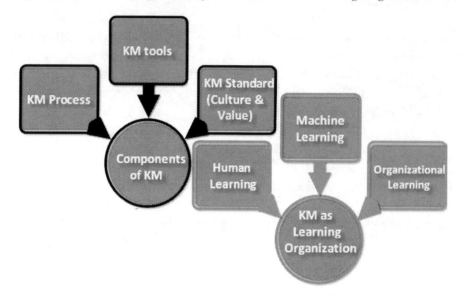

Orientism Management Tools (OMT)

PENTHA ID model 2.0 proposes the design of a focused teamwork environment that enables a flux of collective and individual knowledge paths to foster innovation, imagination, energy, and enthusiasm. This environment is based primarily on an Artificial Intelligence – Tutoring Subsystem, used to identify, monitor and adapt the Orientism Management, working through rules of action, relationship between actions and cognitive content, adaptation and personalization of the decision pathways.

The proposed platform is organic in it's make up and allow for unpredictable interactions due to a connectivist and autopoietic nature of a design. Multiple contexts and communities need to be allowed, to garner context and understanding, in one environment of UI.

It is a next-generation intelligent knowledge management environment, a mash between PLE (Personal Learning Environment), PKE (Personal Knowledge Environment), and PWE (Personal Work Environment), able to support social networking activities as well as collaborative learning, supported by an intelligent system based on artificial intelligence tools

Each user needs to build, store and organize information and knowledge in the way that best helps them.

Human Intelligence (HI) is leveraging the life's experience, education and knowledge by engaging the user in a journey to share their life knowledge and better understand their life passion and purposes.

Users needs to interact with topic/issues/events/people/products.

Collaborative strategies are crucial, in relation with the training objectives and path, as well as the availability of adequate networking facilities for group interactions, within the virtual knowledge space, and the possibility to create communities of practice, a dynamic-, synergistic- and collaborative construction of significant knowledge. It suggests several activities, such as Community Laboratory, Group Laboratory (Project Work), Community online sessions, Community Tutoring (in synchronous and asynchronous modes), specifically assessed. The approach is implementing a specific dedicated KM platform to monitor the knowledge path.

Orientism Management (OM)

Specific Technical Assets:

- Content Management System
- Document Management System
- E-learning applications (in accordance to the user behaviours, role, profile, preferences and personal requirements)
- Creating, Sharing, Re-using, and Management of Knowledge Objects (personal/social e-portfolio)
- Content Ranking based on Human Preference,
- Content Relevance based on User Participation and Selection
- Conceptual managing tool
- Narrative Environment
- Semantic Search Engine
- Gamification
- Intelligent Monitoring, Rule Engine based
- Intelligent Tutoring System/Decision support (Cognitive Tutoring)
- Database design to object-oriented
- Online Analytical Processing (OLAP)
- Model-View-Controller based user interface
- Groupware system
- Knowledge templates for self learning/teaching/CRM dynamic paths
- Video broadcasting tool (with Chat, Raise Hand functionality and event scheduler, real-time collaborative whiteboards)
- Social Content Viewer (eReader)
- Annotations tools
- Enhanced Dashboard analytics
- Intranet/Extranet

Basically, in the HSB-KT theory, the multi-agent environment is an entity comprised of dynamical continuous interaction among Inductive, Deductive and Socioductive thinking. The latter one is a powerful approach to sharing and discovering a whole array of options, leading to more informed decision-making and a more intimate, expansive and dynamic understanding of the culture and context in which the agents work. It is called also as Know Where learning or Middle Up – Down thinking. It represents the whole and interactive entity of three KM dimensions: Technology (KM Tools), Processes (KM Process Framework), and People (KM Standard Culture and Value) (see Figures 6 and 7).

According to it, OM tools need to be associated to the "physical" dimension of the life/work (hardware) (defined as "KM with low consciousness"), comparable to the social environment through KM tools use (such as IT/ICT, Social Media platforms). It concerns the Hypermedia component of PENTHA model, described in so called "Social dimension".

Specifically, advances in knowledge modeling and representation, the semantic web, data mining, analytics, and open data form a foundation for new models of knowledge development and analysis. The technical complexity of this nascent field is paralleled by a transition within the full spectrum of learning (education, work place learning, informal learning) to social, networked learning. These technical, pedagogical, and social domains must be brought into dialogue with each other to ensure that interventions and organizational systems serve the needs of all stakeholders.

Figure 6. To know what, where, how tools, according to HSB-KM (Source: dall'Acqua, 2014)

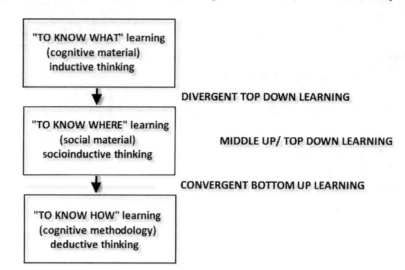

Figure 7. KM tools typologies, according to HSB-KM, (Source: dall'Acqua&Md Santo, 2012)

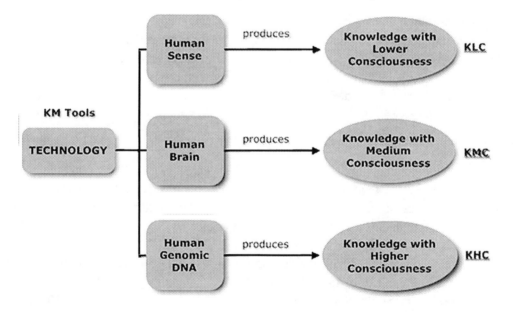

FUTURE RESEARCH DIRECTIONS

PENTHA Model 2.0, applies the Orientism approach to extend the proposed environment to become a "virtual agent arena", able to emulate virtual agents attending a virtual teamwork or activity with a variety of predefined human behaviours, learning behaviours and personal preferences, monitored, individualized and modelled on today's known, typical agents characteristics, agent needs and expectations.

The incoming platform is focused in particular on an innovative approach and concept to allow prospective in-service employees, or apprentices to test their intended work approach in a simulated, near reality "work world" representing known work collaborative environments.

Orientism Management (OM)

This approach is dedicated to allow a professional induction, alleviating today's often expressed concerns of inadequate or insufficient preparation of new entry professionals or allowing a change of role within an organization.

CONCLUSION

The present contribution intends to be useful to employees and/or work/project teams training. Each trainee works as a decision maker, and has to be able to select the information and manage tasks towards a common goal, and to understand what elements are useful to own personal and professional development to optimize performances.

The proposed approach interprets the fluid nature of the decision making process, looking at knowledge and knowledge activities as dynamic, adaptive and self-regulative, based not only on well-known explicit curricular goals, but also on unpredictable interactions and relationships between players. The knowledge process is emerging in human and biological, social and cultural environments. This process is oriented toward the generation of an "order in the chaos" of complex and dynamics management, to orient on the internal "diversity", the variety of backgrounds, interests, knowledge, skills and the whole personality of the trainees, individually or within in a work team.

ACKNOWLEDGMENT

The author wishes to express sincere esteem and gratitude to Dr. Md Santo (Indonesia), awarded and international Knowledge Management expert, founder of Nature Knowledge Theory (NKT), to have inspired the scientific base of the complex concept and to be a valuable research partner in innovative projects.

Also, the author gratefully acknowledges the great support of her colleague, Steve Mackenzie, Team Leader of Distance Learning Designers at De Montfort University (UK), to have reviewed some key aspects of the approach, suggesting valuable optimizations.

REFERENCES

Bandler, R., Robert, A., & Fitzpatrick, O. (2013). *An Introduction To Nlp*. New York: Harper Collins Publishers.

Cheong, R. K. F., & Tsui, E. (2010). The Roles and Values of Personal Knowledge Management: An exploratory study. *VINE The Journal of Information and Knowledge Management System, 40*(2), 204–227.

Cheong, R.K.F., & Tsui, E. (2011). From Skills and Competencies to Outcome-based Collaborative Work: Tracking a Decade's Development of Personal Knowledge Management (PKM) Models. *Knowledge and Process Management: The Journal of Corporate transformation, 18*(3), 175-193.

dall'Acqua, L. (2009). Specification and cognition for an adaptive and intelligent e-learning environment. In *Proceedings of World Conference on E-Learning in Corporate, Government, Healthcare and Higher Education AACE 2009* (pp. 2485-2493). Academic Press.

dall'Acqua, L. (2011). Didactical suggestion for a Dynamic Hybrid Intelligent e-Learning Environment (DHILE) applying the PENTHA ID Model. In *AIP, Conference Proceedings, Special Edition of the WCECS2010* (Vol. 1373, pp. 159-173). Academic Press.

dall'Acqua, L. (2014). Needs and strategies of KM in a multi-user environment: PENTHA Model view and analysis. *Jekpot KM19*.

dall'Acqua, L., & Santo, M. (2012). New interpretative paradigms to understand and manage the unpredictability of the dynamics of learning in a complex multi-user knowledge environment. In *Proceedings of Artificial Intelligence Workshop 2012 on Collaboration and Intelligence in Blended Learning* (pp. 92-9). Academic Press.

dall'Acqua, L., & Santo, M. (2014). Orientism, the basic pedagogical approach of PENTHA ID Model vs. 2, to manage decisions in unpredictability conditions. In *Proceedings of World Congress on Engineering and Computer Science WCECS2014* (vol. 1, pp. 316-21). Academic Press.

Downes, S. (2010). *The role of the Educator in PLE World*. Retrieved (9 Jan 2012), Retrieved from http://www.slideshare.net/Downes/the-role-of-the-educator-in-a-ple-world

Gagné, R. M. (1985). The Condition of Learning and Theory of Instruction. New York: CBS College Publishing.

Gardner, H., & Hatch, T. (1989). Multiple intelligences go to school: Educational implications of the theory of multiple intelligences. Educational Researcher, 18(8), 4–9.

Goldsmith, M., Morgan, H., & Ogg, A. (2004). Effectively Influencing Up:Ensuring That Your Knowledge, Makes a Difference, Marshall Goldsmith. Published in Leading Organizational Learning. Jossey-Bass.

Gurteen, G., & Remenyi, R. (2007). *The Knowledge-Café. If only we knew what we know*. Retrieved from: http://www.slideshare.net/dgurteen/introduction-to-the-knowledge-cafe

Hannafin, M. J., Land, S., & Oliver, K. (1999). Open learning environments: Foundations and models. Reigeluth, 3, 115-140.

Jonassen, D. H. (1999). Designing constructivist learning environments. Reigeluth, 2, 215-239.

Knowledge Cafés, Talks and Workshops Website. (n.d.). Retrieved from http://forwardnetworking.com/knowledge-cafes/

Marschark, M., Lang, H. G., & Albertini, J. A. (2002). Educating Deaf Students: From Research to Practice. Oxford University Press.

Santo, M. (2012). *Knowledge Management Product*. Retrieved from http://mobeeknowledge.ning.com/page/knowledge-management-km-nature-knowledge-theory-nkt-product-knowl

Santo, M., dall'Acqua, L., & Kristinawati. (2014). *New Integrated Formal Science (NIFS) and Personal Knowledge Management (PKM) for K-12 Education*. NKI – SONO Consortium for Educators and Scientists (NSCES) with the School of Business and Management – Bandung Institute of Techn. Retrieved from http://tinyurl.com/kpcyn3u

Nardi, B. (1999). Context and consciousness: Activity theory and human-computer interaction. Cambridge, MA: MIT Press.

Nelson, L. M. (1999). Collaborative Problem Solving. Reigeluth, 241-267.

Regional Gurteen Community Cafes Website. (n.d.). Retrieved from http://www.gurteen.com/gurteen/gurteen.nsf/id/kcafes

Reigeluth, C. M., et al. (2006). Creating shared visions of the future for K-12 education: A systemic transformation process for a learner-centered paradigm. *The Journal of Educational Alternatives, 3*(1), 34-66.

Reigeluth, C. M. (2004). Elaboration Theory. In Education and Technology: An Encyclopedia. Santa Barbara, CA: ABC-Clio.

Reigeluth, M. (1999). Instructional-Design Theories and Models: A New Paradigm of Instructional Theory. Hillsdale, NJ: Lawrence Erlbaum Assoc.

Sandberg, J. A. (1994). Educational paradigms: issues and trends. In Proceedings of Lessons from learning. (IFIP TC3/WG3.3 Working Conference 1993). Academic Press.

Schank, R. C., Berman, T. R., & Macpherson, K. A. (1999). Learning by Doing. Reigeluth, 3, 160-181. doi:10.1017/CBO9780511527920.011 doi:10.1017/CBO9780511527920.011

KEY TERMS AND DEFINITIONS

Coaching: A method in which the Trainer actively supports the Trainee, motivating, analyzing performance, providing feedback, reflection on assignment, stimulating discussion about the method adopted. It mainly focuses on KMM, KMF and KMU.

Exploring: A method which forces the Learners/Users to solve problems with new or alternative solutions. The construction of knowledge occurs through the observation and the transformation of experience. It mainly focuses on KMU.

Fading: A method for adjusting and adapting the learning path according to the achievements of the Learner until the proof of his positive capability in full autonomy. It mainly focuses on KMF, KMW, KMU, KMA, KMS.

Forming: A method concerning a topic introduction to make the Learner/User aware. It mainly focuses on KMC/l.

Modelling: A method for which the Tutor demonstrates how to perform a task. It mainly focuses on KMC/m.

Narrating: A method concerning two different aspects: a) the basic idea of the tutoring aspect is to introduce a topic to attract the attention of Learners/Users, the appreciation of different learning styles and different forms of intelligence; b) the basic idea of the learning aspect is to encourage the Learners to verbalize their experiences. It mainly focuses on KMC/h, KMF and KMU.

Norming: A method to optimize high performing, effective behaviors. It mainly focuses on KMM.

Orientism: Is a new multi-dimensional KM approach to improve the people's ability to manage decisions and own change of perspective, according to natural, social, artificial environments, in personalized multi-user dynamic, assigned value to multiple reference points and multi-interpreting paradigms.

PENTHA Model: Is an Istructional/Knowledge Design Model focused on designing the KM environment, defining the (didactical) rules for an Intelligent Tutoring System, facilitating person's change and enhancement.

Performing: A method to push a user on motivation and attitude in a performance. It mainly focuses on KMC/m and KMW.

Reflecting: A method which pushes to compare own difficulties with an Expert / Tutor and encourages them to perform pull actions. Reflection is the vehicle for critical analysis, problem-solving, synthesizing of opposing ideas, evaluation, identifying patterns and creating meanings. It mainly focuses on KMF and KMU.

Scaffolding: A method focuses on favouring the adaptation of the knowledge/learning path taken, a reflection on the actions developed by the Learner/User stimulated by the Tutor. It mainly focuses on KMC/m, KMU and KMP.

Storming: A method concerning effective communication, conflict resolution. It mainly focuses on KMP and KMA.

APPENDIX: TABLES

Table 1. Variables (vertices) and domains

Vertices' name	Domains
Profession vertex	the Work, the Skills, the Action, the Future of people
Vision vertex	the Future, the Purpose, the Awareness, the Energy of people.
Passion vertex	the Energy, the Spirit, the Love, the Action of people.
Vocation vertex	the Spirit, the Love, the Awareness, the Role of people
Mission vertex	the Role, the Work, the Love, the Purpose of people

Table 2. Factors (relationship between vertices)

Relationship's name	Involved Vertices
Spirit factor	Passion/Vocation (pink link)
Energy factor	Passion/Vision (green link)
Love factor	Passion/Mission (orange link)
Action factor	Passion/Profession (red link)
Awareness factor	Vision/Vocation (brown link)
Purpose factor	Vision/Mission (azure link)
Future factor	Profession/Vusion (yellow link)
Work factor	Profession/Mission (violet link)
Skills factor	Vocation/Profession (blue link)
Role factor	Vocation/Mission (black link)

Table 3. 10 KM typologies (OM model) with related focused tutoring modes

Knowledge Management	Learning	To empower	According to	Focused Tutoring Modes
with (Low) Consciousness KMC/l	*to know what*	Energy, Action, Future	Passion, Vision, Profession	Forming
with (Medium) Consciousness KMC/m	*to know how*	Role, Skills, Work	Vocation, Profession, Mission	Scaffolding, Modeling, Performing
with (High) Consciousness KMC/h	*to know where*	Work, Action, Love	Profession, Mission, Passion	Narrating
with Meaning KMM	*to know why*	Work, Purpose, Future	Profession, Vision, Mission	Coaching, Norming
with Feeling KMF	*to know moving*	Role, Love, Spirit	Vocation, Mission, Passion	Coaching, Reflecting, Fading, Narrating
with Will KMW	*to know experiencing*	Action, Skills, Spirit	Passion, Profession, Vocation	Fading, Performing
with Understanding KMU	*to know enabling*	Awareness, Skills, Future	Vision, Vocation, Profession	Coaching, Narrating, Exploring, Reflecting, Scaffolding, Fading
with Personalization KMP	*to know changing*	Role, Awareness, Purpose	Vocation, Mission, Vision	Storming, Scaffolding
with Availability KMA	*to know opening*	Awareness, Energy, Spirit	Vision, Vocation, Passion	Storming, Fading
with Synergy KMS	*to know devoting*	Purpose, Energy, Love	Passion, Vision, Mission	Fading

Chapter 11
Relationship between Knowledge Management and Academic Integrity in a Middle Eastern University

Judith Mavodza
Zayed University, UAE

ABSTRACT

The difference between knowledge sharing as enabled in a knowledge management (KM) environment, and academic honesty continuously needs clarification and reinforcement in academic institutions. Teaching includes getting students to realize that knowledge is an asset that can be ethically used for creativity and innovation, resulting in the enhancement of the corporate image and effectiveness of a university. Studies have confirmed that academic dishonesty is an ethical challenge facing many academic institutions of higher learning. In the Middle East, the use of English as a second language is often cited as a contributing factor to students' plagiarizing, but the problem extends to the use of Arabic language sources too. Conflicts in approach may arise because KM works well in an environment of sharing, and yet acknowledging academic productivity of others may not always happen spontaneously. This is a challenge faced in MOOCs and by institutions of higher learning the world over.

INTRODUCTION

In the United Arab Emirates (UAE) education system, as in most countries around the world, academic integrity is considered as very important in determining the quality of students and faculty that come out of a university. According to Kirk (2010, p. 41), among UAE plans is an emphasis on the significance of "academic integrity policies to give value to awarded degrees". One of the UAE Ministry of Higher Education Strategic goals for 2011-2013 is to "support scientific research and encourage innovation". Supporting innovation carries with it a KM agenda. The National Qualifications Authority (2013a, p. 11) of the UAE, in a document giving an overview of performance in the education system clearly explains

DOI: 10.4018/978-1-4666-9607-5.ch011

that a knowledge agenda implies a shift in the education system, mainly in the teaching-learning process. Because the current information environment broadly uses internet based applications that come in a variety of formats, academic institutions concern themselves with how the availability of these resources impact teaching and learning. This chapter uses a knowledge management (KM) approach in discussing the academic integrity topic. The view is that good academic conduct or academic integrity helps students learn, and the academe guides them in order to attain high quality qualifications. Thus, the better the quality of perceived products of a university, the more likely employers are encouraged to provide internship opportunities, hire the graduating students, and the more the reputation of the university is perceived to be superior. The discussion that results is about its corporate image – making a case for aligning higher education policy with how teaching and learning is taking place at an individual institution. From this introduction, it is evident that there are both individual, organizational, and national aspects involved. The individual is the student and the educator, while the organization is the academic institution.

BACKGROUND

In discussing KM and academic integrity, there is the requirement to understand the concepts and how applicable they are. While KM has widely been used in business, the use of its principles in academic library environments has been limited but appears to be more comprehensive than other models that focus only on regular library functions such as circulation, or technical services, or reference in that interactivity and the needs of the library users are of paramount importance. In approaching the academic integrity topic, use of KM practices is discussed in this chapter with the implication of institutional overall systemic change in teaching, learning, and library support because the latter does not stand independent of the university for which it has been set up. The change is designed to amplify the quality of academic products of a university for its marketability. Faculty are therefore expected to be qualified to meet the challenge. Thus, revelations of the proliferation of fraudsters selling fake academic qualifications in the UAE as has already been happening in other parts of the world, such as reported in *Khaleej Times* by Croucher (26 April 2009) and in *Gulf News* by Farooqui (28 May 2014) make both academic institutions and employers concerned and stay on the look-out for these. Employers want only the genuinely qualified, while universities want to have faculty who are qualified to teach and research for the education of appropriately qualified new professionals.

Academic Integrity

Academic integrity in this chapter is used interchangeably with academic honesty or good academic conduct. Discussing it includes dialogue on the responsibilities and accountability of faculty and of students. The concept is broad and includes ethical use of information and resources while acknowledging the original source of the information used. It also includes originality and creativity that is central to academic culture. On the other hand, academic dishonesty (a big part of general academic misconduct) includes cheating, plagiarism, falsification or fabrication of data or information, copying without acknowledging, submitting outsourced assignments, "using someone else's language, ideas, or other original material without acknowledging its source" (Correa, 2011, p. 66). Lack of information about academic integrity, or societal emphasis on getting certificates regardless of cost, are sometimes the issue too, rather than the likelihood of students being generally prone to experimenting with academic dishonesty.

Admittedly, a discourse surrounding individual ethical behavior is connected to individual character. Roig (1997) who is subsequently quoted in reference to a UAE academic institution by Wheeler and Anderson (2010, p. 169) suggests that "individual, pedagogical, and institutional factors can all influence the incidence of plagiarism. Students themselves can be impacted by a wide range of factors including their educational conditioning, cultural background, motivation, language skill, peer pressure, gender, issues with time management, ability, and even the subject being studied". Then again, major challenges arise when faculty is not sure about academic integrity, citation and referencing conventions, and respect for intellectual property since that affects the way they guide students.

In this chapter, the discussion relates to a generic UAE academic institution of higher learning associated with teaching, learning, and research. The concept is ingrained in the UAE Ministry of Higher Education and Scientific Commission for Academic Accreditation (2011b, section 5.11, p16) documents. The reason for putting it in context is to avoid assuming meanings or definitions that may possibly be inapplicable. The subject of relevance is constantly referred to in the sections that follow.

Knowledge Management

The proposal in this chapter is about the use of KM principles in reinforcing academic integrity and enhancing the way an academic library can ideally participate in the community that it exists to support, as well as highlighting the practices that foster the environment for it. Cognizance has to also be taken that both KM concepts and the academic integrity culture cannot be introduced or enhanced in any academic institution by the library alone. As such, the discussion pertains primarily to the academic institutions and then explains the role of the library. There is therefore merit in considering the use of KM tools and principles in confronting the academic integrity debate within the context of the mission and values of the institution.

The discussion is grounded in theoretical literature on KM, and explains how libraries can take advantage of tools available in the modern information environment. These include computers, laptops, printers, scanners, handheld or mobile devices, which may not necessarily have been originally created for KM, but expedite its practice. It also discusses the evolving functions of librarians, and then suggests the implications and recommendations, for an academic library nurturing use of the knowledge asset. A KM environment recognizes knowledge as an asset where beneficiaries must necessarily have knowledge choices, access to information and data, storage capabilities, and sharing that are critical processes to its success. Processes fundamental to KM are knowledge creation, knowledge storage and retrieval, knowledge transfer and application (Takeuchi, 2001).

The KM general guiding principles, or accepted guidelines, as laid out by Davenport and Prusak (1998, p. 24) are that knowledge originates and resides in people's minds; that it is important to identify key knowledge workers who can be effectively brought together in a fusion; that knowledge sharing requires trust; that knowledge sharing must be encouraged and rewarded; that it is important to emphasize the creative potential inherent in the complexity and diversity of ideas, seeing differences as positive, rather than sources of conflict, and avoiding simple answers to complex questions; that technology enables new knowledge behaviors; that management support and resources are essential; that knowledge initiatives should begin with a pilot program; that quantitative and qualitative measurements are needed to evaluate the initiative; and that knowledge is creative and should be encouraged to develop in unexpected ways.

KM perspectives are based on a variety of disciplines where it was realized that knowledge is a valuable asset if tapped into and used effectively. It first appeared in 1997 (Jashapara, 2005) as industry was beginning to realize the importance of both tacit or implicit (intellectual capital) and explicit knowledge. It is founded on the expansion of capitalist economies, computerization of industrial work, and economic competition. Lightfoot (2011, p. 3) points out that this phenomenon is an expression of the "Western concept of knowledge and Western cultural ideals". It is emphasized in current literature due to the fact that in the modern information environment, information and knowledge play a critical role in leveraging the operational advantages of an organization against its competitors (Davenport & Prusak, 1998; Drucker, 1999; White, 2004). In the domain of universities, competition is in terms of student enrolment and retention, the ability to attract high caliber faculty, the image and reputation of the university as reflected by its products, national- regional and world rankings, and facilities available. For the library, competition is with alternative sources of information and methods of information dissemination and consumption which the academic community is now exposed to, as well as its mission. Accompanying this information environment are information use issues that include privacy, ownership and ethics.

Essential to KM is the time value relevance of information in the sense that sharing information and being informed ahead of time enables proactivity. However, a research study on developing a KM strategy for the Arab world by Skok and Tahir (2010, p. 10) suggests that "ethno-centric research on knowledge sharing shows a strong disparity between a typical western firm and an Arab one, and how the western based KM literature should be applied cautiously in a non-western setting". In fact, Lightfoot (2011, p.7) points out that "governments in the Arabic-speaking world need to be confident about the sort of knowledge economy they are seeking to promote". The implication of these comments is that ideas or approaches that work can be useful if tailored to appropriately suit different environments, hence the mention of pilot programs that Davenport and Prusak (1998) suggest. This extends to academic institutions in that their strategic direction has to be in tandem with the country's education policies rather than KM solely as applied to Western academic institutions.

KM practice is driven by competitive pressures and the need to manage an organization's intangible assets more efficiently. It fundamentally refers to changes that enhance competitive advantage and maximizing profits (Davenport & Prusak, 1998; Drucker, 1999; White, 2004). This is applicable to an education establishment that has a long-term investment in human capital development at its core. An active library would be the nerve center in supporting and enabling creativity and innovativeness. According to Broadbent (1998, p.24), KM:

rests on utilizing and exploiting the organization's information (which needs to be managed for this to occur); and the application of people's competencies, skills, talents, thoughts, ideas, intuitions, commitments, motivations, and imaginations.

The point is reflected that information is passive by nature, whereas knowledge is a dynamic and active resource residing in people's minds (Davenport & Prusak, 1998; Nonaka & Takeuchi, 1995; Polanyi, 1962). This dynamism and active nature is part of what the modern university focusses on cultivating.

The approaches or models that are covered in literature originate mainly from Japan, Europe, and the United States industries (Lloria, 2008; Lightfoot, 2011; McAdam & McCreedy, 1999). These are intellectual theories, and knowledge creation theories. Lloria (2008) proposes a synthesis that puts KM into three schools. These are the economic (commercial) school that regards knowledge as a part of material wealth, the techno- centric school that focuses on technology in controlling and protecting information and knowledge, and the behavioral school that concentrates on the way that humans react to the environment including intellectual and social interaction through social media. They closely resemble the categories of McAdam and McCreedy (1999) who group KM into the knowledge model, the intellectual model, and the socially constructed model; and Lightfoot (2011) who categorizes it in learning, creative, and openness approaches. These are not rigid categories, but a way of understanding KM practices that institutions need to be aware of as they seek to use some of them to benefit practical situations that involve their nurturing the management and use of the knowledge assets they have. Such benefits include the spirit of collaboration, knowledge sharing, innovativeness, and the institutional cultural change that can occur when an institution deliberately choses to use the KM approach or when it is implementing KM practices. That is a process of enhancing the quality of products coming out of a university.

KM RELEVANCE IN LIBRARIES

Modern libraries facilitate access to information and knowledge resources, a situation that has arisen out of the need to serve web savvy digital natives who are prone to use cloud computing and web 2.0 technologies (such social media technologies as blogs and wikis, instant messaging (IM) chat, tagging, real simple syndication (RSS) feeds, Google maps and Google documents, Google hangouts and video sharing, photos, social office suites and podcasts). These technologies can actually be utilized in support of organizational KM. Guidance on sharing sources and resources ethically is what libraries assist with in the form of information literacy (IL) instruction. The assumption is that individuals that are information literate appreciate the importance of quality information, and know how to retrieve and use it. In the process, they potentially can be effective creators of valuable information, and subsequently knowledge. According to Peterson (2007), the UAE government maintains open and progressive policies towards ICT technology adoption – whether in schools, homes, business's or government. The Government of Abu Dhabi Economic Vision 2030 (2008) has:

a focus on information and communications technology (ICT) to keep Abu Dhabi at the forefront of technological advancement and to ensure its population is fully wired into the global economy

This KM technology approach has the potential to facilitate sharing of resources in educational institutions for academic research. In a UAE industry study, Siddique (2012, p. 710) explains that KM initiatives are still in their infancy stages. As such, the approach is not always clearly understood on different levels, and there also needs to be a realization that IT solutions are enablers rather than the approach. The significance of this conclusion is that the introduction of KM approaches and academic integrity efforts that are intended to guide graduates who eventually join the UAE industry have to be carefully crafted for relevance and effectiveness. This is elaborated upon by Wheeler and Anderson (2010, p. 166) in their research on how to deal with "plagiarism in a complex information society". They acknowledge the importance of applying academic integrity expectations within the UAE based on properly and appropriately educating students about it and what it implies.

It is increasingly evident that social media technologies and innovation are used for educational purposes as pointed out by Tynes (2007, p. 576) that "adolescent participation in social online environments (such as social networking spaces, chat rooms and discussion boards) can foster learning that reinforces and compliments what is taught in traditional classrooms. Many spaces offer training in how to develop critical thinking and argumentation skills". It is thus critical for librarians and faculty to support students in efficiently and effectively using new communication technologies as these unfold. The context of this suggestion is that the Emirates Telecommunications Regulatory Authority ICT survey of 2012 indicated that 72% of UAE households have internet connectivity in their homes, and 99.9% of the UAE population use mobile phones (Telecommunications Regulatory Authority, 2012, p.5). It is therefore useful for educators to take advantage of these networked spaces to provide resources that guide students and faculty about honest academic practice. In this instance, educators have to take on the education-related responsibility since it is not easy for parents to determine how much influence they can have on children's internet use habits. The book entitled *Arab World Unbound: Tapping into the Power of 350 Million Consumers* by Mahajan (2012) gives accounts of how internet and the web have become a way of life for the youth in the Gulf Region, much like in most parts of the world where connectivity is habit. The result has been an erosion of parents' role in their children's character building. However, having choices is one of the KM processes, hence the importance of providing everyone with the choice to use the library guides provided.

Many libraries in the Western hemisphere have started creating spaces for knowledge creation, such as information commons, learning commons, maker spaces, and hacker spaces. Rather than sustain a complete focus on discouraging learners from academic dishonesty, the shift is towards creativity and channeling creative capabilities that enable innovativeness. Maker spaces are areas in the library that have been re-modeled to enable tech-infused informal hands-on learning that is innovation–driven (Loertscher, 2012). In the same league, hacker spaces "are a location where people with common interests, usually in computers, technology, science or digital or electronic art can meet, socialize and/ or collaborate, sharing resources and knowledge to build or make things" (Norman, 2012, p. 100). In these spaces, learning opportunities are created with the collaboration of faculty and librarians to facilitate creation and creativity and support a culture of innovation – innovation, or the capacity to use the imagination to create new things, being a cornerstone of a KM approach. The ground has already been laid in the UAE by the annual Innovator event (www.innovator.ae) in partnership with academic institutions to enhance innovativeness. At the moment its academic partners include Al Ain University of Science and Technology, Abu Dhabi University, American University of Sharjah, Ajman University of Science and Technology, Canadian University of Technology, Higher Colleges of Technology, Khalifa University, Petroleum Institute, Rochester Institute of Technology Dubai, United Arab Emirates University, University of Sharjah, and Zayed University. This is a possible opportunity for the libraries in the universities mentioned to either lend themselves as resource pools, or more importantly, mirror similar practices for purposes of broadening innovativeness opportunities.

There is also the reality that creativity does not always happen in an obvious manner. That means these investments in time and resources have to be continuously monitored and evaluated for viability. Additionally, where knowledge assets have been identified, it is essential to be clear about which kind of knowledge asset is most appropriate to facilitate which type of knowledge creation process. The implication, for the library, is to therefore continuously find ways of re-tooling in order to remain relevant and proactive in the interest of meeting or anticipating these new needs and demands that result from a knowledge-based academic environment. The hacker spaces, maker spaces, and learning commons depend on the existing networked academic environment, support resources, and circumstances to enable the spirit of creativity and innovation.

USE OF A KM APPROACH IN ENHANCING ACADEMIC INTEGRITY

Among the tools that libraries make use of are desktop computers, laptops, printers including 3-D ones, scanners, handheld or mobile devices, i.e. tablets, smart phones and many other smart devices. The humans who have access to these complete the equation. Technologically, these are KM enabling. In terms of service provision, it is possible to maximize the use of technology to make the library the educational and learning space of choice for most students and faculty with the use of these collaboration and information sharing tools. That is an environment conducive to the formation of communities of self-selected participants in creating projects. These are based on collaboration and information sharing enabled by the evolving spaces inside the library, e.g. information commons, learning commons. Then again, in support of good academic practice, it is necessary for the library to have a clear statement of its mission, vision, and strategic objectives, all embedded and shared in the context of the parent university's values. That way it is well positioned to support academic integrity during the creation of the said projects, for value enhancement that adds to recognizable quality of qualifications attained at the university.

In the UAE, competition for international recognition and effectiveness in producing graduates who measure up to the national manpower requirements are major instigators driving universities to focus on how to fit in a globalized world. Faculty work more effectively if they are knowledgeable about good quality academic behavior and feel confident in dealing with academic integrity issues, especially backed by institutional leaders and managers. There may not be any value in creating an academic integrity policy and honor code that has no followers. Research on faculty response to ethical issues at an American university in the Middle-East by Tabsh, El Kadi and Abdelfatah (2012, p. 319) revealed that:

some faculty participants were unaware of the university's code of ethics; several of the faculty surveyed stated that they would ignore violations of an ethical code of conduct committed by colleagues; and there was no definite trend observed between the responses of faculty based on their discipline.

From these findings, it is a cause for concern that some individuals in faculty ranks were not aware of their university's academic integrity provisions. The results are suggestive of the fact that the place where the research was performed does indeed have an ethical code of conduct. Even when it is an expectation that faculty be concerned about academic integrity provisions in their place of work and beyond, making it part of the faculty orientation process to provide academic integrity information, expectations and obligations needs to be made clear.

Accompanying this need for reinforcement and support is the importance of promoting KM approaches, given the reality that students and faculty are not expected to be passive absorbers of information and knowledge as provided on university websites. They all become better academics if they have a certain level of commitment to the initiatives too. By suggesting that a "blend of personal responsibility, effort, self-control, and academic engagement" contribute towards the practice of academic honesty, Hensley (2013, p. 24) explains that both faculty and students are participants in embracing the culture of and norms for academic honesty. One has to always be careful to avoid the assumption that everything that is taught as good academic conduct will be adhered to. Rather, individual, environmental, and situational factors influence the way that taught behavior patterns are accepted.

Discussing a KM approach and academic integrity is based on the recognition of the diversity of institutions, disciplines, employees/ staff, and students (no one approach fits all). That is necessary, for example, in instituting assessments that are in context, and putting in place plagiarism support and detection resources that are relevant and useful. That can be done through sharing any implementation details of existing exemplary academic integrity policies and establishing or initiating appropriate guidance for good academic practice. It is also possible to explore ways to extend best practices for identified student and faculty groups. Faculty have the added responsibility to mentor students with their academically honest practices as suggested by Gray and Jordan (2012) who view professors as major players in shaping student ethical behavior.

The implications of providing guidance inside a university that is developing or engaging in efforts to maximize use of knowledge assets for purposes of supporting educational research include training and educating library users, educational leaders and managers. This is enhanced by establishing protocols for rewarding knowledge sharing and making KM a career-enhancing activity. The library can play a part in showcasing the instructional and research capabilities of faculty. This is part of the process of enabling the development of communities of good academic practice that demonstrate academic integrity, i.e., the development of collective intelligence can be the result of this KM practice.

With information flow as an essential KM element, the question of "fair use" is central to the work of faculty, librarians, and the university's legal office so that institutional policy on copyright and academic integrity is clearly spelt out. To achieve this partly implies knowledge sharing and the need for institutional management support. This is because creating an environment that includes the electronic storage and management of information and knowledge such as in the use of Blackboard (or Moodle, and such others) course management system, for example, requires the involvement of network administrators to collaboratively work with various departments, including input from the library. That demands the institutionalization of protocols for storage, access, and disposition of the documents and records. This reinforces the suggestions from a study by Hamid *et al.*, (2007) at National Library of Malaysia (NLM) that revealed that a clear organizational strategy and the right understanding of KM potentials and challenges could be described as the basic formula for success.

If librarians and faculty together guide students in finding and accessing materials, there is the potential to encourage discussions about ethical and legal issues associated with acquiring and using borrowed text, images, and a whole range of material that users have access to in a Web 2.0 environment, as well as clarifying issues relating to internet security, privacy, and appropriate social network use too. Reliance on Internet and the Web means that the university has to monitor the implications of using the cloud, especially concerning privacy and control of data, given the fact that IT components such as clients, servers, storage and networks, when an organization can be virtualized. Essentially, this cloud computing concept provides new opportunities for library application development as libraries gradually evolve from information to knowledge commons spaces. To make the processes work, trust and respect for colleagues and systems to get such projects up and running, as well as trustworthiness all round is very important, and thus taking the discussion back to professional ethics.

KM relies on trust (Davenport & Prusak, 1998, p. 35). However, from his conceptual paper, Mutula (2011, p. 261) points out that "despite the increasing adoption of digital scholarship strategies among universities, ethics and trust issues are not being addressed". Ethics signifies academic and professional honesty, and trust points to how much anyone can be sure that academic work that has been accomplished in an online environment genuinely belongs to the author rather than from unacknowledged sources. One of the reasons revealed for this shortcoming is the absence of institutionalized strategies for dealing with the challenge. Thus, an approach for verifying originality or curbing cheating/dishonesty in online courses is a useful addition to the overall teaching process to sustain quality and integrity in higher education.

Universities in the UAE, as in most universities internationally, have websites that are dedicated to explaining academic integrity and everything that accompanies its existence. Recognition, understanding, and use of such information is the question. The example of the study by Tabsh, El Kadi, and Abdelfatah (2012) demonstrates this. But then the challenge is not unique to the UAE, but best practices for coping with it are useful if taken heed of, used, and reinforced consistently. What they all aim for is to enable the development of novel capabilities in both teaching practice and student learning. In other words, the ideal to strive for is an environment that enables the conversion of knowledge from one form to another, resulting in knowledge creation that is central to successful KM practice.

RELATIONSHIP OR LINKAGE BETWEEN ACADEMIC INTEGRITY AND THE KNOWLEDGE CONVERSION PROCESS

KM literature on knowledge creation centers around four patterns of interaction in the name of the socialization-externalization-combination- internalization (SECI) model of Nonaka (1994), and Nonaka and Takeuchi (1995). They suggest that these concepts are based on information flow, with information management tools being a subset of KM tools. The creation of new knowledge as expressed by the SECI model is dependent on the interaction between tacit and explicit knowledge that Nonaka and Takeuchi (1995) present as modes of knowing. Tacit knowledge is unwritten and resides in people's minds, often reflected as the skills or competencies that an individual possesses (Polanyi, 1962). Its contextual expression manifests itself as "know-how". Then again, explicit knowledge exists where guidance is available and predictable. The implication of this explanation is that explicit knowledge largely relies on being tacitly understood and applied in tasks or assignments at hand. This can be a catalyst for creating new knowledge that is essential in innovation. In the context of the SECI model, socialization refers to the transformation of tacit or implicit knowledge to tacit knowledge; internalization refers to the transformation of tacit knowledge to explicit knowledge; combination refers to the transformation of explicit knowledge to explicit knowledge; and internalization is when explicit knowledge is being articulated and applied as tacit knowledge. The relevance of a knowledge creation process to academic integrity and vice versa lies in the importance of new knowledge and its value to the quality enhancement of academia.

The SECI process is an ever repeating, spiraling, and interactive knowledge creation one (Ngulube & Lwoga, 2007; Nonaka, 1994), rather than processes happening in a mutually exclusive linear fashion. The interaction between tacit and explicit knowledge does not happen in specific predetermined percentage proportions or patterns. Using the spiral imagery on the SECI model (depending on the online *Oxford English Dictionary* definition of a spiral) implies that the process is a winding one in a continuous and gradually widening (or tightening) curve. It either revolves around a central fixed point on a flat plane or about an axis so as to form a cone. Relating to the subject matter of the current discussion, it is an intricate process grounded on the university's mission and goals. Once adopted, the SECI spiral is therefore not a single time activity with no relation to the past or future, but a continuous and dynamic process that requires constant review of the interaction between tacit and explicit knowledge in order for the practice to remain relevant. It is the institution that decides what type of spiral works best for it. Nonaka (1994, p. 15) points out that the spiral "illustrates the creation of a new concept in terms of a continual dialogue between tacit and explicit knowledge". In the framework of teaching, learning, library use and academic integrity, the SECI processes can be applicable or interpreted as discussed in the sections that follow.

Socialization

Socialization happens when acquired information and knowledge is shared through social interaction such as in group projects. One of the ways to encourage good academic practice has been found to be through the use of group-based activities to facilitate student understanding of concepts. Similarly, the socialization process from a teaching perspective refers to the interaction of teams that are in place to discover and share important knowledge on how to teach effectively, particularly in the current information environment that has produced globalization-specific demands on the academe. Thus, academic institutions benefit from collaboration between or among students or students and faculty, as well as among faculty. That is because sharing information reduces ignorance – and ignorance is an enabler of plagiarism and/ or academic dishonesty.

Hensley (2013), and Wheeler and Anderson (2010) suggest that academic dishonesty or cheating sometimes happens as a coping mechanism because of concerns about grades or a lack of confidence in academic skills. What is important is being mentored by a faculty member or a peer, or observation and behavior modeling. In fact, Thomas, Raynor and McKinnon (2013, p. 4) conclude that this method is very productive "within a collectivist culture, such as the UAE, [*as*] this places the tasks and assessment firmly within the students' 'real life' context". But then Piascik and Brazeau (2010, p. 1) express the concern that students may have in recent years been "taught too well to work in groups and collaborate, and they may not know when to stop doing group work and start doing individual work". Hensley (2013), and Thomas, Raynor and McKinnon (2013) take heed of the self-perpetuating nature of academic dishonesty if practiced among peers, but are positive that helping students develop a culture of academic honesty also impacts their academic behavior constructively. Using the results of a study in Lebanon, McCabe, Feghali and Abdallah (2008, p. 463) found that:

student academic dishonesty shows a significant positive relationship with the perceived perception of peers' behavior and significant inverse relationships with the certainty of being reported, perceived understanding/acceptance of academic integrity policies on campus, and the perceived severity of penalties for violations of these policies

Wheeler and Anderson (2010, p. 169) add to this discussion by suggesting that "the line between collaboration and cheating during assessed tasks is blurred, and if this is not explicitly dealt with by assessors, it will inevitably result in misunderstandings as to what is acceptable".

Literature points to the fact that as students work in groups, helping them to become aware of how to effectively use such resources as electronic plagiarism detection tools helps. The way to do it is to use an educative approach rather than punitive one (Thomas & Sassi, 2011). This is even more effective if organization-wide approaches to plagiarism prevention are put in place so that they are introduced as supporting good academic practice rather than uncoordinated haphazard efforts towards policing academic misconduct, or even ignoring instances of undesirable academic conduct.

Externalization

Externalization happens when tacit knowledge that has been explained clearly becomes explicit knowledge. From an institutional perspective, when meetings or workshops are made available to encourage dialogue among professionals, then it is highly likely that tacit knowledge is expressed. This contributes to creating documented sources of information that reflect the conversion of tacit to explicit knowledge, e.g. guides and manuals, and such others. In the context of library use, if users are supported in collaborating or working in groups to give each other support in information acquisition, and information flow is encouraged, that may reduce the likelihood of plagiarism because of a good understanding of given tasks, using the available information. The products that result from their collaborative efforts are expressive of their ability to convert the acquired knowledge into tangible original student assignments (or recognizable scholarly publications on the part of faculty). Hensley (2013) explains that unrestrained motivation to be a high achiever may be a strong reason to cheat in an academic set-up, overshadowing ethical considerations. The debate becomes one of motivation and ethics, implying a more wholesome approach to support in modifying behavior towards good practice (good academic practice being an expression of externalization).

If procedures for developing students' understanding of academic integrity, and skills for academic honesty are put in place seamlessly, that may support the generation of good academic practice. With diversity in student bodies and academic disciplines, intervention strategies such as creating an online tutorial and introducing an electronic tool for plagiarism detection that the students can use at any time enhances awareness. This reduces instances such as revealed in a study at Wollongong University in Dubai by Koshy (2008) where students were concentrating on avoiding text-matching in Turnitin, rather than use the tool as a guide in developing originality of ideas expressed.

Combination

Combination takes place when information from various sources is integrated or put together to form new knowledge. This can include what students have learnt inside and outside the classroom, i.e. one form of explicit knowledge obtained for purposes of converting or transforming it into another form of explicit knowledge. It can enable plagiarism as there may be a tendency to cite or acknowledge in an incomplete manner, and more so when texts are combined from the same or different sources without attribution. Sometimes students "do not think copying homework answers is wrong when it is done with technology" (Piascik & Brazeau, 2010, p. 1). A literature review focusing on e-cheating in the UAE by Khan (2010, p.321) reveals similar conclusions that point to the fact that "copying or downloading movies and music has become rampant among the younger generation in the country" as well as by Wheeler and Anderson (2010, p. 168) in reference to UAE tertiary level students, 40% of whom do not view cutting and pasting as cheating. It is even more complicated with the use of translated texts that plagiarism detection software fails to identify, or more in some disciplines than in others. That is why it is useful to link assessments and academic integrity as a way to unveil and encourage originality and authenticity in individual work. Piascik and Brazeau (2010, p. 1) suggest that "it is important in any educational program for the instructor to provide the purpose of an assignment as well as directions for its completion at the time it is assigned".

Commitment by faculty and librarians to assist students, as well as respect of personal meaning of knowledge by students form a combination that enables effective use of lessons given and received. That is why Nonaka (1994, p. 20) notes that there is a problem if dialogue between tacit and explicit knowledge does not exist, and "a lack of commitment and neglect of the personal meaning of knowledge might mean that pure combination becomes a superficial interpretation of existing knowledge…". In efforts to modify behavior towards a culture of academic integrity, the aim is not to achieve a perfunctory or sketchy interpretation, but an adoption of correct skills that form the basis for revisions in teaching and academic productivity methods. This is a gradual process that takes both the learners and the educators through layers of schooling, revision, and re-visiting of the methods used. Research that combines information from various sources is a major component of how teaching is done so that when experimentation happens, it is only to the benefit of the teaching and learning environment. That kind of research has to necessarily also include investigations into how academic integrity is integrated into institutional culture since it happens in an institutional context.

Internalization

Internalization becomes possible when attained knowledge is internalized as an individual understands concepts and does not need to plagiarize. The individual and/ or group is/ are able to reflect on the attained and available knowledge so that they can recognize connections or patterns. At this stage, individuals can be said to have learned, but that cannot be viewed as the end of a process. The result is a respect for intellectual property and the desire to have it protected, which Mutula (2011) suggests is a basis for trust in digital research environments. This is reflected if an individual has benefitted from the socialization and externalization processes, and is thus discovering knowledge that is useful, sharing it and knowing how to use it constructively. The realization of the benefits of good academic conduct as it impacts long-term human capital development is an ideal that most academic institutions aim for their student and faculty to develop.

In addition to adopting a culture of academic honesty, a varied assortment of activities can be created to assess and uncover/ demonstrate students' understanding of plagiarism. This helps educators in designing assessments that enable the reduction of plagiarism, and in creating resources to support the development of students' skills for good academic practice. The study by Thomas, Raynor, and McKinnon (2013, p.9) at Zayed University, for example, reveals that a group oral exam was tolerated better and was found to provide culturally resonant means of assessment which also promotes academic integrity within the Arabian Gulf socio-cultural context. Hensley (2013) also views the placing of value on learning, developing, or collaborating as contributory to reducing the likelihood of cheating.

IMPORTANCE OF CONTINUED ACADEMIC INTEGRITY DISCUSSIONS

The quality of products of a university affect its corporate image and effect on university marketing culture in an environment of global competition. Ethical considerations are important because it is the responsibility of academic institutions to educate about and reinforce in students the culture of good academic practice. In their research, Tsokris and Struminger (2013) conclude that academic misconduct influences professional integrity. These authors suggest that "one of the most important roles of an educator is to assist students in developing a set of ethical standards that will guide their personal and professional decision-making abilities as they enter the workforce"(Tsokris & Struminger, 2013, p. 22). Stout (2011, p. 300), for example, argues that "academic integrity on police programmes should be conceptualised and taught as a matter of professional ethics". This argument is a result of the importance of instilling the academic integrity culture as a precursor to reliable ethical behavior in the work place.

The same argument is presented by Piascik and Brazeau (2010) referring to pharmacy graduate students and the responsibility they have in becoming honest professionals after their studies. Essentially, all disciplines need to produce graduates who are professionally reliable, knowledgeable, and dependable.

Khan (2010, p.321) alludes to UAE- related studies that have shown that those students who are piracy inclined while in schools or universities do take these attitudes into the next phase of their lives – the workforce. Cogdell and Aidulis (2008, p. 38) suggest that "students should learn about plagiarism in the context of professional ethics and an ethical attitude should be promoted throughout their study". The use of KM tools and principles provides an opportunity for public and private providers of higher education to collaborate on issues of academic integrity so that they provide consistent messages and approaches in dealing with the issue.

While there is evidence that institutions of higher learning in the UAE are aware of academic integrity matters, it is important that the policies be in sync with local culture in order for them to be well understood and in compliance with internationally acceptable good academic conduct. In that respect, if local librarians work with international academic integrity organisations such as the International Center for Academic Integrity (ICAI), and PlagiarismAdvice.org, that may help in localizing practices. With policies in place, making them known to the entire academic community is important. The library is one of the essential organs of an academic institution in its information literacy (IL) program to give guidance on academic honesty. Possible use, by all libraries in the region, of such a research network as Ankabut (2012) can facilitate and enable the creation and accessibility of policies that are in the context of the Arabian Gulf. This is because Ankabut (2012) electronically interconnects education institutions, and is a reliable space to create resources for academic integrity that all institutions can tap from. The interconnectivity is an instance of a KM enabled environment. The implication is that there has to be a champion (s) who takes up the task of creating the resource and at the same time be ready to share as is essential in KM practice. In a discussion on copyright protection in the Arabian Gulf that includes the UAE, Price (2011, p.298) concludes that:

the areas of great challenge will not be in the enactment of the laws or the acceptance of the principles behind them, but the establishment of the national and regional intellectual property infrastructures, and the skills development of the human resource quantum to give effect to these national needs and aspirations. In all states, the practical application of compliance obligations through effective enforcement has been, and continues to be, the most difficult area with which to contend

There is therefore merit in discussing academic integrity as it applies to places where the concept is not necessarily original and yet important.

ACADEMIC DISHONESTY IN A GEOGRAPHIC AND/ OR LINGUISTIC CONTEXT

Literature reveals that all students require guidance when it comes to awareness of academic integrity, resulting in many universities and colleges adopting honor codes (Thomas, Raynor & McKinnon, 2013). The degrees to which academic dishonesty is discovered may vary, but all students need assistance in reducing it. An investigation by Ely, Henderson, and Wachsman (2013) affirms the fact that although it is not an only solution, when a university has an honor code, that discourages students from academic dishonesty. Concurring with Wheeler and Anderson (2012), the author of this chapter believes that this could be enhanced by the university instituting a program for teaching academic writing skills which is a requirement in most jobs that the students are getting ready for.

Geographic considerations do not seem to be predominant but very relevant. This is because of the fact that, as explained by Hensley (2013, p. 24), "students' inner worlds shape their actions, so it is no surprise that beliefs, values, and priorities influence cheating behaviour". In that sense, if beliefs and values are products of one's cultural/ social background, then there is reason to believe that suggested solutions to the challenge work more effectively if contextualized. In fact, Thomas, Raynor and McKinnon (2013, p. 3) point out that "it is important to appreciate the possibility that cheating will be defined differently within differing cultural contexts". While Farrell (2010) acknowledges that this challenge is not unique to Lebanon, an interview with an individual from one of the ghost/ shadow writing agencies in Beruit, for example, admits that "there are between 200 and 250 people who work in the same organization I do. We do work for students at Lebanese universities, but also for students in Spain and South America." These remarks elucidate further the universality of the problem of cheating in academic situations, aggravated by the complexity of defining it meaningfully.

There have been debates relating to the likelihood of people from some cultures being more likely to plagiarize than others, but especially those who are non-native English speakers (NNES). While this may be discussable, Wheeler and Anderson (2010, p. 171) point out that "plagiarism may indicate a deficit in appropriate skills and not intentional academic dishonesty". What is important is to give consistent guidance on what academic honesty means, beginning with education that a student receives during school years before university and continue throughout university studies. Wheeler and Anderson (2012) have concluded from their study that in the UAE there is room for improvement in the schools so that the culture of academic integrity can be reinforced as students pursue further studies and enter university. Menzel (2012, p.24) believes in ethical behavior being learned behavior that can be re-learned and modified. Strategies to enhance this behavior may not necessarily transform unethical individuals who are inherently dishonest, but they can facilitate decisions that reflect institutional values and purpose. This very discussion suggests putting as much academic integrity emphasis on student and academic groups in the UAE just as anywhere else worldwide.

Ready and easy access to the internet is a major influence on the tendency to copy and paste, though not necessarily the most compelling reason for academic dishonesty. Though internet connectivity in the UAE is high, Hensley (2013, p. 23) actually points out that "cheating existed prior to the digital age and, further, not all students who could cheat choose to do so." In fact, it is useful and practical for academic institutions to review their academic integrity policies so that teaching practices and outcomes are tailored to suit specific environments, especially with the support of institutional leadership. Swan (2014), for example, cites the provost of Zayed University as having "promised to tackle claims of plagiarism, lowering of standards and bullying made by disgruntled lecturers and students".

PUBLISH OR PERISH APPROACH AND ACADEMIC INTEGRITY

The mark of a university that is worth its value is expressed to a substantial extent by the quality of students and faculty associated with it. Scholarly productivity and publishing is one of the recognized methods of evaluating that quality because it is associated with the creation and expression of new and or innovative ideas. It is currently widely acknowledged that faculty who do not publish are expected to be expressing their academic prowess in other ways, depending on the field they are specialized in. Whichever way one considers it, in many instances academic productivity is expected for successful evaluations for appointment, grant funding, and promotion. Norvaiša (2011, p. 120) points out that "in some countries, assessment of the research output produced by research institutions for the purpose of funding, award of positions, promotions, or national prizes tends to attach more weight to the number of publications in journals with high Impact Factor rather than to the quality of the performed research".

Measures for quantitatively analyzing academic literature, such as the impact factor, and altmetrics of publications are used to monitor and evaluate where an academic's work is published. This does not necessarily coincide with the quality of an individual paper or if its results/ hypotheses are proven. According to Thompson Reuters publishers (2014), the impact factor is a measure that is used as one of several "quantitative tools for ranking, evaluating, categorizing, and comparing journals; it is a measure of the frequency with which the "average article" in a journal has been cited in a particular year or period". The citations are sometimes skewed because of excessive self-citing, or citations by a group of colleagues for the sake of boosting the citation statistics as expressed in the research by Norvaiša (2011, p. 127) that "one is attempting to change some bibliometric indicators, rather than seek to improve a research quality". According to Altmetrics.org (2014), the other direction that these measures are taking is altmetrics which is the "creation and study of new metrics based on the Social Web for analyzing, and informing scholarship". EBSCOhost, one of the major academic resource providers, owns Plum Altmetrics which measures research impact by "gathering metrics around artifacts such as articles, clinical trials, blog posts, grants, books, theses/dissertations, webpages and more. These metrics are then categorized into Usage, Captures, Mentions, Social Media and Citations" (McEvoy, 2014). Weaknesses and shortcomings of these methods have been discussed in several platforms. Gibney (2013), for example, reports that "the Wellcome Trust and the Higher Education Funding Council for England are among the bodies calling for the use of the journal impact factor in funding, appointment and promotion decisions to be scrapped". While these innovations and discussions are happening, pressure on academics to be productive still continues.

Spooner (2014) bemoans "how peer-review practices, once meant to ensure quality and rigour, have been completely subverted by the "audit culture" so pervasive at institutions of higher learning the globe over". By this is meant that the expectation for faculty to be productive - or otherwise perish – can lead individuals into desperate measures to fulfill requirements. They ultimately concentrate on publishing only in certain journals because of their high impact factor. This becomes attractive ground for predatory companies that promise academic output for sale, encouraging academic corruption. It is much like the challenge that students find themselves exposed to as mentioned earlier in the academic integrity description part close to the beginning of this chapter. That is a weakness of using " statistics that are inherently unfair and easy to manipulate" Norvaiša (2011, p. 127). Creativity and innovativeness suffer because it is not so much the quality and value of the contribution as being known to have published in a famous journal that matters.

If the notion that teaching and reinforcing academic integrity guidance to students makes a difference is true, then by the time that some of them become members of faculty, they will be in a position to understand the culture better, i.e. transferring their knowledge to their work responsibilities. However, the results of the Tabsh, El Kadi and Abdelfatah (2012) study where faculty were found to be in need of more direction as far as institutional academic integrity issues were concerned suggests that this is an area that continues to require reinforcement. Use of the available academic integrity resources provided by their university is minimal. As applicable to academic institutions in the UAE and around the world, instances like this further put into question the quality of faculty productivity, if it is taking place, and the guidance they are providing to their students. This extends to occurrences when faculty sometimes fail to acknowledge student input in research projects, which is an infringement of intellectual property. As these questions arise, one can allude to the SECI process by suggesting that it is useful to put emphasis on enhancing faculty capabilities by proper institutional orientation and control mechanisms, recognizing faculty effort and rewarding it, and encouraging cross-discipline collaborative projects that encourage creativity. In the process, there may gradually be room for faculty exploring the shortcomings of professionals who have graduated from their departments when the instances come to light.

Having put forward this discussion about challenges with the "publish or perish" approach, it is clear that instilling good academic conduct has to be targeted at the entire academic community – students and faculty. That way the practice becomes more about clarification of and guidance surrounding the norms and culture of good academic behavior than solely punishing unacceptable behavior in the academe. For as long as academics are publishing, regardless of quality (caring only for the name of the journal where articles are published), then primarily it is publishers who benefit the most. The onus therefore is on the academe to focus on its intended mandate rather than principally that of the publishing industry. Learned academically ethical behavior seems to require continuous reinforcement and a degree of motivation to adopt it, hence this discussion.

RECENT DEVELOPMENTS

Besides e-learning that is conducted via electronic media (online *Oxford English Dictionary*), a recent development in the academic environment are Massive Online Open Courses (MOOCs). These are an addition to e-learning but intended for wider audiences that can be international and more diverse than previous models. The online *Oxford English Dictionary* defines a MOOC as "a course of study made available over the Internet without charge to a very large number of people: anyone who decides to take a MOOC simply logs on to the website and signs up". While this definition stands, the model keeps evolving as the creators and users increasingly understand the implications of using it. Some have adopted commercial models, while others have become affiliated to universities and more moving towards being credit-rated to make them viable. *The National* (2013) suggested that EdX, a United States MOOC education platform, was in discussion with some Middle Eastern education institutions including those in the UAE to introduce the use of a MOOC in Arabic language courses. While this phenomenon is not a widely current practice in the UAE, the report signifies the potential for the approach being increasingly thought about. This is reflected in *The National* (2014) report that suggests that "Dubai's Media City is keen to work with local universities and colleges to provide the services and equipment needed to develop these online courses". In the context of this new approach to teaching and learning, academic integrity guidance remains very important especially as the approach is dependent on online instruction and completion of tasks.

In higher education, there is usually the question of how it is verifiable who is taking the online assessments. Faculty who create MOOC modules can collaborate with librarians towards guiding skill development in MOOCs. Examples of how this collaboration works are demonstrated by institutions such as FutureLearn (2014) working together with established universities as well as the British Library. Other examples are Pathways to Information Leadership (P2IL) (2014) which is a collaboration between Aberystwyth University, Emerald Group Publishing and the Association of Information Management (ASLIB); and Coursera (2014) partnering with a wide variety of prestigious universities. In terms of enforcing the correct norms, some universities that offer MOOCs and e-learning are beginning to implement secure and convenient series of assessment strategies for online courses. Examity, for example, is a proctoring service for online assessments of both MOOC and traditional online courses. According to the *Professional Services Close – Up* trade journal (2014), when implemented, students are required to register with Examity to complete exams. Proctors watch and record students' online assessments in real time via web cams and desktop sharing. This helps universities stay ahead of accreditation requirements and ensure the integrity of assessment results. It is therefore important that investigations into more innovative and educative methods of making sure that academic integrity is maintained remain alive. It is in the context of finding appropriate and innovative approaches to educating students that Thomas, Raynor and McKinnon (2013) deduce from their Zayed University study that the use of vivas or unannounced oral exams can contribute towards higher integrity in exams.

Other developments in the library world are maker spaces, and hacker spaces that are being put into practice to enable creativity and collaboration. These may be in the form of student groups collaborating, or student-faculty collaboration. They offer an opportunity to guide students towards originality. These are approaches to meeting the learning styles of library patrons while encouraging creativity. However, there is not necessarily a clear picture of how to enforce academic integrity in these circumstances.

IMPLICATIONS FOR LIBRARIANS

The developments in the teaching and learning world, impacted by technological changes, have resulted in re-thinking a pedagogical framework of new teaching and learning approaches and academic integrity. The discontinuous information environment has created conditions for curriculum revisions emphasizing collaborative efforts of library and faculty. In essence, this situation requires a transliterate academic librarian. Transliteracy refers to "the ability to read, write and interact across a rang-e of platforms, tools, and media from signing and orality through handwriting, print, TV, radio and film, to digital social networks" (Newman, *et al.* 2011). Serving transliterate students requires a librarian who is ready to meet the challenge so as to contribute towards empowering library users with requisite IL skills. As expressed by Gogan and Macus (2013, p.42), "at a time when technologies change at a rapid pace, the ability to create a space where students can acquire meaning is the charge of the transliterate school librarian".

In UAE academic libraries and institutions, it is not out of context to aim for the use of the KM principles that are suggested by Davenport and Prusak (1998, p. 24) to strategically position themselves in a changing information environment. That is because the initiative is a step that the UAE government is interested in as exemplified by the case study of the Emirates ID knowledge management experience. According to the Emirates Identity Authority (2013), a library was:

established in order to provide access to documents and releases electronically, depending on the iGrafx software and the mark of excellence system, which includes all the Emirates ID's methodologies and procedures related to the method of engineering graphics on its internal site, thereby allowing all its employees to access the approved operations, methodologies and documents via a dedicated link as a channel complementary to the library.

The above case study demonstrates that use of a KM approach is feasible. KM theory, with its emphasis on enhancing performance, is suited for current library practice that focuses on providing user-oriented services. The library should champion and strengthen the existing KM environment and information technologies to maximize the use of information and knowledge. The process has to start from somewhere as is suggested by Nonaka (1994, p. 14) in the statement that "innovation produced by one part of the organization in turn creates a stream of related information and knowledge, which might then trigger changes in the organization's wider knowledge systems". As far as the current discussion goes, that part of the organization may very well be the library.

Considering use of KM practices implies that librarians have to deal with a broader range of information resources and services than traditionally. In the process they get to participate in a culture and environment for active learning and information sharing (especially when they are a part of larger institutions which affect the way the library operates). They also have to collaborate much more proactively and deeply with other libraries, information technology services, and users in order to enhance the quality and value of the service they are able to provide. Establishing a principle of collaboration so as to influence institutional culture and using every interaction, whether face-to-face or virtual, as an opportunity to acquire and share knowledge creates an enabling environment for benefitting from knowledge assets. However, it is essential to protect and secure information and knowledge assets to prevent knowledge loss, abuse, and misuse.

There is a lot of information and knowledge that the library should centrally store and give access to for the benefit of the academic community. This puts a requirement on it to build knowledge gateways. The use of these gateways enables information flow that is essential for innovation and the creation of new knowledge. This coincides with intentions expressed in the UAE about developing innovation and creativity within young learners (Lightfoot, 2011). It might also be worthwhile to look into the establishment of a program for creating an institutional repository or repositories to collect knowledge assets for the benefit primarily of students. In fact, since the library functions as a cost center of the university, this is a way to create value to justify receiving continued and increasing institutional support in the face of other competing sources of information.

Competition is the major instigator driving any university and its library to work towards enabling and nurturing student capabilities for creativity and authentic innovativeness in the current knowledge-based environment. The implication of this approach is that institutional leaders and managers need to support it. The library is enabled to play the role of advocate and be central in promoting, encouraging and supporting an environment of good academic practice if the entire university is involved.

CONCLUSION

The ground is fertile for the use of KM principles to strategically position academic institutions and their libraries in the UAE in a changing information environment. KM theory, with its emphasis on creativity and innovativeness, is suited for current library practice that focuses on user-oriented services. As a part of an academic institution, the library should be exemplary in championing and strengthening the existing KM practices and use of information technologies to maximize the use of information and knowledge, especially in academic integrity initiatives and guidance. Ripple effects include an enhanced quality of student projects, recognition for the university – highlighting its corporate image, and the likelihood of the university attracting high caliber faculty and researchers, and the plausibility of industry's willingness to partner – enhancing student chances of good careers. The efforts could very well be applicable to any university and any library in the world, suggesting the commonality of the concerns involved with academic institutions in the UAE and elsewhere. What varies is how different places cope with the challenges they face.

For libraries, the use of KM practices implies dealing with a broader range of information resources and services than traditionally. That way, academic integrity concerns become more elaborate and require more educated approaches by both librarians and faculty. This includes the use of documents, websites, videos and video clips, online communication, and so on. In the process, a culture and environment for active learning and information sharing in a variety of disciplines develops. In line with the processes of the SECI model, librarians also have to collaborate much more proactively and deeply with other libraries, information technology services, and users in order to enhance the quality and value of the service they are able to provide, including experiences and methods of handling academic integrity matters. Establishing a tradition of collaboration so as to influence institutional culture and using every interaction, whether face-to-face or virtual, as an opportunity to acquire and share knowledge, creates an enabling environment for benefitting from using and creating knowledge assets.

Librarians possess skills that are vital in KM, however, they have to widen their skills set and think more openly so as to understand the changing information environment and its implications. A KM approach to teaching and learning requires the involvement of the library. The success of this approach depends on systemic change within the institution, not isolated change in library service. This calls for an organization to create an academic integrity awareness inventory, a knowledge needs analysis, and an analysis of the flow of that knowledge to help in developing appropriate institution-wide policies and practices for proper and well informed good academic behavior, collaborating and sharing, and developing an enabling institutional culture that includes organizational learning for KM. Though it would be a gradual process, chances of adopting and using some of the KM practices in UAE universities are high because the vision of the country supports it.

The library is well placed to centrally store and give access to information and knowledge for the benefit of the academic community. At the same time, it is necessary for it to build knowledge gateways and procedures for using it ethically, sometimes taking advantage of available information sharing networks. The use of these gateways creates an environment suitable for innovation and the creation of new knowledge. The library is also in a position to support KM approaches as they are nurtured in students in preparation for the business environment they join when they complete their studies.

REFERENCES

Altmetrics.org. (2014). *About altmetrics*. Retrieved from http://altmetrics.org/about/

Broadbent, M. (1998). The phenomenon of knowledge management: What does it mean to the information profession. *Information Outlook*, *2*(5), 23–36.

Cogdell, B., & Aidulis, D. (2008). Dealing with plagiarism as an ethical issue. In T. S. Roberts (Ed.), *Student plagiarism in an online world: problems and solutions* (pp. 38–59). Hershey, PA: IGI Global. doi:10.4018/978-1-59904-801-7.ch004

Correa, M. (2011). Academic dishonesty in the second language classroom: Instructor's Perspectives. *Modern Journal of Language Teaching Method*, *1*, 65–79.

Coursera. (2014). *Meet our partners*. Retrieved on 22 September 2014 from https://www.coursera.org/about/partners

Croucher, M. (26 April 2009). Revealed: FAKE Degrees. *Khaleej Times*. Retrieved on 31 May 2014 from http://www.khaleejtimes.com/DisplayArticle08.asp?xfile=data/theuae/2009/April/theuae_April612.xml&section=theuae

Davenport, T. H., & Prusak, L. (1998). *Working knowledge: how organizations manage what they know*. Boston: Harvard Business School Press.

Drucker, P. (1999). Knowledge–worker productivity: The biggest challenge. *California Management Review, 41*(2), 79–94. doi:10.2307/41165987

Ely, J. J., Henderson, L., & Wachsman, Y. (2013). Testing the effectiveness of the university honor code. *Academy of Educational Leadership Journal, 17*(4), 95–104.

Emirates Identity Authority. (2013). *Emirates ID showcases its knowledge management experience to Zakat Fund delegation*. Retrieved on 2 June 2014 from http://www.id.gov.ae/en/media-centre/news/2013/3/4/emirates-id-showcases-its-knowledge-management-experience-to-zakat-fund-delegation.aspx

Farooqui, M. (2014). Fake degree racket in UAE exposed. *Gulf News*. Retrieved on 31 May 2014.from http://m.gulfnews.com/news/uae/crime/fake-degree-racket-in-uae-exposed-1.1339968

Farrell, S. (2010). How much would you pay for your degree? *Now Reports*. Retrieved on 31 May 2014 from http://mobile.mmedia.me/lb/en/reportsfeatures/how_much_would_you_pay_for_your_degree

FutureLearn. (2014). *Featured courses*. Retrieved on 22 September 2014 from https://www.futurelearn.com/

García, G. M. J., Hernández, G. G. J., & Hernández, R. J. G. (2014). Knowledge management through the Material Handling Manager. In *Proceedings ICIL'2014*. University of Zagreb.

Gibney, E. (2013). Great and good reject journal impact factor. The Times Higher Education Supplement: THE, (2101), 8.

Gogan, B., & Marcus, A. (2013). Lost in transliteracy. *Knowledge Quest, 41*(5), 40–45.

Government of Abu Dhabi. (2008).The Abu Dhabi Economic Vision 2030. Retrieved from http://gsec.abudhabi.ae/Sites/GSEC/Content/EN/PDF/Publications/economic-vision-2030-full-version,property=pdf,bereich=gsec,sprache=en,rwb=true.pdf

Gray, P. W., & Jordan, S. R. (2012). Supervisors and academic integrity: Supervisors as exemplars and mentors. *Journal of Academic Ethics, 10*(4), 299–311. doi:10.1007/s10805-012-9155-6

Hamid, S., Nayan, J. M., Bakar, Z. A., & Norman, A. N. (2007). *Knowledge management adoption and implementation readiness: a case study of the National Library of Malaysia*. Paper presented at the Building an Information Society for All, Petaling Jaya, Malaysia.

Hensley, L. (2013). To cheat or not to cheat: A review with implications for practice. *The Community College Enterprise, 19*(2), 22–34.

Hernández, J. G., García, M. J., & Hernández, J. G. (2012). Dynamic knowledge: Diagnosis and Customer Service. In N. Delener (Ed.), *Service Science Research, Strategy, and Innovation: Dynamic Knowledge Management Methods* (pp. 558–584). Hershey, PA: IGI Global; doi:10.4018/978-1-4666-0077-5.ch030

Jashapara, A. (2005). The emerging discourse of knowledge management: A new dawn for information science research? *Journal of Information Science, 31*(2), 136–148. doi:10.1177/0165551505051057

Khan, Z. R. (2010). E-cheating in the UAE: a critical review of existing literature. In Proceedings of the 2010 International Conference on e-Learning, e-Business, Enterprise Information Systems, & e-Government (pp. 320-324). CSREA Press. Retrieved from http://ro.uow.edu.au/cgi/viewcontent.cgi?article=1172&context=dubaipapers

Kirk, D. (2010). The development of higher education in the United Arab Emirates. The Emirates Occasional Papers, 74, 1-57.

Koshy, R. (2008). A case of miscommunication? Obstacles to the effective implementation of a plagiarism detection system in a multicultural university. University of Wollongong Working Paper Series, UOWD-RSC WP-76, 12 June 2008: WP 76/2009.

Lightfoot, M. (2011). *Promoting the Knowledge Economy in the Arab World*. SAGE Open; doi:10.1177/2158244011417457

Lloria, M. B. (2008). A review of the main approaches to knowledge management. *Knowledge Management Research & Practice, 6*(1), 77–89. doi:10.1057/palgrave.kmrp.8500164

Loertscher, D. V. (2012). Maker spaces and the learning commons. *Teacher Librarian, 40*(1), 45–46, 63.

Mahajan, V. (2012). *Arab World unbound: Tapping into the power of 350 million consumers*. Somerset, NJ: John Wiley & Sons.

Maracine, V., & Scarlat, E. (2009). Dynamic Knowledge and Healthcare Knowledge Ecosystems. *Electronic Journal of Knowledge Management, 7*(1), 99–110.

McAdam, R., & McCreedy, S. (1999). The process of knowledge management within organizations: A critical assessment of both theory and practice. *Knowledge and Process Management, 6*(2), 101–113. doi:10.1002/(SICI)1099-1441(199906)6:2<101::AID-KPM53>3.0.CO;2-P

McCabe, D., Feghali, T., & Abdallah, H. (2008). Academic dishonesty in the Middle East: Individual and contextual factors. *Research in Higher Education, 49*(5), 451–467. doi:10.1007/s11162-008-9092-9

McEvoy, K. (2014). *PlumX Includes Usage Statistics from EBSCO Databases*. Retrieved from http://www.ebscohost.com/newsroom/stories/plumx-includes-usage-statistics-from-ebsco-databases

Menzel, D. C. (2012). *Ethics management for public administrators: building organizations of integrity*. Armonk, NY: M.E. Sharpe, Inc.

Mutula, S. M. (2011). Ethics and trust in digital scholarship. *The Electronic Library, 29*(2), 261–276. doi:10.1108/02640471111125212

National Qualifications Authority. (2013). *The UAE education system overview of performance in education*. Retrieved from file:///D:/Documents/Downloads/The%20UAE%20Education%20System%20Report%20(3).pdf

Newman, B. (2011). Beginner's Guide to Transliteracy. *Libraries and Transliter*acy. Retrieved from http://librariesandtransliteracy.wordpress.com/beginners-guide-to-transliteracy/

Ngulube, P. & Lwoga, E. (2007). Knowledge management models and their utility to the effective management and integration of indigenous knowledge with other knowledge systems. *Indilinga - African Journal of Indigenous Knowledge Systems, 6*(2), 117 - 131.

Nonaka, I. (1994). A dynamic theory of organizational knowledge creation. *Organization Science, 5*(1), 14–37. doi:10.1287/orsc.5.1.14

Nonaka, I., Reinmoller, P., & Senoo, D. (1998). The 'ART' of Knowledge: Systems to Capitalize on Market Knowledge. *European Management Journal, 16*(6), 673–684. doi:10.1016/S0263-2373(98)00044-9

Nonaka, I., & Takeuchi, H. (1995). *The knowledge-creating company: how Japanese companies create the dynamics of innovation*. New York: Oxford University Press.

Nonaka, I., Toyama, R., & Konno, N. (2000). SECI, Ba and leadership: A unified model of dynamic knowledge creation. *Long Range Planning, 33*(1), 5–34. doi:10.1016/S0024-6301(99)00115-6

Nonaka, I., & Von Krogh, G. (2009). Tacit knowledge and knowledge conversion: Controversy and advancement in organizational knowledge creation theory. *Organization Science, 20*(3), 635–652. doi:10.1287/orsc.1080.0412

Norman, M. (2012). Frail, fatal, fundamental: The future of public libraries. *Australasian Public Libraries and Information Services, 25*(2), 94–100.

Norvaiša, R. (2011). Journal impact factor and academic ethics. *Mokslo Ir Technikos Raida, 3*(2), 120–128. doi:10.3846/est.2011.10

Oxford English Dictionary. (2014). *Spiral*. Oxford, UK: Oxford University Press.

Pathways to Information Leadership. (n.d.). *About Pathways*. Retrieved on 22 September 2014 from https://infoleader.org/about-pathways

Peterson, J. D. (2007). *The Information and communication technology landscape in the United Arab Emirates: National ICT Policies*. Retrieved on 1 May 2014 from http://www1.american.edu/carmel/jp2450a/2.htm

Piascik, P., & Brazeau, G. A. (2010). Promoting a culture of academic integrity. *American Journal of Pharmaceutical Education, 74*(6), 1–113. doi:10.5688/aj7406113 PMID:21045955

Polanyi, M. (1962). *Personal knowledge: towards a post-critical philosophy*. Chicago: University of Chicago Press.

Price, D. (2011). Politics, piracy and punishment: Copyright protection in the Arabian Gulf. *The Journal of World Intellectual Property, 14*(3/4), 276–300. doi:10.1111/j.1747-1796.2011.00419.x

Professional Services Close - Up. (2014). *Technology-based online proctoring decreases cheating on college finals*. Jacksonville, FL: Close-Up Media.

Roig, M. (1997). Can undergraduate students determine whether text has been plagiarized? *The Psychological Record, 47*(1), 113–123.

Siddique, M. C. (2012). Knowledge management initiatives in the United Arab Emirates: A baseline study. *Journal of Knowledge Management, 16*(5), 702–723. doi:10.1108/13673271211262763

Skok, K., & Tahir, S. (2010). Developing a knowledge management strategy for the Arab World. *EJISDC, 46*(7), 1–11.

Spooner, M. (2014, April 30). *Universities are confusing accountability with accountancy: how the 'audit culture' is ruining the academy and harming society in the process*. Retrieved from http://www.universityaffairs.ca/universities-are-confusing-accountability-with-accountancy.aspx

Stout, B. (2011). Professional ethics and academic integrity in police education. *Policing: An International Journal of Police Strategies & Management, 5*(4), 300–309. doi:10.1093/police/par036

Swan, M. (2014). *Zayed University provost promises to tackle plagiarism and poor standards complaints*. Retrieved on 1 June 2014 from http://www.thenational.ae/uae/education/zayed-university-provost-promises-to-tackle-plagiarism-and-poor-standards-complaints

Swartz, L. B., & Cole, M. T. (2013). Students' perception of academic integrity in online business education courses. *Journal of Business and Educational Leadership, 4*(1), 102–112.

Tabsh, S. W., El Kadi, H. A., & Abdelfatah, A. S. (2012). Faculty response to ethical issues at an American university in the Middle-East. *Quality Assurance in Education, 20*(4), 319–340. doi:10.1108/09684881211263957

Takeuchi, H. (2001). Towards a universal management concept of knowledge. In I. Nonaka & D. J. Teece (Eds.), *Managing industrial knowledge: creation, transfer and utilization* (pp. 315–329). London: Sage. doi:10.4135/9781446217573.n16

Telecommunications Regulatory Authority, UAE. (2012). *ICT in the UAE- Household Survey, 2012*. Retrieved from file:///D:/Documents/Downloads/Household%20Survey-2012-English.pdf

The National. (2013). Interest in Arabic courses online. The National.

The National. (2014). Online courses make big strides. The National.

Thomas, E. E., & Sassi, K. (2011). An ethical dilemma: Talking about plagiarism and academic integrity in the digital age. *English Journal, 100*(6), 47–53.

Thomas, J., Raynor, M., & McKinnon, M. (2013). Academic integrity and oral examination: An Arabian Gulf perspective. *Innovations in Education and Teaching International*, 1–11.

Thompson Reuters publishers. (2014). *The Thompson Reuters impact factor*. Retrieved from http://wokinfo.com/essays/impact-factor/

Tsokris, M., & Struminger, S. (2013). Does academic misconduct influence professional integrity? *Access, 27*(4), 22–23.

Tynes, B. M. (2007). Internet safety gone wild?: Sacrificing the educational and psychological benefits of online social environments. *Journal of Adolescent Research, 22*(6), 575–584. doi:10.1177/0743558407303979

UAE Ministry of Higher Education and Scientific Commission for Academic Accreditation. (2011a). Retrieved on 6 May 2014 from www.caa.ae/caa/images/Guides-IA.pdf

UAE Ministry of Higher Education and Scientific Commission for Academic Accreditation. (2011b). Retrieved on 6 May 2014 from www.caa.ae/caa/images/Guide-RA.pdf

Wheeler, D., & Anderson, D. (2010). Dealing with plagiarism in a complex information society. *Education. Business and Society: Contemporary Middle Eastern Issues, 3*(3), 166–177. doi:10.1108/17537981011070082

White, T. (2004). *Knowledge management in an academic library: based on the case study "KM within OULS"*. Paper presented at the 70th IFLA General Conference and Council, Buenos Aires. Retrieved on 6 May 2014 from http://ora.ox.ac.uk/objects/uuid:62836c4d-10c1-4636-b97c-07a88890fa8a/datastreams/JOURNAL

KEY TERMS AND DEFINITIONS

Academic Ethics: The use of moral principles in accomplishing academic tasks.
Academic Integrity: An expression of honesty in the execution of academic work.
Corporate Image: The mental picture that comes up at the mention of the name of an organization.
Knowledge Conversion: The process of transforming one type of knowledge to another that enables innovativeness and creativity.
Knowledge Management: Use of knowledge to achieve organizational objectives.
Publish or Perish: The approach by the academe to push academics to be productive or else risk losing appropriate academic status, appointment, grant funding, and promotion.
Transliteracy: The ability to understand and communicate across different platforms.

Section 3
New Product Development and Managing Innovation

Chapter 12
Managing Innovation within Organizations

Achilleas Boukis
Sussex University, UK

ABSTRACT

The management of innovation projects within organisations forms the focal point of this chapter. First, the role of various intra-organizational contingencies that affect innovation performance is addressed. Second, several appropriate management practices are identified which play an important role for innovation success. Third, various ways that customer knowledge can successfully be integrated in innovation efforts are discussed. Fourth, top management's role in innovation projects is analysed. Fifth, the importance of interfirm collaborative partnerships for innovation success is described. Finally, various innovation benefits are identified so that organizations are able to prioritize between different innovation outcomes.

1. INTRODUCTION

The role of innovation is pivotal for organizational performance as it can provide the organization with a sustainable competitive advantage and contribute to its long-term success. Managing both successfully and resourcefully innovation activities constitutes a difficult task in the sense that a number of intra-organizational parameters should be taken into account in order to ensure innovation success along with organizational effectiveness. As a result, the need to view innovation as a management process within the context of the organisation arises. This chapter tackles the difficult issue of managing innovation within organisations. To do this, it is necessary to understand the strategies as well as the patterns of interactions and behaviours which represent the organisation. A number of internal parameters critical for innovation success are discussed such as:

- The role of organizational structure for innovation success
- The impact of intra-organizational relationships on innovation
- The use of various knowledge management strategies

DOI: 10.4018/978-1-4666-9607-5.ch012

- The integration of customer knowledge to innovation efforts
- Top management's role in product innovation success
- How interfirm collaboration and networks can contribute to innovation success
- Various benefits that can be reaped from innovation activities

Before analysing each of the aforementioned aspects of the innovation process, the role of contingency theory needs to be discussed in order to provide a more comprehensive understanding of how the internal organizational environment can actually influence the innovation process.

1.1 The Value of Contingency Theory for Innovation

Contingency theory has been one of the major streams of thinking about organizational structures and strategic actions. A considerable volume of research has been conducted using contingency theory as the principal framework, relating the task environment to organizational characteristics or to strategic management. Contingency theory states that there is no one best way to act, and that any one way of acting is not equally effective under all circumstances (Galbraith, 1973). Organizational theorists suggest that there is no one universally optimal approach to management for all organizations. On this basis, the appropriate organizational structure, strategies and management style depend on a set of contingent and dynamic factors.

Drazin and Van de Ven (1985) note the "fit-as-mediation" view which posits that managers choose organizational structures, processes, and strategies that reflect the dynamic circumstances of their organization. As the organization is essentially an "information-processing network", the objective of organizational design is to "achieve an efficient correspondence between the information-processing requirements of its strategic contingencies and the information-processing capabilities of its integration mechanisms" (Galbraith, 1973, p. 6). For example, the need for interfunctional collaboration during innovation requires higher resource interdependency and enhanced info-processing capability to manage the acquired knowledge. Thus, increased collaboration represents a critical contingent factor of innovation and firms need to provide structural mechanisms to put such willingness into action (De Luca and Atuahene-Gima, 2007). Moreover, the knowledge exchange among units is often ambiguous and uncertain because of the diversity of functional information, backgrounds and thought worlds of innovation actors. As a result, increasing knowledge exchange during innovation within the firm is dependent on strategic collaboration among functions which dictates the type and degree of integration mechanisms adopted to disseminate knowledge across the organization (De Luca and Atuahene-Gima, 2007). In fact, the higher the fit between existing organizational structure and processes and innovation strategy, the higher the odds for innovation success (Olson et al., 2005). For these reasons, it is obvious why intra-organizational environment should be thoroughly examined before selecting and implementing any innovation management strategies.

2. KEY ISSUES IN INNOVATION MANAGEMENT

Innovation management is a key parameter of success, as it deals with several issues raised during the product development process. While management in general involves coping with uncertainty, sometimes trying to reduce uncertainty, the *raison d'être* of managers involved in innovation is to lead with the aim of developing something different and innovative (Hammedi, Van Riel and Sasovova, 2011). The management of the innovation process requires the effective collaboration between different functions. Managing innovation projects involves a series of interactions among different functional units as well as the use of various management strategies. When it comes to manage innovation initiatives, three important issues should primarily be taken into account. The first one is related to the high amount of uncertainty that inherently exists within innovation efforts. Hence, managing uncertainty is a central feature of new product development as it affects the innovation outcomes. Second, maintaining a sustainable competitive advantage not only requires the achievement of higher organizational effectiveness but also the enhancement of organizational learning (Jiménez-Jiménez and Sanz-Valle, 2011; Blindenbach-Driessen et al., 2010). As a result, promoting resource allocation efficiency and improving employees' knowledge, skills and abilities (KSAs) are two interdependent goals of the product development process. Third, creating value for the customers should be a key objective of any innovation initiative and, therefore, capturing customer needs and emerging market trends during the development of new products will enable innovation success (Carbonell et al., 2009).

2.1 Managing Different Types of Innovation Uncertainty

Innovation activities inherently entail higher levels of uncertainty and complexity, as developing new ideas and service offerings is often an unstructured and fuzzy process which requires creativity and out-of-the box thinking. Uncertainty results from the fact that, on the one hand, all the necessary info is rarely available, and, on the other, knowing about the future is always incomplete. Different types of uncertainty may exist during the innovation process (Wang et al., 2008) such as technological uncertainty, market uncertainty, regulatory uncertainty, managerial uncertainty and social/political uncertainty. Dealing with these types of uncertainty remains a key issue in innovation management in order to improve the chances for success. The most important aspects of uncertainty are discussed in next:

- **Technological Uncertainty:** Innovators encounter technological uncertainty, both in product design and production processes. The uncertainty related to product design is dependent on the newness of the technology while production process uncertainty refers to a diverse collection of processes, techniques and knowledge that are used to produce products and services. Technology also produces uncertainty associated with the skills and knowledge required to succeed in using new technology (Harris & Woolley 2009).
- **Market Uncertainty:** The idea of innovation implies that it serves the needs of a specific target market. The market environment for innovation includes the needs of customers, the actions of competitors and the prices of substitutive commodities. The uncertainty regarding the demand for the innovation, the unknown consumer behaviour and the hidden customer needs were recognized as the main sources of uncertainty caused by the market (Corrocher & Zirulia 2010).
- **Regulatory Uncertainty:** Regulations play an important role in innovations. An unclear regulatory environment creates fields of opportunity in which the innovator can create his own rule. On the contrary, a highly regulated environment for innovation consists of laws and regulations for innovation activities. Constraining regulations are typical in settings like environment or health. Enabling regulations refer to legislation that supports the innovation processes (York & Venkatraman, 2010) and may relate to intellectual property rights that promote the fair sharing of benefits that arise from the development of a given innovation. One type of uncertainty in the

innovation process relates to the issue of whether the developed concept qualifies for intellectual property protection, such as a patent or trade mark. On the other hand, regulations may have detrimental side effects on the innovation process, as changes in regulations were seen as factors that increase environmental complexity and turbulence, which, in turn, increases innovation uncertainty.

- **Social and Political Uncertainty:** The innovation process does not occur in a vacuum, but instead social interactions among different stakeholders and innovation actors with different background, various viewpoints and often conflicting priorities take place. These interactions are a significant source of uncertainty, as the diversity of interests amongst members of an organization is revealed. Equally important, most decisions relating to the development of innovation take place under high levels of uncertainty and complexity. Although decisions can be improved with more effective information exchange and use, they are often influenced by political struggling, battles for resources and subjective value judgements between different functions or departmental representatives who promote their own personal agenda (De Clercq et al., 2009). Therefore, managing innovation projects is often beholden to political struggling and may prove a hard task to achieve.

- **Managerial Uncertainty:** Managing innovations differs from managing routine tasks. Routine tasks usually imply high level of standardization and stability whereas innovations require autonomy, unstructured tasks, and creative thinking. In practice, there can be managerial uncertainties about the staffing of the project team, the required resources and competencies, the management of relationships with the rest of the organization and co-operation with other team participants (Ortt & Smits 2006). Therefore, it can be argued that managing innovations challenges the traditional way of thinking and requires effective leadership on behalf of the project manager (Gebert et al., 2010).

Figure 1. Types of uncertainty

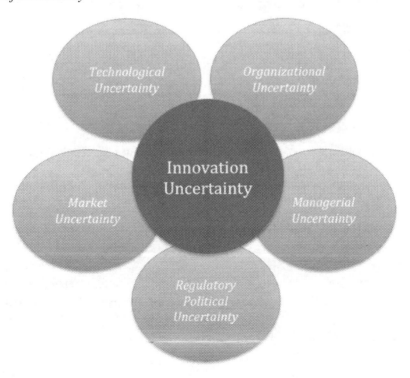

2.2 Achieving Both Organizational Effectiveness and Organizational Learning

Within organisations there is a fundamental tension between the need for stability and the need for creativity. On the one hand, companies require to maintain some level of stability as well as to develop standardized processes with the aim of accomplishing daily tasks in a more efficient and quick way. For example, the processing of cheques by banks every day or the delivery of supplies to retail outlets all over the country demand high levels of efficiency and control. On the other hand, companies also need to innovate and develop new ideas and service offerings in order to remain competitive within an increasingly turbulent global environment (Jiménez-Jiménez and Sanz-Valle, 2011). Organization's success and survival is driven from their capability to innovate, as several short-term (e.g. market success) and long-term benefits (e.g. sustainable competitive advantage) can be reaped through developing new and innovative products. Scholars identify that achieving concurrently multiple NSD goals is often not easy. Due to resource constraints or other intra-organizational contingencies, serving incompatible priorities such as aiming at both cost efficiency as well as enhancing the organization's knowledge base is hard to be achieved (Blindenbach-Driessen et al., 2010).

The concurrent achievement of these complementary goals poses one of the most fundamental problems for innovation management today. Without this emphasis on cost reductions a firm's costs would simply spiral upwards and the firm's products and services would become uncompetitive. On the other hand, organizational learning is a basis for gaining a sustainable competitive advantage and a key variable in the enhancement of organizational performance (Jiménez-Jiménez and Sanz-Valle, 2011). Firms that are able to learn stand a better chance of sensing events and trends in the marketplace. As a consequence, learning organizations are usually more flexible and faster to respond to new challenges than competitors which enable them to maintain long-term competitive advantages. For example, think of any company from P&G to Sony. They have to ensure that their products are carefully manufactured to precise specifications and that they are delivered for customers on a consistent way. In addition, if companies do not make room for creativity and innovation it is very likely that their competitors will outperform them. Hence, here is the dilemma:

- How do firms maximize resource efficiency on the one hand and also expand their organizational knowledge base on the other?

As usual with dilemmas the answer is difficult and has to do with balancing activities and strategic orientations. The firm needs to ensure there is a constant pressure to improve effectiveness in its operations while at the same time it needs to provide room for new product development and nurture a learning orientation. Companies that have the capabilities to achieve an optimized mix between these two orientations will have more chances to remain successful.

2.3 Creating Value for Customers

During the previous decades companies were mostly concerned with productivity gains through passing on tasks from the organization to the consumer and focus on developing innovative products/services using their own capabilities. Traditionally, innovation was a job exclusively for the research and development department of an organization. These workers were triggered by technology without often having adequate knowledge of the external market. The need for monitoring customer preferences and emerging market trends as well as the introduction of online platforms has led to a wider range of interaction possibilities between consumers and manufacturers (Nambisan, 2009). A shift around the 90s to a more active participation of the customers to the innovation process begins as customers are considered as key contributors to innovation success with companies realizing that their participation in various innovation stages enhances the odds of success and promotes the innovativeness of the new offerings. Contemporary consumers are involved in the product development process of businesses with the aim of creating products with higher value that can better satisfy their individual needs (Porter and Kramer, 2011). The current innovation process acknowledges the importance of integrating customer knowledge during new product development and relies increasingly on the contribution of costumers' ideas, insights and knowledge particularly during the earlier innovation stages. Customers are seen as an important and valuable source of product innovation. The inclusion of customers in new product development is becoming a trend for many organizations and is often referred to as "customer co-creation" (Mahr et al., 2013). Companies aim to discover customers' ideas, comments and knowledge that might help them develop and commercialize new product concepts. Co-creating new products with customers' participation can provide companies with a competitive advantage since not only they are able to meet customer needs more successfully but also may enhance customers' perceived value by setting as co-creators of new products and services.

3. ORGANIZATIONAL CHARACTERISTICS AND INNOVATION SUCCESS

The existing structure of an organization can clearly influence the way new products are developed. As innovation success requires high cooperation among functions, the extent that interfunctional development teams are used is positively associated with innovation success (Melton & Hartline, 2013). Second, given the dominant role of Information Technology for monitoring customer needs and ensuring effective info exchange, integrating IT systems during development efforts can significantly contribute to innovation success. Third, the organization's structure also affects innovation activities, as various structural characteristics may enhance or inhibit innovation.

3.1 Managing Interfunctional Development Teams

The creation of new products is a multidisciplinary process that demands interaction and close collaboration of different organizational functions (García, Sanzo & Trespalacios, 2008). For example, executives from the marketing department, operations and finance may need to form an interfunctional development team with the aim of completing the development of a new retail banking product. Interfunctional integration refers to the degree to which employees between different functions cooperate in conducting specific innovation tasks and reflects the recognition by functional units of their interdependence and their need to cooperate for the benefit of the organization. The need for interfunctional cooperation stems from the complex interdependencies among members of functional groups working together on project teams and greater interdependence requires a greater cooperation effort. Indeed, firms identified as having best practices in innovation tend to employ interfunctional integration more extensively than other firms (Melton and Hartline, 2013).

Managing successfully the integration of employees from different functions during innovation efforts becomes substantial as innovation activities create high task interdependencies and require intense info exchange. Interfunctional teams tend to be more effective when they have a shared or common goal and exhibit greater integration, since without it, each function develops its own perceptions and "thought worlds," which lead to interpretive barriers among them during the innovation process. Their use also facilitates the dissemination of novel market and customer information among different functions, offering this way significant advantage for the innovation process e.g. increasing communication frequency and information flow in the organization (Cuijpers, Guenter & Hussinger, 2011). Third, info exchange within interfunctional teams helps employees to achieve a shared understanding about the new product and enhances consistency among decision-making throughout the process. Finally, the use of interfunctional development teams can lead to a more effective and more efficient use of resources, as it can reduce coordination problems between different organizational units in the innovation pipeline (Troy, Hirunyawipada & Paswan, 2008).On the contrary, the lack of interfunctional collaboration will hinder the diffusion of new knowledge produced during innovation projects, undermining the extension of the organizational knowledge base and the effective use of organizational resources (Froehle et al., 2000).

3.2 IT Systems and Innovation Success

The adoption of organization-wide Information Technology (IT) systems on firms and the way they operate has been one of the most noticeable changes within organisations of the early twenty-first century. IT solutions have been adopted by the majority of large private sector firms and many public sector organisations with the aim of improving their organizational effectiveness as well as enhance their innovation capabilities (Zhou, & Wu, 2010). This growing trend can offer some significant advantages to organizations. The principal benefits that can arise the integration of IT to innovation initiatives are linked to gains in the efficiency and effectiveness of the process coupled with more accurate and timely information. Some of the potential benefits of using IT during innovation are:

- More efficient innovation sharing and use and reduction of costs to several procedures
- Better monitoring and cooperation between functions and different company departments
- Modification and adaptation abilities accordingly to company and market requirements
- More competitive and efficient entrance to electronic markets and electronic commerce
- Access to globalisation and integration to the global economy
- Inventory visibility and better decision support
- Active technology for market research and media environment

However, the impact of these systems on a firm's innovative capability may be under scrutiny. For example, in some highly creative working environments, where previously autonomous and creative minds were free to explore, employees are now being restricted to what's on offer via 'pull-down' menus. In fact, the use of highly formalized IT infrastructure may reduce the richness of information content and increase info overload when informal communication processes get increasingly replaced by standardised data exchanges. In addition, integrating IT systems to innovation activities may not easily fit any organisation and often require a reconfiguration of existing processes and routines (Karimi, & Konsynski, 2003).

Managing Innovation within Organizations

3.3 Structural Characteristics

The question as to which organizational structures are more supportive to innovation has been in the research agenda for several years. Burns and Stalker (2011) argue that the environment in which the firm operates determines the optimal structure of the organisation. They considered two types of structure at the opposite ends of a spectrum that ranges from organic to mechanistic and suggested that the organic form will work best when the external environment is dynamic, turbulent or hostile (Bodewes, 2002). Within more turbulent, complex and uncertain environments, static organizational frameworks with rigid division and specialization of labor cannot provide the flexibility and agility needed to maintain competitiveness. Organization and communication structures that encourage and make use of experience-based learning, open knowledge sharing, and interpersonal interactions – such as project teams, problem solving groups, and informal chats – can contribute positively to the performance of innovative activities (Alonso, Dessein and Matouschek, 2008).

Generally it can be stated that innovation is enhanced by organic structures rather than mechanistic ones. Innovation is increased by the use of highly participative structures and empowered cultures. For instance, an idea champion should be part of the total innovation; at the very least he/she must be allowed to follow the progress of the innovation. This builds involvement via ownership and enhances attachment and commitment at the organisational level. There is also a strong case here to let the individual lead the project in a total sense from beginning to end (Van der Panne, Van Beers, & Kleinknecht, 2003).

Despite these two different orientations of an organization's structure, a number of other structural characteristics can affect innovation performance (Bodewes, 2002):

- **Formalization:** The extent to which an organization's policies, job descriptions and rules are explicitly articulated. High levels of formalized innovation activities are often associated with decreased creativity and innovativeness. A high degree of formalization may actually lead to reduced innovativeness because employees are used to behaving in a certain manner. A formalized structure is associated with reduced motivation and job satisfaction as well as a slower pace of decision making (Mom, Van Den Bosch, & Volberda, 2009). The service industry is particularly susceptible to problems associated with high formalization, as employees cannot deviate from the designated process e.g. front-line staff who are listening to a customer's problems may need

Table 1. Characteristics of Organic and Mechanistic Structure

Organic structures	Mechanistic structures
freedom from rules; non-hierarchical	rigid departmental separation and functional specialization
participative and informal interactions	little individual freedom of action
many views considered	hierarchical
face to face interpersonal communication	bureaucratic
inter-disciplinary teams and higher cross-functional cooperation	many rules and set procedures
emphasis on creativity and out-of-the-box thinking	formal reporting
Bidirectional information flow; fluid and flexible info exchange	long decision chains and slow decision-making process
Flexibility with respect to changing needs	Communication via formalized channels

to take action, but the answer may not be specified in any procedural guidelines or rulebook. On the other hand, some amount of formalization is required, as formal planning facilitates the clear sense of direction which is essential to the competitive prosperity of an organization.
- **Centralisation:** Refers to the decision-making activity and the location of power within an organisation (Alonso, Dessein and Matouschek, 2008). The more decentralised an organisation the fewer levels of hierarchy are usually required. Decentralized structures will be more responsive to a changing marketplace, given that they remain more flexible. A decentralized approach is more efficient during innovation because not everything has to be reported to the firm's senior levels which results in saving time and money. A decentralized approach inevitably produces more conflicts than centrally managed innovations do and as a result partners are unable to align strategically and coordinated development activity falters. On the other hand, a centralized approach can resolve conflicts in the network and coordinate all the activities that are necessary for successful innovation. The control leads to a more common understanding and shared principles about the various tasks of an innovation project. A centralized organization has the structural capacity to facilitate interactions between the partners in the innovation network (Alonso, Dessein and Matouschek, 2008).
- **Organisational Size:** A proxy variable for more meaningful dimensions such as economic and organisational resources, including number of employees and scale of operation. Below a certain size, however, there is a major qualitative difference. A small business with fewer than 20 employees differs significantly in terms of resource needs from an organisation with thousands of employees. Large organizations are more inclined to innovate because they are better able to finance R&D internally and to reap the rewards from innovation. Second, scale economies in R&D can be easier achieved, in that it may take a firm of a certain size to be able to finance a particular R&D project, or because returns from R&D are higher if the innovator has a large volume of sales over which to spread the fixed cost of an innovation. Larger firms can diversify the risks of performing R&D by maintaining a diversified portfolio of R&D projects. Finally, large firms may be in a better position to exploit the results of its research efforts (Terziovski, 2010).

Some counterarguments to those in favour of large firms being the most efficient innovators have also been offered. A firm already in possession of high market share may be less motivated to innovate because it feels less threatened by rivals, or because sales of new products may be at the expense of the sales from existing products. Given that in large organizations there are more people involved in decisions and there is a longer chain of command, there might be a managerial coordination inefficiency and loss of flexibility. Third, firms may become bureaucratic as they grow large and actors may be less motivated in innovating as they do not have as much personal benefit from their efforts as do researchers in smaller firms and often their ideas get lost in the shuffle in a large than in a small firm (Vaona & Pianta, 2008).

3.4 Organizational Idiosyncrasies

Apart from the critical role of organizational structure, IT technology and the use of interfunctional teams, organizational idiosyncrasies constitute another important parameter of success during innovation. Organizational idiosyncrasies capture organizational processes and routines, conditions and contingencies that characterize the internal environment of an organization and influence its performance.

In the case of innovation, two aspects of the internal environment are considered as key determinants of success; the extent that a market orientation is nurtured within the organization as well as the existence of a culture supportive for innovation (Tajeddini, Trueman, & Larsen, 2006).

Promoting a Market Orientation Philosophy

Customer needs and expectations evolve over time and responsiveness to changing market needs often calls for the introduction of new products and services. Delivering consistently high quality products and services and responsiveness to changing marketplace needs become important for the success of contemporary organizations. Market orientation (MO) has been described as the implementation of marketing activities designed to satisfy customer needs better than competitors do and is a cultural orientation which sets customer satisfaction at the centre of business operations with the aim of producing superior value for customers and outstanding performance for the firm. Despite some variability in conceptualizations of market orientation, it typically focuses on three components customer focus, competitor focus and interfunctional coordination. Kohli and Jaworski (1990) define market orientation in terms of three dimensions:

- The generation of market information about needs of customers and external environmental factors
- The dissemination of such information among organizational functions and
- The development and implementation of strategies in response to the information

These elements include continuous and systematic information gathering regarding customers and competitors, cross-functional sharing of information and coordination of activities, and responsiveness to changing market needs. Adopting a Market Orientation is associated with higher organizational performance and profitability, innovation success and higher organizational learning (Slater & Narver, 1995). Scholars suggest that the importance of market orientation for organizational performance depends on environmental conditions (Augusto and Coehlo, 2009). Organizations in more competitive and dynamic environments are expected to be more market oriented in order to act proactively to constantly changing environmental conditions. On the other hand, companies with high levels of customer focus have been associated with the creation of me-too products and less radical innovations.

Building a Culture Supportive for Innovation

Organizations nowadays are under constant pressure to remain competitive in an increasingly demanding business environment. To meet this challenge, top management should learn to inspire their organizations to new levels of inventiveness in everything that they do. Much can be done by most organizations to boost their overall innovation (Martins & Terblanche, 2003). It starts with learning to tap into the creative potential of all the employees and their knowledge about customers, competitors, and processes, and the key is to adopt the right organizational climate. The formation and development of a culture supportive for innovation also remains a key issue in most contemporary organizations. As innovation activities cover the entire range of activities necessary to provide value to customers and a satisfactory return to the business, a culture or a shared climate should be shaped and developed within the company in order to constantly drive the creation of value for customers and innovative service offerings (McLaughlin et al., 2009). Companies like Apple, 3M and Honda, have successfully nurtured a highly innovative culture.

4. INTRA-ORGANIZATIONAL PARAMETERS OF INNOVATION SUCCESS

Due to a highly competitive and dynamic environment, organizations must become more flexible and adaptive. The use of multidisciplinary interfunctional structures has become a vital asset for innovation success and the effective collaboration between actors from different functions remains a key determinant of successful innovations. In this context, the importance of interactions and relationships between functions and team participants during innovation initiatives should be further analyzed:

- The role of internal dynamics should be addressed, as the amount and the type of conflicts and the climate among team participants may affect the performance of the team.
- The existence of political activity and trust between different departments and functions also remains critical, as often innovation actors promote the agenda and the interests of their own department, ignoring other's department needs.
- Top management's contribution to innovation success should be described, as their knowledgeability and leadership pattern affect team performance.

4.1 Internal Dynamics

Innovation results are highly dependent on relationships between participants from different functional units. This emphasis is understandable since sharing and using info can be more easily achieved when there is a positive internal climate and harmonic interpersonal relationships (Gebert, Boerner and Kearney, 2010). Managing successfully innovation teams remains a key priority for project managers as high levels of conflicts and mistrust within the development team are considered as the main causes for the poor results in innovation efforts (Vermeulen, 2004). Conflict constitutes an inevitable and commonplace element in teams' dynamics during innovation activities, as it is endemic among employees when they work together under conditions of high task interdependence and uncertainty. In fact, most innovation projects have some form of disharmony and thus, dealing with different types of conflict during innovation initiatives is critical (De Clercq et al., 2009).

Relationship conflict involves disagreements based on personal issues that are not related to work and is related to interpersonal incompatibilities among team members including tension, animosity and annoyance among members within a team. Innovation actors experiencing high relationship conflict tend to become preoccupied with activities such as reducing threat and coalition building and feel decreased satisfaction (Jehn, 1995). In general, due to interpersonal tensions and annoyance within innovation teams, trust in exchange relationships will be reduced and team members' comfort in sharing ideas, challenging each other, accepting others' opinions or offering alternatives are negatively influenced (DeDreu, 2006).

On the other hand, *task conflict* describes disagreement about the work that is being done in the group and exists when there are disagreements among team members about the content of the tasks being performed including differences in viewpoints, ideas and opinions (Jehn, 1995). Task conflict at a moderate level may enhance performance through discussions and debates that improve decision-making and the quality of the outcomes and foster learning as well as the development of new and highly creative insights. Moreover, task conflict may prove beneficial for innovation performance in the sense that cognitive disagreements among NSD participants can enhance their understanding of other functions' needs as well as their willingness to contribute to a more rationalized allocation of resources (Declercq et al., 2009).

Managing Innovation within Organizations

A third important antecedent of team performance is *team climate*. Performance in innovation teams is not straightforward and teamwork involves social and psychological processes that can influence the generation, evaluation, acceptance and implementation of new ideas. For example, team members are unlikely to generate and communicate novel and unusual ideas if they expect these to be criticized. Rather, what is required is a team and organizational environment that allows creative ideas to be openly communicated, fairly evaluated and properly implemented. Innovation can be encouraged in a team climate where creative ideas are supported, can be presented without fear of reprisal and where team members are focused on achieving both organizational and task objectives (Sarin, & O'Connor, 2009). A satisfactory climate supports team members in their search for novel strategies by facilitating access to necessary information and by encouraging team members to think creatively and to develop new approaches to known problems. Furthermore, a positive team climate incorporates the provision of sufficient opportunity for team participants to experiment with new ideas, thus allowing for phases of individual thought and work which are necessary to better leverage individual creative ability. Hence, creating a harmonic internal team climate may allow the team to be more innovative as a unit or may promote the innovativeness of participants within the team (Weiss et al., 2011).

4.2 Interfunctional Relationships

As organizations need to ensure cross-functional cooperation and integration during innovation efforts so as to achieve higher effectiveness and create more innovative products, considerable attention should be devoted to the importance of interdepartmental relationships during innovation interactions. Creating and sustaining harmonic relationships between various organizational functions involved to innovation will help the organization better dealing with political struggling, conflicts and battles for resources that arise within innovation (De Clercq et al., 2009).

Innovation activities depend to a large extent, on whether the relationships between functions are built on a basis of mutual trust. Quite often, performing basic development activities (i.e. info exchange) is highly dependent on the existence of trust, as interfunctional actors who take part in development projects that contain trust are more willing to share ideas and relevant information or clarify problems. Trust's importance during innovation increases, as it inherently entails high levels of uncertainty and relies heavily on the integration of employees from different functions (Dayan and Di Benedetto, 2010). Participants' perceived trustworthiness can positively influence innovation performance, as it makes it possible that the areas do not mistrust the information or decisions brought forward by the personnel belonging to another functional unit. Trust can be a mechanism that reduces conflict levels during innovation whereas the lack of trust causes employees to withhold information and this hinders the processes of knowledge articulation, internalization and reflection (Dayan et al., 2009).

Political activity is also a reality of organizational life and constitutes one of the options for those who wish to influence decision-making. Political activity is fuelled by conditions such as uncertainty about decisions, ambiguity about expectations, role stressors and competition for scarce resources, conditions that appear quite often in an innovation context. Intense political struggles may ultimately hinder the success of innovation strategies and politicking among departments, aimed at acquiring resources for the own department rather than a fair sharing of resources across departments, may decrease the effectiveness of an innovation strategy. When team participants act as representatives of their own department and promote its interests at the expense of other functions, they may affect the effectiveness of the decision making process due to the lack of effective info exchange between competing functions or due to the distortion of related info (Ferris et al., 2002). High levels of political activity may render employees more suspicious of the motives, intentions and prospective actions of their colleagues. Not surprising, though, employees' willingness to engage in various forms of spontaneous sociability such as sharing useful information during group discussions diminishes and personal agendas are posited ahead of organizational goals (Vermeulen, 2004). Under such circumstances, organizational learning is anticipated to be impaired and employees become less motivated to exercise responsible restraint in the use of organizational resources.

4.3 Top Management's Role in Product Innovation Success

It is well recognized that the top management of an organization is responsible for the firm's key strategic decisions. Top management involvement to innovation represents an important form of corporate commitment to the firm's strategic effort and has been positively linked to performance during innovation initiatives. Senior executives' engagement to innovation is a key organizational resource as their know-how and understanding are usually of a tacit nature and result from their past engagement in project experiences. The extant literature stresses the value of senior executives particularly in high uncertainty projects, including visioning to guide the innovation program; championing innovation efforts during critical development stages and participating in daily activities directly or indirectly as project reviewers.

Scholars also highlight project manager's role for daily project activities and define his/her key responsibilities as understanding the multi-languages of different departments, dealing with engineering issues, communicating effectively inside the team as well as outside, while guarding the concept, and resolving conflicts. A project manager should possess the required knowledge of the market and the technology involved in order to add to the success of the innovation project (Hammedi et al., 2011). Another important aspect of project manager's work-role is to effectively manage team participants and ensure that their actions are aligned with superordinate goals. The role of top managers in the innovation efforts of their firms is *sine qua non*, which is to say, there is no innovation without leadership. Senior management play a pivotal role in enhancing or hindering organisational innovation (Smith, & Tushman, 2005). In next we briefly mention some of their major innovation tasks:

- *Nurture a culture and shape a climate that promotes innovation at every level.* In order to build a successful and sustainable culture of innovation, leadership needs to accomplish two broad tasks. First, leaders need to be acutely aware of the impact of their role model behaviour on innovation participants. The second factor is the ability of leaders to deal with high levels of uncertainty and ambiguity as well as stimulate creativity (Martins & Terblanche, 2003). Innovation cannot be promoted without out of the box thinking, ideas' exchange and creative thinking. Tolerance of ambiguity allows space for risk taking, and exploration of alternative solution spaces which do not always produce business results.
- *Empower employees to innovate.* This is one of the most effective ways for leaders to mobilise the energies of people to be creative. Combined with leadership support and commitment, empowerment gives people freedom to take responsibility for innovation. Empowerment in the presence of strong cultures that guide actions and behaviour produces both motivation and enthusiasm for consistent work towards an innovative goal. Employees themselves are able to devise ways that

allow them to innovate and accomplish their tasks. The only serious problem with empowerment occurs when it is provided in an organisation without a strong value system capable of driving activities in a unified and aligned manner to the super-ordinate goals of the organisation.

- *Assess risk tolerance.* Employees need to know the level of risks that they can take safely. This helps them to define the space within which they are allowed to act in an empowered manner. For example, employees need to understand how much time they can spend on their pet projects, and how much effort they need to ensure that their "routine" operations are not made sub-optimal (Ahmed, 1998). In this way, understanding of risk provides clear definition of the priority and space for innovative actions. Without knowing that risk tolerance exists within the organisation, employees tend not to be willing to try and innovate, or engage in activities that are a departure from tradition.
- *Clarify accountability.* A very common problem in empowered innovation is that everyone is encouraged to participate in cross-functional process involvement, to an extent that almost everybody loses track of who is accountable for what. The result of this unrestricted and uncontrolled empowerment may be detrimental for innovation activities. As new processes are put in place then new forms of behavioural guidance must be provided and must be accompanied by redefinitions of individual responsibility (Ahmed, 1998).
- *Provide balanced autonomy.* Autonomy is defined as having control over means as well as the ends of one's work. This concept appears to be one of central importance within innovation activities. There are two types of autonomy: strategic and operational and autonomy. Whereas the first one is related to freedom to set one's own agenda, operational autonomy captures the freedom to attack a problem, once it has been set by the organisation, in ways that are determined by the individual self. Operational autonomy encourages a sense of the individual and promotes entrepreneurial spirit, whereas strategic autonomy is more to do with the level of alignment with organisational goals. It appears that firms that are most innovative emphasise operational autonomy but retain strategic autonomy for top management. Top management appear to specify ultimate goals to be attained but there after provide freedom to allow individuals to be creative in the ways they achieve goals.
- *Individualized recognition.* Rewarding individuals for their contribution to organisational performance is widely used by corporations. Recognition can take many forms so rewards can be either extrinsic or intrinsic. Extrinsic rewards are associated with benefits like pay increases, bonuses and shares and stock options. Intrinsic rewards are those that are based on internal feelings of accomplishment by the recipient. Innovative companies appear to rely more on personalised intrinsic awards, both for individuals as well as for groups. Less innovative companies tend to place almost exclusive emphasis on extrinsic awards. It appears that when individuals are motivated more by intrinsic desires than extrinsic desires then there is greater creative thought and action (Hartmann, 2006). Nevertheless, it has to be stated that extrinsic rewards have to be present at some basic level in order to ensure that individuals are at least comfortable with their salary. Extrinsic rewards promote competitive behaviours which disrupt workplace relationships, inhibit openness and learning, discourage risk-taking, and can effectively undermine interest in work itself. When extrinsic rewards are used, individuals tend to channel their energies in trying to get the extrinsic reward rather than unleash their creative potential (Ahmed, 1998).

5. THE ROLE OF KNOWLEDGE MANAGEMENT STRATEGIES

Knowledge management is crucial for fostering sustainable competitive advantage and remains an issue of heightened importance for organizations, as increasing competition and the vast amount of available info renders it one the most critical organizational strategies. Organizations that are aware of their knowledge resources possess a valuable and unique resource that is difficult to imitate. Hence, knowledge management includes all the activities that utilize knowledge to accomplish the organizational objectives in order to face the environmental challenges and maintain a sustainable competitive advantage in the market place. Knowledge can be distinguished in two different types – tacit and explicit knowledge. Tacit knowledge is the personal and context-specific knowledge of a person which is bound to the individual and is thus difficult to formalize and communicate. In contrast, explicit knowledge can be codified, stored and disseminated. It is not bound to a person and has primarily the character of data. Based on this classification, two different knowledge management strategies have been discussed in the literature for sharing tacit and explicit knowledge respectively: a *codification* and a *personalization* strategy.

5.1 Codification Strategy

A codification strategy has the objective to collect knowledge, store it in databases, and provide the available knowledge in an explicit and codified form. The design of databases, document management and workflow management can be considered as part of this knowledge strategy. The objective of the codification strategy is to transfer, communicate, and exchange knowledge via knowledge networks such as discussion forums (Hansen et al., 1999). However, a codification strategy can increase info overload in the form of large directories of unprocessed documents or unread mail. Given that explicit knowledge is easily imitable and highly mobile, the involuntary transfer of strategic know-how (e.g. blueprints) to competitors is also a possibility. Additionally, in fast-changing industries such as information technology, explicit knowledge rapidly becomes obsolete. More importantly, codified knowledge needs remarkable investments in IT for creating and maintaining repositories, expert systems and web pages (Storey and Kahn, 2010).

5.2 Personalization Strategy

A personalization strategy involves both formal (e.g., project meetings) and informal mechanisms (e.g., short conversations) and results in the sharing of tacit knowledge, which is hard to articulate, acquire, and store within individuals without direct personal experience. Direct interactions between people, corporate yellow pages that provide information about which expertise resides in whom, communities-of-practice, storytelling and setting up shared physical and virtual spaces that inspire constructive interactions are common practices related to this strategy (Hansen et al., 1999). The focus of this approach is not to store knowledge, but to use information technology to help people communicate their knowledge. In this case, knowledge is considered to be closely tied to its owners and conditions are created to ensure its movement between them. As a result, the risk of imitation is lowered. Moreover, applying a personalization approach is highly favourable to creativity and is relevant where products and services are customized and innovative solutions need to be delivered fast (Hansen et al., 1999). However, this strategy also invokes some concerns. First, people are reluctant to share knowledge with each other due to their fear of losing status and power. This restricts the movement of knowledge even within the organization and necessitates due attention towards social and cultural issues. Second, employee turnover implies loss of valuable and complex tacit knowledge that could not anyway be captured by codification and this suggests that people retention strategies need to be given due importance, in conjunction with personalization.

5.3 Using Knowledge Management Strategies within Innovation

Extant research notes that companies will favour the use of either a codification strategy or a personalization strategy. Firms that rely on solely one strategy or another may miss some of the benefits of their joint adoption, as both strategies are likely to reinforce each other. Whereas a codification strategy is suggested to enhance more innovation stage proficiency, the adoption of a personalization strategy remains a key contributor of innovation success. A personalization strategy encourages the accumulation of tacit knowledge whereas a codification strategy favours explicit knowledge, but both strategies are required in a company attempting to expand its knowledge base. Storey and Kahn (2010) display the direct impact of both knowledge management strategies on the level of task knowledge created within innovation. Both knowledge management strategies are anticipated to directly increase organizational learning from innovation efforts because both strategies aim to acquire, capture, and distil knowledge, thereby increasing the amount of knowledge available to the firm.

6. INTEGRATING CUSTOMER KNOWLEDGE TO INNOVATION PROJECTS

In recent years, a growing stream of research has displayed the importance of integrating customer knowledge within the new product development process. Integrating customer knowledge within the development of new products/services constitutes a key priority for a number of reasons. Unless companies understand hidden customer needs and wants they are unlikely to deliver higher value to their customers. Second, the ability to proactively collect, analyze, disseminate and act on customer information is expected to provide organizations with a competitive advantage which remains hard to imitate. Having accurate info about emerging market trends and customers future needs the risk of a product failure is significantly reduced. Customer knowledge can primarily be incorporated within product development either directly through engaging customers to the development process or indirectly through integrating contact employees or sales reps within the innovation projects (Alam, 2013).

6.1 Contact Employee Engagement to Development Teams

Contact staff is a primary company resource as it is in a better position to collect and report customer info which, in turn, can be a basis of new concepts and ideas. Being ''boundary spanners'' between the employing organization and the customers being served, contact employees typically have detailed insights in how a company's current offering satisfy customer needs and can quickly identify areas for improvement and potential pitfalls. Contact employee participation to innovation initiatives can enhance the transfer of important customer intelligence and market info to other team participants (Cadwallader et al., 2010). This knowledge transfer of valuable info and experiences will not only add to the extent of each participant's individual learning but will also augment organizational knowledge due to the diffusion of customer-related knowledge across different organizational functions and echelons. In overall, contact employees can become a valuable source of new ideas and a resource in planning how to successfully deliver and implement a package of new core and augmented product. Researchers emphasize the involvement of contact employees in the innovation process and illustrate the firm's benefits in the development stages when contact employees can define employee training needs, predict customer reactions to promotions, suggest ways of altering technical support processes to increase efficiency and advise on how to best sequence the introduction of the new product.

Within services, contact employee involvement is even more pivotal during innovation efforts. For example, service testing and personnel training reduce the risk of service delivery process failure because employees become familiar with the content and activities of the new service prior to launch. Contact employee integration on service innovation is associated with higher technical quality of the new service, radicalness and service marketability (Lages and Piercy, 2012). Contact employees often have in depth knowledge of how customers judge the quality of a new service and their involvement in the service innovation process has proved beneficial in terms of valuable ideas for new services and process improvements Contact employees' accumulated knowledge from customers related to service defections could be helpful to improve on service offerings, avoiding this way the similar service failures and reducing development costs. In addition, the process of delivering market and customer-related knowledge creation captured by contact staff and connecting it to an organization's knowledge system can add significantly to the development of new services and can extend existing organizational knowledge base (Melton and Hartline, 2010).

6.2 Customer Participation in Product Development

As innovating is essential for securing and expanding a company's position in the market, organizations need to understand customer preferences and attitudes towards existing and new products. Not until recently, companies realize the benefits from customer participation in various stages of the innovation process. This integration of customers into the innovation process provides a better understanding of customers' product requirements (Alam, 2006). One of the key reasons that trigger customer integration is the high failure rate of innovative products. Customer integration can reduce this rate: customers know what they want and need and thus guarantee that new products developed accordingly will satisfy the market. At the same time, customers constitute a reliable buyer potential. In addition, a nearly customer integration minimizes the risk of a later change of construction due to customers' wishes and so prevents an increase in costs and a reduction of profits caused by a delayed market introduction. These recognized positive effects of customer integration have led to the almost general consensus that customer knowledge is an indispensable prerequisite for a successful early innovation phase where it has the biggest impact on R&D activities (Alam, 2006). Equally important is the fact involving customer know how in the development of product innovations prompts a higher degree of product newness, reduces innovation risks, and leads to more precise resource spending.

However, growing experience with customer integration has shown that the involvement of customers may entails negative side effects and risks as well, such as dependence on customers or loss of know-how among other unwelcome aspects (Gassmann, Kausch, & Ellen, 2010). A company that does not select the right customers or fails to find appropriate ways to integrate them will not develop effective product innovations because they are too attentive to the needs of current customers. Second, selecting customers who actually contribute to NPD is, in practice, very challenging, because companies have

Managing Innovation within Organizations

no guarantee of finding the right partner, and the negative consequences of a poor collaboration can be significant. Some authors find that customer integration into NPD leads only to incremental improvements of existing solutions instead of radically new products, as customers are notoriously lacking in foresight (Melton and Hartline, 2010).

7. STRATEGIC ALLIANCES AND NETWORKS DURING INNOVATION

Faced with increased and globalized competition as well as relative lack of resources to develop new products, several companies have started to share their resources and expertise to develop new product with the aim of achieving economies of scale and gaining access to new technology and markets (Teng, 2007). For many firms the thought of sharing ideas and technology in particular with another company is precisely what they have been trying to avoid doing since their conception, due to the lack of trust to other collaborative partners. However, as the cost of building and sustaining the necessary technical expertise and specialised equipment is rising dramatically, even the largest corporations cannot maintain because they lack sufficient technical capabilities to adapt to fast-paced market dynamics (Todeva & Knoke, 2005). Strategic alliances provide an opportunity for both large and small high-technology companies to expand into new markets by sharing skills and resources. On the one hand, it allows large firms to access the subset of expertise and resources that they desire in the smaller firm, while the smaller company is given access to its larger partner's massive capital and organisational resources.

The formation of strategic alliances means that strategic power often resides insets of firms acting together. The development of cell phones, aircraft manufacture and motor cars are all dominated by global competitive battles between groups of firms. For example, the success of the European Airbus strategic alliance has been phenomenal. Formed in 1969 as a joint venture between the German firm MBB and the French firm Aerospatiale, it was later joined by CASA of Spain and British Aerospace of the United Kingdom. The Airbus A300 range of civilian aircraft achieved great success in the 1990s securing large orders for aircraft ahead of its major rival Boeing.

7.1 Types of Strategic alliances during innovation

Strategic alliances usually occur *intra-industry* or *inter-industry*. For example, the three US automobile manufacturers have formed an alliance to develop technology for an electric car. The UK pharmaceutical giant GlaxoSmithKline has established many *inter-industry* alliances with a wide range of firms from a variety of industries; it includes companies such as Matsushita, Canon, Fuji and Apple. Alliances can range from a simple handshake agreement to mergers, from licensing to equity joint ventures. Moreover, they can involve a customer, a supplier or even a competitor. Research on collaborative activity has been hindered by a wide variety of different definitions. There are six generic types of strategic alliance (Trott, 2008):

- **Licensing:** A relatively common and well-established method of acquiring technology. It may not involve extended relationships between firms but increasingly licensing another firm's technology is often the beginning of a form of collaboration. There is usually an element of learning required by the licensee and frequently the licensor will perform the role of 'teacher'.

- **Supplier Relations:** Many firms have established close working relations with their suppliers, and without realising it may have formed an informal alliance. Usually these are based on cost benefits to a supplier. These benefits might include lower production costs that might be achieved if a supplier modifies a component so that it 'fits' more easily into the company's product or reduced R&D expenses based on information from a supplier about the use of its product (Helper and Sake, 2012).
- **Joint Venture:** A joint venture is usually a separate legal entity with the partners to the alliance normally being equity shareholders. With a joint venture, the costs and possible benefits from an R&D research project would be shared. They are usually established for a specific project and will cease on its completion. For example, Sony-Ericsson is a joint venture between Ericsson of Sweden and Sony of Japan. It was established to set design manufacture and distribute cell phones.
- **Collaboration (Non-Joint Ventures):** The absence of a legal entity means that such arrangements tend to be more flexible. This provides for the opportunity to extend the cooperation over time if so desired. Frequently these occur in many supplier relationships, but they also take place beyond supplier relations. Many university departments work closely with local firms on a wide variety of research projects where there is a common interest. For example, a local firm may be using a carbon-fibre material in manufacturing. The local university chemistry department may have an interest in the properties and performance of the material.
- **R&D Consortia:** A consortium describes the situation where a number of firms come together to undertake what is often a large-scale activity. The rationale for joining a research consortium includes sharing the cost and risk of research, pooling scarce expertise and equipment, performing pre-competitive research and setting standards.
- **Industry Clusters:** Clusters are geographic concentrations of interconnected companies, specialised suppliers, service providers and associated institutions in a particular field that are present in a nation or region. It is their geographical closeness that distinguishes them from innovation networks. Clusters arise because they increase the productivity with which companies can compete (Bell, 2005). The development and upgrading of clusters is an important agenda for governments, companies and other institutions. Cluster development initiatives are an important new direction in economic policy, building on earlier efforts in macroeconomic stabilisation, privatisation, and market opening and reducing the costs of doing business.

8. MEASURING INNOVATION PERFORMANCE

As it is difficult to manage what cannot be measured, assessing the extent of innovation success or failure plays a key role in translating an organization's innovation strategy into desired behaviours and results and in achieving long-term success. A number of authors report several dimensions of innovation performance. Some subjective measures of innovation performance include time, cost, budget, market success, ROI, schedule, stage proficiency etc whereas objective proxies include team performance or relationship effectiveness between team participants (Blindenbach-Driessen, Van Dalen, & Van Den Ende, 2010). Moreover, scholars identify short-term (e.g. project efficiency) and long-term (e.g. competitive advantage) performance measures. The achievement of both organizational effectiveness and organizational learning is considered as key issue for innovating companies. Organizational learning is associated with long-term benefits for service firms in terms of expanding their knowledge base and

Managing Innovation within Organizations

maintaining a sustainable competitive advantage and not only adds to tacit and explicit organizational knowledge but also enhances individual experience that can be proved crucial in the long-term (Jiménez-Jiménez, & Sanz-Valle, 2011). Resource allocation effectiveness is also pivotal as scarce resources can impede the execution of many parallel projects.

8.1 Organizational Learning

In today's service-oriented and knowledge-based economies, organizations are quickly realizing that they can no solely compete on past success factors but should promote knowledge management and foster individual learning. Organizational learning is the process by which the firm develops new knowledge and insights from the common experiences of people in the organization with the potential of influencing behaviours and improving the firm's capabilities. Firms that are able to learn stand a better chance of sensing events and trends in the marketplace. As a consequence, learning organizations are usually more flexible and faster to respond to new challenges than competitors which enable them to maintain long-term competitive advantages. Learning is vital to the survival of the organization and critical particularly during innovation as it steers the transformation of technological and market information into new products. Some studies propose that organizational learning drives innovation (Jiménez-Jiménez and Sanz-Valle, 2011).

Organizational learning is related to direct experience, experiences of others and the existing knowledge base of the organization and involves the contributions of different individuals and groups towards organizational problems. Thus, an organization's ability to learn depends on the experience and actions of employees and teams within the organization. Individual's contributed knowledge base produces greater efficiency and reduced development time (Froehle et al., 2000). The knowledge that is created within interfunctional development teams is the result of a process involving the acquisition, the distribution and the use of existing knowledge (Stevens and Dimitriades, 2011) so as to reduce project uncertainty and to lead eventually to the creation of new knowledge for the firm.

8.2 Resource Allocation Effectiveness and Efficiency

Competing in rapidly changing markets often requires the ability to quickly develop and deploy new products and solutions. Services firms pursuing a strategy reliant upon innovation are under constant pressure to employ more effective methods and make more efficient use of their resources (Henard and Szymanski, 2001). Allocation of resources deals not only with the expenditure of funds but also with the allocation of personnel, other support services, infrastructure, and info. Given the notion that the human factor is the most important and most scarce resource within innovation projects, efficient human resource allocation in innovation projects has significant implications for innovation performance (Kleinschmidt et al., 2010). Optimizing the resource allocation process during innovation activities is crucial for a number of reasons:

- The effective fit of employees with different educational backgrounds, expertise and often conflicting priorities can influence innovation success
- Effective info exchange and use between different departments reduces uncertainty and enhances innovation actors' learning.

- A provision of resource slack can significantly increase innovation-related costs, withdrawing resources from other critical organizational activities.

9. LIMITATIONS AND CHALLENGES

This chapter aims at providing a brief overview of the importance of the internal organizational environment for product innovation success. Of course, future scholars should provide more explicit knowledge regarding ways to improve the product development process (e.g. effective process control and evaluation of process quality) and its scope (e.g. organizational forms to enhance market focus and/or integration of NPD with other business objectives). Despite the role of various intra-organizational determinants, the effect of the external organizational environment, emerging customer trends and changing market conditions are also pivotal for new product success. Moreover, more research is needed regarding the difference between success and failure factors of incremental and radical innovation. Finally, understanding how to influence success through effective strategies and launch planning processes is also an importance aspect of innovation that needs further consideration (e.g. accelerate rate of market acceptance). Future research should look into these aspects of innovation in order to provide practitioners with a comprehensive understanding of the innovation process.

REFERENCES

Ahmed, P. K. (1998). Culture and climate for innovation. *European Journal of Innovation Management*, *1*(1), 30–43. doi:10.1108/14601069810199131

Alam, I. (2013). Customer interaction in service innovation: Evidence from India. *International Journal of Emerging Markets*, *8*(1), 41–64. doi:10.1108/17468801311297273

Alonso, R., Dessein, W., & Matouschek, N. (2008). When does coordination require centralization? *The American Economic Review*, *98*(1), 145–179. doi:10.1257/aer.98.1.145

Blindenbach-Driessen, F., Van Dalen, J., & Van Den Ende, J. (2010). Subjective Performance Assessment of Innovation Projects*. *Journal of Product Innovation Management*, *27*(4), 572–592. doi:10.1111/j.1540-5885.2010.00736.x

Bodewes, W. E. (2002). Formalization and innovation revisited. *European Journal of Innovation Management*, *5*(4), 214–223. doi:10.1108/14601060210451171

Burns, T., & Stalker, G. M. (2011).Mechanistic and Organic Systems of Management. *Sociology of Organizations: Structures and Relationships*, 14.

Carbonell, P., & Rodríguez-Escudero, A. I. (2009). Relationships among team's organizational context, innovation speed, and technological uncertainty: An empirical analysis. *Journal of Engineering and Technology Management*, *26*(1), 28–45. doi:10.1016/j.jengtecman.2009.03.005

Carbonell, P., Rodríguez-Escudero, A. I., & Pujari, D. (2009). Customer Involvement in New Service Development: An Examination of Antecedents and Outcomes*. *Journal of Product Innovation Management, 26*(5), 536–550. doi:10.1111/j.1540-5885.2009.00679.x

Corrocher, N., & Zirulia, L. (2010). Demand and innovation in services: The case of mobile communications. *Research Policy, 39*(7), 945–955. doi:10.1016/j.respol.2010.04.008

Cuijpers, M., Guenter, H., & Hussinger, K. (2011). Costs and benefits of inter-departmental innovation collaboration. *Research Policy, 40*(4), 565–575. doi:10.1016/j.respol.2010.12.004

Dayan, M., & Di Benedetto, C. A. (2010). The impact of structural and contextual factors on trust formation in product development teams. *Industrial Marketing Management, 39*(4), 691–703. doi:10.1016/j.indmarman.2010.01.001

Dayan, M., Di Benedetto, C. A., & Colak, M. (2009). Managerial trust in new product development projects: Its antecedents and consequences. *Research Management, 39*(1), 21–37.

De Clercq, D. D., Menguc, B., & Auh, S. (2009). Unpacking the relationship between an innovation strategy and firm performance: The role of task conflict and political activity. *Journal of Business Research, 62*(11), 1046–1053. doi:10.1016/j.jbusres.2008.10.021

De Dreu, C. K. (2006). When too little or too much hurts: Evidence for a curvilinear relationship between task conflict and innovation in teams. *Journal of Management, 32*(1), 83–107. doi:10.1177/0149206305277795

Drazin, R., & Van de Ven, A. H. (1985). Alternative forms of fit in contingency theory. *Administrative Science Quarterly, 30*(4), 514–539. doi:10.2307/2392695

Ferris, G. R., Perrewé, P. L., & Douglas, C. (2002). Social effectiveness in organizations: Construct validity and research directions. *Journal of Leadership & Organizational Studies, 9*(1), 49–63. doi:10.1177/107179190200900104

Froehle, C. M., & Roth, A. V. (2007). A Resource-Process Framework of New Service Development. *Production and Operations Management, 16*(2), 169–188. doi:10.1111/j.1937-5956.2007.tb00174.x

Froehle, C. M., Roth, A. V., Chase, R. B., & Voss, C. A. (2000). Antecedents of new service development effectiveness an exploratory examination of strategic operations choices. *Journal of Service Research, 3*(1), 3–17. doi:10.1177/109467050031001

Galbraith, J. R. (1973). *Designing complex organizations*. Addison-Wesley Longman Publishing Co., Inc.

García, N., Sanzo, M. J., & Trespalacios, J. A. (2008). New product internal performance and market performance: Evidence from Spanish firms regarding the role of trust, interfunctional integration, and innovation type. *Technovation, 28*(11), 713–725. doi:10.1016/j.technovation.2008.01.001

Gebert, D., Boerner, S., & Kearney, E. (2010). Fostering team innovation: Why is it important to combine opposing action strategies? *Organization Science, 21*(3), 593–608. doi:10.1287/orsc.1090.0485

Hammedi, W., Van Riel, A. C., & Sasovova, Z. (2011). Antecedents and Consequences of Reflexivity in New Product Idea Screening. *Journal of Product Innovation Management, 28*(5), 662–679.

Harris, E., & Woolley, R. (2009). Facilitating innovation through cognitive mapping of uncertainty. *International Studies of Management & Organization, 39*(1), 70–100. doi:10.2753/IMO0020-8825390104

Hartmann, A. (2006). The role of organizational culture in motivating innovative behaviour in construction firms. *Construction Innovation: Information, Process. Management, 6*(3), 159–172.

Henard, D. H., & Szymanski, D. M. (2001). Why some new products are more successful than others. *JMR, Journal of Marketing Research, 38*(3), 362–375. doi:10.1509/jmkr.38.3.362.18861

Jehn, K. A. (1995). A multimethod examination of the benefits and detriments of intragroup conflict. *Administrative Science Quarterly, 40*(2), 256–282. doi:10.2307/2393638

Jiménez-Jiménez, D., & Sanz-Valle, R. (2011). Innovation, organizational learning, and performance. *Journal of Business Research, 64*(4), 408–417. doi:10.1016/j.jbusres.2010.09.010

Kleinschmidt, E., De Brentani, U., & Salomo, S. (2010). Information Processing and Firm-Internal Environment Contingencies: Performance Impact on Global New Product Development. *Creativity and Innovation Management, 19*(3), 200–218. doi:10.1111/j.1467-8691.2010.00568.x

Kohli, A. K., & Jaworski, B. J. (1990). Market orientation: The construct, research propositions, and managerial implications. *Journal of Marketing, 54*(2), 1–18. doi:10.2307/1251866

Luca, L. M. D., & Atuahene-Gima, K. (2007). Market knowledge dimensions and cross-functional collaboration: Examining the different routes to product innovation performance. *Journal of Marketing, 71*(1), 95–112. doi:10.1509/jmkg.71.1.95

Mahr, D., Lievens, A., & Blazevic, V. (2013). The Value of Customer Cocreated Knowledge during the Innovation Process. *Journal of Product Innovation Management*.

Martins, E. C., & Terblanche, F. (2003). Building organisational culture that stimulates creativity and innovation. *European Journal of Innovation Management, 6*(1), 64–74. doi:10.1108/14601060310456337

McLaughlin, P., Bessant, J., & Smart, P. (2008). Developing an organisation culture to facilitate radical innovation. *International Journal of Technology Management, 44*(3), 298–323. doi:10.1504/IJTM.2008.021041

Melton, H. L., & Hartline, M. D. (2010). Customer and frontline employee influence on new service development performance. *Journal of Service Research, 13*(4), 411–425. doi:10.1177/1094670510369378

Melton, H. L., & Hartline, M. D. (2013). Employee Collaboration, Learning Orientation, and New Service Development Performance. *Journal of Service Research, 16*(1), 67–81. doi:10.1177/1094670512462139

Mom, T. J. M., van den Bosch, F. A. J., & Volberda, H. W. (2009). Understanding variation in managers' ambidexterity: Investigating direct and interaction effects of formal structural and personal coordination mechanisms. *Organization Science, 20*(4), 812–828. doi:10.1287/orsc.1090.0427

Nambisan, S. (2009). *Virtual customer environments: IT-enabled customer co-innovation and value co-creation* (pp. 109–127). NY: Springer.

Nonaka, I., & Takeuchi, H. (1995). *The knowledge-creating company*. New York: Oxford University Press.

Olson, E. M., Slater, S. F., & Hult, G. T. M. (2005). The performance implications of fit among business strategy, marketing organization structure, and strategic behavior. *Journal of Marketing, 69*(3), 49–65. doi:10.1509/jmkg.69.3.49.66362

Ortt, J. R., & Smits, R. (2006). Innovation management: Different approaches to cope with the same trends. *International Journal of Technology Management, 34*(3), 296–318. doi:10.1504/IJTM.2006.009461

Porter, M. E., & Kramer, M. R. (2011). Creating shared value. *Harvard Business Review, 89*(1/2), 62–77.

Sarin, S., & O'Connor, G. C. (2009). First among Equals: The Effect of Team Leader Characteristics on the Internal Dynamics of Cross-Functional Product Development Teams*. *Journal of Product Innovation Management, 26*(2), 188–205. doi:10.1111/j.1540-5885.2009.00345.x

Slater, S. F., & Narver, J. C. (1995). Market orientation and the learning organization. *Journal of Marketing, 59*(3), 63–74. doi:10.2307/1252120

Smith, W. K., & Tushman, M. L. (2005). Managing strategic contradictions: A top management model for managing innovation streams. *Organization Science, 16*(5), 522–536. doi:10.1287/orsc.1050.0134

Stevens, E., & Dimitriadis, S. (2011). Learning strategies, behaviours and outputs during the service innovation process. *International Journal of Innovation and Learning, 10*(3), 285–309. doi:10.1504/IJIL.2011.042082

Storey, C., & Hull, F. M. (2010). Service development success: A contingent approach by knowledge strategy. *Journal of Service Management, 21*(2), 140–161. doi:10.1108/09564231011039268

Storey, C., & Kahn, K. B. (2010). The role of knowledge management strategies and task knowledge in stimulating service innovation. *Journal of Service Research, 13*(4), 397–410. doi:10.1177/1094670510370988

Storey, C., & Kelly, D. (2001). Measuring the performance of new service development activities. *Service Industries Journal, 21*(2), 71–90. doi:10.1080/714005018

Tajeddini, K., Trueman, M., & Larsen, G. (2006). Examining the effect of market orientation on innovativeness. *Journal of Marketing Management, 22*(5-6), 529–551. doi:10.1362/026725706777978640

Terziovski, M. (2010). Innovation practice and its performance implications in small and medium enterprises (SMEs) in the manufacturing sector: A resource-based view. *Strategic Management Journal, 31*(8), 892–902.

Tidd, J., & Bodley, K. (2002). The influence of project novelty on the new product development process. *R & D Management, 32*(2), 127–138. doi:10.1111/1467-9310.00245

Trott, P. (2008). Innovation Management and New Product Development. Harlow: Pearson Education Ltd.

Troy, L. C., Hirunyawipada, T., & Paswan, A. K. (2008). Cross-functional integration and new product success: An empirical investigation of the findings. *Journal of Marketing, 72*(6), 132–146. doi:10.1509/jmkg.72.6.132

Van der Panne, G., Van Beers, C., & Kleinknecht, A. (2003). Success and failure of innovation: A literature review. *International Journal of Innovation Management, 7*(03), 309–338. doi:10.1142/S1363919603000830

Vaona, A., & Pianta, M. (2008). Firm size and innovation in European manufacturing. *Small Business Economics*, *30*(3), 283–299. doi:10.1007/s11187-006-9043-9

Vermeulen, P. (2004). Managing product innovation in financial services firms. *European Management Journal*, *22*(1), 43–50. doi:10.1016/j.emj.2003.11.012

Wang, C. H., Lu, I. Y., & Chen, C. B. (2008). Evaluating firm technological innovation capability under uncertainty. *Technovation*, *28*(6), 349–363. doi:10.1016/j.technovation.2007.10.007

Weiss, M., Hoegl, M., & Gibbert, M. (2011). Making Virtue of Necessity: The Role of Team Climate for Innovation in Resource-Constrained Innovation Projects. *Journal of Product Innovation Management*, *28*(s1), 196–207. doi:10.1111/j.1540-5885.2011.00870.x

York, J. G., & Venkataraman, S. (2010). The entrepreneur–environment nexus: Uncertainty, innovation, and allocation. *Journal of Business Venturing*, *25*(5), 449–463. doi:10.1016/j.jbusvent.2009.07.007

Zhou, K. Z., & Wu, F. (2010). Technological capability, strategic flexibility, and product innovation. *Strategic Management Journal*, *31*(5), 547–561.

Chapter 13
Start-Up:
A New Conceptual Approach of Innovation Process

Joana Coutinho Sousa
Unlimited-Hashtag, Portugal

Jorge Gaspar
Unlimited-Hashtag, Portugal

ABSTRACT

Nowadays, we are witnessing an increase of innovation both on start-up and SME. The implementation of innovation has a strong impact in the knowledge of economy. The ability of human being in creating it can be defined as a basic skill in a global economy, involving learning as an essential dynamism of the competition. Furthermore, the research and development activities are very important not only for universities and companies but also for the global economy. This paper presents a new conceptual approach for innovation process in start-ups and a new methodology to know how long the innovation process must take. The conceptual approach proposed is divided into seven interactive steps: 1) Have an idea (product, service, process, business/marketing; 2) Analyze the state-of-the-art and the market; 3) R&D activities and Intellectual Property; 4) Listen the market; 5) Define a flexible business plan; 6) Find a business partner; and 7) Go-to-market. Regarding the time of innovation, the presented methodology is based on five Porter's Forces.

INTRODUCTION

Nowadays, we are witnessing an increase of innovation both on start-up and SME. The implementation of innovation has a strong impact in the knowledge of economy. The ability of human being in creating new knowledge can be defined as a basic skill in a global economy, which involves learning as an essential dynamism of the competition. On the other hand, the research and development activities are very important not only for universities and companies but also for the global economy. Following this and taking into account the need of developing standards and guidelines for innovation, the OCDE has

DOI: 10.4018/978-1-4666-9607-5.ch013

been working on developing and updating a set of documents to help the innovators and the innovative companies to work better. As result of this work, two manuals were created: Frascati Manual (OCDE, 2002) and Oslo manual (OCDE, 2005). The first presents standards for measuring the R&D activities and provides a set of definitions and recommendations to classify R&D activities. The second one, the Oslo Manual, provides guidelines for measuring and interpreting the information about innovation. Both manuals are specially worked for SMEs.

Davenport (DTH, 2013) have published a book presenting a general approach about innovation process; however, this book is focus on combining the information technology with resource management in order to get innovation in the company and improve its business. Also, Davila (DT et. al, 2012) has presented a formal innovation process, but just applied on well established companies such as HP, Toshiba, among others.

All available guidelines and works present innovation process approaches for SME suggesting how the organization can be manage and structure in order to make a good and sustainable innovation.

However, these guidelines are not applicable for someone that wants to start a business focus on innovation. Start-ups have not a mature organizational structure to implement those guideline. Furthermore, people without knowledge about business and innovation don't know how to start, what are the steps to assure that idea is really novel, and what are the steps to put verify if the idea is viable and how to put it in the market. This way, there is a need to provide some guideline about innovation process in start-ups.

But first it is important to define what is innovation since sometimes the word innovation is misunderstood.

The innovation consists of a complex process. We need to create new ideas, but these ideas need to be exploited in the market, they need to have impact, bringing new opportunity of changings.

The innovation corresponds to the implementation of a new solution for the market or company. Oslo manual has updated the types of innovation, and according to it there are four (OCDE, 2005): a) product, b) process, c) organization and d) marketing. However, it is very important to note that there is, at least, more one type: e) Business model. The difference between innovation in marketing and business model is little, because the business model is part of marketing; however, it is not totally clear in Oslo Manual. Thus, this Chapter will also introduce a new type of innovation the "Business Model", which will be defined in Background topic.

Currently, many people (scientists, industries, policy makers, potential entrepreneurs) fight for doing innovation, but in most of the cases there is no strategy about it and, consequently, they are not able to translate science in market applications.

Funding programmes for research and innovation has been launching. In Europe, for example, in last 10 years, two programmes were worked (FP7 and Horizon 2020). Even helping into making science, these programmes fail concerning innovation. This happens because there is no tool and guidelines to help people to translate new ideas to market. We are able to develop the ideas but we are weak in the implementation. Furthermore, these programmes are very focused on technology, and innovation is more than technology. We can change the world using new technology, but also how to make business. Industries can be more productive if they innovate in production process, start-ups can gain more notoriety if they can change the marketing methodologies, and for example the industry of the security of personal data can change its business model, attracting more people and gain their trust.

Start-Up

The main goal of this Chapter is to suggest an approach for innovation process, particularly for start-ups, whose don't have money and, when getting, they are not able to waste it. This Chapter presents a new conceptual approach about the innovation process in start-ups, which is divided into seven interactive steps. Furthermore, the Chapter also presents a method to evaluate qualitatively the time of the innovation process, based on Five Porter's Forces (MP, 2008).

Thus, the seven steps of the innovation process are divided into four phases: *Start, Develop, Business Plan* and *Go-to-Market*. Each phase of the innovation process corresponds to one topic on this Chapter.

The *Start* involves step 1 - "Have a new idea" (product, service, process, marketing and business)" and step 2 - "Analyzed the sate-of-the-art and the market". During this topic a discussion about what is an innovative idea and what are the different types of innovation will be presented. Furthermore, how we can know the market and its needs will be also described.

Based on the outputs of Start phase, the *Develop* phase consists of developing R&D activities and Intellectual Property (IP) (step 3) and step 4 – "Listen the Market". In Develop phase will discuss what are the types of R&D activities and which are those that make sense to apply for creating a start-up, and how intellectual property can be done and its importance in innovation. In order to know if developments are in the right path, it is also important to implement some small pilots. Step 4 - "Listen the market" describes the importance of market to orientate the R&D activities and to gain sensibility about how much the market is willing to pay or how market will consume the solution (input for step 5). This is very important for the success of the solution on the market. There is innovation if we are able to put a new idea on the market; otherwise the new idea is just an invention.

In the innovation careful with the development costs and scability of the solution but also the internalization of it is needed. Development costs and scability have impact on the return of investment (ROI). Since in Develop phase some market feedback about the price and/or how it will consume the solution will get, now it is the right time to define the business plan. However, the business plan must be flexible and must be updated frequently whenever new market opportunities arise. New market opportunities can imply some adjustments in the novel solution (Develop phase). During *Flexible Business Plan* phase the description of some tools and methodologies of how to make a flexible business plan will be presented.

When finished the Develop phase and the Flexible Business plan phase, i.e., when the final functional prototype is achieved and during the definition of business plan (step 5), to test it in a semi-real environment is necessary. For that, the implementation a pilot is needed. This pilot must be performed in collaboration with a good business partner (step 6), namely with a potential customer of the solution. This will help not only to test the solution but also to have the feedback of a real customer and improvements that must be made based on that feedback. Based on this, Flexible Business Plan topic will also present some guidelines of how can find business partner and how can implement a pilot in order to test the novel idea.

Finally, *Go-to-market* phase and step 7 is the final step of innovation process. This step must be started when the other steps are concluded and must follow the defined business plan (Flexible Business Plan phase). It is very important to note that even in this last step, during it step 5 must be continually monitored and updated and sometimes step 3 must be also updated with new features, according to the market feedback.

At the end a method for evaluating the time of innovation process is presented through Time of Innovation Process topic.

Background

What is innovation? How we can innovate?

During the last years, many definitions of innovation were presented.

Oslo Manual presents innovation as an implementation of new or significantly improved product (service), or process, or marketing method or organizational method for company, market or world.

Following this, innovation is a new idea that is implemented and it will be impact, i.e, we make innovation when we try to put a new idea in the real-environment; otherwise it is an invention.

After defining innovation, Oslo Manual (OCDE, 2005) divides innovation into four types: product (service), process, marketing and organization. The definition of each one is presented in Table 1.

However, it is very important to note that there is, at least, more one type: Business model. The difference between innovation in marketing and business model is little, because the business model is part of marketing; however, it is not totally clear in Oslo Manual. Thus, the Table 1 must be updated with the innovation in Business Model, as defined in Table 2.

Table 1. Definitions of innovation, according to Oslo Manual (OCDE, 2005)

Type of Innovations	Definition
Product	Product innovation is the introduction of a new good or service or significantly improvements concerning its features. The improvements include technical specifications, components, materials, incorporated software, easy-to-use or other functional features.
Process	Process innovation consists of implementing a new production or distribution method or significant improvements. These improvements are techniques, equipment and/or software.
Marketing	Marketing innovation is the implementation of a new marketing method with significant changes on product conception and package, product position, promotion or price definition. Innovation in marketing concerns on overcoming the customer needs, open new markets or product re-position, aiming to increase sales.
Organizational	Organizational innovation is the implementation of new organizational method in the business of the company, work organization or external relationships. These innovations aim to improve the company performance, decreasing administrative and transaction costs, stimulating the satisfaction of workplace (and so the work productivity).

Table 2. Update to definition of the types of innovation

Type of Innovations	Definition
Business Model	Business model innovation is the design and implementation of a new model to make business and money in a specific market or product. These innovations include to interact more with customer, giving him some power and involving him in the process in order to feel part of the process.
Product	Product innovation is the introduction of a new good or service or significantly improvements concerning its features. The improvements include technical specifications, components, materials, incorporated software, easy-to-use or other functional features.
Process	Process innovation consists of implementing a new production or distribution method or significant improvements. These improvements are techniques, equipment and/or software.
Marketing	Marketing innovation is the implementation of a new marketing method with significant changes on product conception and package, product position, promotion or price definition. Innovation in marketing concerns on overcoming the customer needs, open new markets or product re-position, aiming to increase sales.
Organizational	Organizational innovation is the implementation of new organizational method in the business of the company, work organization or external relationships. These innovations aim to improve the company performance, decreasing administrative and transaction costs, stimulating the satisfaction of workplace (and so the work productivity).

Even dividing the innovation in types, the innovation can results from the combination of the types of innovation. For example, the innovation can involves new features for a product, but at the same time, the product innovation can be combined with business model innovation.

The definition of the types of innovation is very important since most of the times people think that the innovation is related to a new product or service. Furthermore, the business model innovation and marketing innovation is very important since these types of innovation can change the business and how make business currently, providing new ways to overcome some issues in the market, specially for costumer.

Another important issue in innovation is the research and development (R&D) activities. According to Frascati Manual (OCDE, 2002), the R&D activities are divided into three categories, as defined in Table 3.

The innovation is the result of translating science into innovation. During this process, all types of R&D activities are very important; however during the innovation process the most important R&D activities are Applied and Experimental because, in these types of R&D, the prototype presents a level of maturity that allows starting a market research and testing it in the market. Furthermore, it is also very important to note that R&D activities are applied not only to product but also to the other types of innovation. R&D activity allows to research for new benefits for the market and to improve the market in several branches.

During the innovation process, the identification and registration of the intellectual property is very important. According to World Intellectual Property Organization (WIPO) (WIPO, 2003) definition, IP refers to the creation of inventions, literacy and artistic works, designs, symbols, names and images. The IP is divided into three categories: patents, copyright and trademarks.

The registration of IP must be taken into account in innovation, since it is a way to protect good ideas and it is also a way to gain notoriety and a possibility of making money from licensing.

Recently, the concept of Open Innovation has been increased in the innovation community.

Open Innovation does present as an accelerator of the innovation using the knowledge and so a faster path to put innovative solutions in the market. In fact, from Open Innovation novel applications, namely related to technology, are appearing. For example, most of the applications we use (YouTube, Facebook, Google, Python, among other) provide Application Programming Interface (API) for program free or open source tools. These APIs and tools allow developers to implement other applications and sometimes innovative applications based on the provider's technology.

Based on the definitions and information provided before, it seems that the tools to make innovation are met. However, this is not totally true. Even having that information, people, in most of the cases, do

Table 3. The definition of the types of R&D activities, according to Frascati Manual (OCDE, 2002)

Type of R&D	Definition
Basic	Basic Research consists of theoretical work to firstly get knowledge about specific phenomena or observable fact and then generate a theory about that, without any particular application.
Applied	Applied research is the original investigation aiming to acquire new knowledge. This type of research is directly related to a specific practical objective.
Experimental	Experimental research is a systematic work based on existing knowledge gained from research or practical experience. This type of research is related to producing new material, products or devices, to installing new processes, systems and services, or to improving substantially those already produced or installed.

not make innovation; they make inventions. This occurred because there is a lack of guidelines concerning the innovation process. In innovation, people are focusing on developing new prototypes, and they think that at the end the success is guarantee. But no. Why? They forgot the market. They forgot to make a market research; they forgot to evaluate the level of innovation comparing with the existing solutions; they forgot to listen the market during the R&D activities; they forgot to design a good business plan, and so? They go to market without any market strategy and, worse, they don't know the needs of the market.

In fact, in literature, guidelines (CPI, 2014) about the whole process of innovation are not totally available; and this could be a problem to decrease the success of the innovation.

This way, this chapter presents a new approach for innovation process for start-ups, providing information about all steps that must be followed. Furthermore, the chapter also presents a method for evaluating the time of the innovation process based on Five Porter's Forces (MP, 2008).

The aim of the Chapter is to contribute for the innovation community, proving the innovative entrepreneurs with guidelines of the innovation process and, consequently, helping them into increase the probability of success in the market concerning their innovations.

The Start

Step 1: To Have an Idea

The innovation process starts with "To have an idea" (Step 1).

The idea can be generated from two ways: 1) a problem was identified and so it is need to overcome it or 2) simply an idea was created and then a problem will be identified and overcome. Figure 1 illustrates this.

Figure 1. Flow for step 1 – To Have an idea.

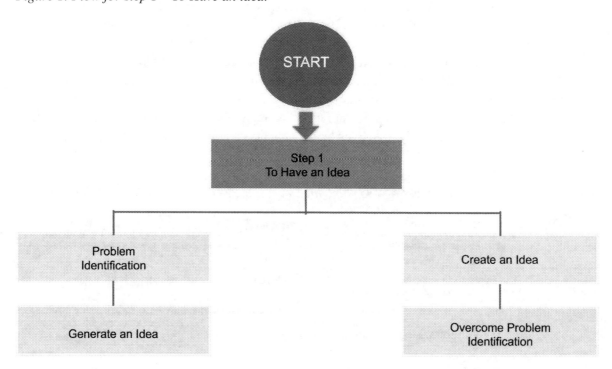

Start-Up

Even generating idea from two ways, the next sub-steps are common, i.e., from the dream (the idea) the design of it must be done. This will involve structuring the idea: identifying the main features, the benefits and how to make money from it. After that, the clarification about the type of innovation it is also very important. Figure 2 is an update of Figure 1.

Most of the times, new ideas are related to technological solutions; however it is important to note that innovation covers many areas of expertise: product, process, organization, marketing and business model.

So, how we can clarify the type of innovation?

After defining the features and business goals of the idea, to define why the idea is different is needed. For that, based on knowledge, the identification of the features that are novel must be listed. These features must be crossed with the innovation definitions according Table 1, aiming to clarify the innovation type.

Depending on the features, the innovation can be one or more types. This clarification is important since it is the starting point for studying the market and the state-of-the art. It is really novel? Where the

Figure 2. Updated flow for to have an idea, showing how to design the idea.

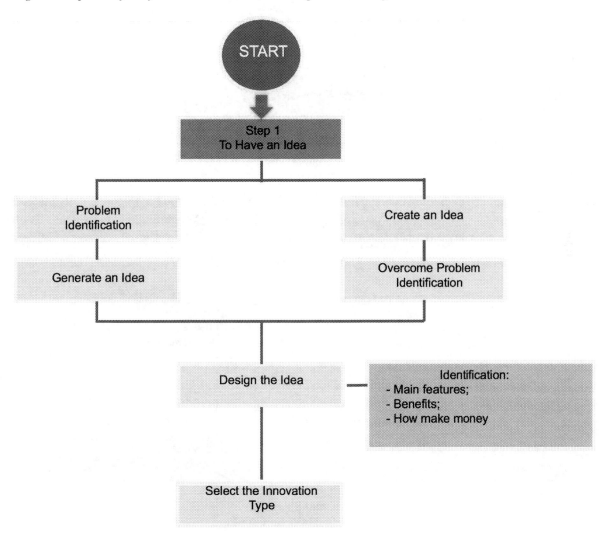

idea is different? How it will bring add-value for the market/customers. The definition of the innovation type will clarify the points where the idea will be new or where the idea will/can introduce significant improvements.

For example, an idea for product innovation implies that the idea must introduce in the market significant changings in technical specifications, components, materials, software, user-interface or other functional features. On the other hand, strategy innovation implies that you will introduce new methodologies of business and marketing, involving new business models, new ways or significant improvements on product design, package or promotion.

Figure 3. represents the step 1 of the innovation process.

Figure 3. Representation of the whole process for step 1 in innovation process.

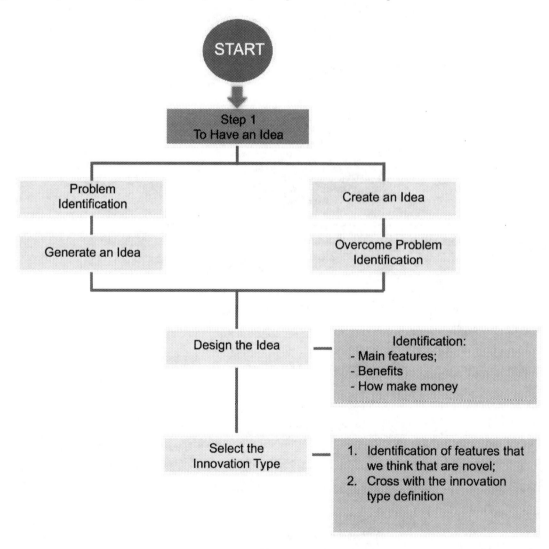

Step 2: Analyse the State-of-the-Art (SOA) and the Market

The second step of the innovation process is to analyse the state-of-the-art (SOA) and the market.

The SOA will provide scientific and technical information about the current situation of development regarding to science, product, process, business, marketing, methodology, among others. The SOA must include not only technical-scientific papers but also patents. Patents are very important since if there is a registration of a patent related to our idea, rights and licenses rise.

There are many tools for making a good SOA. For example, google scholar is a good and reliable tool to search for scientific papers according to specific keywords. This tool provides a digital path to get full papers or abstracts from scientific journals or magazines. For searching patents, google patent is also a good tool. Once more, from specific keywords patents can be reached and read. These are just two examples; however, there are other tools.

When finishing this investigation, the current situation must be listed in order to differentiate our solution rather SOA. For that, to list the main features of our solution, the SOA and patents will help to organize the information and cross it. This will support the innovative entrepreneur to know how his solution is different.

Investigation related to market must be done and it is mandatory. The name of this is market research.

Market research is a way of collecting information about existing solutions, the customers, their needs and beliefs and challenges. This way, market research will provide:

- Market information (prices, supply and demand situation and the understanding of social, technical an legal aspects);
- Market segmentation, which consists of dividing the market or targets in clusters with similar characteristics. The segmentation could be done base on some variables such as: geographic, personality, demographic, technographic (consumer behaviour), psychographic and gender. Also for B2B firmographics (organizational behaviour) is also used;
- Market competition: who are our competitors and what they are doing. Learn from our competitors is very important in order to drive our idea and to increase the probability of success. Furthermore, blogs, magazines, news, among media means must be followed over the time in order to assure that we know the current situation of the market and so to be easier improve our solution and define the business goals.
- Market trends, which are the upward or downward movement of the market in a certain time must be evaluated since trends will have impact in our solution and business goals;
- Market size (current customers and potential customers)
- Market Value (the available market and the future market)

From the market research, a list of market characteristics crossed with the main features of our solution must be listed in order to evaluate the level of innovation of our solution. This evaluation must be done also taking into account the SOA study.

Figure 4. represents the step 2 of the innovation process.

According to the evaluation, the level of innovation must be classified into five categories: "No innovation", "Low", "Medium", "High" and "Disruptive".

Figure 4. Representation of the sub-steps of step 2 in the innovation process

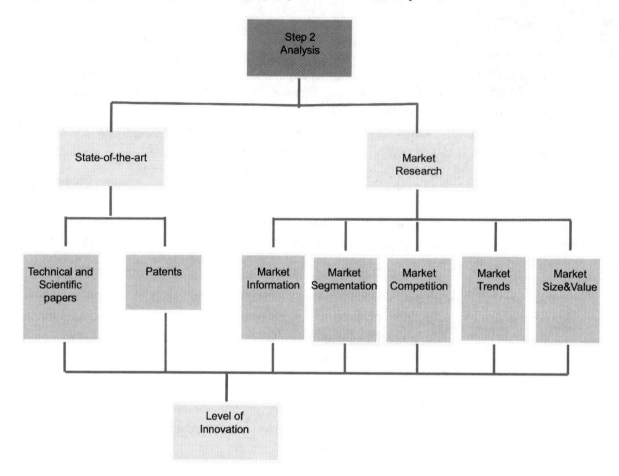

Thus, if the classification is "No innovation" the innovation process must be stopped; otherwise the features that were considered as innovative in step 1 must be updated in accordance with the results of the analysis of the state-of-the-art and market.

Figure 5. illustrates the whole flow for step 1 and step 2 that are the start for generating an innovative idea in a start-up.

This step will be the input for the third step, i.e., to implement R&D activities and to verify the possibility of intellectual property – Develop phase.

Develop

Taking into account the inputs of step 1 and 2, the third step is to start the project development and the IP registration.

Step 3

R&D Activities

Figure 5. The whole flow for step 1 and step 2 concerning the phase 1 - The start in innovation process.

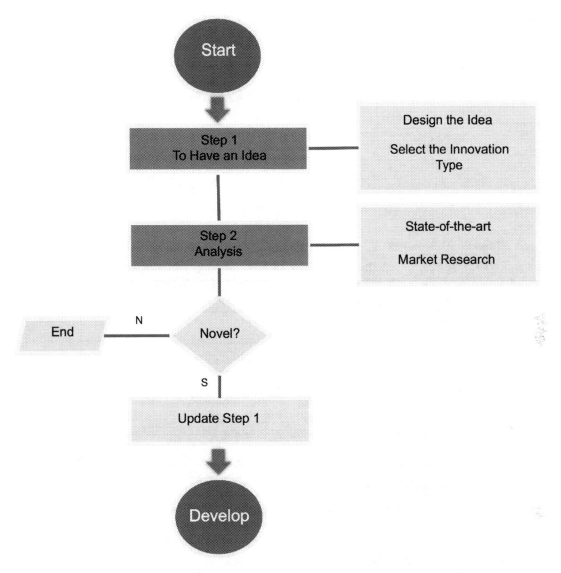

Research and experimental development (R&D) comprise creative work undertaken on a systematic basis in order to increase the stock knowledge, including knowledge of man, culture and society, and the use of this stock knowledge to devise new applications – Fracasti Manual. (OCDE, 2002)

R&D activities are classified into three categories: basic research, applied research and experimental research. The definition of each one is presented in the Table.

According to the definitions of Table and since the goal is to create a start-up, the idea defined in step 1, if it involves R&D activities, the development of it must be focused on applied or experimental research. The choice will have impact on the development process and, consequently, in the time-to-market. This last one is crucial to consider because in innovation the time is fatal, and if the innovative entrepreneur is slow in to put the novel solution in the market, a business opportunity can fail.

The development of R&D activities is a dynamic phase. Throughout R&D process the solution development is needed but the analysis of SOA and market (step 2) must continue in order to know how science and market are progressing and according to that, updating the R&D work.

In order to better manage the work, firstly a plan must be designed. This plan must include:

- Goals of the solution;
- Features;
- Tasks need to be perform;
- Start date to begin the task and due date to finish task;
- Milestones to achieve;
- Equipment or Tools need;
- Costs.

In fact the points listed above are the basis of a project management planning. When those points are defined, the project gantt must be drawn. This gantt is very important since it provides an image of all tasks that must be accomplished and the time of the development.

Figure 6. represents the R&D planning.

During the project plan, two considerations must be taken into account: Open Innovation and Budget.

Open Innovation

Figure 6. Representation of the R&D project planning.

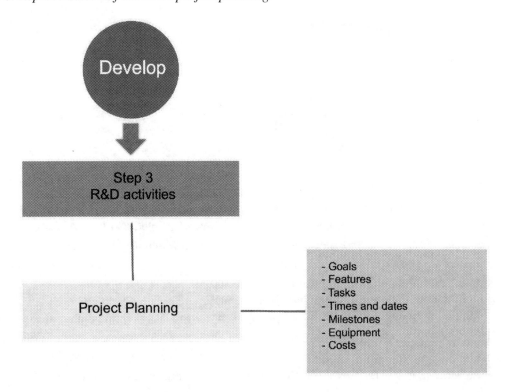

Open innovation is the use of purposive inflows and outfolows of knowledge to accelerate internal innovation, and expand market for external use innovation, respectively. [This paradigm] assumes that firms can and should use external idea as well as internal idea, and internal and external paths to market, as they look to advance their technology – Henry Chesbrough

The use of Open Innovation brings several advantages, such as (CH, 2003):

- R&D costs can be decreased;
- There is a potential to improve the development;
- Customers can be incorporated in a early stage of the development process;
- Synergies between internal and external innovations can be made.

However, the Open Innovation is associated with some risks that must be viewed as challenges and not necessarily as disadvantages, such as (CH, 2003):

- There is a possibility of sharing information that is not intended (see IP section);
- To lose competitive advantage as a consequence of revealing the intellectual property (see IP section);
- To lose the control of the innovation.

If the innovative entrepreneur knows those risks and if he choses for Open Innovation, he must perform a contingency plan in order to assure that the level of those risks are very low.

Furthermore, and related to tools, open source must be chosen. Depending on the idea and the type of innovation, there are several open source tools with high quality and performance. These tools will also help to reduce both development and deployment costs.

Budget

The budget is concerning to the costs of the development. The costs should include human resources, equipment, tools, software, licensing, among others.

In innovation and also in start-ups the project cost is, in the most of the times, neither planned nor analysed; however, this will be one the main important issues to analyse the economic-value of the solution.

The budget will provide a total value spent for developing a certain solution and so it will have impact in the return-of-investment (ROI). Taking into account that in innovation market, the lifecycle of a certain novel product is approximately two years, the finance goal will establish the break-even before that. This will have impact in the price of the solution and so in the sales volume. So, using the information from step 2, namely, market analysis, the innovative entrepreneur must know if the target (consumer) is or not price-sensitive. This is important because if the customer is price-sensitive, the verification of the break- before two years is important in order to assure the success of the project and the success of making money with innovation.

Thus, to make a forecast of the budged and its update during the development is also needed.

After planning the project, the development can start.

The development in this phase must follow the designed plan, and tasks and costs must be updated. This update is very important in order to have an overview of the project progress.

During the development there are two other steps needed to be in consideration: Intellectual property (IP) and Market Feedback (step 4).

Intellectual Property (IP)

According to WIPO definition (NF, 2010), IP refers to the creation of inventions, literacy and artistic works, designs, symbols, names and images. The IP is divided into three categories: patents, copyright and trademarks. The importance of IP is huge (NF, 2010):

- It provides the exclusive rights for using and exploiting inventions;
- It gives the opportunity to license or sell the invention;
- It empowers the negotiation;
- It reinforces the company notoriety;
- It avoids the competitors to copy;
- It enhances the transfer of technology;
- It provides the importance to understand the commercial value of IP assets when developing a business plan;
- It is an instrument for obtaining business financing from institutional and private investors.

This way, IP has value because it can (NF, 2010):

- Be legally protected;
- Create income;
- Be valued;
- Attract investors;
- Boost R&D.

Protecting the results of innovative projects can assure the maximization of its value, taking into account the competition and the position of the solution in the market. IP can also help to define new business strategies to elaborate and negotiate contracts of knowledge transfer.

Thus, taking into account the value of IP and following the patent research performed in step 2 (SOA analysis), during the development activities, the identification of IP opportunity concerning to the solution must be made. This step must be performed as soon as possible in order to protect and be possible presenting the idea/the results in conferences without problems. The following Figure 7 represents Step 3.

As referred at the beginning of this topic, the development is a dynamic phase. This dynamism is related not only to the development activities (including the IP registration) but also the market feedback, which is crucial for updating or improving the solution, thinking in the market success. Thus, the step 4 of the innovation process is "Listen the Market".

Step 4: Listen the Market

In order to know if the developments are in the right path concerning the market needs, the implementation of small pilots is important. The aim of these pilots is not launch the solution but test the prototype

Start-Up

Figure 7. Representation of the step 3 in the innovation process.

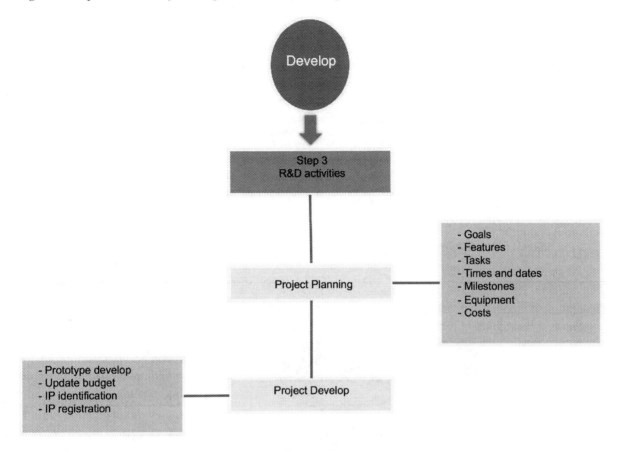

in a controlled environment (as a proof-of-concept) in order to collect feedback from customers (their acceptation) and how much they are willing to pay. Thus, this feedback will provide information for:

- **The Development (Step 3):** The acceptation of the concept and its feedback concerning its functionality must be used as input to improve the solution. Some features will be removed, others updated and others added. This aims to fit the solution to the real needs of the market and so to try becoming the solution realistic, increasing the potential to have a viable business;
- **The Market (Step 5):** How much the customers are willing to pay and how they will consume the solution are important issues to design a good business plan. Furthermore, these inputs will provide information for the calculation of ROI and, consequently, the real viability of the business in two years.

These points are very important for the success of the solution on the market.

Listen the market can be considered the last step of the development activity. From here, prototype will be improved and guidelines for designing the business plan are available. There is innovation if we are able to put an innovative idea on the market; otherwise the new idea is just an invention.

Figure 8. Presents all step of the develop phase.

Figure 8. Representation of the step 3 and 4 concerning the Phase 2 - Develop in innovation process.

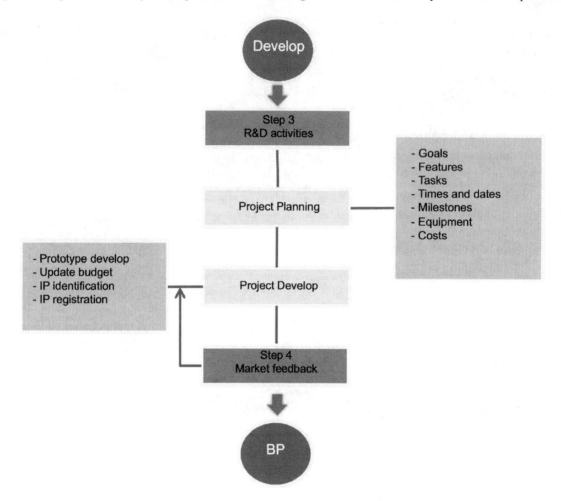

Flexible Business Plan

[The Business Plan is] a written document describing the nature of the business, the sales and marketing strategy, and the financial background, and containing a projected profit and loss statement – Entrepreneur site.

The lack of a business plan is the main reason for the failure of several start-ups. The business plan will provide a mean to design the business strategy but also how to implement it. Business plan must be updated during the implementation in order to keep it up-to-date according to the changes happened in the go-to-market (Step 7).

This way, the definition of a flexible business plan is the step 5 of the innovation process.

Step 5: Define Flexible Business Plan

Generally, a business plans consists of:

Start-Up

Chapter 1: Title Page and Contents
Chapter 2: Executive Summary
Chapter 3: Description of the Business
Chapter 4: Description of the product or service
Chapter 5: Market Analysis
Chapter 6: Competitive analysis
Chapter 7: Marketing Plan
Chapter 8: Operations and Management
Chapter 9: Financial Components of Business Plan

There are many templates for making a business plan; however, before starting with this document, some important steps must be performed in order to support and help on the document:

1. Update market analysis (step 2 – market research);
2. Based on 1), define the markets (countries) to commercialize;
3. Study the chosen markets;
4. Describe the benefits of the new solution for those markets (update step 1 – features and its benefits);
5. Define a price based on market feedback (step 4);
6. Calculate the shared quote to achieve;
7. Define the channels used for putting the solution on the market;
8. Define the channels for communicating;
9. Fill the business plan canvas;
10. Find a business partner (step 6);
11. Do the business plan document.

During this phase, there are some tools and methods can help in filling each point listed before. Following, some points will be briefly discussed.

Define the Markets (Countries) to Commercialize

The definition of markets (2) to commercialize the solution must be based on the market analysis performed in step 2 – market research. This should be done because it provides information about which are the best markets and why. The analysis can be made in accordance with infinite variables. Here the innovative entrepreneur must be creative in to find those variables according to the analysis and he must cross the information about the market. Furthermore, the definition of those variables will provide valuable information for studying the chosen markets (3. Study the chosen markets).

Furthermore, the internationalization of the solution is also very important, because it can expand the business and increase the sales. However, the internationalization is not a simple process. When choosing the markets and countries, the culture of different countries must be taking into account. This is important because both price and solution might be adjusted according to each country. Thus, culture information will be an input for the business plan, which must be flexible and be updated frequently whenever new market opportunities arise. New market opportunities can also imply some adjustments in the solution (step 3) and, consequently, in the business plan.

Study the Chosen Markets

The study of market (3) must answer to the following questions:

Question 1: How the market is characterized?
Question 2: What is the total value of the market (€)?

Regarding the *Question 1*, the answer can be getting from the analysis of the Porter's Five Forces (MP, 2008) and Ansoff matrix.

Porter's Five Forces shape every industry, and helps determine and industry's weaknesses and strengths based on:

- Competition in the industry;
- Potential of new entrants into industry;
- Power of suppliers;
- Power of customers;
- Threat of substitutes products/services.

The Ansoff matrix is the model used to determine the growing opportunities of business. This is made based on the following matrix (Table 4):

Concerning Question 2, many methodologies can be applied; however, to get the answer for this question, the innovative entrepreneur must answer to:

Question 2.1: Total turnover generated in said market (€)?
Question 2.2: Total number of clients/customers?

Define A Price Based On Market Feedback (Step 4)

The definition of the price is an important issue in the business.

In innovation, care with customers and their behaviour related to price (price-sensitive or not) but also the development cost and the scability of the solution are important issues, whose are inputs to define a price.

Development costs and scability have impact on the return-of-investment (ROI); on the other hand, the sales are making if the customer purchase, so, the price must be defined, namely based on what customers are willing to pay and how they will consume the solution (step 4).

Based on this, the final ROI can be calculated and the economic viability of the solution will be transparent. One important issue must be noted: the life cycle of an innovative solution is between 2-3 years. So, the break-even must be achieved ate the middle of the cycle; otherwise the business viability

Table 4. Ansoff matrix

		Products	
		Existing	News
Market	Existing	*Market Penetration*	*Product Development*
	News	*Market Development*	*Diversification*

Start-Up

can be compromised, namely because the solution after 2-3 years probably will be obsolete for the market. Even so, the price must be defined on the market feedback and not in the development costs. To define a price based on development costs can be the beginning of the end.

Calculate the Shared Quote to Achieve

Define business goals is mandatory.

Business goals will be translate in the shared quote.
Thus, the calculus of shared quote (6) will use some information about:

- Total turnover generated in the market;
- Total number of clients/customers, and
- Price of the solution.

Furthermore, based on the characterization of the market (Question1), the innovative entrepreneur will make a forecast about the number of customers he will achieve in first year. Then, according to it and multiplying by the price of solution, the innovative entrepreneur will have the business goal in euros. In order to get the shared quote, the business goal will be divided by the Total turnover generated (Question 2) in the market.

This way, for calculating the shared quote, the following questions must be answered:

Question 3: What is the business goal (€)?
Question 4: What is the shared quote (%)?

Marketing Strategy

Regarding points 7 and 8, channels and communication, respectively, the philosophy is to minimize marketing costs, but maximizing marketing results. Thus, digital marketing and online tools for selling presents a good way to achieve the business goal at the beginning.

According to Smart Insights and TFM&A 2014 report (CD, 2014), 58% of the respondents are convinced that the investment in digital marketing can deliver and 56% said the business has potential for improving

This way, using digital marketing involves:

- Website (Desktop experience);
- Mobile (Mobile site and/or apps);
- Landing pages;
- Email marketing;
- Social media marketing;
- Content marketing;
- Paid digital media.

Business Plan Canvas

The Business Model Canvas (BMC) (Strategyzer, 2015) is a strategic management template for developing new or documenting existing business models. The BMC consists of nine blocks, describing the value's proposition, infrastructure, customers and finances. The Nine blocks are:

1. Customer Segments: this must be filled with the information from market research about the customers;
2. Value proposition: this must be filled with the benefits of the solution;
3. Channels: this must be filled with the channels to put the solution on the markets and the channels to communicate and promote the solution;
4. Customer Relationships: this must be filled using the information of how costumer will consume the solution;
5. Revenue Streams: this must be filled how the innovative entrepreneur will make money with the solution;
6. Key Activities: this must be filled with strategic activities needed to deliver the proposition (e.g. find a business partner (step 6);
7. Key resources;
8. Key Partnerships;
9. Cost Structure.

BMC is the most popular tool for business model innovation, namely because it provides: focus, flexibility and transparency.

It is a tool to have a good overview of the business and a great support to start writing the business plan document.

Step 6: Find a Business Partner

When step 3 is finished, i.e, when the final functional prototype is done, to test it in a scalable and semi-real environment is needed. For that the implementation of a pilot is mandatory.

This phase corresponds to the step 6 of the innovation process, and it is advised to perform the pilot in collaboration with good business partner. This business partner is not a venture capital but also a potential customer of the solution. Thus, the identification of the customers and study the market is very important in order to know what type of business partner must be found.

Making a pilot with a potential customer will help not only to test the solution but also to have feedback from a real customer. This feedback must be used to improve the solution (step 3) and also the business plan (points 9 and 11).

Furthermore, involving a good potential costumer in an early stage, the quality of the solution can be guarantee and the probability of the success in market can be increased.

A good business partnership can be used to promote the solution and, consequently, to gain notoriety in the market and start attracting other customers.

Figure 9. illustrates the flow of Business Plan phase.

Start-Up

Figure 9. The flow of BP phase, involving step 5 and step 6 of the innovation process

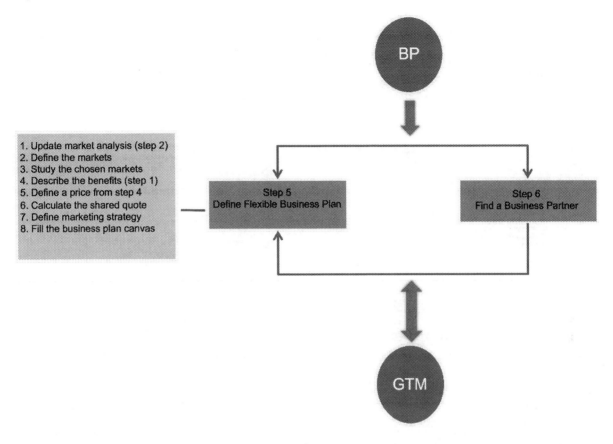

GO-TO-MARKET

Go-to-market (GTM) is the final step in the innovation process. It's the time of making money.

This step must start when the other steps are concluded and must follow the defined business plan (step 5).

It is very important to note that even in this last step, during it step 5 must be continually monitored and updated and sometimes step 3 must be also updated with new features, according to the market feedback.

The go-to-market must follow the defined business strategy and the innovative entrepreneur must be prepared to fight with obstacles, competitors, among others, and psychologically prepared to the failure. Remember that just 1% of the innovation have success.

The main market must be well worked and then, the other markets. It is also very important to continue listen the market feedback and adjust the strategy. Basically, this is the harder phase but the most funny. Don't lose the north is the most important think and follow the feelings as well.

Figure 10. represents the whole innovation process.

Figure 10. The whole innovation process and the corresponding steps

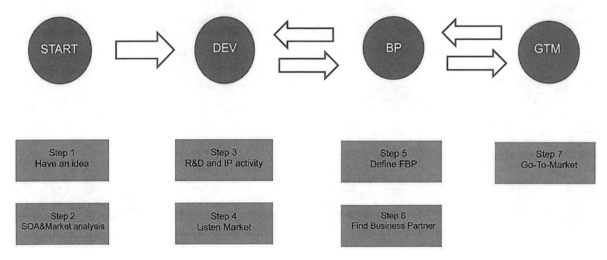

TIME OF INNOVATION PROCESS

One important issue in the innovation process is the time, i.e, how long innovation process must take?

Even being important and with high impact in the innovation, in fact there is no a corrected and an exact answer for the question. Generally, the answer is: as soon as possible.

Even so, some inputs could help in this question.

As described in this chapter, innovation can be done from product, process, organization, marketing and strategy. Depending on each one and the complexity of the innovation, one variable can support in to know how long the innovation process must take: the market.

The step 2 of innovation process involves a market research in order to get information of the market where the new idea will be commercialize. Information about market is its characterization. As mentioned before, the market characterization can be done from 5 Porter's Forces (MP, 2008). These forces will provide data about market behavior and, most important, the level of competition.

In case of a market with high competition the innovation is a mean for an organization get differentiation from competitors. On the other hand, markets with high competition reveals to be faster and so the time to put novel products/services is short. Thus, for these types of markets, the innovation process must take lesser time than other markets.

This way, for this proposed method, to make a good market research is very important in order to know the market and the customers needs. Furthermore, this is just one variable to provide a qualitative measurement for the time of innovation process; however, the complexity of novel solutions and the development activities are variables that will have impact in the time of the innovation process.

Figure 11. represents the whole innovation process and the corresponding time.

SOLUTIONS AND RECOMMENDATIONS

The biggest problem of innovation is to translate science into innovation.

Start-Up

Figure 11. The whole innovation process and the corresponding time of Innovation Process

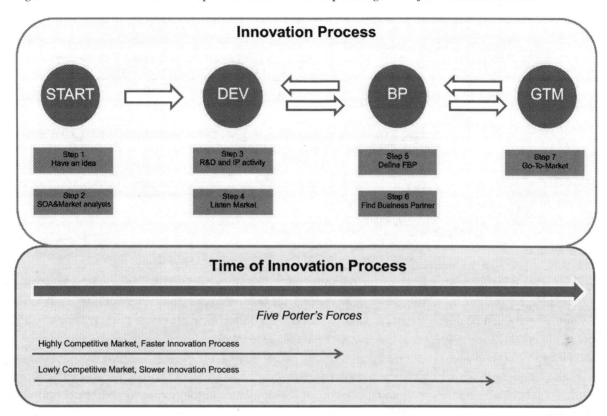

There are some drivers aiming to overcome this problem: books explaining the types of innovation and how to measure it and some guidelines about the maturity levels of technology. Even having information about innovation, in fact there is a lack of a proposed approach concerning the innovation process, namely for innovative entrepreneur. And this is the point of innovation.

Nowadays, people thing that having a new idea is enough to consider innovation; however making innovation is not simple. From the idea to go-to-market, several steps must be taken, namely the market research, the intellectual property research and registration, the market feedback during the development activities and the design of a good business plan. These things seem to be common sense; but people jump most of them. In most of the times, the focus of the innovative entrepreneur is to develop the idea, forgetting the market, but it is the market that will dictate the success of the innovation.

This situation happens because there are no guidelines about how to make innovation. Making innovation is not an exact science and there is no a correct answer; however guide the innovative entrepreneur must be done in this process.

Taking into account this issue, this chapter proposes guidelines for making innovation, especially dedicated for start-ups, where the resources are low and, consequently, to make errors is low. Thus, the chapter presents an approach of innovation process for start-ups. This approach aims not only to guide the innovative entrepreneur, presenting the several steps of the innovation process, but also explain them and sometimes to provide some tools that can help in the innovation process.

Furthermore, the last issue discussed in this chapter is how long the innovation process must take. The literature answer as soon as possible; however this time is important since if we are dealing with competitive markets the innovation process must be faster because the business opportunities for that are also faster. This way, this chapter tries to presents a method to evaluate that from the Five Porter's Forces (MP, 2008). This issue and the presented method for evaluate the time of innovation process are new in the innovation community and could be a great starting point to formulate other methodologies or to improve the presented in this chapter.

The expectation of the presented approach in the preceding section is to help the innovative entrepreneur in evaluating the idea concerning innovation, but also in trying to provide a support for driving the science to innovation, using the good science to make the difference in market and so in our lives.

FUTURE RESEARCH DIRECTIONS

The chapter proposes an approach for innovation process in start-ups. This approach is designed based on information available about innovation, compiling them and to provide guidelines for the innovative entrepreneur for making innovation. This way, the chapter presents a new model for making innovation that must be studied deeply. This study consists of taking a cluster of start-ups and implementing this model, studying the impact of it, i.e, how this approach can increase the success of innovation in start-ups.

The expected results are the proposed process can help in increasing the success of innovation; however other results can arise. For example, implementing this process and following closely the start-ups, the model can be adjusted according to the results of the study and so to provide an update not only for this model but also a great contribution for innovation communities.

This way, the presented approach for innovation process in start-ups can be considered the basis to make more and better and to help more and more to make real and good innovation.

Another point the must be studied deeply is how long the innovation process must take. The chapter presents a method; however other variables must be taking into account. Thus, it is also important to design a strategy for measuring the time of process innovation in order to help the innovative entrepreneur.

CONCLUSION

Nowadays, we are witnessing an increase of innovation both on start-up and SME. The implementation of innovation has a strong impact in the knowledge of economy. The ability of human being in creating new knowledge can be defined as a basic skill in a global economy, which involves learning as an essential dynamism of the competition. On the other hand, the research and development activities are very important not only for universities and companies but also for the global economy.

The innovation consists of a complex process. We need to create new ideas, but these ideas need to be exploited in the market, need to have impact, bring a new opportunity of changing. The innovation corresponds to the implementation of a new solution for the market or company. There are five types of innovation: a) product, b) process, c) organization, d) marketing and e) Business model.

Currently, many people (scientists, industries, policy makers, potential entrepreneurs) fight for doing innovation, but in most of the cases there is no strategy about it and, consequently, they are not able to translate science in market applications.

This situation happens because there are no guidelines about how to make innovation in start-ups. Making innovation is not an exact science and there is no a correct answer; however guide the innovative entrepreneur must be done in this process.

Taking into account this issue, this chapter proposes guidelines for making innovation, especially dedicated for start-ups, where the resources are low and, consequently, to make errors is low. Thus, the chapter presents an approach of innovation process for start-ups, which are divided into four phases, corresponding to seven interactive steps.

Thus, the chapter proposed that innovation process is divided into:

Phase 1: The Start
Phase 2: Develop
Phase 3: Flexible Business Plan
Phase 4: Go-to-market.

The Phase 1 – The start corresponds to the step 1 – To have an idea and step 2 – SOA and Market analysis. The Phase 2 – Develop consists of step 3 – R&D activities and IP registrations and step 4 – market feedback. The Phase 3 – Flexible Business Plan involves the step 5 – define a business plan according to the market research made in step 1, and market feedback in phase 2, and step 6 – find a business partner in order to help in testing the solution but also to promote it. Finally, Phase 4 – Go-to-market presents some insights about the commercialization of the solution.

At the end of the chapter, the time of the innovation process is discussed, presenting a potential method for measuring qualitatively how long the innovation process must take.

From this approach, the expectation is to increase not only the success of innovation, but also to guide the innovative entrepreneur in the process of innovation, making good innovation and changing the market and our lives.

REFERENCES

Chesbrough, H. (2003). *Open Innovation: The new imperative for creating and profiting from technology*. Boston: Harvard Business School Press.

CPI. (2014). *The Innovation Process*. Retrieved on October 29, 2014, from http://www.uk-cpi.com/news/the-innovation-process/

Davenport, T. H. (2013). *Process Innovation: reengineering work through information technology*. Havard Business Press.

Davila, T., Epstein, M., & Shelton, R. (2012). Making Innovation Work: How to manage it, measure it and profit from it (updated ed.). Upper Saddle River, NJ: FT Press.

International Bureau of WIPO. (2003). *What is Intellectual Property?* WIPO Pub: No. 450.

Nadi, F. (2010). *The importance of Intellectual Property (IP) for Economic Growth and Business Competitiveness*. WIPO.

OCDE. (Ed.). (2002). *Frascati Manual.* OCDE.

OCDE. (Ed.). (2005). Oslo Manual (3rd ed.). OCDE and Eurostat.

Porter, M. (2008). The Five Competitive Forces that Shape Strategy. *Harvard Business Review*.

Strategyzer. (2015). *The Business Model Canvas.* Retrieved on April 11, 2015, from http://www.businessmodelgeneration.com/canvas/bmc

KEY TERMS AND DEFINITIONS

BMC: Business Model Canvas
BP: Business Plan
FBP: Flexible Business Plan
GTM: Go-To-Market
IP: Intellectual Property
Innovation Process: The steps and phases needed to achieve the innovation, from the novel idea to market.
Innovative Entrepreneur: Someone who exercises initiative by organizing a innovative venture to take benefit of an opportunity and, as the decision maker, decides what, how, and how much of a good or service will be produced. An innovative entrepreneur supplies risk capital as a risk taker, and monitors and controls the business activities, namely in innovation. The entrepreneur is usually a sole proprietor, a partner, or the one who owns the majority of shares in an incorporated venture.
ROI: Return-of-Investment
Start-up: Early stage in the life cycle of an enterprise where the entrepreneur moves from the idea stage to securing financing, laying down the basis structure of the business, and initiating operations or trading.
SOA: State-of-the-art

Chapter 14
Learning, Using, and Retaining Deep Domain Expertise:
Working in Smart R&D Organizations

Anders Hemre
interKnowledge Technologies, Sweden

ABSTRACT

New product development is a knowledge intensive undertaking. It involves creative exploration, skilled task execution and complex problem solving. For such activities to be effective, relevant domain expertise is required. Knowledge and expertise are not the same. Expertise is not the expert's knowledge, but the superior ability to put acquired knowledge and experience to work in a professional domain. Knowledge can be transferred, but expertise has to be learned. Organizations need to be aware of the difference when making deliberate efforts to maximize the operational value of their knowledge and expertise. This chapter explains the nature of domain expertise, how it is acquired and its crucial role in new product development.

INTRODUCTION

The long term success of businesses to a large extent relies on product and service innovation and the development of professional expertise in related areas. Over a long period of time a great deal of expertise has been gained in many important business, technology and management disciplines.

New Product Development (NPD) is a complex, high value undertaking with both uncertainty and risk involved. Expertise is obviously an important enterprise asset that needs to be engaged and brought to bear on key product and technology issues. Experts and master practitioners thus play important roles in high-performing technology firms. At the same time, managing creativity, learning and expertise has remained a challenge also to organizations which have adopted traditional Knowledge Management (KM) practices. Many have continued to experience less than expected returns on their knowledge assets. Valuable as it is, like tacit knowledge, expertise is also intangible and volatile.

DOI: 10.4018/978-1-4666-9607-5.ch014

With a proper understanding of expertise and expert behaviour, NPD organizations will be better equipped to make deliberate use of their expert resources. Conversely, with insufficient or less utilized expertise, organizations may be under-performing in key disciplines and ultimately fail to deliver on their mandates. As knowledge and expertise are different in nature, organizations need to go beyond traditional knowledge management practices and find ways to also learn, use and retain deep domain expertise.

BACKGROUND

The organizational performance of an enterprise is determined both by the maturity of its practices and by the expertise of its workforce. Organizational maturity is demonstrated by the scope and consistency of both work and management practices and their impacts on enterprise mission delivery. The development of expertise depends on more than just acquiring experience. Reaching a level of expert performance requires *deliberate practice*, i.e. a practice involving self-regulated learning and improvement (Ericsson, 2006). Characteristics of deep expertise include speed of decision making, superior context awareness, extrapolation & discrimination ability, pattern recognition and a high degree of tacit knowledge (Leonard & Swap, 2005).

The management of R&D organizations faces the same general challenges as those experienced in most other types of enterprises. There are, however, some important characteristics of R&D operations. One is the need to accommodate both improvements to existing product lines and the turning of emergent technologies into new high value products and services. Another is the need to maintain a high throughput in the new product development process, while at the same time make sufficient room for individual and organizational learning. Work teams are important learning environments. In e.g. agile development projects, team members grow their expertise more by acts of knowing or "knowing in practice" than by knowledge codification and transfers (Choo, 2014).

New product development projects can be executed in a wide range of environments including start up ventures, small to medium enterprises and large multi-national firms. The organization of work increasingly involves various levels of cooperation and collaboration internally or across firm boundaries. Typically, large NPD organizations are product focused, process driven and project centered. These different operating environments have their specific circumstances and challenges. What they have in common is that organizational performance to a large extent depends on the level of professional expertise in specific technology and management disciplines. In addition, key organization and management issues include access to experts and the development of expertise by non-expert practitioners (O'Dell & Trees, 2014). In multi-project environments, there is an increased need for experts to engage in mentoring and coaching activities and take responsibility for the stewarding of knowledge (Miranda, 2003). Expertise is both knowledge and thinking skills. Learning through mentoring therefore involves protégés and experts developing a practice of thinking "aloud" about a problem or situation and making considerations and judgments visible (McDermott, 2012).

Today most NPD organizations have adopted standard practices. These typically involve handling explicit customer requirements, preparing design specifications and using a stage gate model to manage individual product development projects. Despite its considerable merits, this approach does not quite guarantee a superior organizational performance in the long run. Rapid market and emerging technol-

Learning, Using, and Retaining Deep Domain Expertise

ogy developments put additional requirements on R&D organizations to build knowledge centric, collaborative and well networked operations consistently capable of turning new technology, market and customer knowledge into competitive products. Facing these challenges, smart R&D organizations need to understand a crucial element of new product development – how their experts think and work.

HOW EXPERTS THINK AND WORK

The Nature of Expertise

Expertise is demonstrated by the effectiveness and fluency in complex problem solving, by the superior skill in performing a task and by the ability to see high value opportunities through a wide range of perspectives and a rich repertoire of insights. It's the superior ability of experts to recognize patterns, combine knowledge objects and see promising pathways, which explains the level of performance recognized as expertise.

Experts certainly have deep knowledge, but their expertise resides also in what they pay attention to, the way they think about complex problems and in their intuitive perception of underlying factors that impact a situation. Figure 1 shows a high level representation of expert thinking skills. Experienced professionals know - and know how to analyze - their domain. Experts also do, but they have acquired a deeper know-how enabling them to see further, consider more options and identify useful relationships.

Experts generally share these thinking skills with non-experts, but in a given situation they are able to draw on more of these and perform them better. Expert thinking also relies on the perception of subtle cues, intuition and pattern recognition originating in subsidiary awareness – all contributing to the difficulty of teaching expertise.

Figure 1. Expert thinking skills

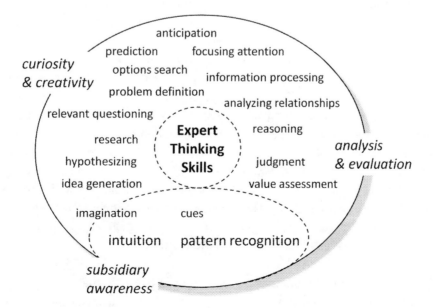

In expert teams, collective efficacy depends on many of the same group dynamics generally found in teams, but to a larger extent on shared mental models, effective feedback and team self-correction (Burke et al., 2006).

Domain expertise is acquired through deliberate practice, i.e. professional work involving self-observation, feedback, reflection, learning and improvement. Learning expertise thus involves not only the accumulation of knowledge through study and experience, but also the development of meta-cognitive skills. Deliberate practice leading to domain expertise typically also includes a repeated involvement with new challenges and complex problems (Cokely et al., 2007). Individual performance improvement as a function of time may of course vary and talent plays a role as well in the pursuit of expertise.

The time it takes to become an expert has been debated. The often quoted 10 year figure originated largely from studies of proficiency in disciplines such as chess and musical performance, where the level of expertise can be observed and determined with relative ease. Even though R&D too is both analytical and creative it doesn't necessarily follow that the time required to achieve expertise in R&D would be the same. It is clear though that acquiring domain expertise in any professional field requires years of deliberate practice and represents a significant investment both by the individual experts and by the firms and organizations in which they work.

The need for deliberate practice suggests that expertise develops in learning organizations. Practices in e.g. the software industry are aiming towards superior design, good engineering and imaginative testing. The quality paradigm, as exemplified by the Capability Maturity Model, explicitly focuses on the process of creating software and systems rather than on the products or objects of design. The learning mandate for software firms is then to deliberately use a higher level of organizational and process maturity to create and maintain conditions conducive to the development and growing of professional expertise and capitalize on this opportunity by also applying the necessary organizational learning techniques.

An important quality of software design and engineering expertise is the ability to make abstractions, i.e. to separate functionality from implementation. Expert software architects can break a problem down into related pieces of functionality rather than related pieces of implementation. They are able to locate patterns from which it is possible to define very useful functional components that work at multiple levels. Most software engineers learn a language and programming techniques fairly quickly given enough dedication. Expertise goes further. The intuitive feeling for making superior design choices, the ability to make the right abstractions and the skill of creating high performance functionality are harder to learn and requires having a combination of talent and experience – or mentoring by someone who has.

Like in many other professions, software expertise comes in different flavors. Some individuals are very good at the architectural level while being less proficient hands-on. There are others who are very good at implementing a solution once they know what to do. Others yet are very good at identifying design or coding errors or show their expertise in effective collaboration and team work.

Expert software developers not only demonstrate superior design strategies and broad, active problem searches in testing. They also function well in cooperative work settings suggesting that software expertise is not only a matter of domain knowledge and task performance, but also requires social and communication skills (Niessen et al., 2006). The same can be argued in many other fields of R&D as well.

Expert Performance in New Product Development

Data communication and computer technologies are widely used in telecommunications. During the design of a network product, a telecom company incorporates a commercial database product. To support the design effort, the company hires an expert on this particular product. After experiencing system related problems, they realize they should instead first have consulted a general database or system expert, who could have suggested that a commercial database should not have been used in this type of application. Even within the same technology area, expertise is domain or application specific.

Developing compact, oil-free compressors for the Heating, Ventilation and Air Conditioning (HVAC) industry requires expertise in both high precision mechanical engineering and fast electronic control systems. Faced with the market introduction of a new product, production ramp-up and relocating the business along with a continued R&D effort all at the same time, a HVAC company recognizes the critical need to manage knowledge and expertise. The company discovers it is difficult to accelerate learning through management interventions, in particular when both experts and learning practitioners feel insecure about the future. With expertise at risk, they also realize that they don't know how unique their expertise really is and whether it could be rebuilt by hiring new experts.

As a result of acquiring new product development mandates and reorganizing, a large R&D organization within a global technology company experiences difficulties with communication and a growing lack of cooperation and collaboration within the organization. This also results in a certain loss of expertise awareness, leading to questions about the availability and location of individuals with specialized product knowledge or technology expertise. It was decided to introduce a tool to help identify knowledgeable individuals and provide users with easy access to expertise. Despite the considerable virtues of the chosen technology, it remained a challenge to engage experts. The technology based knowledge sharing effort had to be expanded to include social components and was further developed to understand community dynamics and expert behaviour. Organizational learning certainly occurred, but for various reasons the outcome remained mixed.

The examples above illustrate the diversity of challenges organizations face when dealing with learning, knowledge and expertise.

NPD organizations operate by turning technology and management knowledge into strategies, products and processes. Also, the basic operational characteristics of *innovation* and *new product development* are different and therefore require different approaches. Organizations need to strike a balance between such opposite operational aspects as e.g. learning and teaching, creativity and conformance, people and process focus and guide organizational transitions between these different modes of operation.

The most common reason for organizational learning deficiency is simply lack of time. Project deadlines and customer commitments take precedence over reflection and learning. There is a mutually dependent relationship between learning and improvement such that they are both in certain respects a prerequisite for one another. If e.g. 100% of lead time improvement is allocated back to lead time reduction, there may be no time left for learning and improvement in other critical areas of performance. It may be better if some freed up time was instead used for ideation purposes or for improvement in product quality. Such considerations require both management and technology expertise. Organizations that are highly streamlined, optimized for efficiency and heavy on processes usually have a bigger difficulty with learning and change than organizations with the opposite characteristics. Maintaining the right balance is a difficult challenge. Being aware of the issue is at least a first step towards finding the best way forward. Understanding cause and effect relationships, building feedback loops into the management system, investing in human capital and increasing social connectivity throughout the organization, must all be part of the capabilities of any firm that is concerned about its future. Building these "soft" capabilities increases the robustness also of the R&D enterprise.

In new product development, problems can typically be classified as complex, complicated or critical depending on e.g. technological uncertainties, the number of design components or time constraints involved. Different kinds of problems would require different kinds of knowledge-based approaches. Table 1 shows how knowledge applies in the NPD process.

Complex problems may require new knowledge or new ways of using existing knowledge to be solved. Complicated problems are problems with many aspects or details involved, but which may not require any new knowledge or any fundamentally new work methods. Critical problems are problems that have to be solved under time constraints and may involve external commitments. Solutions for managing knowledge and expertise must be applied with these classifications in mind to be fully effective.

In R&D, domain expertise is often a prerequisite for making useful contributions to innovation. In the non-linear and fuzzy front end of the innovation process, experts contribute both in the creative effort and in the evaluation and evolution of new ideas suggested by others. Turning raw ideas into rich ideas is typically a collaborative effort requiring experts to engage in idea reviews, idea ratings and positioning decisions. Individual experts may also be involved in a multitude of special tasks such as technology intelligence, third party product evaluations, due diligence and patent applications. With multiple roles and many connections with different professionals, experts need strong social and communication skills in order for their expertise to create maximum organizational value. Also, senior R&D managers often no longer have first-hand experience of the technologies they must manage and therefore need to rely on expert advice. It follows that in this role, experts need to form particularly effective and productive relationships with senior product and project managers.

Smart R&D organizations use their experts' time efficiently. Idea campaigns and tournaments are organized innovation challenges with relatively short time durations and focused on predetermined business opportunities or technology problems. Well-articulated innovation challenges motivate creative thinking and facilitate collaborative ideation. As contributions would cluster in particular business or technology areas, the evaluation of ideas could be performed by a single team of experts and managers, making the review cycle more efficient. Not everyone can be expected to have ideas about everything. Ideation should focus on active solicitation of ideas from groups and individuals who are likely to have ideas about a particular problem or opportunity. In the product domain, this translates to people with sufficient technology expertise or application/user experience from the areas concerned.

Table 1. Knowledge applications in the NPD process

	New Product Development		
	Early/Front end	**Middle**	**Late/Back end**
Practice	Research Product strategy Requirements Management	Design, engineering & testing Project management	Product introduction Technical support
Problem	Complex problems	Complicated problems	Critical problems
Knowledge	Tacit knowledge Domain expertise	Tacit & explicit knowledge Domain expertise	Explicit knowledge Domain expertise
Application	Creative inquiry Sense making Reviews	Problem finding Problem solving Knowledge sharing	Knowledge transfer Problem solving
	Competitive intelligence, intellectual property rights, due diligence, process management, competence & resource management, quality management		

NPD organizations need to recognize how their knowledge assets are utilized in the work process including e.g. knowledge, competence and expertise. Even though such assets are intangible and volatile they can be managed and a first step in doing so is simply to make them more visible from an organizational design point of view and to make their operational roles better defined. Figure 2 shows the knowledge architecture of new product development.

Judging the performance of the organization, and therefore the effectiveness of its design, would have to include questions such as:

- What knowledge do we have of product xyz?
- How good are we at complex problem solving?
- How well do we manage communication and information?
- What level of expertise do we have in project management?

Answers to such questions can then be used to guide efforts involved in e.g. determining the scope and staffing of a project office, the use of communities of practice for collaboration and knowledge sharing or the introduction of a coaching and mentoring program for project managers. In this way a mission centric approach will help build appreciation of knowledge. It will also increase the understanding of the role of knowledge in the business and the flow of knowledge in the business process.

Organizations are complex webs of value chains and value networks, where it is usually neither fair nor fully possible to isolate a particular function or capability and compute its value. Each capability, function or even individual certainly provides value to the organization, but only because of the contributions of everything and everybody else. The value of expertise generally depends on how deep it is, how engaged it is and how critical it is to the organization. Applied, it would be associated with the value of new opportunities, the value of problem resolutions and the value of a superior performance

Figure 2. Knowledge architecture of the NPD organization

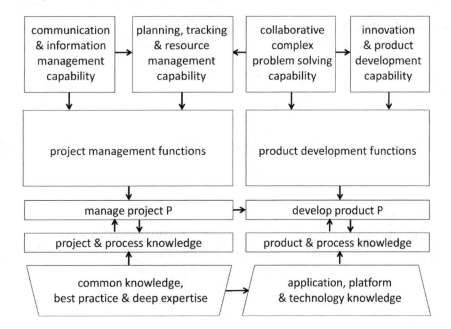

of professional tasks in various parts of the NPD process. Benefits will materialize through intermediary outcomes such as broader and deeper analysis, better sense making, or faster and better decision making. Expertise, if effectively leveraged, will result in smarter products, increased productivity and superior customer value.

SOLUTIONS AND RECOMMENDATIONS

Traditional management practices focus on the capacity to execute and deliver on commitments. Equally important, though often less visible, areas include strategy, business recipe, organizational competence and knowledge base as well as capacities for innovation, learning and change. Building such capacities, or intangible assets, is of prime importance in managing the R&D enterprise and to a large extent determines its performance and sustainability.

The R&D enterprise is a knowledge creating and opportunity rich environment. It needs to be managed with focus on strategy and innovation and with a commitment to deliver on mandates. Robust R&D also involves knowledge based decision-making and competence based performance through superior execution of key disciplines.

Companies should not only create career paths for experts. They should also make deliberate efforts to learn, use and retain expertise through the design of the NPD process and by social engineering. This could either align with a stage gate process or be organized separately. Beyond informal networks and ad-hoc activities, such designs could involve e.g. mandatory knowledge sharing, in-project learning, mentoring, patent activities and the inclusion of experts in formal networks and communities. Figure 3

Figure 3. Learning points in NPD projects

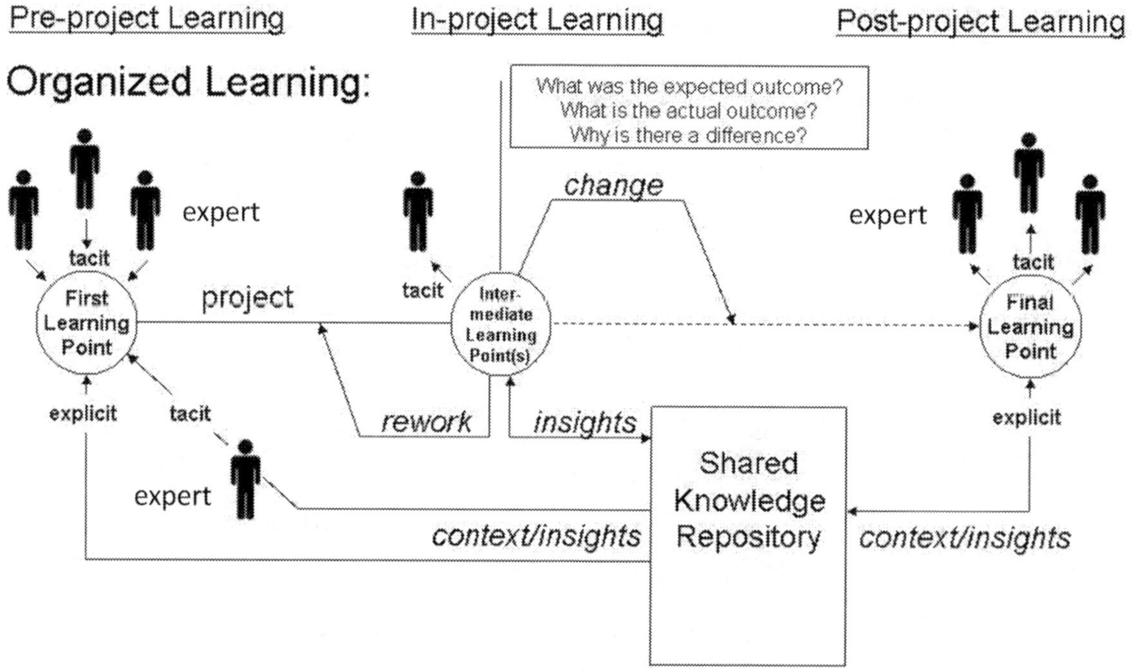

shows the possibility of introducing distinct learning points in NPD projects. Collecting lessons learned at the end of projects and saving those in a knowledge repository rarely benefits individuals other than those involved at the time of compiling the lessons. A first learning point at the beginning of a project would provide opportunities for experts to share insights in context and discuss how these apply to the new project.

There are many stages along the route to deep expertise involving novices, journeymen and master practitioners. To maintain competitive continuity, companies need to have a system for learning and growing expertise in critically important areas such as project management, product technologies, engineering methods and system testing. Trying to preserve and replicate expertise by simply asking experts to share what they know often falls short of expectations. Like tacit knowledge, expertise is difficult to articulate, codify and transfer. It can, however, be learned.

Learning expertise from experts would involve not only a transfer of knowledge but also an effort to understand the options experts see, the considerations they make and what they focus on in real problem situations. Effectively learning expertise relies on creating opportunities and circumstances for deliberate practice through *guided problem solving*, where knowledge can be shared in context and learners can compare their own attempts with how experts analyze situations, choose strategies and make judgment calls. Rather than trying to capture knowledge starting with the expert's point of view, to increase the learning practitioner's experience, learning needs to start from the learners' point of view. Learning expertise should thus begin with the current problems and challenges faced by the learning practitioner and let the expert guide the problem solving. Much like in musical master classes, experts teach their expertise by observing performance, giving feedback and demonstrating how it's done.

Also, to accommodate innovation and to make sufficient room for experts to engage, it is critically important that organizations learn to work with a certain amount of slack. This would call for extra room above and beyond current assignments for experts and others to engage in e.g. idea campaigns, internal think tanks and communities of practice.

Like other professionals, experts may work alone or in collaboration with others. In organizations that use social exchanges for knowledge sharing as part of their learning architecture, experts can connect in different ways with global, regional or local communities. Figure 4 shows a community based learning and collaboration architecture.

Building communities are ways for organizations to connect people and create environments for learning, creative thinking and sharing. From an organizational point of view, introducing communities is thus an example of using social engineering to increase connectivity and improve people's access to information and expertise. In R&D, communities would typically form around scientific topics, new technologies or engineering disciplines. It would be important that such communities include experts as members or at least have access to designated experts.

Expertise is often viewed mainly as proficiency in task execution or problem solving, but is also an important ingredient in successful ideation and idea management. Wanting more ideas must translate into having more ideas to evolve and evaluate. This involves a trade-off between ease of contribution (more ideas) and effort to evaluate (more time required by experts and managers). To stimulate creativity, ideation teams should include diversity in *experience, perspective, expertise* and *thinking styles*. Teams may e.g. include patent engineers (they have seen and reviewed many ideas) and competitive intelligence specialists (they maintain an external view).

Figure 4. Organizational learning and collaboration architecture

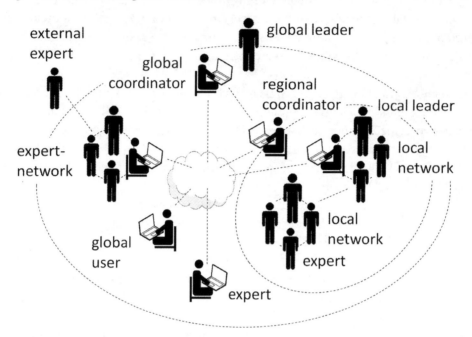

To be useful, expertise needs to be fully engaged. Experts need to be known and available. In large and geographically dispersed organizations, social technology can be used to find experts on specific topics and provide an environment for interactive dialogue. To promote the usage of such technologies, various social techniques could be employed, including the solicitation of contributions through personal invitations including e.g. a reference to a submitted idea. Both experts and managers may need to communicate the need for comments and reviews of ideas that they have submitted, as people may feel unsure about criticizing ideas submitted by experts and managers or ideas promoted by senior management.

It may be necessary to determine whether an ideation tool should be open and used for everything or be limited to new product ideas or perhaps be segmented into different idea applications (products, services, processes…). Most commercial idea management tools include the capability to facilitate idea campaigns, i.e. ways to organize and plan campaigns as well as capture and help evolve ideas emerging from campaigns. This would involve a process of migrating ideas from the initial repository to a managed idea portfolio by way of expert reviews or expert mediated collaborations.

The use of structured thinking guides based on e.g. mind mapping technology provides a way to assist with the comprehensive analysis of complex areas. Such tools could be used by experts and participants in master classes and workshops to help guide the thinking process and capture new ideas. Figure 5 shows an integrated tools environment where experts can engage in ideation, knowledge support and peer activities.

Even though technology is necessary and useful it does not appear that its specific design is a highly significant factor for success. User uptake is basically determined by human factors such as mindset, willingness to change ways of working, understanding the role of knowledge in the business and the flow of knowledge in the business process. These fundamental issues therefore need to be addressed before technology solutions are deployed. Technology must obviously be evaluated on its functional

Figure 5. Integrated tools environment

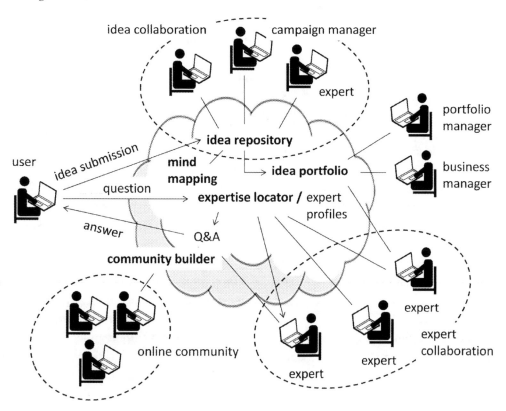

merits, but just as importantly on user acceptance. An integrated solution, a simple user interface and no steep learning curve combined with business relevance and content value are the most important user oriented characteristics to consider.

FUTURE RESEARCH DIRECTIONS

New product development requires a range of professional skills. The disciplines of project management and software engineering have been studied rather extensively (Gillard, 2009), (Graziotin, 2014). Other key NPD disciplines should be investigated to determine domain specific characteristics of expertise and what constitutes the most effective ways of learning and exploiting expertise. Comparing different disciplines as well as different industries would provide further information about the development of expertise by deliberate practice in new product development.

Experts are expected to develop their domain expertise through deliberate practice. As the use of expertise in organizations also requires social and communication skills, further studies should be made of the impact of social engineering on the learning and use of expertise in R&D organizations.

Research has been done on learning processes in networked environments, e.g. the use of networked reflection in the Norwegian electronics industry (Gausdal, 2008). The growing use of networking, co-development and open innovation concepts calls for further studies of how firms can capitalize on co-operative environments for the development of expertise in the R&D and NPD domains.

CONCLUSION

R&D organizations must show excellent performance on existing technology management responsibilities, focus on cost & efficiency and be creative and innovative to secure future competitiveness - all at the same time. In smart R&D organizations, effort must be made to build and leverage human capital and establish close relations between functions through open and effective communication, mutual understanding of the respective areas and agreements regarding the "rules of the game", e.g. how customer commitments are made, how risk is managed and how changes are made to product design and project content. In this broader R&D perspective, domain experts play multiple roles.

R&D is knowledge intensive and the discipline of Knowledge Management (KM) has been practised in research and development for quite some time. Although related, knowledge and expertise are not the same and smart R&D organizations find ways to also work effectively with deep domain expertise. Codification and sharing of knowledge does not provide an effective way of learning expertise. Special efforts are required to create conditions for deliberate practice of key disciplines in new product development.

To fully capitalize on the development of technology and management expertise, organizations should also develop their social engineering skills. Experts not only need to deepen and grow their expertise, but also need to build and maintain productive relationships with managers, practitioners and other experts.

Technology is useful, but solutions for managing knowledge and expertise need to be managed with a sufficient understanding of expertise and expert behaviour. A well integrated tools environment increases the probability of sufficient user uptake. With the help of sufficient slack, social engineering and appropriate knowledge technologies, organizations will be able to orchestrate a *productive interplay* between creativity, expertise and management – the most important organizational characteristic of well performing, innovative enterprises.

REFERENCES

Burke, C. S., Fiore, S. M., Goodwin, G. F., Rosen, M. A., & Salas, E. (2006). The making of a dream team: When expert teams do best. In K. A. Ericsson (Ed.), *The Cambridge Handbook of Expertise and Expert Performance* (pp. 439–453). New York, NY: Cambridge University Press.

Choo, M. (2014). *Exploring Knowing in Practice.* (Unpublished master's thesis). Linnaeus University, Kalmar, Sweden.

Cokely, E. T., Ericsson, K. A., & Prietula, M. J. (2007, July-August). The making of an expert. Boston. *Harvard Business Review*, 114–121.

Ericsson, K. A. (2006). The influence of experience and deliberate practice on the development of superior expert performance. In K. A. Ericsson (Ed.), *The Cambridge Handbook of Expertise and Expert Performance* (pp. 683–703). New York, NY: Cambridge University Press. doi:10.1017/CBO9780511816796.038

Gausdal, A.H. (2008, May). Developing regional communities of practice by network reflection: the case of the Norwegian electronics industry. *Entrepreneurship & Regional Development*, 209-235.

Gillard, S. (2009). Soft Skills and Technical Expertise of Effective Project Managers. *Issues in Informing Science and Information Technology*, 6, 723–729.

Graziotin, D. (2014). *Recent trends in agile processes and software engineering research - XP 2014 conference report*. Retrieved January 11, 2015 from https://thewinnower.com//papers/recent-trends-in-agile-processes-research-in-software-engineering-and-extreme-programming-xp-2014-conference-report

Leonard, D., & Swap, W. (2005). *Deep Smarts*. Boston, MA: Harvard Business School Press.

McDermott, R. (2012). *Getting the most from your mentor*. Retrieved on December 15, 2012 from http://www.nasa.gov/pdf/703218main_48i_mentor.pdf

Miranda, E. (2003). *Running the successful hi-tech project office*. Boston, MA: Artech House.

Niessen, C., Sonnentag, S., & Volmer, J. (2006). Expertise in software design. In K. A. Ericsson (Ed.), *The Cambridge Handbook of Expertise and Expert Performance* (pp. 373–387). New York, NY: Cambridge University Press.

O'Dell, C., & Trees, L. (2014). *How Smart Leaders Leverage Their Experts*. Retrieved on December 19, 2014 from http://www.apqc.org/knowledge-base/download/309016/K04979_How_Smart_Leaders_Leverage_Their_Experts.pdf

KEY TERMS AND DEFINITIONS

Deliberate Practice: A practice involving self-regulated learning and improvement.

Expertise: The ability of a person to demonstrate superior performance in a professional domain or discipline.

Knowledge: The internal representation of truth as justified true belief.

New Product Development: The core business process of an organization to create products, which are new to the business or new to the market.

Organizational Learning: The deliberate effort by an organization to acquire knowledge as a way to change behaviour or improve performance.

Product: A designed, useful application of technology.

Technology: The application of scientific and technical knowledge in the creation of products, processes or services.

Chapter 15
Creating Product Innovation Strategies through Knowledge Management in Global Business

Kijpokin Kasemsap
Suan Sunandha Rajabhat University, Thailand

ABSTRACT

This chapter aims to create product innovation strategies through knowledge management (KM) in global business, thus explaining the theoretical and practical concepts of product innovation strategy and KM; the significance of product innovation strategies and KM in global business; and the creation of product innovation strategies through KM in global business. The capability of product innovation strategies and KM is significant for modern organizations that seek to serve suppliers and customers, increase business performance, strengthen competitiveness, and attain regular success in global business. Modern organizations should establish a strategic plan to create product innovation strategies through KM. The chapter argues that creating product innovation strategies through KM has the potential to improve organizational performance and achieve strategic goals in global business.

INTRODUCTION

Product innovation is important to the growth, success, and survival of firms (Deng, Hofman, & Newman, 2013). Product innovation is a key to organizational renewal and success (Slater, Mohr, & Sengupta, 2014). The challenges of successfully developing new products have received considerable attention from a variety of marketing, strategic, and organizational perspectives (Bohlmann, Spanjol, Qualls, & Rosa, 2013). Supply chain partner innovativeness enhances a firm's innovation strategy which positively influences innovation performance (Oke, Prajogo, & Jayaram, 2013). To develop successful new products, new product development (NPD) managers need to have a thorough understanding of the consumer adoption process, specifically in how consumers evaluate the new products (Mugge & Dahl, 2013).

NPD is a knowledge-intensive activity which involves the active inward and outward technology transfer (Frishammar, Lichtenthaler, & Rundquist, 2012). The development of new products requires

DOI: 10.4018/978-1-4666-9607-5.ch015

organizational resource sufficiency for the process to be systematically conducted (Cunha, Rego, Oliveira, Rosado, & Habib, 2014). While an organization can choose to develop an innovation internally or externally, the internal knowledge development and external knowledge acquisition tend to interact with each other in the innovation process (Xu, Wu, & Cavusgil, 2013). Innovation has positive performance implications (Stock & Zacharias, 2013). Inventive collaborations with users enhance corporate product innovation and that the benefits are greatest in new technology areas and in the generation of radical innovations (Chatterji & Fabrizio, 2014).

Although product innovation is a key tool for firms competing in the marketplace, innovating firms often fail to obtain economic returns from their product innovations (Su, Xie, Liu, & Sun, 2013). Organizational knowledge creation, as reflected in NPD, is a vital process for firms to gain competitive advantage (Akbar & Tzokas, 2013). Knowledge and innovation play a certain role in regional economic growth (Šipikal & Buček, 2013). Innovative product development is highly dependent on new product ideas and product information (Neumann, Riel, & Brissaud, 2013). Understanding the conditions under which organizational groups operate is basic for successfully managing innovation (Koch, 2012).

The strength of this chapter is on the thorough literature consolidation of product innovation strategies and KM. The extant literatures of product innovation strategies and KM provide a contribution to practitioners and researchers by describing a comprehensive view of the functional applications of product innovation strategies and KM to appeal to the different segments of product innovation strategy and KM in order to maximize the business impact of product innovation strategies and KM in global business.

BACKGROUND

Both theoretical and conceptual understanding of innovation has developed significantly since the early 1980s (Hong, Oxley, & McCann, 2012). Localization of knowledge flows has been extensively examined in the literature on innovation (Fabrizio & Thomas, 2012). From a customer's perspective, a more innovative product tends to have uncertain benefits and requires customers to learn new behaviors (Bohlmann et al., 2013). Attempting to move away from the commodity-based products into the higher value-added products remains one of the key challenges for research and development (R&D) managers (Simms & Trott, 2014). To minimize the risk associated with innovation, most scholars agree that firms should engage simultaneously in two types of activities (i.e., exploring new alternatives and exploiting existing competencies) (Dahlin, 2014).

The information and communications technology sector embodies the wide-ranging opportunities for innovation-driven value creation and structural upgrading among the interdependent industries and economies (Wattanapruttipaisan, 2014). Established firms will gain valuable innovative insights by working with user innovators (Smith & Shah, 2013). Many manufacturing firms have initiated their product innovation processes toward transferring knowledge with external partners in the markets for technology (Lichtenthaler, 2013). Firms in the future must be excellent in developing commodities or innovative functional products (Storm, Lager, & Samuelsson, 2013). Consumer acceptance of new products is the key to new product success and requires the effective implementation of market launch activities (Kuester, Homburg, & Hess, 2012).

CREATING PRODUCT INNOVATION STRATEGIES THROUGH KNOWLEDGE MANAGEMENT IN GLOBAL BUSINESS

This section explains the theoretical and practical concepts of product innovation strategy and KM; the significance of product innovation strategies and KM in global business; and the creation of product innovation strategies through KM in global business.

Concept of Product Innovation Strategy

Innovation is the outcome of successful strategies, investment, and relationships which companies actively seek and develop in the marketplace (Conte & Vivarelli, 2014). Innovation can be divided into technological innovations in the form of new products and services and non-technological innovations in the form of marketing changes (Mohnen & Hall, 2013). Innovation is defined through product and process development (Halilem, Amara, & Landry, 2014). Innovation is central to the survival and growth of firms (Ganotakis & Love, 2012). Many innovation studies have focused on a narrow concept of technological innovation such as the generation of patents and the introduction of new products (Tödtling & Grillitsch, 2014).

Globalization drives firms to develop product innovation through their global supply chains (Jean, Sinkovics, & Hiebaum, 2014). Patel et al. (2014) explained that being able to internationally launch new products is critical for technology-based ventures to recoup the high costs of R&D and to fully exploit their innovations. Formal technological innovation fully mediates the relation between prior knowledge and the introduction of viable new products and services (Tang & Murphy, 2012). Jaspers et al. (2012) suggested that technologies from different industries are increasingly combined to create new products and services.

It is very important to understand the interaction and the critical points during dynamic phases of innovation processes (Mäkimattila, Melkas, & Uotila, 2013). Implementation of best practices such as predevelopment market planning and cross-functional teams have been positively correlated with product and project success over a variety of measures (Marion, Friar, & Simpson, 2012). Material resources are recognized as the key driver in innovation project performance (Weiss, Hoegl, & Gibbert, 2013). The effects of innovation-oriented values and norms on product program innovativeness are fully mediated by cultural artifacts (Stock, Six, & Zacharias, 2013). The offshoring firms on average employ a higher share of R&D and design personnel, introduce new products more frequently to the market, and invest more frequently in advanced process technologies compared to non-offshoring firms (Dachs, Ebersberger, Kinkel, & Som, 2015).

Product innovation is a key factor for successful market entry (Becker & Egger, 2013). Jepsen et al. (2014) indicated that an ever-increasing standard of living is pushing firms to develop products and services that are profitable and socially responsible. Pullen et al. (2012) stated that the small and medium-sized enterprises (SMEs) must innovate for organizational survival with the appropriate degree of product innovation, focusing on core competences for efficiency matters. Innovation performance is higher in SMEs that are proactive in strengthening their relationships with innovative suppliers, users, and customers (Lasagni, 2012). Product innovation moderates the mediating effect of knowledge integration mechanisms on product innovation performance (Tsai, Hsu, & Fang, 2012).

Key employees can play an important role in the development and diffusion of new products, processes, and technologies (Rese, Gemünden, & Baier, 2013). Yang et al. (2012) indicated that innovation is an organization's spanning process that must continually change in response to, and in anticipation of, changing business environments. Innovation is one of the key drivers of success that a firm must utilize to develop a competitive advantage (Moon, Miller, & Kim, 2013). Internal innovation efforts and cooperation with local suppliers positively affect the creation of new products (Belso-Martinez & Molina-Morales, 2013). In order to increase their innovation capability, many organizations make the effort to actively change their R&D working practices (Nilsson & Ritzén, 2014).

Castaño-Martínez (2012) analyzed the determinants of product innovation (e.g., human capital, technology, the degree of market competition, and economic performance) in the case of entrepreneurs from the transformation industries, using a model estimated via the partial least square method, to establish whether these determinants change according to whether they are found in developed or developing countries. The positive impact of product design is influenced by brand strength (Landwehr, Wentzel, & Herrmann, 2012). Integrating suppliers into NPD projects offers manufacturers the potential for substantial improvements in the new product being designed (Salvador & Villena, 2013). Established literature on NPD management recognizes top management involvement (TMI) as one of the most critical success factors (Felekoglu & Moultrie, 2014). Interorganizational NPD teams with business customers are rapidly becoming more prevalent (Stock, 2014).

Preventing the imitation of products and their underlying characteristics is a key source of competitive advantage (Lawson, Samson, & Roden, 2012). Hollen et al. (2013) stated that technological process innovation to improve resource productivity and environmental performance has become of pivotal importance. The different technological innovation capabilities have a positive impact on product innovation, beginning with the linkage capability, and then moving to the production capability, and ending with the investment capability (Shan & Jolly, 2013). Contextual ambidexterity is of paramount importance for new product innovation and organizational success, particularly in high-tech firms operating in a dynamic environment (Wang & Rafiq, 2014). Contextual ambidexterity is grounded in organizational culture; and existing research has not crystallized what kind of organizational culture enables contextual ambidexterity and consequently new product innovation (Wang & Rafiq, 2014). Resource flexibility and coordination flexibility have positive moderating effects on the relationship between ambidexterity and NPD performance (Wei, Yi, & Guo, 2014).

Concept of Knowledge Management

Knowledge management (KM) is rapidly disseminated in both academic circles and the business world (Park, Jang, Lee, Ahn, & Yoon, 2013). Knowledge is the most important asset for an organization to create value and sustainable competitive advantage (Chen, 2012). KM becomes a key organizational capability for creating competitive advantage (Kale & Karaman, 2012). KM should be coherent and based on the firm's strategy (Bagnoli & Vedovato, 2014). Effective KM frequently leads to creative value-added innovations and consequently raises competitiveness of its products and services (Kim, 2014).

Globalization has resulted in the use of knowledge as competitive weapon in modern organizations (Chu, Kumar, Kumar, & Khosla, 2014). With the advances in information technology and its increasing impact on humans and society, there has been an expanding need to spread knowledge from domain to domain (Hvannberg, 2015). Effective KM should be coherent and based on organizational strategy

(Bagnoli & Vedovato, 2014). While KM-related business strategy is important, the knowledge-sharing behavior of knowledge workers is a critical enabler of effective KM and organizational performance (Chu et al., 2014).

Kasemsap (2014a) explained that KM, strategic orientation, and organizational innovation have a positive impact on organizational performance. Organizational learning is systematically correlated with KM in global business (Kasemsap, 2014b). KM is primarily concerned with the accumulation, sharing, utilization, internalization, and use of knowledge assets throughout the organization (Kasemsap, 2015a). Project-based organizations should develop and maintain a positive working culture in utilizing KM to reach project objectives and goals (Kasemsap, 2015b). Using data mining methods for business intelligence makes it easier for the users to promote its overall contribution to the KM process (Kasemsap, 2015c).

Managing knowledge constitutes one of the major strategic advantages of an organization (Lunnan & Zhao, 2014). One of the most important aspects of KM is to create a system that is capable of providing mechanisms and methodologies allowing the right knowledge to be at the right place and at the right person as well as at the right time within an enterprise (Oztemel & Arslankaya, 2012). Organizations serve as the knowledge repositories (Holcombe, 2013). Executives and managers inform their decision making with the streams of information, which they manage and generate to build organizational knowledge and value for practice effectiveness (Stipp & Kapp, 2012).

The success of knowledge processes often relates to organizational cultural characteristics (Mueller, 2015). The reuse of knowledge and information arising from the different phases of a product's lifecycle is crucial for a company in order to achieve competitive advantage (Ahmed-Kristensen & Vianello, 2015). To leverage their knowledge resources, many organizations deploy KM systems, which contain at their core a knowledge repository (Ravindran & Iyer, 2014). The integration of business process management and KM helps companies to improve temporal, qualitative and cost aspects of the provision of goods and services and to increase their innovative capacities (Schmid & Kern, 2014). Practices of knowledge sharing relate to communication, observation, artifacts, and human resource practices (Mueller, 2015).

Recent KM research focuses on promoting the knowledge sharing and reusing among the people (Liu & Wang, 2015). Supporting inter-team knowledge sharing is fundamental in scaling agility across the entire organization, and is regarded as the new horizon for agile software development (Santos, Goldman, & de Souza, 2015). The analytic hierarchy process (AHP) can be a useful guide in the decision-making process of KM implementation (Anand, Kant, Patel, & Singh, 2015). Introducing knowledge sharing to an organization must address blockages in the learning flows caused by fragmentation within the community of action research (Massingham, 2015). The main value of knowledge is its usefulness in solving problems (Gillberg & Vo, 2014).

KM encompasses not only the related notions of knowledge transfer and knowledge sharing, but also the entire knowledge acquisition and utilization process, beginning with locating and capturing knowledge (Choo & Bontis, 2002; Takeuchi & Nonaka, 2004). The evaluation of KM has become increasingly significant (Liu & Abdalla, 2013). Park et al. (2013) indicated that managing knowledge is effectively critical to the competitive power of an organization. KM has attracted an increasing number of researchers since the concept was born (Li, Guo, Zhi, Han, & Liu, 2013). Knowledge, organizational innovation and entrepreneurship are regarded as new driving forces for economic growth (Feldmann & Audretsch, 1999). In order to sustain competitive advantage in the global economy, organizations must shift their focus to knowledge-based economic activities (Audretsch & Thurik, 2000).

KM is utilized by a large number of research disciplines (Ackerman, Dachtera, Pipek, & Wulf, 2013). Knowledge is bound to individual or collective actions (Ozel, 2012). KM processes are the activities or initiatives an organization puts in place to enable and facilitate the creation, sharing and use of knowledge for organizational benefit (Chen, 2012). Knowledge-based approaches to the organization offer the valuable insights into some of the central issues of governance and organizational design (Grant, 2013). The three key factors affecting the conduct of business include human, knowledge, and the environment (Intezari & Pauleen, 2014). Knowledge infrastructure and process capabilities are highly correlated (Cho & Korte, 2014). Knowledge culture is recognized as a favorable antecedent of KM (Mueller, 2012).

Knowledge is viewed as a sustainable basis of competitive advantage that many organizations possess (Kim, Song, Sambamurthy, & Lee, 2012). Knowledge is the preeminent resource of firms that wish to remain globally competitive (Kedia, Gaffney, & Clampit, 2012). Noruzy et al. (2013) stated that organizational learning positively affects KM in the manufacturing firms. There is an increasing need for usable tools to support knowledge elicitation, knowledge formalization, and KM (Catenazzi & Sommaruga, 2013). Knowledge must be integrated throughout organization to facilitate the strategic renewal process (Lionzo & Rossignoli, 2013).

Internal knowledge exchange acts as a crucial predictor of management innovation (Černe, Jaklič, & Škerlavaj, 2013). Tsai et al. (2013) indicated that knowledge sharing is the behavior of disseminating acquired knowledge to other members of an organization. Knowledge sharing in academia has become a rising concern (Ramayah, Yeap, & Ignatius, 2013). Collaboration and education are the major concepts of knowledge sharing (Meese & McMahon, 2012). Angelstam et al. (2013) stated that the collaboration, communication, and dissemination of knowledge are the meaningful management features.

An increasing number of organizations are focusing on communities of practice (CoPs) orientated KM studies and the links between KM and organizational business strategy (Chu et al., 2014). CoPs are accepted as the best educational practice and distinct from organizational structures while implementing KM (Chu, Khosla, & Nishida, 2012). McKellar et al. (2014) defined CoPs as the major parts of health care, education, and business. CoPs aim to bring various professionals into a working relationship around their common interests (Harris, 2014). Participation in knowledge-building communities is organized through learning the moves of such games (Bielaczyc & Ow, 2014). CoPs in KM are the formalized processes coupled with technological artifacts to build the groups of people who effectively share knowledge across boundaries (Su, Wilensky, & Redmiles, 2012).

Knowledge is gained through the tacit learning and explicit learning of the specific individuals (Carson & Gilmore, 2001; Wong & Radcliffe, 2000). Knowledge can be transferred by organizational individuals through the acquisition of a new worker who brings in knowledge and experience into the organization and the exchange of information between the existing employees and external contacts. Exploiting external source of knowledge is a key practice concerning their resource constraints (Desouze & Awazu, 2006). Desouze and Awazu (2006) stated that socialization is a dominant factor in the KM cycle.

Manufacturing companies need the internal capabilities for managing technology transfer (Lichtenthaler, 2013). Organizations of different kinds, from structured companies up to social networks or virtual communities, are becoming increasingly aware of the need to collect, organize, mobilize, and increase the expertise and knowledge which characterize their ability to stay alive, adapt, and evolve in a turbulent context (Simone, Ackerman, & Wulf, 2012). The integration of business process management (BPM) and KM helps organizations improve the temporal, qualitative, and cost aspects of the provision of goods and services and to increase their innovative capacities (Schmid & Kern, 2014). Organizations need to put more tangible effort to improve their organizational knowledge implementation level such as establishing systematic measurement system and assigning more resources including people, time, and money (Kim, 2014). The structure of knowledge system is a crucial component to make knowledge system effective and acceptable to organizational users (Turchetti & Geisler, 2013). Zhang et al. (2012) stated that human resources and knowledge are the valuable assets for enterprises.

Organizational KM systems should support the informal knowledge seeking activities and collaboration among the knowledge sharers (Spence & Reddy, 2012). Swarnkar et al. (2012) suggested that knowledge sharing is a major challenge for collaborative networks and is essential to improve the productivity and quality of decisions taken by both collaborative networks and their member organizations. KM strategy and intellectual capital effectively enhance firm performance (Ling, 2013). Certain studies have found a significant link between KM and firm performance (Chuang, Liao, & Lin, 2013). There is a critical need to design learning environments that foster the creative thinking in students, particularly in the area of collaborative creativity (West, 2014). It is crucial to negotiate a legitimate knowledge system which should include both expert and local knowledge (Giordano, Preziosi, & Romano, 2013).

Modern agricultural business will profit in many aspects from information sharing and knowledge exchange, involving the public-private collaboration (Bernardi, 2013). Tengo et al. (2014) stated that the indigenous and local knowledge systems can provide the useful knowledge to enhance the understanding of governance of biodiversity and ecosystems for human well-being. Organizational learning and employees' competence are better managed through projects (Breunig & Hydle, 2013). Organizations specializing in project management may manage a project for the benefits of the third party, using the client's technical knowledge and the principles of work (Stoshikj, Kryvinska, & Strauss, 2014). The applications of individual learning and computer-supported knowledge building are important in global education (Zhao & Chan, 2014). Sung et al. (2012) stated that there is a need to investigate the alternative paradigms for knowledge and information acquirement.

Leaders of economies, industries, and organizations are interested in finding new and better ways to create and apply knowledge. The strategies, methods, and tools of KM will change, but the timeless principles will remain unchanged toward improving organizational performance in a growing knowledge economy. Individuals who wish to successfully participate in the rapidly growing global knowledge economy must consider the development of their personal KM competencies as an essential life skill for the twenty-first century. Those individuals and organizations that can best sense, become quickly alerted to, find, organize, and apply knowledge, with a much faster response time, will simply leave the competition far behind.

Global KM is becoming a reality. The growing knowledge economy becomes the most successful and sustainable economy in the world. Effective KM, at all levels, for the individual, team, organization, and global community will naturally become mainstream and ordinary, as the only way to successfully develop and grow for the future. All of KM goals can be achieved through the good knowledge leadership that understands the unchanging principles for knowledge toward transforming individuals and organizations to become more responsive in the growing knowledge economy.

Significance of Product Innovation Strategies and Knowledge Management in Global Business

As development cycles continue to shorten, competition in the industry intensifies, and a new insight is needed to better understand how increased competition can affect the gains from innovations (Talay, Calantone, & Voorhees, 2014). Large organizations typically focus on enhancing their ability to manage their core businesses, with an emphasis on cost reduction, quality improvements, and incremental innovation in the existing products and processes (O'Connor & Rice, 2013). A firm's ability to manage team dynamics toward generating creative new products and marketing programs constitutes a dynamic capability that can provide a competitive advantage over the competition (Im, Montoya, & Workman, 2013).

The topic of innovation has received a great attention in the economic literature (Murro, 2013). Innovation is one of the most important issues facing business today (Kang & Montoya, 2014). Madrid-Guijarro et al. (2013) stated that innovation is positively associated with organizational performance during the economic expansion and recession years. It is essential for organizations to align the internal research and development strategies with knowledge available in the supply network in order to gain superior innovation performance (Narasimhan & Narayanan, 2013). External sourcing has direct effects on both product innovation and process innovation, with an indirect effect on sales growth (Uhlaner, van Stel, Duplat, & Zhou, 2013).

Innovation performance mediates the interaction of innovation strategy execution and environmental uncertainty on firms' revenue growth. The decision makers' experiences influence innovation decisions toward recognizing the role of passion in the product innovation context (Klaukien, Shepherd, & Patzelt, 2013). Formal R&D management in knowledge-intensive business services is positively related to dynamics in strategic decision making in terms of market positioning and to innovation success (Teirlinck & Spithoven, 2013). The in-house R&D, technology transfer, technology spillover, and the back-propagation of user innovations are the effective sources of technological product and process (TPP) innovation (Liang & Zhang, 2012).

The specificities of the organization of small businesses recognize their strengths and weaknesses in their efforts at innovation (Martínez-Román & Romero, 2013). Small firms rely mainly on the CEO's individual knowledge for developing innovations (Andries & Czarnitzki, 2014). Füller et al. (2012) indicated that the virtual customer integration and the open innovation are considered as the appropriate method to improve the success of NPD. Various innovation measurement mechanisms are used in different departments in the R&D organization, reflecting the diverse views of what constitutes innovation that dominate in each group, as well as the group's level of involvement in the on-going building of innovation capability (Nilsson & Ritzén, 2014). NPD speed improves successful outcomes (Cankurtaran, Langerak, & Griffin, 2013).

Product innovation has a mediating effect on the relationship between different technological innovation capabilities and organizational performance (Shan & Jolly, 2013). Process innovation shows a positive effect on employment, especially for SMEs, while the effect of product innovation is not significant (Triguero, Córcoles, & Cuerva, 2014). The integration of environmental sustainability issues into NPD programs in terms of product design leads to the creation of new opportunities for firms, such as the development of new markets, technologies, and product perspectives (Dangelico, Pontrandolfo, & Pujari, 2013). Firms should be functionally involved in NPD when they introduce a new core product, and even more so if the complementary products are new (van den Ende, Jaspers, & Rijsdijk, 2013).

It is increasingly common to source knowledge for new product ideas from a wide range of actors located outside of organizational boundaries (Salge, Farchi, Barrett, & Dopson, 2013). The full benefits of knowledge exchange realize only when the organization's knowledge protection mechanisms are sufficiently strong, allowing for the safe knowledge exchange between rivals (Ritala & Hurmelinna-Laukkanen, 2013). Customer co-creation during the innovation process is considered as a major source for the organization's competitive advantage (Mahr, Lievens, & Blazevic, 2014). Rass et al. (2013) explained that the implementation of open innovation instruments strengthens an organization's social capital toward increasing organizational performance.

Strategic flexibility provides firms with an ability to create new market opportunities, product, and technological arenas, and to deliver successful new products in modern business (Kandemir & Acur, 2012). Stanko et al. (2012) suggested that the relationships among speed to market, quality, and costs are important to executives and managers as they attempt to set organizational goals for NPD teams, to allocate resources for NPD, and to create positional advantage in the global marketplace. Strategic planning and innovativeness appear to positively affect technological, market, and NPD-marketing alignment (Acur, Kandemir, & Boer, 2012).

Most companies are focused on producing a product or service for customers. However, one of the most significant keys to value creation comes from placing emphasis on producing knowledge. The production of knowledge needs to be a major part of overall product innovation strategies. One of the biggest challenges behind KM is the dissemination of knowledge. People with the highest knowledge have the potential for the high levels of value creation. Modern organizations need to build a new culture that promotes knowledge sharing and constant learning while preserving and recording appropriate information. This is essential in order for corporate knowledge to be effectively retained and enhanced. KM is about managing relationships within the organization. Collaborative tools (e.g., intranets, balanced scorecards, data warehouses, customer relationship management, and expert systems) are used to establish these relationships toward creating product innovation strategies.

Creation of Product Innovation Strategies through Knowledge Management in Global Business

Although a vast stream of research has studied how strategic and tactical launch decisions affect the performance of new products and services, some issues still need the theoretical and empirical investigation (Frattini, Dell'Era, & Rangone, 2013). As different types of knowledge may have different effects on new product positional advantage, knowledge portfolio management in concert with the firm's strategic orientation is required for new product success (Kim, Im, & Slater, 2013). A firm's ability to keep up with the competition in the innovation perspective is a significant driver of survival in the global marketplace (Talay et al., 2014). Product innovation research should more explicitly differentiate between firms of different sizes, rather than prescribing large firm best practices to small firms (Berends, Jelinek, Reymen, & Stultiëns, 2014).

Launching new products with novel characteristics enables firms to temporarily steal market share from rivals (Greenhalgh & Rogers, 2012). Firms need to handle both a larger number of sources for innovation and more different types of innovations (Björk, 2012). New product novelty and meaningfulness are recognized to enhance new product advantage in terms of product differentiation and customer satisfaction, both of which contribute to new product performance (Kim et al., 2013). Creative ideas provide the seed for successful service innovations (Schuhmacher & Kuester, 2012). Regarding product innovation, nanotechnologies are able to fulfill the different needs of food companies, especially with respect to improving food safety and sensory features (Nardone, Seccia, & Maruotti, 2013).

A focus on technology boosts innovation in manufacturing firms (Spanjol, Mühlmeier, & Tomczak, 2012). The new technology-based firms need to find an optimal balance between exploration and exploitation in their innovation activities (Saemundsson & Candi, 2014). The stimulation of creativity enhances innovation (Çokpekin & Knudsen, 2012). The generation of creative ideas and their manifestation as new products are the fundamental innovation activities of product-innovation teams (Im et al., 2013). Considering that product development is a fundamental activity in a market economy (Viswanathan & Sridharan, 2012). Executives and managers are encouraged to integrate the domain-specific knowledge and general knowledge from NPD to reap additional benefits in profiting from investments in innovation and technology (Frishammar et al., 2012).

Information implementation and speed to market practically mediate the relationship between team sense-making capability and new product success (Akgün, Keskin, Lynn, & Dogan, 2012). Critical to the development of new products is the management of the front-end phase, which crucially determines the eventual fate of a new product idea (Akbar & Tzokas, 2013). The culture emerges as an important moderating factor toward weakening effect sizes for individualistic countries, strengthening effects for risk-averse countries, and highlighting the importance of investigating the culture's role in product innovation studies (Evanschitzky, Eisend, Calantone, & Jiang, 2012).

Firms should generate more new products for long-term success in global business (Durmuşoğlu, Calantone, & McNally, 2013). Satisfying customer demands is a distinct challenge for product designers because firms must develop a clear understanding of what aspects of design the customer wants (Moon et al., 2013). Knowledge sharing mediates the relationship between green requirements and new green product success as well as that between green requirements and green product and process innovations (Wong, 2013). SMEs will have better NPD results if they improve their relationships with laboratories and research institutes (Lasagni, 2012). Customer integration during innovation development can enhance organizations' innovation performance (da Mota Pedrosa, 2012).

When firms open new market, technological, and product arenas, they can easily foresee their new demands and changes and successfully deliver new products, meeting customer demands, and offering benefits such as quality, cost, and timeliness (Kandemir & Acur, 2012). Over the course of an NPD process, managers learn about a new product project as to ensure successful launch (Jespersen, 2012). Customer co-created knowledge is described into its key value dimensions of relevance, novelty, and costs (Mahr et al., 2014). Buyer–supplier communication, suppliers' anticipated long-term returns, suppliers' trust of a buyer, and supplier–buyer interdependence play a significant role in changing supplier attitudes toward co-innovation and supplier involvement in a buyer's NPD (Yeniyurt, Henke, & Yalcinkaya, 2014).

Regarding a dynamic oligopoly model, the increasing portion of the inverted U-shaped relationship reflects the changes in the firm's investment policy functions, whereas the decreasing portion arises from the industry transiting to states with fewer firms and wider quality gaps (Goettler & Gordon, 2014). The inverted U-shaped relationship is found between the institutional diversity of a firm's foreign markets and its product innovation success (Wu, 2013). Liu et al. (2014) empirically explored the 308 high-technology Chinese firms and suggested that unabsorbed slack is more strongly positively related with product innovation than is absorbed slack in the high-technology settings. Knowledge exchange results in management innovation through the developed information technology systems that enable information and knowledge to flow within an organization (Černe et al., 2013). Application development, as an institutionalized function in the process industries, focuses on bridging the gap between a product supplier's knowledge of the product's performance scope and the customer's knowledge of its own production process requirements (Lager & Storm, 2013).

Chai et al. (2012) explained that the formalized development process, knowledge sharing across platform-based products, the continuity of platform-based product development teams, and the existence of a champion in platform-based product development enhance the product platform competency. Firms should actively manage the flow of ideas from the front-end innovation activities into the more formal development programs in global business (Markham, 2013). Firms that combine the internally developed technology with a new brand achieve the greater market acceptance for their product innovation during emergent stages (Patel & Haon, 2014). Formal R&D management in small firms in knowledge-intensive business services can be related to more complex linkages between internal innovation strengths and opportunities in the firm's external environment (Teirlinck & Spithoven, 2013).

Firms should prepare for diversification by gaining power in the domestic market and more importantly that they do so by adopting specific innovation and learning efforts (Cirera, Marin, & Markwald, 2012). Accessing the knowledge contained in user-generated innovations enriches the product development outcomes of established firms (Smith & Shah, 2013). Minimizing the risks associated with innovation is most likely to occur when firms follow the path of innovation that generates novel solutions that simultaneously exploit knowledge and resources available to the firms (Dahlin, 2014).

In the growing knowledge economy, the key purpose of KM for creating product innovation strategies is to enhance knowledge processing. Modern organizations will have recognized this purpose when they indicate problems that need solving as they occur; they have effective information location and retrieval channels to enhance individual decision making; they embrace effective knowledge creation processes; and they ensure that created knowledge is shared with and integrated across the whole of the organization. Methods that can help organizations achieve effective KM goals include making better use of collaboration and communication tools; creating and promoting internal COPs; and fostering the identity of virtual teams.

FUTURE RESEARCH DIRECTIONS

The strength of this chapter is on the thorough literature consolidation of product innovation strategies and KM. The extant literatures of product innovation strategies and KM provide a contribution to practitioners and researchers by describing a comprehensive view of the functional applications of product innovation strategies and KM to appeal to the different segments of product innovation strategy and KM in order to maximize the business impact of product innovation strategies and KM in global business. The classification of the extant literature in the domains of product innovation strategies and KM will provide the potential opportunities for future research. Future research direction should broaden the perspectives in the implementation of product innovation strategies and KM to be utilized in the knowledge-based organizations.

Practitioners and researchers should acknowledge the applicability of a more multidisciplinary approach toward research activities in creating product innovation strategies and KM in terms of KM-related variables (e.g., knowledge-sharing behavior, knowledge creation, organizational learning, learning orientation, and motivation to learn). It will be useful to bring additional disciplines together (e.g., strategic management, marketing, finance, and human resources) to support a more holistic examination of product innovation strategies and KM in order to combine or transfer existing theories and approaches to inquiry in this area.

CONCLUSION

This chapter aimed to create product innovation strategies through KM in global business, thus explaining the theoretical and practical concepts of product innovation strategy and KM; the significance of product innovation strategies and KM in global business; and the creation of product innovation strategies through KM in global business. KM is applied across the world in all industries and sectors. Effective KM is the key driver of new knowledge and new ideas to the innovation process, innovative products, services, and solutions. The purpose of KM must not be to just become more knowledgeable, but to be able to create, transfer and apply knowledge with the purpose of better achieving objectives.

More individuals, teams, organizations, and interorganizational networks will be restructuring and renewing themselves with the primary purpose of profitably trading their knowledge to add even higher value, predominantly on the World Wide Web toward creating product innovation in global business. Every organization needs to invest in creating and implementing the best knowledge networks, processes, methods, tools, and technologies. This will enable them to learn, create new knowledge, and apply the best knowledge much faster. Organizations should promote a culture of product innovation and KM regarding the utilization of open communication, shared support, and collaboration. Product innovation strategies and KM efficiently support each other and together to achieve planned goals. Organizations should consider product innovation strategies and KM as the major assets and organizational resources for producing the high-technology goods and services in order to gain sustainable competitive advantage in modern organizations.

The capability of product innovation strategies and KM is significant for modern organizations that seek to serve suppliers and customers, increase business performance, strengthen competitiveness, and attain regular success in global business. Thus, it is fundamental for modern organizations to investigate their product innovation strategies and KM applications, develop a strategic plan to constantly analyze their practicable advancements, and directly respond to product innovation strategies and KM needs of customers. Creating product innovation strategies through KM has the potential to enhance organizational performance and reach sustainable competitive advantage in the digital age.

REFERENCES

Ackerman, M. S., Dachtera, J., Pipek, V., & Wulf, V. (2013). Sharing knowledge and expertise: The CSCW view of knowledge management. *Computer Supported Cooperative Work*, *22*(4/6), 531–573. doi:10.1007/s10606-013-9192-8

Acur, N., Kandemir, D., & Boer, H. (2012). Strategic alignment and new product development: Drivers and performance effects. *Journal of Product Innovation Management*, *29*(2), 304–318. doi:10.1111/j.1540-5885.2011.00897.x

Ahmed-Kristensen, S., & Vianello, G. (2015). A model for reusing service knowledge based on an empirical case. *Research in Engineering Design*, *26*(1), 57–76. doi:10.1007/s00163-014-0184-6

Akbar, H., & Tzokas, N. (2013). An exploration of new product development's front-end knowledge conceptualization process in discontinuous innovations. *British Journal of Management*, *24*(2), 245–263. doi:10.1111/j.1467-8551.2011.00801.x

Akgün, A. E., Keskin, H., Lynn, G., & Dogan, D. (2012). Antecedents and consequences of team sensemaking capability in product development projects. *R&D Management*, *42*(5), 473–493. doi:10.1111/j.1467-9310.2012.00696.x

Anand, A., Kant, R., Patel, D. P., & Singh, M. D. (2015). Knowledge management implementation: A predictive model using an analytical hierarchical process. *Journal of the Knowledge Economy*, *6*(1), 48–71. doi:10.1007/s13132-012-0110-y

Andries, P., & Czarnitzki, D. (2014). Small firm innovation performance and employee involvement. *Small Business Economics*, *43*(1), 21–38. doi:10.1007/s11187-014-9577-1

Angelstam, P., Elbakidze, M., Axelsson, R., Dixelius, M., & Törnblom, J. (2013). Knowledge production and learning for sustainable landscapes: Seven steps using social-ecological systems as laboratories. *Ambio*, *42*(2), 116–128. doi:10.1007/s13280-012-0367-1 PMID:23475650

Audretsch, D., & Thurik, R. (2000). Capitalism and democracy in the 21st century: From the managed to the entrepreneurial economy. *Journal of Evolutionary Economics*, *10*(1), 17–34. doi:10.1007/s001910050003

Bagnoli, C., & Vedovato, M. (2014). The impact of knowledge management and strategy configuration coherence on SME performance. *Journal of Management & Governance*, *18*(2), 615–647. doi:10.1007/s10997-012-9211-z

Becker, S. O., & Egger, P. H. (2013). Endogenous product versus process innovation and a firm's propensity to export. *Empirical Economics*, *44*(1), 329–354. doi:10.1007/s00181-009-0322-6

Belso-Martinez, J. A., & Molina-Morales, F. X. (2013). Non-linear relationships of internal and external resources on a firm's innovation: The case of the Spanish Vinalopó footwear cluster. *Growth and Change*, *44*(3), 494–521. doi:10.1111/grow.12017

Berends, H., Jelinek, M., Reymen, I., & Stultiëns, R. (2014). Product innovation processes in small firms: Combining entrepreneurial effectuation and managerial causation. *Journal of Product Innovation Management*, *31*(3), 616–635. doi:10.1111/jpim.12117

Bernardi, A. (2013). iGreen–Intelligent technologies for public-private knowledge management in agriculture. *KI - Künstliche Intelligenz*, *27*(4), 347–350.

Bettiol, M., Di Maria, E., & Grandinetti, R. (2012). Codification and creativity: Knowledge management strategies in KIBS. *Journal of Knowledge Management*, *16*(4), 550–562. doi:10.1108/13673271211246130

Bidmeshgipour, M., Ismail, W. K. W., & Omar, R. (2012). Knowledge management and organizational innovativeness in Iranian banking industry. *Knowledge Management and E-Learning*, *4*(4), 481–499.

Bielaczyc, K., & Ow, J. (2014). Multi-player epistemic games: Guiding the enactment of classroom knowledge-building communities. *International Journal of Computer-Supported Collaborative Learning*, *9*(1), 33–62. doi:10.1007/s11412-013-9186-z

Björk, J. (2012). Knowledge domain spanners in ideation. *Creativity and Innovation Management*, *21*(1), 17–27. doi:10.1111/j.1467-8691.2012.00627.x

Bohlmann, J. D., Spanjol, J., Qualls, W. J., & Rosa, J. A. (2013). The interplay of customer and product innovation dynamics: An exploratory study. *Journal of Product Innovation Management, 30*(2), 228–244. doi:10.1111/j.1540-5885.2012.00962.x

Borges, R. (2013). Tacit knowledge sharing between IT workers: The role of organizational culture, personality, and social environment. *Management Research Review, 36*(1), 89–108. doi:10.1108/01409171311284602

Breunig, K. J., & Hydle, K. M. (2013). Remote control: Measuring performance for value creation and governance of globally distributed knowledge work. *Journal of Management & Governance, 17*(3), 559–582. doi:10.1007/s10997-011-9194-1

Cankurtaran, P., Langerak, F., & Griffin, A. (2013). Consequences of new product development speed: A meta-analysis. *Journal of Product Innovation Management, 30*(3), 465–486. doi:10.1111/jpim.12011

Carson, D., & Gilmore, A. (2000). SME marketing management competencies. *International Business Review, 9*(3), 363–382. doi:10.1016/S0969-5931(00)00006-8

Castaño-Martínez, M. S. (2012). Product innovation and R&D policy: The case of the transformation industries in developed and developing. *The International Entrepreneurship and Management Journal, 8*(4), 421–436. doi:10.1007/s11365-012-0228-1

Catenazzi, N., & Sommaruga, L. (2013). Generic environments for knowledge management and visualization. *Journal of Ambient Intelligence and Humanized Computing, 4*(1), 99–108. doi:10.1007/s12652-011-0097-4

Černe, M., Jaklič, M., & Škerlavaj, M. (2013). Management innovation in focus: The role of knowledge exchange, organizational size, and IT system development and utilization. *European Management Review, 10*(3), 153–166. doi:10.1111/emre.12013

Chai, K. H., Wang, Q., Song, M., Halman, J. I. M., & Brombacher, A. C. (2012). Understanding competencies in platform-based product development: Antecedents and outcomes. *Journal of Product Innovation Management, 29*(3), 452–472. doi:10.1111/j.1540-5885.2012.00917.x

Chai, S., & Kim, M. (2012). A socio-technical approach to knowledge contribution behavior: An empirical investigation of social networking sites users. *International Journal of Information Management, 32*(2), 118–126. doi:10.1016/j.ijinfomgt.2011.07.004

Chatterji, A. K., & Fabrizio, K. R. (2014). Using users: When does external knowledge enhance corporate product innovation? *Strategic Management Journal, 35*(10), 1427–1445. doi:10.1002/smj.2168

Cho, T., & Korte, R. (2014). Managing knowledge performance: Testing the components of a knowledge management system on organizational performance. *Asia Pacific Education Review, 15*(2), 313–327. doi:10.1007/s12564-014-9333-x

Choo, C., & Bontis, N. (2002). *The strategic management of intellectual capital and organizational knowledge*. New York, NY: Oxford University Press.

Chu, M. T., Khosla, R., & Nishida, T. (2012). Communities of practice model driven knowledge management in multinational knowledge based enterprises. *Journal of Intelligent Manufacturing, 23*(5), 1707–1720. doi:10.1007/s10845-010-0472-6

Chu, M. T., Kumar, P., Kumar, K., & Khosla, R. (2014). Mapping knowledge sharing traits to business strategy in knowledge based organisation. *Journal of Intelligent Manufacturing, 25*(1), 55–65. doi:10.1007/s10845-012-0674-1

Chuang, S. H., Liao, C., & Lin, S. (2013). Determinants of knowledge management with information technology support impact on firm performance. *Information Technology Management, 14*(3), 217–230. doi:10.1007/s10799-013-0153-1

Cirera, X., Marin, A., & Markwald, R. (2012). Firm behaviour and the introduction of new exports: Evidence from Brazil. *IDS Working Papers, 2012*(390), 1–105.

Çokpekin, Ö., & Knudsen, M. P. (2012). Does organizing for creativity really lead to innovation? *Creativity and Innovation Management, 21*(3), 304–314. doi:10.1111/j.1467-8691.2012.00649.x

Connell, J., & Voola, R. (2013). Knowledge integration and competitiveness: A longitudinal study of an industry cluster. *Journal of Knowledge Management, 17*(2), 208–225. doi:10.1108/13673271311315178

Conte, A., & Vivarelli, M. (2014). Succeeding in innovation: Key insights on the role of R&D and technological acquisition drawn from company data. *Empirical Economics, 47*(4), 1317–1340. doi:10.1007/s00181-013-0779-1

Corfield, A., Paton, R., & Little, S. (2013). Does knowledge management work in NGOs? A longitudinal study. *International Journal of Public Administration, 36*(3), 179–188. doi:10.1080/01900692.2012.749281

Cunha, M. P., Rego, A., Oliveira, P., Rosado, P., & Habib, N. (2014). Product innovation in resource-poor environments: Three research streams. *Journal of Product Innovation Management, 31*(2), 202–210. doi:10.1111/jpim.12090

da Mota Pedrosa, A. (2012). Customer integration during innovation development: An exploratory study in the logistics service industry. *Creativity and Innovation Management, 21*(3), 263–276. doi:10.1111/j.1467-8691.2012.00648.x

Dachs, B., Ebersberger, B., Kinkel, S., & Som, O. (2015). The effects of production offshoring on R&D and innovation in the home country. *Economia e Politica Industriale, 42*(1), 9–31. doi:10.1007/s40812-014-0001-2

Dahlin, E. C. (2014). The sociology of innovation: Organizational, environmental, and relative perspectives. *Social Compass, 8*(6), 671–687. doi:10.1111/soc4.12177

Dangelico, R. M., Pontrandolfo, P., & Pujari, D. (2013). Developing sustainable new products in the textile and upholstered furniture industries: Role of external integrative capabilities. *Journal of Product Innovation Management, 30*(4), 642–658. doi:10.1111/jpim.12013

Denford, J. S. (2013). Building knowledge: Developing a knowledge-based dynamic capabilities typology. *Journal of Knowledge Management, 17*(2), 175–194. doi:10.1108/13673271311315150

Deng, Z., Hofman, P. S., & Newman, A. (2013). Ownership concentration and product innovation in Chinese private SMEs. *Asia Pacific Journal of Management, 30*(3), 717–734. doi:10.1007/s10490-012-9301-0

Desouza, K. C., & Awazu, Y. (2006). Knowledge management at SMEs: Five peculiarities. *Journal of Knowledge Management, 10*(1), 32–43. doi:10.1108/13673270610650085

Durmuşoğlu, S. S., Calantone, R. J., & McNally, R. C. (2013). Ordered to innovate: A longitudinal examination of the early periods of a new product development process implementation in a manufacturing firm. *Journal of Product Innovation Management, 30*(4), 712–731. doi:10.1111/jpim.12016

Evanschitzky, H., Eisend, M., Calantone, R. J., & Jiang, Y. (2012). Success factors of product innovation: An updated meta-analysis. *Journal of Product Innovation Management, 29*, 21–37. doi:10.1111/j.1540-5885.2012.00964.x

Fabrizio, K. R., & Thomas, L. G. (2012). The impact of local demand on innovation in a global industry. *Strategic Management Journal, 33*(1), 42–64. doi:10.1002/smj.942

Feldman, M. P., & Audretsch, D. B. (1999). Innovation in cities: Science based diversity, specialization and localized competition. *European Economic Review, 43*(2), 409–429. doi:10.1016/S0014-2921(98)00047-6

Felekoglu, B., & Moultrie, J. (2014). Top management involvement in new product development: A review and synthesis. *Journal of Product Innovation Management, 31*(1), 159–175. doi:10.1111/jpim.12086

Ferguson, S., Burford, S., & Kennedy, M. (2013). Divergent approaches to knowledge and innovation in the public sector. *International Journal of Public Administration, 36*(3), 168–178. doi:10.1080/01900692.2012.749278

Frattini, F., Dell'Era, C., & Rangone, A. (2013). Launch decisions and the early market survival of innovations: An empirical analysis of the Italian mobile value-added services (VAS) industry. *Journal of Product Innovation Management, 30*, 174–187. doi:10.1111/jpim.12070

Frishammar, J., Lichtenthaler, U., & Rundquist, J. (2012). Identifying technology commercialization opportunities: The importance of integrating product development knowledge. *Journal of Product Innovation Management, 29*(4), 573–589. doi:10.1111/j.1540-5885.2012.00926.x

Füller, J., Matzler, K., Hutter, K., & Hautz, J. (2012). Consumers' creative talent: Which characteristics qualify consumers for open innovation projects? An exploration of asymmetrical effects. *Creativity and Innovation Management, 21*(3), 247–262. doi:10.1111/j.1467-8691.2012.00650.x

Ganotakis, P., & Love, J. H. (2012). The innovation value chain in new technology-based firms: Evidence from the U.K. *Journal of Product Innovation Management, 29*(5), 839–860. doi:10.1111/j.1540-5885.2012.00938.x

Gillberg, C., & Vo, L. C. (2014). Contributions from pragmatist perspectives towards an understanding of knowledge and learning in organisations. *Philosophy of Management, 13*(2), 33–51. doi:10.5840/pom201413210

Giordano, R., Preziosi, E., & Romano, M. (2013). Integration of local and scientific knowledge to support drought impact monitoring: Some hints from an Italian case study. *Natural Hazards, 69*(1), 523–544. doi:10.1007/s11069-013-0724-9

Goettler, R. L., & Gordon, B. R. (2014). Competition and product innovation in dynamic oligopoly. *Quantitative Marketing and Economics, 12*(1), 1–42. doi:10.1007/s11129-013-9142-2

Grant, R. M. (2013). Reflections on knowledge-based approaches to the organization of production. *Journal of Management and Governance, 17*(3), 541–558. doi:10.1007/s10997-011-9195-0

Greenhalgh, C., & Rogers, M. (2012). Trade marks and performance in services and manufacturing firms: Evidence of Schumpeterian competition through innovation. *The Australian Economic Review, 45*(1), 50–76. doi:10.1111/j.1467-8462.2011.00665.x

Halilem, N., Amara, N., & Landry, R. (2014). Exploring the relationships between innovation and internationalization of small and medium-sized enterprises: A nonrecursive structural equation model. *Canadian Journal of Administrative Sciences, 31*(1), 18–34. doi:10.1002/cjas.1272

Harris, B. (2014). Creating communities of practice to improve the educational and mental health contexts of bilingual/bicultural youth: A case study from Colorado. *Contemporary School Psychology, 18*(3), 187–194. doi:10.1007/s40688-014-0023-9

Holcombe, R. G. (2013). Firms as knowledge repositories. *The Review of Austrian Economics, 26*(3), 259–275. doi:10.1007/s11138-011-0165-1

Hollen, R. M. A., Van Den Bosch, F. A. J., & Volberda, H. W. (2013). The role of management innovation in enabling technological process innovation: An inter-organizational perspective. *European Management Review, 10*(1), 35–50. doi:10.1111/emre.12003

Hong, S., Oxley, L., & McCann, P. (2012). A survey of the innovation surveys. *Journal of Economic Surveys, 26*(3), 420–444. doi:10.1111/j.1467-6419.2012.00724.x

Huang, H. L. (2014). Performance effects of aligning service innovation and the strategic use of information technology. *Service Business, 8*(2), 171–195. doi:10.1007/s11628-013-0192-z

Hvannberg, E. T. (2015). Identifying and explicating knowledge on method transfer: A sectoral system of innovation approach. *Universal Access in the Information Society, 14*(2), 187–202. doi:10.1007/s10209-013-0340-1

Im, S., Montoya, M. M., & Workman, J. P. Jr. (2013). Antecedents and consequences of creativity in product innovation teams. *Journal of Product Innovation Management, 30*(1), 170–185. doi:10.1111/j.1540-5885.2012.00887.x

Intezari, A., & Pauleen, D. J. (2014). Management wisdom in perspective: Are you virtuous enough to succeed in volatile times? *Journal of Business Ethics, 120*(3), 393–404. doi:10.1007/s10551-013-1666-6

Jaspers, F., Prencipe, A., & van den Ende, J. (2012). Organizing interindustry architectural innovations: Evidence from mobile communication applications. *Journal of Product Innovation Management, 29*(3), 419–431. doi:10.1111/j.1540-5885.2012.00915.x

Jean, R. J., Sinkovics, R. R., & Hiebaum, T. P. (2014). The effects of supplier involvement and knowledge protection on product innovation in customer-supplier relationships: A study of global automotive suppliers in China. *Journal of Product Innovation Management, 31*(1), 98–113. doi:10.1111/jpim.12082

Jepsen, L. B., Dell'Era, C., & Verganti, R. (2014). The contributions of interpreters to the development of radical innovations of meanings: The role of "Pioneering Projects" in the sustainable buildings industry. *R&D Management, 44*(1), 1–17. doi:10.1111/radm.12035

Jespersen, K. R. (2012). Stage-to-stage information dependency in the NPD process: Effective learning or a potential entrapment of NPD gates? *Journal of Product Innovation Management, 29*(2), 257–274. doi:10.1111/j.1540-5885.2011.00894.x

Kale, S., & Karaman, E. A. (2012). A diagnostic model for assessing the knowledge management practices of construction firms. *KSCE Journal of Civil Engineering, 16*(4), 526–537. doi:10.1007/s12205-012-1468-x

Kandemir, D., & Acur, N. (2012). Examining proactive strategic decision-making flexibility in new product development. *Journal of Product Innovation Management, 29*(4), 608–622. doi:10.1111/j.1540-5885.2012.00928.x

Kang, W., & Montoya, M. (2014). The impact of product portfolio strategy on financial performance: The roles of product development and market entry decisions. *Journal of Product Innovation Management, 31*(3), 516–534. doi:10.1111/jpim.12111

Kapyla, J. (2012). Towards a critical societal knowledge management. *Journal of Intellectual Capital, 13*(3), 288–304. doi:10.1108/14691931211248873

Kasemsap, K. (2014a). Strategic innovation management: An integrative framework and causal model of knowledge management, strategic orientation, organizational innovation, and organizational performance. In P. Ordóñez de Pablos & R. Tennyson (Eds.), *Strategic approaches for human capital management and development in a turbulent economy* (pp. 102–116). Hershey, PA: IGI Global. doi:10.4018/978-1-4666-4530-1.ch007

Kasemsap, K. (2014b). The role of knowledge sharing on organisational innovation: An integrated framework. In L. Al-Hakim & C. Jin (Eds.), *Quality innovation: Knowledge, theory, and practices* (pp. 247–271). Hershey, PA: IGI Global. doi:10.4018/978-1-4666-4769-5.ch012

Kasemsap, K. (2015a). Developing a framework of human resource management, organizational learning, knowledge management capability, and organizational performance. In P. Ordoñez de Pablos, L. Turró, R. Tennyson, & J. Zhao (Eds.), *Knowledge management for competitive advantage during economic crisis* (pp. 164–193). Hershey, PA: IGI Global. doi:10.4018/978-1-4666-6457-9.ch010

Kasemsap, K. (2015b). The roles of information technology and knowledge management in project management metrics. In G. Jamil, S. Lopes, A. Malheiro da Silva, & F. Ribeiro (Eds.), *Handbook of research on effective project management through the integration of knowledge and innovation* (pp. 332–361). Hershey, PA: IGI Global. doi:10.4018/978-1-4666-7536-0.ch018

Kasemsap, K. (2015c). The role of data mining for business intelligence in knowledge management. In A. Azevedo & M. Santos (Eds.), *Integration of data mining in business intelligence systems* (pp. 12–33). Hershey, PA: IGI Global. doi:10.4018/978-1-4666-6477-7.ch002

Kedia, B., Gaffney, N., & Clampit, J. (2012). EMNEs and knowledge-seeking FDI. *Management International Review, 52*(2), 155–173. doi:10.1007/s11575-012-0132-5

Kim, N., Im, S., & Slater, S. F. (2013). Impact of knowledge type and strategic orientation on new product creativity and advantage in high-technology firms. *Journal of Product Innovation Management, 30*(1), 136–153. doi:10.1111/j.1540-5885.2012.00992.x

Kim, S. B. (2014). Systematic analyses on knowledge implementation steps and themes at the organizational level. *KSCE Journal of Civil Engineering, 18*(2), 444–453. doi:10.1007/s12205-014-1191-x

Kim, S. B. (2014). Impacts of knowledge management on the organizational success. *KSCE Journal of Civil Engineering, 18*(6), 1609–1617. doi:10.1007/s12205-014-0243-6

Kim, Y. J., Song, S., Sambamurthy, V., & Lee, Y. L. (2012). Entrepreneurship, knowledge integration capability, and firm performance: An empirical study. *Information Systems Frontiers, 14*(5), 1047–1060. doi:10.1007/s10796-011-9331-z

Klaukien, A., Shepherd, D. A., & Patzelt, H. (2013). Passion for work, nonwork-related excitement, and innovation managers' decision to exploit new product opportunities. *Journal of Product Innovation Management, 30*(3), 574–588. doi:10.1111/jpim.12010

Koch, A. H. (2012). Authority and managing innovation: A typology of product development teams and communities. *Creativity and Innovation Management, 21*(4), 376–387. doi:10.1111/caim.12001

Kuester, S., Homburg, C., & Hess, S. C. (2012). Externally directed and internally directed market launch management: The role of organizational factors in influencing new product success. *Journal of Product Innovation Management, 29*, 38–52. doi:10.1111/j.1540-5885.2012.00968.x

Lager, T., & Storm, P. (2013). Application development in process firms: Adding value to customer products and production systems. *R&D Management, 43*(3), 288–302. doi:10.1111/radm.12013

Landwehr, J. R., Wentzel, D., & Herrmann, A. (2012). The tipping point of design: How product design and brands interact to affect consumers' preferences. *Psychology and Marketing, 29*(6), 422–433. doi:10.1002/mar.20531

Lasagni, A. (2012). How can external relationships enhance innovation in SMEs? New evidence for Europe. *Journal of Small Business Management, 50*(2), 310–339. doi:10.1111/j.1540-627X.2012.00355.x

Lawson, B., Samson, D., & Roden, S. (2012). Appropriating the value from innovation: Inimitability and the effectiveness of isolating mechanisms. *R & D Management, 42*(5), 420–434. doi:10.1111/j.1467-9310.2012.00692.x

Lee, J., & Fink, D. (2013). Knowledge mapping: Encouragements and impediments to adoption. *Journal of Knowledge Management, 17*(1), 16–28. doi:10.1108/13673271311300714

Lerro, A., Iacobone, A. F., & Schiuma, G. (2012). Knowledge assets assessment strategies: Organizational value, processes, approaches and evaluation architectures. *Journal of Knowledge Management, 16*(4), 563–575. doi:10.1108/13673271211246149

Li, C., Guo, F., Zhi, L., Han, Z., & Liu, F. (2013). Knowledge management research status in China from 2006 to 2010: Based on analysis of the degree theses. *Scientometrics, 94*(1), 95–111. doi:10.1007/s11192-012-0858-7

Li, X., Li, L., & Chen, Z. (2014). Toward extenics-based innovation model on intelligent knowledge management. *Annals of Data Science, 1*(1), 127–148. doi:10.1007/s40745-014-0009-5

Liang, H., & Zhang, Z. (2012). The effects of industry characteristics on the sources of technological product and process innovation. *The Journal of Technology Transfer, 37*(6), 867–884. doi:10.1007/s10961-011-9206-y

Lichtenthaler, U. (2013). The collaboration of innovation intermediaries and manufacturing firms in the markets for technology. *Journal of Product Innovation Management, 30,* 142–158. doi:10.1111/jpim.12068

Lim, S. Y., & Suh, M. (2015). Product and process innovation in the development cycle of biopharmaceuticals. *Journal of Pharmaceutical Innovation, 10*(2), 156–165. doi:10.1007/s12247-015-9214-9

Ling, Y. H. (2013). The influence of intellectual capital on organizational performance: Knowledge management as moderator. *Asia Pacific Journal of Management, 30*(3), 937–964. doi:10.1007/s10490-011-9257-5

Lionzo, A., & Rossignoli, F. (2013). Knowledge integration in family SMEs: An extension of the 4I model. *Journal of Management and Governance, 17*(3), 583–608. doi:10.1007/s10997-011-9197-y

Liu, H., Ding, X. H., Guo, H., & Luo, J. H. (2014). How does slack affect product innovation in high-tech Chinese firms: The contingent value of entrepreneurial orientation. *Asia Pacific Journal of Management, 31*(1), 47–68. doi:10.1007/s10490-012-9309-5

Liu, X. J., & Wang, Y. L. (2015). Semantic-based knowledge categorization and organization for product design enterprises. *Journal of Shanghai Jiaotong University (Science), 20*(1), 106–112. doi:10.1007/s12204-015-1596-9

Liu, Y., & Abdalla, A. N. (2013). Evaluating the managerial behavior of managing knowledge in Chinese SMEs. *Information Technology Management, 14*(2), 159–165. doi:10.1007/s10799-013-0157-x

Lonnqvist, A., & Laihonen, H. (2013). Managing regional development: A knowledge perspective. International. *Journal of Knowledge-Based Development, 4*(1), 50–63. doi:10.1504/IJKBD.2013.052493

Lunnan, R., & Zhao, Y. (2014). Regional headquarters in China: Role in MNE knowledge transfer. *Asia Pacific Journal of Management, 31*(2), 397–422. doi:10.1007/s10490-013-9358-4

Madrid-Guijarro, A., García-Pérez-de-Lema, D., & Van Auken, H. (2013). An investigation of Spanish SME innovation during different economic conditions. *Journal of Small Business Management, 51*(4), 578–601. doi:10.1111/jsbm.12004

Mahr, D., Lievens, A., & Blazevic, V. (2014). The value of customer cocreated knowledge during the innovation process. *Journal of Product Innovation Management, 31*(3), 599–615. doi:10.1111/jpim.12116

Mäkimattila, M., Melkas, H., & Uotila, T. (2013). Dynamics of openness in innovation processes: A case study in the Finnish food industry. *Knowledge and Process Management, 20*(4), 243–255. doi:10.1002/kpm.1421

Marion, T. J., Friar, J. H., & Simpson, T. W. (2012). New product development practices and early-stage firms: Two in-depth case studies. *Journal of Product Innovation Management, 29*(4), 639–654. doi:10.1111/j.1540-5885.2012.00930.x

Markham, S. K. (2013). The impact of front-end innovation activities on product performance. *Journal of Product Innovation Management, 30*, 77–92. doi:10.1111/jpim.12065

Martínez-Román, J. A., & Romero, I. (2013). About the determinants of the degree of novelty in small businesses' product innovations. *The International Entrepreneurship and Management Journal, 9*(4), 655–677. doi:10.1007/s11365-013-0269-0

Martinkenaite, I. (2012). Antecedents of knowledge transfer in acquisitions. *Baltic Journal of Management, 7*(2), 167–184. doi:10.1108/17465261211219796

Massingham, P. (2015). Knowledge sharing: What works and what doesn't work: A critical systems thinking perspective. *Systemic Practice and Action Research, 28*(3), 197–228. doi:10.1007/s11213-014-9330-3

Matayong, S., & Mahmood, A. K. (2013). The review of approaches to knowledge management system studies. *Journal of Knowledge Management, 17*(3), 472–490. doi:10.1108/JKM-10-2012-0316

McGurk, J., & Baron, A. (2012). Knowledge management: Time to focus on purpose and motivation. *Strategic HR Review, 11*(6), 316–321. doi:10.1108/14754391211264776

McKellar, K. A., Pitzul, K. B., Yi, J. Y., & Cole, D. C. (2014). Evaluating communities of practice and knowledge networks: A systematic scoping review of evaluation frameworks. *EcoHealth, 11*(3), 383–399. doi:10.1007/s10393-014-0958-3 PMID:25023411

Meese, N., & McMahon, C. (2012). Knowledge sharing for sustainable development in civil engineering: A systematic review. *AI & Society, 27*(4), 437–449. doi:10.1007/s00146-011-0369-8

Mohnen, P., & Hall, B. H. (2013). Innovation and productivity: An update. *Eurasian Business Review, 3*(1), 47–65.

Moilanen, M., Østbye, S., & Woll, K. (2014). Non-R&D SMEs: External knowledge, absorptive capacity and product innovation. *Small Business Economics, 43*(2), 447–462. doi:10.1007/s11187-014-9545-9

Moon, H., Miller, D. R., & Kim, S. H. (2013). Product design innovation and customer value: Cross-cultural research in the United States and Korea. *Journal of Product Innovation Management, 30*(1), 31–43. doi:10.1111/j.1540-5885.2012.00984.x

Mueller, J. (2012). The interactive relationship of corporate culture and knowledge management: A review. *Review of Managerial Science, 6*(2), 183–201. doi:10.1007/s11846-010-0060-3

Mueller, J. (2015). Formal and informal practices of knowledge sharing between project teams and enacted cultural characteristics. *Project Management Journal, 46*(1), 53–68. doi: 10.1002/pmj.21471

Mugge, R., & Dahl, D. W. (2013). Seeking the ideal level of design newness: Consumer response to radical and incremental product design. *Journal of Product Innovation Management, 30*, 34–47. doi:10.1111/jpim.12062

Murro, P. (2013). The determinants of innovation: What is the role of risk? *The Manchester School, 81*(3), 293–323. doi:10.1111/j.1467-9957.2012.02286.x

Myers, P. S. (2012). *Knowledge management and organizational design.* London, UK: Routledge.

Narasimhan, R., & Narayanan, S. (2013). Perspectives on supply network–enabled innovations. *Journal of Supply Chain Management, 49*(4), 27–42. doi:10.1111/jscm.12026

Nardone, G., Seccia, A., & Maruotti, G. (2013). How nanotechnologies can contribute to innovation in food firms in Europe. *EuroChoices, 12*(2), 21–26. doi:10.1111/1746-692X.12026

Neumann, M., Riel, A., & Brissaud, D. (2013). IT-supported innovation management in the automotive supplier industry to drive idea generation and leverage innovation. *Journal of Software: Evolution and Process, 25*(4), 329–339.

Nilsson, S., & Ritzén, S. (2014). Exploring the use of innovation performance measurement to build innovation capability in a medical device company. *Creativity and Innovation Management, 23*(2), 183–198. doi:10.1111/caim.12054

Noruzy, A., Dalfard, V. M., Azhdari, B., Nazari-Shirkouhi, S., & Rezazadeh, A. (2013). Relations between transformational leadership, organizational learning, knowledge management, organizational innovation, and organizational performance: An empirical investigation of manufacturing firms. *International Journal of Advanced Manufacturing Technology, 64*(5/8), 1073–1085. doi:10.1007/s00170-012-4038-y

Oke, A., Prajogo, D. I., & Jayaram, J. (2013). Strengthening the innovation chain: The role of internal innovation climate and strategic relationships with supply chain partners. *Journal of Supply Chain Management, 49*(4), 43–58. doi:10.1111/jscm.12031

Ozel, B. (2012). Collaboration structure and knowledge diffusion in Turkish management academia. *Scientometrics, 93*(1), 183–206. doi:10.1007/s11192-012-0641-9

Oztemel, E., & Arslankaya, S. (2012). Enterprise knowledge management model: A knowledge tower. *Knowledge and Information Systems, 31*(1), 171–192. doi:10.1007/s10115-011-0414-4

Panahi, S., Watson, J., & Partridge, H. (2012). Social media and tacit knowledge sharing: Developing a conceptual model. *World Academy of Science. Engineering and Technology, 64*, 1095–1102.

Pandey, S. C., & Dutta, A. (2013). Role of knowledge infrastructure capabilities in knowledge management. *Journal of Knowledge Management, 17*(3), 435–453. doi:10.1108/JKM-11-2012-0365

Park, M., Jang, Y., Lee, H. S., Ahn, C., & Yoon, Y. S. (2013). Application of knowledge management technologies in Korean small and medium-sized construction companies. *KSCE Journal of Civil Engineering, 17*(1), 22–32. doi:10.1007/s12205-013-1607-z

Park, M., Lee, K. W., Lee, H. S., Jiayi, P., & Yu, J. (2013). Ontology-based construction knowledge retrieval system. *KSCE Journal of Civil Engineering, 17*(7), 1654–1663. doi:10.1007/s12205-013-1155-6

Patel, C., & Haon, C. (2014). Internally versus externally developed technology and market acceptance of innovations: The complementary role of branding. *European Management Review, 11*(2), 173–186. doi:10.1111/emre.12029

Patel, P. C., Fernhaber, S. A., McDougall-Covin, P. P., & van der Have, R. P. (2014). Beating competitors to international markets: The value of geographically balanced networks for innovation. *Strategic Management Journal, 35*(5), 691–711. doi:10.1002/smj.2114

Pérez-López, S., & Alegre, J. (2012). Information technology competency, knowledge processes and firm performance. *Industrial Management & Data Systems, 112*(4), 644–662. doi:10.1108/02635571211225521

Pullen, A., de Weerd-Nederhof, P. C., Groen, A. J., & Fisscher, O. A. M. (2012). SME network characteristics vs. product innovativeness: How to achieve high innovation performance. *Creativity and Innovation Management, 21*(2), 130–146. doi:10.1111/j.1467-8691.2012.00638.x

Purcarea, I., Espinosa, M., & Apetrei, A. (2013). Innovation and knowledge creation: Perspectives on the SMEs sector. *Management Decision, 51*(5), 1096–1107. doi:10.1108/MD-08-2012-0590

Rabeh, H. A. D., Jimenéz-Jimenéz, D., & Martínez-Costa, M. (2013). Managing knowledge for a successful competence exploration. *Journal of Knowledge Management, 17*(2), 195–207. doi:10.1108/13673271311315169

Ramayah, T., Yeap, J. A. L., & Ignatius, J. (2013). An empirical inquiry on knowledge sharing among academicians in higher learning institutions. *Minerva, 51*(2), 131–154. doi:10.1007/s11024-013-9229-7

Rass, M., Dumbach, M., Danzinger, F., Bullinger, A. C., & Moeslein, K. M. (2013). Open innovation and firm performance: The mediating role of social capital. *Creativity and Innovation Management, 22*(2), 177–194. doi:10.1111/caim.12028

Ravindran, S., & Iyer, G. S. (2014). Organizational and knowledge management related antecedents of knowledge use: The moderating effect of ambiguity tolerance. *Information Technology Management, 15*(4), 271–290. doi:10.1007/s10799-014-0190-4

Rese, A., Gemünden, H. G., & Baier, D. (2013). "Too many cooks spoil the broth": Key persons and their roles in inter-organizational innovations. *Creativity and Innovation Management, 22*(4), 390–407. doi:10.1111/caim.12034

Ritala, P., & Hurmelinna-Laukkanen, P. (2013). Incremental and radical innovation in coopetition: The role of absorptive capacity and appropriability. *Journal of Product Innovation Management, 30*(1), 154–169. doi:10.1111/j.1540-5885.2012.00956.x

Ruiz-Jimenez, J. M., & Fuentes-Fuentes, M. (2013). Knowledge combination, innovation, organizational performance in technology firms. *Industrial Management & Data Systems, 113*(4), 523–540. doi:10.1108/02635571311322775

Saemundsson, R. J., & Candi, M. (2014). Antecedents of innovation strategies in new technology-based firms: Interactions between the environment and founder team composition. *Journal of Product Innovation Management, 31*(5), 939–955. doi:10.1111/jpim.12133

Salge, T. O., Farchi, T., Barrett, M. I., & Dopson, S. (2013). When does search openness really matter? A contingency study of health-care innovation projects. *Journal of Product Innovation Management, 30*(4), 659–676. doi:10.1111/jpim.12015

Salvador, F., & Villena, V. H. (2013). Supplier integration and NPD outcomes: Conditional moderation effects of modular design competence. *Journal of Supply Chain Management, 49*(1), 87–113. doi:10.1111/j.1745-493x.2012.03275.x

Santos, V., Goldman, A., & de Souza, C. R. B. (2015). Fostering effective inter-team knowledge sharing in agile software development. *Empirical Software Engineering, 20*(4), 1006–1051. doi:10.1007/s10664-014-9307-y

Schmid, W., & Kern, E. M. (2014). Integration of business process management and knowledge management: State of the art, current research and future prospects. *Journal of Business Economics, 84*(2), 191–231. doi:10.1007/s11573-013-0683-3

Schuhmacher, M. C., & Kuester, S. (2012). Identification of lead user characteristics driving the quality of service innovation ideas. *Creativity and Innovation Management, 21*(4), 427–442. doi:10.1111/caim.12002

Shan, J., & Jolly, D. R. (2013). Technological innovation capabilities, product strategy, and firm performance: The electronics industry in China. *Canadian Journal of Administrative Sciences, 30*(3), 159–172. doi:10.1002/cjas.1256

Simms, C. D., & Trott, P. (2014). Barriers to the upgrade cycle in a commodity process industry: Evidence from the UK packaging industry. *R&D Management, 44*(2), 152–170. doi:10.1111/radm.12047

Simone, C., Ackerman, M., & Wulf, V. (2012). Knowledge management in practice: A special issue. *Computer Supported Cooperative Work, 21*(2/3), 109–110. doi:10.1007/s10606-012-9161-7

Šipikal, M., & Buček, M. (2013). The role of FDIs in regional innovation: Evidence from the automotive industry in Western Slovakia. *Regional Science Policy & Practice, 5*(4), 475–490. doi:10.1111/rsp3.12022

Slater, S. F., Mohr, J. J., & Sengupta, S. (2014). Radical product innovation capability: Literature review, synthesis, and illustrative research propositions. *Journal of Product Innovation Management, 31*(3), 552–566. doi:10.1111/jpim.12113

Smith, S. W., & Shah, S. K. (2013). Do innovative users generate more useful insights? An analysis of corporate venture capital investments in the medical device industry. *Strategic Entrepreneurship Journal, 7*(2), 151–167. doi:10.1002/sej.1152

Spanjol, J., Mühlmeier, S., & Tomczak, T. (2012). Strategic orientation and product innovation: Exploring a decompositional approach. *Journal of Product Innovation Management, 29*(6), 967–985. doi:10.1111/j.1540-5885.2012.00975.x

Spence, P. R., & Reddy, M. (2012). Beyond expertise seeking: A field study of the informal knowledge practices of healthcare IT teams. *Computer Supported Cooperative Work, 21*(2/3), 283–315. doi:10.1007/s10606-011-9135-1

Stanko, M. A., Molina-Castillo, F. J., & Munuera-Aleman, J. L. (2012). Speed to market for innovative products: Blessing or curse? *Journal of Product Innovation Management, 29*(5), 751–765. doi:10.1111/j.1540-5885.2012.00943.x

Stipp, K. F., & Kapp, S. A. (2012). Building organizational knowledge and value: Informed decision making in Kansas children's community-based mental health services. *Community Mental Health Journal, 48*(1), 1–11. doi:10.1007/s10597-010-9334-0 PMID:20623189

Stock, R. M. (2014). How should customers be integrated for effective interorganizational NPD teams? An input-process-output perspective. *Journal of Product Innovation Management, 31*(3), 535–551. doi:10.1111/jpim.12112

Stock, R. M., Six, B., & Zacharias, N. A. (2013). Linking multiple layers of innovation-oriented corporate culture, product program innovativeness, and business performance: A contingency approach. *Journal of the Academy of Marketing Science, 41*(3), 283–299. doi:10.1007/s11747-012-0306-5

Stock, R. M., & Zacharias, N. A. (2013). Two sides of the same coin: How do different dimensions of product program innovativeness affect customer loyalty? *Journal of Product Innovation Management, 30*(3), 516–532. doi:10.1111/jpim.12006

Storm, P., Lager, T., & Samuelsson, P. (2013). Managing the manufacturing–R&D interface in the process industries. *R & D Management, 43*(3), 252–270. doi:10.1111/radm.12010

Stoshikj, M., Kryvinska, N., & Strauss, C. (2014). Efficient managing of complex programs with project management services. *Global Journal of Flexible Systems Management, 15*(1), 25–38. doi:10.1007/s40171-013-0051-8

Su, N. M., Wilensky, H. N., & Redmiles, D. F. (2012). Doing business with theory: Communities of practice in knowledge management. *Computer Supported Cooperative Work, 21*(2/3), 111–162. doi:10.1007/s10606-011-9139-x

Su, Z., Xie, E., Liu, H., & Sun, W. (2013). Profiting from product innovation: The impact of legal, marketing, and technological capabilities in different environmental conditions. *Marketing Letters, 24*(3), 261–276. doi:10.1007/s11002-012-9214-1

Sung, R. C. W., Ritchie, J. M., Lim, T., & Kosmadoudi, Z. (2012). Automated generation of engineering rationale, knowledge and intent representations during the product life cycle. *Virtual Reality (Waltham Cross), 16*(1), 69–85. doi:10.1007/s10055-011-0196-8

Swarnkar, R., Choudhary, A. K., Harding, J. A., Das, B. P., & Young, R. I. (2012). A framework for collaboration moderator services to support knowledge based collaboration. *Journal of Intelligent Manufacturing, 23*(5), 2003–2023. doi:10.1007/s10845-011-0528-2

Takeuchi, H., & Nonaka, I. (2004). *Hitotsubashi on knowledge management.* Singapore: John Wiley & Sons.

Talay, M. B., Calantone, R. J., & Voorhees, C. M. (2014). Coevolutionary dynamics of automotive competition: Product innovation, change, and marketplace survival. *Journal of Product Innovation Management, 31*(1), 61–78. doi:10.1111/jpim.12080

Tang, J., & Murphy, P. J. (2012). Prior knowledge and new product and service introductions by entrepreneurial firms: The mediating role of technological innovation. *Journal of Small Business Management, 50*(1), 41–62. doi:10.1111/j.1540-627X.2011.00343.x

Teirlinck, P., & Spithoven, A. (2013). Formal R&D management and strategic decision making in small firms in knowledge-intensive business services. *R&D Management, 43*(1), 37–51. doi:10.1111/j.1467-9310.2012.00701.x

Tengo, M., Brondizio, E. S., Elmqvist, T., Malmer, P., & Spierenburg, M. (2014). Connecting diverse knowledge systems for enhanced ecosystem governance: The multiple evidence base approach. *Ambio*, *43*(5), 579–591. doi:10.1007/s13280-014-0501-3 PMID:24659474

Tödtling, F., & Grillitsch, M. (2014). Types of innovation, competencies of firms, and external knowledge sourcing: Findings from selected sectors and regions of Europe. *Journal of the Knowledge Economy*, *5*(2), 330–356. doi:10.1007/s13132-012-0139-y

Triguero, A., Córcoles, D., & Cuerva, M. C. (2014). Persistence of innovation and firm's growth: Evidence from a panel of SME and large Spanish manufacturing firms. *Small Business Economics*, *43*(4), 787–804. doi:10.1007/s11187-014-9562-8

Tsai, K. H., Hsu, T. T., & Fang, W. (2012). Relinking cross-functional collaboration, knowledge integration mechanisms, and product innovation performance: A moderated mediation model. *Canadian Journal of Administrative Sciences*, *29*(1), 25–39. doi:10.1002/cjas.192

Tsai, M. T., Chang, H. C., Cheng, N. C., & Lien, C. C. (2013). Understanding IT professionals' knowledge sharing intention through KMS: A social exchange perspective. *Quality & Quantity*, *47*(5), 2739–2753. doi:10.1007/s11135-012-9685-4

Tsai, M. T., Chen, K. S., & Chien, J. L. (2012). The factors impact of knowledge sharing intentions: The theory of reasoned action perspective. *Quality & Quantity*, *46*(5), 1479–1491. doi:10.1007/s11135-011-9462-9

Turchetti, G., & Geisler, E. (2013). The nature of knowledge and the platform and matrix solutions in the design of knowledge management systems. *Journal of Management and Governance*, *17*(3), 657–671. doi:10.1007/s10997-011-9199-9

Uhlaner, L. M., van Stel, A., Duplat, V., & Zhou, H. (2013). Disentangling the effects of organizational capabilities, innovation and firm size on SME sales growth. *Small Business Economics*, *41*(3), 581–607. doi:10.1007/s11187-012-9455-7

van den Ende, J., Jaspers, F. P. H., & Rijsdijk, S. A. (2013). Should system firms develop complementary product? A dynamic model and an empirical test. *Journal of Product Innovation Management*, *30*(6), 1178–1198. doi:10.1111/jpim.12053

Viswanathan, M., & Sridharan, S. (2012). Product development for the BoP: Insights on concept and prototype development from university-based student projects in India. *Journal of Product Innovation Management*, *29*(1), 52–69. doi:10.1111/j.1540-5885.2011.00878.x

Wang, C. L., & Rafiq, M. (2014). Ambidextrous organizational culture, contextual ambidexterity and new product innovation: A comparative study of UK and Chinese high-tech firms. *British Journal of Management*, *25*(1), 58–76. doi:10.1111/j.1467-8551.2012.00832.x

Wattanapruttipaisan, T. (2014). Competition policy and intellectual property rights in the information and communications technology sector: Policy implications and options for ASEAN. *Asian-Pacific Economic Literature*, *28*(1), 1–28. doi:10.1111/apel.12048

Wei, Z., Yi, Y., & Guo, H. (2014). Organizational learning ambidexterity, strategic flexibility, and new product development. *Journal of Product Innovation Management, 31*(4), 832–847. doi:10.1111/jpim.12126

Weiss, M., Hoegl, M., & Gibbert, M. (2013). The influence of material resources on innovation projects: The role of resource elasticity. *R&D Management, 43*(2), 151–161. doi:10.1111/radm.12007

West, R. E. (2014). Communities of innovation: Individual, group, and organizational characteristics leading to greater potential for innovation. *TechTrends, 58*(5), 53–61. doi:10.1007/s11528-014-0786-x

Wong, S. K. S. (2013). Environmental requirements, knowledge sharing and green innovation: Empirical evidence from the electronics industry in China. *Business Strategy and the Environment, 22*(5), 321–338. doi:10.1002/bse.1746

Wong, W. L. P., & Radcliffe, D. F. (2000). The tacit nature of design knowledge. *Technology Analysis and Strategic Management, 12*(4), 493–512. doi:10.1080/713698497

Wu, J. (2013). Diverse institutional environments and product innovation of emerging market firms. *Management International Review, 53*(1), 39–59. doi:10.1007/s11575-012-0162-z

Xu, S., Wu, F., & Cavusgil, E. (2013). Complements or substitutes? Internal technological strength, competitor alliance participation, and innovation development. *Journal of Product Innovation Management, 30*(4), 750–762. doi:10.1111/jpim.12014

Yang, Y., Wang, Q., Zhu, H., & Wu, G. (2012). What are the effective strategic orientations for new product success under different environments? An empirical study of Chinese businesses. *Journal of Product Innovation Management, 29*(2), 166–179. doi:10.1111/j.1540-5885.2011.00900.x

Yeniyurt, S., Henke, J. W., & Yalcinkaya, G. (2014). A longitudinal analysis of supplier involvement in buyers' new product development: Working relations, inter-dependence, co-innovation, and performance outcomes. *Journal of the Academy of Marketing Science, 42*(3), 291–308. doi:10.1007/s11747-013-0360-7

Zhang, L., Wang, H., Cao, X., Wang, X., & Zhao, K. (2012). Knowledge management component in managing human resources for enterprises. *Information Technology Management, 13*(4), 341–349. doi:10.1007/s10799-012-0127-8

Zhao, K., & Chan, C. K. K. (2014). Fostering collective and individual learning through knowledge building. *International Journal of Computer-Supported Collaborative Learning, 9*(1), 63–95. doi:10.1007/s11412-013-9188-x

KEY TERMS AND DEFINITIONS

Business Process Management: The activity undertaken by businesses to identify, evaluate, and improve business processes.

Community of Practice: The self-organized network of peers with diverse skills and experience in an area of practice.

Knowledge Management: The strategies and processes designed to identify, capture, structure, value, leverage, and share an organization's intellectual assets to enhance its performance and competitiveness.

New Product Development: The process of developing a new product or service for the marketplace.

Organizational Innovation: The process of translating an idea or invention into the product or service that creates organizational value.

Organizational Learning: The organization-wide continuous process that enhances its collective ability to accept, make sense of, and respond to the internal and external change.

Product Innovation: The development and market introduction of the new, redesigned, and improved product or service.

Research and Development: The systematic activity combining both basic and applied research toward creating new goods and knowledge.

Chapter 16
Innovation Landscape Idea to Product Development

Alok Kumar Goel
CSIR Human Resource Development Centre, India

Puja Singhal
Amity University, India

ABSTRACT

This study seeks to address various phases, challenges and the principles influencing transforming an idea into a product innovation. This study is particularly relevant in light of the driving role given to small scale enterprises by the supporting policies and practices in the process of transforming India into an innovation-oriented nation and leading 'Make in India' program. Based on a multi-disciplinary the framework discussed in this study highlights a number of internal processes and external network attributes, their interactions and moderating relationships as related to their impact on Indian small scale enterprises' product innovation capabilities. This study offers an overview of the factors that affect product innovation capabilities, with particular reference to entrepreneurial orientation of Indian Small and Medium Enterprises (SMEs). This study showcase provocative views that considers the concept of innovation ecosystem and new product development central to its philosophy and objectives.

INTRODUCTION

In the present knowledge economy, innovation has become the key to national growth and competitiveness. Innovation is the means by which the entrepreneur creates new wealth-producing resources with enhanced potential for creating wealth (Drucker, 1985). Organizational growth depends on innovations moving quickly through the organization and employees need broad and deep expertise to develop the integrated solutions demanded by customers. Innovation can be seen as the combined activity of generating creative ideas and the subsequent successful exploitation of these concepts for benefit. The present study is a burning example of entrepreneurial orientation which first transformed an idea into innovation than a tangible product. This chapter entails the success story of an innovator as to how he always searches for change and exploits it as an opportunity.

DOI: 10.4018/978-1-4666-9607-5.ch016

This case study aims to explore the complementary nature of entrepreneurship and innovation through an exploratory study and develops an integrative framework of the interaction between entrepreneurship and innovation. Who are entrepreneurs? How do entrepreneur manage to identify and exploit interesting business ideas? What are their entrepreneurial processes, and how do they define the basis of their firms' competitive edge? What is the Indian Government supporting schemes to promote small enterprises with innovative products in their bid to export their product and earn foreign exchange for the country? This paper seeks to answer these questions by case illustration of Embarc Information Technology (P) Ltd, an Indian SME. The study took a qualitative approach in exploring the synergies between entrepreneurship and innovation and in analyzing the factors that foster the interaction between the two. The purpose was to better understand the complementary nature of entrepreneurship and innovation through an exploratory study of the journey of an innovator to his entrepreneurial venture and to develop an integrative framework of the interaction between entrepreneurship and innovation.

SMEs, due to their small size and scarcity of necessary resources orient them towards looking for external partners in order to be innovative (Dahlander and Gann 2010, Lee et al. 2010, Rahman and Ramos 2010). Entrepreneurial orientation of SME owner plays a vital role in adopting open innovation strategies. This entrepreneurial orientation is also a antecedent for open innovation process in SMEs (Ju, P.H. et al. 2013) and SMEs having external networks are prone to be more innovative (Brunswicker and van de Vrande 2014). When companies aspire for innovation they typically go through four phases: orientation, exploration, selection and engagement (Roijakkers et.al. 2014). Each of these phase accrue value addition in innovation efforts of the company especially once the requisite knowledge network is established.

Semi-structured interviews were conducted to collect case data, with an interview guide to ensure uniform coverage of the research themes (Grawitz, 1996). This type of interview is appropriate in an exploratory research context, as open-ended questions allowed the authors to gain deeper understanding of the techno-entrepreneur, its entrepreneurial process, and the factors on which he based the competitiveness of his firm (Rubin and Rubin, 1995). These interviews were carried out with the entrepreneur at Embarc's offices located at NSEZ, Noida and Agra, India. Each interview lasted approximately one hour and was recorded. The materials were then analyzed using the methods suggested by Yin, R.K. (1994).

ABOUT THE ORGANIZATION

Embarc Information Technology (P) Ltd. is an ISO 9001:2008 certified software and hardware company established in 1994 by SB. It is headquartered in Noida, India and has development centre in Bangalore. Embarc is active in more than 90 Countries. It is engaged in every aspect of software & hardware development for Geo-positioning devices. Their solutions are rugged, technically robust and functionally rich having quality and reliability. Embarc is pioneer in GPS, tracking, navigation, security and have developed an innovative product Find'n'Secure.

Engineers all over the world have been engaged since long in finding a user friendly way to keep a track of a moving vehicle but have not met with much success. Behold an Indian whiz guy from the city of Taj Mahal, Agra, Mr. SB for achieving a major breakthrough in this field. Mr. SB was able to develop a highly sophisticated and innovative satellite-based automatic vehicle tracking system Find'n'Secure that once installed can keep track of the vehicle in any part of the world. This innovative system not only revolutionized the whole scenario in the automobile world but also paved way for bringing safety and security to other moving vehicles like trains, aeroplanes, ships and boat etc. as well. In his journey to innovate the tracking software Mr. SB's goal was to develop such a system where the user may track the details of their vehicles – their location, movement route, speed, halts and time taken in a particular journey.

THE INNOVATION JOURNEY

According to Drucker (1985) Innovation is the specific tool of entrepreneurs, the means by which they exploit change as an opportunity for a different business or a different service. It is capable of being presented as a discipline, capable of being learned, capable of being practiced. Entrepreneurs need to search purposefully for the sources of innovation, the changes and their symptoms that indicate opportunities for successful innovation and they need to know and to apply the principles of successful innovation. It is interesting to know as to how the idea of developing GPS tracking device for vehicles was turned into a reality.

The story as to how Mr. SB got the idea to develop this innovative product is also very interesting. The authors examined the entrepreneurial process followed by Mr. SB, Managing Director, Embarc to create Find'n'Secure. In the first part of the interviews, Mr. SB was asked to give a detailed history of how he built his firm, from the time he first had the idea until the time the Find'n'Secure was actually launched. The information collected was analyzed, and the process reconstructed. An analysis of the reconstruction reveals that the Embarc has gone through following six phases:

Emergence of the Business Idea:

Mr. S.P.Bagga, who was a very close friend of SB, owns a big transport company which has 64 trucks and a fleet of cars. He was fed up with the fraudulent ways of some of his unscrupulous drivers who were bent upon cheating him by submitting false reports of mileage they had actually covered. Mr. Bagga decided to take the help of SB because he knew his potential. The main requirement of Mr. Bagga was that some sort of device might be fitted in every vehicle which could help him monitor the movement of the vehicle through his laptop or even mobile whereby at the end of the day the errant driver might be confronted with the print out of the journey the driver had actually undertaken alongwith the real time of the journey.

Mr. SB had envisaged for a long time to develop an innovative GPS tracking and security system which aimed at offering innovative and cost effective tracking and security solutions comprising of hardware as well as software which could provide a perfect way to track and manage user's entire fleet of vehicles. This incident had sparked the idea in his mind to develop such a product.

Needs analysis: SB held brainstorming sessions with his peers, friends and professionals to find the ways and means as to how to give concrete shape to his brainchild, i.e. "Find'n'Secure". Although Mr. SB was busy in a different project yet he promised Mr. Bagga to turn the idea into a product in real time. It was like a challenge to him. He knew he could do it because his earlier project was also GPS linked. SB started the work in right earnestness. He consulted his friends also who were in the same trade. He put all his assistants to focus only on finding ways and means so that the idea could become a reality. In fact SB put his heart and soul into the new project because there was no question of looking back.

Innovation Landscape Idea to Product Development

Figure 1. Conceptual framework - Innovation Process for Find'n'Secure
(*Source: Authors, Dr. Alok Kumar Goel and Dr. Puja Singhal, 2015*)

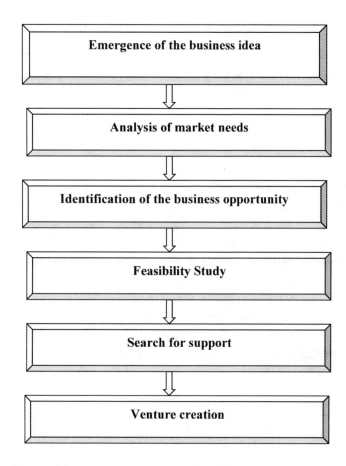

There was a time when he became desperate but then dedication and devotion brought a ray of hope and ultimately success came his way. It took about one and a half years for the project to turn into a reality. It was like a dream come true. His hard work had paid dividends.

This phase of the process differed significantly from the market survey phase of more traditional entrepreneurial processes. In a typical market survey, the product or service is already identified, and the goal is to see whether or not there is a big enough market for it, and on what conditions future customers would buy the product. According to Drucker (1985) the Innovator here in this case SB, must look at every unexpected success with the questions: (1) What would it mean to the Innovator if he exploited it? (2) Where could it lead him? (3) What would Innovator have to do to convert it into an opportunity? And (4) How do he go about it? This means, first, that Innovator need to set aside specific time in which to discuss unexpected successes; and to think through how it could be exploited. Mr. SB took into consideration the prevailing global scenario and security threats to address such needs into the unique features of "Find'n'Secure".

Identifying the opportunity: In his journey to innovate the tracking device Mr. SB's main objective was to utilize GPS and GIS technologies to make GPS tracking system applicable particularly in the field of Automatic Vehicle Location and Security. In the present case the opportunity could be given a concrete shape because the entrepreneur SB had assessed the market needs and chalked out a plan to address those needs in the form of "Find'n'Secure", an innovation in the field of vehicle tracking.

Project Feasibility: This phase looks at need as a source of innovation, and indeed as a major innovative opportunity as an old proverb says, "Necessity is the mother of invention." SB took the final decision of going ahead to start the production of "Find'n'Secure" in the wake of positive results of his interviews and brain storming sessions with cross sections of professionals and the market. This process led him to confirm the feasibility of the project. By the end of this decisive step, which confirmed the feasibility of the business opportunity, he had definitely decided to go into business. It was result of the firm decision of SB to go in for production that problems like obtaining finance, finding appropriate personnel to man the project and right place to locate his firm, etc. became his next agenda to solve.

Prototype and venture into the market: SB carried out extensive research and development culminating in a product prototype that was then tested with a certain number of potential clients. As the project entailed highly technical support, it became extremely difficult for SB to find a technically sound and competent team at Agra. Therefore, he had to plan to shift his base to Bangalore which was technically savvier and IT friendly where a team of competent professionals started working to develop the innovative tracking system.

A new GPS enabled vehicle tracking device was a reality which could be fitted in any vehicle. Mr. Bagga was the happiest man on the earth. He had already incurred heavy losses due to not being able to counter check the claims of the drivers. But now time had changed SB fitted the device in Mr. Bagga car first. The results were fantastic and encouraging. He could not believe his eyes. Not only the route covered by the car could be monitored but in case of emergency like theft even fuel supply or ignition could be stopped simply by clicking a button. It was unbelievable yet it was a reality. SB installed the vehicle location tracking device in all his trucks and monitor the movement of all his trucks whether they were in Delhi or Mumbai. The drivers who were used to adopt unfair means were taken aback when confronted with the proof of their real movements.

The story did not end there. In fact it was the beginning of a new era which would leave it imprints even on the coming generations. It was a case of great transformation of an idea into a product. Knowledge-based innovation is the "super-star" of entrepreneurship. It is what people normally mean when they talk of innovation. SB had to find partners to fund the business and to refine the technological and marketing aspects of the business concept program. When he planned to bring this innovative Automatic Vehicle Location (AVL) device out in the market, the Indian Innovators Association, a non-profit organization of innovators formed to help other innovators, came forward to fund his research to develop the device.

Product Innovation (Find'n'Secure)

Find'n'Secure is an innovative product and extremely advanced automatic vehicle location and security device. It is a unique way for companies and individuals to monitor and control their cars, jeeps, trucks and other vehicles to their precise details while sitting in office. It also enables the user to monitor the movements of their employees, children, pets, spouse, containers or any other asset accurately. Global Positioning System (GPS) tracking system of Find'n'Secure enables users to monitor the movements of their employees, drivers, vehicles or any other asset accurately through GPS tracking system.

It uses a combination of GPS location technology, wireless communication network and different mapping utilities publicly available to provide accurate location of the object in any part of the globe with ability to completely control the same. Find'n'Secure Automatic Location System consists of a AVL unit, a two way communications link between the tracker and the user and a web based tracking software for tracking, monitoring and control. This Automatic Vehicle Location device receives location coordinates from the GPS satellites and transmits them to a web server through the GPRS (General Packet Radio Service) network. The communication system is usually a cellular network similar to the one used by your cellular phone.

The data can also be analyzed for over-speeding, extra-stopping, maintenance planning and other uses. A virtual geo-fence can also be created and when the vehicle enters or leaves the geo-fence, an SMS alert will be received on the mobile. An additional and unique feature of the device is that it can immobilize the vehicle by cutting the ignition or the fuel pump by remote in case of theft. An emergency button sends panic signals or a distress message to the call centre. During an interview Mr. SB told that there is also a provision for battery backup good enough to last 16 hours, after the main battery has been disconnected. This system will work across the globe.

How Find'n'Secure Works

Find'n'Secure automatic location unit is discreetly kept in pocket (Personal Tracker) or installed inside the vehicle (Vehicle unit). Location data is computed by the unit using signals received from GPS satellite. It processes the location data and transmits it via communication network to the web server and from there it is accessed by the call centre or the user on his PC or mobile phone. The user or the call centre can also control the vehicle from his PC / Mobile phone, if required. This system is of great value to the fleet managers because it enables them to view real time location of the vehicles by looking at the area map on their PC / mobile phone. A fleet manager may also take control of the fleet through geofencing (by demarcating specific geographical area for a vehicle on the computer screen) and if the vehicle violates the defined route, he can stop the vehicle from moving. Information retrieved about the actual operation of the fleet is summarized through system generated reports that should help in improving management decisions for cost reduction and increased profitability of the business.

Main advantages of Find'n'Secure vehicle tracking system is:

1. Find'n'Secure is a fully automatic unique GPS Monitoring System which makes recovery of stolen vehicles possible even up to 99%.
2. User could see a moving target (e.g., a car, a bus, a truck, a trailer, a container etc.) real time on internet enabled PC/PDA.
3. User could see group of vehicles together on the same screen with position automatically being updated in real time.
4. Based on true GPS satellite signals and works throughout the globe where cellular coverage is available.
5. Ability to overlay custom maps over Google Maps for those areas which currently do not have street level coverage in Google Maps.
6. Ability to set up Geographical Virtual fence simply by clicking on the map (Automatic alerts are released when the vehicle enters or leaves the geofence).
7. User could Lock / unlock doors of the vehicle from computer / mobile and even switch off engine / fuel pump in case of theft.

8. User could press panic button in case of emergency for automatic distress message to Call center / mobile.
9. It works even when battery is disconnected and insurance premium discounts may apply on account of these unique features of our automatic vehicle location system.
10. Many useful reports like distance travelled in a day for a given period, over speeding, places visited, vehicle group summary, current fleet status, speed analysis etc. may be drawn at the click of the mouse.
11. Hardware may be shifted from one vehicle to another with ease and automatically locates nearest vehicle from a group of vehicles to be deployed to a desired location.
12. Greater number of pickups and deliveries in a day on account of efficient fleet monitoring thereby increased on time performance.

THE CURRENT BODY OF KNOWLEDGE

GPS Tracking System

The Global Positioning System (GPS) is a satellite-based navigation system made up of a network of 24 satellites placed into orbit by the U.S. Department of Defense. GPS works in any weather conditions, anywhere in the world, 24 hours a day. GPS satellites circle the earth twice daily and transmit signal information. GPS receivers use the information to calculate the user's location by the method of triangulation. Basically, the GPS receiver compares the time a signal was transmitted by a satellite with the time it was received. The time difference tells the GPS receiver how far away the satellite is. The receiver must lock on to the signal of at least three satellites to calculate a 2-D position, the latitudinal and longitudinal position, and track movement. Using four or more satellites, the receiver can determine the user's 3-D position, the latitude, longitude, and altitude. Once the position has been determined, the GPS unit can calculate other information such as speed, track, trip distance, bearing and more.

GPS Tracking Unit

A GPS tracking unit is a device that uses the Global Positioning System to determine the precise location of a vehicle, person, or any other asset to which it is attached and to record the position of the asset at regular intervals. The recorded location data can be stored within the tracking unit, or it may be transmitted to a central location data base, or internet-connected computer, using a cellular, radio, or satellite modem embedded in the unit. This allows the asset's location to be displayed against a map backdrop either in real-time or when analysing the track later, using customized software. Most common application of GPS tracking system is applied for tracking of moving objects, such as, vehicles. It is a unique way for companies and individuals to monitor and control their cars, jeeps, trucks and other vehicles to their precise details by sitting in the office.

Geofence

A Geofence is a virtual perimeter on a geographic area using location-based service, so that when the geofencing device enters or exits the defined area, a notification is generated. The notification may be sent to a cell phone, email, Personal Digital Assistant (PDA) or Find'n'Secure tracking software. It includes complete information such as the time, date and location that the virtual boundary was crossed, allowing for an immediate investigation or response to the situation.

Indian Electronics and IT Sector

Electronics and Information Technology is the fastest growing segment of Indian industry both in terms of production and export. The Government of India has announced promotion of IT as one of the five priorities of the country. Imparting greater transparency to business procedures and integration with global market are seen as the hallmark of new industrial, trade and fiscal policies of Indian Government. India's Electronics and IT export has been growing at an annual average growth rate of 18 percent during the past five years.

How does Find'n'Secure Works?

Find'n'Secure Automatic Location unit is discreetly kept in pocket (Personal Tracker) or installed inside the vehicle (Vehicle unit). Location data is computed by the unit using signals received from GPS satellite. It processes the location data and transmits it via communication network to the web server and from there it is accessed by the call centre or the user on his PC or mobile phone. The user or the call centre can also control the vehicle from his PC / Mobile phone, if required. This system is of great value to the fleet managers because it enables them to view real time location of the vehicles by looking at the area map on his PC / mobile phone. A fleet manager may also take control of the fleet through geofencing (by demarcating specific geographical area for a vehicle on the computer screen) and if the vehicle violates the defined route, he can stop the vehicle from moving. Information retrieved about the actual operation of the fleet is summarized through system generated reports that should help in improving management decisions for cost reduction and increased profitability of the business. In case of theft of a vehicle, the options of "Blow horn" and "Open Doors" may be triggered which will attract the attention of passers by. Further, the vehicle will come to a grinding halt by opting the "Engine Block" feature on the computer screen of the software. This way, the vehicle may be saved from theft/robbery. On the other hand, the personal tracker is of immense help in the personal security of an individual as through it, the actual movements of an individual may be viewed in the area map on a PC / mobile phone.

Unique Innovative Features

- Real time tracking in group as well as individual modes
- Support Google maps and Microsoft Virtual Earth
- Complete control of the vehicle through the web
- Find closest tracker to a desired destination using locator tool
- View tracker history for a given period
- Know estimated time of arrival
- Route Optimization
- Enhanced animated view to traverse the travelled path through history tool
- Real time graphic representation of distance and speed
- Create polygon and circular Geofences using Geofence tool

- Schedule time specific Geofences activation/deactivation
- Multi-lingual & time zone support

Application of Find'n'Secure

- Transportation – Real time fleet management
- Public Transportation – Tracking of buses, trucks, trailers, vans, taxis, tankers etc.
- Family - Tracking of children, spouse, elderly person, Alzheimer's patients, pet etc.
- Special Equipments - Tracking of expensive construction and farm equipments
- Security - Tracking of criminals on parole, detective agencies can use it for tracking suspects.
- Emergency Services - Police / Fire / Paramedics etc.
- Railways - Real time tracking of movements of trains
- Military and Logistics
- Forestry, Oil and Gas Explorations
- Wild Life - Tracking of tigers, horses, cattle and other animals
- Tracking of trains, ships and aeroplanes.

SUPPORT FROM GOVERNMENT POLICIES

The primary responsibility of promotion and development of SMEs is of the State Governments. However, the Government of India, supplements the efforts of the State Governments through various initiatives. The role of the Ministry of MSME and its organizations is to assist the States in their efforts to encourage entrepreneurship, employment and livelihood opportunities and enhance the competitiveness of MSMEs in the changed economic scenario. The schemes undertaken by the Ministry and its organizations seek to facilitate/provide: i) adequate flow of credit from financial institutions/banks; ii) support for technology up-gradation and modernization; iii) integrated infrastructural facilities; iv) modern testing facilities and quality certification; v) access to modern management practices; vi) entrepreneurship development and skill up-gradation through appropriate training facilities; vii) support for product development, design intervention and packaging; viii) welfare of artisans and workers; ix) assistance for better access to domestic and export markets and x) cluster-wise measures to promote capacity building and empowerment of the units and their collectives.

In view of the great potential of earning foreign exchange by the export of vehicle tracking device Find'n'Secure to foreign countries, the Indian Government under its MSME promotional scheme has allotted built-up space to Embarc Information (P) Ltd. in Noida Special Economic Zone (NSEZ) to carry out production activities. As per the Govt. policies the units located in NSEZ have been exempted from paying income tax, sales tax, excise duty etc. As a result of this incentive from the Govt. Mr. SB has been able to export his device to more than 40 countries earning precious foreign exchange for the country in the process.

Besides this support from the Govt., Electronics and Computer Software Export Promotion Council (ESC), a Govt. of India sponsored body has provided significant support to Mr. SB to enable him to participate in international exhibitions, conferences and industry level talks. With this Govt. support through

ESC, Embarc has been able to showcase his innovation in several countries. This support from ESC has also helped Mr. SB to establish joint ventures through MOU and marketing and business tie-ups. Indian enterprises will depend on the extent to which they will be able to identify and exploit technological opportunities to create new or significantly improved products and to successfully commercialize them, referred to as technological entrepreneurship capabilities.

CONCLUSION

The study has found that entrepreneurial orientation and new product development are positively related to each other and interact to help an organization to flourish; entrepreneurship and innovation are complementary, and a combination of the two is vital to product innovation and sustainability in today's dynamic and changing environment; entrepreneurship and innovation are not confined to the initial stages of a new venture; rather, they are dynamic and holistic processes in entrepreneurial and innovative organizations.

The study reveals that knowledge-based product innovation needs certain specific requirements and these requirements differ from those of any other kind of innovation. knowledge-based innovation requires careful analysis of all the necessary factors, whether knowledge itself, social, economic or perceptual factors. The analysis must identify what factors are not yet available so that the entrepreneur can decide whether these missing factors can be produced-whether the innovation had better be postponed as not yet feasible. In the study the innovator SB take care of this aspect and thought proactively for what his knowledge-based innovation required. The second requirement of knowledge-based innovation is a clear focus on the strategic position. Finally, the knowledge-based innovator, here in this case is Mr. SB and especially the one whose innovation is based on technological knowledge - needs to learn and to practice entrepreneurial management. In fact, entrepreneurial orientation is more crucial to knowledge-based innovation than to any other kind (Drucker, 1985).

The present paper illustrates successful journey as to how an idea converted in to product innovation and analyzed it vis-à-vis the innovation principles propounded by Drucker(1985). Knowledge-based innovation differs from all other innovations in its basic characteristics: time span, casualty rate, predictability, and in the challenges it poses to the entrepreneur. This exploratory study contributes to an understanding of the existing theories and practices of entrepreneurial orientation and innovation. Its most important contribution certainly lies in highlighting the knowledge creation process. This study will certainly be of interest to researchers working on business idea exploration and also to new product development.

As the study used evidence based research method and drawn inferences from case study. This research approach is especially appropriate in new topic areas and such methods are used to drive new theories (Eisenhardt, 1989), but some characteristics that lead to strengths in theory building from case studies also lead to weaknesses. Theorists working from case data can lose their sense of proportion as they confront vivid, voluminous data. In order to generalize research outcomes there is a need to apply empirical research methods followed by quantitative studies involving large samples in various industries and countries to determine the relative importance of factors, to build path models to understand chains of effects and to formally test for context dependencies. This study leaves several issues for discussion.

NOTE

This manuscript is written solely for educational purposes and is not intended to represent successful or unsuccessful managerial decision making. The authors may have disguised names; financial and other recognizable information to protect confidentiality.

ACKNOWLEDGMENT

The authors express their thanks to the Managing Director of Embarc Information Technology (P) Ltd. for his full support and permission to develop this chapter. We sincerely thank Prof. G.D. Sardana and Prof. Tojo Thatchenkery and grateful to the reviewers for their many valuable suggestions to develop this manuscript.

REFERENCES

Antoncic, B., & Prodan, I. (2008). Alliances, corporate technological entrepreneurship and firm performance: Testing a model on manufacturing firms. *Technovation*, *28*(5), 257–265. doi:10.1016/j.technovation.2007.07.005

Brunswicker, S., & Vrande, V. V. (2014). Exploring Open Innovation in Small and Medium-Sized Enterprises. In New Frontiers in Open Innovation. Oxford Publications. doi:10.1093/acprof:oso/9780199682461.003.0007

Dahlander, L., & Gann, D. M. (2010). How open is innovation? *Research Policy*, *39*(6), 699–709. doi:10.1016/j.respol.2010.01.013

Drucker, P. (1985). *Entrepreneurship and Innovation: Practice and Principles*. New York, NY: HarperBusiness.

Eisenhardt, K. M. (1989). Building Theories from Case Study Research. *Academy of Management Review*, *14*(4), 532–550.

Grawitz, M. (1996). *Me'thodes des Sciences Sociales* (10th ed.). Paris: Dalloz.

Ireland, R. D., Hitt, M. A., Camp, S. M., & Sexton, D. L. (2001). Integrating entrepreneurship actions and strategic management actions to create firm wealth. *The Academy of Management Executive*, *15*(1), 49–63. doi:10.5465/AME.2001.4251393

Ju, P. H., Chen, D.-N., Yu, Y.-C., & Wei, H.-L. (2013). Relationships among Open Innovation Processes, Entrepreneurial Orientation, and Organizational Performance of SMEs: The Moderating Role of Technological Turbulence. In *Perspectives in Business Informatics Research - 12th International Conference, BIR 2013*. Warsaw, Poland: Springer.

Lee, S., Park, G., Yoon, B., & Park, J. (2010). Open innovation in SMEs - An intermediated network model. *Research Policy*, *39*(2), 290–300. doi:10.1016/j.respol.2009.12.009

Rahman, H., & Ramos, I. (2010). Open Innovation in SMEs: From closed boundaries to networked paradigm. *Issues in Informing Science and Information Technology, 7*, 471–487.

Roijakkers, N., Zynga, A., & Bishop, C. (2014). Getting Help from Innomediaries. In H. Chesbrough, W. Vanhaverbeke, & J. West (Eds.), *New Frontiers in Open Innovation* (pp. 135–156). Oxford Publications. doi:10.1093/acprof:oso/9780199682461.003.0013

Rubin, H.-J., & Rubin, I.-S. (1995). *Qualitative Interviewing: The Art of Hearing Data*. London: Sage Publications.

Yin, R. K. (1994). *Case Study Research: Design and Method* (2nd ed.). Thousand Oaks, CA: Sage Publications.

Compilation of References

3MCulture. (2009). *3M – A Culture of Innovation*. Retrieved from http://www.3m.com/us/office/ postit/pastpresent/history_cu.html

Abello, J., Resende, M. G. C., & Sudarsky, S. (2002). Massive quasi-clique detection. doi:10.1007/3-540-45995-2_51

Aboelmaged, M. G. (2014). Predicting e-readiness at firm-level: An analysis of technological, organizational and environmental (TOE) effects on e-maintenance readiness in manufacturing firms. *International Journal of Information Management*, *34*(5), 639–651. doi:10.1016/j.ijinfomgt.2014.05.002

Ackerman, M. S., Dachtera, J., Pipek, V., & Wulf, V. (2013). Sharing knowledge and expertise: The CSCW view of knowledge management. *Computer Supported Cooperative Work*, *22*(4/6), 531–573. doi:10.1007/s10606-013-9192-8

Acur, N., Kandemir, D., & Boer, H. (2012). Strategic alignment and new product development: Drivers and performance effects. *Journal of Product Innovation Management*, *29*(2), 304–318. doi:10.1111/j.1540-5885.2011.00897.x

Agrawal, R., & Srikant, R. (1994). Fast algorithms for mining association rules. In *Proceedings of 1994 International Conference Very Large Data Bases* (VLDB'94).

Ahmed-Kristensen, S., & Vianello, G. (2015). A model for reusing service knowledge based on an empirical case. *Research in Engineering Design*, *26*(1), 57–76. doi:10.1007/s00163-014-0184-6

Ahmed, P. K. (1998). Culture and climate for innovation. *European Journal of Innovation Management*, *1*(1), 30–43. doi:10.1108/14601069810199131

Akbar, H., & Tzokas, N. (2013). An exploration of new product development's front-end knowledge conceptualization process in discontinuous innovations. *British Journal of Management*, *24*(2), 245–263. doi:10.1111/j.1467-8551.2011.00801.x

Akgün, A. E., Keskin, H., Lynn, G., & Dogan, D. (2012). Antecedents and consequences of team sensemaking capability in product development projects. *R&D Management*, *42*(5), 473–493. doi: 10.1111/j.1467-9310.2012.00696.x

Alam, I. (2013). Customer interaction in service innovation: Evidence from India. *International Journal of Emerging Markets*, *8*(1), 41–64. doi:10.1108/17468801311297273

Alavi, M., & Leidner, D. E. (2001). Review: knowledge management and knowledge management systems: conceptual foundations and research issues. *Management Information Systems Quarterly*, *25*(1), 107–136. doi:10.2307/3250961

Alonso, R., Dessein, W., & Matouschek, N. (2008). When does coordination require centralization? *The American Economic Review*, *98*(1), 145–179. doi:10.1257/aer.98.1.145

Altmetrics.org. (2014). *About altmetrics*. Retrieved from http://altmetrics.org/about/

Compilation of References

Anand, A., Kant, R., Patel, D. P., & Singh, M. D. (2015). Knowledge management implementation: A predictive model using an analytical hierarchical process. *Journal of the Knowledge Economy*, *6*(1), 48–71. doi:10.1007/s13132-012-0110-y

Anderson, C. (2009). *Free: the future of a radical price*. New York: Hyperion.

Anderson, R. D., Jerman, R. E., & Crum, M. R. (1998). Quality Management influences on logistics performance. *Transportation Research Part E, Logistics and Transportation Review*, *34*(2), 137–148. doi:10.1016/S1366-5545(98)00008-8

Andries, P., & Czarnitzki, D. (2014). Small firm innovation performance and employee involvement. *Small Business Economics*, *43*(1), 21–38. doi:10.1007/s11187-014-9577-1

Angelstam, P., Elbakidze, M., Axelsson, R., Dixelius, M., & Törnblom, J. (2013). Knowledge production and learning for sustainable landscapes: Seven steps using social-ecological systems as laboratories. *Ambio*, *42*(2), 116–128. doi:10.1007/s13280-012-0367-1 PMID:23475650

Antoncic, B., & Prodan, I. (2008). Alliances, corporate technological entrepreneurship and firm performance: Testing a model on manufacturing firms. *Technovation*, *28*(5), 257–265. doi:10.1016/j.technovation.2007.07.005

Anttonen, M. (2010). Greening from the Front to the Back Door? A Typology of Chemical and Resource Management Services. *Business Strategy and the Environment*, *19*, 199–215.

Aral, S., Dellarocas, C., & Godes, D. (2013). Introduction to the Special Issue—Social Media and Business Transformation: A Framework for Research. *Information Systems Research*, *24*(1), 3–13. doi:10.1287/isre.1120.0470

Audretsch, D., & Thurik, R. (2000). Capitalism and democracy in the 21st century: From the managed to the entrepreneurial economy. *Journal of Evolutionary Economics*, *10*(1), 17–34. doi:10.1007/s001910050003

Bagnoli, C., & Vedovato, M. (2014). The impact of knowledge management and strategy configuration coherence on SME performance. *Journal of Management & Governance*, *18*(2), 615–647. doi:10.1007/s10997-012-9211-z

Bagozzi, R. P., & Yi, Y. (1998). On evaluation of structural equations models. *Journal of the Academy of Marketing Science*, *16*(1), 74–94. doi:10.1007/BF02723327

Baker, P. (2004). Aligning Distribution Centre Operations to Supply Chain Strategy. *International Journal of Logistics Management*, *15*(1), 111–123. doi:10.1108/09574090410700266

Baltatzis, G., Ormrod, D. G., & Grainger, N. (2008). Social networking tools for internal communication in large organizations: Benefits and barriers. *ACIS 2008 Proceedings*, 86.

Bandler, R., Robert, A., & Fitzpatrick, O. (2013). *An Introduction To Nlp*. New York: Harper Collins Publishers.

Bandyopadhyay, S., Sinha, & Rao. (2006). *Social Network Analysis, a handbook*. Sage Publications Inc.

Barreto, O. E. A. (2012). *Gestión del conocimiento a través del Gerente de Proyectos de un modelo logístico*. (Magister dissertation). Universidad Metropolitana, Caracas, Venezuela.

Batagelj, V., & Mrvar, A. P. (2003). Analysis and visualization of large networks. In M. Junger & P. Mutzel (Eds.), *Graph Drawing Software*. Springer Verlag.

Baumgartner, H., & Homburg, C. (1996). Applications of structural equation modelling in marketing and consumer research: A review. *International Journal of Research in Marketing*, *13*(1), 139–161. doi:10.1016/0167-8116(95)00038-0

Bayo-Moriones, A., & Lera-Lopez, F. (2007). A firm level analysis of determinants of ICT adoption in Spain. *Technovation*, *27*(6/7), 352–366. doi:10.1016/j.technovation.2007.01.003

Becker, S. O., & Egger, P. H. (2013). Endogenous product versus process innovation and a firm's propensity to export. *Empirical Economics*, *44*(1), 329–354. doi:10.1007/s00181-009-0322-6

Belso-Martinez, J. A., & Molina-Morales, F. X. (2013). Non-linear relationships of internal and external resources on a firm's innovation: The case of the Spanish Vinalopó footwear cluster. *Growth and Change*, *44*(3), 494–521. doi:10.1111/grow.12017

Bennett, J., Owers, M., Pitt, M., & Tucker, M. (2010). Workplace impact of social networking. *Property Management*, *28*(3), 138–148. doi:10.1108/02637471011051282

Berends, H., Jelinek, M., Reymen, I., & Stultiëns, R. (2014). Product innovation processes in small firms: Combining entrepreneurial effectuation and managerial causation. *Journal of Product Innovation Management*, *31*(3), 616–635. doi:10.1111/jpim.12117

Berendt, B. (2005). The semantics of frequent subgraphs: Mining and navigation pattern analysis. In Proceedings of WebKDD. Chicago: Academic Press.

Bergkvist, L., & Rossiter, J. R. (2007). The predictive validity of multiple-item versus single-item measures of the same constructs. *JMR, Journal of Marketing Research*, *44*(2), 175–184. doi:10.1509/jmkr.44.2.175

Bernardi, A. (2013). iGreen–Intelligent technologies for public-private knowledge management in agriculture. *KI - Künstliche Intelligenz*, *27*(4), 347–350.

Berners-Lee, T., Hendler, J., & Lassila, O. (2001). The semantic Web. *Scientific American*, *279*(5), 34–43. doi:10.1038/scientificamerican0501-34 PMID:11681174

Bettiol, M., Di Maria, E., & Grandinetti, R. (2012). Codification and creativity: Knowledge management strategies in KIBS. *Journal of Knowledge Management*, *16*(4), 550–562. doi:10.1108/13673271211246130

Bhagwat, R., & Sharma, M. K. (2007). Information system architecture: A framework for a cluster of small- and medium-sized enterprises (SMEs). *Production Planning and Control*, *18*(4), 283–296. doi:10.1080/09537280701248578

Bharadwaj, A. S. (2000). A resource-based perspective on information technology capability and firm performance: An empirical investigation. *Management Information Systems Quarterly*, *24*(1), 169–196. doi:10.2307/3250983

Bidmeshgipour, M., Ismail, W. K. W., & Omar, R. (2012). Knowledge management and organizational innovativeness in Iranian banking industry. *Knowledge Management and E-Learning*, *4*(4), 481–499.

Bielaczyc, K., & Ow, J. (2014). Multi-player epistemic games: Guiding the enactment of classroom knowledge-building communities. *International Journal of Computer-Supported Collaborative Learning*, *9*(1), 33–62. doi:10.1007/s11412-013-9186-z

Binney, D. (2001). The Knowledge Management spectrum–understanding the KM landscape. *Journal of Knowledge Management*, *5*(1), 33–42. doi:10.1108/13673270110384383

Björk, J. (2012). Knowledge domain spanners in ideation. *Creativity and Innovation Management*, *21*(1), 17–27. doi:10.1111/j.1467-8691.2012.00627.x

Blindenbach-Driessen, F., Van Dalen, J., & Van Den Ende, J. (2010). Subjective Performance Assessment of Innovation Projects*. *Journal of Product Innovation Management*, *27*(4), 572–592. doi:10.1111/j.1540-5885.2010.00736.x

Board of Innovations. (2011). *Open Innovation and Crowd-sourcing Examples*. Retrieved 12 November 2014 from, http://www.boardofinnovation.com/list-open-innovation-crowdsourcing-examples/

Bodewes, W. E. (2002). Formalization and innovation revisited. *European Journal of Innovation Management*, 5(4), 214–223. doi:10.1108/14601060210451171

Bohlmann, J. D., Spanjol, J., Qualls, W. J., & Rosa, J. A. (2013). The interplay of customer and product innovation dynamics: An exploratory study. *Journal of Product Innovation Management*, 30(2), 228–244. doi:10.1111/j.1540-5885.2012.00962.x

Borgelt, C., & Berthold, M. R. (2002). Mining molecular fragments:Finding relevant substructures of molecules. In *Proceedings of 2002 International Conference on Data Mining* (ICDM'02). Academic Press.

Borges, R. (2013). Tacit knowledge sharing between IT workers: The role of organizational culture, personality, and social environment. *Management Research Review*, 36(1), 89–108. doi:10.1108/01409171311284602

Bower, B. (2010). *Wired Science Online: No Lie! Your Facebook Profile Is the Real You*. Retrieved from http://www.wired.com/wired-science/2010/02/no-lie-your-facebook-profile-is-the-real-you/

Bradford, M., Earp, J. B., & Grabski, S. (2014). Centralized end-to-end identity and access management and ERP systems: A multi-case analysis using the technology organization environment framework. *International Journal of Accounting Information Systems*, 15(2), 149–165. doi:10.1016/j.accinf.2014.01.003

Brandes, U., & Erlebach, T. (Eds.). (2005). Network Analysis: Methodological Foundations. Lecture Notes in Computer Science, 3418.

Brandes, U., Kenis, P., & Wagner, D. (2003). Communicating centrality in policy network drawings. *IEEE Transactions on Visualization and Computer Graphics*, 9(2), 241–253. doi:10.1109/TVCG.2003.1196010

Brandes, U., & Wagner Visone, D. (2003). Analysis and visualization of social networks. In M. Junger & P. Mutzel (Eds.), *Graph Drawing Software* (pp. 321–340). Berlin: Springer Verlag.

Breunig, K. J., & Hydle, K. M. (2013). Remote control: Measuring performance for value creation and governance of globally distributed knowledge work. *Journal of Management & Governance*, 17(3), 559–582. doi:10.1007/s10997-011-9194-1

Bridges, K. (2013). Use of Social Media by Catholic Organizations. *New Theology Review*, 26(1), 1–10.

Brinkley, I., Fauth, R., Mahdon, M., & Theodoropoulou, S. (2009). *Knowledge workers and knowledge work; A Knowledge Economy Programme Report*. London: The Work Foundation.

Brito. (2012, January 4). *Lessons from IBM: 4 Barriers To Social Business Adoption*. Retrieved from http://www.socialbusinessnews.com/lessons-from-ibm-4-barriers-to-social-business-adoption/

Broadbent, M. (1998). The phenomenon of knowledge management: What does it mean to the information profession. *Information Outlook*, 2(5), 23–36.

Broder, A., Kumar, R., Maghoul, F., Raghavan, P., Rajagopalan, S., Stat, R., & Tomkins, A. (2000). Graph Structure in the Web: Experiments and models. In *Proceedings of the World Wide Web Conference*. Amsterdam, The Netherlands: Academic Press. doi:10.1016/S1389-1286(00)00083-9

Brunswicker, S., & Vrande, V. V. (2014). Exploring Open Innovation in Small and Medium-Sized Enterprises. In New Frontiers in Open Innovation. Oxford Publications. doi:10.1093/acprof:oso/9780199682461.003.0007

Brzozowski, M. J. (2009, May). WaterCooler: exploring an organization through enterprise social media. In *Proceedings of the ACM 2009 International Conference on Supporting group work* (pp. 219-228). ACM. doi:10.1145/1531674.1531706

Buck, E. (2013, July 30). *Can I dismiss for an employee for making comments on a social media?* Retrieved from http://fpmblog.co.uk/2013/07/30/can-i-dismiss-for-an-employee-for-making-inappropriate-comments-on-a-social-media-site/

Bunke, H. (1997). On a Relation between Graph Edit Distance and Maximum Common Subgraph. *Pattern Recognition Letters, 18*(8), 689–694. doi:10.1016/S0167-8655(97)00060-3

Burke, C. S., Fiore, S. M., Goodwin, G. F., Rosen, M. A., & Salas, E. (2006). The making of a dream team: When expert teams do best. In K. A. Ericsson (Ed.), *The Cambridge Handbook of Expertise and Expert Performance* (pp. 439–453). New York, NY: Cambridge University Press.

Burns, T., & Stalker, G. M. (2011).Mechanistic and Organic Systems of Management. S*ociology of Organizations: Structures and Relationships*, 14.

Burns, M. J., Craig, R. B. Jr, Friedman, B. D., Schott, P. D., & Senot, C. (2011). Transforming enterprise communications through the blending of social networking and unified communications. *Bell Labs Technical Journal, 16*(1), 19–34. doi:10.1002/bltj.20483

Cankurtaran, P., Langerak, F., & Griffin, A. (2013). Consequences of new product development speed: A meta-analysis. *Journal of Product Innovation Management, 30*(3), 465–486. doi:10.1111/jpim.12011

Carbonell, P., & Rodríguez-Escudero, A. I. (2009). Relationships among team's organizational context, innovation speed, and technological uncertainty: An empirical analysis. *Journal of Engineering and Technology Management, 26*(1), 28–45. doi:10.1016/j.jengtecman.2009.03.005

Carbonell, P., Rodríguez-Escudero, A. I., & Pujari, D. (2009). Customer Involvement in New Service Development: An Examination of Antecedents and Outcomes*. *Journal of Product Innovation Management, 26*(5), 536–550. doi:10.1111/j.1540-5885.2009.00679.x

Carneiro, A. (2000). How does knowledge management influence innovation and competitiveness? *Journal of Knowledge Management, 4*(2), 87–98. doi:10.1108/13673270010372242

Carr. (2011). 10 Enterprise Social Networking Obstacles. *InformationWeek*. Retrieved from http://www.informationweek.com/social-business/social_networking_private_platforms/10-enterprise-social-networking-obstacle/232301139

Carroll, D. (2009). *United Breaks Guitars*. Retrieved from http://www.davecarrollmusic.com/ story/united-breaks-guitars/

Carson, D., & Gilmore, A. (2000). SME marketing management competencies. *International Business Review, 9*(3), 363–382. doi:10.1016/S0969-5931(00)00006-8

Castaño-Martínez, M. S. (2012). Product innovation and R&D policy: The case of the transformation industries in developed and developing. *The International Entrepreneurship and Management Journal, 8*(4), 421–436. doi:10.1007/s11365-012-0228-1

Catenazzi, N., & Sommaruga, L. (2013). Generic environments for knowledge management and visualization. *Journal of Ambient Intelligence and Humanized Computing, 4*(1), 99–108. doi:10.1007/s12652-011-0097-4

Černe, M., Jaklič, M., & Škerlavaj, M. (2013). Management innovation in focus: The role of knowledge exchange, organizational size, and IT system development and utilization. *European Management Review, 10*(3), 153–166. doi:10.1111/emre.12013

Chai, K. H., Wang, Q., Song, M., Halman, J. I. M., & Brombacher, A. C. (2012). Understanding competencies in platform-based product development: Antecedents and outcomes. *Journal of Product Innovation Management, 29*(3), 452–472. doi:10.1111/j.1540-5885.2012.00917.x

Compilation of References

Chai, S., & Kim, M. (2012). A socio-technical approach to knowledge contribution behavior: An empirical investigation of social networking sites users. *International Journal of Information Management*, *32*(2), 118–126. doi:10.1016/j.ijinfomgt.2011.07.004

Chakrabarti, S. (2000). Data mining for hypertext: A tutorial survey. *SIGKDD Explorations*, *1*(2), 1–11. doi:10.1145/846183.846187

Chan, F. T. S., Chong, A. Y.-L., & Zhou, L. (2012). An empirical investigation of factors affecting e-collaboration diffusion in SMEs. *International Journal of Production Economics*, *138*(2), 329–344. doi:10.1016/j.ijpe.2012.04.004

Chang, I., Hsin-Ginn, H., Ming-Chien, H., Ming-Hui, L., & David, C. Y. (2007). Factors affecting the adoption of electronic signature: Executives' perspective of hospital information department. *Decision Support Systems*, *44*(1), 350–359. doi:10.1016/j.dss.2007.04.006

Chan, R. C. H., Chu, S. K. W., Lee, C. W. Y., Chan, B. K. T., & Leung, C. K. (2013). Knowledge management using social media: A comparative study between blogs and Facebook. *Proceedings of the American Society for Information Science and Technology*, *50*(1), 1–9.

Chatterji, A. K., & Fabrizio, K. R. (2014). Using users: When does external knowledge enhance corporate product innovation? *Strategic Management Journal*, *35*(10), 1427–1445. doi:10.1002/smj.2168

Chatti, A., Klamma, R., Jarke, M., & Naeve, A. (2007). *The Web 2.0 driven SECI model based learning process*. Paper presented at the International Conference of Advanced Learning Technologies (ICALT-2007), Japan. doi:10.1109/ICALT.2007.256

Chen, M., & Chen, A. (2005). Integrating option model and knowledge management performance measures: An empirical study. *Journal of Information Science*, *31*(5), 381–393. doi:10.1177/0165551505055402

Cheong, R. K. F., & Tsui, E. (2010). The Roles and Values of Personal Knowledge Management: An exploratory study. VINE The Journal of Information and Knowledge Management System, 40(2), 204–227.

Cheong, R.K.F., & Tsui, E. (2011). From Skills and Competencies to Outcome-based Collaborative Work: Tracking a Decade's Development of Personal Knowledge Management (PKM) Models. *Knowledge and Process Management: The Journal of Corporate transformation,18*(3), 175-193.

Chesbrough, H. (2003). *Open Innovation: The new imperative for creating and profiting from technology*. Boston: Harvard Business School Press.

Cholette, S., & Venkat, K. (2009). The energy and carbon intensity of wine distribution: A study of logistical options for delivering wine to consumers. *Journal of Cleaner Production*, 1–13.

Chong, A. Y. L., & Chan, F. T. S. (2012). Radio Frequency Identification (RFID) in the healthcare industry: A multi-stage diffusion analysis. *Expert Systems with Applications*, *39*(10), 8645–8654. doi:10.1016/j.eswa.2012.01.201

Choo, M. (2014). *Exploring Knowing in Practice*. (Unpublished master's thesis). Linnaeus University, Kalmar, Sweden.

Choo, C., & Bontis, N. (2002). *The strategic management of intellectual capital and organizational knowledge*. New York, NY: Oxford University Press.

Cho, T., & Korte, R. (2014). Managing knowledge performance: Testing the components of a knowledge management system on organizational performance. *Asia Pacific Education Review*, *15*(2), 313–327. doi:10.1007/s12564-014-9333-x

Chou, T. C., Chang, P. L., Tsai, C. T., & Cheng, Y. P. (2005). Internal learning climate, knowledge management process and perceived knowledge management satisfaction. *Journal of Information Science*, *31*(4), 283–296. doi:10.1177/0165551505054171

Chua, A. Y. K. (2006). Starting a Community-of-practice at Holden College: A Reflection of the Experience. *OR Insight*, *19*, 3–8.

Chuang, S. H., Liao, C., & Lin, S. (2013). Determinants of knowledge management with information technology support impact on firm performance. *Information Technology Management*, *14*(3), 217–230. doi:10.1007/s10799-013-0153-1

Chu, M. T., Khosla, R., & Nishida, T. (2012). Communities of practice model driven knowledge management in multinational knowledge based enterprises. *Journal of Intelligent Manufacturing*, *23*(5), 1707–1720. doi:10.1007/s10845-010-0472-6

Chu, M. T., Kumar, P., Kumar, K., & Khosla, R. (2014). Mapping knowledge sharing traits to business strategy in knowledge based organisation. *Journal of Intelligent Manufacturing*, *25*(1), 55–65. doi:10.1007/s10845-012-0674-1

Churchill, G. A. (1979). A paradigm for developing better measures of marketing constructs. *JMR, Journal of Marketing Research*, *16*(1), 64–73. doi:10.2307/3150876

Cirera, X., Marin, A., & Markwald, R. (2012). Firm behaviour and the introduction of new exports: Evidence from Brazil. *IDS Working Papers*, *2012*(390), 1–105.

Clauset, A., Mewman, M., & Moore, C. (2004). *Finding community structure in very large networks*. Arxiv preprint cond-mat/0408187.

Clauset, A., Moore, C., & Newman, M. E. J. (2008). Hierarchical structure and the prediction of missing links in networks. *Nature*, *453*(7191), 98–101. doi:10.1038/nature06830 PMID:18451861

Cogdell, B., & Aidulis, D. (2008). Dealing with plagiarism as an ethical issue. In T. S. Roberts (Ed.), *Student plagiarism in an online world: problems and solutions* (pp. 38–59). Hershey, PA: IGI Global. doi:10.4018/978-1-59904-801-7.ch004

Cohen, W. M., & Levinthal, D. (1990). Absorptive capacity: A new perspective on learning and innovation. *Administrative Science Quarterly*, *35*(1), 128–152. doi:10.2307/2393553

Cokely, E. T., Ericsson, K. A., & Prietula, M. J. (2007, July-August). The making of an expert. Boston. *Harvard Business Review*, 114–121.

Çokpekin, Ö., & Knudsen, M. P. (2012). Does organizing for creativity really lead to innovation? *Creativity and Innovation Management*, *21*(3), 304–314. doi:10.1111/j.1467-8691.2012.00649.x

Collins, C. J., & Smith, K. G. (2006). Knowledge exchange and combination: The role of human resource practices in the performance of high-technology firms. *Academy of Management Journal*, *49*(3), 544–560. doi:10.5465/AMJ.2006.21794671

Colomo-Palacios, R., Fernandes, E., Sabbagh, M., & Amescua-Seco, A. (2012). Human and intellectual capital management in the cloud: Software vendor perspective. *Journal of Universal Computer Science*, *18*(11), 1544–1557.

Connell, J., & Voola, R. (2013). Knowledge integration and competitiveness: A longitudinal study of an industry cluster. *Journal of Knowledge Management*, *17*(2), 208–225. doi:10.1108/13673271311315178

Conte, A., & Vivarelli, M. (2014). Succeeding in innovation: Key insights on the role of R&D and technological acquisition drawn from company data. *Empirical Economics*, *47*(4), 1317–1340. doi:10.1007/s00181-013-0779-1

Cook & Holder. (2007). Mining Graph Data, Electrical Engineering and Computer Science. John Wiley & Sons, Inc.

Cook, N. (2008). *Enterprise 2.0: How social software will change the future of work*. Gower Publishing, Ltd.

Cordella, L. P., Foggia, P., Sansone, C., & Vento, M. (2001). An improved algorithm for matching large graphs. In *Proceedings of the 3rd IAPR-TC-15 International Workshop on Graph-based Representations*.

Compilation of References

Corfield, A., Paton, R., & Little, S. (2013). Does knowledge management work in NGOs? A longitudinal study. *International Journal of Public Administration, 36*(3), 179–188. doi:10.1080/01900692.2012.749281

Corneil, D. G., & Gotlieb, C. C. (1970). An efficient algorithm for graph isomorphism. *Journal of the ACM, 17*(1), 51–64. doi:10.1145/321556.321562

Correa, M. (2011). Academic dishonesty in the second language classroom: Instructor's Perspectives. *Modern Journal of Language Teaching Method, 1*, 65–79.

Corrocher, N., & Zirulia, L. (2010). Demand and innovation in services: The case of mobile communications. *Research Policy, 39*(7), 945–955. doi:10.1016/j.respol.2010.04.008

Coursera. (2014). *Meet our partners*. Retrieved on 22 September 2014 from https://www.coursera.org/about/partners

Coye Cheshire. (2011). *Enterprise Social Software: Addressing Barriers to Adoption*. Retrieved on October 29, 2014, from http://www.ischool.berkeley.edu/programs/mims/projects/2011/enterprise

CPI. (2014). *The Innovation Process*. Retrieved on October 29, 2014, from http://www.uk-cpi.com/news/the-innovation-process/

Cressey, P., & Kelleher, M. (2003). The Conundrum of the Learning Organisation - Instrumental and Emancipatory Theories of Learning. In B. Nyhan, P. Cressey, M. Kelleher & R. Poell (Eds.), Learning Organisations: European perspectives, theories and practices. Luxembourg: CEDEFOP.

Croucher, M. (26 April 2009). Revealed: FAKE Degrees. *Khaleej Times*. Retrieved on 31 May 2014 from http://www.khaleejtimes.com/DisplayArticle08.asp?xfile=data/theuae/2009/April/theuae_April612.xml&section=theuae

Cuijpers, M., Guenter, H., & Hussinger, K. (2011). Costs and benefits of inter-departmental innovation collaboration. *Research Policy, 40*(4), 565–575. doi:10.1016/j.respol.2010.12.004

Cummings, J. N. (2004). Work groups, structural diversity, and knowledge sharing in a global organization. *Management Science, 50*(3), 352–264. doi:10.1287/mnsc.1030.0134

Cunha, M. P., Rego, A., Oliveira, P., Rosado, P., & Habib, N. (2014). Product innovation in resource-poor environments: Three research streams. *Journal of Product Innovation Management, 31*(2), 202–210. doi:10.1111/jpim.12090

Curtis, L., Edwards, C., Fraser, K. L., Gudelsky, S., Holmquist, J., Thornton, K., & Sweetser, K. D. (2010). Adoption of social media for public relations by nonprofit organizations. *Public Relations Review, 36*(1), 90–92. doi:10.1016/j.pubrev.2009.10.003

da Mota Pedrosa, A. (2012). Customer integration during innovation development: An exploratory study in the logistics service industry. *Creativity and Innovation Management, 21*(3), 263–276. doi:10.1111/j.1467-8691.2012.00648.x

Dachs, B., Ebersberger, B., Kinkel, S., & Som, O. (2015). The effects of production offshoring on R&D and innovation in the home country. *Economia e Politica Industriale, 42*(1), 9–31. doi:10.1007/s40812-014-0001-2

Daft, R. L., & Lengel, R. H. (1986). Organizational information requirements, media richness and structural design. *Management Science, 32*(5), 554–571. doi:10.1287/mnsc.32.5.554

Dahlander, L., & Gann, D. M. (2010). How open is innovation? *Research Policy, 39*(6), 699–709. doi:10.1016/j.respol.2010.01.013

Dahlin, E. C. (2014). The sociology of innovation: Organizational, environmental, and relative perspectives. *Social Compass, 8*(6), 671–687. doi:10.1111/soc4.12177

dall'Acqua, L. (2009). Specification and cognition for an adaptive and intelligent e-learning environment. In *Proceedings of World Conference on E-Learning in Corporate, Government, Healthcare and Higher Education AACE 2009* (pp. 2485-2493). Academic Press.

dall'Acqua, L. (2011). Didactical suggestion for a Dynamic Hybrid Intelligent e-Learning Environment (DHILE) applying the PENTHA ID Model. In *AIP, Conference Proceedings, Special Edition of the WCECS2010* (Vol. 1373, pp. 159-173). Academic Press.

dall'Acqua, L. (2014). Needs and strategies of KM in a multi-user environment: PENTHA Model view and analysis. *Jekpot KM19*.

dall'Acqua, L., & Santo, M. (2012). New interpretative paradigms to understand and manage the unpredictability of the dynamics of learning in a complex multi-user knowledge environment. In *Proceedings of Artificial Intelligence Workshop 2012 on Collaboration and Intelligence in Blended Learning* (pp. 92-9). Academic Press.

dall'Acqua, L., & Santo, M. (2014). Orientism, the basic pedagogical approach of PENTHA ID Model vs. 2, to manage decisions in unpredictability conditions. In *Proceedings of World Congress on Engineering and Computer Science WCECS2014* (vol. 1, pp. 316-21). Academic Press.

Dangelico, R. M., Pontrandolfo, P., & Pujari, D. (2013). Developing sustainable new products in the textile and upholstered furniture industries: Role of external integrative capabilities. *Journal of Product Innovation Management, 30*(4), 642–658. doi:10.1111/jpim.12013

Darroch, J., & McNaughton, R. (2002). Examining the link between knowledge management practices and types of innovation. *Journal of Intellectual Capital, 3*(3), 210–222. doi:10.1108/14691930210435570

Davenport, T. H. (2013). *Process Innovation: reengineering work through information technology*. Havard Business Press.

Davenport, T. H., & Prusak, L. (1998). *Working knowledge: how organizations manage what they know*. Boston: Harvard Business School Press.

Davenport, T. H., & Prusak, L. (2001). *Conocimiento en acción. Cómo las organizaciones manejan lo que saben*. Buenos Aires: Editorial Prentice Hall.

Davila, T., Epstein, M., & Shelton, R. (2012). Making Innovation Work: How to manage it, measure it and profit from it (updated ed.). Upper Saddle River, NJ: FT Press.

Davis, F. D. (1989). Perceived usefulness, perceived ease of use, and user acceptance of information technology. *Management Information Systems Quarterly, 13*(3), 319–340. doi:10.2307/249008

Davis, F. D., Bagozzi, R. P., & Warshaw, P. R. (1989). User acceptance of computer technology: A comparison of two theoretical models. *Management Science, 35*(8), 982–1003. doi:10.1287/mnsc.35.8.982

Dayan, M., & Di Benedetto, C. A. (2010). The impact of structural and contextual factors on trust formation in product development teams. *Industrial Marketing Management, 39*(4), 691–703. doi:10.1016/j.indmarman.2010.01.001

Dayan, M., Di Benedetto, C. A., & Colak, M. (2009). Managerial trust in new product development projects: Its antecedents and consequences. *Research Management, 39*(1), 21–37.

de Brito, M. P., Flapper, S. D. P., & Dekker, R. (2002). *Reverse logistic: a review of case studies*. SMG Working paper EI 2002-21, Econometric Institute Report, Erasmus University.

De Clercq, D. D., Menguc, B., & Auh, S. (2009). Unpacking the relationship between an innovation strategy and firm performance: The role of task conflict and political activity. *Journal of Business Research*, *62*(11), 1046–1053. doi:10.1016/j.jbusres.2008.10.021

De Dreu, C. K. (2006). When too little or too much hurts: Evidence for a curvilinear relationship between task conflict and innovation in teams. *Journal of Management*, *32*(1), 83–107. doi:10.1177/0149206305277795

Delery, J. E., & Doty, D. H. (1996). Modes of theorizing in strategic human resource management: Test of universalistic contingency, and configurational performance predictions. *Academy of Management Journal*, *39*(4), 802–835. doi:10.2307/256713

Denford, J. S. (2013). Building knowledge: Developing a knowledge-based dynamic capabilities typology. *Journal of Knowledge Management*, *17*(2), 175–194. doi:10.1108/13673271311315150

Deng, Z., Hofman, P. S., & Newman, A. (2013). Ownership concentration and product innovation in Chinese private SMEs. *Asia Pacific Journal of Management*, *30*(3), 717–734. doi:10.1007/s10490-012-9301-0

Dennis, A. R., & Kinney, S. T. (1998). Testing media richness theory in the new media: The effects of cues, feedback, and task equivocality. *Information Systems Research*, *9*(3), 256–274. doi:10.1287/isre.9.3.256

Desikan, P., & Srivastava, J. (2004). Mining Temporally Evolving Graphs. In Proceedings of WebKDD.

Deskmag, C. E. (2012). *The 2nd Global Coworking Survey*. Retrieved from http://www.deskmag.com/en/first-results-of-global-coworking-survey-171

Desouza, K. C., & Awazu, Y. (2006). Knowledge management at SMEs: Five peculiarities. *Journal of Knowledge Management*, *10*(1), 32–43. doi:10.1108/13673270610650085

Devaraj, S., & Kholi, R. (2003). Performance impacts of information technology: Is actual usage the missing link? *Management Science*, *49*(3), 273–289. doi:10.1287/mnsc.49.3.273.12736

Dholokia, R. R., & Kshetri, N. (2004). Factors impacting the adoption of the internet among SMEs. *Small Business Economics*, *23*(4), 311–322. doi:10.1023/B:SBEJ.0000032036.90353.1f

Díaz, A., Álvarez, M., & González, P. (2004). *Logística inversa y medio ambiente*. Madrid: McGraw Hill.

Diestel, R. (2000). *Graph Theory*. New York: Springer.

Dilenschneider, C. (n.d.). *Inspiring Institutions to Embrace Social Strategies: A Formula for Change*. Retrieved July 28, 2014, from http://colleendilen.com/2011/06/13/inspiring-institutions-to-embrace-social-strategies-a-formula-for-change/

DiMicco, J. M., Geyer, W., Millen, D. R., Dugan, C., & Brownholtz, B. (2009, January). People sensemaking and relationship building on an enterprise social network site. In *System Sciences, 2009. HICSS'09. 42nd Hawaii International Conference on* (pp. 1-10). IEEE.

DiMicco, J., Millen, D. R., Geyer, W., Dugan, C., Brownholtz, B., & Muller, M. (2008, November). Motivations for social networking at work. In *Proceedings of the 2008 ACM Conference on Computer Supported Cooperative Work* (pp. 711-720). ACM. doi:10.1145/1460563.1460674

Dispatch, C. (2010). *One of the Best Values Around– Only in the Dispatch*. Retrieved from http://www.dispatch.com/live/content/faq/exclusive.html

Downes, S. (2010). *The role of the Educator in PLE World*. Retrieved (9 Jan 2012), Retrieved from http://www.slideshare.net/Downes/the-role-of-the-educator-in-a-ple-world

Drazin, R., & Van de Ven, A. H. (1985). Alternative forms of fit in contingency theory. *Administrative Science Quarterly, 30*(4), 514–539. doi:10.2307/2392695

Drucker, P. F. (2001). The next society - A survey of the near future. *The Economist, 361*(8246), 1-5.

Drucker, P. (1985). *Entrepreneurship and Innovation: Practice and Principles.* New York, NY: HarperBusiness.

Drucker, P. (1999). Knowledge–worker productivity: The biggest challenge. *California Management Review, 41*(2), 79–94. doi:10.2307/41165987

Du Plessis, M. (2007). The role of knowledge management in innovation. *Journal of Knowledge Management, 11*(4), 20–29. doi:10.1108/13673270710762684

Dumbill, E. (2012). *What is big data?* [Online] Available from: http: //radar. oreilly.com /2012/01/ what-is-big-data.html

Durmuşoğlu, S. S., Calantone, R. J., & McNally, R. C. (2013). Ordered to innovate: A longitudinal examination of the early periods of a new product development process implementation in a manufacturing firm. *Journal of Product Innovation Management, 30*(4), 712–731. doi:10.1111/jpim.12016

Efimova, L. (2004). *Discovering the iceberg of knowledge work: A weblog case.* Retrieved from https://doc.telin.nl/dsweb/Get/Document-34786/

Eisenhardt, K. M. (1989). Building Theories from Case Study Research. *Academy of Management Review, 14*(4), 532–550.

Eisenhardt, K. M. (1989). Building theories from case study research. *Academy of Management Review, 14*(4), 532–550.

Electronic Frontier Foundation. (2010). *Panopti- click.* Retrieved from https://panopticlick.eff.org/

El-Shinnawy, M., & Markus, M. L. (1997). The poverty of media richness theory: Explaining people's choice of electronic mail vs. voice mail. *International Journal of Human-Computer Studies, 46*(4), 443–467. doi:10.1006/ijhc.1996.0099

Ely, J. J., Henderson, L., & Wachsman, Y. (2013). Testing the effectiveness of the university honor code. *Academy of Educational Leadership Journal, 17*(4), 95–104.

Emirates Identity Authority. (2013). *Emirates ID showcases its knowledge management experience to Zakat Fund delegation.* Retrieved on 2 June 2014 from http://www.id.gov.ae/en/media-centre/news/2013/3/4/emirates-id-showcases-its-knowledge-management-experience-to-zakat-fund-delegation.aspx

Ericsson, K. A. (2006). The influence of experience and deliberate practice on the development of superior expert performance. In K. A. Ericsson (Ed.), *The Cambridge Handbook of Expertise and Expert Performance* (pp. 683–703). New York, NY: Cambridge University Press. doi:10.1017/CBO9780511816796.038

Etzioni, O. (1996). The World Wide Web: Quagmire or Gold Mine? *Communications of the ACM, 39*(11), 65–68. doi:10.1145/240455.240473

Evanschitzky, H., Eisend, M., Calantone, R. J., & Jiang, Y. (2012). Success factors of product innovation: An updated meta-analysis. *Journal of Product Innovation Management, 29*, 21–37. doi:10.1111/j.1540-5885.2012.00964.x

Fabrizio, K. R., & Thomas, L. G. (2012). The impact of local demand on innovation in a global industry. *Strategic Management Journal, 33*(1), 42–64. doi:10.1002/smj.942

Facebook. (2010). *Facebook Statistics.* Retrieved from http://www.facebook.com/press/info. php?statistics

Farooqui, M. (2014). Fake degree racket in UAE exposed. *Gulf News.* Retrieved on 31 May 2014.from http://m.gulfnews.com/news/uae/crime/fake-degree-racket-in-uae-exposed-1.1339968

Farrell, S. (2010). How much would you pay for your degree? *Now Reports*. Retrieved on 31 May 2014 from http://mobile.mmedia.me/lb/en/reportsfeatures/how_much_would_you_pay_for_your_degree

Farzan, R., DiMicco, J. M., Millen, D. R., Dugan, C., Geyer, W., & Brownholtz, E. A. (2008, April). Results from deploying a participation incentive mechanism within the enterprise. In *Proceedings of the SIGCHI Conference on Human Factors in Computing Systems* (pp. 563-572). ACM. doi:10.1145/1357054.1357145

Fee. (2013). Retrieved from http://mashable.com/2013/06/14/enterprise-social-networks/

Feldman, M. P., & Audretsch, D. B. (1999). Innovation in cities: Science based diversity, specialization and localized competition. *European Economic Review*, *43*(2), 409–429. doi:10.1016/S0014-2921(98)00047-6

Felekoglu, B., & Moultrie, J. (2014). Top management involvement in new product development: A review and synthesis. *Journal of Product Innovation Management*, *31*(1), 159–175. doi:10.1111/jpim.12086

Ferguson, S., Burford, S., & Kennedy, M. (2013). Divergent approaches to knowledge and innovation in the public sector. *International Journal of Public Administration*, *36*(3), 168–178. doi:10.1080/01900692.2012.749278

Ferris, G. R., Perrewé, P. L., & Douglas, C. (2002). Social effectiveness in organizations: Construct validity and research directions. *Journal of Leadership & Organizational Studies*, *9*(1), 49–63. doi:10.1177/107179190200900104

Fiddler, L. (2000). *Facilitators and Impediments to the Internal Transfer of Team-Embodied Competences in Firms Operating in Dynamic Environments*. (Tesis Doctoral, Boston University). Proquest Dissertation Abstracts.

Focardi, G., & Salati, L. (2015). A New Approach to Knowledge Sharing, the Multifactory Model. In O. Teràn & J. Aguilar (Eds.), *Social Benefits of Freely Accessible Technologies and Knowledge Resources*. IGI Global. doi:10.4018/978-1-4666-8336-5.ch009

Forcier, E., Rathi, D., & Given, L. (2014). Tools of Engagement for Knowledge Management: Using Social Media to Capture Non-Profit Organizations' Stories. *Proceedings of the Annual Conference of the Canadian Association for Information Science*. Retrieved from http://www.cais-acsi.ca/ojs/index.php/cais/article/view/823

Fornell, C., & Larcker, F. D. (1981). Evaluating structural equation models with unobservable variables and measurement error. *JMR, Journal of Marketing Research*, *18*(1), 39–50. doi:10.2307/3151312

Fox, S. (2000). Communities of practice, foucault and actor network theory. *Journal of Management Studies*, *37*(6), 853–867. doi:10.1111/1467-6486.00207

Frattini, F., Dell'Era, C., & Rangone, A. (2013). Launch decisions and the early market survival of innovations: An empirical analysis of the Italian mobile value-added services (VAS) industry. *Journal of Product Innovation Management*, *30*, 174–187. doi:10.1111/jpim.12070

Frishammar, J., Lichtenthaler, U., & Rundquist, J. (2012). Identifying technology commercialization opportunities: The importance of integrating product development knowledge. *Journal of Product Innovation Management*, *29*(4), 573–589. doi:10.1111/j.1540-5885.2012.00926.x

Froehle, C. M., & Roth, A. V. (2007). A Resource-Process Framework of New Service Development. *Production and Operations Management*, *16*(2), 169–188. doi:10.1111/j.1937-5956.2007.tb00174.x

Froehle, C. M., Roth, A. V., Chase, R. B., & Voss, C. A. (2000). Antecedents of new service development effectiveness an exploratory examination of strategic operations choices. *Journal of Service Research*, *3*(1), 3–17. doi:10.1177/109467050031001

Füller, J., Matzler, K., Hutter, K., & Hautz, J. (2012). Consumers' creative talent: Which characteristics qualify consumers for open innovation projects? An exploration of asymmetrical effects. *Creativity and Innovation Management, 21*(3), 247–262. doi:10.1111/j.1467-8691.2012.00650.x

FutureLearn. (2014). *Featured courses.* Retrieved on 22 September 2014 from https://www.futurelearn.com/

Gagné, R. M. (1985). The Condition of Learning and Theory of Instruction. New York: CBS College Publishing.

Galbraith, J. R. (1973). *Designing complex organizations.* Addison-Wesley Longman Publishing Co., Inc.

Ganotakis, P., & Love, J. H. (2012). The innovation value chain in new technology-based firms: Evidence from the U.K. *Journal of Product Innovation Management, 29*(5), 839–860. doi:10.1111/j.1540-5885.2012.00938.x

Gantz, J. F., Chute, C., Manfrediz, A., Minton, S., Reinsel, D., Schlichting, W., & Toncheva, A. (2008). *The diverse and exploding digital Universe.* An IDC White paper. Framingham, MA: IDC

García, M. J., Hernández, G. J., & Hernández, J. G. (2013). Enterprise diagnosis and the STOILMo. In Delener et al. (Eds.), Fifteenth annual International Conference Global Business And Technology Association. GBATA.

García, C. M., Escobet, T., & Quevedo, J. (2010). PHM Techniques for Condition-Based Maintenance based on Hybrid System Model Representation.*Annual Conference of the Prognostics and Health Management Society.*

García, G. M. J., Hernández, G. G. J., & Hernández, R. J. G. (2014). Knowledge management through the Material Handling Manager. In *Proceedings ICIL'2014.* University of Zagreb.

García, G. M. J., Hernández, G. G. J., & Hernández, R. J. G. (2014a). A Methodology of The Decision Support Systems applied to other projects of Investigation. In *Encyclopedia of Information Science and Technology* (3rd ed.). Hershey, PA: IGI Global.

García, G. M. J., Hernández, G. G. J., & Hernández, R. J. G. (2014b). Knowledge management through the Material Handling Manager. In G. Dukic (Ed.), *Proceedings ICIL'2014.* University of Zagreb.

García, N., Sanzo, M. J., & Trespalacios, J. A. (2008). New product internal performance and market performance: Evidence from Spanish firms regarding the role of trust, interfunctional integration, and innovation type. *Technovation, 28*(11), 713–725. doi:10.1016/j.technovation.2008.01.001

Gardner, H., & Hatch, T. (1989). Multiple intelligences go to school: Educational implications of the theory of multiple intelligences. Educational Researcher, 18(8), 4–9.

Gausdal, A.H. (2008, May). Developing regional communities of practice by network reflection: the case of the Norwegian electronics industry. *Entrepreneurship & Regional Development,* 209-235.

Gebert, D., Boerner, S., & Kearney, E. (2010). Fostering team innovation: Why is it important to combine opposing action strategies? *Organization Science, 21*(3), 593–608. doi:10.1287/orsc.1090.0485

Gibbs, J. L., & Kraemer, K. L. (2004). A cross-country investigation of the determinants of scope of e-commerce use: An institutional approach. *Electronic Markets, 14*(2), 124–137. doi:10.1080/10196780410001675077

Gibney, E. (2013). Great and good reject journal impact factor. The Times Higher Education Supplement: THE, (2101), 8.

Giles, J. (2005). *Nature International Weekly Journal of Science – Special Report: Internet encyclopedias go head to head.* Retrieved from http://www.nature.com/nature/journal/v438/ n7070/full/438900a.html

Gillard, S. (2009). Soft Skills and Technical Expertise of Effective Project Managers. *Issues in Informing Science and Information Technology, 6,* 723–729.

Gillberg, C., & Vo, L. C. (2014). Contributions from pragmatist perspectives towards an understanding of knowledge and learning in organisations. *Philosophy of Management, 13*(2), 33–51. doi:10.5840/pom201413210

Giordano, R., Preziosi, E., & Romano, M. (2013). Integration of local and scientific knowledge to support drought impact monitoring: Some hints from an Italian case study. *Natural Hazards, 69*(1), 523–544. doi:10.1007/s11069-013-0724-9

Gnoni, M. G., & Rollo, A. (2010). A scenario analysis for evaluating RFID investments in pallet management. *International Journal of RF Technologies, 2*, 1–21.

GNP. (2013). *Tem(p)i e luoghi del lavoro flessibile*. Retrieved from http://www.giornatanazionaledellaprevidenza.it/terza-giornata-gnp2013

Goel, A. K., Sharma, G. R., & Rastogi, R. (2010). Knowledge management implementation in NTPC: An Indian PSU. *Management Decision, 48*(3), 383–395. doi:10.1108/00251741011037756

Goel, A., Gupta, N., & Rastogi, R. (2010b). Role of virtual organization in knowledge management. In *Management: Concepts, cases & models*. Excel Publishers.

Goel, A., Rana, G., & Rastogi, R. (2009). Knowledge management implementation in Indian public sector. In *Enhancing organizational performance through strategic initiatives*. Macmillan Publishers India Ltd.

Goel, A., & Rastogi, R. (2011). Knowledge sharing and competitiveness: a study from Indian IT industry. In *Positive initiatives for organizational change and transformation*. Macmillan Publishers India Ltd.

Goettler, R. L., & Gordon, B. R. (2014). Competition and product innovation in dynamic oligopoly. *Quantitative Marketing and Economics, 12*(1), 1–42. doi:10.1007/s11129-013-9142-2

Gogan, B., & Marcus, A. (2013). Lost in transliteracy. *Knowledge Quest, 41*(5), 40–45.

Goldenberg, A., & Moore, A. (2004). Tractable learning of large Bayes net structures from sparse data. In *Proceedings of the 6th International Conference on Machine Learning*. doi:10.1145/1015330.1015406

Gold, S., & Seuring, S. (2011). Supply chain and logistics issues of bio-energy production. *Journal of Cleaner Production, 19*(1), 32–42. doi:10.1016/j.jclepro.2010.08.009

Goldsmith, M., Morgan, H., & Ogg, A. (2004). Effectively Influencing Up:Ensuring That Your Knowledge, Makes a Difference, Marshall Goldsmith. Published in Leading Organizational Learning. Jossey-Bass.

Gooderham, P. N. (2007). Enhancing knowledge transfer in multinational corporations: A dynamic capabilities driven model. *Knowledge Management Research & Practice, 5*(1), 34–43. doi:10.1057/palgrave.kmrp.8500119

Google. (2009). *Corporate Information – Com- pany Overview*. Retrieved from http://www. google.com/corporate/index.html

Google. (2010). *Google Books Settlement Agreement*. Retrieved from http://books.google.com/ googlebooks/agreement/faq.html

Government of Abu Dhabi. (2008).The Abu Dhabi Economic Vision 2030. Retrieved from http://gsec.abudhabi.ae/Sites/GSEC/Content/EN/PDF/Publications/economic-vision-2030-full-version,property=pdf,bereich=gsec,sprache=en,rwb=true.pdf

Granovetter, M. (1983). The strength of weak ties: A network theory revisited. *Sociological Theory, 1*(1), 201–233. doi:10.2307/202051

Grant, R. M. (2000). Shifts in the world economy: the drivers of knowledge management. In C. Despres & D. Chauvel (Eds.), Knowledge Horizons: the present and the promise of knowledge management (pp. 27-53). Butterworth-Heinemann. doi:10.1016/B978-0-7506-7247-4.50005-7

Grant, R. M. (2013). Reflections on knowledge-based approaches to the organization of production. *Journal of Management and Governance*, *17*(3), 541–558. doi:10.1007/s10997-011-9195-0

Grawitz, M. (1996). *Me'thodes des Sciences Sociales* (10th ed.). Paris: Dalloz.

Gray, P. W., & Jordan, S. R. (2012). Supervisors and academic integrity: Supervisors as exemplars and mentors. *Journal of Academic Ethics*, *10*(4), 299–311. doi:10.1007/s10805-012-9155-6

Graziotin, D. (2014). *Recent trends in agile processes and software engineering research - XP 2014 conference report*. Retrieved January 11, 2015 from https://thewinnower.com//papers/recent-trends-in-agile-processes-research-in-software-engineering-and-extreme-programming-xp-2014-conference-report

Greenhalgh, C., & Rogers, M. (2012). Trade marks and performance in services and manufacturing firms: Evidence of Schumpeterian competition through innovation. *The Australian Economic Review*, *45*(1), 50–76. doi:10.1111/j.1467-8462.2011.00665.x

Grundstein, M. (2008). Assessing Enterprise's Knowledge Management Maturity Level. *International Journal of Knowledge and Learning*, *4*(5), 415–426. doi:10.1504/IJKL.2008.022060

Guerrero, M. L. E., Hernández, G. G. J., García, G. M. J., & Hernández, R. J. G. (2014). Indicators and the Picking manager of the Logistic Model Based on positions. In *Proceedings ICIL'2014*. University of Zagreb.

Gupta, A. K., & Govindarajan, V. (2000). Knowledge flows within multinational corporations. *Strategic Management Journal*, *21*(4), 473–496. doi:10.1002/(SICI)1097-0266(200004)21:4<473::AID-SMJ84>3.0.CO;2-I

Gurteen, G., & Remenyi, R. (2007). *The Knowledge-Café. If only we knew what we know*. Retrieved from: http://www.slideshare.net/dgurteen/introduction-to-the-knowledge-cafe

Gu, V. C., Cao, Q., & Duan, W. (2012). Unified modeling language (UML) IT adoption — A holistic model of organizational capabilities perspective. *Decision Support Systems*, *54*(1), 257–269. doi:10.1016/j.dss.2012.05.034

Hair, J. F., Celsi, M., Money, A., Samouel, P., & Page, M. (2011). *Essentials of business research methods* (2nd ed.). Armonk, NY: ME Sharpe.

Halilem, N., Amara, N., & Landry, R. (2014). Exploring the relationships between innovation and internationalization of small and medium-sized enterprises: A nonrecursive structural equation model. *Canadian Journal of Administrative Sciences*, *31*(1), 18–34. doi:10.1002/cjas.1272

Hamıd, S., Nayan, J. M., Bakar, Z. A., & Norman, A. N. (2007). *Knowledge management adoption and implementation readiness: a case study of the National Library of Malaysia*. Paper presented at the Building an Information Society for All, Petaling Jaya, Malaysia.

Hammedi, W., Van Riel, A. C., & Sasovova, Z. (2011). Antecedents and Consequences of Reflexivity in New Product Idea Screening. *Journal of Product Innovation Management*, *28*(5), 662–679.

Han, J., Pei, J., & Yin, Y. (2000). Mining frequent patterns without candidate generation. In *Proceedings of 2000 ACM-SIGMOD International Conference on Management of Data* (SIGMOD'00). Dallas, TX: ACM.

Hannafin, M. J., Land, S., & Oliver, K. (1999). Open learning environments: Foundations and models. Reigeluth, 3, 115-140.

Compilation of References

Hansen, M. T., Nohria, N., & Tierney, T. (1999). What's your strategy for managing knowledge? *Harvard Business Review*, (March-April), 106–116. PMID:10387767

Harris, B. (2014). Creating communities of practice to improve the educational and mental health contexts of bilingual/bicultural youth: A case study from Colorado. *Contemporary School Psychology*, *18*(3), 187–194. doi:10.1007/s40688-014-0023-9

Harris, E., & Woolley, R. (2009). Facilitating innovation through cognitive mapping of uncertainty. *International Studies of Management & Organization*, *39*(1), 70–100. doi:10.2753/IMO0020-8825390104

Hartmann, A. (2006). The role of organizational culture in motivating innovative behaviour in construction firms. *Construction Innovation: Information, Process. Management*, *6*(3), 159–172.

Henard, D. H., & Szymanski, D. M. (2001). Why some new products are more successful than others. *JMR, Journal of Marketing Research*, *38*(3), 362–375. doi:10.1509/jmkr.38.3.362.18861

Hensley, L. (2013). To cheat or not to cheat: A review with implications for practice. *The Community College Enterprise*, *19*(2), 22–34.

Hernández, J. G., García, M. J., Hernández, G. J., & De Burgos, J. (2011). Once Erres (11-Rs) en la Logística Inversa. In Actas CAIP'2011. Universitat de Girona.

Hernández, J. G., García, M. J., & Hernández, J. G. (2012a). Dynamic knowledge: Diagnosis and Customer Service. In N. Delener (Ed.), *Service Science Research, Strategy, and Innovation: Dynamic Knowledge Management Methods* (pp. 558–584). Hershey, PA: IGI Global; doi:10.4018/978-1-4666-0077-5.ch030

Hernández, R. J. G., García, G. M. J., & Hernández, G. G. J. (2012b). The Utilization manager and logistic flow. In *Proceedings ICIL'2012*. University of Zagreb.

Hernández, R. J., García, G. M., & Hernández, G. G. (2013). Enterprise logistics, indicators and Physical distribution manager. *Research in Logistics & Production*, *3*(1), 5–20.

Holcombe, R. G. (2013). Firms as knowledge repositories. *The Review of Austrian Economics*, *26*(3), 259–275. doi:10.1007/s11138-011-0165-1

Holder, L. B., Cook, D. J., & Djoko, S. (1994). Substructure discovery in the subdue system. In *Proceedings of AAAI'94 Workshop Knowledge Discovery in Databases* (KDD'94). Seattle, WA: AAAI.

Hollen, R. M. A., Van Den Bosch, F. A. J., & Volberda, H. W. (2013). The role of management innovation in enabling technological process innovation: An inter-organizational perspective. *European Management Review*, *10*(1), 35–50. doi:10.1111/emre.12003

Holtzblatt, L. (2013). Evaluating the Uses and Benefits of an Enterprise Social Media Platform. *Journal of Social Media for Organizations*, *1*(1).

Hong, S., Oxley, L., & McCann, P. (2012). A survey of the innovation surveys. *Journal of Economic Surveys*, *26*(3), 420–444. doi:10.1111/j.1467-6419.2012.00724.x

Hong, W., & Zhu, K. (2006). Migrating to internet-based e-commerce: Factors affecting e-commerce adoption and migration at the firm level. *Information & Management*, *43*(2), 204–221. doi:10.1016/j.im.2005.06.003

Howkins, J. (2005). Enhancing creativity. In Creative Industries. A symposium on culture based development strategies. New Delhi: Malvika Singh Editor.

Hsu, P.-F., Ray, S., & Li-Hsieh, Y.-Y. (2014). Examining cloud computing adoption intention, pricing mechanism, and deployment model. *International Journal of Information Management*, *34*(4), 474–488. doi:10.1016/j.ijinfomgt.2014.04.006

Huan, J., Wang, W., & Prins, J. (2003). Efficient Mining of Frequent Subgraph in the Presence of Isomorphism. In *Proceedings of 2003 International Conference on Data Mining* (ICDM'03). doi:10.1109/ICDM.2003.1250974

Huang, H. L. (2014). Performance effects of aligning service innovation and the strategic use of information technology. *Service Business*, *8*(2), 171–195. doi:10.1007/s11628-013-0192-z

Huang, J., Baptista, J., & Galliers, R. D. (2013). Reconceptualizing rhetorical practices in organizations: The impact of social media on internal communications. *Information & Management*, *50*(2–3), 112–124. doi:10.1016/j.im.2012.11.003

Hunt, C. (2013). *4 Big Barriers to Social Media Adoption: Key Research Findings*. Retrieved July 28, 2014, from http://www.recruitingblogs.com/profiles/blogs/4-big-barriers-to-social-media-adoption-key-research-findings

Huy, L. V., Rowe, F., Truex, D., & Huynh, M. Q. (2012). An empirical study of determinants of e-commerce adoption in smes in vietnam an economy in transition. *Journal of Global Information Management*, *20*(3), 23–54. doi:10.4018/jgim.2012070102

Hvannberg, E. T. (2015). Identifying and explicating knowledge on method transfer: A sectoral system of innovation approach. *Universal Access in the Information Society*, *14*(2), 187–202. doi:10.1007/s10209-013-0340-1

Iannone, F., & Thore, S. (2010). An economic logistics model for the multimodal inland distribution of maritime containers. *International Journal of Transport Economics*, *37*(3), 281–326.

Ibragimova, B., Ryan, S. D., Windsor, J. C., & Prybutok, J. C. (2012). Understanding the Antecedents of Knowledge Sharing: An Organizational Justice Perspective. Informing Science: the International Journal of an Emerging Transdiscipline, 15, 183–205.

IEEE. (2014). ieee.bigdata.tutorial.1.1slides.pdf. IEEE.

Ilgin, M. A., & Gupta, S. M. (2010). Environmentally conscious manufacturing and product recovery (ECMPRO): A review of the state of the art.[PubMed]. *Journal of Environmental Management*, *91*(3), 563–591. doi:10.1016/j.jenvman.2009.09.037

Im, S., Montoya, M. M., & Workman, J. P. Jr. (2013). Antecedents and consequences of creativity in product innovation teams. *Journal of Product Innovation Management*, *30*(1), 170–185. doi:10.1111/j.1540-5885.2012.00887.x

Infosys. (2013). *Infosys – Connect Architecture, Big Data Spectrum*. Infosys Ltd.

Inokuchi, A., Washio, T., & Motoda, H. (2000). An apriori-based algorithm for mining frequent substructures from graph data. In *Proceedings of 2000 European Symposium Principle of Data Mining and Knowledge Discovery* (PKDD'00). doi:10.1007/3-540-45372-5_2

International Bureau of WIPO. (2003). *What is Intellectual Property?* WIPO Pub: No. 450.

Intezari, A., & Pauleen, D. J. (2014). Management wisdom in perspective: Are you virtuous enough to succeed in volatile times? *Journal of Business Ethics*, *120*(3), 393–404. doi:10.1007/s10551-013-1666-6

Ireland, R. D., Hitt, M. A., Camp, S. M., & Sexton, D. L. (2001). Integrating entrepreneurship actions and strategic management actions to create firm wealth. *The Academy of Management Executive*, *15*(1), 49–63. doi:10.5465/AME.2001.4251393

Jack, E. P., Powers, T. L., & Skinner, L. (2010). Reverse logistics capabilities: Antecedents and cost savings. *International Journal of Physical Distribution & Logistics Management*, *40*(3), 228–246. doi:10.1108/09600031011035100

Compilation of References

Järvinen, J., & Koskinen, L. (2001). *Industrial Design as a Culturally Reflexive Activity in Manufacturing*. Saarijärvi, Finland: Gummerus Printing.

Jashapara, A. (2005). The emerging discourse of knowledge management: A new dawn for information science research? *Journal of Information Science, 31*(2), 136–148. doi:10.1177/0165551505051057

Jaspers, F., Prencipe, A., & van den Ende, J. (2012). Organizing interindustry architectural innovations: Evidence from mobile communication applications. *Journal of Product Innovation Management, 29*(3), 419–431. doi:10.1111/j.1540-5885.2012.00915.x

Jean, R. J., Sinkovics, R. R., & Hiebaum, T. P. (2014). The effects of supplier involvement and knowledge protection on product innovation in customer-supplier relationships: A study of global automotive suppliers in China. *Journal of Product Innovation Management, 31*(1), 98–113. doi:10.1111/jpim.12082

Jehn, K. A. (1995). A multimethod examination of the benefits and detriments of intragroup conflict. *Administrative Science Quarterly, 40*(2), 256–282. doi:10.2307/2393638

Jeney, A. (2014). Impacto del Gerente de Sistemas de Información y Redes del Modelo *Logístico Basado en Cargos en la gestión del conocimiento de una organización, medido a través de una Matriz De Ponderación*. (Magister dissertation). Universidad Metropolitana, Caracas, Venezuela.

Jensen, D., & Neville, J. (2002). *Data Mining in Social Networks*. Paper presented at the Workshop on Dynamic Social Network Modeling and Analysis, Washington, DC.

Jepsen, L. B., Dell'Era, C., & Verganti, R. (2014). The contributions of interpreters to the development of radical innovations of meanings: The role of "Pioneering Projects" in the sustainable buildings industry. *R&D Management, 44*(1), 1–17. doi:10.1111/radm.12035

Jespersen, K. R. (2012). Stage-to-stage information dependency in the NPD process: Effective learning or a potential entrapment of NPD gates? *Journal of Product Innovation Management, 29*(2), 257–274. doi:10.1111/j.1540-5885.2011.00894.x

Jiménez-Jiménez, D., & Sanz-Valle, R. (2011). Innovation, organizational learning, and performance. *Journal of Business Research, 64*(4), 408–417. doi:10.1016/j.jbusres.2010.09.010

Jonassen, D. H. (1999). Designing constructivist learning environments. Reigeluth, 2, 215-239.

Jones, C. (2010, January). *Organization Culture: Barriers to 2.0 Adoption*. Retrieved from http://sourcepov.com/2010/01/11/culture/

Ju, P. H., Chen, D.-N., Yu, Y.-C., & Wei, H.-L. (2013). Relationships among Open Innovation Processes, Entrepreneurial Orientation, and Organizational Performance of SMEs: The Moderating Role of Technological Turbulence. In *Perspectives in Business Informatics Research - 12th International Conference, BIR 2013*. Warsaw, Poland: Springer.

Kale, S., & Karaman, E. A. (2012). A diagnostic model for assessing the knowledge management practices of construction firms. *KSCE Journal of Civil Engineering, 16*(4), 526–537. doi:10.1007/s12205-012-1468-x

Kandemir, D., & Acur, N. (2012). Examining proactive strategic decision-making flexibility in new product development. *Journal of Product Innovation Management, 29*(4), 608–622. doi:10.1111/j.1540-5885.2012.00928.x

Kang, W., & Montoya, M. (2014). The impact of product portfolio strategy on financial performance: The roles of product development and market entry decisions. *Journal of Product Innovation Management, 31*(3), 516–534. doi:10.1111/jpim.12111

Kanter, B. (2009, April). *What lies beneath social media stress, fear, and barriers to adoption in nonprofits? - Beth's Blog: Nonprofits and Social Media*. Retrieved October 29, 2014, from http://beth.typepad.com/beths_blog/2009/04/what-lies-beneath-social-media-stress-fear-and-barriers-to-adoption-in-nonprofits.html

Kapyla, J. (2012). Towards a critical societal knowledge management. *Journal of Intellectual Capital, 13*(3), 288–304. doi:10.1108/14691931211248873

Kärkkäinen, H., Jussila, J., & Väisänen, J. (2010, October). Social media use and potential in business-to-business companies' innovation. In *Proceedings of the 14th international academic mindtrek conference: Envisioning future media environments* (pp. 228-236). ACM. doi:10.1145/1930488.1930536

Kasemsap, K. (2014a). Strategic innovation management: An integrative framework and causal model of knowledge management, strategic orientation, organizational innovation, and organizational performance. In P. Ordóñez de Pablos & R. Tennyson (Eds.), *Strategic approaches for human capital management and development in a turbulent economy* (pp. 102–116). Hershey, PA: IGI Global. doi:10.4018/978-1-4666-4530-1.ch007

Kasemsap, K. (2014b). The role of knowledge sharing on organisational innovation: An integrated framework. In L. Al-Hakim & C. Jin (Eds.), *Quality innovation: Knowledge, theory, and practices* (pp. 247–271). Hershey, PA: IGI Global. doi:10.4018/978-1-4666-4769-5.ch012

Kasemsap, K. (2015a). Developing a framework of human resource management, organizational learning, knowledge management capability, and organizational performance. In P. Ordoñez de Pablos, L. Turró, R. Tennyson, & J. Zhao (Eds.), *Knowledge management for competitive advantage during economic crisis* (pp. 164–193). Hershey, PA: IGI Global. doi:10.4018/978-1-4666-6457-9.ch010

Kasemsap, K. (2015b). The roles of information technology and knowledge management in project management metrics. In G. Jamil, S. Lopes, A. Malheiro da Silva, & F. Ribeiro (Eds.), *Handbook of research on effective project management through the integration of knowledge and innovation* (pp. 332–361). Hershey, PA: IGI Global. doi:10.4018/978-1-4666-7536-0.ch018

Kasemsap, K. (2015c). The role of data mining for business intelligence in knowledge management. In A. Azevedo & M. Santos (Eds.), *Integration of data mining in business intelligence systems* (pp. 12–33). Hershey, PA: IGI Global. doi:10.4018/978-1-4666-6477-7.ch002

Kedia, B., Gaffney, N., & Clampit, J. (2012). EMNEs and knowledge-seeking FDI. *Management International Review, 52*(2), 155–173. doi:10.1007/s11575-012-0132-5

Kelly, K. (2008). *Better Than Free* [e-Book]. Retrieved from http://changethis.com/search?action=search&query=better+than+free

Khan, Z. R. (2010). E-cheating in the UAE: a critical review of existing literature. In Proceedings of the 2010 International Conference on e-Learning, e-Business, Enterprise Information Systems, & e-Government (pp. 320-324). CSREA Press. Retrieved from http://ro.uow.edu.au/cgi/viewcontent.cgi?article=1172&context=dubaipapers

Kietzmann, J. H., Hermkens, K., McCarthy, I. P., & Silvestre, B. S. (2011). Social media? Get serious! Understanding the functional building blocks of social media. *Business Horizons, 54*(3), 241–251. doi:10.1016/j.bushor.2011.01.005

Kim, N., Im, S., & Slater, S. F. (2013). Impact of knowledge type and strategic orientation on new product creativity and advantage in high-technology firms. *Journal of Product Innovation Management, 30*(1), 136–153. doi:10.1111/j.1540-5885.2012.00992.x

Kim, S. B. (2014). Impacts of knowledge management on the organizational success. *KSCE Journal of Civil Engineering, 18*(6), 1609–1617. doi:10.1007/s12205-014-0243-6

Compilation of References

Kim, S. B. (2014). Systematic analyses on knowledge implementation steps and themes at the organizational level. *KSCE Journal of Civil Engineering, 18*(2), 444–453. doi:10.1007/s12205-014-1191-x

Kim, Y. J., Song, S., Sambamurthy, V., & Lee, Y. L. (2012). Entrepreneurship, knowledge integration capability, and firm performance: An empirical study. *Information Systems Frontiers, 14*(5), 1047–1060. doi:10.1007/s10796-011-9331-z

Kirk, D. (2010). The development of higher education in the United Arab Emirates. The Emirates Occasional Papers, 74, 1-57.

Klaukien, A., Shepherd, D. A., & Patzelt, H. (2013). Passion for work, nonwork-related excitement, and innovation managers' decision to exploit new product opportunities. *Journal of Product Innovation Management, 30*(3), 574–588. doi:10.1111/jpim.12010

Kleinberg, J. M. (1999). Authoritative sources in a hyperlinked environment. *Journal of the ACM, 46*(5), 604–632. doi:10.1145/324133.324140

Kleinberg, J., & Lawrence, S. (2001). The Structure of the Web. *Science*, 294–322. PMID:11729296

Kleinschmidt, E., De Brentani, U., & Salomo, S. (2010). Information Processing and Firm-Internal Environment Contingencies: Performance Impact on Global New Product Development. *Creativity and Innovation Management, 19*(3), 200–218. doi:10.1111/j.1467-8691.2010.00568.x

Knowledge Cafés, Talks and Workshops Website. (n.d.). Retrieved from http://forwardnetworking.com/knowledge-cafes/

Koch, A. H. (2012). Authority and managing innovation: A typology of product development teams and communities. *Creativity and Innovation Management, 21*(4), 376–387. doi:10.1111/caim.12001

Kohli, A. K., & Jaworski, B. J. (1990). Market orientation: The construct, research propositions, and managerial implications. *Journal of Marketing, 54*(2), 1–18. doi:10.2307/1251866

Kolari, P., & Joshi, A. (2004). Web mining: Research and Practice. *IEEE Computational Science & Engineering, 6*(4), 49–53. doi:10.1109/MCSE.2004.23

Koplowitz, R. (2010). *Enterprise Social Networking 2010 Market Overview.* Forrester Research.

Koshy, R. (2008). A case of miscommunication? Obstacles to the effective implementation of a plagiarism detection system in a multicultural university. University of Wollongong Working Paper Series, UOWD-RSC WP-76, 12 June 2008: WP 76/2009.

Kuan, K. Y., & Chau, Y. K. (2001). A perception model for EDI adoption in small businesses using a technology-organization-environment framework. *Information & Management, 38*(1), 507–521. doi:10.1016/S0378-7206(01)00073-8

Kubica, J., Goldenberg, A., Komarek, P., & Moore, A. (2003). A comparison of statistical and machine learning algorithms on the task of link completion. In *Proceedings of the KDD Workshop on Link Analysis for Detecting Complex Behavior.*

Kuester, S., Homburg, C., & Hess, S. C. (2012). Externally directed and internally directed market launch management: The role of organizational factors in influencing new product success. *Journal of Product Innovation Management, 29*, 38–52. doi:10.1111/j.1540-5885.2012.00968.x

Kumar, R., Novak, J., & Tomkins, A. (2006). Structure and evolution of online social networks. In *KDD '06: Proceedings of the 12th ACM SIGKDD international conference on Knowledge discovery and data mining.* New York: ACM. doi:10.1145/1150402.1150476

Kumar, R., Raghavan, P., Rajagopalan, S., & Tomkins, A. (1999). Trawling the web for emerging cyber-communities. *Computer Networks, 31*(11-16), 1481–1493. doi:10.1016/S1389-1286(99)00040-7

Kuramochi, M., & Karypis, G. (2001). Frequent Subgraph Discovery. In *Proceedings of 2001 International Conference on Data Mining* (ICDM'01). doi:10.1109/ICDM.2001.989534

Lager, T., & Storm, P. (2013). Application development in process firms: Adding value to customer products and production systems. *R&D Management, 43*(3), 288–302. doi:10.1111/radm.12013

Landwehr, J. R., Wentzel, D., & Herrmann, A. (2012). The tipping point of design: How product design and brands interact to affect consumers' preferences. *Psychology and Marketing, 29*(6), 422–433. doi:10.1002/mar.20531

LaPaugh, A. S., & Rivest, R. R. (1978). *The subgraph homeomorphism problem.Annual ACM Symposium on Theory of Computing, Proceedings of the tenth annual symposium on Theory of Computing*, San Diego, CA.

Lasagni, A. (2012). How can external relationships enhance innovation in SMEs? New evidence for Europe. *Journal of Small Business Management, 50*(2), 310–339. doi:10.1111/j.1540-627X.2012.00355.x

Lawson, B., Samson, D., & Roden, S. (2012). Appropriating the value from innovation: Inimitability and the effectiveness of isolating mechanisms. *R & D Management, 42*(5), 420–434. doi:10.1111/j.1467-9310.2012.00692.x

Le-Anh, T., Koster, R. B. M., & Yu, Y. (2010). Performance evaluation of dynamic scheduling approaches in vehicle-based internal transport systems. *International Journal of Production Research, 48*(24), 7219–7242. doi:10.1080/00207540903443279

Lee, J., & Fink, D. (2013). Knowledge mapping: Encouragements and impediments to adoption. *Journal of Knowledge Management, 17*(1), 16–28. doi:10.1108/13673271311300714

Lee, S., Park, G., Yoon, B., & Park, J. (2010). Open innovation in SMEs - An intermediated network model. *Research Policy, 39*(2), 290–300. doi:10.1016/j.respol.2009.12.009

Legris, P., Ingham, J., & Collerette, P. (2003). Why do people use information technology? A critical review of the technology acceptance model. *Information & Management, 40*(3), 191–204. doi:10.1016/S0378-7206(01)00143-4

Leite, P. R. (2003). *Logística reversa. Meio ambiente e competitividade*. Prentice Hall.

Leonard, D., & Swap, W. (2005). *Deep Smarts*. Boston, MA: Harvard Business School Press.

Leonardi, P. M., Huysman, M., & Steinfield, C. (2013, October). History, and Prospects for the Study of Social Technologies in Organizations. *Journal of Computer-Mediated Communication, 19*(1), 1–19. doi:10.1111/jcc4.12029

Lerro, A., Iacobone, A. F., & Schiuma, G. (2012). Knowledge assets assessment strategies: Organizational value, processes, approaches and evaluation architectures. *Journal of Knowledge Management, 16*(4), 563–575. doi:10.1108/13673271211246149

Lessig, L. (2004). *Free Culture: How Big Media Uses Technology and the Law to Lock Down Culture and Control Creativity*. New York: The Penguin Press.

Liang, H., & Zhang, Z. (2012). The effects of industry characteristics on the sources of technological product and process innovation. *The Journal of Technology Transfer, 37*(6), 867–884. doi:10.1007/s10961-011-9206-y

Lian, J., Yen, D., & Wang, Y. (2014). An exploratory study to understand the critical factors affecting the decision to adopt cloud computing in Taiwan hospital. *International Journal of Information Management, 34*(1), 28–36. doi:10.1016/j.ijinfomgt.2013.09.004

Li, C., Guo, F., Zhi, L., Han, Z., & Liu, F. (2013). Knowledge management research status in China from 2006 to 2010: Based on analysis of the degree theses. *Scientometrics, 94*(1), 95–111. doi:10.1007/s11192-012-0858-7

Compilation of References

Lichtenthaler, U. (2013). The collaboration of innovation intermediaries and manufacturing firms in the markets for technology. *Journal of Product Innovation Management, 30*, 142–158. doi:10.1111/jpim.12068

Lightfoot, M. (2011). *Promoting the Knowledge Economy in the Arab World.* SAGE Open; doi:10.1177/2158244011417457

Lim, S. Y., & Suh, M. (2015). Product and process innovation in the development cycle of biopharmaceuticals. *Journal of Pharmaceutical Innovation, 10*(2), 156–165. doi:10.1007/s12247-015-9214-9

Ling, Y. H. (2013). The influence of intellectual capital on organizational performance: Knowledge management as moderator. *Asia Pacific Journal of Management, 30*(3), 937–964. doi:10.1007/s10490-011-9257-5

Lin, H. F. (2007a). A stage model of knowledge management: An empirical investigation of process and effectiveness. *Journal of Information Science, 33*(6), 643–659. doi:10.1177/0165551506076395

Lionzo, A., & Rossignoli, F. (2013). Knowledge integration in family SMEs: An extension of the 4I model. *Journal of Management and Governance, 17*(3), 583–608. doi:10.1007/s10997-011-9197-y

Lipschutz, S. (1997). Schaum's outline on Data Structures. Tata McGraw-Hill Publishing Company Limited.

Liu, H., Ding, X. H., Guo, H., & Luo, J. H. (2014). How does slack affect product innovation in high-tech Chinese firms: The contingent value of entrepreneurial orientation. *Asia Pacific Journal of Management, 31*(1), 47–68. doi:10.1007/s10490-012-9309-5

Liu, X. J., & Wang, Y. L. (2015). Semantic-based knowledge categorization and organization for product design enterprises. *Journal of Shanghai Jiaotong University (Science), 20*(1), 106–112. doi:10.1007/s12204-015-1596-9

Liu, Y., & Abdalla, A. N. (2013). Evaluating the managerial behavior of managing knowledge in Chinese SMEs. *Information Technology Management, 14*(2), 159–165. doi:10.1007/s10799-013-0157-x

Li, X., Li, L., & Chen, Z. (2014). Toward extenics-based innovation model on intelligent knowledge management. *Annals of Data Science, 1*(1), 127–148. doi:10.1007/s40745-014-0009-5

Lloria, M. B. (2008). A review of the main approaches to knowledge management. *Knowledge Management Research & Practice, 6*(1), 77–89. doi:10.1057/palgrave.kmrp.8500164

Loertscher, D. V. (2012). Maker spaces and the learning commons. *Teacher Librarian, 40*(1), 45–46, 63.

Lonnqvist, A., & Laihonen, H. (2013). Managing regional development: A knowledge perspective. International. *Journal of Knowledge-Based Development, 4*(1), 50–63. doi:10.1504/IJKBD.2013.052493

López-Nicolás, C., & Meroño-Cerdán, Á. L. (2011). Strategic knowledge management, innovation and performance. *International Journal of Information Management, 31*(6), 502–509. doi:10.1016/j.ijinfomgt.2011.02.003

Lopez-Nicolas, C., & Soto-Acosta, P. (2010). Analyzing ICT adoption and use effects on knowledge creation: An empirical investigation in SMEs. *International Journal of Information Management, 30*(6), 521–528. doi:10.1016/j.ijinfomgt.2010.03.004

Luca, L. M. D., & Atuahene-Gima, K. (2007). Market knowledge dimensions and cross-functional collaboration: Examining the different routes to product innovation performance. *Journal of Marketing, 71*(1), 95–112. doi:10.1509/jmkg.71.1.95

Lucio-Nieto, T., Colomo-Palacios, R., Soto-Acosta, P., Popa, S., & Amescua-Seco, A. (2012). Implementing an IT service information management framework: The case of COTEMAR. *International Journal of Information Management, 32*(6), 589–594. doi:10.1016/j.ijinfomgt.2012.08.004

Luna, J. J. (2009). Metrics, Models, and Scenarios for Evaluating PHM Effects on Logistics Support. *Proceedings of Annual Conference of the Prognostics and Health Management Society.*

Lunnan, R., & Zhao, Y. (2014). Regional headquarters in China: Role in MNE knowledge transfer. *Asia Pacific Journal of Management, 31*(2), 397–422. doi:10.1007/s10490-013-9358-4

Madrid-Guijarro, A., García-Pérez-de-Lema, D., & Van Auken, H. (2013). An investigation of Spanish SME innovation during different economic conditions. *Journal of Small Business Management, 51*(4), 578–601. doi:10.1111/jsbm.12004

Maes, P., & Mistry, P. (2009). *Retrieved from TED talks – Pattie Maes and Pranav Mistry demo SixthSense*. Retrieved from http://www.ted.com/talks/pat- tie_maes_demos_the_sixth_sense.html

Mahajan, V. (2012). *Arab World unbound: Tapping into the power of 350 million consumers*. Somerset, NJ: John Wiley & Sons.

Mahr, D., Lievens, A., & Blazevic, V. (2013). The Value of Customer Cocreated Knowledge during the Innovation Process. *Journal of Product Innovation Management.*

Mahr, D., Lievens, A., & Blazevic, V. (2014). The value of customer cocreated knowledge during the innovation process. *Journal of Product Innovation Management, 31*(3), 599–615. doi:10.1111/jpim.12116

Maineri, M. (2013). *Collaboriamo! come i social media ci aiutano a lavorare e a vivere bene in tempo di crisi*. Milano: Hoepli.

Mäkimattila, M., Melkas, H., & Uotila, T. (2013). Dynamics of openness in innovation processes: A case study in the Finnish food industry. *Knowledge and Process Management, 20*(4), 243–255. doi:10.1002/kpm.1421

Maniam, A. (2004). *Graph-based click-stream mining for categorizing browsing activity in the World Wide Web*. (Master's Thesis). University of Texas at Arlington.

Manyika, J. (2014). *Big data: The next frontier for innovation, competition, and productivity*. Retrieved from http://www.mckinsey.com/insights/mgi/research/technology_and_innovation/big_data_the_next_frontier_for_innovation

Maracine, V., & Scarlat, E. (2009). Dynamic Knowledge and Healthcare Knowledge Ecosystems. *Electronic Journal of Knowledge Management, 7*(1), 99–110.

Marion, T. J., Friar, J. H., & Simpson, T. W. (2012). New product development practices and early-stage firms: Two in-depth case studies. *Journal of Product Innovation Management, 29*(4), 639–654. doi:10.1111/j.1540-5885.2012.00930.x

Markham, S. K. (2013). The impact of front-end innovation activities on product performance. *Journal of Product Innovation Management, 30*, 77–92. doi:10.1111/jpim.12065

Marlow, D. C. (2009). *Primates on Facebook*. Retrieved from http://www.economist.com/sciencetechnology/displayStory.cfm?story_id=13176775

Marschark, M., Lang, H. G., & Albertini, J. A. (2002). *Educating Deaf Students: From Research to Practice*. Oxford University Press.

Martínez-Román, J. A., & Romero, I. (2013). About the determinants of the degree of novelty in small businesses' product innovations. *The International Entrepreneurship and Management Journal, 9*(4), 655–677. doi:10.1007/s11365-013-0269-0

Martinkenaite, I. (2012). Antecedents of knowledge transfer in acquisitions. *Baltic Journal of Management, 7*(2), 167–184. doi:10.1108/17465261211219796

Martins, E. C., & Terblanche, F. (2003). Building organisational culture that stimulates creativity and innovation. *European Journal of Innovation Management*, *6*(1), 64–74. doi:10.1108/14601060310456337

Massingham, P. (2015). Knowledge sharing: What works and what doesn't work: A critical systems thinking perspective. *Systemic Practice and Action Research*, *28*(3), 197–228. doi:10.1007/s11213-014-9330-3

Matayong, S., & Mahmood, A. K. (2013). The review of approaches to knowledge management system studies. *Journal of Knowledge Management*, *17*(3), 472–490. doi:10.1108/JKM-10-2012-0316

Matschke, C., Moskaliuk, J., & Cress, U. (2012). Knowledge exchange using Web 2.0 technologies in NGO's. *Journal of Knowledge Management*, *16*(1), 159–176. doi:10.1108/13673271211199007

McAdam, R., & McCreedy, S. (1999). The process of knowledge management within organizations: A critical assessment of both theory and practice. *Knowledge and Process Management*, *6*(2), 101–113. doi:10.1002/(SICI)1099-1441(199906)6:2<101::AID-KPM53>3.0.CO;2-P

McCabe, D., Feghali, T., & Abdallah, H. (2008). Academic dishonesty in the Middle East: Individual and contextual factors. *Research in Higher Education*, *49*(5), 451–467. doi:10.1007/s11162-008-9092-9

McDermott, R. (2012). *Getting the most from your mentor*. Retrieved on December 15, 2012 from http://www.nasa.gov/pdf/703218main_48i_mentor.pdf

McEneaney, J. E. (2001). Graphic and Numerical Methods to assess Navigation in Hypertext. *International Journal of Human-Computer Studies*, *55*(5), 761–786. doi:10.1006/ijhc.2001.0505

McEvoy, K. (2014). *PlumX Includes Usage Statistics from EBSCO Databases*. Retrieved from http://www.ebscohost.com/newsroom/stories/plumx-includes-usage-statistics-from-ebsco-databases

McGurk, J., & Baron, A. (2012). Knowledge management: Time to focus on purpose and motivation. *Strategic HR Review*, *11*(6), 316–321. doi:10.1108/14754391211264776

McKellar, K. A., Pitzul, K. B., Yi, J. Y., & Cole, D. C. (2014). Evaluating communities of practice and knowledge networks: A systematic scoping review of evaluation frameworks. *EcoHealth*, *11*(3), 383–399. doi:10.1007/s10393-014-0958-3 PMID:25023411

McLachlin, R., & Larson, P. D. (2011). Building humanitarian supply chain relationships: Lessons from leading practitioners. *Journal of Humanitarian Logistics and Supply Chain Management*, *1*(1), 32–49. doi:10.1108/20426741111122402

McLaughlin, P., Bessant, J., & Smart, P. (2008). Developing an organisation culture to facilitate radical innovation. *International Journal of Technology Management*, *44*(3), 298–323. doi:10.1504/IJTM.2008.021041

Meese, N., & McMahon, C. (2012). Knowledge sharing for sustainable development in civil engineering: A systematic review. *AI & Society*, *27*(4), 437–449. doi:10.1007/s00146-011-0369-8

Melton, H. L., & Hartline, M. D. (2010). Customer and frontline employee influence on new service development performance. *Journal of Service Research*, *13*(4), 411–425. doi:10.1177/1094670510369378

Melton, H. L., & Hartline, M. D. (2013). Employee Collaboration, Learning Orientation, and New Service Development Performance. *Journal of Service Research*, *16*(1), 67–81. doi:10.1177/1094670512462139

Mendelzon, A., Michaila, G., & Milo, T. (1996). Querying the WWW. In *Proceedings of the International Conference on Parallel and Distributed Information Systems*, (pp. 80–91). Academic Press.

Menzel, D. C. (2012). *Ethics management for public administrators: building organizations of integrity*. Armonk, NY: M.E. Sharpe, Inc.

Meo, R., Lanzi, P. L., Matera, M., & Esposito, R. (2004). Integrating web conceptual modelling and web usage mining. In Proceedings of WebKDD.

Meroño-Cerdan, A., Soto-Acosta, P., & Lopez-Nicolas, C. (2008). ª). Analyzing collaborative technologies' effect on performance through intranet use orientations. *Journal of Enterprise Information Management*, *21*(1), 39–51. doi:10.1108/17410390810842246

Meroño-Cerdan, A., Soto-Acosta, P., & Lopez-Nicolas, C. (2008b). How do collaborative technologies affect innovation in SMEs? *International Journal of e-Collaboration*, *4*(4), 33–50. doi:10.4018/jec.2008100103

Messmer, B. T. (1995). *Efficient Graph Matching Algorithms for Pre-Processed Model Graphs*. (Ph.D. Thesis). Institut fur Informatik und Angewandte Matheatik, Universitat Bern, Switzerland.

Micelli, S. (2011). *Futuro artigiano*. Venezia: Marsilio Editore.

Microsoft. (2009). Oil and Gas Pros View Social Media as Important for Productivity, Collabora- tion; Yet Few Firms Have Tools in Place. *New Survey Reports*. Retrieved from http://www.microsoft.com/presspass/press/2009/feb09/02-18OGSocialMediaPR.mspx

Miller, A. (2011). Cultural Barriers to Organizational Social Media Adoption. *Social Knowledge: Using Social Media to Know What You Know*, 96-114.

Milton, N. (2012). *Quantified KM success story number 30: Halliburton Electronic Technicians Community*. Retrieved on November 12, 2014, from http://www.nickmilton.com/2012/05/quanitified-km-success-story-number-30.htmlnumberixzz3HcelCSrV

Minbaeva, D. B. (2005). HRM practices and MNC knowledge transfer. *Personnel Review*, *34*(1), 125–144. doi:10.1108/00483480510571914

Minbaeva, D. B., Pedersen, T., Björkman, I., Fey, C. F., & Park, H. J. (2003). MNC knowledge transfer, subsidiary absorptive capacity, and HRM. *Journal of International Business Studies*, *34*(6), 586–599. doi:10.1057/palgrave.jibs.8400056

Miranda, E. (2003). *Running the successful hi-tech project office*. Boston, MA: Artech House.

Mohnen, P., & Hall, B. H. (2013). Innovation and productivity: An update. *Eurasian Business Review*, *3*(1), 47–65.

Moilanen, M., Østbye, S., & Woll, K. (2014). Non-R&D SMEs: External knowledge, absorptive capacity and product innovation. *Small Business Economics*, *43*(2), 447–462. doi:10.1007/s11187-014-9545-9

Moloney. (2011). *12 Social Business Predictions for 2012*. Retrieved from https://blogs.perficient.com/portals/2011/12/21/12-social-business-predictions-for-2012/

Mom, T. J. M., van den Bosch, F. A. J., & Volberda, H. W. (2009). Understanding variation in managers' ambidexterity: Investigating direct and interaction effects of formal structural and personal coordination mechanisms. *Organization Science*, *20*(4), 812–828. doi:10.1287/orsc.1090.0427

Moon, H., Miller, D. R., & Kim, S. H. (2013). Product design innovation and customer value: Cross-cultural research in the United States and Korea. *Journal of Product Innovation Management*, *30*(1), 31–43. doi:10.1111/j.1540-5885.2012.00984.x

Moy, M. (2005). Using TMODS to run the Best Friends Group Detection Algorithm. 21st Century Technologies Internal Publication.

Mueller, J. (2015). Formal and informal practices of knowledge sharing between project teams and enacted cultural characteristics. *Project Management Journal*, *46*(1), 53–68. doi: 10.1002/pmj.21471

Mueller, J. (2012). The interactive relationship of corporate culture and knowledge management: A review. *Review of Managerial Science*, *6*(2), 183–201. doi:10.1007/s11846-010-0060-3

Mugge, R., & Dahl, D. W. (2013). Seeking the ideal level of design newness: Consumer response to radical and incremental product design. *Journal of Product Innovation Management*, *30*, 34–47. doi:10.1111/jpim.12062

Murro, P. (2013). The determinants of innovation: What is the role of risk? *The Manchester School*, *81*(3), 293–323. doi:10.1111/j.1467-9957.2012.02286.x

Mutula, S. M. (2011). Ethics and trust in digital scholarship. *The Electronic Library*, *29*(2), 261–276. doi:10.1108/02640471111125212

Myers, P. S. (2012). *Knowledge management and organizational design*. London, UK: Routledge.

Nadi, F. (2010). *The importance of Intellectual Property (IP) for Economic Growth and Business Competitiveness*. WIPO.

Nahapiet, J., & Ghoshal, S. (1998). Social capital, intellectual capital, and the organizational advantage. *Academy of Management Review*, *23*, 242–266.

Nambisan, S. (2009). *Virtual customer environments: IT-enabled customer co-innovation and value co-creation* (pp. 109–127). NY: Springer.

Narasimhan, R., & Narayanan, S. (2013). Perspectives on supply network–enabled innovations. *Journal of Supply Chain Management*, *49*(4), 27–42. doi:10.1111/jscm.12026

Nardi, B. (1999). Context and consciousness: Activity theory and human-computer interaction. Cambridge, MA: MIT Press.

Nardone, G., Seccia, A., & Maruotti, G. (2013). How nanotechnologies can contribute to innovation in food firms in Europe. *EuroChoices*, *12*(2), 21–26. doi:10.1111/1746-692X.12026

National Qualifications Authority. (2013). *The UAE education system overview of performance in education*. Retrieved from file:///D:/Documents/Downloads/The%20UAE%20Education%20System%20Report%20(3).pdf

Nelson, L. M. (1999). Collaborative Problem Solving. Reigeluth, 241-267.

Neuburger. (2008, October 15). *Teacher Fired for Inappropriate Behavior on MySpace Page | Mediashift | PBS*. Retrieved from http://www.pbs.org/mediashift/2008/10/teacher-fired-for-inappropriate-behavior-on-myspace-page289/

Neumann, M., Riel, A., & Brissaud, D. (2013). IT-supported innovation management in the automotive supplier industry to drive idea generation and leverage innovation. *Journal of Software: Evolution and Process*, *25*(4), 329–339.

Newman, B. (2011). Beginner's Guide to Transliteracy. *Libraries and Transliteracy*. Retrieved from http://librariesandtransliteracy.wordpress.com/beginners-guide-to-transliteracy/

Newman, M., & Girvan, M. (2004). Finding and evaluating community structure in networks. *Physical Review E: Statistical, Nonlinear, and Soft Matter Physics*, *69*, 26–113. PMID:14995526

Ngulube, P. & Lwoga, E. (2007). Knowledge management models and their utility to the effective management and integration of indigenous knowledge with other knowledge systems. *Indilinga - African Journal of Indigenous Knowledge Systems*, *6*(2), 117 - 131.

Niessen, C., Sonnentag, S., & Volmer, J. (2006). Expertise in software design. In K. A. Ericsson (Ed.), *The Cambridge Handbook of Expertise and Expert Performance* (pp. 373–387). New York, NY: Cambridge University Press.

Nijssen, S., & Kok, J. A. (2004). Quickstart in frequent structure mining can make a difference. In *Proceedings of 2004 ACM SIGKDD International Conference on Knowledge Discovery in Databases* (KDD'04). Seattle, WA: ACM.

Nilsson, S., & Ritzén, S. (2014). Exploring the use of innovation performance measurement to build innovation capability in a medical device company. *Creativity and Innovation Management*, *23*(2), 183–198. doi:10.1111/caim.12054

Nonaka, I. (1990). *A theory of organizational knowledge creation*. Nihon Keizai Shimbun-sha.

Nonaka, I. (1994). A dynamic theory of organizational knowledge creation. *Organization Science*, *5*(1), 14–37. doi:10.1287/orsc.5.1.14

Nonaka, I., & Konno, N. (1998). The concept of ba: Building a foundation for knowledge creation. *California Management Review*, *40*(3), 40–54. doi:10.2307/41165942

Nonaka, I., Reinmoller, P., & Senoo, D. (1998). The 'ART' of Knowledge: Systems to Capitalize on Market Knowledge. *European Management Journal*, *16*(6), 673–684. doi:10.1016/S0263-2373(98)00044-9

Nonaka, I., & Takeuchi, H. (1995). *The knowledge-creating company*. New York: Oxford University Press.

Nonaka, I., & Takeuchi, H. (1995). *The knowledge-creating company: how Japanese companies create the dynamics of innovation*. New York: Oxford University Press.

Nonaka, I., & Takeuchi, H. (1995). *The knowledge-creating company: How Japanese companies create the dynamics of innovation*. Oxford University Press.

Nonaka, I., & Takeuchi, N. (1995). *The Knowledge Creating Company*. Oxford, UK: University Press.

Nonaka, I., Toyama, R., & Konno, N. (2000). SECI, Ba and leadership: A unified model of dynamic knowledge creation. *Long Range Planning*, *33*(1), 5–34. doi:10.1016/S0024-6301(99)00115-6

Nonaka, I., & Von Krogh, G. (2009). Tacit knowledge and knowledge conversion: Controversy and advancement in organizational knowledge creation theory. *Organization Science*, *20*(3), 635–652. doi:10.1287/orsc.1080.0412

Nordström, K. A., & Ridderstrale, J. (2007). *Funky Business Forever: How to enjoy capitalism*. Pearson Education.

Norman, M. (2012). Frail, fatal, fundamental: The future of public libraries. *Australasian Public Libraries and Information Services*, *25*(2), 94–100.

Noruzy, A., Dalfard, V. M., Azhdari, B., Nazari-Shirkouhi, S., & Rezazadeh, A. (2013). Relations between transformational leadership, organizational learning, knowledge management, organizational innovation, and organizational performance: An empirical investigation of manufacturing firms. *International Journal of Advanced Manufacturing Technology*, *64*(5/8), 1073–1085. doi:10.1007/s00170-012-4038-y

Norvaiša, R. (2011). Journal impact factor and academic ethics. *Mokslo Ir Technikos Raida*, *3*(2), 120–128. doi:10.3846/est.2011.10

O'Dell, C., & Trees, L. (2014). *How Smart Leaders Leverage Their Experts*. Retrieved on December 19, 2014 from http://www.apqc.org/knowledge-base/download/309016/K04979_How_Smart_Leaders_Leverage_Their_Experts.pdf

O'Dell, C., & Grayson, C. J. (1998). If only we knew what we know: Identification and transfer of internal best practices. *California Management Review*, *40*(3), 154–170. doi:10.2307/41165948

Öberg, Ch., Huge-Brodin, M., & Björklund, M. (2012). Applying a network level in environmental impact assessments. *Journal of Business Research*, *65*(2), 247–255. doi:10.1016/j.jbusres.2011.05.026

OCDE. (Ed.). (2002). *Frascati Manual*. OCDE.

OCDE. (Ed.). (2005). Oslo Manual (3rd ed.). OCDE and Eurostat.

Compilation of References

OECD. (2004). *The significance of knowledge management in the business sector.* OECD.

Oke, A., Prajogo, D. I., & Jayaram, J. (2013). Strengthening the innovation chain: The role of internal innovation climate and strategic relationships with supply chain partners. *Journal of Supply Chain Management, 49*(4), 43–58. doi:10.1111/jscm.12031

Olson, E. M., Slater, S. F., & Hult, G. T. M. (2005). The performance implications of fit among business strategy, marketing organization structure, and strategic behavior. *Journal of Marketing, 69*(3), 49–65. doi:10.1509/jmkg.69.3.49.66362

Ortt, J. R., & Smits, R. (2006). Innovation management: Different approaches to cope with the same trends. *International Journal of Technology Management, 34*(3), 296–318. doi:10.1504/IJTM.2006.009461

O'Sullivan, D., & Dooley, L. (2010). Collaborative innovation for the management of information technology resources. *International Journal of Human Capital and Information Technology Professionals, 1*(1), 16–30. doi:10.4018/jhcitp.2010091102

Oxford English Dictionary. (2014). *Spiral.* Oxford, UK: Oxford University Press.

Ozel, B. (2012). Collaboration structure and knowledge diffusion in Turkish management academia. *Scientometrics, 93*(1), 183–206. doi:10.1007/s11192-012-0641-9

Oztemel, E., & Arslankaya, S. (2012). Enterprise knowledge management model: A knowledge tower. *Knowledge and Information Systems, 31*(1), 171–192. doi:10.1007/s10115-011-0414-4

Palfrey, J., & Gasser, U. (2008). *Born Digital: Understanding the First Generation of Digital Natives.* Cambridge, MA: Basic Books.

Panahi, S., Watson, J., & Partridge, H. (2012). Social media and tacit knowledge sharing: Developing a conceptual model. *World Academy of Science. Engineering and Technology, 64*, 1095–1102.

Panahi, S., Watson, J., & Partridge, H. (2013). Towards tacit knowledge sharing over social web tools. *Journal of Knowledge Management, 17*(3), 379–397. doi:10.1108/JKM-11-2012-0364

Pandey, S. C., & Dutta, A. (2013). Role of knowledge infrastructure capabilities in knowledge management. *Journal of Knowledge Management, 17*(3), 435–453. doi:10.1108/JKM-11-2012-0365

Park, M., Jang, Y., Lee, H. S., Ahn, C., & Yoon, Y. S. (2013). Application of knowledge management technologies in Korean small and medium-sized construction companies. *KSCE Journal of Civil Engineering, 17*(1), 22–32. doi:10.1007/s12205-013-1607-z

Park, M., Lee, K. W., Lee, H. S., Jiayi, P., & Yu, J. (2013). Ontology-based construction knowledge retrieval system. *KSCE Journal of Civil Engineering, 17*(7), 1654–1663. doi:10.1007/s12205-013-1155-6

Patel, C., & Haon, C. (2014). Internally versus externally developed technology and market acceptance of innovations: The complementary role of branding. *European Management Review, 11*(2), 173–186. doi:10.1111/emre.12029

Patel, P. C., Fernhaber, S. A., McDougall-Covin, P. P., & van der Have, R. P. (2014). Beating competitors to international markets: The value of geographically balanced networks for innovation. *Strategic Management Journal, 35*(5), 691–711. doi:10.1002/smj.2114

Pathways to Information Leadership. (n.d.). *About Pathways.* Retrieved on 22 September 2014 from https://infoleader.org/about-pathways

Pérez-López, S., & Alegre, J. (2012). Information technology competency, knowledge processes and firm performance. *Industrial Management & Data Systems, 112*(4), 644–662. doi:10.1108/02635571211225521

Peterson, A. J. (2005). *An examination of reverse logistics factor impacting the 463-L pallet program*. (Master dissertation). Air University, Dayton, OH.

Peterson, J. D. (2007). *The Information and communication technology landscape in the United Arab Emirates: National ICT Policies*. Retrieved on 1 May 2014 from http://www1.american.edu/carmel/jp2450a/2.htm

Petrescu, M. (2013). Marketing research using single-item indicators in structural equation model. *Journal of Marketing Analytics*, *1*(2), 99–117. doi:10.1057/jma.2013.7

Piascik, P., & Brazeau, G. A. (2010). Promoting a culture of academic integrity. *American Journal of Pharmaceutical Education*, *74*(6), 1–113. doi:10.5688/aj7406113 PMID:21045955

Pishvaee, M. S., Farahani, R. Z., & Dullaert, W. (2010). A memetic algorithm for bi-objective integrated forward/reverse logistics network design. *Computers & Operations Research*, *37*(6), 1100–1112. doi:10.1016/j.cor.2009.09.018

Podsakoff, P. M., Mackenzie, S. B., Lee, J., & Podsakoff, N. P. (2003). Common method biases in behavioral research: A critical review of the literature and recommended remedies. *The Journal of Applied Psychology*, *20*(5), 879–903. doi:10.1037/0021-9010.88.5.879 PMID:14516251

Pokharel, S., & Mutha, A. (2009). Perspectives in reverse logistics: A review. *Resources, Conservation and Recycling*, *53*(4), 175–182. doi:10.1016/j.resconrec.2008.11.006

Polanyi, M. (1962). *Personal knowledge: towards a post-critical philosophy*. Chicago: University of Chicago Press.

Poon, W.-Y., Leung, K., & Lee, S.-Y. (2002). The comparison of single item constructs by relative mean and relative variance. *Organizational Research Methods*, *5*(3), 275–298. doi:10.1177/1094428102005003005

Porter, M. (2008). The Five Competitive Forces that Shape Strategy. *Harvard Business Review*.

Porter, M. E. (1985). *Competitive Advantage*. New York: Free Press.

Porter, M. E., & Kramer, M. R. (2011). Creating shared value. *Harvard Business Review*, *89*(1/2), 62–77.

Pot, F. (2011). *Social innovation of work and employment, Challenge Social Innovation*. Paper presented at the meeting workshop: Social innovation at work, Wien, Austraia.

Price, D. (2011). Politics, piracy and punishment: Copyright protection in the Arabian Gulf. *The Journal of World Intellectual Property*, *14*(3/4), 276–300. doi:10.1111/j.1747-1796.2011.00419.x

Prins, J., Yang, J., Huan, J., & Wang, W. (2004). Spin: Mining maximal frequent subgraphs from graph databases. In *Proceedings of 2004 ACM SIGKDD International Conference on Knowledge Discovery in Databases* (KDD'04). Seattle, WA: ACM.

Professional Services Close - Up. (2014). *Technology-based online proctoring decreases cheating on college finals*. Jacksonville, FL: Close-Up Media.

ProQuest Case Study. (2014). *Using the Oscillation Principle for Software Development Conversations Matter Blog*. Retrieved on 21 November 2014 from http://www.nancydixonblog.com/

Pullen, A., de Weerd-Nederhof, P. C., Groen, A. J., & Fisscher, O. A. M. (2012). SME network characteristics vs. product innovativeness: How to achieve high innovation performance. *Creativity and Innovation Management*, *21*(2), 130–146. doi:10.1111/j.1467-8691.2012.00638.x

PulsePoint. (2012). *The Economics of A Fully Engaged Enterprise*. Retrieved July 28, 2014, from http://www.pulsepointgroup.com/services/social-media-accelerator

Purcarea, I., Espinosa, M., & Apetrei, A. (2013). Innovation and knowledge creation: Perspectives on the SMEs sector. *Management Decision, 51*(5), 1096–1107. doi:10.1108/MD-08-2012-0590

Rabeh, H. A. D., Jimenéz-Jimenéz, D., & Martínez-Costa, M. (2013). Managing knowledge for a successful competence exploration. *Journal of Knowledge Management, 17*(2), 195–207. doi:10.1108/13673271311315169

Raghavan, P. (2002). Social networks: From the web to the enterprise. *IEEE Internet Computing, 6*(1), 91–94. doi:10.1109/4236.989007

Rahman, H., & Ramos, I. (2010). Open Innovation in SMEs: From closed boundaries to networked paradigm. *Issues in Informing Science and Information Technology, 7*, 471–487.

Rai, R. K. (2011). Knowledge management and organizational culture: A theoretical integrative framework. *Journal of Knowledge Management, 15*(5), 779–801. doi:10.1108/13673271111174320

Ramayah, T., Yeap, J. A. L., & Ignatius, J. (2013). An empirical inquiry on knowledge sharing among academicians in higher learning institutions. *Minerva, 51*(2), 131–154. doi:10.1007/s11024-013-9229-7

Ramdani, B., Chevers, D., & Williams, D. (2013). SMEs adoption of enterprise applications: A technology-organisation-environment model. *Journal of Small Business and Enterprise Development, 20*(4), 89–115.

Rana, G., & Goel, A. (2014). Ethan learns to be a learning organization. *Human Resource Management International Digest, 22*(6), 12–14. doi:10.1108/HRMID-08-2014-0114

Rana, G., & Goel, A. (2015). Stars of the future give Bhushan Power and Steel the edge. *Human Resource Management International Digest, 23*(1), 15–17. doi:10.1108/HRMID-12-2014-0158

Rao, B., & Mitra, A. (2014a). *An approach to study properties and behavior of Social Network using Graph Mining Techniques*. In DIGNATE 2014: ETEECT 2014, India.

Rao, B., & Mitra, A. (2014b). A new approach for detection of common communities in a social network using graph mining techniques. In *High Performance Computing and Applications (ICHPCA), 2014 International Conference on*. doi: .2014.7045335 doi:10.1109/ICHPCA

Rao, B., & Mitra, A. (2014c). An Approach to Merging of two Community Sub-Graphs to form a Community Graph using Graph Mining Techniques. *2014 IEEE International Conference on Computational Intelligence and Computing Research* (ICCIC-2014). IEEE.

Rao, B., & Mitra, A. (2014d). *An Approach of Mining Big-Data from a very large community graph for analysing of economic standard of communities using Distributed Mining Techniques*. CCSN 2014, Puri, India.

Rapp, A., Beitelspacher, L. S., Grewal, D., & Hughes, D. E. (2013). Understanding social media effects across seller, retailer, and consumer interactions. *Journal of the Academy of Marketing Science, 41*(5), 547–566. doi:10.1007/s11747-013-0326-9

Rass, M., Dumbach, M., Danziger, F., Bullinger, A. C., & Moeslein, K. M. (2013). Open innovation and firm performance: The mediating role of social capital. *Creativity and Innovation Management, 22*(2), 177–194. doi:10.1111/caim.12028

Rastogi, P. N. (2000). Knowledge management and intellectual capital - The new virtuous reality of competitiveness. *Human Systems Management, 19*(1), 39–48.

Rathi, D., Given, L., Forcier, E., & Vela, S. (2014). Every Task its Tool, Every Tool its Task: Social Media Use in Canadian Non-Profit Organizations. *Proceedings of the Annual Conference of the Canadian Association for Information Science*. Retrieved from http://www.cais-acsi.ca/ojs/index.php/cais/article/view/905

Ravasz, E., & Barabasi, A.-L. (2003). Hierarchical Organization In Complex Networks. *Physical Review, 67*. PMID:12636753

Ravindran, S., & Iyer, G. S. (2014). Organizational and knowledge management related antecedents of knowledge use: The moderating effect of ambiguity tolerance. *Information Technology Management, 15*(4), 271–290. doi:10.1007/s10799-014-0190-4

Ravi, V., Shankar, R., & Tiwari, M. K. (2005). Analyzing alternatives in reverse logistics for end-of-life computers: ANP and balanced scorecard approach. *Computers & Industrial Engineering, 48*(2), 327–356. doi:10.1016/j.cie.2005.01.017

Rayward, W. B. (1975). *The Universe of Information: The Work of Paul Otlet for documentation and International Organisation*. Chicago, IL: University of Chicago.

Regional Gurteen Community Cafes Website. (n.d.). Retrieved from http://www.gurteen.com/gurteen/gurteen.nsf/id/kcafes

Reigeluth, C. M. (2004). Elaboration Theory. In Education and Technology: An Encyclopedia. Santa Barbara, CA: ABC-Clio.

Reigeluth, C. M., et al. (2006). Creating shared visions of the future for K-12 education: A systemic transformation process for a learner-centered paradigm. *The Journal of Educational Alternatives,3*(1), 34-66.

Reigeluth, M. (1999). *Instructional-Design Theories and Models: A New Paradigm of Instructional Theory*. Hillsdale, NJ: Lawrence Erlbaum Assoc.

Rese, A., Gemünden, H. G., & Baier, D. (2013). "Too many cooks spoil the broth": Key persons and their roles in inter-organizational innovations. *Creativity and Innovation Management, 22*(4), 390–407. doi:10.1111/caim.12034

Research Team. (2012, May 14). *How Domino's and Dell Rebuilt Trust After a Social PR Crisis*. Retrieved from http://pivotcon.com/how-dominos-and-dell-rebuilt-trust-after-a-social-pr-crisis/

Riesen, K., Jiang, X., & Bunke, H. (2010). Exact and Inexact Graph Matching: Methodology and Applications. In Managing and Mining Graph Data. Academic Press.

Ritala, P., & Hurmelinna-Laukkanen, P. (2013). Incremental and radical innovation in coopetition: The role of absorptive capacity and appropriability. *Journal of Product Innovation Management, 30*(1), 154–169. doi:10.1111/j.1540-5885.2012.00956.x

Rivas, M. (2011). *From creative industries to the creative place. refreshing the local development agenda in small and medium size towns*. URBACT creative clusters project final report.

Roig, M. (1997). Can undergraduate students determine whether text has been plagiarized? *The Psychological Record, 47*(1), 113–123.

Roijakkers, N., Zynga, A., & Bishop, C. (2014). Getting Help from Innomediaries. In H. Chesbrough, W. Vanhaverbeke, & J. West (Eds.), *New Frontiers in Open Innovation* (pp. 135–156). Oxford Publications. doi:10.1093/acprof:oso/9780199682461.003.0013

Roth, A., & Kaberger, T. (2002). Making transport systems sustainable. *Journal of Cleaner Production, 10*(4), 361–371. doi:10.1016/S0959-6526(01)00052-X

Rubin, H.-J., & Rubin, I.-S. (1995). *Qualitative Interviewing: The Art of Hearing Data*. London: Sage Publications.

Ruggles, R. (1998). The state of the notion: Knowledge management in practice. *California Management Review, 40*(3), 80–89. doi:10.2307/41165944

Compilation of References

Ruiz-Jimenez, J. M., & Fuentes-Fuentes, M. (2013). Knowledge combination, innovation, organizational performance in technology firms. *Industrial Management & Data Systems, 113*(4), 523–540. doi:10.1108/02635571311322775

Saemundsson, R. J., & Candi, M. (2014). Antecedents of innovation strategies in new technology-based firms: Interactions between the environment and founder team composition. *Journal of Product Innovation Management, 31*(5), 939–955. doi:10.1111/jpim.12133

Safko, L. (2010). *The social media bible: tactics, tools, and strategies for business success.* John Wiley & Sons.

Salge, T. O., Farchi, T., Barrett, M. I., & Dopson, S. (2013). When does search openness really matter? A contingency study of health-care innovation projects. *Journal of Product Innovation Management, 30*(4), 659–676. doi:10.1111/jpim.12015

Salvador, F., & Villena, V. H. (2013). Supplier integration and NPD outcomes: Conditional moderation effects of modular design competence. *Journal of Supply Chain Management, 49*(1), 87–113. doi:10.1111/j.1745-493x.2012.03275.x

San Martín, S., López-Catalán, B., & Ramón-Jerónimo, M. A. (2012). Factors determining firms' perceived performance of mobile commerce. *Industrial Management & Data Systems, 112*(6), 946–963. doi:10.1108/02635571211238536

Sandberg, J. A. (1994). Educational paradigms: issues and trends. In Proceedings of Lessons from learning. (IFIP TC3/WG3.3 Working Conference 1993). Academic Press.

Santo, M. (2012). *Knowledge Management Product.* Retrieved from http://mobeeknowledge.ning.com/page/knowledge-management-km-nature-knowledge-theory-nkt-product-knowl

Santo, M., dall'Acqua, L., & Kristinawati. (2014). *New Integrated Formal Science (NIFS) and Personal Knowledge Management (PKM) for K-12 Education.* NKI – SONO Consortium for Educators and Scientists (NSCES) with the School of Business and Management – Bandung Institute of Techn. Retrieved from http://tinyurl.com/kpcyn3u

Santos, V., Goldman, A., & de Souza, C. R. B. (2015). Fostering effective inter-team knowledge sharing in agile software development. *Empirical Software Engineering, 20*(4), 1006–1051. doi:10.1007/s10664-014-9307-y

Sarin, S., & O'Connor, G. C. (2009). First among Equals: The Effect of Team Leader Characteristics on the Internal Dynamics of Cross-Functional Product Development Teams*. *Journal of Product Innovation Management, 26*(2), 188–205. doi:10.1111/j.1540-5885.2009.00345.x

Schank, R. C., Berman, T. R., & Macpherson, K. A. (1999). Learning by Doing. Reigeluth, 3, 160-181. doi:10.1017/CBO9780511527920.011 doi:10.1017/CBO9780511527920.011

Schmid, W., & Kern, E. M. (2014). Integration of business process management and knowledge management: State of the art, current research and future prospects. *Journal of Business Economics, 84*(2), 191–231. doi:10.1007/s11573-013-0683-3

Schuhmacher, M. C., & Kuester, S. (2012). Identification of lead user characteristics driving the quality of service innovation ideas. *Creativity and Innovation Management, 21*(4), 427–442. doi:10.1111/caim.12002

Sethi, V., & King, W. (1994). Development of Measures to Assess the Extent to Which an Information Technology Application provides Competitive Advantage. *Management Science, 40*(12), 1601–1627. doi:10.1287/mnsc.40.12.1601

Shang, S. S. C., Lin, S., & Wu, Y. (2009). Service innovation through dynamic knowledge management. *Industrial Management & Data Systems, 109*(3), 322–337. doi:10.1108/02635570910939362

Shan, J., & Jolly, D. R. (2013). Technological innovation capabilities, product strategy, and firm performance: The electronics industry in China. *Canadian Journal of Administrative Sciences, 30*(3), 159–172. doi:10.1002/cjas.1256

Sharif, M., Davidson, R., & Troshani, I. (2013). Exploring Social Media Adoption in Australian Local Government Organizations. *CONF-IRM 2013 Proceedings.* Retrieved from http://aisel.aisnet.org/confirm2013/29

Shevtshenko, E., Bashkite, V., Maleki, M., & Wang, Y. (2012). Sustainable design of material handling equipment: A win-win approach for manufacturers and customers. *Mechanika*, *18*(5), 561–568. doi:10.5755/j01.mech.18.5.2703

Siddique, M. C. (2012). Knowledge management initiatives in the United Arab Emirates: A baseline study. *Journal of Knowledge Management*, *16*(5), 702–723. doi:10.1108/13673271211262763

Sila, I. (2013). Factors affecting the adoption of B2B e-commerce technologies. *Electronic Commerce Research*, *13*(2), 199–236. doi:10.1007/s10660-013-9110-7

Silverman. (2013, September 10). *4 Big Barriers to Social Media Adoption: Key Research Findings*. Retrieved from http://denovati.com/2013/09/barriers-to-social-media-adoption

Simms, C. D., & Trott, P. (2014). Barriers to the upgrade cycle in a commodity process industry: Evidence from the UK packaging industry. *R&D Management*, *44*(2), 152–170. doi:10.1111/radm.12047

Simone, C., Ackerman, M., & Wulf, V. (2012). Knowledge management in practice: A special issue. *Computer Supported Cooperative Work*, *21*(2/3), 109–110. doi:10.1007/s10606-012-9161-7

Sinclair, N. (2006). *Stealth KM: Winning knowledge management strategies for the public sector*. Db Butterworth Heinemann.

Šipikal, M., & Buček, M. (2013). The role of FDIs in regional innovation: Evidence from the automotive industry in Western Slovakia. *Regional Science Policy & Practice*, *5*(4), 475–490. doi:10.1111/rsp3.12022

Skok, K., & Tahir, S. (2010). Developing a knowledge management strategy for the Arab World. *EJISDC*, *46*(7), 1–11.

Slater, S. F., Mohr, J. J., & Sengupta, S. (2014). Radical product innovation capability: Literature review, synthesis, and illustrative research propositions. *Journal of Product Innovation Management*, *31*(3), 552–566. doi:10.1111/jpim.12113

Slater, S. F., & Narver, J. C. (1995). Market orientation and the learning organization. *Journal of Marketing*, *59*(3), 63–74. doi:10.2307/1252120

Sloan, T. W. (2011). Green renewal: Incorporating environmental factors in equipment replacement decisions under technological change. *Journal of Cleaner Production*, *19*(2-3), 173–186. doi:10.1016/j.jclepro.2010.08.017

Smith, S. W., & Shah, S. K. (2013). Do innovative users generate more useful insights? An analysis of corporate venture capital investments in the medical device industry. *Strategic Entrepreneurship Journal*, *7*(2), 151–167. doi:10.1002/sej.1152

Smith, W. K., & Tushman, M. L. (2005). Managing strategic contradictions: A top management model for managing innovation streams. *Organization Science*, *16*(5), 522–536. doi:10.1287/orsc.1050.0134

Soto-Acosta, P., Colomo-Palacios, R., & Perez-Gonzalez, D. (2011). Examining whether highly e-innovative firms are more e-effective. *Informatica*, *35*(4), 481–488.

Soto-Acosta, P., & Meroño-Cerdan, A. (2006). An analysis and comparison of web development between local governments and SMEs in Spain. *International Journal of Electronic Business*, *4*(2), 191–203. doi:10.1504/IJEB.2006.009790

Soto-Acosta, P., & Meroño-Cerdan, A. (2008). Analyzing e-Business value creation from a resource-based perspective. *International Journal of Information Management*, *28*(1), 49–60. doi:10.1016/j.ijinfomgt.2007.05.001

Spanjol, J., Mühlmeier, S., & Tomczak, T. (2012). Strategic orientation and product innovation: Exploring a decompositional approach. *Journal of Product Innovation Management*, *29*(6), 967–985. doi:10.1111/j.1540-5885.2012.00975.x

Spence, P. R., & Reddy, M. (2012). Beyond expertise seeking: A field study of the informal knowledge practices of healthcare IT teams. *Computer Supported Cooperative Work*, *21*(2/3), 283–315. doi:10.1007/s10606-011-9135-1

Compilation of References

Spooner, M. (2014, April 30). *Universities are confusing accountability with accountancy: how the 'audit culture' is ruining the academy and harming society in the process*. Retrieved from http://www.universityaffairs.ca/universities-are-confusing-accountability-with-accountancy.aspx

Srivastava, J., Cooley, R., Deshpande, M., & Tan, P.-N. (2000). Web usage mining: Discovery and applications of usage patterns from web data. *SIGKDD Explorations, 1*(2), 1–12. doi:10.1145/846183.846188

Srivastava, S. K. (2007). Green supply-chain management: A state-of-the- art literature review. *International Journal of Management Reviews, 9*(1), 53–80. doi:10.1111/j.1468-2370.2007.00202.x

Stanko, M. A., Molina-Castillo, F. J., & Munuera-Aleman, J. L. (2012). Speed to market for innovative products: Blessing or curse? *Journal of Product Innovation Management, 29*(5), 751–765. doi:10.1111/j.1540-5885.2012.00943.x

Steinicke, S., Wallenburg, C. M., & Schmoltzi, Ch. (2012). Governing for innovation in horizontal service cooperations. *Journal of Service Management, 23*(2), 279–302. doi:10.1108/09564231211226141

Stevens, E., & Dimitriadis, S. (2011). Learning strategies, behaviours and outputs during the service innovation process. *International Journal of Innovation and Learning, 10*(3), 285–309. doi:10.1504/IJIL.2011.042082

Stipp, K. F., & Kapp, S. A. (2012). Building organizational knowledge and value: Informed decision making in Kansas children's community-based mental health services. *Community Mental Health Journal, 48*(1), 1–11. doi:10.1007/s10597-010-9334-0 PMID:20623189

Stock, R. M. (2014). How should customers be integrated for effective interorganizational NPD teams? An input-process-output perspective. *Journal of Product Innovation Management, 31*(3), 535–551. doi:10.1111/jpim.12112

Stock, R. M., Six, B., & Zacharias, N. A. (2013). Linking multiple layers of innovation-oriented corporate culture, product program innovativeness, and business performance: A contingency approach. *Journal of the Academy of Marketing Science, 41*(3), 283–299. doi:10.1007/s11747-012-0306-5

Stock, R. M., & Zacharias, N. A. (2013). Two sides of the same coin: How do different dimensions of product program innovativeness affect customer loyalty? *Journal of Product Innovation Management, 30*(3), 516–532. doi:10.1111/jpim.12006

Storey, C., & Hull, F. M. (2010). Service development success: A contingent approach by knowledge strategy. *Journal of Service Management, 21*(2), 140–161. doi:10.1108/09564231011039268

Storey, C., & Kahn, K. B. (2010). The role of knowledge management strategies and task knowledge in stimulating service innovation. *Journal of Service Research, 13*(4), 397–410. doi:10.1177/1094670510370988

Storey, C., & Kelly, D. (2001). Measuring the performance of new service development activities. *Service Industries Journal, 21*(2), 71–90. doi:10.1080/714005018

Storm, P., Lager, T., & Samuelsson, P. (2013). Managing the manufacturing–R&D interface in the process industries. *R & D Management, 43*(3), 252–270. doi:10.1111/radm.12010

Stoshikj, M., Kryvinska, N., & Strauss, C. (2014). Efficient managing of complex programs with project management services. *Global Journal of Flexible Systems Management, 15*(1), 25–38. doi:10.1007/s40171-013-0051-8

Stout, B. (2011). Professional ethics and academic integrity in police education. *Policing: An International Journal of Police Strategies & Management, 5*(4), 300–309. doi:10.1093/police/par036

Strategyzer. (2015). *The Business Model Canvas*. Retrieved on April 11, 2015, from http://www.businessmodelgeneration.com/canvas/bmc

Straub, D. W. (1989). Validating instruments in MIS research. *Management Information Systems Quarterly, 13*(2), 147–169. doi:10.2307/248922

Su, N. M., Wilensky, H. N., & Redmiles, D. F. (2012). Doing business with theory: Communities of practice in knowledge management. *Computer Supported Cooperative Work, 21*(2/3), 111–162. doi:10.1007/s10606-011-9139-x

Sung, R. C. W., Ritchie, J. M., Lim, T., & Kosmadoudi, Z. (2012). Automated generation of engineering rationale, knowledge and intent representations during the product life cycle. *Virtual Reality (Waltham Cross), 16*(1), 69–85. doi:10.1007/s10055-011-0196-8

Su, Z., Xie, E., Liu, H., & Sun, W. (2013). Profiting from product innovation: The impact of legal, marketing, and technological capabilities in different environmental conditions. *Marketing Letters, 24*(3), 261–276. doi:10.1007/s11002-012-9214-1

Swan, M. (2014). *Zayed University provost promises to tackle plagiarism and poor standards complaints*. Retrieved on 1 June 2014 from http://www.thenational.ae/uae/education/zayed-university-provost-promises-to-tackle-plagiarism-and-poor-standards-complaints

Swan, J., Newell, S., Scarbrough, H., & Hislop, D. (1999). Knowledge Management and Innovation: Networks and networking. *Journal of Knowledge Management, 3*(4), 262–275. doi:10.1108/13673279910304014

Swarnkar, R., Choudhary, A. K., Harding, J. A., Das, B. P., & Young, R. I. (2012). A framework for collaboration moderator services to support knowledge based collaboration. *Journal of Intelligent Manufacturing, 23*(5), 2003–2023. doi:10.1007/s10845-011-0528-2

Swartz, L. B., & Cole, M. T. (2013). Students' perception of academic integrity in online business education courses. *Journal of Business and Educational Leadership, 4*(1), 102–112.

Szulanski, G. (1996). Exploring internal stickiness: Impediments to the transfer of best practices within the firm. *Strategic Management Journal, 17*(S2), 27–43. doi:10.1002/smj.4250171105

Tabsh, S. W., El Kadi, H. A., & Abdelfatah, A. S. (2012). Faculty response to ethical issues at an American university in the Middle-East. *Quality Assurance in Education, 20*(4), 319–340. doi:10.1108/09684881211263957

Tajeddini, K., Trueman, M., & Larsen, G. (2006). Examining the effect of market orientation on innovativeness. *Journal of Marketing Management, 22*(5-6), 529–551. doi:10.1362/026725706777978640

Takeuchi, H. (2001). Towards a universal management concept of knowledge. In I. Nonaka & D. J. Teece (Eds.), *Managing industrial knowledge: creation, transfer and utilization* (pp. 315–329). London: Sage. doi:10.4135/9781446217573.n16

Takeuchi, H., & Nonaka, I. (2004). *Hitotsubashi on knowledge management*. Singapore: John Wiley & Sons.

Talay, M. B., Calantone, R. J., & Voorhees, C. M. (2014). Coevolutionary dynamics of automotive competition: Product innovation, change, and marketplace survival. *Journal of Product Innovation Management, 31*(1), 61–78. doi:10.1111/jpim.12080

Tang, J., & Murphy, P. J. (2012). Prior knowledge and new product and service introductions by entrepreneurial firms: The mediating role of technological innovation. *Journal of Small Business Management, 50*(1), 41–62. doi:10.1111/j.1540-627X.2011.00343.x

Teh, P., & Yong, Ch. (2011). Knowledge sharing in IS personnel: Organizational Behavior's Perspective. *Journal of Computer Information Systems, 51*(4), 11–21.

Compilation of References

Teirlinck, P., & Spithoven, A. (2013). Formal R&D management and strategic decision making in small firms in knowledge-intensive business services. *R&D Management, 43*(1), 37–51. doi:10.1111/j.1467-9310.2012.00701.x

Telecommunications Regulatory Authority, UAE. (2012). *ICT in the UAE- Household Survey, 2012.* Retrieved from file:///D:/Documents/Downloads/Household%20Survey-2012-English.pdf

Tengo, M., Brondizio, E. S., Elmqvist, T., Malmer, P., & Spierenburg, M. (2014). Connecting diverse knowledge systems for enhanced ecosystem governance: The multiple evidence base approach. *Ambio, 43*(5), 579–591. doi:10.1007/s13280-014-0501-3 PMID:24659474

Teo, T. S. H., Ranganathan, C., & Dhaliwal, J. (2006). Key dimensions of inhibitors for the deployment of web-based business-to-business electronic commerce. *IEEE Transactions on Engineering Management, 53*(3), 395–411. doi:10.1109/TEM.2006.878106

Terziovski, M. (2010). Innovation practice and its performance implications in small and medium enterprises (SMEs) in the manufacturing sector: A resource-based view. *Strategic Management Journal, 31*(8), 892–902.

The National. (2013). Interest in Arabic courses online. The National.

The National. (2014). Online courses make big strides. The National.

Thite, M. (2004). Strategic Positioning of HRM of knowledge-based organizations. *The Learning Organizations: An International Journal, 11*(1), 28–44. doi:10.1108/09696470410515715

Thomas, E. E., & Sassi, K. (2011). An ethical dilemma: Talking about plagiarism and academic integrity in the digital age. *English Journal, 100*(6), 47–53.

Thomas, J. C., Kellogg, W. A., & Erickson, T. (2001). The knowledge management puzzle: Human and social factors in knowledge management. *IBM Systems Journal, 40*(4), 863–884. doi:10.1147/sj.404.0863

Thomas, J., Raynor, M., & McKinnon, M. (2013). Academic integrity and oral examination: An Arabian Gulf perspective. *Innovations in Education and Teaching International*, 1–11.

Thompson Reuters publishers. (2014). *The Thompson Reuters impact factor.* Retrieved from http://wokinfo.com/essays/impact-factor/

Tidd, J., & Bodley, K. (2002). The influence of project novelty on the new product development process. *R & D Management, 32*(2), 127–138. doi:10.1111/1467-9310.00245

Tiwana, A. (2003). *The knowledge management toolkit: Orchestrating IT, strategy and knowledge platforms.* Prentice-Hall.

Tödtling, F., & Grillitsch, M. (2014). Types of innovation, competencies of firms, and external knowledge sourcing: Findings from selected sectors and regions of Europe. *Journal of the Knowledge Economy, 5*(2), 330–356. doi:10.1007/s13132-012-0139-y

Tomasini, R. M., & Van Wassenhove, L. N. (2009). From preparedness to partnerships: Case study research on humanitarian logistics. *International Transactions in Operational Research, 16*(5), 549–559. doi:10.1111/j.1475-3995.2009.00697.x

Tornatzky, L. G., & Fleischer, M. (1990). *The process of technological innovation.* Lexington, MA: Lexington Books.

Treem, J. W., & Leonardi, P. M. (2012). Social Media Use in Organizations: Exploring the Affordances of Visibility, Editability, Persistence, and Association (SSRN Scholarly Paper No. ID 2129853). Rochester, NY: Social Science Research Network. Retrieved from http://papers.ssrn.com/abstract=2129853

Triguero, A., Córcoles, D., & Cuerva, M. C. (2014). Persistence of innovation and firm's growth: Evidence from a panel of SME and large Spanish manufacturing firms. *Small Business Economics, 43*(4), 787–804. doi:10.1007/s11187-014-9562-8

Tripathy, B. K., & Mitra, A. (2012). An algorithm to achieve k-anonymity and l-diversity anonymisation in social networks. IEEE – CASoN, Brazil. doi:10.1109/CASoN.2012.6412390

Trott, P. (2008). Innovation Management and New Product Development. Harlow: Pearson Education Ltd.

Troy, L. C., Hirunyawipada, T., & Paswan, A. K. (2008). Cross-functional integration and new product success: An empirical investigation of the findings. *Journal of Marketing, 72*(6), 132–146. doi:10.1509/jmkg.72.6.132

Tsai, K. H., Hsu, T. T., & Fang, W. (2012). Relinking cross-functional collaboration, knowledge integration mechanisms, and product innovation performance: A moderated mediation model. *Canadian Journal of Administrative Sciences, 29*(1), 25–39. doi:10.1002/cjas.192

Tsai, M. T., Chang, H. C., Cheng, N. C., & Lien, C. C. (2013). Understanding IT professionals' knowledge sharing intention through KMS: A social exchange perspective. *Quality & Quantity, 47*(5), 2739–2753. doi:10.1007/s11135-012-9685-4

Tsai, M. T., Chen, K. S., & Chien, J. L. (2012). The factors impact of knowledge sharing intentions: The theory of reasoned action perspective. *Quality & Quantity, 46*(5), 1479–1491. doi:10.1007/s11135-011-9462-9

Tsai, W. (2001). Knowledge transfer in intraorganizational networks: Effects of network position and absoptive capacity on business unit innovation and performance. *Academy of Management Journal, 40*(5), 996–1004. doi:10.2307/3069443

Tsokris, M., & Struminger, S. (2013). Does academic misconduct influence professional integrity? *Access, 27*(4), 22–23.

Tsui, A. S., Pearce, J. L., Porter, L. W., & Tripoli, A. M. (1997). Alternative approaches to the employee-organization relationship: Does investment in employees pay off? *Academy of Management Journal, 40*(5), 1089–1121. doi:10.2307/256928

Turchetti, G., & Geisler, E. (2013). The nature of knowledge and the platform and matrix solutions in the design of knowledge management systems. *Journal of Management and Governance, 17*(3), 657–671. doi:10.1007/s10997-011-9199-9

Twaróg, S., Szoltyseck, J., & Otreba, R. (2012). Shaping alumni's sensitivity to issues of social logistics. In *Proceedings of the Management, Knowledge and Learning International Conference 2012*.

Tynes, B. M. (2007). Internet safety gone wild?: Sacrificing the educational and psychological benefits of online social environments. *Journal of Adolescent Research, 22*(6), 575–584. doi:10.1177/0743558407303979

UAE Ministry of Higher Education and Scientific Commission for Academic Accreditation. (2011a). Retrieved on 6 May 2014 from www.caa.ae/caa/images/Guides-IA.pdf

UAE Ministry of Higher Education and Scientific Commission for Academic Accreditation. (2011b). Retrieved on 6 May 2014 from www.caa.ae/caa/images/Guide-RA.pdf

Uhlaner, L. M., van Stel, A., Duplat, V., & Zhou, H. (2013). Disentangling the effects of organizational capabilities, innovation and firm size on SME sales growth. *Small Business Economics, 41*(3), 581–607. doi:10.1007/s11187-012-9455-7

Uziene, L. (2010). Model of organizational intellectual capital measurement. *The Engineering Economist, 21*(2), 151–159.

van den Ende, J., Jaspers, F. P. H., & Rijsdijk, S. A. (2013). Should system firms develop complementary product? A dynamic model and an empirical test. *Journal of Product Innovation Management, 30*(6), 1178–1198. doi:10.1111/jpim.12053

Van der Panne, G., Van Beers, C., & Kleinknecht, A. (2003). Success and failure of innovation: A literature review. *International Journal of Innovation Management, 7*(03), 309–338. doi:10.1142/S1363919603000830

Compilation of References

Van der Vorst, J. G. A. J., Tromp, S., & Van der Zee, D. (2009). Simulation modelling for food supply chain redesign; Integrated decision making on product quality, sustainability and logistics. *International Journal of Production Research*, *47*(23), 6611–6631. doi:10.1080/00207540802356747

Van Gent, S. H., Megens, C. J. P. G., Peeters, M. M. R., Hummels, C. C. M., Lu, Y., & Brombacher, A. C. (2011). *Experiential Design Landscapes as a Design Tool for Market Research of Disruptive Intelligent Systems.1st Cambridge Academic Design Management Conference*.

Vanetik, N., Gudes, E., & Shimony, S. E. (2002). Computing Frequent Graph Patterns from Semistructured Data. In *Proceedings of 2002 International Conference on Data Mining* (ICDM'02). doi:10.1109/ICDM.2002.1183988

Vaona, A., & Pianta, M. (2008). Firm size and innovation in European manufacturing. *Small Business Economics*, *30*(3), 283–299. doi:10.1007/s11187-006-9043-9

Vermeulen, P. (2004). Managing product innovation in financial services firms. *European Management Journal*, *22*(1), 43–50. doi:10.1016/j.emj.2003.11.012

Vestal, W. (2003). Ten traits for a successful Community of Practice. *KM Review*, *5*(6), 6.

Vismara, L., Di Battista, G., Garg, A., Liotta, G., Tamassia, R., & Vargiu, F. (2000). Experimental studies on graph drawing algorithms. *Software, Practice & Experience*, *30*(11), 1235–1284. doi:10.1002/1097-024X(200009)30:11<1235::AID-SPE339>3.0.CO;2-B

Viswanathan, M., & Sridharan, S. (2012). Product development for the BoP: Insights on concept and prototype development from university-based student projects in India. *Journal of Product Innovation Management*, *29*(1), 52–69. doi:10.1111/j.1540-5885.2011.00878.x

Von Krogh, G. (2012). How does social software change knowledge management? Toward a strategic research agenda. *The Journal of Strategic Information Systems*, *21*(2), 154–164. doi:10.1016/j.jsis.2012.04.003

Walling, S. (2009). *Becoming an open enterprise: five lessons from Booz Allen Hamilton*. Retrieved November 13, 2014, from http://Readwrite.com/2009/06/26/Becoming-An-Open-Enterprise-Five-Lessons-From-Booz

Wang, C. H., Lu, I. Y., & Chen, C. B. (2008). Evaluating firm technological innovation capability under uncertainty. *Technovation*, *28*(6), 349–363. doi:10.1016/j.technovation.2007.10.007

Wang, C. L., & Rafiq, M. (2014). Ambidextrous organizational culture, contextual ambidexterity and new product innovation: A comparative study of UK and Chinese high-tech firms. *British Journal of Management*, *25*(1), 58–76. doi:10.1111/j.1467-8551.2012.00832.x

Wang, Y. M., Wang, Y. S., & Yang, Y. F. (2010). Understanding the determinants of RFID adoption in the manufacturing industry. *Technological Forecasting and Social Change*, *77*(5), 803–815. doi:10.1016/j.techfore.2010.03.006

Wang, Y., & Ahmed, P. (2009). The moderating effect of the business strategic orientation on e-commerce adoption: Evidence from UK family run SMEs. *The Journal of Strategic Information Systems*, *18*(1), 16–30. doi:10.1016/j.jsis.2008.11.001

Wang, Y., & Haggerty, N. (2009). Knowledge transfer in virtual settings: The role of individual virtual competency. *Information Systems Journal*, *19*(6), 571–593. doi:10.1111/j.1365-2575.2008.00318.x

Wan, J., Zhang, H., Wan, D., & Huang, D. (2010). Research on knowledge creation in software requirement development. *Journal of Software Engineering & Applications*, *3*(05), 487–494. doi:10.4236/jsea.2010.35055

Wattanapruttipaisan, T. (2014). Competition policy and intellectual property rights in the information and communications technology sector: Policy implications and options for ASEAN. *Asian-Pacific Economic Literature*, *28*(1), 1–28. doi:10.1111/apel.12048

Weiss, M., Hoegl, M., & Gibbert, M. (2011). Making Virtue of Necessity: The Role of Team Climate for Innovation in Resource-Constrained Innovation Projects. *Journal of Product Innovation Management*, *28*(s1), 196–207. doi:10.1111/j.1540-5885.2011.00870.x

Weiss, M., Hoegl, M., & Gibbert, M. (2013). The influence of material resources on innovation projects: The role of resource elasticity. *R&D Management*, *43*(2), 151–161. doi:10.1111/radm.12007

Weiss, R., Velez, B., & Sheldon, M. (1996). HyPursuit: A hierarchical network search engine that exploits context-link hypertext clustering. In *Proceedings of the Conference on Hypertext and Hypermedia*. doi:10.1145/234828.234846

Wei, Z., Yi, Y., & Guo, H. (2014). Organizational learning ambidexterity, strategic flexibility, and new product development. *Journal of Product Innovation Management*, *31*(4), 832–847. doi:10.1111/jpim.12126

Wenger, E., McDermott, R., & Synder, W. (2002). Cultivating Communities of Practice: A guide of Managing Knowledge. Boston: Harvard Business School Press.

Wenger, E. C., & Snyder, W. M. (2000). Communities of Practice: The Organizational Frontier. *Harvard Business Review*, *78*(1), 139–146. PMID:11184968

West, R. E. (2014). Communities of innovation: Individual, group, and organizational characteristics leading to greater potential for innovation. *TechTrends*, *58*(5), 53–61. doi:10.1007/s11528-014-0786-x

Wheeler, D., & Anderson, D. (2010). Dealing with plagiarism in a complex information society. *Education. Business and Society: Contemporary Middle Eastern Issues*, *3*(3), 166–177. doi:10.1108/17537981011070082

White, T. (2004). *Knowledge management in an academic library: based on the case study "KM within OULS"*. Paper presented at the 70th IFLA General Conference and Council, Buenos Aires. Retrieved on 6 May 2014 from http://ora.ox.ac.uk/objects/uuid:62836c4d-10c1-4636-b97c-07a88890fa8a/datastreams/JOURNAL

Wiig, K. M. (2000). Knowledge Management: an Emerging Discipline Rooted in a Long History. In Knowledge Horizons: the present and the promise of knowledge management (pp. 3-26). Butterworth-Heinemann. doi:10.1016/B978-0-7506-7247-4.50004-5

Wilken, C. V., & Ramsell, P. (2004). Building Effective Communities. In E. Truch (Ed.), *Leveraging Corporate Knowledge* (pp. 55–60). Burlington, VT: Gower Publishing.

Wong, S. K. S. (2013). Environmental requirements, knowledge sharing and green innovation: Empirical evidence from the electronics industry in China. *Business Strategy and the Environment*, *22*(5), 321–338. doi:10.1002/bse.1746

Wong, W. L. P., & Radcliffe, D. F. (2000). The tacit nature of design knowledge. *Technology Analysis and Strategic Management*, *12*(4), 493–512. doi:10.1080/713698497

Wu, J. (2013). Diverse institutional environments and product innovation of emerging market firms. *Management International Review*, *53*(1), 39–59. doi:10.1007/s11575-012-0162-z

Xanthopoulos, A., & Iakovou, E. (2009). On the optimal design of the disassembly and recovery processes.[PubMed]. *Waste Management (New York, N.Y.)*, *29*(5), 1702–1711. doi:10.1016/j.wasman.2008.11.009

Xavier, W. S., & Martins, R. S. (2011). Logistic strategy and organizational structure in Brazilian Small and Medium-sized Enterprises (SMEs). *Organizations and Markets in Emerging Economies*, *2*(4), 91–116.

Xu, S., Wu, F., & Cavusgil, E. (2013). Complements or substitutes? Internal technological strength, competitor alliance participation, and innovation development. *Journal of Product Innovation Management, 30*(4), 750–762. doi:10.1111/jpim.12014

Xu, S., Zhu, K., & Gibbs, J. (2004). Global technology, local adoption: A cross-country investigation of Internet adoption by companies in the United States and China. *Electronic Markets, 14*(1), 13–24. doi:10.1080/1019678042000175261

Yan, X., & Han, J. (2002). gSpan: Graph-based substructure pattern mining. In *Proceedings of 2002 International Conference on Data Mining* (ICDM'02).

Yan, X., Zhou, X. J., & Han, J. (2005). Mining closed relational graphs with connectivity constraints. In *Proceedings of 2005, ACM SIGKDD International Conference on Knowledge Discovery in Databases* (KDD'05). doi:10.1145/1081870.1081908

Yang, Y., Wang, Q., Zhu, H., & Wu, G. (2012). What are the effective strategic orientations for new product success under different environments? An empirical study of Chinese businesses. *Journal of Product Innovation Management, 29*(2), 166–179. doi:10.1111/j.1540-5885.2011.00900.x

Yeniyurt, S., Henke, J. W., & Yalcinkaya, G. (2014). A longitudinal analysis of supplier involvement in buyers' new product development: Working relations, inter-dependence, co-innovation, and performance outcomes. *Journal of the Academy of Marketing Science, 42*(3), 291–308. doi:10.1007/s11747-013-0360-7

Yin, R. K. (1989). *Case Study Research: Design And Methods (Applied Social Research Methods)*. Sage Publication.

Yin, R. K. (1994). *Case Study Research: Design and Method* (2nd ed.). Thousand Oaks, CA: Sage Publications.

York, J. G., & Venkataraman, S. (2010). The entrepreneur–environment nexus: Uncertainty, innovation, and allocation. *Journal of Business Venturing, 25*(5), 449–463. doi:10.1016/j.jbusvent.2009.07.007

Youndt, M. A., Snell, S. A., Dean, J. W. Jr, & Lepak, D. P. (1996). Human resource management, manufacturing strategy and firm performance. *Academy of Management Journal, 39*(4), 836–866. doi:10.2307/256714

Zágarra, C., & García-Falcón, J. M. (2003). Factors favoring knowledge management in work teams. *Journal of Knowledge Management, 7*(2), 81–93. doi:10.1108/13673270310477306

Zaiane, O. R., & Han, J. (1995). Resource and knowledge discovery in global information systems: A preliminary design and experiment. In *Proceedings of the 2nd International Conference on Knowledge Discovery and Data Mining*.

Zaki, M. J. (2002). Efficiently Mining Frequent Trees in a Forest. In *Proceedings of the 7th International Conference on Knowledge Discovery and Data Mining*. doi:10.1145/775047.775058

Zander, U., & Kogut, B. (1995). Knowledge and the speed of transfer and imitation of organizational capabilities: An empirical test. *Organization Science, 6*(1), 76–92. doi:10.1287/orsc.6.1.76

Zapata, L., Rialp, J., & Rialp, A. (2009). Generation and transfer of knowledge in IT-related SMEs. *Journal of Knowledge Management, 13*, 246–256.

Zhang, L., Wang, H., Cao, X., Wang, X., & Zhao, K. (2012). Knowledge management component in managing human resources for enterprises. *Information Technology Management, 13*(4), 341–349. doi:10.1007/s10799-012-0127-8

Zhao, K., & Chan, C. K. K. (2014). Fostering collective and individual learning through knowledge building. *International Journal of Computer-Supported Collaborative Learning, 9*(1), 63–95. doi:10.1007/s11412-013-9188-x

Zhou, K. Z., & Wu, F. (2010). Technological capability, strategic flexibility, and product innovation. *Strategic Management Journal, 31*(5), 547–561.

Zhu, K., & Kraemer, K. (2005). Post-adoption variations in usage and value of e-business by organizations: Cross-country evidence from the retail industry. *Information Systems Research*, *16*(1), 61–84. doi:10.1287/isre.1050.0045

Zhu, K., Kraemer, K. L., & Xu, S. (2006). The process of innovation assimilation by firms in different countries: A technology diffusion perspective on e-business. *Management Science*, *52*(10), 1557–1576. doi:10.1287/mnsc.1050.0487

Zhu, K., Kraemer, K. L., Xu, S., & Dedrick, J. (2004). Information technology payoff in e-business environments: An international perspective on value creation of e-business in the financial services industry. *Journal of Management Information Systems*, *21*(1), 17–54.

Zhu, K., Kraemer, K., & Xu, S. (2003). Electronic business adoption by European firms: A cross-country assessment of the facilitators and inhibitors. *European Journal of Information Systems*, *12*(4), 251–268. doi:10.1057/palgrave.ejis.3000475

Zhu, Y., Li, Y., Wang, W., & Chen, J. (2010). What leads to the post-implementation success of ERP? An empirical study of the chinese retail industry. *International Journal of Information Management*, *30*(3), 265–276. doi:10.1016/j.ijinfomgt.2009.09.007

About the Contributors

Alok Kumar Goel is working at CSIR-Human Resource Development Centre, Ghaziabad, India and Visiting Scholar at Hasselt University Belgium, Europe. He pursued PhD in the area of Knowledge Management from Indian Institute of Technology Roorkee, India. Dr. Goel holds a Bachelor's degree in Mechanical Engineering, a Bachelor's degree in Law and a Master's degree in Management. Dr. Goel is recipient of 2013 Emerald/EFMD Outstanding Doctoral Research Award in the Knowledge Management category. His research interests include human resource management, social media, innovation and knowledge management. Dr. Goel has published numerous articles and book chapters on knowledge management, human capital creation and innovation management. Outlets for his research work include among others Emeralds' Management Decision, Strategic HR Review, Human Resource Management International Digest, Emerald Emerging Markets Case Studies, Inderscience International Journal of Indian Culture and Business Management and Sage South Asian Journal of Business and Management Cases, etc. He is an active member of Indian Society for Training & Development and National HRD Network.

Puja Singhal is presently associated with Amity University, Noida, India as Ph.D Coordinator of Amity College of Commerce and Finance. She is Gold medalist in Economics and worked in the projects of V.V.Giri National Labour Institute, India .She also holds Higher Diploma in Software Engineering. She is a Research Guide, with several years of academic and research experience. She has authored various books, and has to her credit various research papers in national and International journals. She is also involved in PAN – African E-learning Project. She also received the best paper award in International Conference held at India Habitat Center, New Delhi, India. She presented her paper at European Conference on Learning Innovation and Quality held at Belgium .She has visited various European countries like Belgium, Holland, Switzerland for her research work. Her present research fields are Social Media, E-learning, and Innovation in education. She is an active member of All India Management Association, Planetary Scientific Research Centre.

* * *

Achilleas Boukis is a Lecturer in Marketing at Sussex university, UK. He has also worked as Research Fellow in the ALARM Research Centre and the Department of Marketing and Communication at Athens University of Economics and Business. He received his Ph.D. from Strathclyde University and also holds an MSc with in Marketing and Communication from Athens University of Economics and Business and a BSc in Business Administration from the same university. His main research interests lie within the services marketing area. Moreover, he is interested in luxury branding, internal brand management, service encounter and innovation management. He has published his research in academic journals such as Journal of Strategic Marketing, Journal of Services Marketing, Managing Service Quality and International Journal of Retail and Distribution Management. Achilleas Boukis has also presented his research at international conferences such as EMAC, AMS and AMA. He also serves as an ad-hoc referee in several academic journals. Currently, he is the module leader for Marketing Research and supervises dissertations for Master's students.

Luisa dall'Acqua is a senior Cognitive Scientist, Knowledge Management Researcher, Instructional Technologist and Designer, with special interest for didactic and cognitive engineering in multi-agent systems. She owns academic and professional specializations in Psycho-/ Sociological Science, Logic, E-Learning and KM (Techniques and Technologies), technologies and programming projects in support of the educational and research environment at educational institutions and agencies. Since 1990 she performed teaching activities, with (e-)tutoring/coaching experiences towards students (high/higher school), teachers in service, and international professionals; and since 2003 she was member of intl. project and research teams (US, Europe, Asia). She holds a master degree (DL) in Philosophy, a master (MU2) in E-learning Technologies, a PhD in Institutional Sociology and a second PhD in Psycho-, Sociological Science and eLearning (eLearning and Knowledge Management curriculum). Luisa is author respected international papers and book editions, scientific reviewer for several Intl. Journals, Committee Member for Intl. Workshops/Conferences and Intl.Advisor; Especially, she is author of a Multidimensional Instructional Design Model (PENTHA), an innovative KM approach (Orientism) for education and business context, and a Personal Intelligent Learning/ Knowledge Environment.

Giulio Focardi previously worked as a consultant, and developed several mathematical dynamic models, as a free lance or through consulting companies. He is now CEO of Osun Solutions, an Italian firm that deals with business development and innovation through unconventional and sustainable methods. His research and professional interests are Social Business and Sharing Economy, with particular regard to Social Innovation through Participatory Processes.

María J. García is a Bachelor in Chemistry and have a master in Operations Research. Together others authors had increase their investigations, already above two hundred, mainly in the areas of Evaluation and Management of Projects, Knowledge Management, Managerial and Social Decision making, Risk Management and Operations research, especially in making decision under uncertainty and risk, and multi-criteria decision. They have been presented or published in different countries, having publications and offering their reports, chats or conferences in: Azerbaijan, Finland, Poland, Croatia, Switzerland, Greece, Germany, Italy, Czech Republic, Iceland, Lithuania, Spain, France, Portugal, United States, Panama, Uruguay, Brazil, Mexico, Argentina and Chile besides attending as guest speaker, in reiterated occasions, in lectures to relevant events in Colombia, Peru, Spain and Venezuela. Among other works she is coauthor of: "A Methodology of the Decision Support Systems Applied to Other Projects of Investigation"; "Matrixes of Weighing and catastrophes"; "Mathematical models generators of Decision Support Systems for help in case of catastrophes. An experience from Venezuela".

About the Contributors

Jorge Gaspar holds Degree in Marketing, MSc in Innovation Management with expertise in marketing, business development and innovation. He has more than 15 years of experience in a multinational environment on differentiated markets. Currently, he is Country manager of a multinational company in the health market and partner of a start-up, Unlimited-Hashtag.com. Putting together technological skills with business expertise, Unlimited-Hashtag provides support in innovation process and in technological projects, developing the projects from the idea to go-to-market.

Anders Hemre has extensive experience from the telecommunications industry having worked in various engineering and management capacities at Ericsson in Europe, the Middle East, the Far East and North America. Mr. Hemre previously served as Chief Knowledge Officer at Ericsson Research Canada, where he directed efforts in strategy, organizational learning and knowledge sharing. He has also served as R&D management adviser to the Electronics and Telecommunications Research Institute in Korea and as senior ITU expert to the Bulgarian Ministry of Communications. As adviser, writer and independent researcher he currently specializes in organizational creativity, innovation, R&D and expertise management practices. Mr. Hemre has appeared as panelist, moderator and speaker at numerous international conferences on innovation and knowledge management. He is a MSEE graduate from the Chalmers University of Technology in Gothenburg, Sweden and is a member of the International Society for Professional Innovation Management.

Gilberto J. Hernández is a Bachelor in Chemistry and have a master in Technology of foods. Together others authors had increase their investigations, mainly in the areas of Food technologies, Playful, in particular in the fantastic sports leagues, Knowledge Management, Managerial and Social Decision making, Logistics, Risk Management and Operations research, especially in multi-criteria decision and making decision under uncertainty and risk. They have been presented or published in different countries, having publications and offering their reports, chats or conferences in: Azerbaijan, Finland, Poland, Croatia, Switzerland, Greece, Czech Republic, Spain, Portugal and United States besides attending as guest speaker, in lectures to relevant events in Costa Rica and Venezuela. Among other works he is co-author of: "Enterprise Logistics, Indicators and Physical Distribution Manager"; "Multiatribute Models with Multiplicative factors in the Fantasy Sports"; "The Industrial design manager of LoMoBaP and Knowledge Management"; "Dynamic knowledge: Diagnosis and Customer Service".

José G. Hernández is a Chemical Engineer and has a master in Operations Research. Together others authors had increase their investigations, already above two hundred, mainly in the areas of Knowledge Management, Managerial and Social Decision making, Logistics, Risk Management and Operations research, especially in multi-criteria decision. They have been presented or published in different countries, having publications and offering their reports, chats or conferences in: Azerbaijan, Finland, Poland, Croatia, Switzerland, Greece, Germany, Italy, Czech Republic, Iceland, Lithuania, Spain, France, Portugal, United States, Panama, Paraguay, Uruguay, Brazil, Cuba, Mexico, Argentina and Chile besides attending as guest speaker, in reiterated occasions, in lectures to relevant events in Colombia, Peru, Costa Rica, Brazil, Spain and their own country, Venezuela. Among other works he is coauthor of: "Shelter Selection with AHP Making Use of the Ideal Alternative"; "Teaching Enterprise Logistics through Indicators: Dispatch Manager"; "Multiattribute Model with Multiplicative Factors and Matrixes Of Weighing and the Problem of the Potable Water".

M. K. Prasanna Iyer is Director of PromptKPO, a Knowledge Management Consulting firm. She is adept at building KM systems, aligned with the organization's culture and stakeholder vision. She has been associated with large companies, like Motorola, Tata Advanced Systems, Centre for Good Governance, and so on. Our systems address mapping of expert knowledge, most of it, Tacit Knowledge- and Social Media enables that process through spirit and tools. In these volatile times, speedy responsiveness, coupled with business intelligence is critical in negotiating changes head-on. Sharp focus to enable our customers win, is equally important. These are the guiding principles that model this consultant's assignments.

Kijpokin Kasemsap received his BEng degree in Mechanical Engineering from King Mongkut's University of Technology Thonburi, his MBA degree from Ramkhamhaeng University, and his DBA degree in Human Resource Management from Suan Sunandha Rajabhat University. He is a Special Lecturer at Faculty of Management Sciences, Suan Sunandha Rajabhat University based in Bangkok, Thailand. He is a Member of International Association of Engineers (IAENG), International Association of Engineers and Scientists (IAEST), International Economics Development and Research Center (IEDRC), International Association of Computer Science and Information Technology (IACSIT), International Foundation for Research and Development (IFRD), and International Innovative Scientific and Research Organization (IISRO). He also serves on the International Advisory Committee (IAC) for International Association of Academicians and Researchers (INAAR). He has numerous original research articles in top international journals, conference proceedings, and book chapters on business management, human resource management, and knowledge management published internationally.

T. N. Krishnan is an Associate Professor in the area of Organizational behavior & Human resources at the Indian Institute of Management Kozhikode. His research interests are in the area of careers and talent management. He has done his Fellow Programme in Management from Indian Institute of Management, Ahmedabad and has been a Fulbright Senior Research Fellow. He has several publications in peer reviewed national and international journals.

Amir Manzoor holds a bachelor's degree in engineering from NED University, Karachi, an MBA from Lahore University of Management Sciences (LUMS), and an MBA from Bangor University, United Kingdom. He has many years of diverse professional and teaching experience working at many renowned national and internal organizations and higher education institutions. His research interests include electronic commerce and technology applications in business.

Judith Mavodza is Holder of a Doctor of Literature and Philosophy in Information Science (UNISA) with a Knowledge Management focus, a M.A. in Library and Information Studies (University of London, UCL), and Associate Professor at Zayed University, Abu Dhabi, UAE.

Anirban Mitra is presently associated with VITAM, Berhampur as Associate Professor and Head in the Department of Computer Science & Engineering. He has authored around 40 national and international journal/conference papers and few book chapters to his credit. He is in technical review committee of near about 8 reputed conference and journals. Now, he is handling Industrial projects as an honorary

About the Contributors

consultant and also associated with a funded research project at I.I.T. Kharagpur. He has 08 years plus of regular experience which also includes teaching- as visiting faculty at Khallikote Govt. (Auto.) College and Berhampur University, academic guide, research and handling administrative responsibilities like as a regular Examiner for UG and PG courses. His present research field are Rough sets, Knowledge Representation, Social Network, Data Mining and Graph Mining.

Ernesto López Monterrubio is Project Manager and Knowledge Base creator in the IT department at Vector Casa de Bolsa in 2014.

Flor Morton holds a Ph.D in Management Sciences from EGADE Business School, Tecnologico de Monterrey, Mexico. Graduated with honors of a Major in Marketing from the same University. She has collaborated as a marketing strategist for a marketing solutions agency at diverse projects for national and international companies. Her research dissertation focuses on the influence of touch on consumer behavior in an online context.

Simona Popa is a PhD candidate in the Department of Management and Finance at the University of Murcia, Spain. She holds a BA in Accounting and data management from the University Alexandru Ioan Cuza (Iasi, Romania). Her research interests are in the areas of Management Information Systems, Human-Computer Interaction, Business Information Management, and eBusiness.

Bapuji Rao is an Asst. Prof. in the department of CSE/IT, VITAM, Odisha, India since 2011. Having 10+ years of teaching experience in C, C++, Java, DBMS, IWT, Data Structure using C, DAA, Oracle, and Shell Scripting. Research fields are Algorithms, Social Network, Data Mining, and Graph Mining. Actively researching since 2012. Seven papers have been published in International conferences including two IEEE, one Springer, and one Elsevier. Two papers have been communicated to IJCA and Inderscience IJIM for publication and have been accepted for publication.

Lorenza Victoria Salati uses instruments and methods by visual anthropology as a support to the self-perception of individuals as change makers. She was hired by international and local NGO's and public institutions as media educator and as documentary filmmaker to explore agricultural and ethnic issues in Europe and Africa (Burkina Faso, Mozambique, Senegal). In the meanwhile with these institutional experiences, she started facing up to new communication needs emerging from the Web 3.0. So, she started investigating new forms of expression and innovative methods of storytelling. The main line of research is the definition and transmission of methods and tools that can be used by individuals and organizations to build a strategy of self-representation and self-narration. The goal is to define and share skills and techniques for an effective communication with a bottom up approach, using social networks. Since 2012 she is following and studying the sharing economy phenomenon. Her research is aimed to find practical solutions to the current issues of workers who have to face a completely changed labor market.

Rusnita Saleh is the corresponding author. Rusnita Saleh has been a Knowledge Management practitioner for over 17 years, with a strong focus on institutional learning and development, and especially in the development of communication tools and technologies within organizations. As one of Indonesia's pioneers in the field of Knowledge Management, she has initiated and managed numerous KM projects in a variety of working environments; private sector, government agencies, and international NGOs.

Previously she was the Group Knowledge Management Leader at the National Team for Accelerating Poverty Reduction, an initiative in support of the integration of Indonesia's poverty reduction programs, and reporting to the office of Indonesia's Vice President. She is the author of numerous papers and articles on Knowledge Management, Information Management and Communication, and has lectured and presented on those topics.

Niall Sinclair is recognized as a leading authority on Knowledge Management (KM). He has worked in both private and public sectors around the world. As a senior executive in the Canadian Government he was responsible for Government of Canada KM initiatives, and since leaving public service he has worked with many organizations to help them to understand and implement KM practice, including: NASA, the General Services Administration (US Government), the Pan-American Health Organization, the Public Health Agency of Canada and the Bank of Montreal. Recently he was a Visiting Scholar in KM at Bangkok University, as well as being the Director of KM at the Institute for Knowledge and Innovation, South-East Asia. Niall Sinclair is the author of the KM best-seller "Stealth KM" (Butterworth-Heinemann, 2006), and writes a monthly KM column for the Bangkok Post. He has lectured and presented on KM throughout Asia, North America and Europe.

Pedro Soto-Acosta holds a Ph.D in MIS (with European Ph.D mention) and a Master's in Technology Management from University of Murcia. He received his BA in Business Administration from University of Murcia and his BA in Accounting & Finance in Europe from Manchester Metropolitan University (UK). He attended Postgraduate Courses in Management at Harvard University (USA) and participated in the Leonardo da Vinci Programme in Bradford (UK). His work has been published (or is forthcoming) in Behaviour & Infomation Technology, Computers in Human Behavior, European Journal of Information Systems, European Management Journal, Information Research, Interactive Learning Environments, International Journal of Information Management and Information Systems Managemet, among others. Pedro Soto has won Research Awards such as the ABG Award to Research and Business Spirit, the Best Research Paper Award at Information Systems One World 2007 (ISoneWorld 2007), held in Las Vegas (USA), and the Best Conference Paper Award at BITMED 2009, held in Beijing (China). He was also recipient of the Extraordinary Doctoral Award in Business. He was appointed as the Conference Chair of the International Conferences IASK E-Activity and Leading Technologies (2009, 2010), IASK Global Management 2009 and IASK InterTIC (2009, 2010). He is Editorial Board Member and Associate Editor for several International Journals.

Joana Coutinho Sousa is MSc in Biomedical Engineering with expertise in areas of biomedical engineering, innovation management and marketing strategy. She was R&D project coordinator, management 3 FP7 projects and 5 national funding projects, and in parallel she made research in biomedical signal processing, features extraction, pattern recognition and continuous monitoring patients and Development of new biosignal techniques to be applied on Research, Health and Sport. Currently, she is the innovation sub-director at Edge Innovation, coordinating innovative projects, making innovation management in ICT and Health areas and supporting the creation of start-ups. She is also partner of a start-up, Unlimited-Hashtag.

About the Contributors

Teresa Treviño holds a Ph.D. on Management Sciences and a Master's degree in Marketing from EGADE Business School, Tecnologico de Monterrey, Mexico. She received a major in Information Technologies Management from Tecnologico de Monterrey, Campus Monterrey. Her research interests focuses on Internet Marketing; specifically online communications, social media marketing, and electronic word-of-mouth.

Aparna Venugopal is a Doctoral candidate at the Indian Institute of Management Kozhikode, currently pursuing her thesis in the area of Organizational behavior & Human resources. Her primary research interests fall in the area of ambidextrous organizations, upper echelons perspective, theory of paradox, and technology and innovation management. She holds a bachelors degree in mechanical engineering and a Master's degree in business administration.

Laura Zapata is currently associate professor of Management Department at EGADE Business School and Director of MBA Programs-Monterrey site since 2011. She teaches Business Strategy for the MBA program and Methodology and Strategy for the Doctorate of Business Administration. Her research work focuses in strategic management and knowledge management processes: generation and transfer. She has presented her research work at international conferences and has several publications in international journals such as International Journal of Manpower, Estudios de Administración (Universidad de Chile), European Journal of International Management and Journal of Knowledge Management. She has been distinguished with the 2008 Teaching and Research Award from Tecnológico de Monterrey, and The Carolina Fundation Posdoctorate Fellowship. Since 2009 Dr. Zapata is head of European Studies for Development and Competitiveness Research Chair, and since 2006 she is member of Mexico's National Researchers System (CONACyT).

Index

A

Academic Ethics 264
Academic Integrity 241-243, 245, 247-259, 264
Acquisition 71, 205, 210, 251, 285, 331, 334-335
Adverse Inverse Logistics (AIL) 81

B

Barriers 31-33, 37, 40-42, 148, 163, 174, 193, 196, 200, 272
Benign Inverse Logistics (BIL) 81
Best Practices 1-2, 7, 11, 15, 21, 26, 152, 163, 167, 170, 207, 212, 248-249, 271, 332, 338
Big Data 96-99, 139-142
Bit Matrix 106
BMC 309-310, 316
BP 25, 311, 316
Business Performance 330, 341
Business Process Management 334-335, 356

C

challenge 31, 95, 98, 141, 148, 151-152, 154, 156, 159-160, 163-164, 173, 205-206, 220, 241-242, 248-249, 253-255, 257, 275, 317, 321, 336, 339, 360
Classification and use manager 65, 67, 73
Coaching 230, 237, 318, 323
collaboration 2, 5, 25, 31-32, 35-37, 39-40, 66, 162-163, 168, 177-178, 195, 197-198, 200, 205, 214, 225, 245-247, 250, 256-259, 267-268, 271-272, 276, 283, 293, 310, 318, 320-321, 323, 325-326, 335-336, 340-341
Common Community 94-95, 117-118, 123
Communication 2, 6, 8, 15, 27, 31, 36-37, 54, 150, 176, 194, 197-198, 200, 204-205, 207-208, 210-211, 213-214, 222, 231, 238, 246, 259, 272-273, 309, 320-322, 327-328, 334-335, 339-341, 362-363, 365

Communities of Practice 1, 3, 7, 12, 14, 151, 227, 232, 323, 325, 335
Community Graph 94-95, 104, 116, 118, 123-124, 130-132, 139, 141-142
Community Head 131
Community Number 132
Community of Practice 3, 6, 13, 222, 356
Competition 70, 176, 178-180, 185-186, 192, 209, 244, 247, 252, 258, 277, 280, 283, 291, 304, 312, 314, 333, 336-338
Compilation and reception manager 65
Coordination 154, 196, 272, 274-275, 333
Corporate Image 241-242, 252, 258, 264
Crowdworker 64
culture 6, 8, 13, 29, 31-33, 35-38, 40, 52, 59, 153, 162-164, 168, 186, 207-208, 212, 214, 231, 233, 242-243, 246-247, 250-256, 258-259, 275, 301, 307, 333-335, 338-339, 341
Customer 5, 24-25, 28, 32, 34-35, 37, 50, 66, 69, 73, 80, 92, 138, 141, 153, 181, 184-185, 266, 268, 270-272, 275, 281-283, 286, 293, 303, 308, 310, 318-319, 321, 324, 328, 331, 337-339

D

Dataset 99, 111-112, 180, 182
Decision Making 162-163, 197, 218, 235, 278, 318, 324, 334, 337, 340, 368
Deliberate Practice 318, 320, 325, 327-329
deployment 41, 155-156, 169-170, 198, 303
Development 3-4, 6-7, 21-24, 29, 37, 40, 46-50, 57-59, 64, 67, 70, 80, 163-164, 169, 186, 219-220, 228, 233, 235, 244, 248-249, 252-253, 256, 267-268, 270-272, 275-278, 281-283, 285-286, 291, 293, 295, 299-305, 308, 312-314, 317-323, 327-334, 336-337, 339-340, 357-359, 362, 366-367
digital technologies 36, 204-206, 208, 214-215
Digraphs 141

Index

E

Economy 47, 54, 57-60, 64, 208, 244-245, 291, 314, 334, 336, 339-340, 358

enterprise 2.0 8

Enterprise Logistics 65-66, 68, 71, 92

enterprise social media 32, 41, 198

Entrepreneur 32, 59, 299, 301, 303, 306-309, 311-316, 358-359, 362, 367

Environment 35, 46-47, 49-50, 57, 60, 64, 66, 73, 85, 92, 141, 149, 151-152, 155, 166, 177-178, 205, 207, 210, 214, 218-220, 223, 231-234, 238, 241-244, 246-250, 252-253, 256-259, 267, 270, 273-277, 286, 293, 305, 310, 324, 326-328, 333, 335, 340, 367

Expert Behaviour 318, 321, 328

Expertise 1, 3, 6, 12, 26, 37, 52, 151, 159-162, 176, 178, 181, 184, 192, 197, 210, 280, 283, 297, 317-329, 335, 358

exploitation 55, 73, 92, 196, 200, 338, 358

exploration 14, 36, 182, 196, 200, 225, 317, 338, 359, 367

Exploring 7, 59, 230, 237, 256, 331, 359

Fading 229-231, 237

F

FBP 316

Flexibility 40, 51, 67, 150, 208-209, 214, 273-274, 310, 333, 338

Flexible Business Plan 291, 293, 306, 315-316

Forming 70, 100, 237

Forums 1, 3, 7-8, 12, 25, 280

Frascati Manual 292, 295

G

Graph Mining 94, 96, 98, 104, 141

GTM 310, 316

Guided Problem Solving 325

I

ICT 233, 245-246

Idea Management 325-326

Ideation 321-322, 325-326

Implementing KM 148-150, 156, 158, 160, 174, 245, 335

incremental innovation 197, 337

Information 3, 5, 8, 17, 25, 31-32, 34, 36-37, 59, 72-73, 77, 92-96, 98-103, 107, 141, 148-150, 154-155, 158-159, 163, 166, 168-171, 173-174, 177-178, 181, 185, 194, 196-197, 199, 204-206, 208, 210-211, 213-214, 219-220, 231-232, 235, 242-253, 256-259, 267, 271-272, 275, 277-278, 280-281, 285, 292, 295-296, 299, 303, 305, 307, 309, 312, 314, 325, 327, 331, 333-336, 338-340, 359-360, 363-366, 368

Innovation 1-2, 9-11, 13, 23-26, 34-37, 40, 46-47, 50, 54, 56-59, 162, 177-179, 193-198, 200, 232, 241, 245-246, 249, 258-259, 266-268, 270-278, 281-286, 291-306, 308, 310-317, 321-322, 324-325, 327, 330-337, 339-341, 357-362, 367

Innovation Communities 26, 314

Innovation Management 267-268, 270

Innovation Process 267-268, 271-272, 282, 286, 291-293, 295-296, 298-301, 304-306, 310-316, 322, 331, 337, 341, 359, 361

Innovative Entrepreneur 299, 301, 303, 307-309, 311-316

Innovativeness 244-246, 255, 258, 264, 271, 277, 330, 332, 338

Integration 95, 160, 169, 178, 181, 183-185, 192, 213, 267, 271-272, 277, 282-283, 286, 332, 334-335, 337, 339, 365

Intellectual Property 35-37, 55, 243, 252-253, 255, 291, 293, 295, 300, 304, 313, 316

Internet 26, 36, 99, 140, 176-179, 181, 184-186, 194, 212, 242, 246, 248, 254, 256

Inverse Logistics 65, 67-69, 71-74, 80-83, 87, 92-93

IP 293, 295, 300, 304, 315-316

K

Knowledge 1-6, 8-9, 12-13, 17-19, 22-23, 25-26, 29, 32-33, 36-41, 46-47, 50-51, 53, 64-65, 67-72, 82-83, 86-87, 92, 94, 96, 99-100, 103-105, 141, 148-152, 154-164, 166-172, 174, 176-181, 183-186, 192-201, 204-215, 218-223, 225, 227-233, 235, 237-238, 242-252, 255, 257-259, 264, 266-268, 270-273, 275, 277-278, 280-282, 284-286, 291-292, 295, 297, 301, 303-304, 314, 317-326, 328-341, 357-359, 364, 367

Knowledge Conversion 249, 264

Knowledge Creation 65, 205, 208, 220, 243-244, 246, 249, 282, 331, 340, 367

Index

Knowledge Dynamic 92
Knowledge exchange 46, 51, 53, 159, 176-181, 183-186, 192, 267, 335-337, 339
Knowledge Management 1, 3-5, 9, 12, 17-18, 29, 65, 67, 69-70, 83, 87, 92, 94, 148-149, 156, 161-164, 166, 170, 176, 193-198, 200-201, 204-205, 211, 213-214, 218-223, 228-232, 235, 241-243, 257, 264, 280-281, 285, 317-318, 328, 330, 332-333, 336, 338, 357
Knowledge transfer process 205-206, 208, 213, 215

L

Leadership 8, 13, 16-17, 21-22, 32, 35, 38, 159, 218-219, 228, 231, 254, 256, 278, 336
Learning 1-3, 6-7, 11-12, 14, 24-25, 32, 40, 59, 153, 159, 164, 214, 218, 220-222, 227-235, 237-238, 241-243, 245-247, 249, 252-253, 255-259, 268, 270, 273, 275-276, 278, 281, 284-285, 291, 314, 317-318, 320-321, 324-329, 334-336, 338, 340, 357
Lessons Learnt 1, 3-4
Litefactory 51, 64
Logistics Model 93
Logistics Model Based on Positions (MoLoBaC) 93

M

Market 34, 36, 46, 50, 52, 54, 56-58, 60, 66, 73, 92, 211, 268, 271-272, 274-275, 278, 280-286, 291-305, 307-316, 318-319, 321, 329, 331-333, 337-340, 357, 361-362, 365
Market Research 295-296, 299, 307, 312, 315
Mechanism 164, 169, 210-212, 222, 250, 277
Modelling 111, 176, 182, 237
MoLoBaC 67-69, 71-73, 79-81, 83, 85-87, 93
MOOCs 241, 256
Multifactory 46-47, 49-51, 53-54, 57-60, 64
Multimediality 219
Multi-User Environments 219

N

Narrating 229-230, 237
New Product Development 268, 270-271, 281, 317-323, 327-330, 357-358, 367
Norming 237

O

Organizational Innovation 334, 357

Organizational Learning 164, 259, 268, 270, 275, 278, 281, 284-285, 318, 320-321, 326, 329, 334-336, 340, 357
organizations 1, 8, 23-27, 29, 31-42, 59, 66, 70-71, 86, 92, 148-152, 155-157, 173-174, 178-179, 185, 193, 195-201, 204-206, 208-209, 213-215, 266-267, 270-272, 274-277, 280-282, 285, 317-323, 325-328, 330, 333-341, 366-367
Orientism 218-219, 221-225, 228, 231-232, 234, 237
Oslo Manual 292, 294

P

PENTHA Model 233-234, 238
Performing 94, 214, 230, 237-238, 277, 319, 328
Process 1, 3-4, 11-12, 25, 29, 35, 39-40, 51, 54, 59, 65, 69-71, 80, 83, 86-87, 92, 95-98, 111, 141, 153, 162, 168-169, 196, 205-206, 208-209, 211, 213-215, 218-219, 222-223, 225, 230-231, 233, 235, 242, 245-250, 252, 256-259, 264, 266-268, 271-272, 278, 281-282, 285-286, 291-302, 304-307, 310-316, 318, 320-324, 326, 329-335, 337, 339-341, 356-362, 366-367
Product 24-26, 34, 36-37, 39-40, 46-47, 50, 54, 56-58, 72-73, 80-81, 92, 153, 160, 193, 267-268, 270-272, 278, 281-283, 286, 291-295, 297-299, 303, 312, 314, 317-323, 325-334, 336-341, 357-362, 366-367
Product Innovation 46-47, 54, 57-58, 271, 278, 286, 295, 298, 330-333, 336-341, 357-358, 362, 367
Publish or Perish 254, 256, 264

R

radical innovation 196, 286
R&D 46, 57, 80, 282, 291-293, 295-296, 300-302, 315, 317-322, 324-325, 327-328, 331-333, 337, 340
Reflecting 29, 230, 238, 337
Research and Development 80, 270, 291, 295, 314, 328, 331, 337, 357, 362
Resource Allocation 268, 285
ROI 284, 293, 303, 308, 316

S

Scaffolding 230-231, 238
Seed Number 132
Sharing Economy 47, 54, 57, 59, 64

Index

SMEs 51, 56, 176-180, 183-186, 292, 332, 337, 339, 358-359, 366
SOA 299, 302, 304, 315-316
Social Business 31, 41, 64
Social Logistics 74, 77, 93
Social Media 1, 4, 7, 9, 11, 21, 23, 26-29, 31-42, 46-47, 54, 57-58, 60, 138, 140-141, 151, 194-200, 231, 233, 244-245, 255
Start-up 291, 293, 300-301, 314, 316
Storming 231, 238, 362
Strategies 13, 35, 39, 42, 57, 59, 109, 113, 149, 158, 163, 220-223, 227, 232, 248, 251, 254, 256, 266-268, 277, 280-281, 286, 304, 320-321, 325, 330-332, 336-338, 340-341, 357, 359
Sustainability 42, 56, 64, 66, 324, 337, 367

T

technological mechanisms 208, 212-213, 215
Technology 17, 24-25, 31, 33, 37-40, 59, 151, 155-156, 160-161, 163, 166, 168, 172, 177-181, 183-185, 192-193, 195, 198, 200, 205, 207-208, 211-215, 226, 231, 233, 243-247, 251, 258-259, 270-272, 274, 278, 280, 283, 292, 295, 303, 312, 317-319, 321-322, 326, 328-331, 333, 335, 337-340, 359, 362, 365-366, 368
Thinking Skills 318-319
Training 2-3, 5, 37, 77, 153, 167, 169, 182, 211, 218, 220, 230-232, 235, 245, 248, 282, 366
Transliteracy 257, 264
Tutoring 229-232, 237-238

U

Utilization 41, 73, 80-81, 87, 334, 341

W

Work Life Balance 64

Become an IRMA Member

Members of the **Information Resources Management Association (IRMA)** understand the importance of community within their field of study. The Information Resources Management Association is an ideal venue through which professionals, students, and academicians can convene and share the latest industry innovations and scholarly research that is changing the field of information science and technology. Become a member today and enjoy the benefits of membership as well as the opportunity to collaborate and network with fellow experts in the field.

IRMA Membership Benefits:

- **One FREE Journal Subscription**
- **30% Off Additional Journal Subscriptions**
- **20% Off Book Purchases**
- Updates on the latest events and research on Information Resources Management through the IRMA-L listserv.
- Updates on new open access and downloadable content added to Research IRM.
- A copy of the Information Technology Management Newsletter twice a year.
- A certificate of membership.

IRMA Membership $195

Scan code to visit irma-international.org and begin by selecting your free journal subscription.

Membership is good for one full year.

www.irma-international.org